READING THE
ALLEGORICAL INTERTEXT

READING THE ALLEGORICAL INTERTEXT

Chaucer, Spenser, Shakespeare, Milton

Judith H. Anderson

Fordham University Press

New York   2008

Copyright © 2008 Fordham University Press

All rights reserved. No part of this publication may be reproduced, stored in a retrieval system, or transmitted in any form or by any means—electronic, mechanical, photocopy, recording, or any other—except for brief quotations in printed reviews, without the prior permission of the publisher.

Library of Congress Cataloging-in-Publication Data

Anderson, Judith H.
  Reading the allegorical intertext : Chaucer, Spenser, Shakespeare, Milton / Judith H. Anderson. — 1st ed.
    p. cm.
  Includes bibliographical references and index.
  ISBN-13: 978-0-8232-2848-5 (pbk : alk. paper)
  1. English literature—History and criticism—Theory, etc. 2. Spenser, Edmund, 1552?–1599. Faerie queene. 3. Chaucer, Geoffrey, d. 1400. Canterbury tales. 4. Shakespeare, William, 1564–1616. King Lear. 5. Milton, John, 1608–1674—Criticism and interpretation. 6. Intertextuality. 7. Symbolism in literature. 8. Influence (Literary, artistic, etc.) I. Title.
  PR21.A85 2008
  820.9′15—dc22

                                                        2008003833

Printed in the United States of America
First edition

For Sarah Massey-Warren,
who will read from within the fullness of
the intertext

Contents

Prior Publication   ix

Introduction: Reading the Allegorical Intertext   1

PART 1: ALLEGORICAL REFLECTIONS OF *THE CANTERBURY TALES* IN *THE FAERIE QUEENE*

1. Chaucer's and Spenser's Reflexive Narrators   27
2. What Comes after Chaucer's *But* in *The Faerie Queene*   42
3. "Pricking on the plaine": Spenser's Intertextual Beginnings and Endings   54
4. Allegory, Irony, Despair: Chaucer's *Pardoner's* and *Franklin's Tales* and Spenser's *Faerie Queene*, Books I and III   61
5. Eumnestes' "immortall scrine": Spenser's Archive   79
6. Spenser's Use of Chaucer's *Melibee*: Allegory, Narrative, History   91

PART 2: AGENCY, ALLEGORY, AND HISTORY WITHIN THE SPENSERIAN INTERTEXT

7. Spenser's *Muiopotmos* and Chaucer's *Nun's Priest's Tale*   109
8. Arthur and Argante: Parodying the Ideal Vision   126
9. Chaucer's *Parliament of Fowls* and Refractions of a Veiled Venus in *The Faerie Queene*   135
10. The Antiquities of Fairyland and Ireland   154
11. *Better a mischief than an inconvenience*: "The saiying self" in Spenser's *View of the Present State of Ireland*   168

PART 3: SPENSERIAN ALLEGORY IN THE INTERTEXTS OF SHAKESPEARE AND MILTON

12. The Conspiracy of Realism: Impasse and Vision in *The Faerie Queene* and Shakespeare's *King Lear*   183

13. *Venus and Adonis*: Spenser, Shakespeare, and the Forms of Desire · 201
14. Flowers and Boars: Surmounting Sexual Binarism in Spenser's Garden of Adonis · 214
15. Androcentrism and Acrasian Fantasies in the Bower of Bliss · 224
16. Beyond Binarism: Eros/Death and Venus/Mars in *Antony and Cleopatra* and *The Faerie Queene* · 239
17. Patience and Passion in Shakespeare and Milton · 259
18. "Real or Allegoric" in Herbert and Milton: Thinking through Difference · 272
19. Spenser and Milton: The Mind's Allegorical Place · 280

Notes · 321

Index · 423

Prior Publication

(in whole or in substantial part)

"Narrative Reflections: Re-envisaging the Poet in *The Canterbury Tales* and *The Faerie Queene*," in *Refiguring Chaucer in the Renaissance*, ed. Theresa M. Krier (Gainesville: University Press of Florida, 1998), 87–105: now entitled "Chaucer's and Spenser's Reflexive Narrators."

"What Comes after Chaucer's *But*: Adversative Constructions in Spenser," in *Acts of Interpretation: The Text in Its Contexts*, ed. Mary J. Carruthers and Elizabeth D. Kirk (Norman, Okla.: Pilgrim, 1982), 105–18: now entitled "What Comes after Chaucer's *But* in *The Faerie Queene*."

"'A Gentle Knight was pricking on the plaine': The Chaucerian Connection," *English Literary Renaissance*, 15 (1985), 166–74: now entitled "'Pricking on the plaine': Spenser's Intertextual Beginnings and Endings" (© Blackwell/Wiley).

"Allegory, Irony, Despair: Chaucer's *Pardoner's* and *Franklin's Tales* and Spenser's *Faerie Queene*, Books I and III," in *Textual Conversations in the Renaissance: Ethics, Authors, and Technologies*, ed. Zachary Lesser and Benedict Robinson (Aldershot, Hampshire, U.K.: Ashgate, 2006), 71–89.

"'Myn auctour': Spenser's Enabling Fiction and Eumnestes' 'immortall scrine,'" in *Unfolded Tales: Studies in Renaissance Romance*, ed. George M. Logan and Gordon Teskey (Ithaca, N.Y.: Cornell University Press, 1989), 16–31: now entitled "Eumnestes' 'immortall scrine': Spenser's Archive."

"Prudence and Her Silence: Spenser's Use of Chaucer's *Melibee*," *ELH*, 62 (1995), 29–46: now entitled "Spenser's Use of Chaucer's *Melibee*: Allegory, Narrative, History" (© Johns Hopkins University Press).

"'Nat worth a boterflye': *Muiopotmos* and *The Nun's Priest's Tale*," *Journal of Medieval and Renaissance Studies*, 1 (1971), 89–106: now entitled "Spenser's *Muiopotmos* and Chaucer's *Nun's Priest's Tale*" (© Duke University Press).

"Arthur, Argante, and the Ideal Vision: An Exercise in Speculation and Parody," in *The Passing of Arthur: New Essays in Arthurian Tradition*, ed.

Christopher Baswell and William Sharpe (New York: Garland, 1988), 193–206: now entitled "Arthur and Argante: Parodying the Ideal Vision" (© Routledge/Taylor and Francis).

"'The 'couert vele': Chaucer, Spenser, and Venus," *English Literary Renaissance*, 24 (1994), 638–59: now entitled "Chaucer's *Parliament of Fowls* and Refractions of a Veiled Venus in *The Faerie Queene*" (© Blackwell/Wiley).

"The Antiquities of Fairyland and Ireland," *JEGP*, 86 (1987), 199–214 (© University of Illinois Press).

"*Better a mischief than an inconvenience*: 'The saiyng self' in Spenser's *View*, or, How many meanings can stand on the head of a proverb?" in *Worldmaking Spenser: Explorations in the Early Modern Age*, ed. Patrick Cheney and Lauren Silberman (Lexington: University of Kentucky Press, 1999), 219–33: now entitled "*Better a mischief than an inconvenience*: 'The saiyng self' in Spenser's *View of the Present State of Ireland*."

"The Conspiracy of Realism: Impasse and Vision in *King Lear*," *Studies in Philology*, 84 (1987), 1–23: now entitled "The Conspiracy of Realism: Impasse and Vision in *The Faerie Queene* and Shakespeare's *King Lear*" (© University of North Carolina Press).

"*Venus and Adonis*: Spenser, Shakespeare, and the Forms of Desire," in *Grief and Gender, 700–1700*, ed. Jennifer C. Vaught, with Lynne Dickson Bruckner (New York: Palgrave Macmillan, 2003), 149–60.

"Flowers and Boars: Surmounting Sexual Binarism in Spenser's Garden of Adonis," *Spenser Studies*, 23 (forthcoming 2008, © AMS Press).

"Acrasian Fantasies: Outsides, Insides, Upsides, Downsides in the Bower of Bliss," in *A Touch More Rare: Harry Berger, Jr., and the Arts of Interpretation*, ed. David Lee Miller and Nina Levine (New York: Fordham University Press, forthcoming 2009): now entitled "Androcentrism and Acrasian Fantasies in the Bower of Bliss."

"Beyond Binarism: Eros/Death and Venus/Mars in Shakespeare's *Antony and Cleopatra* and Spenser's *Faerie Queene*," in *Shakespeare and Spenser: Attractive Opposites*, ed. J. B. Lethbridge (Manchester, U.K.: Manchester University Press, forthcoming 2008).

"Passion and Patience in Shakespeare and Milton," *Spenser Studies*, 21 (2007), 2005–20 (© AMS Press).

Each essay appears herein with the permission of the original publisher and holder of copyright, the latter identical with the publisher unless otherwise indicated.

READING THE
ALLEGORICAL INTERTEXT

Introduction

Reading the Allegorical Intertext

Reading between and among texts is something I have been doing in articles, books, and classrooms over several decades. This kind of reading is a staple of the traditional, centuries-spanning literary survey course, as well as of literature courses more generally. It highlights specifically textual concerns with the generation of meaning. Such intertextual relations can be historicized in the survey of *longue durée*, either exemplarily or thematically, selectively, and therefore rather narrowly. With the latter options, the focus has tended to shift from linguistic text to thematized content and historical context, and from literary writing to other expressions of culture (e.g., science or religion) and of society (e.g., economic or political institutions). These shifts from texts to theme, culture, and society are certainly viable. They have afforded, and continue to afford, intellectual stimulation and enlightenment. But the possibility of a stronger balance between them and the linguistic and rhetorical foci essential to nuanced, critical thinking depends at this point on recognition, reassertion, and reconception of the legitimacy and value of specifically textual concerns. While my own approach to revaluation is initially and recurrently theorized, its strongest allegiance is to practice and demonstration—that is, to textuality as such. Actually reading between texts, and the tangible results of doing so, are the core of my argument. At the same time, however, I want to make visible what such activity contributes and what it produces. In short, I want theoretically to frame and variously and sufficiently to exhibit these throughout.

The title of this volume, *Reading the Allegorical Intertext: Chaucer, Spenser, Shakespeare, Milton*, plays on "surfing the Internet." I conceive the intertext, like the Internet, as a state, or place, of potential, one that can variously be narrowed or expanded, minimized or enlarged. More exactly, the intertext is a convenient term for a relationship or a series of relationships with a single text or multiple texts that enrich and reorient the signification and reception of the text in question. The intertext can be imagined on a continuum between deliberate imitation and intentional allusion, on the one hand, and on the other, an intertextuality in which the unlimited agency of the signifier operates virtually without regard for context, whether sentential and textually specific or broadly cultural, societal, and historical. While authorial agency and linguistic free play are opposing binaries in the abstract, in practice they coexist interestingly, elusively, and indefinitely. The same applies to the coexistence of individual agency with cultural and societal determinism.

Necessarily, as a condition of potentiality and relationship, the intertext, like any good fiction, is conceptually and functionally unstable: it comes into being in the act of reading a text.[1] Within the intertext, fortuitous resonance shades into deliberate control, occasional echo into sustained allusion, and vice versa. Categorically, the borders of the intertext are fuzzy. This is actually one of its conceptual strengths, and it has much to teach us about inherited conventions and individual inflections of meaning and, further, about linguistic play, about textual *containment* (in both the limiting and inclusive senses of this punning word-concept), and about the agency of authors and readers. In the texts of Chaucer, Spenser, Shakespeare, and Milton, "Reading the Intertext" is also for me a way of talking about the history of significant form, particularly allegorical form, that encapsulates and magnifies the workings of signification itself, and it is a way of talking about landmark texts as distinctive outcroppings of culture, at once part of the main and distinct from its mass.

Having employed the still-debated, loosely-used term *intertextuality* two paragraphs earlier, I want to address its import and, in both senses, to *contain* its function in my argument. *Intertextuality* is a term coined by Julia Kristeva in the late 1960s, and as a concept, if not always as a term, it soon had currency in various theories grounded in Saussurian linguistics, perhaps Roland Barthes's being the most familiar variant. The term was also appropriated from Kristeva's Bakhtinian usage to an extreme deconstructive sense of unlimited semiosis, always already deferred. According to Mary Orr, *intertextuality* was now taken to mean *only* "a mosaic of quotations" or "a random juxtaposition and collage of texts," thus displacing Kristeva's emphasis on "the reconstitutive synergies of text" or reducing it to negation, to the death of the author and the annihilation of anything outside the text.[2] Orr, a student of intertextuality, argues that Kristeva's version does not simply signal the verbal mosaic it became for abusive appropriators, but "a logical relationship of 'X and/or not X,' an 'an(d)other,'" or, elsewise, I would add, X and/or not Y (32). The second X in the Kristevan "X and/or not X" and even more clearly in "an(d)other" could have been designated by a Y, although such a change would unfold, and could lessen, her attack on identity—the self-sameness of the textual sign. Designated by X and Y, the structure of Kristevan intertextuality, like *transposition*, her later term for it, is more clearly similar to the structural duplicity of metaphor—like and/or not-like. It resembles a compressed, encapsulated act of translation, whether this act pertains to words as such or to a rhetorical trope, a *translatio*, or metaphor.

In other words, as Graham Allen observes in discussing Kristevan intertextuality, whereas traditional logic derives from "Aristotle's assertion that something is either 'X' or 'not-X,'" poetic, like metaphoric and intertextual, language is double, or both X and not-X (44).[3] Kristeva's later use of the term *transposition* (Latin *transponere*: "to put across," "to transfer") for intertextuality highlights the basic metaphoricity of her concept: metaphor, known also as *translatio* ("translation," from Latin *transferre/translatus*), likewise signifies "a carrying across" or "transfer" from one place or thing to another. In relation to the social positionalities implied by Kristevan *transposition*, consider a similar use of the term *translation* in the early modern period to signify the transfer of an official from one ecclesiastical jurisdiction to another, the transmigration of a soul to heaven, the transformation or refashioning of apparel, the transfer (or alienation) of money or property from one person to another, and the movement of a tradesman from one company to another (e.g., baker to draper), as well as the transfer from one language to another and the transfer from tenor to vehicle (and vice versa) in metaphor. All these translations are transpositions, too. The terms *intertextuality, transposition, and translation* (or *metaphor*) have in doubleness a common core.

The Kristevan addition of a poststructural "and/or" to the traditional X = Y; X does not = Y structure of metaphor (i.e., my love [x] is and is not a rose[y]) only and aptly attributes to metaphor, as to intertextuality, the potential for over- or indeterminacy. Paul Ricoeur cites an expression found in the preambles of Majorcan storytellers, "*Aixo era y no era* (it was and it was not)," in order to express the split reference characteristic of metaphor—a kind of bifocality that differentially doubles and productively disrupts, rather than merely negating, the world as we know it.[4] Properly and historically understood, intertextuality, like metaphor, is potency, not simply cancellation. My use of the term *intertext*, which is less freighted with decades of over- and ill-packed baggage, seeks to recover the vitality of textual exchange. Moreover, it seeks to encompass intertextuality, influence, and imitation, along with other literary relations between and among texts, such as allusion and citation.⁵

Since Kristeva's coinage four decades ago, the term *intertextuality*, when not used loosely, popularly, or, indiscriminately to designate any relationship whatever between words, texts, languages, forms, and genres, has usually carried its narrow, exclusionary, deconstructive sense.⁶ Correlatively, it has been worked to find—in fact to fashion—and demonize an *other*. The leading specters have been *influence* and *imitation*. In practice, I find that both have been denigrated, not because they are opposed to intertextuality, but because they are difficult to separate clearly and cleanly from it in an actual text. The boundaries keep blurring, much as do the not-unrelated boundaries of agency and subjectivity, the latter term implying not only psychic interiority but also cultural and social conditioning or downright subjection.

Orr suggests that influence has been reduced to, and distorted as, merely source hunting and intention, and this might have been the situation in the early years of death-of-the author deconstruction. In recent decades, however, opposition to influence has looked more like a fear of reason (*ratio*, order, form) and a distrust of agency, even when these constructive values are skeptically advanced or realistically qualified, and when form is conceived to be flexible, developmental, or open. Contrary to the misconceiving of *influence* as a closing down of new construction or a freezing of its forms, influence is instead "a metaphor of motions and fluid"—Latin *in*, plus *fluere*, "to flow" (Orr, 15, 93). Like the infusing of spirit, strength, or archival treasures of which Spenser's poet speaks, influence can, and often does, work against stagnation.⁷ Its positive potential is for growth, enrichment, and change.

Imitation, when misconceived, might actually be less a specter than the reflection of a naive assumption about human development, both cognitive and societal.⁸ Even the conception of laddering or constructing with and beyond existing blocks of culture (instruments, artifacts, structures) that is dear to a humanistic cognitive scientist like Andy Clark requires a considerable amount of imitation.⁹ Especially in the Renaissance, imitation is a fact of life, a hallmark of education, and a profound habit of mind. It is no coincidence that this period also produced art at once aesthetically outstanding and critically engaged with a complex world. Perhaps the imitation that is really a bogey for an oversimplified, exclusionary intertextuality is its misrecognition as merely passive copying or exact duplication, whether of a predecessor text, a generic form, or a referential world. In this last instance, a false presumption of the transparency of language is likely the real enemy, rather than imitation as traditionally and constructively understood.

Oft confounding confusion, imitation misrecognized as transparency or duplication is then dubbed *mimesis* in a badly skewed version of the Aristotelian tradition. In effect, this skewing collates the exact imitation of literary predecessors and models with the passive reproduction of things and events. Hidden within such misrecognition is a desire to cancel referentiality *tout court* and more generally to secede from the world of history, which includes cultural precedents and forms, even as these, to a various degree, include history. Orr may have this secession in the back of her mind when she refers to an exclusionary "intertextuality's terrible potential sameness," shut off from what is putatively outside the text (92). To me, this is a sameness in which the present and the past, synchrony and diachrony, are indistinguishable and in which all texts have finally one meaning—in short, merely an inversion of the transcendental signifier, even if now in the service of postmodern gods. This sameness is an old world turned upside-down rather than constructively reinvented.

Ricoeur's use of Aristotle's *Poetics* as a major base text in his trilogy *Time and Narrative* has suggested to me that a reductive skewing of the concept of mimesis also goes hand in hand with a denial of temporality or narrative process to allegory and a denial of temporal configuration to history.[10] When mimesis becomes naively conceived realism, or photocopy, allegory must correlatively become naively conceived Realism, or abstraction. Mind separates from matter, psyche from flesh, concept from history. In a denial of allegorical thinking and allegorical form, binaries thus reign supreme and unchallenged. But here I anticipate the next stage of my argument.

The other term in my title *Reading the Allegorical Intertext* that requires glossing is *allegorical*. From the time of my first book, I have described allegory as a process of thinking.[11] This process combines mind with matter, emblem with narrative, abstraction with history. Its forms are often mythic. Basically it is continued, or moving, metaphor, as classical and early modern rhetoricians have described allegory itself. In Cicero's immensely influential *De Oratore*, for example, Crassus considers allegory an extension of metaphor, which is typically based in a single word, whereas allegory occurs in "a chain of words linked together: ex pluribus [verbis] continuatis connectitur" and thus, in modern terms, in the contiguous relationship that characterizes narrative.[12] Recently, I have been especially interested in allegorical form as a way to engage and exceed binarisms, notably gendered ones, as the later chapters in this volume reflect.

Two treatments of literary allegory are especially important to my conception of this form. From Carolynn Van Dyke, I borrow a semiotic description of allegory as a "synthesis of deictic and nondeictic generic codes."[13] Van Dyke uses *deictic* and *nondeictic* as convenient, summary terms for any number of binaries, such as particular and universal, concrete and abstract, material and moral, natural and emblematic, real and Real. *Deictic* itself signifies "directly pointing out" or "demonstrative." In a linguistic context, it indicates a word that particularizes and points, such as the demonstrative pronoun *this*. It derives from Greek δεικτικός, "able to show, showing directly." By *genre*, Van Dyke intends both "a set of conventions based on an inferable semiotic code" *and* "the texts that realize the code—or realize it to a significant degree" (20–21). While I prefer to sidestep the distracting and tricky question, tangential for my purposes, of whether or in what sense allegory is to be defined as itself a genre, I agree with Van Dyke's acknowledgment of formal variation and development in textual allegories. What Alastair Fowler says most importantly about genre in his capacious *Kinds of Literature* pertains to allegory as well, despite his nebulously characterizing allegory as a mode—a kind of adjectival register comparable to the epigrammatic, georgic, or elegiac.[14] In Fowler's view, what especially characterizes all genres is that they "are continuously undergoing metamorphosis"; thus "the character of genres is that they change" (18, 23).[15] Likewise, with allegory.

In an older study of allegory by Stephen Barney, I have found the conception of an allegorical "boundary case" particularly useful. Barney insists that allegories have a temporal dimension; they require whole fictions, persons engaged in events with beginnings, middles, and ends (further shades of the plot in Aristotelian *mimesis*):

> The boundary case would be a description of a static scene, laden with personification, like an emblem or triumph. If we call such a description an allegory, I propose that we conceive of the scene as a stilled moment in a moving narrative.[16]

Barney concludes by suggesting that we deny the designation *allegory* to the static boundary case, instead using only the adjective *allegorical* for it and thereby observing both its relation to, and its difference from, the temporal, narrative movement of literary allegory, properly defined. Like Barney or, still further back, like Northrop Frye, Van Dyke, too, considers allegory necessarily a narrative form, or as she puts it, "the syntactic codes of narrative, or, less elegantly but more accurately, of the plot" are "fundamental" to allegory.[17] This diegetic character of allegory is a point I would stress, quite in opposition to a number of otherwise enlightening theorists who write of allegory as if it were simply identical with abstraction per se and therefore *other* to narrative, whereas narrative is actually an intrinsic, defining feature of literary allegory.

At one time, I considered enclosing the word *allegorical* within parentheses in the title of this volume as a way of typographically signaling the variousness of my concern with allegory and the conceptual breadth of allegory itself. The claim that all signification is allegorical raises few eyebrows nowadays, but current claimants are likely to add that, once this is said, there is little else to say. That is, while the claim is decidedly worth recognizing, the old crux pertains: if allegory is everywhere, it is nowhere. At the other pole from this totalizing claim, with its extreme sensitivity to the distance between word and thing and to the fictive nature of language, is the limiting and specifying of allegory in ways that reduce, trivialize, or freeze the form. One way to simplify allegory is to assume its structure as a precise equivalent: $X = Y$; Redcrosse is Holiness; allegory is abstraction. Another way is to immobilize this form: $X = Y$, allegory IS; allegory is self-same, identical, non-developing; the allegory IS separate from its narrative. Still another way is to deny complexity, multiplicity, openness, contradiction, and subversion, to allegory: since $X = Y$, irrationality, excess, surface, emotive texturing, and the like are accidental, inessential, illusory—to be dealt with by the reader-as-Procrustes. Conversely, as has been known since ancient times and, as I have earlier noted, allegory is basically a continued form of metaphor that formally partakes of, and structurally participates in, recursive-progressive (dramatic) narrative. Metaphor, the logical structure of which is and is not, carries two terms, which are and/or are not alike: $X = Y$ and/or X does not $= Y$; moreover, these relationships shift and develop over space/time in allegorical narrative. Even allegory as simple as Prudentius' *Psychomachia* or *Everyman* combines terms, levels, codes, dimensions, call them what you will, and does so developmentally.[18] Personification, which is itself a type of metaphor, markedly does so as well when it participates in dramatic narrative.

My use of words like *accidental* and *essential* in recent examples intimates the relevance of a conception of form to allegory, as Gordon Teskey recognizes in his *Allegory and Violence*.[19] Equating allegory with abstraction, however, Teskey assumes that allegorical form is Platonic, not to mention male, indeed violently male. Whether on the basis of intellectual history or of actual allegories—for example, the treatment of form in Spenser's Garden of Adonis—such Platonizing can be neither an unqualified assumption nor a necessary one. The cyclical first stage of Spenser's Garden features a shift in point of view from the seminary of recycling forms to the eternity of matter. Our perspective flips from one side of a single cosmic coin to the other—the view from on high to that from below, from an eternity of forms to one of matter in which forms are debased and transitory.[20] Either view is weighted with value, succession only temporarily affording primacy to the one and finality to the other; cyclical succession and systemic co-operation are conclusive. Deferring an excursus into intellectual history, I'll invoke a statement from Jean-Luc Nancy's philosophy of the image, which suggests where my sense of form is going. According to Nancy, the image, and specifically its surface, is "Not an 'idea' (*idea* or *eidolon*), which is an intelligible form, but a force that forces form to touch itself."[21]

I'm inclined momentarily to be anecdotal, recalling a persistent memory of Michelangelo's sculptures in The Accademia in Florence. While I admired the perfection of Michelangelo's *David* when last in this museum, I was drawn more strongly to his Boboli *Captives*—rough, unfinished, sometimes inchoate forms emerging from massive blocks of stone. Erwin Panofsky's classic discussion of *Captives* reads in them a reinstatement of "Plotinus' allegorical interpretation of the process by which the form of a statue is extricated from the recalcitrant stone."[22] Notable in Panofsky's observation is an emphasis on the straining *emergence*, the torturous *freeing*, of the form from its material prison, rather than on the violent imposition of form on matter. Like Christian hylomorphisms deriving from Aristotle, the particular Neoplatonic lens through which Panofsky views Michangelo's sculptures discovers a role for matter teleologically more informed and less inert than Plato's.[23] Yet more active constructions of matter alternatively applicable to these sculptures can readily be found elsewhere as well, for example, in Renaissance medicine, alchemy, magic, and natural philosophy or science, including vitalism(s). Looking at Michelangelo's *Captives* through my own lenses, what I see, and the sculptures show, is not only struggle but also a kind of organic continuity, an involvement with the substance of the stone, a proximity too massive and powerful ever to be broken. Rather than feeling oppressed, I feel moved, awed—perhaps, in a phonic pun shared by Chaucer and Spenser, even "astonied" (astonished).

Earlier, I suggested that a reductive conception of mimesis correlates with a denial of temporal configuration to history. Insofar as allegory engages history through narrative process, as well as through various kinds of historical allusion and reference ranging from direct names to structural patterns, the vexed question of what history itself might be bears on this form, and vice versa. Discussing allegory in connection with puritanism, or radical Protestant reform, for example, Thomas H. Luxon seeks to show in his book *Literal Figures* that typology, or *figura*, as explained in Erich Auerbach's classic essay on the subject, is a kind of allegory, rather than history as Auerbach argues.[24] In this endeavor, Luxon opposes Barbara Lewalski's firm differentiation of figural typology from allegory—that is, of biblical foreshadowing and fulfillment from what she considers abstraction—and he actually seems to have Auerbach on his side (Luxon, 43).[25] As Auerbach admits, "figural interpretation is 'allegorical' in the widest sense," simply because in it, "one thing stands for another" (54). Auerbach thus signals his own awareness that any form of signification shares common ground with allegory. But instead of stopping with this admission, Auerbach, as earlier intimated, repeatedly and painstakingly also distinguishes figural typology from allegory and claims it for history on the basis of the "full historicity [die volle Innergeschichtlichkeit: 'full authority']" both of the figural "sign and what it signifies."[26] Notably, Auerbach now identifies allegory with abstraction alone, however, and, in another dubious equivalence, also at times with Neoplatonic spiritualism; he similarly conflates literary allegory (allegory as narrative or dramatic form) with allegoresis (allegory as exegesis). In short, his sense of literary allegory is questionable, if not deficient. He would, in effect, consider the deictic grounding of allegory in narrative, in materiality and temporal process, a type of history, and would consider its nondeictic concepts, ideas, and ideals alone, allegory.[27] To the contrary, even aside from the special case of historical allegory, as a form literary allegory is *grounded* in matter and movement.

Reaching behind Lewalski's argument to her Auerbachian source, Luxon, whose sights in *Literal Figures* set finally on the writings of John Bunyan, wants to discredit Auerbach's distinction between typology and allegory not by questioning his use of the latter term, as I do, but by demonstrating that Auerbach empties "out the category of the historically real" and unwittingly equivocates in his use of the terms "*historical, historicity,* and *history*" (43, 51, 61). By stopping with an English translation rather than returning to Auerbach's original German, however, Luxon underestimates Auerbach's subtlety and historical awareness, and he slights both Auerbach's distinction and his argument as a whole by simply assuming a materialist definition of history, apparently untainted by language, text, or Weltanschauung, an innocence of which Auerbach is unlikely to have been guilty.[28] He also misses the anticipation in Auerbach's essay *Figura* of Auerbach's yet more famous study of *Mimesis: The Representation of Reality in Western Literature*, very much the study of a reality that changes, along with and inseparably from its differing representations.[29] Indeed, in *Figura*, Auerbach's combination of *konkret* and *inner* ("concrete" and "inner") with *Geschichtlichen*, "historical truth," or "historical reality," in order to identify and to comprehend his subject, instead of relying on an unprefixed and unsuffixed *Geschichte*, "history," registers his meticulous awareness of the difference between a straightforward historical account and one that manifests a figural (typological) dimension. In what follows, I want to examine Auerbach's distinction between typological history and allegory, briefly considering its relation to mimesis, since this distinction is relevant theoretically to allegory and ultimately to Milton, Bunyan's contemporary.

Roughly in the center of *Figura*, Auerbach concentrates on the figural interpretation of Saints Augustine and Paul, perhaps in this order because of his particular interest in medieval art, focally, in Dante. While stressing the variousness and breadth of Augustine's figural practices, at one point Auerbach summarizes Augustine's method as a metaphorical transfer from time to eternity:

> Even though Augustine rejects abstract allegorical spiritualism and develops his whole interpretation of the Old Testament from the concrete historical reality [konkret Innergeschichtlichen], he nevertheless has an idealism [Idealität] which removes the concrete event [das konkrete Ereignis], completely preserved as it is, from time and *transposes* [*versetzt*] it into a perspective of eternity [English, 42; German, 37: my emphasis].

Translating "konkret Innergeschichtlichen" here as "concrete historical reality" misses the whole point, namely that the historical reality, while tangible, is vitally inner—spiritual and perhaps prophetic or revelatory, if read aright—and that it anticipates, even motivates, the idealistic transposition (*Versetzung*) of the concrete event to the perspective of eternity.[30] A more accurate translation to English of "konkret Innergeschichtlichen," however paradoxical or elusive, is simply "concrete inner history," a profoundly significant history revealing more than places and dates.[31] In a later passage on the Church Fathers but not specifically on Augustine, Auerbach remarks the occurrence of a difference not only between *figura* and fulfillment (*veritas*) but also between *figura* and *historia* or *littera*, "the literal sense of the event related." Here "*figura* is the same literal meaning or event *in reference to the fulfillment cloaked in it*, and this fulfillment itself is *veritas*, so that *figura* becomes a middle term between *littera-historia* and *veritas*" (47: my emphasis on English). The fulfillment cloaked in concrete history looks like the spiritual meaning within it–the *Innergeschichtlichen*, or inner historical truth—a reality at once inside and outside history per se, simultaneously apart from and a part of it. In a way that I applaud, Auerbach is simultaneously characterizing a kind of bifocality and insisting on the substance and significance of appearance and surface, on the inner, deep content of irreducibly material form. Michelangelo's *Captives* come again to mind.

In a passage just before the one in question, Auerbach observes that sometimes there are three stages in Augustine's writings, rather than just two, figure and fulfillment. The three are "the Law or history of the Jews as a prophetic *figura* for the appearance of Christ; the incarnation as fulfillment of this *figura* and at the same time as a new promise of the end of the world and the Last Judgment; and finally, the future occurrence of these events as ultimate fulfillment" (41, 36). For a reader of Augustine's *Confessions*, I would add, these stages correspond to the distension (*distentio*) of past and future, as memory and expectation, presently held in continuity within the attentive mind, the *intentio*. The latter stages constitute the threefold present found in Augustine's dynamic and dialectical understanding of time.[32]

Auerbach's conclusive formulation of the figural view endeavors to balance history with interpretation, the reality of flesh and worldly event with that of the metaphorizing mind. In the European Middle Ages, he explains, the dominant view ("Anschauung") was

> that earthly life is thoroughly real [wirklich], with the reality [Wirklichkeit] of the flesh into which the Logos entered, but that with all its reality [Wirklichkeit] it is only *umbra* and *figura* [shadow and figure] of the authentic, future, ultimate Truth [des Eigentlichen, Zukünftigen, Endgültigen und Wahren], the *real reality* that will unveil and preserve the *figura* [welches, die Figur enthüllend und bewahrend, die *wahre Wirklichkeit* enthalten werde: my emphasis on English and German]. In this way the individual earthly event [jedes irdische Geschehen] is not regarded as a definitive, self-sufficient reality [Wirklichkeit], nor as a link in a chain of development in which single events or combinations of events perpetually give rise to new events, but viewed primarily in immediate vertical connection [ummittelbarren vertikalen Zusammenhang] with a divine order which encompasses it, which on

some future day will itself be concrete reality [Wirklichkeit]; so that the earthly event is a prophecy [Realprophetie] or *figura* of a part of a wholly divine reality [Wirklichkeit] that will be enacted in the future [72, 66].

Two points: the translator's earthly real and his really real, both rendering Auerbach's consistent use of *Wirklichkeit*, strikingly correspond to the real and Real of Van Dyke's conception of allegory; in her conception, allegory even has vertical and horizontal axes, which "continually intersect" as the narrative progresses (45). The translator's effort to clarify Auerbach's usage by adding "concrete" to reality (Auerbach's *Wirklichkeit*) in the final lines actually disregards Auerbach's careful, emphatic, even restrictive use of the German *konkret* ("concrete," "real," "tangible") and inadvertently suggests a confusion not present in the original, despite the translator's understandable wish to negotiate the ambivalent relation of history to truth, and time to eternity.

Treating the Pauline origin of figural interpretation, Auerbach characterizes Paul's transposition of the Old Testament from "a book of the law and history of Israel" to "a promise and prefiguration of Christ" as a combination of "practical politics with creative poetic faith [praktischpolitischen mit den dichterisch gestaltenden Glaubenskräften]" (51, 45). The translator's phrase "creative poetic faith"—more literally, "poetic, formative, belief-force"—is especially noteworthy, given what follows it: Paul's seminal thinking

> transformed the Jewish conception of Moses risen again in the Messiah into a *system* of figural prophecy, in which the risen one both fulfills and annuls [erfüllt und aufhebt] the work of his precursor. What the Old Testament thereby lost as a book of national history, it gained in concrete dramatic actuality [dramatisch-konkreter Aktualität] [51, 45: my emphasis].

Like the transposition from time to eternity or from real to Real in my previous citations, this passage signals the presence of metaphor, indeed a system of metaphor whose description introduces the signature Hegelian word-concept *aufheben*, signifying at once "to raise or uplift," "to preserve," and "to cancel."[33] Thus raised or transposed, as well as partly retained and partly canceled, the precursory Old Testament text becomes one term in an extensive, continued metaphorical structure; it both is and/or is not the other, later New Testament term. Once again, this looks very much like literary allegory, complete with narrative emplotment, so long as allegory is not reduced merely to abstraction or spiritualism—to the nondeictic, or Real alone. Auerbach glimpses the possibility of allegory here but keeps it at arm's length.

Auerbach's suddenly discovering "concrete dramatic actuality" in the systemic, continued metaphorizing of Paul's "creative poetic faith" is at once arresting and revealing.[34] While the whole phrase calls for attention, I'll start with "actuality / Aktualität." This word is extraordinary in the lexicon of Auerbach's *Figura*. As we have seen, Auerbach normally relies on *Wirklichkeit* to designate reality, and often, where the translator offers phrases like "concrete reality," "concrete force," "concrete history," "concrete future," or simply the word "concrete," the German text has other words, which are similar, to be sure, but not identically nuanced in context, such as *sinnlich / -keit* (material, sensuous), *praktisch* (practical, experiential), or *wirklich* (real, true) itself, alone.[35] *Concrete (konkret)* is unambiguously solid, hard—there. What reality is perceived to be and the ways its creative representation, or mimesis, change are, after all, at the center of Auerbach's scholarship, which everywhere registers his care regarding them.

Two other passages in *Figura* cast light on Auerbach's use of "Aktualität" to describe Paul's configuration of the Old Testament and the translator's rendering of it as "actuality." In the first, Auerbach cites in Latin a passage from one of Augustine's sermons, which includes the phrasing "ne substrato fundamento rei gestae," which Auerbach's translator renders, "lest, undermining the foundation of actuality" (39). "Rei gestae" is more literally "of the thing acted" or, somewhat redundantly, "of the thing actually done"— the deed or action. The second passage that concerns me also pertains to Auerbach's lexicon. Having noted that the poles of figure and fulfillment are both "within time, within the stream of historical life," Auerbach adds, "Only the understanding of the two persons or events is a spiritual act [Akt], but this spiritual act [Akt] deals with concrete events [Material des ... Geschehens] whether past, present, or future, and not with concepts or abstractions" (53, 47). In the German text, but not in the English, this act of understanding belongs to the *intellectus spiritualis*, the spiritual, or highest, intellect. Yet the important point for Auerbach is first that it is an act, something experiential or living, and second, that it engages historical persons and events, not merely a-historical abstractions. Actuality for him, as for Aristotle in the *Poetics*, literally and emphatically involves actions—*res gestae*, doings. In short, Auerbach's reference to Paul's *configuration* of the Old Testament as "concrete dramatic actuality [dramatisch-konkreter Aktualität]" looks very much like a memory of, and plausibly an allusion to, Aristotelian mimesis. Auerbach's description of "figural prophecy . . . as a purposive, creative, concrete interpretation of universal history [zielsichere, gestaltende, konkrete Deutung der Weltgeschichte]" only underscores this point (58, 52).

I shall end this excursus on history and allegory by returning to Ricoeur's treatment of *Time and Narrative*, which will serve to illuminate the pertinence of Aristotelian mimesis to Auerbach's view. Ricoeur, introducing his discussion of "mimetic activity (*mimesis*)," first describes this activity as "creative imitation, by means of the plot of lived temporal experience" and adds that it is difficult to distinguish mimesis from "emplotment (*muthos*)" in Aristotle, since Aristotle tends to conflate them (I, 31). He subsequently asserts that Aristotle's significantly entitled *Poetics* "contains just one all-encompassing concept," namely, mimesis, "the [creative] imitating or representing of action in the medium of metrical language," and he also emphasizes that "Imitating or representing is a mimetic [hence constructive] activity inasmuch as it produces something, namely the organization of events by emplotment" (I, 33–34). Still further insisting on the overlap of representation with the organization of action and time, he observes that the subordination of character to action in Aristotle "seals the equivalence" between the "representation of action" and the "organization of events" (I, 37). "The act of emplotment," in short, "extracts a *configuration* from a succession," an arrangement from chronology and a form from time (I, 66: my emphasis).[36]

Not surprisingly, Ricoeur's study of mimesis introduces a comprehensive, sophisticated review of modern theories and practices of history. Among the representative historians and philosophers of history whose work Ricoeur analyzes are Fernand Braudel, Jacques Le Goff, Georges Duby, Karl Hempel, William H. Dray, Georg H. von Wright, Arthur C. Danto, W. B. Gallie, Louis O. Mink, Hayden White, Paul Veyne, and Maurice Mandelbaum. Ricoeur's review intersects with his concepts of "a prefigured time," "a prenarrative quality of experience," and the "symbolic mediation" of all human action (I, 54, 57, 60, 74). His interest focuses on "the configurational [and organizational] operations that connect history to narrative," which, however "tenuous and deeply hidden" they might be, "preserve . . . the historical dimension itself" (I, 227, 230). Glossing this dimension, Ricoeur writes that "History . . . remains historical to the extent that all . . . its objects refer back to first-order entities—peoples, nations, civilizations—that bear the indelible mark of concrete agents' participatory belonging to the sphere of praxis and narrative," that is, of symbolically mediated human action and emplotment.[37] A history (or an ideology) that is so

Introduction   15

purely material as to have eliminated symbolic mediation and configuration is thus illusory, inhuman, and unrealistic.

In a chapter on the "Threefold Mimesis," whose title suggestively recalls the threefold present of Augustinian time treated in Ricoeur's first chapter, Ricoeur's discussion of narrativity and reference returns to his earlier work on metaphor and, for my purpose, further accentuates both the intersection of his analysis with Auerbach's *Figura* and the larger implications of both theories.[38] Ricoeur, writing on metaphor, argues that the referential capacity of language is "not exhausted by descriptive discourse and that poetic [i.e., literary, imaginative, creative] works refer . . . to the world in their own way," namely, through "metaphorical reference" (I, 80). Such reference, as I have previously suggested, is and/or is not; in Ricoeur's formulation, it is also "*as-if*" (I, 45). Recalling Auerbach's use of *aufheben*, such reference at once transposes and raises, partly preserves, and partly cancels.[39] It frees "a more radical power of reference to those aspects of our being-in-the-world that cannot be talked about directly," and the world itself becomes the entirety of "references opened by every sort of descriptive or poetic text" (I, 80). Ricoeur concludes, "Far from producing only weakened images of reality—shadows, as in the Platonic treatment of the *eikon* in painting or writing (*Phaedrus* 274e–77e)—[mimetic] literary works depict reality by *augmenting* it with meanings that themselves depend upon the virtues of abbreviation, saturation, and culmination, as so strikingly illustrated by emplotment" (I, 80).[40] Ricoeur's augmented reality returns us to Paul's configuration of the Old Testament, in Auerbach's view, as "concrete dramatic actuality [dramatisch-konkreter Aktualität]," and more generally to the *transposing* of Auerbach's *konkret Innergeschichtlichen*, via mediating *figurae*, to God's time. As Auerbach himself showed when he read Dante, in the actual practice of transposition (*Versetzung*), materiality, like the stony substance of Michelangelo's *Captives*, can and does assert a claim too strong to be cancelled or broken.

Earlier, I described the intertext as a condition of potentiality and relationship, adding that it comes into being in an act of reading a text. No text speaks to another without a writer, no matter how elusive, at one end, and at the other a reader.[41] For these reasons, textual relations work in more than one way, either from older texts to more recent ones—Chaucer to Spenser or Spenser to Shakespeare, for example—or the reverse: Spenser to Chaucer or Shakespeare to Spenser. T. S. Eliot registers the phenomenon of reversal in "Tradition and the Individual Talent" when he writes, "what happens when a new work of art is created is something that happens simultaneously to all the works of art which preceded it."[42] What happens in the later text can extend, expose, or alter the earlier one interpretively—that is, through perception, or reading.[43] Reflection of one text in another, whether synchronic or diachronic, is also a historically situated reading, or reception, of it, often illuminating precisely for this reason. Interrelating texts, like interrelating philosophical systems or interrelating paintings, afford a way of thinking about significance that does not require on the part of readers a prior translation into another mode or another discourse that is bound to transform the results before they are even established. For writers, as for readers, texts speak directly to texts before and differently from the way they speak when filtered through other codes, structures, and generally more abstractive kinds of interpretation. Specifically fictive, or "poetic," texts speak a language inseparably and significantly bonded to figure and form, including but certainly not limited to traditional generic structures. Such figures and forms are not only cognitive but also imaginative, affective, mnemonic, and variously sensuous—temporal and rhythmic, spatial and imagistic. Such texts are themselves distinctive ways of *perceiving* significance. While they are fabricated from ordinary language and embedded in specific cultures and societies, they are nonetheless a particular, recognizable kind of linguistic form, and, indeed, by this logic, themselves a distinct form of human language and experience.[44]

Reading or, indeed, hearing, the intertext is integral to realization not only of its significance but also of its very existence, a fact helpful in accentuating its instability and relative elusiveness and the necessity of demonstrating its substance persuasively. This recognition of readerly reception, though a truism, bears emphasis. Recognition of any intertext is subject and relative to our familiarity with texts besides the primary one—subject to which other texts we know and to how and how well we know them, as well as to our ability to *share* this textual knowledge with others. A comparative response to a text also makes subtle, as well as more distinct, features accessible to description, rendering them more visible, audible, and, indeed, comprehensible. Here the heightened awareness of the layered complexities of meaning that accumulate and shift over time and the epistemological pleasure of grasping connections that derive from participation in any textual community go some distance toward validating attention to the intertext.[45]

The conceptual and imaginative fertility of the intertext is another of its strengths and attractions. Such intertextuality, by definition involving more than one text and therefore putting more relations in play, *intensifies* awareness of textuality itself, that is, of the condition of knowledge through and within language, surely a vital part of the human condition. Pertinent here is my focus primarily on major, canonical literary writings (perhaps the most major and canonical ones of all in English), rather than on the kinds of writings my other recent books have mainly engaged. Foremost among my reasons for it are their engagement with allegory, their textual complexity and expansiveness, their relative familiarity and importance to any literary tradition in the English language, expressly including an oppositional one, and their practical relevance to the traditional survey course.[46]

In my textual quadrumvirate—Chaucer, Spenser, Shakespeare, Milton—Spenser's writings and especially (but not exclusively) his culturally encyclopedic *Faerie Queene* are *pivotal*. Seldom has a text been more intertextual than this one. Its relations with Chaucer are deep, varied, and defining, perhaps best underwriting my conception of an intertext. With Shakespeare they are recurrent and metamorphic, if more submerged and surprising, and with Milton, they are persistent, critical, and form-bending. While the particular relationship between the Spenserian text and those of the three other writers varies from insistent allusion to chance echo and from single words to large symbolic structures, the plausibility of relationship is always there: explicit statement and precise verbal citation make it a given that Spenser knew Chaucer's writing and that Milton knew Spenser's; Shakespeare's familiarity with Spenser's is also established by specific, recurrent verbal citation. Earlier, I indicated that my strongest allegiances in this book are to practice and demonstration, that reading between texts and the results of doing so are the ground of my own textual pleasure and the core of my argument, even at its most abstractly theorized moments. What follows indicates the directions these readings will take, beginning with the Spenser-Chaucer intertext.

Part 1 offers a series of widely varied reflections of *The Canterbury Tales* in *The Faerie Queene*. Its first two studies treat the narrative personae of Chaucer and Spenser in macro and micro terms: Chaucer's *General Prologue* and *The Faerie Queene* seen from the vantage point of poststructural theory and then from that of linguistic minutiae within Spenser's sixth Proem. My third study, while brief, considers the Chaucerian frame both of *The Faerie Queene* and of Spenser's poetic career, moving from the word "pricking" in the first line of Spenser's opening canto to the final stanzas of his *Mutability*

Cantos and from Chaucer's *Canterbury Tales* to his *Troilus and Criseyde*. Each of these intertextual studies works against the simplistic opposition of sternly moral, allegorical Spenser to wittily ironic, narratively dramatic Chaucer, thus modifying these commonplaces and the tired assumptions underlying them. Taken together, they range over the course of Spenser's romance epic.

The next study, on "Allegory, Irony, Despair," concentrates this revisionary work on the first and last books of Spenser's 1590 edition. It establishes the intertext between Chaucer's *Pardoner's Tale* and Spenser's canto of Despair in Book I and the related intertext between Dorigen's complaints in Chaucer's *Franklin's Tale* and the trio of complaints in the fourth canto of Spenser's Book III: Britomart's, Cymoent's, and Arthur's. This study starts with verbal echoes as a way of suggesting the plausibility of the intertextual context but concentrates instead on relations between Chaucerian and Spenserian texts that are broader—more imaginative and conceptual—than local, and explicitly verbal. As I will show, readers and writers register, remember, and reproduce much else in literary models besides the odd word or phrase. Subtler relations among texts exist and carry meaning: tonal allusions, motifs and images, rhythmic effects, tropes, structural paradigms, ideological formations, and the like. The most historically interesting and engaged interpretations of earlier texts are often found in the texts that reflect and revise not only their content, but also and inseparably their forms, whether these are conceived in philosophical, semiotic, or (analogously) organic terms.

The first of two concluding studies of relations between Chaucer's frame story and Spenser's romance epic, which compose the major Chaucer-Spenser intertext, starts with Spenser's recurring attention to Chaucer's unfinished romances and then moves beyond these to a broader consideration of the Spenserian archive, or "immortall scrine," of written intertexts—words, fragments, whole compositions (II.ix.56). The next study examines the relation of Spenser's Melibee to Chaucer's in the final book of the 1596 *Faerie Queene*, opening out to the relation of Spenser's poem not only to his own poetic beginnings in pastoral, but also to memory, to allegory and narrative, and to history. The implication of allegory in narrative (including the narrator) is an issue recurrent in this part of the volume. Like my study of "Allegory, Irony, Despair," this examination of Book VI will figure recurrently in my final chapter on "Spenser and Milton: The Mind's Allegorical Place."

Part 2, "Agency, Allegory, and History within the Spenserian Intertext," consists of several studies of intertextual relations other than those between *The Faerie Queene* and *The Canterbury Tales*. Further variety in the intertext and a particular focus on questions of agency and cultural influence are my main interests here. Studies in this section treat Spenser's shorter poem *Muiopotmos* and Chaucer's *Nun's Priest's Tale*; then *The Faerie Queene* and, separately, each of the following: Chaucer's *Parliament of Fowls*, La3amon's *Brut*, and Spenser's own *View of the Present State of Ireland*. The last of these studies relates the proverbial expression *Better a mischief than an inconvenience* in Spenser's *View* of Ireland to its broad cultural context, which ranges from law and politics to literature and religion. The first of these studies, an ironic treatment of fate and freedom, determinism and will, generates a Spenserian intertext of allusion and defining contrasts that implies authorial agency, even while questioning the agency of its butterfly-protagonist, and the last instances more strongly the agency of the signifier within a proverbial intertext, in which the writer is every bit as much spoken as speaking. Intervening essays examine the refractive influence of tradition, its productive and its restrictive holds on the present, or, in Chaucer's phrasing, its inherent power, "yfounded stronge."[47]

The second essay in part 2, like the first one, implies authorial agency in order to locate parody in the name of Argante, the sexually perverse giantess of Spenser's third book, whose archival connection with La3amon's Queen of Faerie correlates with larger patterns of parody in *The Faerie Queene*. The less plausible alternative to agency here would be an ironic and inadvertent intertextual enormity, a perversely errant signifier, and this is a possibility lingering in the name of the giantess that cannot be ruled out. Like my chapter on *Muiopotmos*, this one also treats the ambivalence of the natural world for evil or good, pain or pleasure, anarchy or creative energy. Agencies in the remaining two studies of part 2, are tantalizingly mixed or simply elusive. Spenser's Venus and her major Chaucerian antecedent in *The Parliament* offer about as unstable a combination of authorial deliberation and the agency of the signifier—a refracted figure rather than a word in this case—as I can imagine. In effect, this combination is both a skeptical meditation on, and itself a reflection of, the determining force of the cultural past and the agency of the present. Preceding the final study, in which a proverb in Spenser's *View* both speaks and is spoken, "The Antiquities of Fairyland and Ireland" examines the relation between Spenser's fifth book and his *View* of Ireland as itself a reflexive intertext and a meaningful contradiction that to all appearances conveys more than the writer ever intended. In this contradiction, the Spenserian intertext might be said to find a voice all its own. This study of "Antiquities," like chapters 7 and 9 ("*Muiopotmos*" and "Refractions") and the final two chapters in part 1 ("'immortall scrine'"and "*Melibee*"), carries implication for the typological treatment of history, for which material history is the vehicle that remains, that will not be denied, albeit simultaneously and variously the vehicle of other and often higher tenors.

While a number of studies in parts 1 and 2 explicitly engage the subject of allegorical form, and all do so implicitly, part 3, on writings by Shakespeare and Milton, makes allegory a central focus. For both writers, *The Faerie Queene* is a verbally intertextual, as well as an allegorical, or formal, referent. My first study in part 3 considers the ways in which and the extent to which *King Lear* participates in allegorical form. Despite an established but controversial alignment of *Lear* with Beckett's absurdist dramas or, at the alternative extreme, with Dante's *Purgatorio*, its relation to allegory has long proved controversial, largely because of simplistic and unhistorical conceptions of this form. To these, *The Faerie Queene*, the allegorical poem in English par excellence, administers a powerful antidote. Aside from specific echoes and related, interwoven themes and methods, Spenser's romance epic and Shakespeare's tragedy engage and question fundamental binaries in ways that are characteristically salient in Spenserian allegory.

My next two studies of Shakespeare are paired: Shakespeare's epyllion *Venus and Adonis* is read as a seriocomic meditation on the kinds of figures desire generates in the third book of *The Faerie Queene*, and his *Antony and Cleopatra*, is read first in intertextual reference to Shakespeare's own epyllion, which has been seen as a precursor to this play, and then in reference to Spenser's poem, especially the Garden of Adonis. Again the fundamental binaries to which allegory is a formal, cultural corollary are conspicuous: life and death, body and vision, Venus and Mars. As I have earlier observed, however, allegory as process may begin, but it does not stop, with such binaries; instead, when read whole, rather than only through text-bites, it explores, challenges, and can exceed them. Between Shakespeare's epyllion and *Antony and Cleopatra*, I also discuss the surmounting of sexual binarism in Spenser's Garden of Adonis, to which both epyllion and play allude and with which they further relate intertextually, and I examine the gendering of Acrasian fantasies in the Bower of Bliss, whose seductive sorceress has often and variously been compared with Shakespeare's Cleopatra. Here my long-standing conversation with the vitally important critical work of Harry

Berger on language, rhetoric, reading, and all things Spenserian, a conversation that I have often found both inspirationally and oppositionally defining, spills out of the endnotes and into the text. Not surprisingly, it does so in the context of sex and gender. While these chapters on Spenser's Garden and Bower are less focally intertextual than the others in part 3, they are so to an extent in themselves, and within the section as a whole, they are thoroughly so. In addition to providing a point of reference for Shakespeare's writings, Spenser's Garden also makes several appearances in my final chapter on Milton.

The extent to which Milton's *Paradise Lost* participates in allegorical form, like that to which Shakespeare's plays do, is a question entangled in theoretical and historical arguments about what allegory is and how it functions. Milton's epic has been claimed for allegory on disparate grounds ranging from Anne Ferry's "language of metaphor" in the heyday of New Criticism (*pace* Ferry's Romanticized horror of "allegory"), to the unifying, allegorical Idea that Mindele Anne Treip has found more recently in Tasso, to Kenneth Borris' still more recent and didactic application of this idea to the corporate body (a version of the traditional *corpus mysticum*) of the Son.[48] Treip urges as "the direct line of [allegorical] influence, Tasso-Spenser-Milton" (95). In the meantime, Catherine Gimelli Martin's *Ruins of Allegory* has replaced a Spenserian model of allegory, whose example Milton invokes but Martin slights, with a model answering to Walter Benjamin's baroque, Germanic one.[49] Benjamin's Platonized model, derived from the seventeenth-century *Trauerspiel*, or "mourning play," rests on a foundation of ruin, decay, and death.[50] Victoria Silver's *Imperfect Sense*, a perceptive book focused on Milton's irony, that is, on a doubleness that overlaps theoretically with that of allegory, lacks an indexical entry for Spenser. At the same time, the Satanic alternatives in *Paradise Regained*, "Real or Allegoric," which suggest Van Dyke's deictic and nondeictic, or real and Real, loom large in Silver's conception.[51] Within the Milton-Spenser intertext, an issue basic to representation emerges here, and it focally involves an awareness of allegorical form that Spenser made newly significant.

Questions about allegory raised by these studies of Milton, as well as by others on allegory *per se*, provide a constant backdrop for my own study and often come to the fore. They include the following: is early modern allegory in English conceived historically as continued metaphor—Cicero's "chain of words"—within the rhetorical tradition, or does it derive from the informing Idea of allegory, as conceived by sixteenth-century Italian theorists? Conceptually, is allegory the same as abstraction, as Susanne Wofford and

Teskey have argued?[52] Or is it essentially a narrative (or dramatic) form, as posited by Frye, Barney, and Van Dyke, or, instead, a frozen, static one? Is allegory truly metonymic rather than metaphoric at its most radical, as Sayre N. Greenfield maintains, and if so, does not *radical* here mean "reductive," or merely root-like, rather than revolutionary; otherwise put, does allegory merely signal metonymic code rather than metaphoric process?[53] In yet another question, is allegory at bottom a centrifugal or centripetal force? Earlier and current discussions, for all their very considerable strengths, have slighted or been insufficiently sensitive to the dynamic of the Milton-Spenser intertext, which engages and reorients the entire issue of allegory, both its process and its form.

Spenser's engagement of binarism—matter and spirit, in particular—which I consider fundamental to allegory, is thematic, formal, and deliberate. Throughout his writing, his experimental use of form at once participates in binarism and questions or disrupts it. Form in Spenser is reflexive and, as it were, self-conscious. This allegorical engagement of binarism is to a very considerable extent what Shakespeare and Milton find in Spenser and what they engage and develop. Milton may consign the explicit allegory of Sin and Death to hell, but this consignment is more than eloquently allegorical; it also extends way beyond the fabled gates of hell, since it envelops the moving and evolving figure of Satan, who clearly belongs to the narrative. Indeed it does so from the time he conceives s/Sin in heaven, which chronologically precedes his first appearance in the epic. Throughout *Paradise Lost*, Milton, like his avowed "Original," namely Spenser, makes form, both purely verbal and narrative form, speak.[54] Intertextual memory becomes the perceptual basis—literally the allegorized ground—of newly realized and historicized form in *Paradise Lost*.

Most of the essays in this volume have been published individually, although my present introductory chapter, which overarches them and provides a rationale for the volume, and two of the three essays on Milton in part 3, are new; the third of these (actually the first on Milton) has been modified and somewhat expanded. Most other essays have also been modified, sometimes substantially, and the earliest one, on "*Muiopotmos* and *The Nun's Priest's Tale*," has been thoroughly revised to clarify and specify its original implications. As a rule, however, I have not found it necessary or practicable to rewrite so extensively as in the chapter on "*Muiopotmos*" or to update annotations except in the interest of accuracy or important new knowledge.

Comprehensive updating would often have involved my noting another author's more recent publication that overlaps in some significant way with mine and might have included a note to this effect. Blanket excision of repeated points or observations in the essays would have removed needed steps in otherwise autonomous arguments: a large book like this one, which crisscrosses extensive corpora in several centuries, each of which comes trailing historical-cultural contexts and long critical traditions, cannot ask a reader to keep in mind dozens of elaborations that bear crucially on the immediate argument or repeatedly to interrupt the argument to read or reread other chapters. Accordingly, I have tried to strike a balance among allusion to, annotation of, and repetition of my earlier arguments.

My own investment in publishing these various essays engaging the intertext relates more broadly to these considerations. It results from my conviction that together the essays mean a good deal more and to an appreciable extent differently from what each has meant, or now means, alone. Moreover, in integrating essays originally separate, I am able to reflect something of the extraordinary, various, interrelating abundance of these poets, which includes some *discordia concors*—otherness and perhaps even purely logical contradiction within each. If so, albeit still at a respectful critical distance, these essays as a whole approach the capaciousness of poetic thinking without subordinating it to a logical consistency that is at once linearly thesis-driven and culturally gendered, an assertion that will increasingly emerge in the arguments of my chapters themselves, particularly in part 3 of this volume.

For some readers, the real payoff of this volume will come in its chapters on Shakespeare and Milton, which might be said to harvest the arguments of the earlier ones—earlier both as positioned in the volume and, with one notable exception, the chapter on *King Lear*, as originally written. Back reference, both in the text and the notes, abounds in this section. If a reader's interest is solely in Shakespeare or Milton, it would surely be possible to read just the chapters in the part 3, which concentrates on them, but the arguments of each of the chapters in this final part in particular will be significantly advanced, altered, and deepened by a reading of the two earlier parts, to which the late chapters often refer and a grasp of which they largely assume, since sufficiently extensive repetition is simply not a viable option. This volume, in short, attempts as a whole to make available the necessary foundation and background on which the late chapters build and without which they could not have been written.

PART I Allegorical Reflections of *The Canterbury Tales* in *The Faerie Queene*

1. *Chaucer's and Spenser's Reflexive Narrators*

Reports of the "death of the author" in the closing decades of the twentieth century nowadays appear to have been greatly exaggerated. His (sometimes her) presumed demise, to be sure, was strategically useful, not merely in renewing the formalist critique of the intentional fallacy, but also in laying to rest the naive assumption of a unified, autonomous self essentially apart from history and in full control of the unconscious. Arguably, however, it was also misleading and even dangerous, since it tended to trivialize agency, accountability, and any responsibility to history that really matters. In its stead, I have preferred to conceive of the *withdrawal* of (not necessarily by) the author as a *moving* term whose distance from the text varies and shifts, both predictably and unpredictably, and is subject to localized textual evidence, whether literary, historical, or both. Here, it is my intention (for which I trust I'm responsible) to pursue this conception by relating Spenser to Chaucer. I do so first because a narrative voice or narrator is one of the most conspicuous features of Chaucer's writing and one that has dominated much interpretation of it in roughly the past half century, and second because of Spenser's assertion of poetic affinity with what he termed Chaucer's "owne spirit."[1]

Chaucer's *Tales of Sir Thopas* and *Melibee* are the only two *Canterbury Tales* told by a figure representing the poet himself. Together, these *Tales* afford disparate reflections on the poet's craft and the kind of poetry he writes and thus on his identity as a poet: *Sir Thopas* suggests "elvyssh" pleasures, careless play, and a faerie escape from ideological duties; *Melibee* responds to history, responsibility, and prudential care; the one offers recreation, and the other engages the pressures of social reality.[2] Spenser wove memories of *The Tale of Sir Thopas* through the first four books of *The Faerie Queene* and then made the *Melibee* a pretext for the first of the pastoral cantos of Book VI, the crucial canto that precedes and enables the Acidalian vision. Spenser's memories of *Sir Thopas* occur in eroticized contexts: for example, Redcrosse's allusive pricking into the initiation of narrative in Book I and later his reunion with Duessa to consummate his lust, Arthur's dream of the Faerie Queen and his subsequent desire for Florimell, and Scudamour's account in Book IV of his quest for Amoret. Spenser's complementary memories of Chaucer's *Melibee* directly juxtapose imprudent indulgence with its vulnerability to hostile worldly forces. Although explicit memories of *Melibee* are concentrated in the ninth canto of Book VI, their roots reach back to earlier books, notably to the soothing words of Despair in the ninth canto of Book I, and they reach forward to Melibee's capture and death after the Acidalian vision, which Melibee, of course, does not see. Spenser appears to have understood Chaucer's self-representations in terms of the large, symbolic patterns of *The Faerie Queene*, aligning *Sir Thopas* consistently with the pleasure principle and the *Melibee* more specifically, although not exclusively, with its harsh price.[3]

Like Chaucer himself, Spenser also deployed these symbolic valences in connection with his own identity as a poet. For example, the Faerie Queen of Arthur's dream, whose literary origin lies in Chaucer's *Sir Thopas*, affords an ever-elusive alternative to the real Tudor Queen available to direct address in the Proems; the faerie of the dream therefore suggests both a more inaccessible ideal and a fantasized liberation from courtly service to Elizabeth I, including the poetics of courtship. Melibee, the contrasting example, is a pastoral singer who has withdrawn in disillusionment from the court, only to be destroyed by forces alien to his song; his fate suggests that time and history, realities outside the poet's wishes, will nevertheless exact their ruthless due, and it casts a long shadow over the similar withdrawal from court in the 1590s by Colin Clout, Spenser's pastoral speaker and thinly veiled poetic persona.[4]

Spenser's memories of *Sir Thopas* and *Melibee* provide background and motivation for the relation of his poetic identity to the other major locus of Chaucerian self-depiction, hence artistic self-definition, in *The Canterbury Tales*, namely, *The General Prologue*. Along with the *Tales of Sir Thopas* and *Melibee* and the *Retraction*, this *Prologue* is the only sustained instance of Chaucerian self-representation in the Canterbury collection, the Chaucerian text that Spenser's epic recalls again and again. On the face of things, the conspicuous narrator of Chaucer's *Prologue*, who is at once personally allusive and fictive, offers another clarifying reference and likely antecedent for Spenser's narrator. Indeed, if Spenserian narration is to some extent a representation of storytelling and the Spenserian narrator represents the conventional storyteller, as Harry Berger has argued, strikingly similar claims have been made for Spenser's Chaucerian antecedent.[5] On conceptual grounds, which might appeal to an allegorist, such claims as these imply a significant relation between the more fully dramatized Chaucerian narrator and his narration and the more openly rhetorical and abstractive Spenserian forms of these.

A number of other characteristics of *The General Prologue* invite comparison with *The Faerie Queene*, among them its movement from seemingly assured categories and symbols to an increasingly uncertain and self-reflexive awareness of its own construction, an awareness figured first in the narrator's unsteady valuations of the pilgrims and then in his anxiety as he approaches his rendering of the tales themselves:

> But firste I pray you, of youre curtesy
> That ye ne arette it nat my folly
> Thogh that I playnly speke in this matere
> To tellen you her wordes and eke her chere[,]
> Ne thogh I speke her wordes properly[;]
> For this ye knowen as wel as I[:]
> Who shal tellen a tale after a manne
> He mote reherce as nye as euere he canne
> Euerych word, if it be in his charge[,]
> Al speke he neuer so rudely ne large[,]
> Or els he mote tellen his tale vntrewe
> Or feyne thynges, or fynde wordes newe[—]
> He may nat spare al tho he were his brother[;]
> He mote as wel saye o worde as another.[6]

Surely, this narrator protests too much. Again and again, and then yet again, he signals a conclusion, only to continue spinning his apologetic wheels—in fact, for several lines more than I have cited. In order to account for his behavior, we can posit a poet genuinely uncertain about the acceptability of the *Tales* he is about to report; or, recalling the persistence of irony in *The General Prologue*, we can envision a poet who really is not worried at all but still wants to cover himself in case others are, poking fun at the convention of the willing reporter's dubiously sincere apology while he's about it; or we can combine these two figures into a poet who communicates duplicitously through the unstable guise of a narrative persona and therefore both gets to have his worry and to distance himself from it; or, in a final poststructural maneuver, we can forget about the poet altogether and, taking a further plunge into pure textuality, describe the text as the site of awareness, a self-reflexive construct merely figured in an ironized speaker, the text in this case effectually becoming the conscious subject.[7] On numerous occasions, the same interpretive choices play themselves out in *The Faerie Queene*, memorable instances occurring in the Proem to Book V, where the narrator soliloquizes anxiously and at length about the "state of present time," and in the egregiously overwritten description of Una's plight in Book I when Sans Loy assaults her: so penetrating are her "shriekes, and shrieking cryes, . . . That molten starres do drop like weeping eyes; / And *Phoebus* flying so most shamefull sight, / His blushing face in foggy cloud implyes" (vi.6.).[8] The occurrences of such *obvious* candidates for irony are all the more conspicuous in Spenser's writing precisely because they are fewer and farther between than in *The General Prologue*; this is a problematical fact in itself inviting interpretation, and likely related to the generally less fully dramatized form of Spenser's narrative and narrator.

Whether considered book by book or altogether, the general progress of *The Faerie Queene*, which moves from assurance to self-reflexive doubts, also resembles Chaucer's *Prologue* conceptually. With each of Spenser's books, initial assumptions about symbolism are quickly questioned: the bloody cross, the Palmer's rationalizing, Britomart's armor, the merely nominal heroes—that is, the 'mond brothers—of Book IV, the relation of myth and symbol to history in Book V and of pastoral to violence in Book VI. The overall movement from Books I–III, the first installment, to Books IV–VI, the second, is a progression from relative assurance to more pronounced worry and doubt, as well. Although I am not suggesting that the whole movement of Spenser's expansive poem derives from Chaucer's *Prologue*, I think we can observe in them both some similarity of perspective regarding poetic materials, intentions, and achievements, and thus again regarding elements of a *poetic identity*.

The concrete particularity and fictive complexity of portraits in Chaucer's *Prologue* resist consistent allegorical interpretation, but in broad terms these portraits also invite it, since they range from the physical, moral, and spiritual ideality of the knight at the outset to the equally comprehensive and obvious degeneracy of the Pardoner at the end.[9] Moreover, the notoriously ironic non sequiturs of this *Prologue* (e.g., "But for to speke of her conseyence") constitute a form of duplicity, or "other-speech," and they tantalizingly suggest the disruptions of expectation and disjunctions of form associated with allegory proper.[10] If Spenser looked for meaning in Chaucer's *Prologue*, and on the evidence of his writings I imagine he did, the message he found was indirection, whose endlessly ironic techniques were to decenter and define his own doubled and redoubled representations within an allegorical medium, including his own representations as a poet.

In a classic two-pronged consideration of allegory and irony, Paul de Man characterizes "the notion of *dédoublement*, or dividing in two," in a way highly suggestive of the doubled narrative voices of Chaucer and Spenser. *Dédoublement*, which is essential for irony, "sets apart a reflective activity, such as that of the philosopher [or the poet], from the activity of the ordinary self caught in everyday concerns." Reflective activity and the ordinary self are, perhaps, not quite *Sir Thopas* and *Melibee*, eroticized pleasure and harsh reality, but they do not constitute an entirely dissimilar pair, and de Man's development of their valences is further relevant.[11] "The notion of self-duplication or self-multiplication"—*se dédoubler*—de Man continues, is the ironic "relationship, within consciousness, between two selves"; it is an intra- rather than an inter-subjective relationship that realizes "the *distance* constitutive of all acts of reflection" (194–95). The *dédoublement* that is available in a fictive "world constituted out of, and in, language" enables the subject both to differentiate itself from, and to remain within, the [everyday] world (196).

Subsequently, Gordon Teskey makes explicit a connection between allegory and irony that de Man does not fully exploit. He describes irony as allegory's own Other; it underlies and enables allegory in much the same way, I would add, that Hate precedes and enables Love in the cosmic allegory of Spenser's Temple of Venus.[12] As irony underlies allegory, so difference underlies wholeness, and doubleness precedes the conceptualization of oneness, as Una's doubling in the false Una, Duessa's precursor, initiates Una's naming, or cognitive form (I.i.45). In an extension of the relationship between irony and allegory, the irony that pervades Chaucer's self-representations might thus be seen to invite, rather than to exclude, the pervasive allegory that more overtly characterizes Spenser's.

To decenter self-representation through *dédoublement*, however, is not the same as to avoid it entirely. Both Spenser and Chaucer give their narrators a tantalizingly persona(l) dimension that exceeds, but includes, simple use of the first person pronoun. Even before the narrator of the *Tales of Sir Thopas and Melibee* emerges, Chaucer's representative is the more fully (not to say plumply) mimetic figure, an active participant in the pilgrimage and a thoroughly embodied voice, a figure who eats, drinks, and interacts socially with the other pilgrims. Although the narrator is unnamed as a participant within the *Tales* themselves, in the Introduction to *The Man of Law's Tale*, Chaucer is mentioned patronizingly as the teller of lovers' tales "Mo than Ouyde made of mencioun / In his epystels" (xxi^v).[13] Inside manuscript and early printed collections of *The Canterbury Tales*, albeit in paratextual statements that frame segments of the *Tales* themselves, Chaucer is also identified repeatedly by name as the recounter both of two *Tales* and of the pilgrimage as a whole.[14] In more inclusive collections of his poetry, such as the Renaissance editions of his corpus, he is also identified as "Geffray" within *The House of Fame* (cccxvi^v) and named in captions or endnotes as the maker of various other poems.

In comparison, Spenser's name never appears explicitly *within* his poetry, or at least within his English poetry.[15] His Faerie narrator is also a less mimetically embodied figure than Chaucer's Canterbury pilgrim, but like several of Spenser's other speakers, he has nonetheless personalized markers within the fiction itself, for example, "*Mulla* mine" or "my mother Cambridge" (IV.xi.34, 41). At another, considerably more complicated level, Spenser's narrator becomes the socially contextualized speaker of the Proems and the self-citational figure whose words not only recall earlier passages of *The Faerie Queene* but also Spenser's shorter poems, including the personally allusive *Amoretti* and *Epithalamion*, and they likewise image other contours of Spenser's own life, such as his friendship with Ralegh and his final withdrawal to Ireland; and, indeed, in Book VI, the words of the Faerie narrator pass into those of Colin himself.

While the primary narrators of both Chaucer and Spenser acknowledge responsibility for the texts in which they appear, Chaucer's anxious narrator, who disclaims artistic ability, would limit his role to reporting, while Spenser's narrator often identifies himself as the singer of his poem and thereby claims an identity more specifically poetic. Overtly neither a pilgrim nor even a dreamer, Spenser's narrator is more openly the creator of his poem and more openly a fiction. His ambiguous identity as shaper and shaped dovetails suggestively with an increasing cultural concern about the difference between history and poetry, or truth and fiction.[16]

All personalized references, of course, can also be regarded as conventions and potentially as material to be mocked, but there is still an appreciable difference, even within deconstructive norms, between a personally marked text and one lacking such gestures. Form, after all, has significant content. It could be here, in fact, that an internal contradiction arises in any textual theory that indiscriminately levels as convention conspicuous personal signatures in the text. This is merely in practice to discount them in the interest of a meta-narrative characterized by its own self-identity.

Does the absorption of text into meta-narrative, and of personalized reference into convention, leave not a trace behind?

Describing intertextual dialogics, Don Bialostosky remarks that the worst misconception of formalism " 'is to imagine that what does not [directly or explicitly] appear in the text does not impinge upon it.' "[17] While Bialostosky is unlikely to have had the writer specifically in mind, there is no logical reason to exclude him alone, along with his culture, from this statement. Non-exclusion is not the same as attributing ultimate control—originary, causal, intentional, determinative—to the writer, and inclusion of him remains a highly problematical, densely mediated interpretive act, not a literal one.[18] My point is that inclusion remains an interpretive option and one textually grounded—even insistent. The hard question is how to get at it.[19]

There is parody aplenty in *The Faerie Queene*, but reading the Spenserian narrator or, rather, narrators *only* as figures of parody seems to me at odds with the variousness of the poetry itself—perversely, if you will, too self-consistent. Such reading produces a poem that lacks agency and commitment and, more exactly, the urgency and emotional investment of real exploration, including self-questioning. There is too much internal distance in it, if this is a distance always maintained. In Spenser's writing, there is instead an irreducible doubleness—not in the strictly numerical sense, but in the sense of irony, ambiguity, variety, and elusiveness—that nevertheless implicates the poet in suggestive and persistent ways, although it can never be simply equated with him. As already indicated, Chaucer's writing offers a likely precedent for this doubleness, indeed, sometimes this tripleness and quadrupleness, whose conceptual roots emerge in *The General Prologue*.[20]

Within this *Prologue*, the decentering of self-representation is concentrated in techniques of impersonation, by which term I intend a modern dead metaphor that is enlivened—literalized, or more accurately, actively and performatively figuralized—in Chaucer's and Spenser's texts, where one character can literally become—or blend into—another. A second relevant dead metaphor that I would reactivate involves the term "investment." In Chaucer criticism it has been common to debate, then to deny, Chaucer's "investment" in a particular character or tale such as Melibee's, but if "investment" is understood etymologically as a covering or as clothing, as a mask and very possibly an emotionally charged or "invested" (i.e., cathected) one, it offers, along with "impersonation," a specific and suggestive term for discussing Chaucerian and Spenserian storytellers. These storytellers, who dominate *The Canterbury Tales* and appear with a frequency we tend to overlook in *The Faerie Queene*, are at once masks and the ascribed voices that animate them. A mask suggests the same mediation that representation does, but a mask typically has holes and therefore implies something or someone behind it, whether a vacancy, an historical person, or a doubled, deliberately elusive, and fleeting identity, perhaps one that is not unlike the fleeting figure of Arthur's dream or, indeed, not unlike the poet's.[21] A mask could also be a way of representing an identity that is schizophrenic in the currently loosened, unclinical sense—fragmented or momentary, glimpsed, cumulative, multiple, indefinite, and, above all, experimental—even searching.

In *The Faerie Queene*, *mask* is itself a privileged term, occurring in the first line of the Proem to Book I—"Lo I the man, whose Muse whilome did maske"—and later recurring with ironic thematic insistence in the House of Busirane and the fourth and fifth books.[22] In all these instances, the word *mask* is associated with cultural forms—conventional, social, poetic, mythic, personal, and subjective. These are seen to be falsifying but necessary, provisional but also expressive and powerful.[23] Impersonation is likewise an idea—in fact, a conceptual pun—that is introduced early, specifically, and ironically in *The Faerie Queene*. When Archimago, that purveyor of images, separates Redcrosse from Una and masks himself in the sign of Holiness, the armor with the bloody cross, he is said "the person to put on / Of that good knight," namely Redcrosse; thus he literally and duplicitously *impersonates* him, *enacting* the combination of Latin *in* and *persona*, "into the person [of]," an act that Archimago has already anticipated in poisoning the imagination of the Redcrosse Knight. When, after pointedly recalling the first stanza describing Redcrosse, the Spenserian narrator remarks—it cannot be innocently—of Archimago's guise, "*Saint George* himself ye would haue deemed him to be," the whole issue of the reliability or deception of representation is put on the table, and since Archimago is a figure of the Protean poet, the whole issue of self-representation appears here as well (I.ii.11). For Spenser, even more explicitly than for Chaucer, the idea of impersonation is thematized, problematical, and self-reflexive from the start.[24] Moreover, this self-reflection implicates the narrative and the self, or the subjectivity, who in this case, whatever else he is, is the absent-but-not-absent poet.

In Chaucer's *General Prologue* (and in the subsequent *Tales*), there are certain pressure points where the difference between character and characterizer blurs conspicuously, displaying an instability of intention, origin, and identity that is explicitly thematized in the narrator's subsequent apology, which I cited earlier: "Who shal tellen a tale after a manne / He mote reherce as nye as euere he canne / Euerych word." This blending, obvious just often enough to become openly an issue, affords a paradigm of relationship between character and characterizer, mask and masker, voice and projector. This model seems to me to offer the most authentic and suggestive indication we have of the self-reflexive relationship between the narrator of the poem itself and its poet. Throughout the medieval and Renaissance periods, when human beings were thought to share a common essence and the body was supposed to be permeable, its borders open and porous rather than hard-edged, there is considerable historical warrant for such a relationship.[25]

Probably the best known Chaucerian example of paradigmatic blending occurs in the portrait of the Monk. Characterizing the Monk's disregard of monastic rules with increasing engagement and tonal ambiguity (a frequent and psychologically suggestive combination in Chaucerian texts), the narrator remarks of the Monk's dismissal of cloistered confinement,

> And I say his opynyon was good[:]
> Wherto shuld he study, and make him selfe wood
> Upon a boke alway in cloystre to powre
> Or swynke with his handes, or labowre
> As Austyn byd[?] Howe shul the worlde be serued[?][26]
> Let Austyn haue his swinke to hym reserued[!]
> Therefore he was a pryckesour a right.
>
> (B.iii^r)

Whether this passage is mocking or approving, and whether its penultimate line—"Let Austyn haue his swynke to hym reserued"—expresses disapproving mimickery, ambivalent ventriloquism, or the very words of the Monk, is left utterly and deftly unclear.[27] The Monk's attitude speaks through the narrator, and momentarily the narrator's voice enters the role of the Monk, even while the lines framing the passage ensure that the difference between Monk and narrator remain audible and visible. The irreducible doubleness of the passage implies criticism of the Monk but also denies it. What we have here is a version of the blending of one figure with another that Spenser made virtually a hallmark of *The Faerie Queene*, and what is significant in this instance is that the blending involves a relatively mimetic figure of the poet.

The same phenomenon occurs to varying degrees throughout *The General Prologue*, and in the interest of variety, I'll address two other instances of it. The distinction of the first is the narrator's engagement with a good character, the Parson.[28] Reflecting on the relation of the Parson's words to his deeds, the narrator remarks that the Parson explained a relevant biblical passage with a homely proverb:

> And this fygure he radde eke therto[,]
> That if golde ruste, what shulde yron do[?]
> For if a preest be foule, on whom we trust[,]
> No wonder is a leude man to rust[;]
> And shame it is, if a preest take kepe[,]
> To se a shytten shepherde, and a clene shepe.
> (Biv^v)

Again, in the latter half of this passage, the difference between the attitude and even the words of the narrator and those of the pilgrim he describes becomes indistinct, and this momentary indistinction suggests a self-reflexive model for the relationship of the decentered poet himself to his narrator. If read in one direction, namely from Parson to narrator to poet, the model implies that any person behind the mask will be only a recessive figural construct; read in the other, from poet to narrator to Parson, it indicates not only *expression*—literally, a pressing out, a form, a representation in image and word—but also some degree of allegorical projection, however partial, brief, and soon deflected.[29] This latter reading, which starts with an undifferentiated figure of the poet, involves an act of faith in the fact that there actually *was* historically, not an autonomous self, but a poet, a documented and textualized assumption that I do not hesitate to embrace.

My final example of Chaucerian blending occurs in the portrait of the Summoner. Here the narrator reports how the Summoner corrupts justice by reducing it to bribery: he teaches "a good felawe . . . to haue none awe . . . of the archedekyns curse,"

> But if mans soule were in his purse[,]
> For in his purse he shulde ypunysshed be[.]
> Purse is the archedekens hel, sayde he.
> (Bv^v)

The more I look at this passage, the more the two explanatory lines that precede the last, which is a direct quotation of the Summoner's words, sound like the narrator's glossing, and the lines that immediately follow the passage muddy the attribution of attitudes still further. In them, the narrator continues,

> But wel I wote he lyed right in dede[;]
> Of cursyng ou3t eche synful man drede
> For cursyng wol slee, ri3t as assoyling saueth[—]
> And also ware him of a Significauit.
>
> (Bv^v)

Meeting the first three of these lines, which initially seem pious, fearful, and also indignant, a reader is likely to cancel any previous doubt about the identity of the cynical speaker in the lines immediately preceding. "Aha," she concludes, "it was all the Summoner." But then comes the line with a wallop, "And also ware him of a Significauit." The likely speaker of this warning is by all odds the narrator, since the line continues his explanation, even while radically altering its basis. A *significavit* is the sort of writ likely to entail harsh physical punishment, and the one-liner mentioning it casts doubt on the sincerity of the three before it, making their conventional piety sound like the pious lip service that masks a worldly pragmatism wary of fleshly punishment. Their imputed insincerity in turn reaffirms that the cynical assessment of the archdeacon's greed with which all this ambiguity started might as readily belong to the narrator as to the Summoner. Once again, two figures, the narrator and his character—in the dramatic, personal, and graphic senses of this word—have blended. More precisely, their attitudes, or voices, have momentarily become indistinguishable or, from another point of view, they have doubled and become duplicitous. If this duplicity is not Chaucer's as such, being distanced from him through his narrative speaker, it is a *characteristic* trademark of his writing, or poetic identity, and in this way a trace of the poet himself.

Spenser seems to me an incredibly astute student of Chaucer's work, and variously throughout *The Faerie Queene* he—or rather, his narrative voice or attitude—slips ambiguously, duplicitously into a mask or into the techniques of impersonation.[30] This slippage is more indirect and implicit and, like the rest of Spenser's poem, less realistically mimetic than Chaucer's. Recently it caught my attention while I was working on other Spenserian essays, to which it bore an incidental relation. As a critical shorthand, I want to describe the relevant passages in these essays, an exercise that will appropriately be a Spenserian process of reflexive self-citation. One of the passages occurs in an essay on the Giant with the scales in the fifth book of *The Faerie Queene*, who debates with Artegall the justice of the old world order.[31] The leveling Giant's materialistic argument is wholly based on quantity, appearance, and sight: "*Seest* not, how badly all things present bee," he demands and then continues, "The *sea* it selfe doest thou not plainely *see* / Encroch vppon the land there vnder thee?" (V.ii.37: my emphasis). In these lines, the insistent punning (see/sea), which is only nominally and inadvertently the Giant's, is unusually obvious, and it pointedly anticipates the leveling of the Giant himself, who is literally "thrust downe into the deepest maine," and drowned "in the sea" with a narrative irony so pronounced as to be vindictive (V.ii.38, 49). Like Talus' shouldering the Giant from the cliff to the rocks below, this irony participates in violent suppression, as the narrator's subsequent comparison of the Giant to a doomed ship—"misfortunes piteous pray"—which is driven onto the rocks by a "cruell tempest," appears to acknowledge (V.ii.50).

But who is this narrator and what does he have to do with the poet, that is, with an identifiable voice of the text, or with the more specifically personated voice of the fifth Proem, which appears to agree with the Giant? And what is his relation to Artegall, the Giant's virtuous opponent, whose fortunes to this point have often been ironized or strongly ambivalent? Since I read the debate between Artegall and the Giant as a real one with two sides and not merely as a showcase for Artegall's righteousness, these redoubled signs of ironic doubling indicate to me a divided narrator who is invested in both sides and as much engaged in self-debate as is Redcrosse in the encounter with Contemplation. Without turning *The Faerie Queene* into a panorama of direct, neurotic authorial projections or regarding it as an unmediated transcription of Elizabethan culture, we can see in its heightened moments of narrative *dédoublement* a process of self-definition and, again, some trace of the poet's identity.

The second instance of slippage I have recently encountered occurs in Book IV of *The Faerie Queene*, when Scudamour engages Amoret's hand to lead her from the Temple of Venus.[32] Here it is not clear whether the simile "Like warie Hynd within the weedie soyle" refers to Amoret's hand or to Scudamour himself, in either case a problematical reading (IV.x.55). If Scudamour is the more likely referent, despite the fact that a hind is a female deer, the confusion (or conflation) of the roles of hunter and hunted in the simile suggests how much Scudamour, the Knight who compares himself to Orpheus leading Eurydice from hell, is threatened by this Venerean place, to which he has been drawn so unerringly and in poetry of such power. Love and hate are as hard to distinguish here as is the author of their confusion, whether Scudamour, who is the Chaucerian teller of this tale, or the narrator behind him. The appearance of a deer in the canceled ending of Book III, where it images Scudamour, and in the *Amoretti* as well, further enforces its connection with Spenser, the Orphic poet of the *Epithalamion*.³³ Once again, the trace of a poetic identity surfaces in a moment of impersonation, as the narrator's closing line in the Temple episode all but announces: "So ended he his tale, where I this Canto end" (IV.x.58).³⁴ With this line, a specific figure of the figure behind the curtain comes openly into view, and it affirms an allegory of authorship in which the poet himself lies concealed but implicit.

Writing autobiographically, Roland Barthes once asked, "why should I not speak of 'myself' since this 'my' is no longer 'the self'?" Decentered, various, and ungrounded, Barthes' "subject apprehends himself *elsewhere*."³⁵ To apprehend the self is literally to grasp—to seize and arrest it. To the extent that apprehension occurs, its alienated site will preeminently be language, and its means the methods of *dédoublement*, notably including mask and impersonation.

The Bower of Bliss, in which most readers find heightened poetic engagement, affords an especially concentrated example of doubling as Guyon and the Palmer approach Acrasia herself. Their approach is framed by insistent memories of Chaucer's narrative in *The Parliament of Fowls* and therefore of the identity of his poetic narrator, whose character in the *Parliament* resembles the one in *The Canterbury Tales*. Here, "all that pleasing is to liuing eare, / Was there consorted in one harmonee" (II.xii.70). "The ioyous birdes"

> Their notes vnto the voyce attempred sweete;
> Th'Angelicall soft trembling voyces made
> To th'instruments diuine respondence meet.

The sounds of waterfalls "vnto the wind did call: / The gentle warbling wind low answered to all" (xii.71).³⁶ There is no denying the appeal of the narrator's joyous voicing of this place. At this moment we are in a "Paradise" of "melodious sound" and without qualifying reminders of Rhodope, Thessalian Tempe, or "*Eden* selfe" (II.xii.52). Yet the narrator passes next to a critical description of Acrasia, "the faire Witch her selfe." This is his most distanced appraisal of her, and it involves an abrupt and self-reflexive doubling.

Usually unremarked is the fact that this description of Acrasia, which occupies stanzas 72–74 and affords the first immediate vision of her, is specifically the narrator's, since Guyon and the Palmer are not within sight until stanza 76. The narrator attempts objective analysis:

> And all that while, right ouer him she hong,
>   With her false eyes fast fixed in his sight,
>   As seeking medicine, whence she was stong,
>   Or greedily depasturing delight:
>   And oft inclining downe with kisses light,
>   For feare of waking him, his lips bedewd,
>   And through his humid eyes did sucke his spright,
>   Quite molten into lust and pleasure lewd;
> Wherewith she sighed soft, as if his case she rewd.
>   (II.xii.73)

This stanza acknowledges the narrative's implication in Acrasian pleasure more explicitly than the seductive stanzas that precede it, and does so while holding Acrasia at bay. Acrasia's eyes, "fast fixed in his sight," ambiguously and bisexually suggest her sight beholding, his sight beheld, and his sight beholding. In accord with Renaissance medical practices, she seeks healing "whence she was stong," or else she feeds on delight. Thus vulnerable and already wounded, or else consuming, she is variously recipient or seeker. She fears to wake him, yet gets her sustenance through his "humid eyes." The sleeping Verdant has some connection with the vision of Acrasia (in all senses of *vision*), and her fear of waking him implies that they exist for one another in a dream. Acrasia is the dreamer's as the dreamer is hers. No matter how morally the narrative here strives to distance this vision of symbiosis, the poet figuratively—indeed allegorically—acknowledges his implication in its authorship, as, indeed, he must, "The whiles some one did chaunt this louely lay" (74). Tasso's lay it is, but not in English.[37]

When Guyon and the Palmer finally catch up with the narrator, they have crept—the word is Spenser's—through groves and thickets "at last [to] display" Acrasia, Spenserian phrasing that surely sounds prurient enough to compromise their creeping: *display* means "exhibit," but for this etymologically informed poem, it also signifies, for a shocking instant, "fold apart or asunder." Borne on the wings of my allegory of authorship, I am tempted to add that it means "de-implicated," or unfolded in another sense, as well. The reasserted presence of Guyon and the Palmer, with all the de-implicating moral control that it signifies, enables the narrator's second description of Acrasia; the description is emotive, and it alludes to Chaucerian narrative:

> Vpon a bed of Roses she was layd,
>   As faint through heat, or dight to pleasant sin,
>   And was arayd, or rather disarayd,

All in a vele of silke and siluer thin,
That hid no whit her alabaster skin,
But rather shewd more white, if more might bee:
More subtle web *Arachne* can not spin,
Nor the fine nets, which oft we wouen see
Of scorched deaw, do not in th'aire more lightly flee.
                                            (II.xii.77)

More follows, but in a properly sequential reading of the poem, the narrator returns here to an erotic appeal in which the word, let alone the idea, "sin," rhyming with "thin," "skin," and "spin," is barely distinguished. My conclusion from such striking evidence of multiple narrative voices in the Spenserian text would reject both the idea that there is a single Spenserian voice and that there is none. What I want to say instead is that complexity, conflict, and a multidimensional awareness—an awareness subtly, complexly, and equivocably patterned—are characteristic of Spenser's identity as a poet, the details of whose figure—"*Mulla* mine" or "mother Cambridge"—elsewhere gesture pointedly enough toward his life to invite, but not to delimit or define, connections. Thus the poet I describe is a personal, not an impersonal, pronoun, and he is also a figure whose essential humanity may lie—may even lie punningly—precisely in his decenteredness. In Manfred Frank's *Neostructuralism*, it would lie in the determinacy needed even to determine that it is, indeed, indeterminate.[38] And yet it *would* lie there.

2. *What Comes After Chaucer's* But *in* The Faerie Queene

The bearing of an article by Talbot Donaldson called "Adventures with the Adversative Conjunction in *The General Prologue* to *The Canterbury Tales*; or, What's Before the *But*?" on the Proem to Book VI of *The Faerie Queene* is unlikely, indirect, and illuminating. Donaldson's article examines how the illogical use of *but* in Chaucer's *Prologue* indicates the pressures of a mind "made nervous by the complexities of its own discourse, worried by subtle implications dimly perceived but not openly recognized, or harassed by emotional responses to the material it is trying to order." Familiar examples of such subjective usage occur in the portrait of the Prioress: "But, for to speken of her conscience"; in that of the Knight: "His hors were goode, but he was nat gay"; in that of the Wife of Bath: "But she was somdeel deef, and that was scathe."[1] The same article might be seen as further evidence of the presence of a dramatic persona in *The General Prologue*, although Donaldson resolutely avoids making this claim explicitly; he does observe, however, that while "Chaucer's narrator in the Prologue is capable of both logical and illogical *buts* . . . he produces the latter in a majority of two to one—which is one reason why the Prologue is such interesting poetry."[2]

Turning from Donaldson's "Adventures with . . . *But*" to Spenser's sixth Proem, I encountered what seemed a curiously familiar phenomenon, the recurrence of logical and illogical *but* no less than eight times in the twenty-seven lines of stanzas 4 to 6. This recurrence, whether conjunctive (five times) or prepositional (three times), is an intensification of Chaucerian practice in *The General Prologue*, and, as if its cumulative effect on the tone of Spenser's Proem were not already unsettling enough, it is further reinforced by other adversative and concessive constructions (*yet*, four times; *though*, twice) and made still more noticeable by equivocal reference and by lexical ambiguity. Doubleness—duality and, indeed, duplicity—is in the warp and woof of these stanzas:

Stanza 4:

> Amongst them all growes not a fayrer flowre,
>   Then is the bloosme of comely courtesie,
>   Which *though* it on a lowly stalke doe bowre,
>   *Yet* brancheth forth in braue nobilitie,
>   And spreds it selfe through all ciuilitie: (5)
>   Of which *though* present age doe plenteous seeme,
>   *Yet* being matcht with plaine Antiquitie,
>   Ye will them all *but* fayned showes esteeme,
> Which carry colours faire, that feeble ties misdeeme.

Stanza 5:

> *But* in the triall of true curtesie,
>   Its now so farre from that, which then it was,
>   That it indeed is nought *but* forgerie,
>   Fashion'd to please the eies of them, that pas,
>   Which see not perfect things *but* in a glas: (5)
>   *Yet* is that glasse so gay, that it can blynd
>   The wisest sight, to thinke gold that is bras.
>   *But* vertues seat is deepe within the mynd,
> And not in outward shows, *but* inward thoughts defynd.

Stanza 6:

> *But* where shall I in all Antiquity
>   So faire a patterne finde, where may be seene
>   The goodly praise of Princely curtesie,
>   As in your selfe, O soueraine Lady Queene,
>   In whose pure minde, as in a mirrour sheene,   (5)
>   It showes, and with her brightnesse doth inflame
>   The eyes of all, which thereon fixed beene;
>   *But* meriteth indeede an higher name:
> *Yet* so from low to high vplifted is your name.[3]

Occasionally the syntax of this Proem has provoked a passing comment, but to the best of my knowledge the recurrence of *but* and of other related syntactical constructions, all deployed with increasing subjectivity, has never seemed especially significant to readers of Spenser. Yet the fact of such recurrence is truly remarkable, and this feature of the Spenser-Chaucer intertext is what Donaldson's article led me to notice.

Whereas in Chaucer's *General Prologue*, syntax that is illogical in sequence, ambiguous in effect, and subjective in character mainly serves narrative realism—an artful impression of verisimilitude—in Spenser's Proem to Book VI it serves a realism that is essentially conceptual. In the *Prologue* it expresses an illogical or ambiguous relation between one aspect of human behavior or appearance and another; in the Proem it expresses a similar relation between an antique ideal, at once mythic and visionary, and the "forgerie" of present time. In both works, however, such syntax also indicates a dynamic, developing process. Whether seemingly a visual and narrational process (Chaucer) or a visionary and self-expressive one (Spenser), it is thus a truly temporal process, whose meaning is accretive, continuing, and incomplete except when grasped and held as a totality. This process, like the syntax that shapes it, embraces qualifications, contrasts and negations, objections, exceptions, and limitations that cannot be rationalized or otherwise eliminated without distortion. Both processes, or forms, are versions of a poesis that is simultaneously cognitive and affective.

Although I have suggested that the forms of realism served by this process differ in *Prologue* and Proem, I do not want to imply that they exclude one another rigidly. Chaucer's portrait of the Parson, for example, focuses at least nominally on a particular parson, but in more sustained and specific terms it also treats the relation of an ideal to present corruption and in this way resembles Spenser's sixth Proem. When Chaucer's seeming realism is most Spenserian in the *Prologue*, however, his procedures are in some respects least Chaucerian: the portrait of the Parson is virtually devoid of the irony of immediate, dramatized observation. Although it is full of satire of the lazy, self-serving parsons not present dramatically on the pilgrimage, it never satirizes the good Parson himself nor even has a few well-padded belly laughs at his expense, as happens with the Clerk. Curiously enough, these distinctions have a syntactical corollary. The portrait of the Parson is studded with *buts* (seven of the thirty-seven adversative uses of *but* Donaldson finds in *The General Prologue*), but most of these are basically logical rather than illogical uses; for example, "Ful loth were him to cursen for his tithes, / But rather wolde he yiven out of doute" (488–89). Compared with most of Chaucer's other portraits, that of the Parson is also more of a set piece. While effective satire, it is less a process of perceiving the particular Parson than a rational assessment or disciplined statement of the more general gap between parsonical ideal and parsonical reality.

Coincidentally and somewhat superficially, Spenser's Proem to Book VI might resemble the atypically Chaucerian portrait of the Parson, but Spenser is most truly Chaucerian when his perceptual procedures in this Proem resemble those of the illogical and ambiguous observer of other portraits in *The General Prologue*. Further, they are far more typically Chaucerian than they are in the first Proem of *The Faerie Queene*. In this Proem, when Spenser refers to the Queen actually ruling England, his syntax is essentially logical and unambiguous, and his image of her, while iconic, allusive, and laudatory, is, like the brilliance and purity of crystal, atemporal and static. In the sixth Proem, however, the Queen is actually, rather than ideally, realer than in the first, and ambiguous or illogical syntax—the syntax of duplicity, as I shall call it—focuses on her person. This last fact makes Spenser's relation in this Proem to the duplicitous Chaucer of double meanings—the Chaucer of irony, ambiguity, and equivocation—even more pronounced, despite the characteristic differences in form (narrative as against conceptual realism) between their writings that in this instance remain firmly present. When Spenser is most Chaucerian in the Proem to Book VI, he is thus least Spenserian—if by Spenserian we mean the poet of the Proem to Book I, whose conception of the real Queen, the actual Elizabeth, is idealized and, because less complexly human, perhaps poetically less interesting. It should be obvious that I find such a definition of Spenserian far too limited and, indeed, too static, accounting as it does for a very small portion of *The Faerie Queene*.

The first three stanzas of Spenser's Proem to Book VI do little more than hint at the distance between an antique ideal and the present forgery that threatens true vision in stanzas 4 to 6 (cited in full above). But with explicit recognition of this distance only a few lines away, the third stanza glances darkly at trouble in implanting "the sacred noursery / Of vertue" in earth. The poet asks the Muses to reveal to him the nursery of virtue that has been hidden in their keeping from men "Since [ever since or because] it at first was by the Gods with paine [painstakingly, painfully, or along with pain] / Planted in earth."[4] When the nursery of virtue is embedded in earth, its purity—or at least its painlessness—is doubtful, and the origin of its latency—its concealment—is elusive. Yet whether the nursery of virtue is earthly and embedded or latent and visionary, an inclusion of alternatives that the ambiguous syntax of stanza 3 enforces, it was initially derived "From heauenly seedes" and nourished "with carefull labour" by the Muses "Till it to ripenesse grew, and forth to honour burst." The diction of this line suggests the burgeoning of a plant, the opening of a flower, latency revealed, potential fulfilled—ripeness, readiness, presence. That the verb *burst*, the emphatic final word of the stanza, is potentially both a present and a past form (albeit the past tense in stanza 3) reinforces these suggestions and prepares for the use of the present tense throughout the next stanza, perhaps most dramatically in its opening lines: "Amongst them all [blossoms in the nursery] growes not a fayrer flowre, / Then is the bloosme of comely courtesie." Presence, after all, occurs in present time.

It hardly seems accidental, given the associative process of the human mind, that specific reference to the "present age" should come in stanza 4. Here opposition between the present and the past, the actual and the ideal, becomes open. Now "present age" is contrasted directly with "plaine Antiquitie," a mythic time and condition continuous with its origins in "the sacred noursery / Of vertue." Explicit reference to present time entails further syntactical complications, specifically a movement from an ambiguity of continuity and inclusion in stanza 3 (earthly and embedded or latent and visionary) to an ambiguity of discontinuity and fragmentation. This movement is progressive in stanza 4. Twice, once on either side of line 5, the stanza's midpoint, the construction "though . . . Yet" occurs. In the first instance, concession is made to the "lowly stalke" of courtesy's flower, which nevertheless ("Yet") blossoms "in braue nobilitie" and spreads through "all ciuilitie." Thus described, the relation of flower to stalk is less adversative than merely conjunctive and continuous. In the second instance, however, a far more intensely adversative pairing of *though* and *yet* occurs, and the fact that the same construction has already occurred in this stanza makes its recurrence in virtually the same position within the later lines conspicuous. This time concession is not to lowliness but, it would appear, to its opposite, the "present age," seemingly plenteous in courtesy, yet really in an adversative relation to "plaine Antiquitie." This second time, *yet* is a conjunction only in name. Even syntactically the present is "matcht" with the mythic fulfillment of virtue that occupies the first half of the stanza, and the present is found wanting:

> Of which [blossom(s) of courtesy: "all," "it"] though
>   present age doe plenteous seeme,
> Yet being matcht with plaine Antiquitie,
> Ye will them all but fayned showes esteeme,
> Which carry colours faire, that feeble eies misdeeme.

The word *all* occurs both in the first line of stanza 4, where it expresses inclusiveness of reference ("Amongst them all growes not a fayrer flowre"), and in the eighth line, as cited just above, where it participates in duplicity, in the ambiguity of deception. By line 8 earthly reality not only opposes and belies the reality of vision but very nearly obliterates it. The strongest meaning of lines 7 to 9 is that all the blossoms of courtesy in the present age are merely showy pretenses misjudged by the morally insensitive, of whom the present age would appear to consist. Weakly and rather unpersuasively, however, these lines allow a less negative reading. If we take *being* in line 7 to modify *age* rather than *which . . . them all*, the blossoms might still be considered true, albeit subject to misjudgment; in that case their latency would remain relevant, and their virtuous potential would remain real. Alternatively, it is also conceivable, if unlikely, that *being* modifies *Ye* in line 8 and thereby refers essentially to the failures of perception, the misjudgments, of the poet's present audience. Such misjudgments would imply a measure of human control, along with human culpability, and conversely at least some possibility of regeneration. The one fact unambiguously clear at the end of stanza 4, however, is that syntax has become less than tightly logical. Indeed, it has become perplexed and downright treacherous.

The theme of perception might be regarded as the corollary of illogical syntax and especially of adversative constructions in the stanzas that follow. As we have seen, this theme too is introduced in the closing half of stanza 4 and especially in lines 8 to 9 ("seeme," "showes," "eies misdeeme"). Although the *but* in line 8 is a preposition, it is nonetheless significant as an anticipation of a whole chorus of *buts* in stanza 5, whose keynote it thereby intensifies: "But in the triall of true curtesie, / Its now so far from that, which then it was." This *but*, emphasized by its position as the first word of the first line of stanza 5, is clearly the adversative conjunction, yet it is also a dubiously logical use of it. Exactly what the opening of stanza 5 is adverse to is not readily apparent. The opening lines merely heighten the primary meaning of the end of stanza 4: there we read that present courtesy is showy pretense and now that it is so far from what it was "That it indeed is nought but forgerie." In strictly logical terms, the conjunction that opens stanza 5 should be *and* rather than *but*, whose illogical presence is made still more conspicuous by the four *buts* that troop after it in the same stanza. The first of these—"nought but forgerie"—is prepositional or probably so, because when perceived for long in the adversative context of stanza 5, it threatens to become a syntactical pun (i.e., "nought . . . but [is] forgerie"). As used in the line, this prepositional *but* demonstrates its near identity with the adversative conjunction, a historical likeness that the *OED* more than once remarks.[5]

The adversative conjunction that opens stanza 5 ("But in the triall of true curtesie") is truly logical only if we take it to be in opposition to the less likely but more positive readings of the end of stanza 4, which I have detailed above, namely, the possibilities that the latent blossoms of courtesy remain relevant and could be available to an audience deeming rightly. But this logical interpretation seems farfetched at best and entirely inaccessible to one not reading with pickaxe and thumbtacks. It serves mainly to show how much less the poet's syntax responds here to logic than it expresses something like the pressures of a mind "made nervous by the complexities of its own discourse, worried by subtle implications dimly perceived but not openly recognized, or harassed by emotional responses to the material it is trying to order"—Donaldson's characterization of the effect of the illogical use of *but* in Chaucer's *Prologue*. Further, the poet's syntax—or, to speak more sensibly, the poet-speaker of the sixth Proem—appears to do so knowingly. His syntax is not itself the butt of its own illogic, as happens so often when the Chaucerian narrator, the dramatic persona of *The General Prologue*, in perceiving his fellow pilgrims unwittingly expresses the irony and indeed the illogic of being fallibly human. Since irony is a type of ambiguity or double vision, the Chaucerian narrator, unlike the poet of the sixth Proem, more typically embodies a verbal duplicity he does not fully recognize or control.

Roughly the central portion of stanza 5, lines 4 to 7, increasingly extends courtesy into a context of opposition, exception, and limitation, an adversative context in which doubleness and deception, both forms of disunity, are implicit. Predictably in these lines the theme of true or false perception becomes more insistent, and the poet's dis-ease, like the doubleness of his expressions, becomes more pronounced: present courtesy is nothing but forgery,

> Fashion'd to please the eies of them, that pas,
> Which see not perfect things but in a glas:
> Yet is that glasse so gay, that it can blynd
> The wisest sight, to thinke gold that is bras.

In the first two of these lines, however, the courtesy that is fashioned to please begins to sound morally more mixed than simply false and suggests the human condition more than it does the abstraction Falseness. The verb *pas* means either "pass by" or "pass away," and the preposition *but* (potentially an adversative conjunction: i.e., "but see in a glass") means either "except" or "unless." Thus the faulty sight of the heedless is not readily distinguished from the only sight of perfection available in a mortal existence. The clear echo in line 5 of the famed verse from I Corinthians 13:12, "For now we see through a glass darkly," strongly enforces both readings. At the same time it enforces the reality of the gap that has opened between ideal perfection and the conditions of human existence—between virtue visionary and virtue embedded, between the fairest flower of courtesy and the feigned show. In the sixth and seventh lines of this stanza, it is not surprising to find a flicker of sympathy along with great sadness for the gayness of a glass that dazzles the wisest. As perfection becomes more elusive and unearthly, it becomes in a material sense less real.

"But vertues seat is deepe within the mynd, / And not in outward shows, but inward thoughts defynd": these final lines of stanza 5 redefine and relocate virtue in a seeming effort to save its relevance and vitality, its present reality. They do so logically but very abruptly. The two adversative conjunctions within them testify to the discontinuity of "outward shows" and "inward thoughts"—of the mind and the world outside it. If these two realms are related, it is as adversaries now. Even the conjunction *and* in line 9 is drawn into the context of opposition, a logical plus thus becoming in point of illogical fact a minus: "And not." Still, at the end of the stanza, the interior realm, while limited and again hidden, albeit this time "deepe within the mynd," is humanly real. By suddenly and emphatically reinterpreting the hopeless opposition between the ideal or true and the actual or false as an opposition between inner truth and outer falseness, the poet renders truth, living truth, more exclusively subjective. He thus limits but preserves its integrity and does so with an abruptness that is more emphatic than confident or rhetorically persuasive. On the distant horizon, Milton's "paradise within" comes into view.

The *but* with which stanza 6 opens may well be the most suspect adversative in the whole Proem. Having defined virtue as inward in the last two lines of stanza 5 and there having twice asserted the adversative conjunction ("But vertues seat . . . but inward thoughts"), the poet now begins, "But where shall I in all Antiquity / So faire a patterne finde" as in you, "O soueraine Lady Queene"? The reader need only try substituting *and* for this opening *but* to measure the unsettling effect of the poet's echoing all those *buts* in the preceding stanza. *And* would have been immensely more reassuring in tone. Instead, as the line now stands, the initial *but* is openly and insistently adversative.

In stanza 6 the poet introduces the Queen, whose presence in this Proem the earlier Proems have led us to expect, and in this one, as in those earlier, his treatment of her becomes finally the index of the relation of present virtue, living truth, to an ideal and visionary antiquity. In stanzas 6 to 7, which close the sixth Proem, however, this relationship bears only a superficial resemblance to that found in the first two Proems of *The Faerie Queene*, and if aligned with the third Proem, it serves to illuminate the poet's uneasiness with the Queen's bright image at an earlier stage of the poem than is often acknowledged.[6] Largely as a result of the emphatic trio of *buts* in the last two lines of stanza 5 and the first line of stanza 6, the beginning of the latter stanza appears contrived or, to adapt the poet's own words a few lines before, pretentiously "fayned" and excessively showy. *But*, the adversative conjunction between the two stanzas, which is in fact a disjunction, sounds at once forced and uneasy. Scrutinized logically, as perhaps out of politesse or policy it should not be, it suggests that the Queen is somehow adverse to an inward definition of virtue because she is an outward show, a suggestion positively bristling with alarming ambiguity. But an outward show of true virtue alive in the present age is scarcely credible at this stage of the Proem.

Strictly speaking, of course, ambiguity itself is illogical and by its very presence contributes to the irrationality of the *but* with which stanza 6 opens. As Humphrey Tonkin has noticed, the phrasing of the lines this *but* immediately introduces further ensures that we cannot be certain whether the location of the virtuous Queen is in antiquity or in the present: "But where shall I in all Antiquity / So faire a patterne finde . . . As in your selfe"?[7] In other words, we are not really sure about her location in time and place, and hence about her true nature and identity. In view of the poet's nervously studied contrivance in beginning the stanza, scrutiny of his logic seems rather tactless, but failure to scrutinize it is mere complicity. The poet's compliment to the Queen here is courteous in some sense, but it is also ambiguous—neither wholehearted nor single-minded, perhaps despite half himself. It is equivocal, and he seems troubled by the real possibility that there may be in it only a flattering show of true courtesy.[8]

In the eleventh canto of Spenser's Book V an exchange between Artegall, the Knight of Justice, and Burbon, a Knight whose name and story allude to recent French history, provides a relevant gloss on what is happening in stanza 6. Artegall rebukes Burbon for timeserving, and Burbon, for his part, denies that he is false to truth, claiming that, when necessity constrains, "To temporize is not from truth to swerue, / Ne for aduantage terme to entertaine." Artegall's rejoinder is uncompromising: "Fie on such forgerie . . . Vnder one hood to shadow faces twaine. / Knights ought be true, and truth is one in all" (stanza 56). Since Burbon's figure openly embodies contemporary, topical reference, Artegall might as well have said "present forgerie" and thereby have anticipated the poet's disillusioned view in the Proem to Book VI. In this Proem, Artegall's and Burbon's dissenting voices, one pragmatic and expedient and the other idealistic and visionary, have been together submerged rather than silenced or totally separated. It is as if the poet had swallowed both voices, without being himself taken in by either one. Yet knowingly, as a result of this infolding, the poet's own voice, like his syntax, has become fundamentally more duplicitous.

The rest of stanza 6 confirms the essential duplicity of perception in the Proem, but, ironically, in this way duplicity frees the poet to fashion an alternative to it: perfection needs only truth; imperfection needs fiction. The one need only be found, expressed, and celebrated; the other needs to be bettered and transformed or else simply escaped. In the first four lines of the stanza the poet has asked where he can find so fair a pattern "where may be seene / The goodly praise of Princely curtesie" as in the Queen, and he has implied visual, tangibly showy associations both through his diction ("faire ... patterne ... seene") and by directing a rhetorical question with dramatic presence to the Queen. Now, immediately following this direct address to her ("O soueraine Lady Queene"), he suddenly upends the logical assumptions he has invited from the opening word of the stanza ("But") and interiorizes, literally implants, the pattern of courtesy in the Queen's mind, "In whose pure minde, as in a mirrour sheene, / It showes." Evidently queenly virtue is not an "outward show" after all but an inward one, and, assisted by a few more carefully planted verbal echoes, an associative thinker can hardly help adding, an "inward thought," as perhaps the virtuous Queen herself is also to be "defynd." I have earlier observed that inner virtue may be real, but in a limited, partial way.

But queenly virtue is not quite so easily implanted or, for that matter, transformed. The "mirrour sheene" (bright, shining, resplendent) is not so readily kept distinct from the "glasse so gay" in the preceding stanza that dazzles the "wisest sight," including the poet's, perhaps. Distinguishing mirror from glass is made all the more difficult by the acclaim following the assertion that "It [presumably the pattern] showes," namely, "and with her brightnesse doth inflame / The eyes of all, which thereon fixed beene." Although in good Spenserian usage the possessive pronoun *her* means "its" here and refers to the pattern, in the present context it cannot avoid suggesting the Queen herself and thereby drawing our gaze outward. It offers to direct our attention from intangible pattern to tangible sovereign. The verb *inflame* does nothing to counter these merely phenomenal or showy suggestions, and, in conjunction with "The eyes of all," it could be taken to reinforce them. Further, the appearance of *but* as the first word in the next line and as the seeming successor to *inflame* momentarily acts to confirm an impression of excess: "doth inflame . . . But meriteth" something better than inflammation.

The concluding lines of stanza 6—"But meriteth indeede an higher name: / Yet so from low to high vplifted is your name"—extend to the Queen the compliment adversative-concessive. At this point in the Proem *but/yet* is surely a conspicuous combination, and elliptical syntax in the first of these lines renders it all the more so. In addition, the subject of *meriteth* in line 8 is elusive; I take it to be *patterne*, in which case "an higher name" than "Princely curtesie" is the meaning intended. Since the *but* beginning line 8 is clearly adversative, it requires a point of reference earlier in the stanza that is negatived, limited, or otherwise qualified here, and, once we determine that the referent is not in the inflamed eyes of the lines just preceding, thus canceling our momentary impression that it was to be found there, "Princely curtesie" or "praise [praiseworthiness, virtue] of Princely curtesie" five lines earlier becomes the logical candidate. But in this case the rich rhyme between lines 8 and 9 ("name"/"name") actually qualifies sharply the Queen's virtuous status because it suggests a division between "an higher name" and "your name" and therefore implies that the comparative referent in line 8 is the Queen's name: "an higher name than yours" is the logical expectation of the syntax in lines 8 to 9, and the seemingly anticlimactic rich rhyme ensures that we attend closely to the meaning of these lines.[9] Curiously enough, had line 8 begun with *and* rather than *but*, or had line 9 begun with *and* rather than *yet*, or had either line ended differently, both lines might have afforded straightforward adulation. As they stand, however, careful, deliberate, and duplicitous, they fit the larger pattern of stanza and Proem and make editorial tampering unjustified.[10] Forcefully and simultaneously, they suggest both the real imperfection of the Queen's court and its praiseworthy potential, its ever-unrealized worth:

> Then pardon me, most dreaded Soueraine,
>   That from your selfe I doe this vertue bring,
>   And to your selfe doe it returne againe.

In the final stanza of the Proem the Queen and her court are clearly a fiction, idealized and distinct from the present age, a reflection in the inner "mirrour sheene" and not in the outer "glasse so gay." This doubling of the kinds of mirrors (or glasses) is itself a duplicity absent from the first two Proems, but it is also one that clarifies and redeems in the present context:

> Right so from you all goodly vertues well
> Into the rest, which round about you ring,
> Faire Lords and Ladies, which about you dwell,
> And doe adorne your Court, where courtesies excell.

Having finally acknowledged the essential duplicity of the Queen, having realized not only poetically but even syntactically in the Proem that she is Una only in inner vision and dark conceit, the poet can celebrate her truly and faithfully as fiction.

It may be the essential duplicity of human experience—complexity, ambiguity, irony, illogic, deception—that finally brings the major works of Chaucer and Spenser together, different as they remain in some respects, and this duplicity that leads them to employ similar formal techniques. Employment of the techniques and devices of duplicity by both poets—here their deliberate use of illogical syntax and of illogical adversatives in particular—suggests the existence of a linguistic bedrock of comparison that redefines the character of the Chaucer-Spenser intertext and illuminates what Spenser meant in *The Faerie Queene* by describing Chaucer as the "well of English vndefyled" whose spirit survived in Spenser himself (IV.ii.32, 34).

3. *"Pricking on the plaine"*: Spenser's Intertextual Beginnings and Endings

The opening line of the first canto of the first Book of *The Faerie Queene*, "A Gentle Knight was pricking on the plaine," introduces the Chaucerian intertext and does so problematically.[1] I doubt the Spenserian exists who has not heard some medievalist declare, "I could never get over, or never forgive Spenser, his opening line." Yet for years Spenserians themselves, as if conspiring to accept the poet's insensitivity to his own words, totally ignored the "hard begin" of Spenser's best-known Book. By recalling Chaucer's comic *Tale of Sir Thopas*, knight prickant, this remarkably bold and witty beginning serves notice of the extent to which the writings of the medieval poet to whom Spenser affirmed his affinity will pervade, and complicate, his poem.

The problem in Spenser's first line centers on the word "pricking," which has, of course, the perfectly straightforward, innocent meaning, "To spur or urge a horse on; to ride fast," and the *OED* rightly cites Spenser's line as an instance of this meaning.[2] I am unpersuaded, however, that this is the full range of meaning of the word in this line. My argument that it is not so will be circumstantial and eventually circuitous, but such is the difference between lexical definition and poetic usage: literature—especially poetry and even more especially Spenser—is contextual, that is, circumstantial in the extreme.

The work "pricking," already conspicuous as the first verbal action in the opening line of Spenser's story, occurs in a context designed to render its meaning specifically problematical. Pricking emphatically means *fast* riding, even galloping, rather than ambling. It causes some logical distraction, not to mention visual consternation, to learn that "faire beside" the pricking knight a lovely lady rode "Vpon a lowly Asse" and that "by her" side she in turn led a white lamb on a leash and that lagging, but still within sight, a dwarf, loaded down with sleeping bags and provisions, followed on foot. The time is out of joint, or if not the narrative time, then surely the narrative distance and rate. Within the first stanza of canto i alone, the knight's pricking or spurring on his steed is also narratively discontinuous with the steed's displeasure at the "foming bitt." The steed's disdaining control suggests that restraining pressure is being or at least could be applied to the reins and thus that Redcrosse's rear view mirror might eventually show him that he has outpricked Una, her lamb, and her dwarf—left them, I might add allegorically, in his dust.

Besides being narratively incongruous, the word "pricking" has, like the word "shroud" five stanzas later, a resonance and potentially a doubleness of signification that words like "trot," "gallop," or "amble" simply lack.[3] To begin again with the *OED*, the verb "prick" has also the *figurative* meaning "To drive or urge as with a spur; to impel . . . stimulate, provoke."[4] This meaning commonly carries a generalized association with the agency of nature, appetite, or desire. One of Chaucer's best-known lines in the first sentence of *The Canterbury Tales* describes the lovesick little birds that sleep all night with open eye—"So prycketh hem nature in her corages"—and it thereby affords both an example in point and an instance of the fertile and fundamentally Chaucerian association of such pricking with courage or "corage," the seat of vitality, spirit, lustiness, and vigor.[5]

Although the primary source of the lover's song in Spenser's Temple of Venus is Lucretius' hymn to the Goddess of Love, Lucretian sentiments merge more than once with relevant Chaucerian memories of pricking:

> the merry birds, thy prety pages
> Priuily *pricked* with thy *lustfull* powres,
> Chirpe loud to thee out of their leauy cages,
> And thee their mother call to coole their kindly rages.
> (IV.x.45: my emphasis)

Spenser's lines recall the earlier English poet's association of sexual appetite and desire with nature's pricking. Statistically, the greatest numbers of forms of the word "prick" occur in Spenser's second and fourth Books, and it is reasonable that they should do so. Book II is centrally concerned with the tempering of appetite, and Book IV, with the frustration and fulfillment of desire and, more fundamentally, with the natural force and energy of which love is in good part an expression.

Even at a glance through the Spenser *Concordance*, however, two other occurrences of the word "prick" in Book I are particularly striking, both for the suggestiveness of their immediate verbal contexts and for their Chaucerian flavor or resonance. Conveniently, these occurrences associate the Redcrosse Knight with Prince Arthur, an association eventually to prove of some interest for a reading of the first line of canto i in this Book. In canto ix, Arthur comments on the circumstances that led to his dream of the Queen of Faeries:

> It was in freshest flowre of youthly yeares,
>   When courage first does creepe in manly chest,
>   Then first the coale of kindly heat appeares
>   To kindle loue in euery liuing brest.
>   (I.ix.9: my emphasis)[6]

Nearing the dream itself, Arthur explains how on that fateful day he was "prickt forth with iollitie / Of looser life, and heat of hardiment" (12). Arthur's comments align "courage" and "iollitie of looser life" with the force that "pricks" him into his defining experience, the erotic dream of an elf queen. Like *courage*, *jollity* is a richly suggestive word meaning cheerfulness, pleasure, bravery, or lust.[7] Interestingly, it occurs in Chaucer's *Sir Thopas* (lxxxiv^v) and, in adjectival form—"Full iolly knight he seemd"—in the first stanza of Spenser's story that begins with a description of Redcrosse's "pricking on the plaine." The second occurrence of the word "prick" in Book I that is particularly striking in relation to Redcrosse's initial pricking comes in canto x, when Contemplation describes Redcrosse's route from plowman's state to Faerie court: "Till prickt with courage, and thy forces pryde, / To Faery court thou cam'st to seeke for fame" (66). Here again the word "prickt" is aligned with richly charged words—"courage" and "forces pryde"—implying prowess and desire.

A seemingly inevitable extension of lexical meanings of the word "prick" is persuasively documented by Eric Partridge in *Shakespeare's Bawdy*.[8] Counting substantive and verbal examples, Partridge finds that *prick* appears as a pun eight times in Shakespeare's works. Likely the most familiar instance of this Shakespearean pun occurs when Mercutio observes in *Romeo and Juliet*, "the bawdy hand of the dial is now upon the prick of noon" (II.iv.112–13).[9] And somewhere elusively, richly, naughtily, and comically in-between Chaucer's description of those little love sick birds pricked "in her corages" by nature and Shakespeare's more pointed bawdy is Chaucer's notoriously persistent employment of the verb "prick" in the *Tale of Sir Thopas*: for example,

> Sir Thopas fyl in loue longyng,
> And whan he herde the throstel syng
>   He pricked as he were wode
> His faire stede in his prickyng

So swette, that men might him wring
    His sydes were al blode.
Sir Thopas eke so wery was
For prickyng on the softe gras
    So fiers was his corage
That doun he layde him in that place

to dream of the elf queen who will be his "lemman," he hopes, and will sleep, oddly enough, under his "gore" (lxxxiv^v). Inspired, or at least awakened, by the dream, Sir Thopas climbs gracelessly into his saddle and once more "pricketh ouer style and stone / An Elfe quene for to espye." Examples could be multiplied—mercilessly.

For a reader of Chaucer, the word "pricking" has special resonance and, given a suitable context, a particularly strong, metrically mnemonic potential for association with *The Tale of Sir Thopas*. Excepting the *Treatise on the Astrolabe*, in which *prick* has technically delimited meanings, forms of this word occur eight times in *Sir Thopas*, more often than in any other Chaucerian piece. In view of the relative brevity of *Sir Thopas*—roughly two hundred lines—the association of pricking with this *Tale* is readily available, always possible where relevant, and irresistible when invited.

Spenser's own knowledge of Chaucer's *Tale of Sir Thopas* is indisputable, and the ease, detail, and pervasiveness of his borrowings indicate a thorough assimilation of it. In the March Eclogue of *The Shepheardes Calender*, a tale about two comic boors, he uses one of the two (or more) forms of the tail-rhyme stanza found in *Sir Thopas*, and throughout *The Faerie Queene*, he takes individual words or phrases from it—for example, the Squire of Dames's phrase "many a lane" in Book III (vii. 58) and the Giant Disdain's jacket of "checklaton" in Book VI (vii.43).[10] Spenser finds the name Ollyphant in *Sir Thopas*, plausibly also the name Blandamour (spelled Blayndamour in Thynne's *Thopas*) and, probably, by way of Ollyphant's name and lustful nature, the inspiration for Lust's elephantine ears.[11] In addition, of course, there is mention of Sir Thopas as the confounder of Ollyphant in the 1590, although not in the 1596, edition.[12] And finally, there is Prince Arthur's dream of the Faerie Queene in Book I, for which *Sir Thopas* offers as close a source or analogue as centuries of researchers determined to find a more dignified candidate have been able to unearth.[13] I shall return somewhat later to Arthur's dream, which, to my mind, *Sir Thopas* underlies but underlies complexly, for it seems to me most unlikely that Spenser missed the outrageous humor in a Chaucerian *Tale* he knew so well—humor, incidentally, to which Wyatt, Lyly, Drayton, and Shakespeare all responded.[14]

Nor do I think the view that Spenser either ignored this humor or simply moralized it out of existence is remotely adequate to the wit and subtlety of *The Faerie Queene*.

Given the persistence of a misconception of Spenser as moralistic and humorless, a momentary digression is in order. In the twentieth-century revival of interest in Spenser, this misconception starts, representatively but by no means exclusively, with Josephine Waters Bennett's *Evolution of "The Faerie Queene"* (1942), a volume important enough in its time to have been reprinted in 1960. Although Bennett does not suppose Spenser unaware of Chaucer's humor in *Sir Thopas*, she observes that Gabriel Harvey, Spenser's slightly older and somewhat patronizing friend, considered *Sir Thopas* "morall" and that Harvey so labeled it in his marginalia.[15] She also suggests that Harvey's understanding of *Sir Thopas* was influenced by *The Faerie Queene* (19n32). Unfortunately, however, Bennett misinterprets Harvey's marginalium ("morall") on "Chaucer's Tale" in Speght 1598, taking it to refer to *Sir Thopas* rather than to the *Melibeus*. But it is the *Melibeus* that is consistently labeled "Chaucer's Tale" in both Speght and the earlier Thynne family of editions. With equal consistency *Sir Thopas* is called "the Rime of Sir Thopas." In sum, Spenser's alleged moralizing of *Sir Thopas* has no basis in evidence external to the poem, and Bennett's error might be passed over in silence had it not been more recently resuscitated by J. A. Burrow to become a recurrent reference in discussions of the Chaucer-Spenser intertext.[16] On this note, I want to return to the opening of Spenser's first canto to ask what sense a distant echo of *Sir Thopas*—an available resonance, as I have termed it—would make here and in the subsequently unfolding context of Redcrosse's story.

To begin with, a reader who considers the possibility of an echo can do little more with it at the outset of canto i than I already have: that is, to notice resonance and discontinuities and to be mildly puzzled. A similar effect occurs a few stanzas later when a sudden rainstorm is poured by an angry Jove "into his Lemans lap": we have questions and hints, not answers. But once we have grasped the relation of Archimago to Redcrosse and the specifically erotic nature of the dream Archimago provokes, the incongruous—indeed disunified—aspects of our initial impression of Redcrosse become increasingly significant. Increasingly, we realize their potential. Archimago, persistently termed the old man or aged sire, is no more an exclusively external tempter of Redcrosse than the nature of old Adam—the old man as opposed to the new—is external to humankind. The dream Archimago provokes rises out of Redcrosse's own nature, and it reveals the knight's failure to reconcile the pricking of his "corage" with his faith, the force and the energy of his human nature with the form and purity of truth. The word "prick"—conspicuous in the first line of Redcrosse's story and discontinuous with the immediate narrative context—foreshadows this larger, moral discrepancy, making it both more comprehensible and more inevitable–ironically, if perversely enough, more natural.

Prince Arthur's dream of the Faerie Queen adds another dimension to our initial impression of Redcrosse. As Patricia Parker has shown, Arthur's dream is loaded with verbal memories of Redcrosse's earlier dream of a false Una.[17] Within Spenser's first Book itself, therefore, an element of parody, asking for interpretation, underlies Arthur's dream. Allusions to three of Chaucer's stories increase this parody and simultaneously our awareness of the human complexity—possible futility and positive comedy—that underlie, enrich, and also threaten the ideal vision. Perhaps the most striking of the Chaucerian allusions in Arthur's experience is to *The Tale of Sir Thopas*, but there are also pervasive recollections of Chaucer's *Troilus and Criseyde* and one strong echo of *The Wife of Bath's Prologue*. The recollections of *Troilus* glance at a love story with a bright beginning and a blighted end.[18] The echo of the Wife's *Prologue*—"no fort can be so strong / Ne fleshly brest can armed be so sound, / But will at last be wonne with battrie long" (ix.11)—recalls her mock harangue on behalf of hapless husbands one through three: "She may no while in chastite abyde / That is assayled on euery syde . . . men may nat kepe a castel wal / It may so long assayled be ouer all" (xli^r).[19] The memory of Chaucer in Spenser's lines thus glances both at the failure of human virtue and at the comic vitality of a thoroughly untamed virago.

Skeptical distancing of Arthur's ideal vision is to an extent inevitable in these Chaucerian allusions, but rather than merely mocking this vision, the delicate layering of parody that underlies it also deepens our awareness of its human relevance. Much the same kind of ironic resonance and specifically Chaucerian parody underlie both outset and end of *The Faerie Queene*, both the ambiguously "gentle" knight's "pricking on the plaine" and the poet's farewell to this world and this poem in the final stanzas of the Mutability Cantos. Like Arthur's dream, the Chaucerian resonance that thus frames the entirety of the poem we have is informed with the ambivalent potency of the physical world, the potency of natural appetite and natural time.[20]

In the interest of a specifically Spenserian closure, which is, like circle and cycle, properly circuitous, I want to extend these observations on the Chaucerian frame of *The Faerie Queene* to the Chaucerian character of

Spenser's poetical career as he himself evidently framed it. Spenser's poetic début, *The Shepheardes Calender*, like his grand finale, *The Faerie Queene*, recalls Chaucer at its outset and again at its end, and together these two poems, one pastoral and one romance epic, enclose the poet's progress.[21] In *The Calender*, Immerito's initial address and final farewell to his poem—"Goe little booke" and "Goe lyttle Calender"—allude simply and umistakably to Chaucer's *Troilus*: "Go lytel booke, go my lytel tregedye"

> But subiecte ben vnto al poesye
> And kysse the steppes, where as thou seest pace
> Of Vergyl, Ovyde, Homer, Lucan, and Stace.
> (ccxviii^v)

Spenser similarly cautions his *Calender* not to match with the "poesye" of his predecessors "But [to] followe them farre off, and their high steppes adore."

In the penultimate stanza of the Mutability Cantos, as John Pope, quoting Talbot Donaldson, has written, Spenser's profoundly ambiguous lines on the doubleness of the human condition again recall the ending of Chaucer's *Troilus*.[22] But with benefit of a fuller Chaucerian intertext, they do so more subtly and richly. Condemning the world in lines which, in Donaldson's words, "poignantly enhance the very thing that he is repudiating," Chaucer cautions "yonge fresshe folkes, he or she" to think "al nys but a fayre / This worlde that passeth sone, as floures fayre" (ccxviii^v).[23] Spenser's lines speak similarly of loveliness and loss, of pleasure and futility:

> Which makes me loath this state of life so tickle
> And loue of things so vaine to cast away;[24]
> Whose flowring pride, so fading and so tickle,
> Short *Time* shall soon cut down with his consuming sickle.

Thus alluding at once to the ending of Chaucer's *Troilus* and recalling, through the further significance of such allusion, the end of Spenser's own *Calender*, the final stanzas of Mutability come full circle, even as they appear to signal the conscious nature of the poet's intention to end. These stanzas simultaneously continue and conclude, defeat time and acknowledge its destructive power.[25] Their irreducible ambiguity is far distant from the narrative discontinuities at the outset of the poem, but circuitously, through a matrix of association and resonance, they lead us back to beginnings.

4. *Allegory, Irony, Despair: Chaucer's* Pardoner's *and* Franklin's Tales *and Spenser's* Faerie Queene, *Books I and III*

In the following chapter about allegory, irony, and despair in *The Pardoner's Tale* and Book I of *The Faerie Queene* and in *The Franklin's Tale* and Book III, I start with verbal echoes as a way of suggesting the plausibility of an interpretive context, but concentrate instead on intertextual relations between Chaucerian and Spenserian texts that are broader—more imaginative and conceptual—than local and explicitly verbal. Whether in art or life, readers and writers register, remember, and imitate much else in literary models besides the odd word or phrase, as I have noted in my introduction.¹ Both subtler and more extensive relations among texts manifestly exist and convey meaning: tonal allusions, motifs and images, rhythmic effects, tropes, structural paradigms, ideological formations, and the like. Such relations are significant in culture and relevant to its historical expressions, and their observation not only modifies and enhances previously recognized dimensions of meaning but also discovers new ones. The most complex and compelling interpretations of earlier texts are to be found in writers who imitate and revise, not only their content, but also and inseparably their forms. In Gerald Bruns's words, such a later text can elicit from the earlier one "that which remains unspoken."² Particularly in the Renaissance, with its desire to recover the past, to return *ad fontes*, to the fountains and sources—to the deep "well," in Spenser's word for his Chaucerian source—writers tried actually to converse with their predecessors, as Petrarch did literally in his letters to classical authors such as Cicero and Livy. Their conversations with their deepest sources were touched by the primary sense of the word *converse* in the Renaissance itself: "to live with," "to dwell among." What follows listens to the conversation between Spenser's texts and Chaucer's.

Theresa Krier has recently suggested an allusion to *The Pardoner's Tale* in *The Faerie Queene*, Book IV, occurring in lines that A. C. Hamilton's second edition cross-references with the temptation of Despair in Book I (ix.46, vs. 1–2, 47, vs. 7–8).[3] The allusive lines, spoken by the Spenserian narrator, are these:

> O Why doe wretched men so much desire,
>   To draw their dayes vnto the vtmost date,
> And doe not rather wish them soone expire,
>   Knowing the miserie of their estate,
>   And thousand perills which them still awate,
> Tossing them like a boate amid the mayne,
> That euery houre they knocke at deathes gate?
>   (IV.iii.1)[4]

Where Hamilton hears the despairing Spenserian questions "Why then doest thou, O man of sin, desire / To draw thy dayes forth to their last degree" and "Is it not better to doe [i.e., to die] willinglie, / Then linger till the glasse be all out ronne," Krier hears within the Chaucer-laden context of Book IV an allusive memory of the old man's knocking on his "moodres gate"—Mother Earth—in *The Pardoner's Tale*.[5] In the early cantos of Book IV, Krier has in mind Spenser's explicit invocation of "Dan *Chaucer*, well of English vndefyled," numerous verbal echoes and narrative memories of Chaucer's poems, and the more generalized incorporation of chthonic mothers that invites the memory of Mother Earth here.[6] I would accept both Hamilton's and Krier's recollections—the one of Despair and the other of the Pardoner—and would further suggest that their coincidence is (even literally) predictable from the vantage point of the first book of Spenser's epic romance. Awareness of Chaucer's *Pardoner's Tale* and especially of its "olde man" is brooding and pervasive through much of Book I. It begins with the old man Archimago and climaxes in the related character of Despair. Conspicuously and ironically, it involves the Redcross Knight's recurrent encounters with mirrors of himself that he fails to recognize and the progressive identification of sleep, or rest, with death.

An older Chaucer criticism, as Marshall Leicester has distilled it, identifies the Pardoner as "the *eunuchus non dei*, the embodiment of the *vetus homo*, the Old Man whose body is the body of this death and who is guilty of sinning against the Holy Ghost."[7] Specifically, this is the Bible's Old Man who fails to put on the New, as urged in Ephesians 4:22–24. Criticism has also established that the "olde man," as well as the three rioters, is an aspect or a reflection of the Pardoner.[8] More than the Pardoner fully realizes, he meets himself in his tale about the search for Death. Like the Pardoner, the rioters, too, gamble, overplay their hands, and through greed indeed find death, but the more secret, less openly motivated parallels between the Pardoner's "olde man" and the Pardoner himself are the unforgettable ones, at once more poignant and more terrible. This restless, haunting product of the Pardoner's imagination not only enables the rioters to achieve their desire for Death, but also expresses his own death wish:

> Thus walke I lik a restles caityfe
> And on the ground, which is my mothers gate
> I knocke with my staffe erlyche and late
> And say, leue mother let me in
> Lo howe I vanisshe, flesshe, bloode and skyn
> Allas, whan shal my bones ben at reste[?][9]

Chaucerians have referred the restless wish of the "olde man" to Augustinian despair, which is the inverse of pride, an abyss of guilt at once self-centered, self-tormenting, and self-destructive.[10] In relation to the Pardoner, Leicester cites a modern description of such despair from Kierkegaard's *Sickness unto Death* that is sufficiently suggestive in relation to Spenser's figure Despair to bear repeating:

> Literally speaking, there is not the slightest possibility that anyone will die from this sickness or that it will end in physical death. On the contrary, the torment of despair is precisely this inability to die. . . . If a person were to die of despair as one dies of a sickness, then the eternal in him . . . must be able to die in the same sense as the body dies of sickness. But this is impossible; the dying of despair continually converts itself into a living. The person in despair cannot die; "no more than the dagger can slaughter thoughts" can despair consume the eternal, the self at the root of despair, whose worm does not die and whose fire is not quenched. . . . [This] is precisely the torment, is precisely what keeps the gnawing alive and keeps life in the gnawing . . . [that he] cannot reduce himself to nothing [48].

Similarly, Spenser's Despair, having failed at the last minute to secure the death of Redcrosse, tries to hang himself, "But death he could not worke himselfe thereby; / For thousand times he so himselfe had drest, / Yet nathelesse it could not doe him die" (I.ix.54).

Whereas critics of Chaucer have reproached the rioters for taking the boy's personification of death literally, it might more accurately be said that the rioters take this personification realistically in the substantive, Platonic sense.[11] Of course, with consummate irony, the rioters eventually do achieve death as a physical reality, though only with their own extinction. But before then, rushing off to slay the thief Death, they look less like a trio of literalists than like three drunks entering a fantasy world, or, as it turns out, an allegory. Once in this fictive world—part deictic and part nondeictic, part real and part Real[12]—they don't understand the significance of the "olde man" and his allegorically resonant directions, but they do recognize that he has some connection with the Death they seek. They remark his odd appearance, "al forwrapped saue thy face," and his "great age" and later, after he has spoken, they accuse him of being Death's "espye," one "of his assent," and even like Death himself, a "thefe" (lxxviii^{r-v}). That "espye" in its cognate verbal form can mean "to lie in ambush for" or "to set a snare for" and "to discover (a person or thing that is concealed)," "to discover or disclose (a person) as to identity or condition," is surely more relevant to the rioters' meeting with the "olde man" than they recognize, even as their words, responding to the old man's and highlighting their ironic resonance, cue readers further into the allegory.[13]

The "olde man" himself conveys a spooky excess of significance, even while his figure is insistently natural—real in this lower-case sense. This synthesis of deictic with nondeictic is very much part of his power and, paradoxically, of the resemblance to him of Spenser's more abstract figure Despair, a point to which I shall return later. Here, I would emphasize again that everything about the "olde man" works on a natural, or deictic, level. Even his most hauntingly resonant words evoke the image of a frail old man steadying his steps with a cane or staff as he walks—tap, tap, tap, or, "knocke, knocke, knocke." His words project the thoughts that match his deictic movement and appearance, much as might the words of a personifier of animal-stories for children. The technique is dramatic, imaginative, and poignantly empathetic. Little wonder the rioters do not recognize the old man's full meaning: this is not the boy's stylized picture of an emblematic, nondeictic Death brandishing dart or spear, but death in a living form, the death wish arising from despair. We hear the affective power of this figure, as figure, resisting single-minded translation to the containment of an abstractive and bloodless system, be it psychoanalytical or theological, or both.

What I have called an excess of significance in or about the old man's figure, however, starts with the very suddenness of his appearance. Coming up over a stile, the "olde man" is initially, so to speak, right in the rioters' faces. Spookily wrapped up, aged but willing to walk all the way to India, and conceiving, if only in a manner of speaking, of a bargain of youth for age that sounds odd, if not unnatural, the "olde man" delivers directions to the rioters that are about as loaded with nondeictic meaning as anything Spenser ever wrote: his directions feature a "croked way," as distinct from a straight one, and the archetypal tree associated with the Fall and more generally—via Servius on Vergil's *silva* ("wood, forest")—associated with matter itself, with the root beneath the tree, *radix malorum*, which takes form in this *Tale* as gold florins and fleshly *cupiditas* and thus as the greed that motivates the Pardoner's entire sermon.[14] Oblivious to obvious moral and spiritual meaning, as well as to the old man's pious warnings, the vice-ridden rioters achieve the death of the body that is denied the "olde man." The Pardoner, their creator, enters the allegory with them, as earlier he might have been said to have entered the tavern, where his vivid dramatizations of life cross into direct discourse:

> By goddes preciouse herte, and his nayles
> And by the blode of Christ, that is in hayles
> Seuene is my chaunce, and thyn is fyue and thre
> By goddes armes, if thou falsly play me
> This daggar shal thorowe thyn herte go.
> (lxxviii[r])

But all the Pardoner achieves in his allegory—I think without fully realized awareness—is an expression of his otherwise repressed death wish. His fragmented personality, much remarked by modern psychoanalytic interpreters, achieves ironic wholeness, a wholeness that is not wholeness, in the sharing of this wish by teller, "olde man," and unruly rioters. This self-canceling wholeness realizes content subversively latent in allegorical form itself, in its contradictory impulses to inclusion and division. Such latency is not characteristically *expressed*, as it is both here and in Spenser's first Book.

Allegory often projects elements of a complex whole, such as a person or human consciousness, as separate personifications, as in the instance of both the "olde man" and the rioters, who mirror the Pardoner in some respect. It also combines temporal narrative with non-temporal abstraction to produce an analytical and exploratory *process*. The more allegorical the text, the more these characteristics will be evident in it, or tautologically, vice versa. In Spenser's first Book, unmistakably an allegory from its outset, the Pardoner's "presence" is a memory—refracted, progressive, elusive, persistent.[15] It is recurrently evoked by the text through the sheer weight of repeated coincidence in meaning arising within a shared technique, the weight of a particular traditional content merging with a particular conventional form. With respect to content, the Bible and Augustine especially are common cultural denominators in both texts, and allegorical projection or mirroring is common in both with respect to form. Spenser's avowed awareness of Chaucer's poetry, which is prominent in Book I, as in all but one of the other books of *The Faerie Queene*, is itself a relevant factor and *a condition of plausible interpretation*.

In Book I, while Archimago's temptation of Redcrosse is a consequence of the events it follows—his entrance into the Wandering Wood and his battle with the serpent-woman Error—it marks the first clear failing of the Knight's faith and the beginning of his descent to despair, the ironic nadir of his quest for holiness and wholeness in a self-contradictory allegorical medium. If, as some argue, this medium is a stand-in for meaning itself in this life, then Spenser's poem focuses more specifically on a potential that is present more latently and fleetingly in Chaucer's. Archimago, whose name suggests imagination, the image-making faculty, and its product or "chief image," is a shape shifter and impersonator, an artist who manipulates the imaginations of others to produce tempting but guilty illusions. Dressed as a hermit, "Bidding his beades," framing his stories of "saintes and Popes" with "*Aue-mary*'s," he is a representative of the Catholic Church and one who, like the Pardoner, can "file his tongue as smooth as glas" (i.30, 35). He is pointedly called "the old man," the *vetus homo*, a reference reinforced by "aged sire," and he turns out to be on a continuum with the fallen nature of everyman, who is figured in this book by the Redcross Knight (ii.5). Archimago is the first of many figures who mirror Redcrosse in such a way that we understand them to be at once inside and outside him, an ironic realization that Archimago's actual impersonation of Redcrosse brings home. His figure suggests that Spenser may have read the Pardoner's story of the "olde man" and the rioters in much the same way, and two additional considerations enforce this possibility. The false dream Archimago gets from the Cave of Morpheus—that is, from sleep, or, Redcrosse's merely but thoroughly natural condition—conspicuously alludes to Chaucer's *Book of the Duchess* and likewise indicates that Spenser either read Chaucer's poem allegorically or found in it the potential thus to repackage it. Earlier, the description of the Wandering Wood noticeably includes Chaucer's wood in *The Parliament of Fowls* among its sources, and the subsequent motif spanning Book I that associates trees with the nature of flesh begins here. Fradubio, the tree man physically rooted in bad faith, is a particularly and ironically telling mirror of Redcrosse and a memorable embodiment of this archetypal arboreal motif, coincidentally present in *The Pardoner's Tale* as well.

Allegory, Irony, Despair: Chaucer and Spenser 67

As Redcrosse progresses in bad faith, the resemblance of his situation to the Pardoner's develops further. Redcrosse's inconclusive battle with Sans Joy, who figures his own joylessness and the emotional condition of his eventually conscious despair, leads under the aegis of Pride, the deceptively showy surface of restless, inner discontent, to the bottom of hell. Implicitly, this hell is within Redcrosse, whose joylessness takes him there in the night. It is a subterranean hell that explicitly evokes the descent into earthly matter (including the flesh) in Vergil's sixth book, as glossed by Servius, and Redcrosse's descent occurs while he is in bed and presumably dreaming, as before at Archimago's hermitage. Within the infernal precincts of this hell, natural rest moves closer to the "deadly sleepe" first witnessed in that hermitage and then more openly in the poignant speeches of Despair (i.36, cf. 32):

> Is not short paine well borne, that brings long ease,
> And layes the soule to sleepe in quiet graue?
> Sleepe after toyle, port after stormie seas,
> Ease after warre, death after life does greatly please.
> (I.ix.40)[16]

At "the furthest part" of Hell, a "Deepe, dark, vneasie, dolefull, comfortlesse" cave much like Despair's, the tale of Aesculapius' reuniting the scattered members of Hippolytus signals the restoration to wholeness not of Redcrosse but ironically of Sans Joy, his joylessness, the sickness of spirit gnawing within him (v.36–39).[17] Since the story of Hippolytus also reads as an account of jealousy and betrayal from either Redcrosse's or Una's different points of view, it serves as a reflection of and on their division "into double parts" at Archimago's hermitage, even while holding both parts in unholy communion (ii.9).[18] Like the Pardoner's, this Aesculapian wholeness is not wholeness, but a perverse reunion of Redcrosse's parts, and it fulfills the psychic fragmentation Redcrosse embraced when, abandoning Una, he took up with Duessa, double being or duplicity (Latin *duo*, "two," and *esse*, "to be").

When Despair finally takes form as a character in Book I, his appearance mirrors that of the miserable Redcross Knight when he emerges from Orgoglio's dungeon: "A ruefull spectacle of death and ghastly drere," Redcrosse has "sad dull eyes deepe sunck in hollow pits," "bare thin cheekes," and "rawbone armes," all reflected in the face of Despair, whose "hollow eyne / Lookt deadly dull, and stared as astound; / His raw-bone cheekes through penurie and pine, / Were shronke into his iawes, as he did neuer dine" (viii.40–41; ix.35). In the dungeon Redcrosse has explicitly wished for physical death in order to escape his living one, his "hollow, dreary, murmuring voyce" resounding, "O who is that, which brings me happy choyce / Of death, that here lye dying euery stound" (viii.38)?

The Knight's Despair combines elements of the Pardoner with those of the "olde man." Despair is a preacher who, like the Pardoner, preys on guilt and manipulates the imagination with a finely tuned psychological finesse. He plants traps easy to see through, if only his victim were confident of salvation and deaf to the appeal of repose he offers. Repeatedly, he calls Redcrosse's failings to mind, rubbing salt in the wound of his diseased conscience, and he drives him to desperation by picturing vividly the torments of the damned. His counsel is deadly in every sense, and, as we have seen, like the Pardoner's "olde man," he explicitly embodies a death-wish, which is paradoxically a wish for the death that can never die, which is described so fittingly by Kierkegaard.

Above all, Despair is an artist with words. This is the deepest source of his affective power and of his reality (small *r*) as a temptation, despite the openness of his evil intent and even of his name. While clearly a nondeictic abstraction, Despair is heard and felt as a deictic experience. Rightly described as "charmed," "inchaunted," and "bewitch[ing]," the cadences of Despair have an arresting, hypnotic attraction (ix.30, 48, 53). The resonance of his words, like those of the Pardoner's "olde man," is moving and hauntingly memorable and may also be the deepest source of his likeness to this aged precursor in Chaucer:

> Who trauels by the wearie wandring way,[19]
>   To come vnto his wished home in haste,
>   And meetes a flood, that doth his passage stay,
>   Is not great grace to help him ouer past,
>   Or free his feet, that in the myre sticke fast?
> . . . .
>
> He there does now enioy eternall rest
>   And happie ease, which thou doest want and craue,
>   And further from it daily wanderest:
>   What if some litle paine the passage haue,
>   That makes fraile flesh to feare the bitter waue?
>   Is not short paine well borne, that brings long ease,
>   And layes the soule to sleepe in quiet graue?
>   Sleepe after toyle, port after stormie seas,
> Ease after warre, death after life does greatly please.
>   (I.ix.39–40)

Striking testimony to the comforting appeal of the last four lines, which I cited earlier by themselves, is to be found in their having been a staple of British military funerals during the twentieth century.[20]

Coming face-to-face with Despair is a new experience for Redcrosse, even though he has earlier been depressed and has even wished for death. Building on the foundation of Redcrosse's earlier feelings, Despair newly tempts the Knight to a conscious, willful disbelief in his own salvation. Significantly, Despair's is the first cave that Redcrosse actually enters voluntarily, while awake, and with Una. The marked contrast of this situation with those at or in earlier caves or cave-like enclosures—Error's, Morpheus,' Night's, Aesculapius,' Orgoglio's—signals the difference in meaning. Likewise, the naming of Despair outright even before he appears and the simple fact that he has an English name advertising, rather than half masking, his full identity differentiate the kind and level of experience he embodies from those embodied by Archimago, Lucifera, Sans Joy, and Orgoglio. In this striking respect, Despair resembles the Pardoner, who not merely discloses but even insists on his own vice, fraud, and malice, yet whose sermon, especially the words of its "olde man," touches and disturbs us.

It would be easy, if unimaginative, to see this resemblance, this defiance of our wariness, as Spenser's effort to overgo Chaucer: after all, what could be a greater accomplishment than to make us feel the appeal of a figure as physically ugly and unqualifiedly evil as Despair? It would be equally easy, and to my mind more inviting, more generous, and more plausible, to see it as homage to the Chaucerian "well of English" and deep tonal source from within the relatively more abstract and analytical form Spenser chooses to speak to his audience. Is this not the sort of homage artists often pay their precursors, sometimes acknowledging their influence or inspiration in the title of a painting or poem? Looked at this way, a central thread of the narrative fabric in Book I becomes an intensification and more extensive examination not alone of a Chaucerian theme, despair, but also of Chaucerian character, irony, and allegorical reflection. While very much a new creation and a different sort of poem, Book I becomes also a reading of Chaucer and a text in the history of interpretation, as well as in the history of form. The relation between *The Pardoner's Tale* and Book I likewise becomes an intertextuality that is truly inter-text, *text* being understood as a whole.

Gerald Bruns observes of a manuscript culture, which was still very much alive in Spenser's time, that the appropriation and "embellishment" of another text "is an art of disclosure, as well as an art of amplification. Or rather, amplification is not merely supplementation but also interpretation: the act of . . . eliciting from it [the earlier text] that which remains unspoken" (55–56). To a considerable extent, his observation applies to the relation between *The Pardoner's Tale* and Book I: the "olde man" haunts the imagination of Book I and what is implicit in the form of the Pardoner's allegory becomes focal there. But this application is by no means an isolated instance of broader imaginative and conceptual relations aside from, but not excluding, specific verbal echoes between Chaucer's poems and Spenser's epic romance. Further to exemplify and to explore this fact, I will pursue the suggestive bearing of *The Franklin's Tale* on Book III, which, like that of *The Pardoner's Tale* on Book I, ought to be apparent but has not proved so. This relationship, too, involves allegory, irony, and despair.

Once again, a verbal echo offers an initial clue but affords only information of a general sort. In the first canto of Book III, when Britomart rebukes six knights trying to force Redcrosse to exchange the love of Una for that of Malecasta, her words closely recall the Franklin's: "Ne may loue be compeld by maisterie; / For soone as maisterie comes, sweet loue anone / Taketh his nimble wings, and soone away is gone" (25).[21] This allusion to Chaucer fits Spenser's immediate context, invites us to think of *The Franklin's Tale* as Britomart's quest begins, and appears to require no further explanation. In due course, a number of other memories in Book III add to its Chaucerian cast, recalling tales of desire and marriage similarly appropriate to its subject matter: notably, memories of *The Tale of Sir Thopas*, *The Wife's Prologue*, and old January and young May in *The Merchant's Tale*, who are prototypes of Malbecco and Hellenore.[22]

Given these Chaucerian memories, I would look more closely at a motif, a technique and tonal allusion, and a subgenre in the fourth canto of Book III. This is the canto of generic complaints, first Britomart's, then Cymoent's, and finally Arthur's, each complaint inviting comparison with the others. Britomart's comes when she reaches the seacoast in her restless quest for Artegall. It is the place to which "her grieuous smart," a love wound that makes her feel "nought but death her dolour mote depart" seems naturally to draw her. There, she sits upon "the rocky shore," and

> hauing vewd a while the surges hore,
> That gainst the craggy clifts did loudly rore,
> And in their raging surquedry disdaynd,

That the fast earth affronted them so sore,
And their deuouring couetize restraynd,
Thereat she sighed deepe, and after thus complaynd.
(III.iv.6–7)

In the Petrarchan complaint she then utters, the sea of passion within mirrors that without her. Like the Petrarchan religion of love itself, her woes as a near-hopeless lover reflect the images of religious despair, here those of storm and shipwreck associated by Augustine and others, via the Vulgate's Psalm 101 and the "profundum marum" of the Vulgate's Psalm 67:23, with the abyss of despair.[23]

Britomart pleads first with the sea and later with the "God of winds" that the billows might abate, for otherwise her

feeble vessell crazd, and crackt
Through thy strong buffets and outrageous blowes,
Cannot endure, but needs it must be wrackt
On the rough rocks, or on the sandy shallowes.
(III.iv.9–10)

Reminiscent of Petrarch's sonnet 189 as Britomart's complaint is, this Petrarchan subtext has no "craggy clifts" or "rough rocks" awaiting the storm-tossed ship. But her lament finds a parallel to them in the lovelorn Dorigen's fear of "the grysly rockes blake" in *The Franklin's Tale*, where Dorigen stands on a cliff overlooking the sea and casts "her eyen downwarde fro the brinke" (lxi^r).[24] "Fro the brinke" is suggestively suicidal, hence despairing, and from it she pleads, "But thilke god, that made the wynde to blowe / As kepe my lorde,"

And wolde god that all these rockes blake
Were sonken in to hell for his sake.
These rockes slee myn hert for feare.
(lxi^v)[25]

Earlier, Dorigen's extensive complaint about the rocks questions the wisdom and motives of God as creator and provider:

Eterne god, that through thy purueyaunce
Ledest this worlde, by certayne gouernaunce
In ydel, as men sayn, doste thou nothing make
But lorde, these grisly fendely rockes blake
That semen rather a foule confusyon

Of werke, than a fayre creacion
Of suche a parfyt god, wyse and ful stable
Why haue ye wrou3t this werke unresonable:
For by this werke, north, south, west, ne este
There nys fostred, man, byrde, ne beste
It dothe no good, but anoyeth
Se ye nat lorde, howe mankinde it distroyeth[?]
                                          (lxi^{r-v})

When Dorigen's unwelcome wooer Aurelius later underwrites the illusion by which the rocks disappear, an appalled Dorigen herself declares "such a mister or meruayle . . . ayenst the processe of nature" (lxiii^v). Thus trapped and punished through an artful illusion for her "unnatural" wish to get rid of the rocks, she is ironically "astonyed," turned to stone herself, in this favorite Spenserian pun.[26]

Dorigen's plight has been variously interpreted in the latter half of the twentieth century. For example, Elaine Tuttle Hansen first sees Dorigen's complaint about the rocks and God as meant by the *Tale* (implicitly by the Franklin and complicity by Chaucer) to indicate "the inappropriateness and irrationality of such intense desire in a woman [for her husband's safe return]." Hansen later makes the metafictional suggestion that the rocks are "a multivalent symbol" among whose significations are "masculine fantasies about the monstrosity of female sexuality, another version of Scylla and Charybdis, and the dangers embodied in Dorigen as heroine that stand in the way of [her husband] Arveragus's return to a chaste wife." In an earlier criticism represented by E. Talbot Donaldson, Dorigen is a naive idealist who resents the rocks because they are not "for the best in the best of all possible worlds." In his view, she subsequently "makes an analogy between . . . [Aurelius'] bad behavior and nature's in allowing the ugly rocks to remain where they are" and thus combines her disapproval of Aurelius' adulterous desire with the rocks symbolizing a natural threat to her love's safe return. In this older, new critical reading, Dorigen is culpable, if only of innocence and foolishness; in the more recent feminist one, she is the pawn in a patriarchal tale and the object over which a homosocial contest in culturally valent "fredom" and true "gentillesse" is waged. In an impressive ideological omnium-gatherum, Stephen Knight describes the overdetermined rocks as "a classic *fin amor* 'impossible task'; a reification of Dorigen's insecurity when she is alone; [and] the key to her challenge . . . to providence [hence to hegemony]." He adds that they also reflect "the water relations of the ur-Dorigen [combined fairy mistress and propertied Breton queen], and in a more contemporary transformation they hinder trade as well as Arveragus' return. . . . Lastly they are a Breton [coastal] reality."[27] What Spenser might have made of Dorigen's "grysly rockes blake" is uncertain, but that he, too, would have seen allegory in the focal motif they constitute seems hardly in doubt.

In view of the "rocky" site of Britomart's Petrarchan complaint and the rocks in it upon which the "God of winds" (for Dorigen, the "god, that made the wynde to blowe") threatens to wreck her vessel, it seems a curious coincidence that, instead of remaining in the endlessly self-enclosed circle of Petrarchan sonneteering, Britomart turns from it in a fit of vengeance actively to pursue her quest by venting her frustration on Marinell, both the "rocky-hart[ed]" son of the sea himself and "loue's enimy," as he is described, and thus associated with the source of her torment (III.iv.26, IV.xii.7, cf. 13).[28] Marinell, whose name signifies "sea" (Latin *mare*) is the son of Dumarin (French "of the sea-farer," or "sailor") and the sea nymph Cymoent (Greek $\kappa \upsilon \mu \alpha$, "wave") and hence by denomination and descent one-sided and self-centered. Violently unhorsed by Britomart, he lies in "deadly stonishment," as deadly still as a stone, and when his mother comes to lament over his fallen body even "the hard rocks could scarse from teares refraine," as happens again much later, when Florimell, in love with "stony heart[ed]" Marinell from the opening of Book III, complains so piteously that "ruth it moued in the rocky stone" of her prison (III.iv.19, 35; IV.xii.5, 13). In contrast to Dorigen, Britomart is empowered to act against the threatening sea-rocks embodied in Marinell—at this point in her career, in any case.

Dorigen's complaint to God about the rocks is not as directly about passionate love, however, as Britomart's is. Nor is the complaint to and about Night that Spenser's Prince Arthur, lovelorn like Dorigen, utters at the end of the same canto that begins with Britomart's complaint. But Arthur, like Dorigen, complains about the natural order.[29] At the same time, the resemblance of Arthur's condition in this canto to Britomart's is enforced, not only by the generic forms of their plaintive utterances, but also by a barrage of specific verbal echoes, which insist on our also noting their relationship. Losing sight of Florimell in the "griesly shadowes" of night, for example, Arthur wanders "Like as a ship, whose Lodestarre suddenly / Couered with cloudes, her Pilot hath dismayd," a recollection of Britomart's similar image in her complaint of Love, her "lewd Pilot," who "saile[s] withouten starres, gainst tide and wind"; this connection is additionally reinforced by the "thousand fancies" and "sad sorrow, and disdaine" that Arthur here inherits from Britomart's earlier behavior in this canto (III.iv.5, 8–9, 15, 52–54). Via Arthur, Britomart is thus further related to Dorigen and indirectly to Dorigen's complaint about nature. In a summary word, canto iv thereby *triangulates* the relation of these three figures.

Arthur's complaint apostrophizes Night as the "foule Mother of annoyance sad, / Sister of heauie death, and nourse of woe," whose ugliness has been thrust down to hell to dwell in "*Herebus* blacke house, / (Blacke *Herebus* thy husband . . .)" (iv.55). Like Dorigen in *The Franklin's Tale*, who asks, "Eterne god, . . . Why haue ye wrought this werke unresonable," Arthur demands of Night, "What had th'eternall Maker need of thee, / The world in his continuall course to keepe, / That doest all things deface?" (iv.56). Arthur's despairing complaint is as impious within a biblical ideology as Dorigen's, but through its immediate affective motivation, loss of the fleeing Florimell, whom he had hoped would turn out to be his elusive elf queen, it is made understandably so, and it is even given a comic cast, since his situation at this point twice allusively recalls that of Chaucer's Sir Thopas.[30] Transferred to a male, and an exemplary one at that, and treated sympathetically, the threat of Dorigen's questioning of God is thus contained: Spenserians have generally found Arthur's question unremarkable, by comparison thus highlighting both the problematical gendering of Dorigen's complaint and the more exclusively erotic focus of Arthur's and Britomart's.[31]

Between Britomart's and Arthur's complaints, the sea nymph Cymoent rushes to the side of her wounded son Marinell, whom she first thinks dead, and laments his demise inconsolably. If her complaint has a topical relation to either of Dorigen's complaints in *The Franklin's Tale*, it involves the despairing instinct for death, submerged within Dorigen's "grysly rockes blake" and openly expressed in the extensive exempla of suicides in her second complaint. In canto iv, this instinct is also found within Britomart's "half-formed death-wish," which, "in the symbolic logic of the poem, . . . directs her steps" to the stony sea coast in the first place.[32] The same instinct is *showcased* in Cymoent's complaint:

> O what auailes it of immortall seed
>   To beene ybred and neuer borne to die?
>   Farre better I it deeme to die with speed,
>   Then waste in woe and wailefull miserie.
>   Who dyes the vtmost dolour doth abye,
>   But who that liues, is left to waile his losse:

> So life is losse, and deathe felicitie.
> Sad life worse then glad death: and greater crosse
> To see friends graue, then dead the graue selfe to engrosse.
>
> (III.iv.38)

My use of the word *showcased* is meant to underline exactly what is special about Cymoent's complaint: its artfulness is on exhibit. A sea nymph, even to Spenser's readers, is a creature of the feigning fancy at its freest, and Cymoent is a figure in idyllic pastoral, of which a whole piscatory subgenre exists. The sea nymph's affecting lines, we might say laconically, are well done. But again and again, they are undercut by the narrator, as happens in the immediate, comic sequel to her complaint. Right after two stanzas of her affective outpourings, further reinforced by her companion nymphs', we get "Thus when they all had sorrowed their fill, / They softly gan to search his griesly wound" (iv.40). The arias completed, pressing matters of life and death now claim attention. If this effect were isolated, we might prefer to ignore it—Homer nodding or some such. But there is an instance of it just before (iv.35) and a still stronger instance in the stanza immediately after the comic sequel just quoted:

> Tho when the lilly handed *Liagore*,
>   (This *Liagore* whylome had learned skill
>   In leaches craft, by great *Appolloes* lore,
>   Sith her whylome vpon high *Pindus* hill,
>   He loued, and at last her wombe did fill
>   With heauenly seed, whereof wise *Paeon* sprong)
> Did feel his pulse.
>
> (III.iv.41)

Between the lilly-handed Liagore's introduction and her actually feeling the severely wounded Marinell's pulse, there is time for a leisurely parenthesis of five lines to review her medical and mythological credentials. This is a form of timing and ironical juxtaposition—a tonal effect, if you will—associated repeatedly, distinctively, and memorably with Chaucer's writing. Perhaps the most notorious instance of it occurs in the description of the Prioress in *The General Prologue*: "But for to speken of her conseyence"—her conscience sandwiched here between ten lines about her table manners and another eight about her kindness to animals. Such *irony of duration and position*, or timing, especially if read aloud, finds a point of reference not only in Chaucerian practice generally, but specifically in the length and sequencing of Dorigen's complaint about threatened and virtuous women.[33]

This second complaint by Dorigen is long, and its many exempla, while at first clear instances of her desire to keep her chastely married body undefiled, become increasingly less relevant to her situation, with the result that for many readers the complaint begins to take on a self-generating, virtuoso life of its own.[34] The narrator's laconic comment after roughly a hundred lines of lamentation, "Thus playned Dorigene a day or twey, / Purposyng euer that she wolde dey," is characteristically Chaucerian and ironic, implying, as it does, that Dorigen's prolixity efficiently defers any danger of action (lxiiii^{r-v}). This undercutting and trivializing of Dorigen's emotion is all the more effective coming right after the most seemingly irrelevant exempla of all to Dorigen's choice between infidelity to her word or to her marriage:

> Oh Thenta quene, thy wifely chastyte
> To alle wiues may a myrrour be.
> The same thing I saye of Bilia,
> Of Rodogone, and eke Valeria.
>
> (lxiiii^{r})

In the words of Robert Burlin, "Lest there be any question of tone here, one need only recall [Germaine] Dempster's description of the magnificent irrelevance . . . to Dorigen's situation" of the three histories breathlessly bundled into one couplet: "'Valeria's glory had consisted in refusing to remarry, Rhodagune's in killing her nurse, and Bilia's in never remarking on the smell of her husband's breath.'"[35]

How to interpret Dorigen's second complaint has predictably become controversial in Chaucer criticism. Most earlier critics see the complaint as parody, whether of rhetorical exempla, of Dorigen, or of the Franklin. Knight, followed by Hansen, finds in it a self-denying cancellation of Dorigen's earlier assertion of a distinct and "critical feminine viewpoint," as when she reproached God for the destructiveness of nature and deflated Aurelius' illicit desire for her married body. Knight argues that her exempla of virgins who prefer suicide to defilement indicate her recoil from sexuality, and since the wives she invokes are predominantly nameless or widowed, she "projects her sense of isolation into non-marriage and unnaming." The notorious exempla in the final lines of her speech (Bilia and company) offer "the same mixture of relevant and urgently irrelevant cases." In support of masculine "hegemony," her earlier challenging viewpoint is thus "foreclosed as she imagines that very viewpoint as manless, nameless, lifeless" (27). In contrast, an exceptional reading of Dorigen's lament is Gerald Morgan's. Invoking classical rhetorical tradition and medieval morality, Morgan mounts a spirited defense of the "truth, propriety and appositeness" of Dorigen's exempla, but he tends to discount their original contexts and disregards the tonal effects of duration and sequencing (84). Perhaps most tellingly of all, Knight observes that a number of medieval scribes found Dorigen's long complaint "as boring as many critics have, and so cut its length" (26, 34n46). From the medieval period to our own, the critical consensus at least acknowledges the problematical character of her complaint, which is too long to ignore and simply too insistent to forget.

Even without regard to the relation between Dorigen's despairing complaint about the rocks and Britomart's and Arthur's paired complaints, Spenser's treatment of Cymoent's complaint in itself is thus suggestively Chaucerian. Like Chaucer, Spenser is inclined to indulge but also to feminize and in some way to distance emotional effusions of the sort Cymoent utters, and if only by way of analogue to or tonal memory of Chaucer's ironical undercutting of Dorigen, as we have just seen, he does so as a sequel to Cymoent's lament. When *The Franklin's Tale* is glimpsed among the texts informing all three complaints in Spenser's fourth canto (Britomart's, Cymoent's, and Arthur's), however, its relation to this canto indicates a dimension of meaning beyond those of localized rhetoric, theme, and source. This is a formal, structural dimension of signification that appreciably modifies our sense of the whole. Recreatively imaginative, idyllically pastoral, indulgent, and comic, the portion of Spenser's fourth canto that belongs to a sea nymph "of immortall seed . . . ybred and neuer borne to die" is not merely self-containing; it also serves to contain the emotional excess on both sides of it, the real suicidal threat of despairing *tristitia* (joylessness, depression). It deflects their very real dangers. Sung in Cymoent's key, the poignant yet nonetheless self-indulging despair of Britomart, linked to Arthur's as well, is showcased in a recreatively artful form and ironized and thus safely contained and deflected. For an analogous moment, Spenser's Anacreontics come to mind: recreative, erotic, impatient, spiteful, and comic, they are an interlude in contrasting form between the *Amoretti* and *Epithalamion*, more serious business both.[36]

Like much of Spenser's Book I, his fourth canto in Book III, read with *The Franklin's Tale*, becomes in still another, larger way an intertextual and meta-originary reading of Chaucer and a text in the history of interpretation and form. The *relatively* more lifelike forms in which Chaucer writes Spenser typically reduces, then magnifies and refocuses, essentializing (or further essentializing) them to various degrees. He separates a single plight or character into several different but related ones, dividing to probe, analyze, clarify, and plumb. In the instance of *The Franklin's Tale*, his reading appears to recognize and respect what is at stake in Chaucer's, implicitly endorsing its ideological requirements in the ironizing of emotional effusion and the containment of religious doubt. At the same time, however, by dividing the whole of Dorigen's emotional plight into three parts, his reinterpretation at least gets free enough of it to follow Britomart, the major figure and central signifier in Book III, beyond despair. This difference is a *result* of such refocusing and magnifying or, in other words, of a process of thought *embodied* in poetic form.

5.   Eumnestes' "immortall scrine": Spenser's Archive

Like Chaucer, Spenser often finds or pretends to find in earlier books the enabling source of his own poetry, and for this reason, among others, he describes Chaucer's writing as the wellhead of his own. A number of Spenser's interpreters have sought the meaning of his deliberate reliance on a written tradition in pure textuality or in its effect on a community of readers.[1] While not rejecting their many valid perceptions, I want to suggest that this reliance also be referred to the claim the Spenserian poet made for it, particularly in *The Faerie Queene*. In Spenser's most massively allusive poem, the significance of earlier works is inseparable from the idea of antiquity, an idea in which these works are themselves implicated. "Whylome as antique stories tellen vs," Spenser wrote in imitation of the beginning of Chaucer's *Knight's Tale*—"Whylom, as olde stories tellen vs"—and thereby he specifically placed Chaucer's work in a tradition of antique writings, even as he recalled Chaucer's own placement of *The Knight's Tale* in such a tradition.[2]

Antiquity, as Spenser develops this idea in *The Faerie Queene*, consists of plain truth and timeless admonitions; it is an idealized place of mythic patterns and an undefiled "well" of simple purity.[3] Antiquity resides in memorial scrolls and permanent records, and these participate in Clio's "volume of Eternitie," a volume that always surpasses yet ever illumines human memory (III.iii.4). For the Renaissance generally and more particularly for Spenser, the sense of a literary tradition and of the words and forms that constitute it is more idealistic and mysterious than in a modern poetics of loss and displacement. It is far more eclectic, including skepticism and doubt but also affirming wisdom, virtue, and truth. Often, as Spenser describes this tradition, it is recorded memory, tied intrinsically to the very idea of words, written records, and the mnemonic working of the human mind.

Predictably, many of the words Spenser uses to describe recorded memory are so revealing as to suggest his selecting them for the reminders—the associations or reminiscences—built into their history. Among these is the arresting word *scrine*, from Latin *scrinium*, which first appears in the Proem to Book I, where the poet asks his muse to "Lay forth out of . . . [her] euerlasting scryne / The antique rolles" of Faerie Land.[4] Cooper's *Thesaurus*, or treasury, of the Roman language defines *scrinium* as "a coffer or other like place wherein jewels or secrete things are kept."[5] Stephanus' *Thesaurus linguae latinae* derives *scrinium* from *secernendum*, "setting apart, secreting, secluding," and defines it as a place in which precious things and mysteries (*secreta*) are preserved and protected (*servantur*).[6] Not surprisingly in view of these definitions, the word *scrine* also carries the more specific meaning "shrine" during the Middle Ages and the Renaissance.[7] Also in view of them, Spenser's description of the rolls that lie in his muse's "euerlasting scryne" as "hidden still"—that is, hidden always, secretly, silently, motionlessly—makes sense, but it is primarily in relation to the sacred meaning "shrine" that the word *everlasting* at this point does so. In the chamber of Eumnestes, or Good Memory, within the brain turret of the House of Alma, the word *still* recurs in the phrase "recorded still" describing Eumnestes' operation and carries with it something of its mysterious force in the first Proem. In connection with Eumnestes' function, the word *scrine* likewise appears, characterized this time not as "euerlasting" but, with added point, as "immortall" (II.ix.56).

Both Cooper and Stephanus include among their examples of the meaning of *scrinium* Catullus' phrase "librariorum . . . scrinia"—the booksellers' containers of manuscripts or rolls.[8] This example bears on the furnishing of Eumnestes' chamber, which is "all . . . hangd about with rolles, / And old records from auncient times deriu'd, / Some made in books, some in long parchment scrolles" (ix.57). The association of *scrinia*, or scrines, with books, records, and sacred relics goes deep into the past. Under the late Roman emperors, there were four types of public scrines for various kinds of historical records (*scrinia libellorum, memoriae, epistularum,* and *epistularum Graecarum*).[9] The scrines of monasteries or churches were the places, whether chests, cupboards, niches, or rooms, where the enabling instruments and authorizing documents that pertained to the rights of the institution were kept. In this context, the scrine is equivalent to the *secretum*, or "secret place," the treasury of the institution and, prior to the establishment of libraries, the depository for books.[10] Isidore of Seville, whose *Etymology* was a notable source for the Renaissance, describes scrines as containers in which books or treasures are protected—"servantur libri vel thesauri"—and explains this to be the reason that those Romans who preserved the sacred books—"libros sacros"—were called *scriniarii*.[11]

From the ancient Roman past, through the Middle Ages, to the Tudor present, the fortunes of the word *scrine* suggest, in addition to its association with books and archives, equally persistent associations with memory or with things worth remembering—things worth keeping *in mind* and things of value: repeatedly and specifically *scrine* is associated with secrecy or seclusion (*secerno, secretum*), with a need to guard or preserve, and with the word and idea of a *thesaurus*, a treasure or a treasury of writing and, more fundamentally, of words. One moves easily, induced by the context of Spenser's usage, from these associations to Sidney's commonplace observation that, "memorie being the onely treasurer of knowled[g]e, those words . . . fittest for memory are likewise most conuenient for knowledge"; and then back in time to Plato's more mystically oriented idea that all knowledge is memorial, a kind of remembering, an idea reflected variously yet in turn by Aristotle, by the Neoplatonists, and by Saint Augustine.[12]

The word *scrine*, in itself and as Spenser employs it, also conveys the idea of communal or racial content—of resources that span generations.[13] Such resources may be accessible to individuals in time but always exceed their direct and specific experience. Here, in connection with Spenser's two uses of *scrine*, one thinks of Bacon's traditional definition of history as both memory and experience, and of Aristotle's and Aquinas' descriptions of experience itself as memory—as the fused product of many generations of memories of many things. When Aquinas considers the intellectual virtue of prudence, whose components the three sages of Alma's brain turret represent, he follows Aristotle in explaining that "*intellectual virtue is engendered and fostered by experience and time*" and that "experience [itself] is the result of many memories." He concludes that "prudence requires the memory of many things," or, as he affirms elsewhere, "prudence requires experience which is made up of *many memories*." Similarly, for Bacon's wise and prudent historian, whose knowledge belongs to the faculty of memory, "history and experience" are "the same thing." Heirs of such definitions, the sages of Alma's brain turret represent imagination, rational judgment, and memory—the last in the figure of Eumnestes; they look in turn to the future, the present, and the historical past and together constitute Spenser's allegory of prudence.[14]

The content of Eumnestes' "immortall scrine" appears to be considerably purer than the books and scrolls, "all worme-eaten, and full of canker holes," that hang about his walls. These physically decrepit records are explicitly contrasted with the disembodied purity and seeming transcendence of the content of memory, which derives from them. Well removed from physical worms, the content of Eumnestes' scrine belongs to a figure "of *infinite* remembrance," who

> things foregone through many ages held,
> Which he *recorded still*, as they did pas,
> Ne suffred them to perish through long eld,
> As all things else, the which this world doth weld,
> But laid them vp in his *immortall scrine*,
> Where they for euer *incorrupted* dweld.
> (II.ix.56: my emphasis)

Like the content of any other shrine, including the body, the temple of the Holy Ghost, it is the content of Eumnestes' scrine—the "precious things and mysteries"—that is immortal, rather than the scrine itself, to which, in a way familiar to readers of *The Faerie Queene*, Spenser transfers the attribute of immortality. The immortal content of this scrine in which the past dwells uncorrupted is not far distant from the figurative use of *scrine* in Nicholas Udall's translation of Erasmus' *Apophthegmes*: "The mynde or solle of manne is couered, and ... housed or hidden within the tabernacle or skryne of the bodye and dooeth in a mannes communicacion clerely appere and euidently shewe itself."[15]

Udall's translation would seem to apply to the House of Alma, to the chamber of Eumnestes, and to Eumnestes' scrine itself, with its transferred epithet "immortall": together, like so many Chinese boxes, these recesses are always receding, always hidden, but always there, always evident, always recorded—in words and (re-*cor*-dari) in the heart. As a gloss on Eumnestes' scrine, Udall's translation also returns us to Stephanus' derivation of *scrinium* from *secernendum*, "setting apart, secreting, secluding," which, along with "The antique rolles, which there [in the muse's scrine of Proem I] lye hidden still," suggests so hauntingly the Proem to Book VI:

> Such secret comfort, and such heauenly pleasures,
>   Ye sacred imps, that on *Parnasso* dwell,
>   And there *the keeping* haue of *learnings threasures*,
>   Which doe all worldly riches farre excell,
>   Into the mindes of mortall men doe *well*,
>   And goodly fury into them *infuse*;
>   Guyde ye my footing, and conduct me well
>   In these strange waies, where neuer foote did vse,
> Ne none can find, but who was taught them by the Muse.

Reuele to me the *sacred* noursery
  Of vertue, which with you doth there *remaine*,
  Where it in siluer bowre does *hidden ly*.
       (1–3; except *Parnasso*, my emphasis)

Secrecy, seclusion, the preservation of learning's treasures, the welling or infusing of them into mortal minds, their sacred source at once immanent and hidden still—all again are present. Though all Spenser's muses are daughters of Dame Memory, his particular muse is most often Clio, History, which is memory itself, and the mnemonic resources this muse preeminently figures are finally the reason that "vertues seat is deepe within the mynd" (5). It is entirely appropriate that Spenser's mnemonic muse and Eumnestes should preside over the same scrine.[16]

The connections between Eumnestes' chamber and the Proem to Book VI lead, as do so often the traces or "tracts" of Spenser's "fine footing," to another, related passage in which the word *permanent* is a deliberately chosen paradigm of the provenance of recorded memory. This passage occurs at the outset of the Mutability Cantos and therefore affords some retrospect on Eumnestes' treasure. In it, Spenser refers to the "antique race" and ancient lineage of Mutability and explains that he has "found it registred of old, / In *Faery* Land mongst records permanent" (vi.2). Like the word *scrine*, the phrase "records permanent" is arresting: a permanent record of change is puzzling on the face of it, albeit on reflection potentially ironic; the word *permanent* itself, moreover, has never appeared before this canto in connection with records or in the entire course of *The Faerie Queene* or, for that matter, with a single, relevant exception, in the rest of Spenser's poetry.

The word *permanent* occurs a total of four times in Spenser's poetry—twice more in later portions of the Mutability Cantos and once in *Amoretti* 79. These other occurrences accentuate the relation of the problematical phrase "records permanent" to Eumnestes' treasure and illuminate its importance. The two later uses of *permanent* in the Cantos come during the trial of Mutability's claims to sovereignty, and both emphasize the cosmic implications of this word. In the first of them, Mutability explicitly aligns permanence with an absence of movement—a stillness—which is only illusory, observing in her opening volley the ways in which "the Earth (great mother of vs all) . . . only seems vnmov'd and permanent" (vii.17). All that springs from the unstable Earth, Mutability maintains, necessarily changes restlessly; not only do the bodies of men "flit and fly: / But eeke their minds (which they immortall call) / Still change and vary thoughts, as new occasions fall" (19).[17] The merely occasional nature of the mind's conceptions, of which its own immortality is clearly one, is the most disturbing extension of Mutability's argument, and it challenges directly the immortality of Eumnestes' treasure.

The final occurrence of *permanent* comes in the summation of Mutability's case: "Then since within this wide great *Vniuerse / Nothing* doth firme and permanent appeare," she concludes, "What then should let, but I aloft should reare / My Trophee, and from all, the triumph beare?" (vii.56: my emphasis on *nothing*). In Mutability's rhetorical question, the implications of impermanence are again comprehensive and total, mocking the ironized unity implicit in *universe* ("one-turning") with negation. Indeed, in the context of Mutability's seemingly overwhelming claims, the pun on the word *nothing*, which Shakespeare was to make so crucial in *King Lear*, momentarily threatens to assert itself: no *thing* is permanent, but nothingness is so.

In *Amoretti* 79, the word *permanent* belongs to a more positive context, yet one that similarly underlines its metaphysical charge. The sonnet links permanence to the characterization of "true beautie" as "free / from frayle corruption," like the "incorrupted," indwelling content of Eumnestes' "immortall scrine." Since *Amoretti* 79 immediately precedes the sonnet in which Spenser mentions having composed six books of *The Faerie Queene*, it is not wholly surprising that much of it should be relevant to my preceding discussion and especially to something permanent or immortal within the virtuous mind. "Men call you fayre, and you doe credit it," the poet begins the sonnet, but he soon observes how

> the trew fayre, that is the gentle wit,
>   and vertuous mind, is much more praysd of me.
> For all the rest, how euer fayre it be,
>   shall turne to nought and loose that glorious hew:
>   but onely that is permanent and free
>   from frayle corruption, that doth flesh ensew.
> That is true beautie: that doth argue you
>   to be diuine and borne of heauenly seed:
>   deriu'd from that fayre Spirit, from whom al true
>   and perfect beauty did at first proceed.
> He onely fayre, and what he fayre hath made,
>   all other fayre lyke flowres vntymely fade.

The concluding couplet is remarkably close to the end of Chaucer's *Troilus*, where the poet admonishes "yonge fresshe folkes" to look to God and think "al nys but a fayre / This worlde that passeth sone, as floures fayre," an ending which, as I have noted in an earlier chapter, the penultimate stanza of the Mutability Cantos similarly recalls.[18]

The distinction throughout *Amoretti* 79 between "vertuous mind" and "glorious hew," permanence and corruption, spirit and flesh, resembles that between the content of Eumnestes' "immortall scrine" and his worm-eaten books; it also accentuates Spenser's care in referring Mutability's lineage to the "records permanent" *in* Faerie Land, rather than to those *of* Faerie Land. Only in Faerie are records permanent, and if we want to know where Faerie is, we need only remember the Proem to Book II, where we learn both that we can trace its whereabouts "By certaine signes here set in sundry place" and that "no body"—that is, no one at all, none bodily, none in bodily form—"can know" where it is. Hardly by coincidence, we learn in this same Proem that *The Faerie Queene,* "this famous antique history," is the "matter of just memory." Records are permanent only in Faerie Land, which is the only place Eumnestes' "immortall scrine" remains, resides, dwells uncorrupted, at once because the muse is the daughter of Memory and because she is also the daughter of Apollo—of poetic creativity—or elsewhere of Jupiter, of enabling power (III.iii.4, IV.xi.10). The content of memory is the source—the spring or well—but memory must be unfolded and its motive potential fulfilled.

Like *scrine*, the word *permanent* comes to Spenser with a significant set of implications—a thesaurus of memories, reminiscences, and associations. The etymological citations of a modern dictionary offer a shortcut to these and an introduction to the freer etymological associations familiar to the Renaissance from Classical sources. *Permanent,* deriving from Latin *per,* "through," and *manere,* "to remain," is cognate to the word *manor,* or "desmesne, domain, area of dominium," which comes from Latin *manere* by way of Old French *manoir,* "to stay or dwell." The Indo-European base of *manere,* namely *men-,* is thought originally to have been identical with the Indo-European homonym *men-,* meaning "to think," which also underlies the word *mind.* The connection between *men-,* "to think," and *men-,* "to remain," is hypothesized to be the idea "stand in thought."[19]

While the finer points of Indo-European bases were hardly available to Spenser, such etymological speculations as those of the Roman Varro were, and they clearly fed the poet's own etymologically oriented and inventive imagination.[20] Like Spenser, Varro connects the ideas of remaining and thinking both with one another and with the idea of remembering or memory. He uses the Latin word *mens,* or "mind," to bridge them: thus, "*meminisse* 'to remember,' [derives] from *memoria* 'memory,' when there is again a motion toward that which *remansit* 'has remained' in the *mens* 'mind': and this may have been said from *manere* 'to remain.'"[21] Developing further the association of *manere*, "remain," with *memoria*, "memory," Varro explains the expression *Mamurius Veturius* as an appellative signifying "memoriam veterem," what Chaucer might have translated as "a memory of olde times," and Spenser as "an antique image."[22]

The rest of Varro's etymologies in this section read like a gloss on Mutability, on Spenser's explicit recognition in the final Cantos that mutability and mortality are part of the abiding records in Faerie Land and of the undying content of human memory: "Et in Arcadia Ego," to quote the title of Panofsky's famous essay on the presence of transience and death in Arcady, the condition he defines as a "retrospective vision of an unsurpassable happiness, enjoyed in the past, unattainable ever after, yet enduringly alive in the memory," and elsewhere as the topos "Sacrosancta Vetustas."[23] Varro's evolving derivations from *memoria*, "memory," also anticipate Spenser's recurrent interest in the idea that "moniments," or monuments, admonish, an idea relevant to Mutability and to the "records permanent" of her "antique race and linage ancient": from *memoria*, Varro explains, comes "*monere* 'to remind,' because he who *monet* 'reminds' is just like a memory. So also the *monimenta* 'memorials' which are on tombs . . . *admonere* 'admonish' the passers-by that they themselves were mortal and that the readers are too. From this, . . . other things that are written and done to preserve their *memoria* 'memory' are called *monimenta* 'monuments.' " My point is not that mutability and mortality have never before been acknowledged as part of the content of memory in *The Faerie Queene* but that they have not been the major focus of attention the way they are in Spenser's last Cantos. For example, both are present, though variously, in Eumnestes' registers, whether "*Briton moniments*" or "*Antiquitie* of *Faerie* lond," and in the admission in the Proem to Book II that "no *body* can know" Faerie's whereabouts, an admission that clearly refers to Faerie as more than simply a written record, the fragile document we hold in our hands or the poem whose location in our bookshelves we know.

Imprinted in the heart and embedded in the mind, enduring, memorial, admonitory, and written in the human past, "records permanent," and "mongst" them the memory of Mutability's origin, are the stuff that Spenser's Faerie romance is made on. The substitution of permanence for Eumnestes' "immortall scrine" may appear at first a real change and a retreat from intimations of visionary transcendence, but like everything else in the Mutability Cantos, it proves on closer inspection also a sign of continuity. If a reminder of mortality is latent in the word *permanent*, one is similarly present not only in immortal but also in *scrine*, meaning "shrine," and specifically in the historical equation of *scrine* with a *feretrum*, or "bier," for the carriage or enclosure of *reliquae sacrae*, "sacred relics"—of what remains, *remanere*, and of what reminds, *rememorare*, *reminisci*.[24] If the claim to spiritual transcendence simultaneously present both in "scrine" and "immortall" is muted in "records permanent," it is, though still more deeply hidden, still there. It remains, and it does so alongside the acknowledgment of death.

Like the resources of memory in Eumnestes' chamber, the House of Alma as a whole combines a number of philosophical traditions, which scholarly studies have gone far to identify.[25] These include both the Aristotelian and Platonic traditions and, where apt, in baptized form. As so often in the crucial centers, the houses or temples, of *The Faerie Queene*, to follow a single, competing doctrine would seem to have been, in Spenser's view, doctrinaire: to know rather than to recover and to renew truth. It would be to short-circuit the *process* of memory, to mummify its secrets and resources rather than to revive and revise them in accessible forms.[26] As Alastair Fowler has argued, some form of Platonized or Neoplatonized reminiscence of truth of the sort present in Macrobius' *Commentary on the Dream of Scipio* was never far from Spenser's mind in Book II, and it would be difficult, in fact simply wrong, not to be reminded of this association by his mystically charged diction in Eumnestes' chamber and, more generally, in connection with that "sacred . . . noursling of Dame Memorie," his Muse (IV.xi.10).[27] But this reminiscence vanishes as quickly as the Graces on Mount Acidale when it is pressed and, even if not pressed, passes elusively within the subsequent movement, the *cursus*, of the poem itself into the demystified memory of an Aristotelian or more materialized system. And yet the inspiriting words recurrently attributed to memory are there still and still are "ment, / T'expresse the meaning of the inward mind" (VI.viii.26).

What is clear is that for Spenser the words and texts of recorded memory hold imprints of truth and sources of wisdom and that the "spirit" of these, infused into the poet, enables his Faerie vision (IV.ii.34). This is the reason he recalls so many overlapping yet various texts, so many "records permanent" of Mutability's true meaning in the final Cantos and, crucially among them, not just Chaucer's *Parliament of Fowls* and *Troilus and Criseyde* but also his translation of Boethius, whose conspicuous references to a source or "well" Chaucer himself recalls near the end of *The Knight's Tale*. "And if," Chaucer's Boethius reads, the "kynge and lorde/ wele and begynnynge" did not govern and constrain all things, "they shulde departen from her

wel/ that is to sayn from her begynnyng and . . . tournen in to nought"
(cclxiv^v). Alluding to this passage, *The Knight's Tale* aligns it more specifically with an acceptance of death:

> It helpeth not/ all gothe that ylke wey
> Than may ye se that al thyng mote dey
> What maketh this/ but Jupiter the kyng?
> That is prince/ and cause of all thyng
> Conuertyng all to his propre w[e]ll[28]
> From whiche it is deryued sothe to tell.
>
> (xlii^v)

Recalling the Boethian well of origin, Nature's judgment on Mutability's claims at the end of Spenser's seventh canto asserts that, though all things change,

> They are not changed from their first estate;
> But by their change their being doe dilate:
> And turning to themselues at length againe,
> Doe work their owne perfection so by fate.
>
> (VII.vii.58)

In Nature's answer, origin and destination, first cause and final effect, are one. The two stanzas of Canto viii, which follow closely on her answer and with which the poem ceases, poignantly express the poet's concern with personal mortality and with an ultimate destination. Their doing so suggests that in framing her answer not only the Boethian well but also Chaucer's adaptation of it in *The Knight's Tale*, which touches more directly on death, is present to the poet's mind and thus that the Chaucerian memory is infolded in the Boethian one.

Within Alma's brain turret in Book II, Eumnestes seeks and reaches what has been lost or *removed* ("laid amis") and does so through the agency of a reminder or recollector, namely Anamnestes, the old man's young page (ix.58). Anamnestes' function corresponds to that which specific words and texts—like those of Chaucer—play for the Faerie poet, and to that which the Faerie poem, in turn, plays for us. Such words and texts are at once the "tract" and the way of tracing back as far as we are able, a process never finished, hence never perfected, until life itself is. Like memory as portrayed in Eumnestes' chamber and more generally like Alma herself, life, as used here, is at once collective and cumulative and individually and therefore partially realized. In this respect, it resembles experience, history, and time.

Spenser appears to have meant his avowed kinship with Chaucer, and especially with Chaucer's romances, as a paradigm of his relation to the recorded sources of memory. Because Chaucer's work, however profoundly human, is not memorably doctrinal or mystical, this paradigm is especially revealing. When Spenser begins his extension of Chaucer's *Squire's Tale*, he fuses *The Knight's Tale* with the Squire's and thus the father's with the son's. Together, these two romance *Tales* become an image of the extension of experience through time, which is generically, although not uniquely, characteristic of romance. In this way Spenser affords us a paradigm of fusing parallel to that he claims between Chaucer's work and his own as-yet-unfinished extension of it and also parallel within the fable of Book IV to the fusing of Priamond's and Diamond's lives into the more cumulative, more complex Triamond. Notably, in characterizing his extension, he hopes not to complete *The Squire's Tale* (as is customarily assumed) but in a more general, more analogous way to follow the "footing" of Chaucer's "feete"—his "tracts" both spiritual and metrical—that he may "meete" the sooner with Chaucer's "meaning," something more deeply hidden toward which the tracks point (IV.ii.34). Gesturing toward and participating in, rather than fully possessing or merely appropriating, are here the mnemonic ideas that sustain and empower. In connection with them, Spenser's particular engagement with Chaucer's *unfinished* romances—*The Squire's Tale* and *The Tale of Sir Thopas*—is indeed remarkable. In the same passage in which Spenser describes *The Squire's Tale* as model and source, he characterizes Chaucer as the "well of English vndefyled" and speaks of the "infusion" of Chaucer's "spirit" into his own. He thus speaks of Chaucer much as he speaks in the sixth Proem of the muse's infusing and welling of "secret comfort, . . . heauenly pleasures," and the fruit of "learnings threasures . . . Into the mindes of mortall men," his own mind most specifically included.

At this point of my argument, it should almost have been predictable (even punningly so) that the root word of *infuse* and of *fons/fontis*, "source or well," would prove to be the same, namely *fundere*, "to pour," a fact available to Renaissance writers: "A *fons* 'spring' is that from which running water [*aqua viva*] *funditur*, 'is poured.'"[29] Running water is moving, changing, hence living (*viva*) water, as Mutability would be among the first to remind us, since "all that moueth [i.e., lieueth] doth mutation loue" (VII.-vii.55). One of the lessons Spenser learned from Chaucer, as he signals conspicuously in Arthur's dream of the Queene of Faerie, in the extension of *The Squire's Tale*, and in the half-jesting reference in the Mutability Cantos to Chaucer's own reference to *De planctu naturae*, is how to treat a source, be it Macrobius, Boethius, Alanus, Lollius, or Chaucer himself—that is, how to imbibe its spirit without being stagnated by its letter, how to use the resources of memory not as museum pieces, as mere authorities, but as the living voices of spirit.[30] Throughout *The Faerie Queene*, Spenser sought the traces of truth and the sources of inspiration, not in an unmediated self but in the cumulative expression of the inward mind inscribed in the human past and present in human records, in human words and texts, from the beginning.

6. *Spenser's Use of Chaucer's* Melibee: *Allegory, Narrative, History*

In an important article on the relation of Spenser's late lyrics to *The Faerie Queene*, Paul Alpers is especially concerned to defend Spenser's Melibee, the kindly old shepherd destroyed in the sixth book by marauding brigands, from other readers' charges of laziness, carelessness, or blindness. In terms of traditional morality, Alpers seeks to defend Melibee from the charge of imprudence in the style of his life. To this end he asserts Melibee's "parity" in Book VI with Colin Clout, Spenser's own pastoral persona, who invokes the celebrated vision of the Muses on Mount Acidale.[1] By "parity," Alpers means that both characters "speak with pastoral authority," and therefore that they share the kind of lyric domain he has earlier defined in a seminal article on *The Shepheardes Calender*.[2]

As Alpers conceives this domain in the earlier article, it is an "'aesthetic space' in terms of rule and authority," and it has "a qualified but nonetheless genuine independence" from history and politics—that is, from a world that is outside the poem, in his view. According to Alpers, its independence resembles the legal concept of *demesne* or, more generally, the implications of the word *domain* itself, a cognate of *demesne* similarly derived from Latin *dominium*. F. W. Maitland explains the legal concept of *demesne* as follows: "the ultimate (free) holder, the person who *stands at the bottom of the scale*, who seems most like an owner of the land, and who *has a general right of doing what he pleases* with it, is said to hold the land in demesne."[3] As Alpers translates this definition to a poetic domain, the freeholder has "a kind of *literary* authority" over his lyric realm—whence the authority he attributes equally to Colin and Melibee, the focal singers of pastoral in Book VI.

Much of Alpers' argument for the parity of these two pastoral figures hinges on their origin as "two kinds of pastoral song" in Vergil's first Eclogue.[4] For Alpers, the name of Spenser's Melibee evidently derives from that of Vergil's exiled Meliboeus, and in Book VI Melibee represents the "wisdom of the *fortunatus senex*," although he must represent it somewhat paradoxically, since he turns out to be considerably less than *fortunatus*. Albeit not in name, Colin similarly derives from Vergil's more fortunate Tityrus in the same eclogue. Together, Vergil's Meliboeus and Tityrus voice two versions of pastoral, the one belonging to the romantic woodlands ("*silvestrem musam*") and the other to the open fields ("*calamo agresti*"). Spenser subsequently realigns these landscapes with Colin and Melibee, giving Melibee the fields, and Colin-Tityrus the "wood / Of matchlesse hight."[5]

I agree that Spenser draws on Vergil's Eclogue and that Melibee and Colin can be paired in the way Alpers outlines, but I also think that their pairing is greatly complicated by other ancestors, particularly by two of the native British ones, whose lineal burden is moral and whose bearing on the pastoral cantos limits their authority. This is particularly true in the case of Melibee, on whom my chapter will focus, since he is the more problematic figure who is sacrificed to enable and to define Colin's paradisal landscape. Yet even in Colin's case, there are qualifying signs that hedge his lyric authority. His name comes directly from moral contexts—from Skelton's moral complaint *Collyn Clout* and from an eclogue by Marot, a poet who figures the moral dilemma of withdrawal and engagement, or—in Annabel Patterson's more politicized phrasing—of accommodation and dissent.[6]

Melibee's name carries a warning still stronger than Colin's. It alludes not only to Vergil's Meliboeus, who is dispossessed of his native lands and driven into exile, but also, with equal clarity, to Chaucer's relentlessly moral tale of a culpable Melibee. Chaucer's Prudence, the wife of Melibee, renders his name, "a man that drynketh hony," indeed, one who has "ydronke so muchel hony of sweete temporeel richesses, and delices . . . of this world," that he is "dronken" and has forgotten the conditions of his creaturely existence.[7] In Chaucer's *Tale*, Melibee is clearly imprudent. Enemies break into his house, beat his wife, and wound his daughter Sophie, because, as Prudence informs him, "thou hast . . . nat defended thyself suffisantly agayns hire assautes" (1422, xci^r). His plight thus bears a suggestive resemblance to that of Spenser's Melibee, whose dwelling the lawless brigands invade and whom they spoil "of all he had." In Spenser, Melibee and his aged wife are then with "his people captiue led away," conspicuous among them, his adopted daughter Pastorella–"little pastoral" (VI.x.39–40).

To borrow Alpers' terminology, Melibee is a poetic freeholder who mistakenly thinks that his only care is to "attend"—ambiguously to tend or merely to expect and await—what is his. As he serenely imagines it,

> The litle that I haue, growes dayly more
> Without my care, but onely to attend it;
> My lambes doe euery yeare increase their score,
> And my flockes father daily doth amend it.
> What haue I, but to praise th'Almighty, that doth send it?
> (VI.ix.21)

The ready ease of Melibee's question intimates its complacency, which is lent a comic cast by the wavering referent of the phrase "my flockes father" (the ram or the deity) and by the disyllabic rhyme (amend it/send it). Unfortunately, Melibee cannot so carelessly maintain his pastoral domain in the face of hostile intruders who imprison, enslave, and destroy its inhabitants (ix.21). Without admitting the inescapability of a reality outside his idyll, he is simply doomed, that is, judged. The judgment is at once cruel and biblically resonant.[8]

Even in summaries so brief and allusive, the invitation to read allegorically and morally is insistent in both Chaucer's and Spenser's tales of Melibee. In addition to basic plot and tropology, further coincidences between the concerns of the two works are distinctive. Both make the *invention*—here understood as the "discovery" *and* the "imposition"—of allegorical meaning problematical. Both make inescapably obvious a strain between a purposeful, conceptualized allegorical interpretation and a more simply and externally fortuitous one. Notoriously, at one point in Chaucer's *Melibee*, for example, Prudence tells her husband that he should be merciful to his enemies and at another that their attack on his daughter is analogous to the assaults of "the three enemys of mankynde—that is to seyn, the flessh, the feend, and the world," whom Melibee has suffered to enter into his "herte wilfully by the wyndowes of . . . [his] body, . . . so that they han wounded . . . [his] soule in fyve places" (1420–22). If we employ an allegorical reading consistently, Prudence is in the curious position of advising Melibee to go easy on the world, the flesh, and the devil when she counsels forgiveness; if we discount her analogy, we fly in the face of Wisdom, *Sophia*, his daughter Sophie's figurative identity.[9] At the outset of the *Tale*, it is Sophie who has been wounded in five places, suggesting the vulnerability of the senses, and in the preceding quotation it is she who explicitly represents Melibee's wounded soul.[10] Given the interpretive strain in the *Tale* between interiorized and exteriorized readings, we have cause additionally to reflect on an analogous disparity between wisdom and prudential knowledge, or, more simply and ethically, between ultimate ends and appropriate means. These are considerations that apply with peculiar force both to the conduct of the good life and to a poetic meant to delight as well as to instruct; thus they also apply to the styles chosen for the complementary arenas of life and poetry. Form again manifests content.

Comparably, in Spenser's sixth book, Melibee's kindness to Pastorella, the foundling whom he has adopted, his hospitality to the errant knight Calidore, and the wisdom evident in his Boethian stoicism—"It is the mynd, that maketh good or ill, / That maketh wretch or happie, rich or poore"—contrast starkly with his harsh fate at the hands of the brigands (VI.ix.30). In an allegorical poem such a fate implies that he has seriously erred in some way, and once this suspicion arises, a likelihood that his resemblance to Chaucer's culpable Melibee increases, many of the verses he sings fall under its shadow. Take these lines characterizing his lifestyle for another striking example:

> To them, that list, the worlds gay showes I leaue,
>   And to great ones such follies doe forgiue,
>   . . . .
>   Me no such cares nor combrous thoughts offend,
>   Ne once my minds vnmoued quiet grieue,
>   But all the night in siluer sleepe I spend,
> And all the day, to what I list, I doe attend.

Sometimes, Melibee adds,

>   I hunt the Fox, the vowed foe
>   Vnto my Lambes, and him dislodge away;
>   Sometime the fawne I practise from the Doe,
>   Or from the Goat her kidde how to conuay;
>   Another while I baytes and nets display,
>   The birds to catch, or fishes to beguyle:
>   And when I wearie am, I downe doe lay
>   My limbes in euery shade, to rest from toyle,
> And drinke of euery brooke, when thirst my throte doth boyle.
>
>   (VI.ix.22–23)

Pondering the intricacies of Melibee's ancestry, I sometimes dally with the surmise that Spenser had somehow seen a manuscript copy of Marlowe's "Passionate Shepherd" and that his treatment of Melibee's fate is the first of the many replies to it, of which his friend Ralegh's is the best known.[11] By Alpers' definition in yet another work, Melibee's is the landscape of idyllic pastoral, which "responds to and is in a sense created by man's desires," and it is woefully vulnerable to assault from other kinds of reality.[12] Like Chaucer's, Spenser's Melibee has drunk too much honey and has forgotten the realities of his creaturely existence. He has blurred the mind's domain, which "maketh good or ill, . . . wretch or happie, rich or poore," with the world's, and his error highlights the division of mind and world that has been an urgent pressure in the poem at least since the outset of Book IV, the beginning of the 1596 installment. Still more to the immediate point, the idyllic landscape at issue *belongs* to Melibee; it is his creation, one that exists in *his* voice, and not in the narrator's. It is where he *lives*, or has his being. In the rhetorical sense, it is, in short, his "place," or topos.

That it is landscape at all is important, since the meaning of landscape itself is an issue in Book VI. The hapless Serena's problems might be said to have started when she carelessly stepped into an allegorical landscape in canto iii: thus "Allur'd with myldnesse of the gentle wether, / And *pleasaunce* of the place," she "Wandred about the fields, as liking led / Her wauering lust [i.e., 'pleasure,' 'delight,' 'desire'] after her wandring sight" (23: my emphasis). She does nothing specifically wrong, but her simplest actions and inactions become morally significant. Landscape in Book VI is not *simply* neutral or innocent; like the landscape of Milton's Eden, it comes charged with meaning. Similarly, Melibee's spending all night in silver sleep or attending all day to what he pleases ("listes," i.e., "lustes"), his laying his limbs in every shade, or drinking from every fountain suggest his vulnerability, his imprudence, his willful misperception of specifically, relevantly allegorical dimensions of meaning.[13]

Alpers has astutely observed that Melibee can have a pastoral voice and "be a pastoral figure [precisely] because he has been at court," and thus, that "having crossed the boundary within which he now dwells," he is "conscious of it and the choice it represents." Indeed, "he is even a figure of the poet," specifically in his pastoral guise, and, in short, he is a "courtly and humanist self-representation."[14] After all, "little pastoral," the courtly scion Pastorella, is Melibee's adopted daughter, not his natural one. But if Melibee is a figure of the poet, the implications of his enlarged consciousness for his care-less way of life are especially worrisome. Melibee may sing of the "sweet peace" of his "natiue home" and of the "lowly quiet life" that he inherits, but he is himself no longer innocent of what Calidore terms "fortunes wrackfull yre" (ix.25, 27). Having sold himself for ten years as a worker in the "Princes gardin," Melibee has been alienated by the "vainenesse" he found there. Thus "Long deluded / With idle hopes" and thoroughly disillusioned with the Court, he has finally returned to his sheep (ix.24–25).

At moments we glimpse in Melibee's figure the shadowy silhouette of an Adam who would return to the Garden; at others, we glimpse a reflection of the courtly poet whose adopted home is the Irish countryside, where "sweet peace" in the sixteenth century is illusory or fleeting. Like Melibee, the Faerie Queen's poet has also withdrawn in disillusionment from the Court and has gone home again to the country, the domain of his own persona Colin Clout. The striking similarities between Melibee's reasons for abandoning the Court, the narrator's apology for Calidore's choosing to do likewise, and, in *Colin Clouts Come Home Again*, Colin's own warnings about the Court offer additional support for the perception of a resemblance between these two singers.[15] Implicit in this perception is an analogy between the pressures on the demesne of an imperiled landholder in troubled Ireland and the pressures on the demesne of pastoral—the pressures, in short, on Colin Clout's home-country.[16]

Hearing the stanzas describing Melibee's idyll, Calidore hangs "still vpon" the shepherd's "melting mouth attent; / Whose sensefull words empierst his hart" (ix.26). Although the word *sensefull* can mean "sensible," in the context of a melting mouth and "pleasing tongue," the meanings "sensuous" and "sensual" are more pertinent and distantly recall the sense wounds of Melibee's Sophie in Chaucer's *Tale*. Between the attractions of Melibee's words and Pastorella's face, Calidore is suggestively described as having "lost himselfe" and having grown "halfe entraunced." Like Melibee's name, "honey drinker" (*mel bibens*) or "honey toned" ($\mu\varepsilon\lambda\iota\beta o\acute{\eta}$), the enchanting power of his melting mouth and "pleasing tongue" stirs memories of other "charmed speeches" in the poem and of another "tongue, like dropping honny, [which] mealt'h / Into the hart" (I.ix.30, 31). I quote, of course, a description of the subtle power of Despair in Book I, which is drawn from the very canto, the ninth, that corresponds to Melibee's pastoral in Book VI. Such coincidences are usually significant in *The Faerie Queene*, and since this one directly precedes another in both books, namely a tenth-canto mount of vision, it is all the more likely to be so.

If even *Acidale*, the name of Colin's visionary mount in Book VI, can hint at *accidia*, sloth or despair, as Renwick and Nelson long ago suggested, and if this Mount can be said to *overlook* the vale, at once in the senses "survey," "look beyond," and "neglect," it is not surprising that a disturbing element of retreat should accrue to Melibee, the pastoral figure who has withdrawn, disillusioned, from the Court. Consider again those famous lines of Despair, "Sleepe after toyle, port after stormie seas, / Ease after warre, death after life does greatly please," in conjunction with snatches of Melibee's song: "And when I wearie am, I downe doe lay / My limbes in euery shade, to rest from toyle," for "Me no such cares nor combrous thoughts offend, / Ne once my minds vnmoued quiet grieue, / But all the night in siluer sleepe I spend." When Calidore hears in such words the promise of a state in which a knight might ever "dwell at ease," free "From all the tempests of these worldly seas, / Which toss the rest in daungerous disease," his response is both ominous and understandable (ix.19).

Spenser's sixth book is well known to be laden with memories of Book I, conspicuous among them not only the tenth-canto mount of vision but also the invocation of the Spenserian poet's pastoral origin and, in the two cantos immediately before Melibee's, the appearance of the "sib to great *Orgolio*" (vii.41). Other memories—for example, of sleep and shade and a carelessly "vnweeting" drink from a weary nymph's fountain—are less distinct, but nonetheless present. Perhaps all these memories have been written into the last book, because, like the first, it fundamentally concerns how we perceive, interpret, and represent what is real.

Herein lies another connection between Spenser's tale of Melibee and Chaucer's. Regardless of what degree of seriousness or satire we attribute to Chaucer's *Melibee* and its companion piece *Sir Thopas*, these are the only two *Canterbury Tales* told by a figure representing the poet himself, and together they afford contrasting meditations on the poet's craft.[17] Not surprisingly in view of the recurrent refractions of *Sir Thopas* throughout *The Faerie Queene*, Spenser's version of Chaucer's *Melibee* continues this meditation. From *The Shepheardes Calender*, which launched Spenser's poetic career, through the epic romance that dominated it, Spenser claimed Chaucer as the "auctour" whose work he emulated "through infusion sweete / Of ... [Chaucer's] owne spirit" (IV.ii.34). Like Spenser's refractions of *Thopas*, his tale of Melibee casts light on what he made of his "auctours" work and hence how he read it.

Both Chaucer's and Spenser's tales of Melibee are in some sense prudential works, and prudence is by definition a virtue committed to time and to memory. According to Aristotle, prudence concerns "what sorts of thing[s] conduce to the good life in general." It therefore pertains to what is "good and expedient" for a person, "not in some particular respect" such as health or strength, but more broadly. Yet prudence, while conducing to the good life, remains a practical, as distinct from a philosophic, wisdom. Its sphere of activity is this world, and it is essentially informed by history. Prudence is "a reasoned and true state of capacity to act with regard to human goods" or, more tellingly, with regard to "the things that are good or bad for Man."[18] Chiefly it involves *how* we ought to achieve a desirable end and thus guides the *means* we choose.[19]

Since prudence is a practical and virtuous guide to the attainment of the good life, it (she in the instance of Chaucer's *Tale*) draws heavily on the resources of traditional wisdom, on the *thesauri* or treasures of time. Indeed, prudence is defined both by Aristotle and Aquinas as an "*intellectual virtue . . . engendered and fostered by experience and time*," that is, by the cumulative memories of many generations about many things. As Chaucer's Prudence puts it, "in olde men is the sapience, and in longe tyme the prudence" (1163, lxxxviii^r). Similarly for Aquinas, prudence at once "requires the memory of many things" and "experience which is made up *of many memories*."[20] It is "a virtue most necessary for human life," for it "learns from the past and present about the future."[21] Appropriately, in Spenser's allegory of prudence in Book II, the sages of Alma's brain turret represent three aspects of prudence, namely, memory, judgment, and foresight, or, as Cicero describes them, "*memoria, intellegentia, providentia*," the faculties by which we discern what has been, what is, and what is yet to come.[22]

Lee Patterson has described Chaucer's *Melibee* as a "prudential florilegi[um]," a fact that is evident enough: the major voice in the *Tale* is that of Prudence, who lectures Melibee tirelessly, and her lectures consist largely of proverbs, apothegms, and other sententious expressions: for resonant examples, "every wys man dredeth his enemy," "weleful is he that of alle hath drede," "the wise man that dredeth harmes, eschueth harmes," "in alle wise flee ydelnesse," "For right as the body of a man may nat lyven withoute the soule, namoore may it lyve withouten temporeel goodes."[23] Prudence might well have added, "Render therefore unto Caesar the things that are Caesar's and unto God the things that are God's."[24] Her lectures afford a sometimes dizzying mix of morally righteous sentiments with worldly wise ones. She can parry quotations with her husband or rise to moral heights—"he that may have the lordeshipe of his owene herte is moore to preyse than he that by his force or strengthe taketh grete citees" (1515, xcii^r). Her copious mode of discourse, which would be right at home in the early modern period, encapsulates the treasures of cultural time and experience and thereby characterizes her prudential and practical nature.[25]

At times the *sententiae* invoked in Chaucer's *Melibee* seem to debate the nature, use, and worth of honey (*mel*) itself. For example, Melibee praises

Prudence's counsel by citing Solomon's view that "wordes . . . spoken discreetly by ordinaunce been honycombes, for they yeven swetnesse to the soule and hoolsomnesse to the body" (1112, lxxxvii^v). But Prudence later rebukes Melibee's indulgence in worldly delights by remembering "the wordes of Ovide, that seith,/ 'Under the hony of the goodes of the body is hyd the venym that sleeth the soule,'" and likewise Solomon, who also "seith, 'If thou hast founden hony, ete of it that suffiseth,/ for if thou ete of it out of mesure, thou shalt spewe'" (1413–16, xci^r). In accordance with Melibee's citation, Prudence's discourse is a spiritual pleasure and a cache of cultural nourishment—indeed, in a traditional mnemonic image, a honeycomb.[26] Digesting her *copia*, however, and noting Melibee's difficulty more often than not in doing the same, readers might also recall the Chaucerian persona's grimly facetious warning on the threshold of his *Tale* that his *Melibee* will contain "somwhat moore / Of proverbes than ye han herd bifoore," and they might understandably, if also perversely, connect these with the very excess of which Prudence speaks, an excess that results in rejection, or "spewing" (955–56, lxxxvi^r). Although so ironic a reading may itself be Melibean, the combination of wisdom and "sensefull" indulgence in Spenser's Melibee suggests a corrective response to an excess perceived as being too one-sidedly moral. Unfortunately, however, the correction introduces as many problems for the portrayal of a honey drinker as it resolves: while Spenser's Melibee is humanly more complex than either main character in Chaucer's *Tale*, his voice is less simply moral (or immoral), and his fate more disturbingly real.

Like the discourse of the characters in Chaucer's *Melibee*, that of Spenser's Melibee is strikingly sententious and at crucial moments specifically proverbial. It is surely significant that he hits his proverbial high point in the stanzas for which he is justly most admired:

> In vaine (said then old *Meliboe*) doe men
>   The heauens of their fortunes fault accuse,
>   Sith they know best, what is the best for them:
>   . . . .
>   For not that, which men couet most is best,
>   Nor that thing worst, which men doe most refuse;
>   But fittest is, that all contented rest
> With what they hold: each hath his fortune in his brest.
>
> It is the mynd, that maketh good or ill,
>   That maketh wretch or happie, rich or poore:

> For some, that hath abundance at his will,
> Hath not enough, but wants in greatest store;
> And other, that hath litle, askes no more,
> But in that litle is both rich and wise.
> For wisedome is most riches; fooles therefore
> They are, which fortunes doe by vowes deuize,
> Sith each vnto himselfe his life may fortunize.
> (VI.ix.29–30)

Both Shakespeare and Milton knew the appeal of these lines, which draw on at least nine proverbial expressions. One, "A man is the architect of his own fortunes," which is particularly attractive in Plautus' version, " 'Nam sapiens quidem pol ipsus fingit fortunam sibi' (For I tell you a man, a wise man, molds his own destiny)," is even repeated: a form of it appears in Melibee's first alexandrine and again in his second. Other proverbs active in these stanzas include "Accusing Fortune is only excusing ourselves," "We desire what is forbidden," "Happy is the man who is content with his own lot," "Good and evil are chiefly in the mind," "The more a man has, the more he desires," "The greatest wealth is contentment with a little," "Wisdom is wealth," and "He is a fool who plans for a fortune by vows."[27]

In the eighteenth century, Thomas Warton suggested that Melibee's last two lines derive from the conclusion of Juvenal's Satire X, known to readers of the Loeb edition as "The Vanity of Human Wishes." In view of Melibee's unfortunate capture and death, Juvenal's concluding lines shade into irony: " 'nullum numen habes, si sit prudentia; nos te, / nos facimus, Fortuna, deam caeloque locamus' (Thou wouldst have no divinity, O Fortune, if we had but . . . [*prudentia*, 'prudence']; it is we that make a goddess of thee, and place thee, in the skies)."[28] The question they raise is whether Melibee, who, like Chaucer's Melibee, embraces the honeyed power of words, but whose aged wife, unlike the wifely Prudence of Chaucer's *Tale*, is noticeably voiceless, really does have prudence.

In sharp contrast to the stanzas just quoted, Melibee's speech in canto ix includes other forms of discourse whose content bypasses a traditional moral and ethical burden. The most striking of these are the idyllic stanzas earlier cited, which include not a single proverb. Memorably attractive as these are and much as they bear a general resemblance to Marlowe's "Passionate Shepherd" and to Tasso's treatment of the old shepherd who comforts Erminia, their honeyed indulgence is distinctively Spenser's, or rather, Melibee's own.[29] Their indulgence and their distance from traditional moral and ethical wisdom urge again the question of Melibee's prudence.

Several statements in Lee Patterson's article on Chaucer's *Melibee* fit Spenser's redaction surprisingly well, and they further suggest how the *Tale* of Chaucer, Spenser's acknowledged "auctour," interacted with his own concerns. In Patterson's view, Chaucer's *Melibee* has an "unrelenting commitment to the historical world." It "describes a world of harsh deeds and serious consequences, in which the man of action must make his way by means of a pragmatic prudence" (159–60). Patterson considers the *Melibee* an educational work, plausibly meant for the young Richard II, and he characterizes the effect of its accumulated *sententiae* as authoritative, disciplinary, and illiberal. But even while the *Melibee* enforces the dominant ideology, it is shot through with pedagogical contradictions. These include opposite directives—on the one hand to examine thoughtfully, on the other merely to memorize—and comic ineffectiveness, since Melibee repeatedly misinterprets the counsel Prudence offers.[30] The *Melibee* thus "represents a writer who may have bowed before his social [ideological?] responsibilities but remains acutely aware of both the cost and the meager returns" of doing so (160).

While Spenser's tale of Melibee may not belong to a genre of educational books meant for aristocratic youths, it does belong to the book of *The Faerie Queene* most explicitly concerned with the rearing of children (Bruin's baby, Tristram, Pastorella) and to one that draws openly on a genre of courtesy books meant for the instruction of courtiers. The concentration of proverbs in Melibee's counsel, however ambivalent their ultimate worth, also reflects conspicuously the logical and rhetorical practices that humanist educators recommended as a primary means of linguistic empowerment.[31] Moreover, in the instance of Melibee's fate, the commitment of this Faerie book to history is inescapably compelling. Here history is understood not only as "a world of harsh deeds and serious consequences" but also as memory and experience—in Cicero's words, as "*vero testis temporum, lux veritatis, vita memoriae, magistra vitae, nuntia vetustatis* [the witness of times past, the light of truth, the life of memory, the guide of life, the messenger of age]."[32] History so characterized is prudential. In *The Faerie Queene*, it specifically includes the memories and experience of earlier books of the poem and the related temporality of narrative, particularly within Book VI itself. Understood in these ways, history bears heavily on an interpretation of Melibee's pastoral authority.

I have noted already the memories of Book I in the canto dominated by Melibee's voice, and these memories extend to other books as well. For example, a memory of Book II, of Guyon's debate with Mammon on the threshold of the latter's Cave, pushes the measure of Melibee's prudence toward a worldly wisdom that is anxious and unillusioned. Guyon's righteous rejection of material wealth and power, which is construed in his faint as a rejection of the material means of existence, has a certain resemblance to Melibee's indignant rejection of the gold Calidore offers him in return for his hospitality (II.vii.8, 10, 16). Extending a "golden guerdon" to Melibee, Calidore tells him it "may perhaps you better much withall, / And in this quiet make you safer liue" (VI.ix.32). Arguably, Calidore offers Melibee the means to protect himself, but Melibee, thrusting away the gold, replies,

> Sir knight, your bounteous proffer
> Be farre fro me, to whom ye ill display
> That mucky masse, the cause of mens decay,
> That mote empaire my peace with daungers dread.
> (VI.ix.33)

In similar terms, Guyon had rejected the "worldly mucke" that "with sad cares [would] empeach our natiue ioyes" (II,vii.10, 15). Melibee, like Guyon in the Cave, thinks he can avoid the ways of the world, and like him, he ironically becomes an "image of mortalitie," a resolutely idealistic but physically fallen monument to the reality of material existence (II.i.57). Melibee's defiance is admirable, but in worldly terms it turns out to be as unrealistic as Guyon's, and in Melibee's world, his situation, or site, in Book VI, this lack of realism is willful.

Like Melibee, the poet who wrote *The Faerie Queene* was a dreamer, but he was also the embattled colonist who wrote *A View of the Present State of Ireland* at just about the time Book VI was being published. As the *View* starkly demonstrates, he had every reason to respect the material underpinnings of power, relevantly including the power of defense. Not so coincidentally, perhaps, defense also occupies a conspicuous but ambiguous position in the counsel of Chaucer's Prudence, where the opposition of material to moral considerations may favor the moral ones but does so in terms that ironically facilitate worldly readings: if a stranger falls into your company, for example, "enquere thanne as subtilly as thou mayst of his conversacion, and of his lyf before, and feyne thy way; say that thou [wolt] thider as thou wolt nat go;/ and if he bereth a spere, hoold thee on the right syde, and if he bere a swerd, hoold thee on the lift syde" (1294–1338, here 1310–12, lxxxx^r; cf.1422, xci^r). Anxious, unillusioned, realistic, prudential: take your pick. The realities of travel in the fourteenth century lie near the surface of Prudence's advice.

In the presentation of Spenser's Melibee, recollections of Book VI itself are among the most immediate and telling memories of our earlier experience of the poem. Grounds for them begin with the first canto, which, like the opening cantos of all the other books in *The Faerie Queene*, signals the appropriate ways of reading and the thematic problems of the current quest. In it, Calidore encounters and overpowers Briana's churl, who has been charged with the shameless task of collecting a mantle of men's beards and ladies' locks. Calidore catches the fleeing churl in the porch of Briana's castle and cleaves

>   his head asunder to his chin.
> The carkasse tumbling downe within the dore
> Did choke the entraunce with a lumpe of sin,
> That it could not be shut, whilest *Calidore*
> Did enter in, and slew the porter on the flore.
>   (VI.i.23)

At this point other defenders of the castle flock about Calidore

>   and hard at him did lay,
> But he them all from him full lightly swept,
> As doth a Steare, in heat of sommers day,
> With his long taile the bryzes brush away.
>   (VI.i.24)

For a moment it all sounds so easy—Calidore's furious violence transmuted with the flick of a steer's tail to a pastoral landscape. But when he encounters Briana in the next stanza, she upbraids him in terms that challenge this transmutation:

> False traytor Knight, (sayd she) no Knight at all,
>   But scorne of armes that hast with guilty hand
>   Murdred my men, and slaine my Seneschall;
>   Now comest thou to rob my house vnmand,
>   And spoile my selfe, that can not thee withstand?
>   (VI.1.25)

Of course, Calidore, though much abashed, denies any shame, imputing it instead to those who first "breake bands of ciuilitie." While the moral strength of his position is clear, it does not cancel the excessive fury in his response or, more importantly for my purpose, the dissonance of the simile of the inoffensive steer with his bloody dispatch of Briana's defenders. The poet's inclusion of Briana's rebuke *insists* on this dissonance, which prefigures major stylistic and thematic movements of Book VI. Two later and relevantly contrasting examples are the transformation of Ariadne's grief and of the violence of the Centaurs and Lapiths into an image of cosmic order on Mount Acidale, and the transformation of Melibee's idyllic landscape into a wasteland. In these examples as well, a peaceful or harmonious fiction opposes a violent actuality. Both assay the relation of artifice, indeed, of anything essentially inward and mind-made, to a force outside the mind's domain (or demesne).

By the time we reach the pastoral cantos of Book VI, large themes and patterns have already been well established. The relation of fortune to human desire, of what is given to what is willed and sought, has been an evolving theme to this point, as has the more specific relation of repose to the threat of external forces.[33] When such focal themes recur in Melibee's landscape, we are likely to remember earlier incidents. For example, when Melibee sings, "But all the night in siluer sleepe I spend," it is a sleepy reader who does not recall that every time characters relax, let alone sleep, in Book VI, they are threatened or actually wounded: thus Aladine, Calepine, Serena (three times), and Arthur himself. That Melibee's unbroken "siluer sleepe" generically recalls other poems praising the country no more neutralizes its diction or insulates it from its present context in Book VI than the virtual identity of the blazon of Serena's physical attractions with the blazons of early modern sonnets alters the transforming fact that in Book VI the blazon of dismemberment figures the perception of cannibals. The sixth book, whose arch-villain is a blatant and beastly misuser of language, is fundamentally about words, about interpretations, and, by a further extension, about poetic forms. The inclusion within the book of conventional forms such as moral proverbs and pastoral lyrics subjects their powers and limitations—their authority—to exploration and assessment. It is supremely appropriate that Chaucer's *Melibee*, the prose work in which the poet examines the demands and costs of historical engagement, should loom large in the genealogy of Spenser's lyrical tale of his own honey drinker.

The larger context of Book VI might be said to encompass its pastoral cantos, as they in turn encompass the vision on Mount Acidale, and as the entire book is encompassed by what is beyond and outside it. On the face of it, such encompassing contexts might seem to resemble those of *The Shepheardes Calender*, the pastoral domain Alpers originally assigns the Spenserian poet, and might seem to be simply more layered and complex than the *Calender is*. Looked at more closely, however, they partake of a difference not simply of density, but also of kind. *The Calender* is not a narrative or allegorical form to anywhere near the extent that Book VI is, and this is a major reason that the poet of *The Calender* presides more easily and fully over his domain than Melibee does. In contrast, the lyric moments of Book VI are embedded in narrative, even as Book VI is embedded in history, the poetry of past times included. The Blatant Beast that rends the poet's rhymes at the end is analogous to the brigands who waste Melibee's landscape, and thus the poem as a whole is analogous to the pastoral cantos (VI.xii.40–41). What is at stake in these cantos is immense, since it involves their relationship not merely to lyric pastoral, but also to memory, to allegorical narrative, and, in a broad sense, to history.

If Chaucer's *Melibee* is a work in which the writer "remains acutely aware of both the cost and the meager returns" of engaging history, then Melibee's fate in Spenser's redaction might similarly be considered the "cost" and Colin's vision on Mount Acidale the "return," which is arguably not so meager. Melibee is sacrificed on the altar of prudence, in this case mainly a blind for harsh realism, in order at once to enable and implicitly to delimit Colin's still greater liberty. Melibee provides both the initial repose and the qualifying conditions that even an imagined, momentary access to a vision like that on Mount Acidale requires. Thus the pastoral cantos of Book VI both affirm the re-creative powers of pastoral and renounce pastoral innocence, a paradoxical conclusion with which Alpers would agree, although for different reasons.[34] Conveniently, it is a conclusion that the depiction of Melibee anticipates and the fate of Melibee seals.

PART 2   Agency, Allegory, and History within
         the Spenserian Intertext

7. *Spenser's* Muiopotmos *and Chaucer's* Nun's Priest's Tale

Most readers would probably agree with the editors of the Spenser *Variorum* that "in writing *Muiopotmos*[: *or The Fate of the Butterflie*] Spenser could hardly have been unconscious of Chaucer's mock-heroic poems, but that he was not engaged in a studied imitation of them."[1] As evidenced in *Muiopotmos*, Spenser's specific interest in *The Nun's Priest's Tale* lies somewhere between sustained allusion and incidental reminiscence; it is persistent but elusive. The relationship between these poems includes but extends beyond general similarities of genre, theme, and plot and the odd detail, such as the name of Clarion, which is likely motivated by that of Chauntecleer.[2] Precisely because the two poems are similar in general ways, their marked differences serve to define their artistic means and moral visions. For a prime example, Spenser significantly varies Chaucer's conspicuous use of rhetoric in relation to the ideologically sensitive themes of fortune and free will. Indeed, we might say of *Muiopotmos*, as has been said of *The Nun's Priest's Tale*, that "the real hero of the poem is rhetoric," yet it is a different type of rhetoric, used for different reasons and with tellingly different effects.[3]

When set beside *Muiopotmos*, *The Nun's Priest's Tale* illuminates the characteristics that make Spenser's poem a Renaissance and, more exactly, a Reformation work. Calvinist thought informs the meaning of Spenser's poem, distinguishing it from Chaucer's, even while casting in suggestive relief the nature of his relation to Chaucer and the uses he made of Chaucer's work. In the *Prologue* of *The Nun's Priest's Tale*, Harry Bailly scorns the Monk's fatalistic stories, which, he remarks, are "nat worth a boterflye" (3980). He measures the Monk's fatalism by a butterfly; in *Muiopotmos*, a butterfly's fate becomes the ambivalent measure of a human being's.

The Nun's Priest's Tale offers a world simultaneously sober and comic, cheerful despite its threats, and despite its pitfalls wonderfully secure.[4] In it, the distinctions between human and animal are constant and definite; in the figure of Chauntecleer we might be aware of a man's "chicken nature," of his feathered wives and feathery rhetoric, of his pride and weakness, but we are never allowed to lose sight of the ridiculous and genuinely risible fact that Chauntecleer is a rooster. The tone of Chaucer's *Tale* never falters; it instructs and alerts but does not puzzle or threaten us. We would not say after reading this *Tale*, "We are as chickens to the gods; they pluck us for their sport."

From the outset of *The Tale*, a moral norm is present in the life of the simple widow, by contrast a reminder both of the Wife of Bath and of the Prioress (4014–16, 4024–36). The villainous fox who lurks in a "bed of wortes" (herbs, cabbages) and the tumultuous hue and cry raised at his heels after he seizes Chauntecleer are tonal corollaries of this norm. The farcical chase of "daun Russell" near the end of the *Tale* engages the entire natural world in an effort to rescue a chicken, or still more ironically, in headlong pursuit of a fowl (Middle English "foul") and a fox. Here the "verray hogges" follow hard after the suggestively (not to say, bawdily) named Malkin, and a reference to peasant rebellion follows—and could only follow—directly after a flash of parodic wit playing on Vergil's use of apian imagery:[5]

> The gees for feere flowen over the trees;
> Out of the hyve cam the swarm of bees.
> . . . .
> Certes, he Jakke Straw and his meynee
> Ne made nevere shoutes half so shrille.
> (4581–85)

In this mock epic chorus from "Old MacDonald," now animated for adults, the fox has real teeth, but there is really no chance of his using them with finality: "Nowe, goode men, I prey yow herkneth alle: / Lo, how Fortune turneth sodeynly / The hope and pryde eek of hir enemy!" (4592–94). Reliably, fortune sides with our rooster-protagonist.

The fox serves as a correlative to Chauntecleer's pride and in this way as an extension of it. Dan Russell comes uninvited, but without Chauntecleer's active cooperation, his flattery would be ineffectual. Chauntecleer's problem lies less in oversight than in willful blindness, and rooster though he be, the judgment on his responsibility comes in a moment of self-recognition: "For he that wynketh, whan he sholde see, / Al wilfully, God lat him nevere thee" (4621–22). Fittingly, the most telling condemnation of Chauntecleer's vanity and pride thus comes from his own beak. Chauntecleer finally controls this situation, because he controls himself.

The moral imperative in Chaucer's *Tale* is clear: the ties between inner blindness and external danger, between folly and vulnerability, between personal culpability and cosmic calamity are direct and rational. Appropriately, the *Tale* ends with a series of morals—first, Chauntecleer's reference to his own free will and to his own blindness (4619–22); then the fox's reference obliquely to God's justice and more directly to his own lack of control: "God yeve hym meschaunce, / That is so undiscreet of governaunce" (4623–24). Finally comes the subtler, more humane morality of the Nun's Priest himself, who begins by repeating what Chauntecleer and the fox have already said (4626–27) and then continues, "But ye that holden this tale a folye, / As of a fox, or of a cok and hen, / Taketh the moralite, goode men" (4628–30). The Priest's use of the word "But," where we should have expected "and," focuses attention on his audience. This shift in point of view is essentially dramatic rather than thematic, and it is thoroughly moral as well. The audience (or readers) presumably are to become self-conscious about their own responses to the *Tale* and aware of their own involvement in its "moralite." If some have thought the *Tale* an irrelevant story about lesser creatures, they have missed the point, and so the Priest wryly suggests that they had best take the "moralite" and, indeed, that they need it. He has first restated the obvious morals of his *Tale*, and then he has brought home to his audience the meaning of "moralite" itself: morality has thus become an act of understanding. The concluding lines of the *Tale* imply that if we were not willfully blind to meaning, as Chauntecleer was, then, perhaps, we might accord with the good will of God:

> For seint Paul seith that al that writen is,
> To oure doctrine it is ywrite ywis;
> Taketh the fruyt, and lat the chaf be stille.
> Now, goode God, if that it be thy wille,
> As seith my lord, so make us alle goode men,
> And brynge us to his heighe blisse! Amen.

Although the Priest's remarks are often ironic and occasionally ambiguous, rhetoric in his *Tale* is clearly controlled and unquestionably full of meaning. Ordinarily response to it (if not analysis of it) is immediate.[6] The Priest's résumé of major theories concerning the relationship of human will to God's foreknowledge, for example, demands attention, even while inviting laughter. The Priest mocks, yet uses these theories, alerting listeners to the theological issues at stake and simultaneously to the ineffectuality of human efforts to resolve them. He first warns that there is a tremendous amount of "altercacioun" and "disputisoun" in the schools about this matter:

> And hath been of an hundred thousand men.
> But I ne kan nat bulte it to the bren
> As kan the hooly doctour Augustyn,
> Or Boece, or the Bisshop Bradwardyn,
> Wheither that Goddes worthy forwityng
> Streyneth me nedely for to doon a thyng,—
> "Nedely" clepe I symple necessitee;
> Or elles, if free choys be graunted me
> To do that same thyng, or do it noght,
> Though God forwoot it er that I was wroght;
> Of if his wityng streyneth never a deel
> But by necessitee condicioneel.
> (4429–40)[7]

This hardly simple Priest's ironic purpose is even more immediately evident in the lament that follows the fox's seizing Chauntecleer, which presents opposing views of Chauntecleer's responsibility for his own misfortune. The first of these resembles the pessimistic and deterministic view of the speaker in *The Monk's Tale*: "O destinee, that mayst nat been eschewed!" (4528); the second suggests with progressive irony that Chauntecleer is to blame for his own fate:

> Allas, that Chauntecleer fleigh fro the bemes!
> Allas, his wyf ne roghte nat of dremes!
> And on a Friday fil al this meschaunce.
> (4529–31)

Almost too casually, the first line suggests that Chauntecleer is at fault—too bad he flew from the beams, but those are the breaks of fortune. The second line ineffectually shifts responsibility from Chauntecleer to his wife: his fate would have been less certain had she taken dreams, not to mention the needs of a rooster's ego, more seriously. The third line, a thoroughgoing anticlimax, compels resistance to its ironic facticity and thereby insists on Chauntecleer's culpability. At the same time, it hints overtly at the underlying reasons for his downfall—what a coincidence that Chauntecleer heeded his wife's scorn rather than his own convictions on Friday, a day important to Venus and, of course, to the willful Old Adam's redemption as well.

In recognizing anticlimax and skillful irony in the third line, we exercise certain assumptions at once about the coherence of rhetoric and about that of the universe in this poem. But it is the poem itself that has consistently invited these assumptions.[8] In the plot, the rhetoric, and the ironic vision of *The Nun's Priest's Tale*, a reader is constantly aware not only of structure, patterns, deft control, but also of the fact that they are coherently significant. Hearing the speaker's voice in this *Tale*, we are likely to feel that we can be reasonably sure of his meaning. A surprising number of half-truths mingle with plain facts in the Priest's lamentation for Chauntecleer, but they are all measured by a single perception and all ironic because of it. Chauntecleer has worked his own misfortune. His willful pride, after all, has clearly preceded his fall.

Like the rhetoric which creates it, the world in *The Nun's Priest's Tale* makes sense, and its total effect is comic and reassuring. This is a world in which "Mordre wol out," sometimes a dangerous world and certainly an ironic one, but finally, at least in this *Tale*, a just and even generous one. Here a person seems essentially free, the responsible agent of his or her own actions; and if this is the way we seem, then for all practical purposes, as the *Tale* concludes, we really must be.

Muiopotmos leaves us with a significantly different set of impressions. In Spenser's poem the world is not merely less secure but actually hostile; at the same time forces external to the psyche, or to the butterfly Clarion, have become more dominant. Although Spenser's poem raises issues of agency and responsibility as explicitly as Chaucer's, the individual will appears to be less determinant in it and, as a result, less free.[9] Taken whole, *Muiopotmos* is less comic and less consistently ironic; its total vision is less assured. In it, the line that separates truths from half-truths has become harder to locate. The sense of a definable reality (truth) is not so firmly and securely present in the later poem.[10]

Two passages from *Muiopotmos* can illustrate and in part account for these impressions. In the first, the distinctions between human being and butterfly are at once greater and lesser, and they prove less constant and definite than their counterparts in Chaucer's poem. For example, there is a notable difference between Chauntecleer's lecturing Pertelote and Clarion's actually donning armor:

> His breastplate first, that was of substance pure,
> Before his noble heart he firmly bound,
> That mought his life from yron death assure,
> . . . .
> And then about his shoulders broad he threw
> An hairie hide of some wilde beast, whom hee
> In saluage forrest by aduenture slew,
> And reft the spoyle his ornament to bee:
> Which spredding all his backe with dreadfull vew,
> Made all that him so horrible did see,
> Think him *Alcides* with the Lyons skin
> When the *Noemean* Conquest he did win.
>   (57–59, 65–72)

The witty analogy between the anatomy of a butterfly (chitinous exoskeleton, fuzzy back) and the military accoutrements of these lines only emphasizes the imposition of human significance. An equivalent situation in *The Nun's Priest's Tale* might have involved Chauntecleer's actually decking himself out as a clerk or eating roast venison rather than worms. Comic incongruity tells heavily in this passage from *Muiopotmos*, which, even when cited in part, as here, prolongs attention to the ill-fitting fact that the Herculean Clarion is a butterfly. The voice of the Spenserian narrator contributes to the playful tone of the passage, while it signals another difference from *The Nun's Priest's Tale*. Within the first seventy-five lines of Chaucer's *Tale*, for example, Chauntecleer is talking to Pertelote, but throughout *Muiopotmos*, we hear only a narrative voice. This difference significantly influences our view of Clarion and the way we read the entirety of Spenser's poem. We are more aware of Clarion as an object and a vehicle of meaning than is the case with the voluble Chauntecleer. Hardly by coincidence, many readers have felt the need to identify the meaning of Clarion as a symbol that is more topical or specific than generically human, a temptation that the more dramatic, more fully animated treatment of Chauntecleer does not so readily provoke.[11] While Spenser is not a more deliberate artist than Chaucer, his portrayal of Clarion is simply more self-consciously, showily, significantly artificial than what is found in Chaucer's *Tale* of a vain, talking rooster. Morally, his portrayal is also more puzzling; for some readers, this is yet another reason to suspect topical reference.

The second passage, taken from one of two central stanzas in *Muiopotmos*, likewise involves incongruity, although this time the incongruity is not so comic. When Clarion sports in the "gay gardins," the narrator asks,

> What more felicitie can fall to creature,
> Than to enioy delight with libertie,
> And to be Lord of all the workes of Nature,
> To raine in th'aire from earth to highest skie . . . ?
> (209–12)

This passage directly follows six stanzas tracing Clarion's flight through the gardens. Suddenly asking a series of rhetorical questions, the narrator reflectively highlights Clarion's activities, momentarily seeming to lose the distinction between human and insect in a way that they are never lost in *The Nun's Priest's Tale*. The dramatic situation in Spenser's passage is also unclear, partly because we are not sure whether the narrator is speaking primarily to his audience or to himself—whether he is reflecting tangentially upon Clarion's activities or in fact (as in effect) directly interpreting them for us. There is no break between these lines and the preceding lines of narrative sufficient to prepare us for the abrupt shift in perspective. As a result of it, we may suddenly find ourselves objecting that perhaps a human being, but surely not Clarion, is lord of the works of nature, and if we object to this miscasting of Clarion, we may realize that we are objecting to one view of our own role as well and that we, like Clarion, are mere creatures.[12] The inappropriate excess of attributing to a butterfly the biblically empowered dominion of humankind over "the fowl of the air . . . and every living thing . . . upon the earth," to which the final lines of the passage allude, spills over, so to speak, on us (Gen. 1:28). The joke is not primarily or even equally on Clarion here but on overweening human pride, and it is precisely because these lines at first make little sense in reference to the butterfly that their significance strikingly emerges. As in *The Nun's Priest's Tale*, morality here involves an act of understanding, but it is no longer an act which, in the same sense at least, can be called dramatic or continuous—indeed, coherent. The shift in point of view is not from tale to audience or even to speaker so much as it is a shift from one plane of reference to another—in a word, from insect to human to God, the only true "Lord of all the workes of Nature," reigning "from earth to highest skie." With this conspicuous shift in register, we recognize that the poem is asking us to read in a different way.

The voice rhetorically questioning Clarion's sport in the gardens belongs to an elusive, shifty narrator who is less personable than Chaucer's and who lacks the expected moral and social identity of a nun's priest. In the latter's *Tale*, insight and irony are also embedded in a surface that in context already makes sense—"*Mulier est hominis confusio*"—even when this sense is arbitrarily kept to a single, simple, surface meaning: Chauntecleer literally flew from the beams on a Friday—right? Or Boethius, Bradwardine, and the lot of them complicate the real issues, or just take the morality, good men—right? In *Muiopotmos*, however, it is not only in the presence of apparent incoherence, but precisely because of it that we achieve insight: Clarion the butterfly is "Lord of all the workes of Nature, / To raine in th'aire from earth to highest skie"—not right at all if taken literally rather than allegorically.

Only such allegorical insight can keep *Muiopotmos* from being a disquieting and thoroughly pessimistic poem.[13] Taken at face value, Clarion's end would be *merely* abrupt, unfair, fatalistic, and ugly. In the last stanza, Aragnoll rushes fiercely from his den to seize "greedelie / On the resistles pray"; then "with fell spight, / Vnder the left wing" he

> . . . stroke his weapon slie
> Into his heart, that his deepe groning spright
> In bloodie streames foorth fled into the aire,
> His bodie left the spectacle of care.

Where the final emphasis in *The Nun's Priest's Tale* falls on Chauntecleer's pride, in *Muiopotmos* it falls on Aragnoll's malice. Throughout Spenser's poem, Clarion is less willful than is Chauntecleer, and at its end, the "fond Flie" never voices a moral: unlike Chauntecleer, he never realizes *our* perceptions. At the same time, however, misguided, prodigal, and wanton as Clarion may be, he never loses the fragile beauty of a butterfly.[14] His excesses qualify but do not destroy it. With Chauntecleer and "daun Russell" as a point of comparative reference, Aragnoll's malice arguably looks less like a correlative to Clarion's pride than to his beauty. Chauntecleer gets caught in ironies that are primarily self-induced; Clarion, in an irony that is primarily cosmic. *Muiopotmos* literally translated means "fly-fate," and in reading the poem it is difficult not to wonder at crucial moments whether we are to the gods as flies are to us.

The irony—or the web—in which Clarion is trapped takes shape in the myth of Astery, which succeeds the mock heroic arming of the butterfly. This little myth is first introduced by an extensive description of Clarion's pretty wings, "siluer bright" and "passing farre / All Painters skill": "Not halfe so manie sundrie colours arre / In *Iris* bowe, ne heauen doth shine so bright, / Distinguished with manie a twinckling starre" (92–94). Little wonder that many a Lady in Court "Beholding them, him secretly enuide" and wished that "Some one that would with grace be gratifide, / From him would steale them priuily away, / And bring to her so precious a pray" (110–12). For these Court Ladies, Clarion is prey, merely something to acquire and possess. Their wishes anticipate Aragnoll's.

On this note, the poem proceeds without pause to the myth of Astery, a *pourquoi* story telling how butterflies came to have such beautiful wings. "Report is" that when the nymph Astery, an especially industrious culler of flowers, was praised by Venus, other nymphs slandered her diligence, enviously claiming that she had received secret help from Cupid. Venus, then remembering Cupid's love for Psyche, became fearful and jealous, flew into a rage, and promptly turned the innocent Astery into a butterfly:

> And all those flowres, with which so plenteouslie
> Her lap she filled had, that bred her spight,
> She placed in her wings, for memorie
> Of her pretended crime, though crime none were:
> Since which that flie them in her wings doth beare.
>   (140–44)

The Court Ladies' cupidity, their mean possessiveness, takes form in the myth of Astery, precipitating the very myth that it introduces. Their envy is both cause and effect of this myth in the poem: they envy Clarion's beautiful wings, which are a direct result of Astery's misfortune, the story of which their envy motivates and introduces. Aragnoll's encircling web is already a-weaving.

The description of Clarion's wings, whose beauty leads to courtly envy and treachery, thus concludes the many stanzas devoted to the arming of the heroic butterfly, one of the most securely comic passages in the poem. Before the myth of Astery, the fully armed Clarion seems poised for flight into genuine mock epic, but after it he travels in an altered context. He soars lightly through the countryside in "franke lustinesse" (pleasure, delight, desire) "That none gainsaid, nor none did him enuie," yet readers now realize that he flies carelessly into a more dangerous and threatening world. Unaccountably, his activities seem to become morally more suspect as well, and soon we hear of his "wauering wit" as he is carried away by "vnstaid desire" to the "riotous excesse" of the "gay gardins." In a few more stanzas we learn of his "glutton sense" and of his spoiling "the pleasures of that Paradise," as he tastes them "at will, / And on their pleasures greedily doth pray" (203–4). Another circle in the web has been completed: now Clarion's behavior mirrors that of the Court Ladies and foreshadows that of Aragnoll himself.

The increasingly moral rhetoric of these stanzas is what stands between Clarion and a thoroughly deterministic view of the world, as does the poem's definitive shift into allegory at their end when the narrator asks abruptly, pointedly, and discontinuously what greater happiness exists than in free delight to be Lord of Nature and "raine in th'aire from earth to highest skie." At the same time, however, the narrator's moral awareness (or conceivably his ironized lack of it) cannot stand between Clarion and his evident fate. On the one hand, Clarion is going wrong, even if he will never know it; on the other, the essential connection lies between ours and the narrator's perceptions and what is lacking in Clarion's. Aragnoll thus becomes an extension of Clarion's lack of awareness rather than of his pride. When Clarion tastes "at will" in the gardens, he seems innately willful—willful by arthropodous instinct, rather than by choice. If Aragnoll realizes anything in Clarion it is therefore primarily weakness and moral void.[15] As opposed to the primary emphasis in *The Nun's Priest's Tale*, and in particular opposition to the significance of "daun Russell," the spider appears to be a force external to the fly.

Clarion belongs to the natural world: unaware, appealing, lovely, and evidently doomed. He is also the victim of this world—a harsh, irrational, unjust world in a way that the Nun's Priest's world is not. The widening gap between our kind of awareness and Clarion's throughout the poem characterizes Spenser's treatment of individual responsibility and accounts for major differences in tone and meaning between his poem and Chaucer's. It accounts as well for some of the reasons Spenser's poem is so clearly a Renaissance and Reformation work. The following pages examine this gap in awareness more fully and then trace its development through passages in *Muiopotmos* in which the poet addresses himself specifically to questions of awareness, will, and fortune.

Despite the prodigality ascribed to Clarion, his guilt is lightly touched upon. Only two stanzas before we hear—or half hear in a single line—that Clarion's "play" is spoiling the pleasures of paradise, the butterfly surveys "euerie flowre and herbe there set in order":

> Now this, now that he tasteth tenderly,
> Yet none of them he rudely doth disorder,

Ne with his feete their silken leaues deface;
But pastures on the pleasures of each place.
(173–76)

The word "pastures" sounds a somewhat incongruous (and Acrasian) note but fails to drown out the delicacy of the lines that it follows; *pastures* (from Latin *pascere,* "to feed") is, after all, a natural word-concept, not *per se* a moral one. Even when we hear explicitly about Clarion's gluttony and greed, numerous verbal attractions modify a negative assessment: notions about "varietie," "sweetnesse," and "play" itself, or the "warme Sunne," "gladfulnes, and kingly ioyaunce." Clarion's paradise is full of verbal melody and imagistic allure: "Coole Violets, and Orpine growing still, / Embathed Balme, and chearfull Galingale, / Fresh Costmarie, and breathfull Camomill" (193–95).[16] As in so many passages of *The Nun's Priest's Tale,*[17] representation of the "gay gardins" involves rhetorical flourishes; indeed, the gardens *are* in some sense such a flourish. Yet the Nun's Priest acts more directly to expose the egotistical pretensions of inflated rhetoric; the gardens have more lyricism than pretension and exaggeration about them. Our sensibilities respond to this lyricism with considerable sympathy, and as in Spenser's Bower of Bliss, they are meant to do so.

The appeal of Clarion and the gardens asks us to see in the butterfly a harmless, naturally innocent, attractive creature. The moral rhetoric in the garden passages and Clarion's history, intertwined with Astery's, remind us that the butterfly's innocence is reckless and, in human terms, deceptive. Clarion's present winged beauty is of mixed birth, formed by Love (Venus), but also by hatred (envy, slander, fear, jealousy). There is an ugly malice in the world to which the unwitting Clarion takes his flight, but ugliness and weakness are found in the unwitting Clarion's history as well.

This tension between innocence and weakness, between attraction and ugliness, is characteristic of Spenser's poetry and of the age in which it was written. It is easy, for instance, to feel the pertinence of Calvin's thought here—both his strong sense of the world's beauty:

> Shall the Lord haue set in flowers so great a beautie, as presenteth it selfe to our eies: shall he haue giuen so great a sweetnesse of sauour as naturally floweth into our smelling: and shall it be vnlawfull either for our eies to take the vse of that beautie, or for our smelling to feele that sweetnesse of sauour?

and his sense of the world's corruption, the result of a past which besmirches the present:

> For because we are naturally inclined to hypocrisie, therefore a certaine vaine resemblance of righteousnes doth abundantly content vs in stead of righteousnes in deed. And because there appeereth nothing among vs, nor about vs, that is not defiled with much filthines, therefore that which is somewhat lesse filthie pleaseth vs as though it were most pure, so long as we hold our selues within the bounds of mans vncleanes.[18]

In Calvinist thought, as received and developed by the reformers of the later sixteenth and seventeenth centuries, the natural world is merely threatening and seductive unless it is seen with a special kind of awareness. If the true Temple is within, an interiorized faith transforms the whole world for the believer. The value of the world is thus relative to belief. At the same time that the natural world becomes more autonomous, more external, more profane, and more scientific (in the modern sense), individual vision becomes potentially more sacred. The unenlightened viewer sees a world which is lovely, to be sure, but essentially misleading or meaningless. The enlightened viewer sees the same world but at once within it and beyond it sees also what is real.[19] Calvin's thinking, of course, like the rest of the Reformation, is saturated in Augustine's; the difference between the two, while largely a matter of tone and emphasis, is yet sufficient in degree and in institutional effect to look like a difference in kind.

I suspect that Reformation thinking, especially Calvin's, lies behind many of the striking features of rhetoric in *Muiopotmos*: for example, behind the lines earlier examined in which a sudden shift in plane of reference is the means by which we achieve insight (209–12). The same thinking even further informs the stanzas that immediately follow this shift and precede the myth of Arachne. In these stanzas the speaker continues to ask and to answer rhetorical questions explicitly about fortune, fate, free will, and the relation of happiness to heavenly powers. Like the Nun's Priest's tongue-in-cheek résumé of theories about the will and his comically ironic remarks about Chauntecleer's fate, these questions raise the major issues at stake, though in a different way. Having asked whether it is not wonderful to be Lord of the works of Nature and then provocatively having added, to be free of all restraints, "To feed on flowres, and weeds of glorious feature, / To take what euer thing doth please the eie," the speaker again has sudden second thoughts and so continues, "But what on earth can long abide in state?" (217). He then concludes anxiously, "That none, except a God, or God him guide, / May them [perils] auoyde, or remedie prouide." In a third stanza he comments on the absolute powers of the gods, who "Warre against vs the vassals of their will," and in a fourth, remembering and then addressing Clarion, "Whose cruel fate is wouen euen now / Of *Ioues* owne hand," he sees that "Nought may thee saue from heauens auengement." Freedom, license, transience, a helpful god or God, servitude to hostile gods, a cruel fate at the hands of a vengeful god—quite a menu of attitudes and interpretive options, but one notably concluding with those enforcing (human) helplessness.

"O destinee, that mayst nat been eschewed! / Allas, that Chauntecleer fleigh fro the bemes!" Spenser might as well have had Chaucer's lines in mind, but if he did, he has significantly enlarged upon them to alter their impact. In contrast to the speed, the sharpness, the ironic condensation of the Chaucerian lines, Spenser's four stanzas raise the issues of fate and agency more gradually and puzzlingly. By the end of them, his speaker in *Muiopotmos* deliberately indulges a fatalistic point of view. His voice totally lacks the tongue-in-cheek quality that characterizes similar passages in *The Nun's Priest's Tale*. He not only expresses some of our own doubts about cosmic justice in *Muiopotmos*, but through the length and apparent seriousness of his reflections, he reinforces them. The determinism of these stanzas becomes important in and for itself, rather than as the view of a dramatized character or as an ironic reflection on the action. Like the "gay gardins," these stanzas do not merely embellish the poem; they become a special, conspicuous part of its meaning.[20]

By the next stanza, the speaker has refocused on his narrative, and once again the plane of reference shifts to develop an alternative approach to Clarion's experience:

> It fortuned (as heauens had behight)
> That in this gardin, where yong *Clarion*
> Was wont to solace him, a wicked wight
> The foe of faire things, th'author of confusion,
> The shame of Nature, the bondslaue of spight,
> Had lately built his hatefull mansion.
>
> (241–46)

For the present, Aragnoll is no further identified, but few readers could miss the obvious allusions to Satan in these lines or the alternative to a thoroughgoing determinism implicit in them.[21] Instead of developing his villain's immediate designs on Clarion, however, the narrator turns next to the myth of Arachne to develop his alternative reading.

This myth explains that Aragnoll hates "the ioyous Butterflie" because his mother Arachne challenged Pallas Athena to match "with her in curious skill / Of workes with loome, with needle, and with quill" (271–72); Arachne realized that the contest was lost when Athena wove a butterfly into her own tapestry:

> And by her silence, signe of one dismaid,
> The victorie did yeeld her as her share:
> Yet did she inly fret, and felly burne,
> And all her blood to poysonous rancor turne.
>
> That shortly from the shape of womanhed
> Such as she was, when *Pallas* she attempted,
> She grew to hideous shape of dryrihed,
> Pined with griefe of follie late repented:
> Eftsoones her white streight legs were altered
> To crooked crawling shankes, of marrow empted,
> And her faire face to fowle and loathsome hewe,
> And her fine corpes to a bag of venim grewe.
> (341–52)

In short, Arachne turns into a spider, mother of Aragnoll, that "cursed creature, mindfull of that olde / Enfestred grudge, the which his mother felt," and so as soon as Aragnoll spies Clarion in the garden, he swells inwardly with "vengefull malice" and starts weaving his web (353–60). History is again at its entangling work.

Clarion's flight through the "gay gardins" falls between the myths of Astery and Arachne, thereby connecting a history of innocence injured unjustly by envy with a history of pride, inner rancor, and "follie late repented"—alternative ways, in effect, of reading the Fall of humankind.[22] Both myths affect our view of Clarion, but in different ways. Most obviously, Arachne wills her own fate, whereas Astery does not. The fact that Spenser reworked Ovid's myth of Arachne to emphasize her malice and guilt makes this contrast even more striking.[23] The fates of Astery and Arachne likewise differ. On the one hand, Astery is changed by Venus into a butterfly, something beautiful within the natural order. By Venus' association of the innocent nymph with Psyche, Cupid's beloved, and thus, as it happens, with the Greek word for mind or soul, namely *psyche*, which is traditionally represented by a butterfly, Astery's end also hints—but only hints, and does so *despite* Venus—at a more positive justice beyond the merely natural order, that is, beyond the order to which the pagan Venus herself belongs.[24] Arachne, on, the other hand, changes, rather than is changed, from a woman to a spider, a poison within the natural order; and if the spider's portrayal alludes to a force beyond nature, it glances, we have seen, at Satan himself (241–46). Thus Astery's fate hints at a primal goodness in nature after all, and Arachne's at a rational explanation of evil. Again, hints.

Throughout *Muiopotmos*, the poet (or the poem, if you will) has adjusted and sometimes disoriented our view of Clarion, variously collapsing or reinforcing the distance between human and butterfly. Now in the myth of Arachne he shifts our perspective for the first time to a decidedly Christian and human context of sin and responsibility, one that can more adequately rationalize Clarion's harsh fate. Prior to the myth of Arachne, we get only an impasse: in human terms, Clarion's play in the gardens is careless, weak, and immoral; but Clarion is a butterfly, and his behavior, like his beauty, is natural; taken together (as, after all, Clarion is in the poem), he looks more fragile than malicious, more weak than corrupt. But as long as we regard the butterfly (the ambiguous *psyche*) as if he were everywhere a constant—somehow a person or a fully dramatized character—and not to a larger extent the poet's creature, or vehicle of meaning, we get only this impasse. The impasse is in the poem, but it is also clear from the poem that we are not supposed to stop with it.[25]

Response to *Muiopotmos* should be both sequential and retrospective, as I have tried to argue it here; our judgment involves the reassessment of earlier responses as well as the development of new ones.[26] By adding more specifically spiritual and moral dimensions to the poem, the myth of Arachne-Aragnoll in effect supersedes (indeed, sublates), although it cannot wholly cancel, doubts the poem itself has raised about the justice of Clarion's fate. The freedom of the butterfly's "will" is never denied in the poem; we are instead asked to see that it really never matters or, more precisely, that it is not really the point.[27] Given Aragnoll (or Satan or any known Evil, it would seem), we realize that a purely natural innocence—the poet's, Clarion's, Astery's, the reader's—is in this world always already tainted and, without a god's or God's help, simply doomed. The myth of Arachne suggests that the poem is essentially aimed at our recognizing this insight and that its pivotal concern is with vision.

The tapestries woven by Arachne and Pallas Athena enforce this impression. Athena evidently wins not simply because she is a better weaver but because she weaves better stories; she sees the world in a different way, and the butterfly is part of her vision. Arachne sees the gods as lusty lovers; she shows Jove as a beast. Athena sees the gods as institutors of fruitful peace (324–28). Whereas Arachne "figur'd how *Ioue* did abuse / *Europa* like a Bull," Athena "made the storie of the olde debate, / Which she with *Neptune* did for *Athens* trie." Athena's story issues in "A fruitfull Olyue tree" and an encompassing "wreathe of Olyues hoarie."[28] She makes, or creates, in a positive light, even if we realize her position also to be self-serving and her purpose to maintain her evidently genuine superiority; Arachne rashly and spitefully, if also truthfully, exposes.[29] Either weaver chooses an emphasis, or an interpretive perspective, and both their choices imply similar options for the poet and his readers.

But it is the wanton, beautiful butterfly in the border of Athena's tapestry that especially dismays Arachne: *wanton*, the word Milton notoriously used to describe Eve's untrammeled tresses, signifies "playful" but also "unrestrained," with the potential to shade into "excessive" and "immoral"—exactly the right descriptor for the evolving figure of Clarion or, alternatively *and* simultaneously, for the changing light in which he is seen. The butterflies in *Muiopotmos* belong to so many Chinese boxes: the butterfly in the tapestry border, the butterfly in the myth of Astery; Clarion, the butterfly whose story connects and encircles the others'. In the context of this poem, the butterfly in Athena's border must point beyond itself, but it persistently remains itself as well, "Fluttring among the Oliues *wantonly,* / That seem'd to liue, so like it was in sight" (331–32: my emphasis).[30] When seen, this butterfly—life-like, lovely, wanton—defeats Arachne's overweening pride, and when seen by her, turns envy to self-poisoning rancor. The myth of Arachne is bordered by the history of Clarion, and so the tapestry might be said to mirror in small Spenser's poem. The tapestry shows human pride defeated by the irreducibly ambivalent sight of a lovely butterfly and an envious human being destroyed by herself: "Yet did she inly fret, and felly burne, / And all her blood to poysonous rancor turne" (343–44). In Chaucer's *Tale*, coincidentally enough, it is when Chauntecleer casts "his ye / Among the wortes on a boterflye" that he suddenly becomes "war of this fox, that lay ful lowe" and thus, as it soon turns out, aware of the pitfall his own foolhardy, heedless pride has readied for him (4463—65). Briefly, the secure vision of the Nun's Priest thus comes contrastingly to mind.

With barely a break Spenser's poem shifts from the myth of Arachne to Aragnoll's ensnaring of Clarion. In its short, swift conclusion, "careles" Clarion wanders "at will . . . In the pride of his freedome principall: / Litle wist he his fatall future woe" (379–81). Clarion now appears at once freer and more fated; his will receives more emphasis at precisely the moment that he fails all the more fatally to exercise it morally. Because Clarion's figure looks both freer and more foolish after the introduction of Aragnoll and Arachne and because of the brief reappearance of genuine mock epic, the butterfly is distanced from us just when we are most aware of the inextricable entanglement of his fate with our own:

> Helpe O thou Tragick Muse, me to deuise
> Notes sad enough, t'expresse this bitter throw:
> For loe, the drerie stownd is now arriued,
> That of all happines hath vs depriued.
> (413–16)

"Foolish . . . without foresight," Clarion flies into Aragnoll's web. Ambiguously, abruptly, appropriately, the end of this poem leaves us looking at a butterfly: "His bodie left the spectacle of care" (440).

Perhaps the upshot of *Muiopotmos* is a series of questions arbitrarily answered, if answered at all. Is this multi-faceted gem of a poem about fate and free will, ideology and agency, innocence and the biblical Fall, or political exposure and prudence? Or is it about inherited forms and present realities or about perspectival poetry and interpretive reading? Is it finally playful or pessimistic, comic or tragic? Are we, indeed, in the end merely flies to the gods? Such questions are not without bearing on a typological reading of history in which, as I observed in my introduction, material history, embodied here in a butterfly, is the vehicle that remains, that will not be denied, even if simultaneously also the vehicle of other and higher tenors.

8. *Arthur and Argante: Parodying the Ideal Vision*

One of the more luridly colorful figures in *The Faerie Queene* is Argante, the aggressively lustful giantess of Book III. She first appears bearing the Squire of Dames "athwart her horse," bound fast "with cords of wire, / Whom she did meane to make the thrall of her desire."[1] Within stanzas, she has discarded the Squire, replacing him with the mightier Sir Satyrane, whom she plucks by the collar right out of his saddle and evidently hopes to subject to her service, for "ouer all the countrey she did raunge, / To seeke young men, to quench her flaming thrust." Whomever she finds most fit "to serue her lust,"

> She with her brings into a secret Ile,
> Where in eternall bondage dye he must,
> Or be the vassall of her pleasures vile.
> (III.vii.50)

The reprehensible Argante is also the twin sister of Ollyphant, or elephant, with whom she is reported to have been locked in sexual intercourse at birth. These incestuous twins are therefore a nightmarish parody of the immaculate birth of the twins Amoret and Belphoebe two cantos earlier. Incest, from Latin *incestus*, is the supreme expression of unchastity, as A. C. Hamilton notes, and this fact emphasizes the parodic relation between Belphoebe, exemplar of chastity in Spenser's poem, and the lascivious Argante.[2]

Spenser takes Ollyphant, the name of Argante's twin brother, from the giant in Chaucer's *Sir Thopas*, a *Tale* on which Spenser drew frequently and specifically in Book I for Prince Arthur's dream of his beloved elf queen, the Queen of Faerie, as I have shown in the third chapter of this volume.[3] In the Letter to Ralegh, Spenser wrote that his own sovereign Queen, Elizabeth, bears two persons, "the one of a most royall Queene . . . the other of a most vertuous and beautifull Lady." "This latter part," he added, "in some places I doe express in Belphoebe," who bodies forth chastity. The former part—"the person of . . . the Queene, and her kingdome in Faery land"—he expresses in the Faerie Queen herself, the idealized figure whom Arthur loves and for whom he searches the length of Spenser's poem.[4] Through both connections, on the one hand, as a parody of Belphoebe's birth, and on the other, in the shared Chaucerian origin of Ollyphant's name and Arthur's vision of the Faerie Queen, the genealogy of Argante thus distantly touches the person of Queen Elizabeth, and its touch leaves the trace of ambivalence.

Argante's own name has never been accounted for satisfactorily, despite its curious coincidence with that of Tasso's male knight, whose spear, like Satyrane's, is mast-sized (vii.40). Whereas most editors pass over the significance of Argante's name in conspicuous silence, Hamilton follows Joel Belson in glossing it as a coinage from Greek *argos* ($ἀργός$) meaning "bright," "shining," "white," or "swift-footed," and related to the Greek words *arges* ($ἀργής$) meaning "bright," "shining," "white," or "vivid," and *argas* ($ἀργᾶς$) meaning "shining" or "white."[5] This gloss, as Belson explains it, seems to me somewhat strained, however, since Argante is said to be afire, not alight, with fury and lust; since her "sun-broad shield" suggests enormousness—indeed enormity—not brilliance; and since her dappled horse, not she, accounts for the speed with which she enters the poem.[6] In fact, if we try to base Argante's name on Greek coinages, the word *argos* ($ἀργός$) or "idle," "yielding no return," seems to me an equally suitable candidate, because we can connect it with Spenser's use of *idle* elsewhere in the poem, meaning "useless" or "degenerate in moral terms" and occasionally punning on *idyll*, or "place of pleasure," a meaning relevant to Argante's island bower, her "secret Ile" of lust.[7]

But I doubt that the primary source of Argante's name is to be found in coinages from Greek. Instead, it is to be found in Arthurian legend. In Laʒamon's *Brut*, King Arthur, mortally wounded at the battle of Camelford, addresses these words to his successor: "And I will fare to Avalun, to the fairest of all maidens, to Argante the queen, an elf most fair, and she shall make my wounds all sound; make me whole with healing draughts." Reinforcing Arthur's words, Laʒamon subsequently adds, "the Britons believe yet that he is alive, and dwelleth in Avalun with the fairest of all elves."[8] While in Laʒamon, two women merely bear Arthur over the sea to Avalon, in Geoffrey of Monmouth, an undoubted Spenserian source, Avalon is specified to be an isle or island and thus the kind of land mass that Spenser's Argante (not to mention Spenser's sovereign) inhabits.[9]

Belson, Hamilton's source in glossing Argante's name, was aware of the occurrence of Argante in Laʒamon's *Brut*, but he refers to it only as an example of his belief that Argante is a variant of the name Morgan in medieval literature, for it is usually Morgan le Fay who reigns in Avalon. Rather than consider the relation of Laȝamon's Argante to Spenser's, Belson is intent on the relation of Spenser's Argante to the "'morgans' or sea women of Breton folklore who were said to dwell in under-sea palaces," and in French folklore were said to have a "craze for human men" that could never be sated because men died at their touch.[10] Unfortunately, Belson's bridge from Spenser's Argante to these frustrated morgans is his belief that the names Argante and Morgan were interchangeable and that Spenser and his readers were aware of this possibility. The only evidence for their interchangeability, however, is the presence of Argante, instead of Morgan, in Laȝamon's *Brut* and the older scholarly speculations of our own century based upon it, which are, to put the matter mildly, highly conjectural.[11] Moreover, the morgans of folklore do not even match Spenser's Argante very closely, for she is an island or land creature, not a sea woman, and at her touch men like Satyrane or the Squire of Dames may get bruised, but they do not perish. In view of these difficulties, it is not surprising that Hamilton adopted Belson's Greek etymology of Argante's name and passed over his hypothesis that Argante is really Morgan and therefore based on the morgans of myth. Yet the facts remain that Spenser uses the name Argante and that the apparent source of this name either is Laȝamon's *Brut* or is represented by it, since a number of scholars argue that Laȝamon drew on Welsh, Irish, or French sources for his poem, which now are lost.[12]

Before I pursue further the relation of Laȝamon's Argante to Spenser's, I should raise more directly the question of whether Spenser might have encountered the *Brut*. Laȝamon's long poem, which contains the first version of Arthur's life in English, is generally considered to be of thirteenth-century origin. Its subject is the history of the Britons, who are depicted as the descendants of Trojan Brutus; about a third of it treats the story of Arthur. Although Laȝamon's Middle English is difficult, it is not inaccessible, and the main argument against the likelihood that Spenser knew it is the absence of a printed edition of it during the Renaissance and its survival to this day in only two Cottonian manuscripts, if modern editions are excepted.[13] Indeed, the main reason that few readers have noticed the coincidence of Argante's presence in Laȝamon and in Spenser is very probably the scarcity of modern editions of the *Brut* until fairly recently.

Yet the provenance of the two known manuscripts of Laȝamon's *Brut* is English, and Laȝamon, an English priest in Worcestershire with ties to Ireland, was presumably drawing on oral and written legend in greatly elaborating his major source, the French *Brut* of Wace. Neither Laȝamon's poem nor his putative sources, therefore, were entirely beyond Spenser's reach, which, Rosemond Tuve has repeatedly assured us, must have extended to manuscript sources.[14] Spenser's demonstrable interests in British history, Arthurian legend, and older poetry in English would surely have recommended Laʒamon's poem to him, had he met it. Noteworthy here, perhaps, is the fact that Spenser's particular interest in the story of Brute (also Brutus in Spenser) was strong enough for him somehow to have produced five Welsh words in two lines of verse, which actually scan, in the account of Brutus Greenshield that Arthur finds in Alma's chamber of memory, amid "rolles,"

> And old records from aunciemt times deriu'd,
> Some made in books, some in long parchment scrolles,
> That were all worme-eaten, and full of canker holes.
> (II.ix.57)[15]

Aside from Spenser's historical interests and the availability or unavailability to him of a manuscript of Laʒamon's *Brut*, there is nothing outside his *Faerie Queene* itself to influence our judgment of the one piece of hard evidence of a relationship between Spenser and Laʒamon that we have—the name Argante. Simply assuming this relationship for the present, I would like to explore its potential for significance in *The Faerie Queene*, to see what kinds of meanings it might release and in what kinds of patterns participate, thereby to measure its plausibility on internal grounds.

From what we have seen already, Spenser's perverse Argante is a simple antitype of the chaste Belphoebe and shares, through the origin of her brother Ollyphant's name, a distant tie to Prince Arthur's vision of the elf queen; and in these radically deflected ways the figure of Argante parodically approaches the idea of Elizabeth I. This is parody that the origin of Argante's name as Laʒamon's elfish queen of fairies enforces so considerably as to alter its status from tentative suggestion to far-reaching and metamorphic fact. With Laʒamon to hand, the very structure of the episodes surrounding the center of Book III, the Garden of Adonis, begins to participate in parody. On both sides of the idealized Garden, there is thwarted love. In the cantos on their far side, such compromised and dishonorable figures as Argante, the Witch and her son, the False Florimell, and the Squire of Dames dominate the scene. On their near side and in sharp contrast are the honorable figures of Belphoebe and Timias, who alludes to Sir Walter Ralegh as conspicuously as Belphoebe does to Elizabeth.[16] From the perspective of the thwarted love of Timias for Belphoebe, plus the recognition of Argante as a monstrous parody of the Faerie Queen, Argante's figure can be read as a terrible reflection of and on Elizabeth's notorious exploitation of courtly flirtation with her younger male courtiers. Here I would emphasize that this reading is unlikely to occur merely on the basis of contrast between Belphoebe and Argante, chastity and unchastity. It is simply not a meaning truly available without reference to La3amon's *Brut*.

If we once recognize in Argante a distorted reflection of the Faerie Queene, we can make sense of other resonances latent and perhaps suppressed in Argante's figure. For example, should we also choose to derive her name secondarily from the Greek coinages I earlier discussed, we can recover a sardonic commentary on the rewards of the courtier's life that is substantially more detailed and realistic than is an animated fantasy of lust. Greek *argos*, meaning "useless" or "yielding nothing," refers to a lack of return on untilled land or to a lack of return of money—to the absence of yield, then, on land or money. We need only connect this word (as I did earlier) with its Greek homonym *argos*, or "shining" and "bright," and thence with the related *arges* and *argas*, "shining," whose root, *arg-*, shared with the latter *argos*, comes in Latin and French to mean "silver" and "money"—*argentum* and *argent/argenté*, respectively—more nearly to suggest Argante's name and to find in the giantess a sour but typically Spenserian reflection on the niggardly rewards of courtiership under Elizabeth's thumb.[17]

As antitype to an idealized elf queen, Argante correlates more generally with the ambivalent treatment of Arthur, at times throughout Spenser's poem but most conspicuously in Book I, when, paradoxically, the poem also most idealizes him. Here, Arthur's figure, embodying in the poem the perfection of all the virtues, is imprinted with complicating, compromising, and completing elements of meaning and history. In the course of the poem, Argante proves to be just one of the skeletons in Prince Arthur's closet.

When Arthur is first introduced, the poet concludes a lengthy description of him by focusing on the wondrous shield he carries, which can dispel illusion and turn men to stone. The shield, we learn, was made anciently for Arthur by Merlin:

> Both shield, and sword, and armour all he wrought
> For this young Prince, when first to armes he fell;
> But when he dyde, the Faerie Queene it brought
> To Faerie lond, where yet it may be seene, if sought.
>
> (I.vii.36)

The "he" who died refers logically and syntactically in the last two of these lines to Arthur, the "he" who fell to arms in the line immediately preceding, rather than to Merlin, and yet the temporal clause, "when he dyde," is the more unsettling precisely because of its initial unobtrusiveness, its insidious subordination, its failed ambiguity.[18] The poet's use of the word *but* ("But when he dyde"), rather than *and*, points up the discontinuity present in Arthur's death, even as the pronoun *he* momentarily masks it, and the combined influence of the two words further contributes to the oddly emphatic, oddly evasive effect. It is as though the poet were simultaneously inviting us to overlook Arthur's death and refusing to let us do so.

Acknowledged to be dead in time even when first introduced in the poem, the young Prince Arthur is conspicuously an image, a poetic figure tied and not tied to British history. His youth itself, not yet possessed of rule, and his romantic quest for an ideal distance him both from the mighty king dominant in legendary history and from the very human and fallible warrior of the Arthurian cycles. At the same time, of course, the figure of Spenser's Arthur is conceived in allusion to British history, not only through his name and descriptive details like the dragon on his helmet, but also through the canto-long catalogue of the British rulers who preceded him, a mnemonic event in which Arthur himself participates in the House of Alma. This Arthur exists in the space between history and imagination, between what has been and what might be, between the forces that engendered the Arthur of legendary history and the glimpse, elusive but inspiring, of the Faerie Queen. He is at once a figure of pure and open potential and, insofar as he is in some sense truly Arthur, a figure embedded in the failures of history.

From this point of view, the complicating and potentially subversive elements of parody in Arthur's dream of the Faerie Queene, which have attracted much attention, make sense. The dream itself alludes to that of Chaucer's comic Sir Thopas; numerous verbal details within it echo the Redcrosse Knight's dream of a false Una earlier in Spenser's poem, and several of its lines recall Chaucer's *Wife of Bath's Prologue* and his *Troilus and Criseyde*, both tales of humanly vital but immoral or ephemeral love.[19] Even as Arthur expresses the Faerie ideal that motivates him, these echoes and allusions parodically qualify his vision, although they do so without destroying or overwhelming its positive force. They both threaten and enrich it by adding dimensions to it that are undeniably present in human history. Without such dimensions, Arthur's dream would not be moored to what has preceded him, whether in Redcrosse's Christian story, in Chaucer's poetic world, in the Arthurian cycles, or in the mythic awareness of the race. With them, the dream has a basis in history and human reality, morally mixed for ill and good as these will always be.

The ambivalences that cluster around Arthur's figure when the poet first describes him similarly indicate parody of various sorts.[20] The dragon on his helmet bespeaks his kinship to Uther Pendragon (or "dragon's head") and reflects the fiery dragon in the sky that foretold Arthur's birth; but in a Book in which cumulative symbols of evil are serpentine forms, it signals as well the demonic force that the figure of Arthur harnesses.[21] In this last sense, Arthur's dragon is like the brazen serpent of Moses in the wilderness, like that in Fidelia's cup, and like those associated with wisdom and healing in classical myth—on the caduceus, for example, or in the figure of Asclepius.

Atop Arthur's crest, "A bunch of haires discolourd diuersly" exactly replicates a line describing Archimago impersonating the Redcrosse Knight and thereby parodically recalls evil illusion more precisely than is ever the case in Arthur's dream. The replicated line charges Arthur's figure with the ambivalent potency earlier possessed only by evil. Arthur's figure, taken whole, redirects this potency, rather than being drawn by its presence into alliance with Archimago's disguise. Arthur's crest itself, for example, is said to be comparable "to an Almond tree ymounted hye . . . Whose tender locks do tremble euery one / At euery little breath, that vnder heauen is blowne" (I.vii 32). Throughout Book I—from the Wandering Wood, to Fradubio's grove, to Orgoglio's fountain of lust and beyond—trees, often trembling, are associated with the theme of fleshly nature and, to this point, only with temptation and failure. Now, however, the trembling of a tree suggests a world in concert with heaven, and specification of it as an almond tree alludes to Aaron's rod in Numbers 17:5–8 that budded and yielded almonds as a sign of his election by God.[22] Like the tree of life into whose balm Redcrosse falls in his final fight with the Dragon, the tree and the theme it embodies are here repossessed by a positive power. And yet, even as they are repossessed, allusive parody is present as both threat and human relevance. Nature redeemed, or repossessed, is not *natura impeccabilis*, nature incapable of sinning, as a traditional Christian theology might put it.

But two parodic touches in the description of Arthur take us closer to Argante. Both suggest pride, which from the beginning of Book I participates in the ambivalent potency of the natural world. This ambivalence underlies and accounts for much Spenserian parody and is, indeed, the axis around which Spenserian types and antitypes revolve. The first of the prideful parodies occurs when Spenser uses the word "haughtie" to describe Arthur's helmet (31). This word recalls Orgoglio's "haughtie eye" some fifteen stanzas earlier and anticipates the evil Dragon's crest in canto xi (15). Sixteenth-century meanings of *haughty* range from negative, through neutral, to positive ones: it can simply mean "high, lofty" in a literal sense or "imposing in aspect"; more positively, it means "high-minded" and "aspiring," exalted in "character, style, or rank"; and yet its earliest meaning, which persists throughout the period, is the one still current, "high in one's own estimation," "proud," and "arrogant."[23] While Arthur's helmet is defensive armor and thereby implies his haughtiness to foes, it also carries his identifying dragon crest and with it once again the trace of a double potential for evil or good. In this, the "haughtie helmet" resembles the word *pride* itself when it first appears in Book I to characterize the trees in the Wandering Wood—those "loftie trees yclad with sommers pride" (i.7). Here, if only for a brief moment before *pride* is described in both the next two lines as an obstruction of heaven's light, it carries the natural and innocent meaning, "prime," "flowering," "splendor," and glances at the ambivalence of the natural world for evil or good, pain or pleasure, anarchy or creative energy.[24]

The second parodic touch of pride in the description of Arthur is more insistent than his haughtiness. It alludes to the House of Pride and specifically to the characterization of Lucifera, that "mayden Queene," whose figure is an early antitype in the poem to that of the virgin Queen, Elizabeth, and therefore potentially a parody of her. Twice in the characterization of Lucifera the phrase "exceeding shone" occurs: thus Lucifera's

> bright blazing beautie did assay
> To dim the brightnesse of her glorious throne,
> As enuying her selfe, that too exceeding shone.
>
> Exceeding shone, like *Phoebus* fairest chylde. . . .
>   (I.iv.8–9)

Like the "glistring gold" of Lucifera and her throne, which is at once an extension of and rival to her discontented self, the "glistring ray" of Arthur's wondrous shield "so exceeding shone . . . That *Phoebus* face it did attaint" (vii.34). That Arthur's pride is in the shield whose power is God's is a meaning that simultaneously carries the promise of redemption and the threat of presumption. It is also a meaning inscribed both in biblical history and in the history of Britain.

My point has been that from an early stage of *The Faerie Queene* parody is evident in connection with Arthur's own idealized figure and with the ideal he pursues, the elf queen of his vision. Argante, as a parody of this queen, is an immensely stronger and more destructive instance of the broader parody whose roots spread over Book I, but she is hardly alien to Spenser's methods or to the ambivalence and oppositions of his points of view, which have become more pronounced by Book III. The potential parody of the virgin Queen present in Lucifera becomes in Book III more directly a criticism of her "ensample dead"—her lifeless or unworldly example—in the person of Belphoebe, and in Book IV it emerges in the loathsome figure of Slander, "that queane [or queen] so base and vilde" (III.v.54, IV.viii.28).[25] As a monstrous fantasy and a fleeting nightmare not quite suppressed, Argante is a shocking parody of the Faerie Queen in Book III but, sadly, once recognized, one that is hard to ignore or forget. As such a parody, moreover, she is an assault on the object of Arthur's quest, and, if we trust the sequence of cantos and books in *The Faerie Queene*, she is an assault from which this quest never fully recovers. Never, after the final half of Book III, is the possibility of Arthur's finding the Faerie Queen in any sense viable.

In my introduction, I observed that the alternative to purposeful Spenserian agency in the naming of Argante would be an inadvertent intertextual enormity, a perversely errant signifier, and that the lingering of this possibility in the name of the Giantess cannot be ruled out. Although in the end I would reiterate this possibility, I have tried to show both the historical plausibility of Spenser's awareness of the Faerie Queen Argante in Laȝamon (or his sources) and the patterns of parody within Spenser's romance epic that indicate his witty, not to say wicked, use of this awareness. The rest is quite simply a reader's choice between enormity and awareness, inadvertence and agency, and in this way, once again very typically Spenserian, as evident also in *Muiopotmos*. On reflection, it is Chaucerian as well, if we think representatively of *The General Prologue*, *The Franklin's Tale*, or the *Troilus*.

9. *Chaucer's* Parliament of Fowls *and Refractions of a Veiled Venus in* The Faerie Queene

The lack of weight most criticism has accorded the relationship between *The Faerie Queene* and Chaucer's *Parliament of Fowls* is surprising: for Spenser, Chaucer was a poet of love, an acknowledged poetic model who "well couth . . . wayle hys woes," and the *Parliament* is Chaucer's formative consideration of the various kinds of love.[1] Recurrently, from the initial canto of Book I through the Mutability Cantos, *The Faerie Queene* recalls Chaucer's poem. The *Parliament* is a text that bears unmistakably, crucially, and complexly on the Spenserian conception of eros and on the broader question of the Renaissance poet's use of the past and particularly of the Middle Ages.

Throughout *The Faerie Queene*, embodied memories of Chaucerian texts contribute to an eroticized poetics, but more clearly and explicitly than other memories, those of the *Parliament* indicate that typically the Chaucerian intertext, the very "well of English," is, like the "welspring" of desire itself, Venerean (IV.ii.32, x.47). Yet the relation of this major Chaucerian precursor to its Elizabethan reflection is as distanced and ironic as it is direct and unqualified. Rather than simply reclaiming or rejecting the past, Spenser continually refracts and revises the forms of its presence. A past form like the *Parliament* is revealed as a cultural constant—recurrent, enduring, and to an extent defining—but it is also resituated and, in the case of the already ambivalent Chaucerian source, revaluated. Paradoxically it is both affirmed and denied, exposed *and* reinstated.[2]

My purpose is to examine this paradox as it applies to the Temple of Venus in Spenser's fourth book, since this is a site that draws on Chaucer's *Parliament of Fowls* in refractive ways that we have not appreciated. Necessarily, much of my evidence for the pervasive influence of the *Parliament* on Spenser's poem and the consequent likelihood of its presence in the Temple of Venus will be cumulative, and my argument, like Spenser's own, will sometimes follow a tangled path. Spenserian memories of the *Parliament* range from virtual quotation to distant reflection and often come entangled in other memories—significantly and importantly in the instances of *Sir Thopas*, Ovid's *Metamorphoses*, the *Amoretti*, and *Epithalamion*. In this tangle they resemble the anti-oedipal rhizome of Deleuze and Guattari, which proves characteristic of such associative flows in the Spenserian text. The more focal and specific memories of the *Parliament* itself might be likened to the rhizomatous bulb, however, which is not only a more substantial form than the random network of roots flowing from it but potentially also one that becomes fully emergent and flowers.[3] In other words, refractive memories of the *Parliament* are by a shift of metaphor and perspective also rhizomatous, my refractive metaphor allowing for, although by no means requiring, a greater measure of teleological control than the vegetal one.

Spenser's best-known uses of the *Parliament* span *The Faerie Queene*, opening its first canto to intimations of eros and occupying a highly charged site in the Mutability Cantos, its putative end. Chaucer's poem is a conspicuous source for the catalogue of trees in the Wandering Wood of Book I, and in the description of "dame Nature" near the poem's end, Spenser specifically invokes it to confirm the difficulty of describing "All her array and vestiments": so hard is this task "That old Dan *Geffrey* (in whose gentle spright / The pure well head of Poesie did dwell) / In his *Foules parley* durst not with it mel" (VII.vii.9). If Spenser had not actually named Chaucer and the *Parliament* in this passage, the *Variorum* annotators, who minimized medieval English influence, would probably have seen no connection worth recording. Although here identified as "The pure well head of Poesie," Chaucer is far less the source for the words and images Spenser uses in describing Nature than the imaginative and conceptual model for his indirection in representing her garments or outermost form. Chaucer inspires an inability topos whose emotive and mystical effect Spenser radically heightens, comparing his own amazement at Nature's appearance to that of the apostles who witnessed the Transfiguration. Very likely Spenser's amazement is not unconnected with the Venerean roots of this transformed figure (or transfigured form) of Nature, which are implicit in the relation of Venus to Nature in Chaucer's text.

Guided by Spenser's actual naming of the *Parliament* in the Mutability Cantos and presumably recognizing that his recourse to it is conceptual, commentators have pointed to the general similarity between Chaucer's depiction of Nature "in a launde, vpon an hyl of floures," encompassed by "halles" and "boures" of branches, and Spenser's description of the earth's spontaneously providing a pavilion and throne of trees for his goddess.[4] Josephine Waters Bennett has further observed the resemblance between the arboreal settings of Nature in both poems and the "pleasant arbour, not by art, / But of the trees owne inclination made," amid the myrtle trees on the Mount of Venus (and Adonis) in Book III (vi. 44).[5] As with the description of Nature herself, this resemblance is conceptual and suggestive rather than verbal and exact, yet it seems in its Venerean context a credible link in a series of arboreal associations relating Spenser's poem to the *Parliament*.

Recollection of the *Parliament* in Books II and IV, especially in the Bower of Bliss and in the Temple of Venus, is more complicated and ambivalent than in the Mutability Cantos or in Book III. The difference, however, cannot satisfactorily be equated with a simple opposition between Nature and Venus or between good and bad Venuses, any more than it can be in Chaucer's *Parliament*. The catalogue of trees at the entrance to the Wandering Wood, which introduces the arboreal imagery associated with fleshly nature and hence with both fallen and redeemed humanity in Book I, cautions against this equation, as does the Venerean nature of the Garden of Adonis and, indeed, of Nature herself. When a poet wants sharply to distinguish figures from one another, he does not go out of his way to make their names, sources, and characteristics overlap, as in these cases.

Chaucer's garden of love in the *Parliament* is at once the approach to the Temple of Venus and the site to which the Dreamer returns to find the "noble goddesse Nature," who is evident to him only after he has seen Venus herself (cclxxx^v). In this garden the air "so attempre was / That neuer was there greuance of hote ne colde / There was eke euery holsome spyce and gras," and it was "euer clere day, and neuer nyght" (cclxxx^r). Similarly, in the Bower of Bliss, "the Heauens alwayes Iouiall" never allow "scorching heat, nor cold intemperate,"

> But the milde aire with season moderate
> Gently attempred, and disposed so well,
> That still it breathed forth sweet spirit and holesome smell.
> (II.xii.51)

More than once in Spenser's description of the Bower, memories of the garden in the *Parliament* are thus explicit and verbally exact. "On euery bough," the Chaucerian narrator hears "the byrdes . . . synge / With voyce of aungel, in her ermony," and he hears "instrumentes, of stringes in accorde . . . playe, a rauysshynge swetnesse," and "Therwith a wynde, vnneth it myght be lesse / Made in the leues grene, a noyse softe / Accordant to the foules songe on lofte" (cclxxx^r). In the Bower, "all that pleasing is to liuing eare, / Was there consorted in one harmonee" (II.xii.70). "The ioyous birdes"

> Their notes vnto the voyce attempred sweete;
> Th'Angelicall soft trembling voyces made
> To th'instruments diuine respondence meet.

The sounds of waterfalls "vnto the wind did call: / The gentle warbling wind low answered to all" (II.xii.71). The initial stage of Chaucer's garden of love is not seen as evil; indeed, the narrator supposes, without evident irony, that its ravishingly sweet sounds are comparable to the best heard by "god, that maker is of al and lorde"(cclxxx^r). Recognizing such a benign source behind Spenser's Bower confirms and complicates still further our response to its undeniable attractions, making all the more shocking the reductive violence of Guyon's wrath.

In one memorable detail of the description of Acrasia herself, Spenser's recollection of Chaucer's Venus is likewise unmistakable. Acrasia's breast is "bare to readie spoyle / Of hungry eies" (II.xii.78), and she is "arayd, or rather disarayd,"

> All in a vele of silke and siluer thin,
> That hid no whit her alablaster skin,
> But rather shewd more white, if more might bee:
> More subtile web *Arachne* can not spin,
> Nor the fine nets, which oft we wouen see
> Of scorched deaw, do not in th'aire more lightly flee.
> (II.xii.77)

Chaucer's erotic and ambivalent Venus, hair unbraided, lies "naked from the brest vnto the hede," as "Men myght her se" (cclxxx^v). The rest of her, the narrator reports with approval, was "couered wel to my pay / Right with a lytel kerchefe of valence / There was no thycker cloth of defence" (cclxxx^v)—that is, "to my pleasure, nothing defended her from sight except a thin kerchief." An editor of the Spenser *Variorum* quotes E. B. Fowler on the similarity of these passages: "The voluptuous appeal of Acrasia's veillike, transparent garment—not emphasized in Tasso—provokes immediate comparison with Boccaccio's description of Venus in *La Teseide* [*sic*]"; as an afterthought he then adds, "Cf. also Chaucer's rendering" (II, 391–92). But Acrasia's veil is not merely unemphasized by Tasso, it is wholly unimagined by him. The *Variorum* editor's comment, although old, fairly represents attention to the bearing of this Chaucerian wellspring on Spenser's poem.

Boccaccio's *Teseida* affords a more problematic candidate for Acrasia's precursor, however, because it is Chaucer's own source for the description of Venus in the *Parliament*, and in treating her he follows Boccaccio more closely than is normally his practice. While I think it likely that Spenser had read the *Teseida*, there is little persuasive evidence that he did so, since he makes no use of it that is not clearly mediated by Chaucer. If at any point he followed Boccaccio directly, he evidently did so with Chaucer firmly in mind. In the present instance, Boccaccio writes of a garment ("*veste*") so thin ("*sottil*") covering the other part ("*l'altra parte*") of Venus that it scarcely concealed anything ("*quasi nulle appena nascondia*").[6] Boccaccio's "*sottil*," or "thin," "subtle," garment became Chaucer's "subtyl coverchef of Valence," a thin woven fabric, and then in Renaissance editions of Chaucer became a "lytel kerchefe of valence." Since Spenser compares Acrasia's veil to a "subtile web," he might here have read his Renaissance Chaucer with Boccaccio in mind, unwittingly deducing from Boccaccio what Chaucer had actually written.[7] But to me, it looks as though Spenser may have had Chaucer and Boccaccio both in mind, as well as the imaginative process by which one poet follows "the footing of . . . [poetic] feete"—in this case the process by which Spenser himself follows Chaucer following Boccaccio (IV.ii. 34). His considerable, emotive elaboration of the subtlety of Acrasia's veil extends the Chaucerian narrator's pleasure at the thin covering to a lingering enactment of his response. In Boccaccio's text there is not so specific an invitation to response and certainly not to lingering, self-indulgent indirection as the one Spenser found in the *Parliament*.

In Book IV of *The Faerie Queene*, memories of the *Parliament*, reinforced by those of Chaucer's *Sir Thopas*, notorious knight prickant, gravitate toward the experience of Scudamour, first in the House of Care and then in the Temple of Venus. Through a series of interlacing, intertextual allusions, memories, and recurrent associations, these Chaucerian works serve to connect Scudamour's erotic experiences with those of Arthur and Redcrosse and thereby reciprocally to relate theirs, through Scudamour's, to the Venerean source in the Temple. Following these entangled connections, we begin to grasp the complexity of the sustained process of assimilation to which the poet of *The Faerie Queene* pointed when, in Book IV, he identified Chaucer's work as an imaginative source for his own (IV.ii.32–34).[8]

Before Spenser's story of Scudamour even reaches the Temple of Venus in Book IV, the fire-hot sighs born of desire and the bitter sorrows caused by jealousy in Chaucer's Temple of Venus have a general relevance to Scudamour's "gealous dread" in the House of Care, where sighs are Care's bellows, and the pain inflicted by "redwhot yron tongs" breaks his sleep (IV.v.38, 44–45). The specific cause of Scudamour's jealousy, the fear that Amoret has been unfaithful, molests his "ydle braine" and makes "him dreame those two disloyall were: / The things that day most minds, at night doe most appeare" (IV.v.43). To paraphrase: "What you think about most in the daytime, you dream about at night"; in a note on this observation, the unregenerate *Variorum* cites Ennius and *The Dream of Scipio*, the latter another major source for Chaucer's *Parliament*. But neither citation—the one about a King's worries and the other about the younger Scipio's dream of Africanus—is as pertinent or memorable as a rhetorically conspicuous stanza in the *Parliament*, whose climax is a lover's dream:

> The wery hunter, slepyng in his bedde
> To wodde ayen his mynde gothe anone
> The juge dremeth, howe his plees be spedde
> The carter dremeth, howe his cartes gone
> The ryche of golde, the knight fight with his fone
> The sike mette he drinketh of the tonne
> The louere met, he hath his lady wonne.
>
>   (cclxxix^v)

Chaucer translated this stanza virtually whole from a common medieval schoolbook, where, suggestively, given Scudamour's *raptus* of Amoret on the Spenserian horizon, it served to introduce the third Book of Claudian's *De Raptu Proserpinae*.[9] As a set piece of amplification that adds virtually nothing to the immediate needs of Chaucer's narrative, this stanza resembles the catalogue of trees that follows it within less than a hundred lines. For a rhetorician (or a rhetorically minded poet), it thus invites an associative link between these two commonplaces, the one about trees and the other about dreaming. Both commonplaces are found together in the *Parliament* in the context of erotic yearning, and, as noted, both recur in Spenserian contexts of erotic anxiety.

The coincidences between these tangled, refracted memories of the *Parliament* and the figure of Scudamour afford a virtual embarrassment of additional associations even before he reaches the Temple of Venus.

Scudamour's dreaming "those two disloyall were" and the narrator's observing what "day most minds, at night do[es] most appeare" so pointedly apply to Redcrosse's situation in the opening cantos of Book I—his battle with Error in the Wandering Wood and his subsequent dream in Archimago's hermitage—that I have often rechecked them to assure myself that the same phrases really are not there. In these opening cantos Redcrosse enters, through the catalogue of trees in the Wandering Wood, an experience of disunity and eventual psychic dismemberment.[10] As earlier noted, Spenser's catalogue of trees alludes to the arboreal setting of the erotic dream in Chaucer's *Parliament*, and it simultaneously evokes another list of trees in Book X of Ovid's *Metamorphoses*, which provides the arboreal setting for Orpheus' songs just after his final loss of Eurydice and just before his dismemberment at the hands of the impassioned Maenads. The threatening context of Ovid's list is relevant to Redcrosse and later to Scudamour when, comparing himself to Orpheus, he leads Amoret from the Temple of Venus.

The dreaming Scudamour is clearly in trouble under Care's roof, and his problems are thus interwoven with those of morally more exemplary figures like Redcrosse in *The Faerie Queene*. To view his travail in this light is to find a cultural resonance, even an urgency, in his story that is not always accorded by modern readers to the potentially parodic figure of "Cupids man" (IV.x.54). It is also to see more clearly the relation between Scudamour's experiences and those of the poet of the *Amoretti* and *Epithalamion*. If Scudamour's comparison of his taking Amoret from the Temple of Venus to Orpheus' leading Eurydice from hell enmeshes him in irony, it also relates him to the self-reflexive Spenserian poet who invoked Orpheus' ill-omened wedding song as a model for his own in the opening stanza of his *Epithalamion*.[11]

The effect of jealous fear on Scudamour as he leaves the House of Care recalls the erotic experiences of Arthur that derive from Chaucer's *Tale of Sir Thopas*, as well as again those of Redcrosse. At once digressive and relevant, this typically Spenserian linkage reinforces the Chaucerian underpinnings of Scudamour's story and sharpens their bearing on the Temple of Venus itself. *Sir Thopas* is the source for Arthur's initial dream of the Faerie Queen; his subsequent frustration at her absence when he loses Florimell in Book III connects him again, unmistakably, both with Sir Thopas and Scudamour and, through Scudamour, with the Temple of Venus.[12] Curiously, it often goes unremarked that Spenser's male figures reflect and reflect on one another no less than do his oft refracting female figures. (Is there a critical tendency to *ascribe* more autonomy, or narrative realism, in Faerie to male figures?)

In an anticipation of Scudamour's plight, Arthur, having outworn the weary night "In restlesse anguish and vnquiet paine" after losing Florimell, "clombe vnto his steed" and went forth "With heauie looke and lumpish pace" (III.iv.61). Similarly Scudamour, his own night spent with Care in "disquiet and hartfretting payne," rises like a "heauie lumpe of lead," the "signes of anguish" on his face. He, too, then "clombe" "Vnto his lofty steede" and fared wearily forth (IV.v.45–46). The critical connection between these passages and *Sir Thopas* begins when Arthur, having abandoned "His wearisome pursuit" of Florimell,

> from his loftie steed dismounting low,
> Did let him forage. Downe himselfe he layd
> Vpon the grassie ground, to sleepe a throw;
> The cold earth was his couch, the hard steele his pillow.
>
> (III.iv.53)

Now fantasies occupy his "idle braine" (iv.54), and he spends the night wishing for his absent Faerie Queen. In comparison, as night approaches in Chaucer's burlesque *Tale*,

> Sir Thopas eke so wery was
> For prickyng on the softe gras
>   So fiers was his corage
> That doun he layde him in that place
> To maken his stede some solace
>   And gaue him good forage.
>
> (lxxxiiii^v)

Both poets in these matched passages even oddly use (or misuse) the word "forage," whose meaning properly refers to dry fodder, rather than to the grazing of fresh grass.[13] For several lines Sir Thopas, like Arthur, next dreams about and wishes for an elf-queen. Then "In to his sadel he clombe anone / And pricketh ouer style and stone" in search of her. Here again in *Thopas* is the distinctive word clomb, or "climbed," which in this context hardly suggests the graceful ascent of a knightly steed and which Spenser similarly employs in describing the lumpish departures of Arthur and Scudamour after their restless nights. These two figures are the chief knights in Spenser's poem who travel primarily in search of a woman, and under the sway of eros both are related tellingly to an undignified Chaucerian past.[14]

Like Britomart pursuing Ollyphant—the destructive fantasy whose name comes from *The Tale of Sir Thopas*—and finding instead Scudamour prostrate on the ground, I am returned again by way of *Thopas* to Scudamour's story in Book IV, where, even as Scudamour begins his account of the Temple of Venus, his own words recall *Sir Thopas*: "Then hearke ye gentle knights and Ladies free, / My hard mishaps, that ye may learne to shonne" (x.3). Behind Scudamour's address to his audience lies that of the comic Chaucerian narrator near the end of the unfinished *Thopas*:

> Nowe holde your mouthe for charite
> Bothe knight and lady fre
> And herkeneth to my spell.
>
> (lxxxv)[15]

The echo is considerably enforced by the Chaucerian request just before it that Scudamour's fellow travelers and travailers in love make of him—"That as we ride together on our way, / Ye will recount . . . All that aduenture" (ix.40)—and by the generally Chaucerian dramatization of Scudamour as the teller of his own tale.[16] This is a kind of autonomy granted so extensively to no other character in the poem, and it enables the doubleness of perspective and narrative distance in the Temple of Venus that are characteristically Chaucerian. Scudamour's tale, like Arthur's quest, is in some sense a continuation of the fragmentary *Sir Thopas*.

Whenever the poet of *The Faerie Queene* thought about love, any kind of love, he evidently thought about Chaucer; the very presence of a Temple of Venus in Spenser's Book IV would appear in itself an invocation of Chaucer, who memorably depicted three such temples: in *The House of Fame* and in *The Knight's Tale*, as well as in the most relevant of these, *The Parliament of Fowls*.[17] Spenser's Temple of Venus and its environs share numerous features with the Temple in the *Parliament*, but most of them do not clearly distinguish Chaucer's influence from that of other works in the tradition of the courts of love. More distinctive for a reader—perhaps I should say "this reader"—of Spenser is the *continuity* of experience within Chaucer's garden of love, including his Temple of Venus.

The *Parliament* is fundamentally concerned with a thoroughly Spenserian subject, namely, the continuity—the impinging, implicating variety—of the forms of love. This is a narrative and temporal continuity that includes seeming opposites and acknowledges the morally mixed nature of human passion. In connection with Spenser's poem, it again suggests why Arthur's dream of the Faerie Queen includes a hobgoblin's garland of Chaucerian references to *The Wife of Bath's Prologue, Troilus,* and *Sir Thopas*; why the poem similarly recalls *Sir Thopas* as Scudamour begins the tale of his journey in IV.x to the "wellspring" of Venerean desire; and why the meaning of the Temple of Venus itself has proved so open to radically different interpretations, ranging from benign to malefic (IV.x.47). In short, it highlights a vision of eros that is realistically and humanly mixed, not a simple affirmation of the cultural forms it assumes, nor yet a simple denial.

At the threshold of the dream in the *Parliament* the narrator confronts a gate into the garden whose contradictory inscriptions indicate the blissful and baleful aspects of love—in Scudamour's terms, the honey and gall. To enter through the gate is to encounter both aspects. Once within the garden, he joyously views the paradisal landscape whose description I quoted earlier in connection with the Bower of Bliss: here trees are "clad with leues, that aye shal last," and there is "swetnesse, euermore ynoughe" (cclxxx^r). Daylight is everlasting and nothing ever dies. But here as well occurs the catalogue of trees upon which Spenser drew to describe the Wandering Wood, and the Chaucerian narrator's perspective in characterizing the human uses to which the trees are put serves as a reminder of a less paradisal existence, for example, "the coffer vnto carayne," the "holme to whyppes lasshe," or "the cypres dethe to playne" (cclxxx^r).

After the catalogue of trees Chaucer's narrator surveys the seemingly innocent and sensuous delights of the garden for four stanzas before noticing "Cupyde our lorde" under a tree with his daughter, who is preparing his arrows, "Some to slee, and some to wounde and carue" (cclxxx^r). Then, without any mention of a change in the narrator's location, he simply becomes aware ("ware") of an assemblage of personifications who represent various expressions of love, ranging from high-minded refinement to mercantilism and including such figures as Pleasure, Desire, Courtesy, Delight, Gentleness, "beaute, with a nyce atyre / And youthe, ful of game and iolyte," Foolhardiness, Flattery, Go-betweens ("Messagery"), and Material Rewards ("mede") (cclxxx^{r-v}). The narrator accomplishes the progression from Cupid to these more elaborate expressions of courtship as if by directing his eyes a few degrees in another direction, although it is also conceivable that they suddenly appear in response to his presence. Next, in another shift of attention, he sees the Temple of Venus, "yfounded stronge"—strongly based or grounded—and dancing around it, "euer, fro yere to yere," a company of women with untressed hair. This Temple, firmly founded, is built to last, and the dance that surrounds it is as unending as the preoccupations of love just outside Spenser's Temple of Venus (IV.x.25). The Temples of both poets are cultural sites, inherited and embedded—"yfounded stronge."

The Temple in the *Parliament* is, more exactly, an image of human passion—sultry, dark, and voluptuous.[18] Within it, Priapus stands sexually erect, and men "try and try" to bedeck him with garlands of fresh flowers, an effort whose symbolism seems clear, and exhausting, enough.[19] As we have seen, Venus lies naked, except for the "lytel kerchefe of valence," and two young folk kneeling before her cry for her help. The Temple is also a place of sorrow, heated by lovers' sighs that fan the flames on its altars. At its entrance Peace sits with a curtain in her hand, probably an image of discretion or secrecy, and Patience sits on a hill of sand, suggesting futility. The personifications "Behest" and "Arte" (Promise and Subtlety or Skill) appear to move in and out of the interior of the Temple, where Riches, Bacchus, and Ceres are also to be found. The broken bows of Diana's votaries hang on the walls, and everywhere are paintings depicting the consuming power of passion—Paris, Semiramis, Hercules, Biblis, Dido, Tristram and Isolde, Troilus, and on and on. Quite a range of possibilities, I might add, though all with unhappy endings.

What I would stress at this point is the seamlessness of the narrative movement through the various stages of the garden and into the Temple itself. There is an easy inevitability, perhaps even a naturalness about it, which continues into the Temple and out of it again. In fact, Chaucer's narrator does not even tell us how he leaves the Temple—whether by retracing his steps or finding an exit on its further side, for example. Instead, with good dream logic, he simply remarks, "Whan I was comen ayen in to the place / That I of spake, that was so sote and grene" (cclxxx^v). The "place," both site and topos, is the paradisal garden described earlier ("That I of spake"); here, only after having been through the Temple and having seen Venus, he now finds the goddess Nature, "vicar of the almyghty lorde," who, like Concord in Spenser's Temple, knits "hote, colde, heuy, lyght, moyst, and drey . . . by euen nombre of accorde" (cclxxxi^r). Throughout the narrator's tour, the only responses he reports are his immense joy on first entering the garden, his pleasure at seeing the transparency of the veil covering Venus, and his desire to solace himself (for any number of reasons) after leaving the Temple.

Besides the narrator's movement, there are other connections between the interior of the Temple and the garden outside. The very dream of the garden is attributed to the power of "Citherea [Venus], thou blysful lady swete / That with thy *fyre bronde*, dauntest whan thee lest," and near the conclusion of the parliament of birds, the formel (female) eagle, aware of the sexual desire that underlies the courtly rhetoric of the tercels, explicitly refuses to serve "Venus, ne Cupyde . . . *as yet*" (cclxxix^v, cclxxxiii^r: my emphasis).[20] In Renaissance editions of the *Parliament* there is an additional connection between Temple and garden: "Cupyde," the first person the narrator sees in the garden, at one point is identified, instead of Chaucer's "Cypride" or Venus, as the figure lying between Bacchus and Ceres in the Temple, thus intimating their cooperation and virtual interchangeability at moments of this experience (cclxxx^v).

When the goddess Nature herself explains in the *Parliament* that the birds mate as she "pricks" them "with pleasaunce," it becomes still more difficult to distinguish her inspiration from that of Venus or, indeed, from that of Spenser's hermaphroditic Venus, who privily pricks "the merry birds" with her "lustfull powres" (cclxxxi^r, IV.x.45). Alanus de Insulis, a major Chaucerian source for the *Parliament*, and John Lydgate, a roughly contemporary reader of it, further encourage our seeing this connection. Alanus, whose "playnte of kynde" Chaucer invokes in describing Nature, recognized Venus and the sexuality she symbolizes as part of the natural process, although he bitterly lamented the extent to which, in a fallen world, she had wandered from her rightful path.[21] Lydgate goes so far as to combine Alanus' Nature with Chaucer's Venus: he recalls how Alanus saw Nature "Clad al in flours and blosmes of a tre . . . in hir moost excellence, / Vpon hir hed a kerche[f] of Valence."[22] Surprising as Lydgate's recollection may be, it is not inexplicable in terms either of the *Parliament* or the "playnte of kynde," the two texts that underlie it, and it curiously anticipates similar refractions of Chaucer's work in *The Faerie Queene*.

Reflecting on Venus' influence in the garden as well as in the Temple of the *Parliament*, J. A. W. Bennett muses, "no one can say where Love that is part of the whole procreative process of Nature becomes that passive self-absorbed divinity who brings not joy but pain"; yet Bennett does his best throughout an otherwise illuminating book to distinguish the two (147). Like a host of subsequent critics, he finally wants Nature and Venus—or at the very least a "good" Venus and a "bad" one—kept sharply and safely distinct. Chaucer's poem, however, insists on their connection, even while insisting on the difference between them. This characteristic Chaucerian doubleness admits both the joyful dream and its disappointing corruption, both fantasied ideal and painful reality. Perhaps this is the profoundly simple point that the gate to the garden adumbrates with its twin inscriptions promising love and hate or bliss and woe.

Visually, the most striking coincidence between the Temples of Venus in Spenser's and Chaucer's poems is the presence of a Venerean goddess in some way veiled. Spenser's, in shape and beauty "Farre passing that, which by surpassing skill / *Phidias* did make in *Paphos* Isle of yore,"

>   much fairer shined,
> But couered with a slender veile afore;
> And both her feete and legs together twyned
> Were with a snake, whose head and tail were fast combyned.
> (IV.x.40)

Notably, the veil is "slender"—thin and transparent—enough for the shape, beauty, and radiance of the statue to shine through effectively, and it is in some limited way "afore" the statue, rather than wholly encompassing her.[23] Apparently, it also stops short of her legs and feet and, as subsequent passages indicate, leaves her face, neck, and shoulders uncovered, much as are those of Chaucer's Venus (42, 56).[24]

Many analogues for this veiled Venus have been suggested, including emblematic, mythological, and philosophical versions of Venus herself and versions of Isis and Cybele, both deities associated with her fertile power.[25] As far as I know, however, none really accounts for the "slender veile afore," whose purpose, the narrator speculates, is to cover her hermaphroditic sexual parts:

> But sooth it was not sure for womanish shame,
> Nor any blemish, which the worke mote blame;
> But for, they say, she hath both kinds in one,
> Both male and female, both vnder one name.
> (IV.x.41)

The narrator's extended speculation insures our attention to the presence of the veil. Yet some of the Venerean analogues for the veil commonly cited are not even visual or iconic, let alone anatomically situated, as, for example, the analogue in Plutarch's *De Iside et Osiride*, where a statue of Minerva-Isis is reported merely to bear the inscription, "my veil no mortal has yet uncovered."[26] Other analogues displace the veil to Venus' head and shoulders, suggesting Cybele, or to her entire body, cap-à-pie, inappropriately suggesting the shrouded Venus Cartari pictures mourning over the body of dead Adonis.[27]

But I am far from denying the relevance of any veiled Venus to the one in Spenser's Temple. The exclusion of multiple meanings is normally not Spenser's way, nor the Renaissance way. In a context where eros and fertility are explicit, however, I do not see how we can overlook connections between the hermaphroditic statue and two other figures actually within *The Faerie Queene* itself, the goddess Nature and Acrasia, both female forms in some memorable way veiled, both with Venerean attributes, and both recalling the *Parliament*. While Spenser's highly and multiply textualized Temple is not presented as a dream, it is a memory—specifically Scudamour's but culturally any reader's—and as such it is subject to the mind's refractions: "a lytel kerchefe [or 'subtyl coverchef'] of valence" crucially positioned on one Venus is not imaginatively so far from "a slender veil afore" to cover "both kinds" of sex in another. This kind of similarity is what Peter Hawkins has called a "recognizable refraction," a manifestation in which we speak less of the presence of the original type than of the "degrees" of its presence.[28] Refraction that is recognizable and demonstrable is a basic principle in reading any intertext, including textualized, as well as graphically textual, images. The striking emphasis at the outset and end of Chaucer's *Parliament* on the reading of "olde bokes," including illustrated ones, in order to learn about love—about generative eros in physical, sociocultural, and specifically poetic senses—is clearly advice that Spenser's practice shows he took to heart: "For out of olde feldes, as men saythe / Cometh al this newe corne, fro yere to yere" (cclxxix^r, cclxxxiii^r).[29]

The "couert vele" in Scudamour's story both conceals and reveals connections.[30] The hermaphroditic "Idol" it covers revises Chaucer's Venus and her descendant Acrasia, assimilating their attraction to Nature's fertility, and yet this veiled image also acknowledges their darker, more threatening power. Spenser's Venus, like the entirety of Chaucer's dream, is thus set between a corrupt Venus and an idealized Nature, between Acrasia's Bower earlier in the poem and Nature's arbor near its end. Again like the earlier poet's dream, the experience over which the hermaphroditic Venus presides, Scudamour's progress through the court-of-love tradition in search of his Amoret, combines joy with pain and anticipated perfection with impending failure. Spenser's Temple, too, in its own way concerns the mixed nature of *amor*, human love.

This Temple is more positively weighted than relatively sinister sites like the Bower of Bliss, the House of Busirane, or even Chaucer's Temple alone, without the surrounding garden. When Scudamour, already having passed through a sensuous paradise that generically resembles Chaucer's garden of love, finally reaches the "purposd place" of his desire, the "temple of great *Venus*," he finds Concord, "Mother of blessed Peace and Friendship trew," rather than Chaucer's Peace of dubious character, sitting at its entrance. Concord, "nourse of pleasure and delight," not only holds all heaven and earth in a harmonious course but also "vnto Venus grace the gate doth open right" (34–35). In effect, she combines the interests of Nature with those specific to Venus. But Spenser's Venus herself combines them: at her appearance "the daedale earth throw[s] forth . . . Out of her fruitfull lap aboundant flowres," and all creatures are inspired "to quench their inward fire" in generation. "The root of all that ioyous is, . . . Mother of laughter, and welspring of blisse," she is the one who at first made "all the world" and "dayly" still repairs it (45–47).

Yet Spenser's Temple is also a more social and, not surprisingly, a more ambivalent place than Nature's seat of judgment or the Garden of Adonis, where emphasis falls on the physical process and cycle of generation. The crowns, chains, and garlands, along with "pretious gifts worth many a pound" that lovers pay, are not far removed from the garlands, Meed, and Riches of Chaucer's dream, and the many lovers lying around the Idol's altar and "piteously complayning" of loss, delay, pride, disdain, or fraud, if not themselves "fraudulently fayning," recall "Bihest" and "Arte" and the pair of pleading lovers within Chaucer's Temple (37, 43). But if, for the moment, we except the effect of Scudamour, who—like Renaissance editions of the *Parliament* mentioned earlier—brings Cupid from outside the Temple into its midst, the Idol's sanctum is painted mainly with positive strokes. The steam that rises from a hundred altars aspires to heaven with "true louers vowes," and it is "through loues constrayning" that an anguished devotee voices the impressive poetry of the Lucretian hymn to Venus that "fill[s]" the Temple with song (38, 43). The Temple is represented as a mysterious center of potency with a magnetic appeal.

What I have called the effect of Scudamour, however, is crucial. The Temple episode is an experience seen from inside and outside, from Scudamour's engaged, admiring point of view and from a more detached, allusive, and ironic one. While neither view cancels the other, their accord is at best uneasy. The distance between them is evident at times throughout the canto and is most pronounced near its end, when Scudamour, emboldened by Venus, leads the unwilling Amoret as his "glorious spoyle" from the Temple (55, 58). Here occurs the heavily ironic passage referenced earlier in which he compares his exploit to Orpheus' rescue of Eurydice from Hades, a comparison that effectually anticipates—and for the reader of Book III recalls—

his subsequent loss of Amoret, even as he asserts the safety and surety of his possession of her. In Scudamour's comparison, love and death, eros and "the Stygian Princes boure," impinge on one another, as they do in the recesses of Chaucer's Temple, where the stories of consuming passion depicted on the walls all end in death.

Yet I doubt that reference in Spenser's Temple to "Th'Elysian fields," site of "lasting blesse," or even to Hades, where the shade of Eurydice dwells, will support Jonathan Goldberg's unqualified assertion that "Love is hell" in Scudamour's eyes, useful as is Goldberg's pessimistic reading in fixing attention on the relation of love and death and heaven and hell in canto x (88–91, IV.x.23). In Chaucer's Temple, a number of the victims of passion—Dido, Tristram, Paris, Helen, Achilles, Cleopatra—are drawn from Dante's circle of the lustful in the *Inferno*; conspicuously, Scudamour refers not to them but instead to Orpheus, who (along with "stout *Aeneas* in the Troiane fyre") is presented as a hero in Spenser's "Hymne in Honovr of Love."[31] Orpheus' *heroism*—albeit in "daring to prouoke the yre / Of damned fiends, to get his loue retyre" (233–35)—is what the Hymn emphasizes, as does the primary meaning of canto x. Spenser's Temple may be a troubling place and at best a morally mixed one, but it is not simply (or simplistically) evil.

Even near the end of the Temple episode, the perspective in which Scudamour's experience appears is not consistently ironic. Just before Venus emboldens him to lead Amoret from the altar, his words momentarily suggest the depth of his own uncertainty and in some sense, perhaps, also his author's:

> but I which all that while
> The pledge of faith, her hand engaged held,
> Like warie Hynd within the weedie soyle,
> For no intreatie would forgoe so glorious spoyle.
>   (IV.x.55)

The hind, or female deer, is a familiar Petrarchan image for the beloved, but its relation to the rest of Scudamour's sentence is awkward and puzzling. The nearest referent for the "warie Hynd" is Amoret's hand, which would become, in this case, a synecdoche for the whole woman. If we take the simile at face value, however, it sorts ill with the woman: Amoret is at this point more exposed than an actual deer would be in the "soyle," or marsh, and "warie" (cognate with "aware," "knowing") is questionable as a description of her frightened, innocent, inexperienced reluctance.[32] The alignment of a "hand," presumably one anxiously sweaty, with "hind in a marsh" is also, in literal terms, distracting (to put it politely). Discounting all these syntactical and figurative qualms, however, we might simply activate the submerged pun on *soyle* as "sexual intercourse" and take Amoret's engaged hand to anticipate this future event.[33]

But syntactical and figurative qualms might also lead us to an alternative reading, since there decidedly is one. The syntactic referent of the hind could be Scudamour himself: "I, who, like a wary hind in safe haven, for no entreaty would relinquish what I had won." Curiously, the comparison of the Knight to a cautious, knowing, (female) deer in a marshy haven makes better sense than does the more immediate reading, and it is supported by the cancelled ending of the 1590 *Faerie Queene*, which similarly compares Scudamour's response to the sight of Amoret to a deer's bathing in a cool marsh after the thirst of a long chase, presumably by dogs. Although not specified as a hind in 1590, the harassed deer is again in a marshy haven suggestively associated with the woman, and corroboration for avoiding a rigid, rote (modern) decorum regarding the gendering of similes can be found in the subsequent comparison of rocky Marinell to "an Hynde whose calfe is falne vnwares / Into some pit, where she him heares complaine" (IV.xii.17). In the Temple of Venus the simile of the deer, if taken to refer to Scudamour, would not be the only expression of his doubt and fear, but partly because an inadvertent expression of these, it would be the most interesting and revealing one. Its confusion of the roles of hunter and hunted would suggest how much the Orphic Knight is threatened by this Venerean place to which he has been drawn so overwhelmingly. Love and hate, bliss and woe, are not easy to distinguish here, nor is the author of their confusion.

Whether conceived before or after the Temple episode, a deer image similar to those describing Scudamour also appears in *Amoretti* 67; this time the deer's role belongs to the woman and conspicuously to a woman whose will, unlike Amoret's, is unforced—free, if only willingly to be "fyrmely tied" and, more ambivalently, to be "wonne with her owne will beguyled"—willingly to be charmed, deceived, or cheated. The difference between Scudamour's force and this freedom is significant, enlightened, even poignant, but it is also limited, and it lends an added edge to the uncertainty of his conclusive attitude in the Temple, whether in the original experience or in the retelling. It is not too farfetched to remember as well the Orphic poet's anxious—or is it reassuring—question before the altar in *Epithalamion*: "Why blush ye loue to giue to me your hand, / The pledge of all our band?" (238–39).[34]

A problem I have with existing interpretations of the Temple, both benign and malefic, is the extent to which they are themselves closed, settled, and determinate—wholly on top of things.[35] For me, the most compelling and balanced interpretation overall remains Harry Berger's, but I am not finally persuaded by the evidence Berger cites that the poem is as fully outside—as critically detached from—the culture it depicts as his reading requires. His reading of the Temple of Venus anticipates his later formulation of the "paradise principle" in *The Shepheardes Calender* and his still more recent work on narrator and narrative in *The Faerie Queene*. In this later work, Berger shifts the claims made in 1968 for the poet to the play of discourses within the poem, which remains essentially free of cultural limitations and commitments.[36] This is not the way I read the uncertainties of Book IV, particularly of its tenth canto. Like Chaucer's *Parliament*, Spenser's Temple is a site of exploration, and it reaches a radically "vnperfite" conclusion in Scudamour's triumph. Although it does not suggest that Spenser was so fully inside his own culture as to have regarded this site uncritically, it is far from suggesting that he was able to stand outside what must have been, and may still be, its inherent power, "yfounded strong." Little familiarity with such works as the *Amoretti* and *Epithalamion* is needed to realize that even after the sudden vanishing of the House of Busirane had been published and hence accomplished, these poems reflect and participate in the erotic discourse of Spenser's culture both self-consciously and unself-consciously. Even sonnets coming late in the *Amoretti* exult, like Scudamour, in spoyle and conquest, if only in the recesses of the mind's "bowre of blisse" (69, 76). What C. S. Lewis famously described as "five centuries of human experience, predominantly painful," does not vanish so quickly.[37]

Scudamour's account of the Temple of Venus has a notoriously problematical relation to the rest of Book IV. In terms of narrative chronology, his account—as, to an extent, Spenser's—belongs to the past and yet is a present and full reassertion, a reliving, of it. Chaucerian irony frames and at times penetrates Scudamour's triumph, but the poetic and erotic impetus of his experience, particularly strong and memorable in the Lucretian hymn to Venus, retains equal if not greater power. This impetus thereby marks a concluding distinction between the Chaucerian and Spenserian tales that is worth noting. Although Amoret's involuntary departure from the Temple contrasts sharply with the female eagle's freedom in the *Parliament* to refuse eros (for a year, at least), Spenser's poem does not invoke this contrast, and the relation between the Temple episode and Chaucer's poem is not precise enough to justify the interpretive emphasis on the contrast that Kent Hieatt proposes, which amounts to an imposition of the earlier poem on the later one (112). The formel's choice produces a deferral in the *Parliament* that hardly aligns with Scudamour's no-win choice between folly and sacrilege, timidity and (over)boldness: "For sacrilege me seem'd the Church to rob, / And folly seem'd to leaue the thing vndone" (x.53). Whatever Scudamour's doubts, once he has advanced as far into an erotic experience as that represented in the Temple, the relevance of the formel's freedom to Amoret's situation is moot. Amoret's lack of freedom is a consequence of Scudamour's impetuous, "throb[bing]" vision of conquest and plunder, and her consent is not an option conceived to be within its "ouer bold" terms (x.53–54).[38]

As in the Mutability Cantos, the correspondence between Spenser's Temple episode and Chaucer's *Parliament*, while demonstrable, is finally less verbal and precise than imaginative and conceptual. Essentially, it amounts to a kind of doubleness, a complexity of vision, that comprehends what the Temple, that construct "yfounded stronge," shares with the self-absorbed passion of Acrasia—or indeed of *Sir Thopas*—and what it shares with the generative vitality of Nature. Whereas in the *Parliament* the role of the loveless narrator is passive, however, that of Scudamour is active and aggressive; more explicitly and urgently, it focuses the question of whether a morally mixed form like the Temple, the cultural expression of a specifically human nature, is also, by a kind of natural necessity, enduring.

10. *The Antiquities of Fairyland and Ireland*

In our century the words *antique* and *antiquity* normally have a resonance different from what they had for late sixteenth-century readers of Spenser's *Faerie Queene*. For us, these words suggest not only age but also antiquation. They signal both the distance of time and that of obsolescence: while something "antique" might be valuable or quaint or interesting, it is not essentially practical or even very useful. This sense of antiquation, which registers a lack of functional relevance, is not unknown to the late sixteenth century or to Spenser, but it is novel and rare rather than usual and standard. It is not the first meaning that springs to a Renaissance specialist's mind when the poet of Faerie characterizes his greatest poem as "antique." But the poet's awareness of the negative sense "antiquation" is hard to discount even in the 1590 installment of *The Faerie Queene* and is increasingly evident in the 1596 one. In the idea of antiquity and more exactly in the word *antique* and its cognates, as Spenser employs them, we can chart a revealing instance of the shifting but developing sense of the past during the period of the English high Renaissance.[1] This is very much an instance in process—unsettled, pronounced, and, for an observer of the early modern sense of history, highly significant. It addresses the early-modern perception of nearness to and distance from antiquity that Elizabeth L. Eisenstein, for one, provocatively questioned some years back in her seminal book *The Printing Press as an Agent of Change: Communications and Cultural Transformations in Early-Modern Europe*.[2]

The *OED* cites only two instances of negative meaning for cognates of *antique* and *antiquity* in or before the sixteenth century and none for these words themselves.[3] The negative sense of both cognates is obsolescence or obsoleteness rather than merely age. The earlier cognate, *antiquate*, a participial adjective, occurs in editions of Tyndale's work dated 1531 and 1573;[4] it means obfuscated through the passage of time, rather than simply useless, and could be related to a specialized medical instance of the same word in the late Middle Ages (ante 1425?), namely, *antiquat*, meaning inefficient through old age rather than useless.⁵ The second negative cognate, the verb *antiquate*, is first noted in Spenser's *View of the Present State of Ireland*, putatively written in 1596. Here Spenser's Irenius, one of his personae, declares certain statutes of Ireland "impertinente and vnnessessarye the which perhaps thoughe at the time of the makinge of them weare verye nedefull, yeat now *thoroughe Change of time are Cleane antiquated and alltogeather idle*."⁶ Linguistically and perceptually this declaration is striking. Irenius' use of *antiquated* to mean thoroughly useless and his awareness of the effects of changing temporal contexts on legal statutes are, for the first time the *OED* records, unmistakably modern. What makes his declaration still more interesting, however, is the fact that the sense of antiquation it expresses is not characteristic of Spenser's use of the idea of antiquity elsewhere and, indeed, conflicts with it.

Spenser, again and again in his poetry and especially in *The Faerie Queene*, employs the adjective *antique*, a sixteenth-century coinage, and, a quarter as often, the older noun *antiquity*. There are sixty-five uses of both words in all, forty-seven of which occur in *The Faerie Queene*. There is nothing like this usage in Shakespeare, for example, whether for frequency, focus, range, or symbolism, and, to my knowledge, there is nothing like it earlier in English literature, even in Chaucer, Spenser's "well of English vndefyled."⁷ The meanings Spenser attributes in his poetry to the words *antique* and *antiquity* range from the historical or simply long-gone past to the pure and visionary, and from a rude and barbarous reality to a mythic golden age. Except in Mammon's wicked mouth, however, they do not include a sense of utter uselessness, worthlessness, or irrelevance. While a number of times in *The Faerie Queene* the words *antique* and *antiquity* are neutral in meaning, merely designating "ancient" or "olden time," and at least once they are touched distinctively by ambiguity, in this poem they generally carry more positive weight.

Antiquity is, after all, in the warp and woof of *The Faerie Queene*, inseparable from its fabric and overall design, and the same is true of Spenser's first important poem, *The Shepheardes Calender*. The verbal medium, the very diction, of both these poems is throughout "antiqued" or made to reflect that of an earlier age. In the Dedicatory Epistle of *The Shepheardes Calender*, the glossator E. K. terms such verbal antiquity "obsolete"—the first use of *obsolete*, incidentally, the *OED* records—but, while thus registering his awareness of the oddity of Spenser's old words, E. K. goes on to justify their appropriateness and usefulness in the poem, even at one point comparing Spenser's practice to Livy's employment of old words "to set forth in hys worke an eternall image of antiquitie."⁸ Such obsoleteness is purposeful and constructive, not "Cleane antiquated and alltogeather idle" like those statutes of Ireland. It is antique but not antiquated, and by virtue of its antiquity it is, according to E. K., authoritative, authentic, and enduring.

E. K.'s Dedicatory Epistle was published seventeen years before the presumptive date of *A View of the Present State of Ireland*. Although, like the *View*, it is written in prose, its purpose differs radically from that of Spenser's political analysis of Ireland. What it shares conspicuously with the *View*, however, is a pronounced concern with "antiquity," an intertextual concern that obviously engaged the author of *The Shepheardes Calender* as well. Also evident when *Calender* and *View* are placed together—chronologically to frame, as it were, *The Faerie Queene*—is a distinction between what is suitable for practical and what for fictional purposes and, more exactly, between what suits political and what suits poetic ends. A distinction in kinds of meaning—hence kinds of truth—here emerges with implications for the worth and authority of antiquity, as well as for the wholeness of truth.⁹

This distinction, whose roots spread back over the entire sixteenth century, aligns with those Sidney and Bacon drew, not long before and not long after century's end, between poetry and history, fiction and factual truth. Like these distinctions, that evident in Spenser's writings is emphatically not simply a distinction between prose and poetry—between the *View* and *The Faerie Queene*, for example.¹⁰ It is a split between two different kinds of purposes and two different ways of interpreting what is real, and it involves the value of antiquity, hardly a concept neatly separable from history. At times this split does involve contradictions between Spenser's prose and poetry, but it also involves their relation: it not only gets into *The Faerie Queene* and pervades the later books, but is also present within the *View* itself, albeit implicitly so.

In the first printed edition of the *View* (1633), which justifiably claims manuscript authority, the persona Irenius, who is more often than not—although neither exclusively nor unqualifiedly—associated with Spenser himself, observes of the implausible Irish claim of descent from one "*Gathelus a Spaniard*" that "the *Irish* doe heerein no otherwise, then our vaine *Englishmen* doe in the Tale of *Brutus*, whom they devise to have first conquered and inhabited this Land, it being as impossible to proove, that there was ever any such *Brutus* of *England*, as it is, that there was any such *Gathelus* of *Spaine*."¹¹ In a different manuscript of some lineal authority, a virtually identical version of this skeptical observation continues, "But hearin theye [the Irish] shewe their great lightnes, which beeinge a barbarous and salvage nation, woulde faine fetche them selves from Spaine Lyke as wee and the French also woulde from the Troians: wherin theye muche deceive them selves in their reckninge."[12] According to Rudolf Gottfried, editor of the *Variorum View*, such denial of the Brutus legend is "undoubtedly" Spenser's, despite its blatant contradiction of two extensive genealogies in Books II and III of *The Faerie Queene*."[13] Nowhere in Spenser's writing is the split between two different versions of truth more obvious than in his treatment of the Brutus legend, first in poetry and then in history. Nowhere else does he so thoroughly debunk popular myths of origin—indeed, popular antiquities—as in the *View*.

But this debunking is not wholly representative of Spenser's attitude toward antiquity in the *View*. Repeatedly, he speaks through Irenius of the need to grasp the antiquity of the Irish—"whence they firste spronge" and what accounts for the origin and unruly persistence of their "olde Customes and Antiquities which they receaue by Continvall tradicion from theire parentes by recordinge of theire bardes and Cronicles in theire songes and by dailye vse and ensample of theire elders."[14] Clearly antiquity illuminates why things are as they are in Ireland and how they got that way. Unlike a modern anthropologist, of course, Spenser's Irenius generally wants to reform or to extirpate Irish "Customes and Antiquities," but this desire does not cancel his perception of their political importance. And even beyond his practical understanding of the antiquities of Ireland, his fascination with them is evident in his recurrent impulse to digress concerning them and in his recurrent promise to devote a separate work to them alone.[15]

Gottfried takes this promise to show that Spenser considered the Irish "antiquities" a "completely separable element, a kind of historical decoration on the façade of the *View*," and he notes in support of his reading the deletion from most manuscripts of "two fairly long" digressions about antiquities "which have survived in single manuscripts" or in a single manuscript and the printed version.[16] These deletions are presumed to be authorial on the basis of Renwick's theory that the variants in question represent an earlier, unrevised version of the *View*.[17] Why the variants were deleted invites further speculation, however, since the kernel of one was reintroduced at a later stage of the best manuscript and the other was replaced or corrected by similar antique material. Indeed, the historical "point" of both deletions—that Irish antiquity is chiefly other-than-Spanish in origin—was not only retained in revised form but was also greatly expanded.[18] Far from being "completely separable" from the *View*, Spenser's antiquities are, where they seem digressive and indulgent, evidence of a tension between practical and poetic purposes that is thus present in this prose work.

A reader of the *View* is frequently aware of Spenser's essentially poetic impulse to *make* meaning out of Irish antiquity, rather than simply to record what is directly relevant to a historical point, and likewise aware of his straining to discipline into history opportunities for the essentially mythopoeic and purely verbal expansiveness that attract him. Even the dialogue form that Spenser employs in the *View* builds into this work both self-conscious questioning and self-conscious affirmation of the value—the usefulness—of his antique material. Thus it at once enables expression of his own anxiety regarding such indulgence and authorizes more of the same. It also provides an instance of what appears to be Spenser's somewhat unsettled and ambivalent sense of antiquity's worth at this point.

To a modern historical temper, Spenser's indulgence is frivolous or merely decorative; to a poetic temper, by no means so sharply, readily, or consistently distinguished from a historical one in the sixteenth century, it is both pleasing and imbued with latent significance. Signs of indulgence appear, for instance, in his revision of the earlier passage treating the legend of Gathelus, now newly and expansively identified as "the sonne of *Cecrops* or *Argus* whoe havinge married the kinge of Egeiptes daughter Thence sayled with her into Spaine and theare inhabited." The same passage continues for some length, indulgently citing additional examples of Irish antiquity whose historical truth Spenser's Irenius finds worthless—the story of "Nemed and his ffower sonnes," for example:

> whoe Comminge out of *Scithia* peopled Irelande and inhabited it with his sonnes Twoe hundred and fiftene yeares till he was ouercome of the Geauntes dwellinge then in Irelande. And at laste quite banished and roted out, After whome twoe hundred yeares the sonnes of one *Dela* beinge Scithians arrived heare againe and possessed the wholle lande of which the yongest called *Slanius* in the end made himself *monarch*. Lastlye of the ffower sonnes of *Milesius* kinge of Spaine which Conquered that Lande from the *Scythyans* and inhabitinge it with Spanniardes called it of the name of the yongest *Heberius Hibernia* [89–90].

All these are "in truethe meare fables and verye Milesian lyes," Irenius fulminates, and then adds, "But yeat vnder these tales yee maye in a manner see the truethe lurke. . . ." As in Spenser's poetry, the tautology of the doubly adversative conjunction *But yeat* is revealingly nervous, indicative not of a totally assured view but of one aware of unsettling complexities in questions of truth and still very much in process.[19]

Spenser's indulgent expansiveness is likewise present in the often fantastic etymologies he everywhere imaginatively accepts from his sources or else imagines outright—the Welsh or British antiquities evident in Irish words and surnames, for example: "As the Tooles are called of the olde Brittishe worde *Tol* that is an hillye Countrie, The Brins of the Brittishe worde Brin That is woddye And the Cavanaghs of Caune that is stronge . . . [and] when anye flyethe vnder the . . . proteccion of [another] . . . againste an enemye he Criethe vnto him Cummericke that is *Britone* helpe, for the Britone is Called in his owne Language *Cumeraigh*" (94–95). Considering the tension between different kinds of purpose and meaning in Spenser's *View of the Present State of Ireland*, I think it hardly coincidental that this last quotation, like the preceding one, should recall the 1596 installment of *The Faerie Queene*, which is presumably close in time to the composition of the *View* itself. The preceding quotation, of course, recalls the sons of Milesio in Book V (iv.7), to which the legend of Milesius has been linked as a source.[20] The latter, etymological quotation recalls the poetic activity of the Marriage of Rivers in Book IV (xi), which ends with the naming of the fifty Nereids, ascribing to them attributes that derive from their Greek names and thus, as Harry Berger has put it, generating a poetic world from the word.[21] As I have remarked before, the relation between Spenser's poetry and prose variously involves the meaning and value of such antiquities.

In the *View*, antiquities include such phenomena as historical origins, customs, manners, laws, stories, etymologies, and myths. In *The Faerie Queene* these same antiquities are represented, but there is an additional and more conspicuous emphasis on the relation of antiquity to the ideal vision, to sagacity and wisdom, to something permanent and venerable. In the course of six books, as the relation of this poem, Spenser's "antique history," to the contemporary world changes, so do the role and significance of antiquity in it (II.Pro.i). In time, "antiquity" becomes for the Faerie poet less simply an ideal and more of a fiction. It becomes more simply an image or fabrication, even while purportedly retaining its proximity to moral truth.

The word *antique* first appears in the Proem to Book I of *The Faerie Queene*, when Spenser asks the poem's Muse to enable the burden of his song by laying out of her "euerlasting scryne / The antique rolles, which there lye hidden still": the phrase "hidden still" is complexly faceted, signifying "now as formerly hidden," "hidden always," "hidden silently, secretly;" "hidden unperturbed, constant, motionless, immutable," and hence "everlasting."[22] Similar memorial rolls appear as the "antique Registers" of Eumnestes, or "Good Memory," in the House of Alma; as the "antique" record of women's martial powers, as the "antique bookes" that record the wondrous generation of Amoret and Belphoebe, and as the "rolles . . . And records of antiquitie" known only to Clio, Muse of history and "sacred . . . noursling of Dame *Memorie*," "heauenly" rolls that, godlike, name and number the floods in the Marriage of Rivers and replenish the poet's wizardly, generative powers. In the end, these rolls appear as the "records permanent" of Fairyland—the records "hidden still"—in which the "antique race" and ancient lineage of Mutability were registered long ago.[23]

The association of Spenser's Faerie subject matter with antiquity, with Clio, and with memory is further enforced by the reiteration of the unusual word *scrine* in connection with Eumnestes' power, as before, in Proem I, with the secrets of Spenser's Muse.[24] This is a connection I have examined in an earlier chapter, which bears brief review here. Eumnestes, custodian of antiquity,

> of infinite remembrance was,
> And things foregone through many ages held,
> Which he recorded *still*, as they did pas,
> Ne suffred them to perish through long eld,
> As all things else, the which this world doth weld,
> But laid them vp in his immortall *scrine*,
> Where they for euer *incorrupted* dweld.
> (II.ix.56: my emphasis)

A *scrine* (Latin *scrinium*) is a "box for the safe-keeping of valuables" and more specifically a "shrine" for holy relics.[25] Thus, for Spenser, antiquity—that is, the material en-rolled in memory, which is the seat of historical awareness and understanding—has not only an enduring authenticating, and authorizing power, as it did for E. K., but in some sense, perhaps always latent, or "hidden still," a sacred one.[26]

While the idea of antiquity, like the material in antique rolls, endures in *The Faerie Queene*, its value is neither wholly secure nor constant. Increasingly it is threatened by antiquation—uselessness, irrelevance, or *idleness*, to use Spenser's own gloss on a worthless antiquity in the *View*. In the Proem to Book II, this threat is little more than a passing shadow, a possibility admitted into the poem but confidently, even playfully, dismissed. Later in Book II, at and in the Cave of Mammon, its power is acknowledged more strongly but is characterized as moral evil and thereby withstood. By Books V and VI, however, the same threat is undeniably a part of contemporary political reality.

Central to Spenser's sense of antiquity in the 1590 installment, the celebrated second Proem first characterizes his poem as this "antique history" and then three stanzas later as "this antique Image." Its initial stanza broaches the matter of idleness directly:

> Right well I wote most mighty Soueraine,
>   That all this famous *antique* history,
>   Of some th'aboundance of an *idle* brain
>   Will iudged be, and painted forgery,
>   Rather then *matter of iust memory*,
>   Sith none, that breatheth liuing aire, does know,
>   Where is that happy land of Faery,
>   Which I so much do vaunt yet *no where* show,
> But vouch *antiquities* which *no body* can know.
>   (II.Pro.i, my emphasis)

The painted forgeries abounding in an idle brain look ahead to the description of Phantastes in the House of Alma, whose chamber swarms with "idle thoughts and fantasies," devices, dreams, "and prophesies; / And all that famed is, as leasings, tales, and lies" (II.ix.51). For a reader of the *View*, they also resemble the idle beliefs and antiquated practices of the Irish, and the punning clause "no body can know"—that is, "no one at all," "none bodily," or "none in bodily form"—finds a distant echo in the tales of Spanish Gathelus or Milesius or Trojan Brutus that no body "can prove."[27] Such insubstantial tales are distinguished in *The Faerie Queene* from the antique registers of Eumnestes, which, including biblical, Classical, and mythological material,[28] are the "matter of iust memory," ancient wisdom and inventions having within them the reflection of a higher truth. The "matter of iust memory" includes, of course, the legend of Brutus (x.9–13).[29]

Spenser's admitting in this Proem the charge of idleness, if only to scorn it, also invites in the context of the Proem's first four lines a momentary connection between the words *antique* and *antic*, meaning "grotesque," "fantastic," or "bizarre." Despite the fact that both *antic* and *antique* were formerly accented on the first syllable, as *antique* is in line 2, Spenser elsewhere distinguishes them, consistently associating *antics* with the words "wild" and "curious."[30] Once made, the lurking shadow of connection exists even within the poem, however, and it threatens to intrude itself even where context rationally excludes it. As earlier with the grotesquely parodic image of a "mayden Queene" present in Lucifera, here the parodic echo of "antic" in Spenser's "antique history" is invited only to be pushed away and shown itself to be, in truth, irrelevant. Yet this echo renders the poet's awareness of possibilities here more complex and his growing acknowledgment of baleful ones as the poem progresses more understandable, in fact, intertextually speaking, pre-dictable.

As we know, moreover, Spenser did need to fend off the charge of antic idleness from none other than his friend Gabriel Harvey, who judged what he first saw of *The Faerie Queene* the fantastic work of "*Hobgoblin* runne away with the Garland from *Apollo*."[31] One easily imagines such a judgment as a motivation behind the Proem to Book II or such another behind it as appears in Harvey's letter to Spenser written from "myne hostisses by the fyersyde, beinge fasteheggid in rownde abowte on every side with a company of honest good fellowes, and at that tyme reasnable honeste quaffers." From this Falstaffian setting, Harvey transmits his fellow drinkers' spirited reply to a letter of complaint from the poet. The reply begins, "Sir, yower newe complaynte of the newe worlde is nye as owlde as Adam and Eve, and full as stale as the stalist fasshion that hath bene in fasshion since Noes fludd. You crie owte of a false and trecherous worlde, and therein ar passinge eloquent and patheticall in a degree above the highest." The letter continues, reminding Spenser of Cain's treachery to his brother and of "ould Grandsier" Adam, so subtly and fraudulently pitched out of Paradise, and it implies strongly throughout that Spenser's complaint to Harvey included a contrast between a presently false and treacherous world and a golden past.[32] Thus Harvey's letter additionally suggests that an ideal image of the past was real enough to Spenser actually to enter into the letters he wrote to his friends.

In view of Spenser's persistent concern with the past—now as source, now as monument, now as ideal—it is not surprising that an idealized image of antiquity should appear full blown and in its characteristic opposition to present time as early as the description of Una's birthplace, Eden, in the twelfth canto of Book I: "For th'antique world excesse and pride did hate; / Such proud luxurious pompe is swollen vp but late" (14). Thus situated,

Spenser's image of Eden provides the immediate antecedent of the references to antiquity in the second Proem. Thinking, perhaps, of the word "nowhere" (Greek *utopia*) in line 8 of this Proem, William Nelson aligns Spenser's idealized antique image—his "happy states"—with Budé's description of More's *Utopia*: "ciuitatem . . . suis utique ritibus bonisque acquiescentem, innocentia beatam, caelestem quodam modo uitam agentem, ut infra caelum, sic supra mundi huius cogniti colluuionem [a commonwealth . . . satisfied with its own goods and customs, blessed in innocence, leading in a certain measure a heavenly life, indeed in a lower world than heaven, but above the impurity of this known world]."[33] This state, Nelson explains, is "the world of nature . . . as it would be were evil absent" (302). As if to confirm this explanation, Spenser's Proem compares the reality of his utopian land to the newly found—indeed, newly realized—lands of the Americas.[34] Now finding true what hitherto existed unrecognized, the poet implies the tangibility of the idealized antique image in a way he will reject in the Proem to Book VI, where, as shown earlier in the present volume, antique virtue is *not* outwardly but only *inwardly* defined.[35]

But even while the Spenserian poet seems to make Faerie spatially credible in the second Proem, temporally he distances it. He knows its reality now in a poem that enshrines an antiquity no body can know. He finds Faerie now, yet in antiquity. The temporal paradox simultaneously succeeds in bringing the ideal close and holding it at a distance. Simultaneously it is past and present, lost and found, truth and fiction, history and image—a description, incidentally, equally applicable to Milton's Eden. Moreover, in the Proem to Book II the antique ideal is directly connected—as reflection and origin, thus as image and history—with present realms and a present ruler, as will not be the case in the Proem to Book V, where Spenser stresses instead the contrast between the "image of the antique world" and the "state of present time" (1). In the second Proem, however, the balance between truth and fiction, continuity and discontinuity, authenticity and antiquation, seems nearly perfect. Disparate realities remain apart yet are continuous. Whatever its final limitations, the potential for further realization, both inner and outer, here seems immense.

But even in Book II the limitations on this potential do not take long to reassert themselves in the more ominously threatening form of the money-god Mammon. Debating with Mammon outside the Cave, Guyon invokes the purity of "The antique world, in his first flowring youth" when "Like Angels life was then mens happy cace" and no man "gan exceed / The

164   *Reading the Allegorical Intertext*

measure of her [the world's] meane and naturall first need," and he soon hears the patronizing reply, "Sonne,"

> leaue the rudenesse of that antique age
> To them, that liu'd therein in state forlorne;
> Thou that doest liue in later times, must wage
> Thy workes for wealth, and life for gold engage.
> (II.vii.16, 18)

In Guyon's exchange with Mammon, two senses of the past sharply conflict, as the antique ideal meets face to face this distinctly modern charge of antiquation. The threat of irrelevance to present time, although resisted by Guyon, here attains a greater and more pointed reality, and Guyon's ultimate victory over it in canto vii is shown to be at once spiritually self-preserving and, as I have argued elsewhere, in a purely natural sense, self-destructive.[36] It is no accident, I suspect, that the word "antique" and its punning antitype "antickes" should appear in consecutive stanzas in Mammon's canto, first in reference to his antic armor and then to the antique shapes stamped on his smelted, New World gold, a monetary materializing of antiquity that is at once familiar and here disturbing. In the shadow of Mammon's Cave, the pun that subverts the antique ideal threatens to be really and overwhelmingly relevant.

In Books V and VI of *The Faerie Queene*, the words *antiquity* and *antique* do not occur outside the two Proems and the extraordinary, mythopoeic canto depicting the antiquity of "Isis Church" (V.vii.arg., 2). Before concluding with the more general relevance of antiquity in these two books, I want to bring some intellectual context to bear on the history of the antique ideal image itself. What I have in mind is to be found in Bacon's *Advancement of Learning*, published in 1605, and Sidney's *Defence of Poesy*, written in the early 1580s but unpublished until 1595, both works to which I have earlier alluded. Together, they address the shifting relation of truth to fiction and history to image in this period that Spenser's sense of antiquity in the *View* and *The Faerie Queene* perceptively epitomizes.[37]

In the *Advancement*, Bacon defines poetry, whether in verse or prose, as "nothing else but Feigned History." His definition is deliberately reductive in order to sharpen a distinction between an idealizing poetic fiction and truth, or in terms of my argument, between poetic image and history:

because the acts or events of *true history* have not that magnitude which satisfieth the mind of man, *poesy* feigneth acts and events greater and more heroical: because *true history* propoundeth the successes and issues of action not so agreeable to the merits of virtue and vice, therefore poesy feigns them more just in retribution, and more according to revealed providence; because true history representeth actions and events more ordinary . . . therefore poesy endueth them with more rareness [202–3, my emphasis].

In Bacon's view, poetry is far more pleasing than "true history" but is also far less truthful. Sidney's view of the relation of poetic fiction, or "feigning," and of history to truth differs markedly from Bacon's. Although he, too, finds history less morally edifying than poetry, his opinion of history, compared to Bacon's, is scornful; for Sidney, the historian is "captived to the truth of a foolish world" and "many times a terror from well-doing, and an encouragement to unbridled wickedness" (111). Conversely for Sidney, the poet's fiction is superior to, and truer than, actual history.

Sidney's and Bacon's opposing views of the relation of fiction and history to truth align themselves suggestively with a number of "antiqued" passages and their antitypes in the last two books of *The Faerie Queene*. The opposed conclusions of Arthur's and Artegall's stories afford an obvious example: Arthur is idealized in stanzas echoing the entry of Redcrosse into Eden—the very prototype of Spenser's antique ideal—and he is granted a triumph that differs remarkably from the messy historical events to which his story refers; in contrast, Artegall is vilified by Detraction, Envy, and the Beast in an outcome blatantly close to actual history and in the face of which an antique ideal of justice fades into irrelevance. The images of Isis and Mercilla afford another example.On the surface, these images are complementary, but examined closely, they are also opposed. In the mythic and ideal Isis, whose priests wear "Mitres shaped like the Moone, / To shew that Isis doth the Moone portend," we find an antique reflection of the living sovereign Elizabeth, albeit a partial one (vii.4). In contrast, the notoriously troubled and troubling presentation of Mercilla alludes flagrantly to the living sovereign and to her actions in history and as it does so casts the shadow—indeed, the obscurity—of antiquation on Isis herself. While the Faerie poet may finally have sympathized with Mercilla's dilemmas in Book V and supported her decisions, he was not self-deceiver enough to see in them the purity, the "plaine . . . patterne," of an antique ideal (VI.Pro.4, 6). By Books V and VI, at least, he knew full well the chasm between the antique ideal and the perturbing reality of political antiquation.

The end of Book VI, Calidore's capture of the Blatant Beast and the Beast's subsequent rending of the "Poet's rime," reiterates the split between an *antiqued* ideal and actuality at the end of Book V. Both endings can be aligned with the possibilities idealizing imagery expresses and with the "constant disappointment" of them in actual time of which Frances Yates writes in *Astraea*; and such "universal possibilities forever betrayed" can in turn be aligned with the opposition of Sidney's idealism and Bacon's material realism.[38] In the course of *The Faerie Queene*, the poet does not relinquish the moral validity of the antique ideal, but by the end of the poem his sense of its relevance to actuality changes considerably. The antique ideal becomes more simply a fiction, a poet's golden image detached from the present realities of time and place to which it was earlier moored, or seemingly moored, in the Proem to Book II. The antique ideal thus becomes, in the modern sense, more nearly and ominously just an antique.

Returning to Tyndale's use of the participial adjective *antiquate*, I can gloss more precisely Spenser's sense of antiquity in the final books of *The Faerie Queene*. Tyndale expounds two consecutive but seemingly opposed verses in St. John's first epistle, which read as follows:

> Brethren, I *write* no new commandment unto you, but *an old commandment* which ye had at the beginning: for an old commandment is the word which ye heard from the beginning [epistle 2:7; Tyndale, 174, my emphasis].

> Again, *a new commandment I write* unto you, which is true in him, and also in you; for the darkness is past, and the true light now shineth [epistle 2:8; Tyndale, 174: my emphasis].

Like the antique memories of Clio and Eumnestes in *The Faerie Queene*, St. John's "beginning," as Tyndale interprets it, refers at once to the individual and to the race. Tyndale takes "the beginning" to signify both each believer's baptism in Christ and the "old commandment . . . given at the beginning of the world, and . . . ever since . . . written in the heart of all that put their hope in God." Tyndale explains the paradoxical newness of this old command as its renovation by Christ, whose teaching dispels the work of sin, forgetfulness, obfuscation, and desuetude. Thus,

> The devil hath sown his darkness in the field where this commandment should grow; and the weeds of men's traditions had overgrown the corn of this old commandment; so that it was *antiquate*, and clean out of knowledge. But Christ, the light of all true doctrine, now shineth; and hath scattered the

darkness, and plucked up the weeds by the roots, and restored this old commandment again [174: my emphasis].

"Antiquate, and clean out of knowledge," the old commandment might have become, but it was never worthless, useless, or irrelevant.

At the end of *The Faerie Queene*, Spenser's intertextualized sense of the idealized antique image closely resembles Tyndale's "antiquate" commandment—obfuscated but not impertinent, obsolescent but not idle. At the end, Spenser's confidence in the efficacy of his poetic enterprise and specifically in its ability to effect reform may falter, but the antique ideal left behind for six books still remains. Like St. John's and Tyndale's commandment, it remains written. Remembering Clio's and Eumnestes' "scrine" and reading historically in terms of it, I should therefore not finally describe antiquity as "left behind" or even as merely "written," but again as *enshrined*—that is, *enscrined*—in *The Faerie Queene*.

11. Better a mischief than an inconvenience: *"The saiyng self"* in Spenser's View of the Present State of Ireland

The phrase "saiyng self" (*sic*) in my title comes from Nicholas Udall's introduction to Erasmus' *Apophthegmes* and refers to the individual apophthegm, or, as we would say, to "the saying itself."[1] To a modern ear, Udall's phrasing also suggests both the self or subject who speaks an apophthegm and the one who is culturally spoken by it, thereby expressing its mixed, unstable ownership and agency. The particular "saiyng self" of Spenser that I intend, "Better a mischiefe then an Inconvenience," occurs strikingly twice in the first half of *A View of the Present State of Ireland*.[2]

This saying, whose glossing I deliberately postpone, stands out in a modern setting first because it is unfamiliar, but the formal and historical contexts in which it occurs in the *View* also draw attention. It may be the only proverb repeated in the *View*—at least it is the only repetition of one to catch my eye in numerous rereadings. First spoken by Spenser's persona Irenius, it is curiously reiterated by Eudoxus, his other persona, some fourteen pages later, soon enough for notice even by the mnemonically challenged modern reader. But this saying also stands out as a prefabricated syntactical unit—an instance of that oddity the frozen syntagm—and it is further notable as an instance of the popular rhetorical figure *paroemia*, the sort of figure that Renaissance editions flagged for emphasis and mnemonic reference with an indexical finger.[3] Of course as a proverb it is even more importantly a cultural nugget—a "gem" to Erasmus—in the cultural code of a society that valued and collected the treasures of prudence and traditional wisdom.[4]

When Irenius initially invokes the saying, he is arguing that English common law is "inconvenient"—that is, unfitting—for Ireland, inasmuch as it was not framed for Irish circumstances.[5] Rejecting a conception of human law in strict accord with abstract justice, he maintains pragmatically that laws are only just if they can prevent current evils and provide for "the safetye of the Comon weale." He then offers an example of how this safety ought to be balanced against an abstract right, explaining, "It is a flatt wronge to punishe the thoughte or purpose of anye before it be acted, ffor trewe Iustice punisheth nothinge but the evill acte or wicked worde, yeat by the lawes of all kingedomes it is a capitall Cryme to devize or purpose the deathe of the kinge" because regicide would more harm the commonweal than subsequent "punishment of the Malefactours coulde remedye." It is to encapsulate this explanation of an exception to the general principle that he concludes, "better is a mischief then an inconvenience" (65–66).

Before dealing fully with the interpretive possibilities that Irenius' concluding proverb embodies, I will need to describe its reiteration by Eudoxus, yet a couple of preliminary observations are possible here. First, the proverb's context suggests that a mischief is a wrong or harm done—in words cited by the *OED* in the relevant entry—"to one or some particular persons" as distinct from a greater harm "to the whole Common-wealth in generall."[6] Second, if we take the word "capital" in Irenius' phrase "capitall cryme" at face value to indicate an offense deserving the death penalty, then his principle of preventive homicide agrees with the published views of Jean Bodin but goes beyond the penalty for such a crime of intention specified in the Statutes of Ireland during the reign of Elizabeth.[7]

In Ireland the statutory penalty for devising the death of the king was forfeiture of all the offender's possessions and "perpetuall imprisonment," although a repeat offense, which could even include *imagining* regicide, brought death.[8] At the beginning of Elizabeth's reign, the Statutes of England imposed the same penalty, but this was later toughened: in the thirteenth year of her reign, the English Parliament made the penalty capital on the first express offense and then, under the ever-increasing apprehension of a Romish threat in the twenty-seventh year (1584–85), on the first imagined offense.[9] In passing it might be noted again, however, that the larger context of Irenius' explanation is the unsuitability of English law for Irish circumstances.[10] The heightened emphasis on an expedient safety in his explanation, in which this statutory contradiction participates, is further accentuated by the gratuitous, intensifying adjective in the phrase "*flatt* wronge" and, for the etymologically-minded, by the macabre connection between the words *capital* and *mischief,* both ultimately deriving from Latin *caput,* "head," or in this case headlessness.[11]

The second time the proverbial saying in question occurs, it comes with a casualness, even a nonchalance, that is suspect. This time, Eudoxus is replying to Irenius' moderating argument that the statutory designation of the Irish practices of "coigny" and "livery" as treason is "inconvenient," that is, "inconsistent with reason" (78–79).[12] Roughly, these practices refer to the tenant's providing lodging, victuals, and fodder for his lord. Eudoxus begins by agreeing that Irish lords are wronged by the punitive statute "since it was an antiente Custome and nothinge Contrarye to lawe, for to the willinge theare is no wronge done"—a principle in common law to this day. Verbally echoing More's *Utopia*, he opines, moreover, that there are "*even heare in Englande* . . . in manye places as lardge Customes." Then he supposes that the purpose of the statute was to forbid the violent taking of victuals from "other mens tennantes againste theire wills" (79: my emphasis). Such taking, he labels "a greate outrage and yeat not so greate . . . as that it shoulde be made Treasone, ffor Consideringe that the nature of Treasone is Concerninge . . . the Prince . . . it is hardelye wrested to make this Treasone, But as you erste saide, *Better a mischiefe then an Inconvenience*" (79–80).

This time, the saying self is even italicized for emphasis, as if to accentuate the discrepancy between Eudoxus' own argument, as well as that of Irenius, and the nugget of proverbial wisdom that concludes it. "Oh, well," Eudoxus seems to be saying, "The statute is totally unjust, but what the hell, bring out the traditional slogans and let's get on with it." Something that exceeds a merely literal reading is clearly occurring. Not only echoing but explicitly asking us to remember Irenius' earlier use of the proverb—"But as you erste saide"—Eudoxus' statement puts a spotlight on it and opens both its use and its meaning in either of its immediate contexts to scrutiny.[13]

This may be the point at which we find out how many meanings can stand on the head of a proverb, in this case the contextualized and specifically intertextualized proverb in question. Since both occurrences of the saying "Better a mischief then an inconvenience" in the *View* involve statutory contexts, legal employment of it in Spenser's historical context is the place to begin. Interestingly, this employment is at odds with that of Irenius and therefore at least on the surface with that of Eudoxus, who invokes Irenius' use of it. In late medieval and sixteenth-century English law, according to J. H. Baker, *Better a mischief than an inconvenience* has "a life of its own"; it is a legal maxim, a codified saying. In it, *inconvenience* means roughly "inconsistency," the idea being that it is preferable "to suffer a mischief in an individual case than the inconvenience which might follow from admitting exceptions to general rules," or, in a modern maxim that similarly opposes equity, "Hard cases make bad law."[14] Norman Doe labels the saying a "late medieval common lawyer's slogan" and similarly interprets *inconvenience* as "inconsistency, [or] not upsetting established practice, [albeit] at the expense of allowing injustice: [thus] 'a mischief will be suffered sooner than an inconvenience'" (155, 173).¹⁵ Here *mischief* again pertains focally to the individual, and *inconvenience* to the law and established practice.

Doe is more expansive, however, noting that while "*mischief* related to abstract right and wrong," rather than to inconsistent results or "inconvenience," it nonetheless involved a "narrower and less moral idea than that of reason or conscience" and "specifically meant being without redress or procedural vexation" (155). In other words, the narrow application of the saying *Better a mischief than an inconvenience* does not align easily with the capital crimes of Spenser's offenders. Despite the more obvious discrepancy between Eudoxus' sense of justice and his ironic use of this saying to terminate discussion, the saying itself fits least well Irenius' endorsement of preventive homicide in the *View*, an injustice that would appear to extend well beyond procedural inequity. Indeed, Irenius' citation of a legal maxim *against exceptions* to justify an *exceptional* law in which an immaterial intention, as distinguished from a material word or deed, brings death is itself noticeably self-contradictory.

Christopher St. German's *Doctor and Student*, an Henrician exposition of common law that was popular with practitioners and lay persons throughout the sixteenth century and beyond, attests to the same narrow legal use of the saying, invoking it conclusively in a question that weighs the face value of a legal document against the "conscience"—the knowledge and awareness—pertaining to its execution. The student's response to this question establishes that the law need only ascertain whether the document at issue is the party's "dede or not/ and not whether the dede were made with conseyence or agaynst conseyence/ and thoughe the partye maye be at a myschyefe thereby/ yet the lawe wyll rather suffre that myschyefe then the sayd inconuenyence."¹⁶ Here again the integrity of (merely) legal principles and procedures—law for law's sake, as it were—is what matters rather than equity or morality; in fact these hardly seem to count. Even the student of law later observes, however, that in the case under consideration the dictates of reason and conscience should on a private basis redress the legal decision, thus underlining the tension between the maxim legally understood and conscience or equity.

In the early 1620s the same legal principles prevail where this maxim occurs. For example, Sir Edward Coke refers a mischief to a "private loss" and an inconvenience to a "public evil" and declares that the former is preferable to the latter. It is an inconvenience, he explains, "that any of the maxims of the law should be broken, though a private man suffer loss."¹⁷ With respect to Spenser's *View*, the intrepretive stakes are therefore these: if a specifically legal meaning limited to procedure and consistency does not restrict the maxim at issue and if the maxim also applies self-contradictorily, as I've suggested, then the invitation in the text to scrutinize this maxim enables the moral and equitable considerations that the accepted legal meaning would otherwise exclude.

Outside contemporary legal sources, the proverb *Better a mischief than an inconvenience* turns out to have led another rich textual life, a condition that further colors and complicates its meaning as a prefabricated unit—an imported whole—in a political tract such as Spenser's *View*. Two relevant instances occur in a commercial document that bears on a legal context—Gerard de Malynes' *Consuetudo, vel Lex Mercatoria: or, The Ancient Law-Merchant*.[18] In the first of these, Malynes, describing an early modern form of insurance against maritime losses, explains that if the insured has "caused himselfe to bee assured" for more than his cargo is worth, then in the event of loss "the last assurors which haue subscribed to the Policie" will be exempt from payment, for "It is better to suffer a mischiefe than an inconuenience" (161, cf. 156).[19] Curiously, the inconvenience this time is to the principle that money is received only for risk taken, and in direct contrast to the instance I cited from *Doctor and Student*, the mischief is against the actual document of insurance in question, which does not correspond to the actual loss. As a consequence "a Law not observed is inferiour to a Custom well observed" (156).[20]

In a second use of the same proverb Malynes, himself a merchant, contends that the disallowing of interest on money in all circumstances, such as the support of orphans or the mechanisms of monetary exchange, is "to remedie a mischiefe [interest, or, 'usury'] with a greater inconvenience" (329). His meaning here is moral or commercial and commonsensible rather than legal and procedural. While he continues to mean an inconvenience to the greater entity or whole and a mischief to the lesser entity or part and to intend the greater good over the lesser, he is no longer within the compass of statutory law.

In connection with usury or the interest on money, the proverb *Better a mischief than an inconvenience* also occurs twice in the learned Thomas Wilson's *Discourse Uppon Usurye* (1572).[21] In the first occurrence, the proverb is implicated in an unprincipled action born of necessity: for princes must do what "they would not of themselves doe yf it were not for very necessity, to avoide a greater inconvenience" (186). Wilson, a member of Parliament, a Master in the Court of Requests, Ambassador to the Netherlands, Secretary of State, Dean of Durham, and author of a Logic and a Rhetoric, obviously knew something of Machiavellian politics as well as of law and religion. One of his personae in the *Discourse*, a temporal or common-law lawyer, observes that a number of statutes have permitted usury, "which I woulde they had contynued, to avoide further evell, for (as we say) bettre it is to suffer a mischiefe then an inconvenience" (237). Although attributed to a lawyer, Wilson's use of the proverb is clearly non-technical, simply privileging the greater good over the lesser. Perhaps more striking is the fact that it is used *against* the current law on the books regarding usury and thus contradicts its proper legal usage in support of statutory integrity.

In a more explicitly political tract, *The Supremacie of Christian Princes* (1573), Bishop John Bridges invokes the same proverb to conclude an argument opposing rebellion against "an heretical, a scismatical, or a symoniacal King." "The lawiers woulde briefly say to this," writes Bridges, "better suffer a mischiefe, than an inconuenience." He adds that even if such an unjust king were considered an inconvenience, "we may not take away one inconuenience with an other greater inconuenience," and recommends instead "conuenient remedies of pacience and constancie."[22] Although Bridges, too, identifies his saying with lawyers, his use of it does not accord with theirs in the narrow senses of procedure and consistency. The inconvenience he envisions is a radical social disruption, rebellion, and his convenient remedies are "fitting" or "appropriate" ones. Of course the lawyers also envisioned radical disruption from a violation of legal formalism and opposed it in the maxim at issue. If Bridges' saying actually originates in the law, it might be seen as an instance of the violence of analogical extension— homologism—that is not unlike one possible reading of Irenius' use of it. To repeat: *one* possible reading.

Better a mischief than an inconvenience also occurs in contemporary literary contexts, where its use gravitates toward a moral rather than strictly legal meaning and further contributes to its instability. For example, in *The Resurrection of Our Lord*, a miracle play dating from the decades 1530 to 1560, the high priests Annas and Caiaphas twice urge the soldiers guarding Christ's tomb to lie about the circumstances in which his body has disappeared, thus suffering the mischief of a falsehood rather than the greater inconvenience of discrediting "Mosyses lawe."[23] Here, in distinction to the saying's force in a legal context, the mischief to be countenanced is clearly immoral and against conscience. In two of John Lyly's plays, the saying appears again, both times with moral coloring. In *Mother Bombie* (1594) it registers the difference between "a little shame" or "mischiefe" and "an infinite griefe" or "continual inconuenience." In *Gallathea*, where the saying refers to the sacrifice of a virgin to appease Neptune, Gallathea's father is accused of "preferring a common inconuenience, before a priuate mischiefe" because he wants to shield his daughter.[24] In *Roaring Girl* (1611), an oblique, reversed version of the saying occurs when Master Gallipot suggests that he report his wife adulterous in order to discourage her supposed former suitor, and she retorts, "You embrace a mischiefe [a worse harm], to preuent an ill [a lesser harm]."[25] From Mistress Gallipot's viewpoint, the "ill" or rival's claim is lesser because she would actually like to be bedded by the supposed suitor. Since she has already told her gullible husband that she was formerly contracted to this supposed rival, the threatened "ill" appears to Gallipot a rightful claim rather than a legally inconsistent one. In this context the saying hardly carries the force of the legal maxim for either Gallipot.

In four other contemporary texts, Lyly's *Euphues and His England* (1580), Brian Melbancke's *Philotimus* (1583), Shakespeare's *Merry Wives of Windsor* (1597–1602), and Gabriel Harvey's "New Letter of Notable Contents, 1593," *Better a mischief than an inconvenience* occurs with a similarly radical modification or even reversal of the legal meaning. Lyly's Camilla, offended by Philautus' letter of love, debates with herself whether she can honorably answer it and then decides that she should "commit an inconuenience," that she "might preuent a mischiefe, chusing rather to cut . . . [him] off short by rigour then to giue . . . [him] any iot of hope by silence" (II, 127). This time the mischief, "harm," "distress," or "evil consequence" is decidedly greater than the inconvenience, which amounts to an "impropriety."[26] Such is also the case in *Philotimus*, when the unfortunate Philotimus, hoping for money to appease his creditors, tells his presumptive benefactor that although he realizes "how litle thou owest me . . . yet must I commit an inconuenience, to preuent a mischiefe, and for aunrient benevolence, craue your benificence." Here again "inconvenience" means "an unseemly act" or, perhaps, even a mere "discomfort."[27] Another variation on the saying, in which the word "extremity" replaces "inconvenience," bears a similar but stronger sense of distress in Shakespeare's *Merry Wives of Windsor*, when Falstaff, offered the option of an indecorous escape in woman's clothing, gasps, "any extremity rather than a mischief" (IV ii 73–74). However demeaning his disguise, it is clearly less of a threat than the mischief he anticipates at the hands of an irate husband.[28]

Spenser's friend Gabriel Harvey actually reverses the proverb in a letter that treats Nashe's attacks on him, for which Nashe at least temporarily appears contrite. Harvey, although highly skeptical and often derisive, presents himself as willing to suppress a counterattack (by the mysterious gentlewoman) long enough to await further signs of Nashe's penitence rather than quash his suspect overtures. For this purpose Harvey cites both the proverb and its inverse, introducing a distinction between its public and private applications: "Howbeit as in some publique causes, better a mischief, then an inconuenience: so in many priuate cases *better an inconuenience, then a mischief.* Though an Orient Gemme be precious, and worthy to be gazed vpon with the eye of Admiration, yet better an Orient Gemme sleepe, then the Penitent man perish."[29] While Harvey's concessive clause ("Howbeit . . . inconuenience") affirms the usual form of the proverb, his reversal of this form in the apodosis of his sentence further destabilizes the proverb's potential as a cultural signifier. It also encapsulates what has appeared to this point in nonlegal sources of the later sixteenth century to be a translation of the legal maxim to a usage that is personal and equitable and thus thoroughly opposite to it. The uncertain ground this "saiyng self" now traverses includes not only the relation of statute to equity and of law to morality but also that of a public domain to private one.

If the saying thus participates in a tension within the law and another between the law and popular usage, its intertextual potential for instability is further intensified both by other legal uses of the terms *mischief* and *inconvenience* and by other nonlegal ones.[30] In law, these terms often appear as a seemingly synonymous pair, their doubling a means of emphasis, as in the phrase "tres-grand mischief & inconuenience."[31] In legislation, *mischief* had sometimes a thoroughly moral and not only a legal connotation, referring, for example, to a harm "'contrary to the pleasure of God'" or to "wilful premeditated murder . . . 'by the laws of God and of natural reason forbidden'" (Doe, 156–57). Specifically within common law, *inconvenience* appears to have had a more stable meaning, but once outside the *practice* of common lawyers, it could appear in legislation describing riot, robbery, and murder (Doe, 167).

Outside legal sources, both words had broader ranges of meaning, as we have already seen reflected to an extent in the saying itself. In the Tudor period, *mischief* could additionally mean anything from "misfortune," "trouble," and "distress" to "disadvantage" and "injury," to "wickedness," "troublemaker," or even "morbidity," while earlier usage, still present in extant documents, further extended the meaning to "need, want, [and] poverty."[32] Besides an inconsistency in law, *inconvenience* applied to any "want of agreement," "incongruity," or "absurdity" with respect to reason or rule; to "moral or ethical unsuitableness" or "unseemly behavior," "impropriety." Like *mischief,* it could also mean "harm," "injury," "misfortune," and "trouble," or "problem" in the sense of an unforeseen obstacle.[33]

In *A View of the Present State of Ireland* occurrences of the word *mischief* and particularly of the word *inconvenience* outside the proverbial saying further bear on a translation of the proverbial "saiyng self." On the few occasions that *mischief* occurs nonproverbially, it indicates "harm" or a synonym for "troublous practize" (74, 144) and therefore does not indicate a more technical legal usage. In contrast to the relative infrequency of *mischief*, *inconvenience* and its cognates weave threadlike through the pages on either side of the two proverbial instances of it, appearing elsewhere in the tract with some regularity as well. Usually they signify an inconsistency with reason, as in the instance of Irish folkmotes or tenancy (131, 134). When the inconsistency relates specifically to the laws, as it often does, it exists between the law and reason or circumstances rather than between legal cases or discordant results in a single case. Thus nowhere does the inconsistency appear to amount to a technically legal meaning.[34] While *inconvenience* sometimes merely indicates "harm," "trouble," or "injury," in adjectival form its other major signification besides "inconsistent" is "unsuitable," or "unfitting," as the native Irish garb and the speaking of Irish by the Old English are said to be.[35] In short, other occurrences of both words in the *View*, a number of them referring to law, offer no evidence for a strictly legal and thereby safely contained interpretation of the proverb, as Irenius invokes it. In no way do they restrict a reading of it open to the moral and ethical ambivalence that Eudoxus' use of it invites. In other words, whether through simple incompetence, moral discomfort, or cultural critique, Spenser's deployment of the proverb "Better a mischief then an inconvenience" in a way that is discrepant with both its legal contexts in the *View* and thus with its use both by Irenius and by Eudoxus questions the meaning of the proverb itself, the circumstances or instances to which it is applied, and the kind of justice they embody. Here the "saiyng self" carries a heavy and equivocal cultural burden.

What else this ambivalence implies, of course, is another issue. More than half a century ago, Raymond Jenkins, later followed by Spenser's biographer Alexander Judson, concluded that Spenser was "very familiar with the operation of the law-courts of Munster," basing his assertion on the discovery that Spenser was deputy clerk of the Council of Munster.[36] The implications of Jenkins' large claim are themselves unclear, however, since they could imply the superficiality of Spenser's legal expertise as easily as the depth of it: not unlike Chaucer's summoner, the far more educated Spenser might well have learned a number of law terms "out of som decree—/ No wonder is, he herde it al the day."[37] In other words, it is possible that Irenius' misuse within a legal context of the saying "Better a mischief then an inconvenience" results from incompetence, his own or Spenser's, although Eudoxus' clearly ironic repetition of the saying inclines against this merely authorial alternative. Moral discomfort, cultural critique, or perhaps some combination of these remain the other interpretive possibilities, and they are the ones supported both by the genuinely dialogic form of the *View*'s review of law and by the more fully contextualized voice of Spenser's epic romance *The Faerie Queene*.[38]

If we think that the poet of Faerie wrote the *View* (and there is considerable verbal evidence that he did), we really should not be surprised that his twin—his duplicitous—personae Irenius and Eudoxus should manage between them to utter a "saiyng self" that lands us in cultural quicksand, even though this possibly bottomless miring directly implicates the special nature of sovereignty, the danger of regicide, and more exactly the threats, including that of the imagination, to Spenser's Queen. The potential for instability and for appropriation in any prefabricated unit of meaning, perhaps any "saiyng self," is a subject of which the poet of *The Faerie Queene* is demonstrably aware. Witness the sophistical use the character Despair makes of the resources of proverbial knowledge drawn from scripture, the Classics, and other traditions or the stichomythic exchange of conflicting, relatively valued sayings between Prince Arthur and Una when they first meet in Book I. Even more to the point is the proverbially expressed conflict in Spenser's Book of Justice between Artegall and Burbon regarding the unity or expedient duplicity of truth itself—a conflict between the saying "To temporize is not from truth to swerue" and the opposite saying "Knights ought be true, and truth is one in all" (V.xi.56).[39] The fundamental *duplicity* or equivocity of culturally empowered sayings in *The Faerie Queene* is another perception that Spenser could have found both in Chaucer, his avowed poetic father, and in such a schoolboy-text as Erasmus' *De copia*, and it may well be one of the features defining the specific voice of Spenser's romance epic.[40]

Still more relevant than the instances in Books I and V that I have cited to the force of the saying at issue in the *View* is the vexed treatment of the execution of Mary Stuart in Spenser's fifth book—the book of Justice. Here, recalling multiple proverbs, the narrator endeavors to balance the claims of justice and mercy, referring first to justice, which "from iust verdict will for nothing start, / But to preserue inuiolated right, / Oft spilles the principall, to saue the part" (V.x.2). Whether justice spills the principal or the principle, a distinction often honored more in the orthographic and orthoepic breach than in the observance, it would seem to align readily both with the consistency that honors the integrity of the legal system over that of the individual life and with the numerically greater part over the numerically lesser one. In contrast with these possibilities, the narrator tells us that the principle of mercy, which is of "So much more . . . powre and art" than justice,

> . . . seekes to saue the subiect of her skill,
> Yet neuer doth from doome of right depart:
> As it is greater prayse to saue, then spill,
> And better to reforme, then to cut off the ill.
> (V.x.2)

How mercy saves rather than spilling and reforms rather than cutting off without departing from "doome of right," the poem does not tell us, and the oft-remarked discrepancy between mercy and Mary-Duessa's fate suggests its inability adequately to do so. The point I would make is that this discrepancy finds a reflection in the odd ambiguity regarding the numerically "greater good" detectable in the exchange first between Irenius' and Eudoxus' deployment of the "saiyng self" and then between their ambivalent, shared legal saying and its broader, moral use in the circumambient culture. It finds another reflection in the image of Malfont, the poet who has been silenced, his tongue nailed to a post for a trespass "adiudged so by law" in the court of Mercilla (V.ix.25). And it finds still another in the uneasy oscillation Debora Shuger has seen emerging in the Renaissance between the "right to life" and the "solidarity of the patriarchal family and tribal community," between the "autonomous subject" and "his archaic subjection to the *mystica conjunctio*," and thus between what I have identified as the individual, private right and the greater, public good in Spenser's deployment of the maxim.[41] Far from being a modern invention, this is an oscillation—indeed, a tension—that traces back at least to the thirteenth century and thus is considerably older than Shuger recognizes.[42]

On the basis of one saying in a tract of 188 *Variorum* pages, I can contribute to discussion of the writer's engagement in the views of his personae, whether direct, ironized, or otherwise mediated by his culture, but I can hardly resolve this issue. What I can conclude is that the immediate or seeming sense of Irenius' conclusive proverb is questioned first by its seeming affirmation but actual derision in Eudoxus' mouth and then by its interplay with the tensions of usage, including voice, in the broader culture. On the basis of what I discovered when I began seriously to wonder about the meaning and function of the saying in question, I would also conclude that we could profitably pay a good deal more attention to the rhetorical and historical details of the *View* before deciding who is saying what in it.

In a chapter like this, I am also struck by the possibility of still another kind of conclusion, a final meaning to stand on the head of my proverb. There was a time when I might have reviewed the historical-cultural materials in this chapter and then have proposed a reading of the passages from the *View* in question without displaying extensive documentation except, radically abbreviated, in the notes. In this way I would have kept my eye firmly on what I determined the text to be. Now I exhibit these materials within the body of the chapter, for they have become a more significant part of its subject, participating in a multiplicity or qualified indeterminacy of self and voice. But this remains an indeterminacy qualified for me, as it has been in this chapter, by its relation to *The Faerie Queene*—by what I shall term the "volume" of this epic romance, not merely its mass but also its specific audibility, the recurrent, demonstrable effect of a rhetoric that is at once communal and distinctive. Moreover, this relative indeterminacy, which first appears so selfless and impersonal as a reading practice, is ultimately dependent on some conception, if only a questioning, of self and voice: conceptually, a self must underlie an indeterminate self, a concept of person must underpin one of impersonality. A characteristic feature of modernity, Anthony Giddens tells us, is self-reflexivity, self-evaluation that is institutionalized and culturally ingrained as never before.[43] In the deliberate exchange between Irenius and Eudoxus and the open-ended exchange with a larger cultural textuality that it extends, I cannot help wondering whether we might be seeing the expression of something at least remotely similar.[44]

PART 3   Spenserian Allegory in the Intertexts of Shakespeare and Milton

12. *The Conspiracy of Realism: Impasse and Vision in*
    The Faerie Queene *and Shakespeare's* King Lear

Despite an established but controversial alignment of *King Lear* with Beckett's absurdist dramas or, at the alternative extreme, with Dante's *Purgatorio*, the relation of *King Lear* to allegory has remained an elusive topic. The interpretive extremes of this pendulum's swing are thus conspicuous, but the nature of the pendulum itself seems under taboo. Those aligning a Dantesque or absurdist work with *Lear* have been interested in such analogous texts primarily as statements of meaning rather than as allegorical forms, that is, as content alone rather than as informed content or as the content of form. Even older critics like A. C. Bradley, W. B. C. Watkins, or Maynard Mack, who are sensitive to the allegorical potencies of Shakespeare's play, are wary of the term *allegory* itself.[1]

For example, Watkins, the author of an old, good, and still suggestive book comparing Shakespeare with Spenser, describes Shakespeare's "mixed technique" of characterization in *Lear* as "a combination of psychological realism and symbolical stylization" (83). Although Watkins conceives of Goneril as "a symbol in the allegory toward which the play tends" (99) and therefore envisions some sort of continuity between symbol and allegory, his categories imply the Romanticist's view that a symbol is somehow really different in kind from and superior to allegory, a view that Paul de Man, for one, cogently showed, long after Watkins wrote, to be fallacious and self-mystifying.[2]

Like Watkins, Bradley, an even older, yet classic, critic of Shakespeare, also seems to think of allegory almost exclusively in the limiting context of characterization in Lear, rather than in terms of the plot or narrative process of the play. His wariness of the term *allegory* is more pronounced and more revealing. Bradley identifies Lear's desire to "anatomise Regan" with a "strain of thought . . . present in some degree throughout the play." In this thinking he finds

> the tendency which, a few years later, produced Ariel and Caliban, the tendency of imagination to analyse and abstract, to decompose human nature

into its constituent factors, and then to construct beings in whom one or more of these factors is absent or atrophied or only incipient. This, of course, is a tendency which produces symbols, allegories, personifications of qualities and abstract ideas; and we are accustomed to think it quite foreign to Shakespeare's genius, which was in the highest degree concrete.... [But,] while it would be going too far to suggest that he was employing *conscious symbolism or allegory* in King Lear, it does appear to disclose a mode of imagination not so very far removed from the mode with which, we must remember, Shakespeare was perfectly familiar in Morality plays and in the *Fairy Queen* [212–13: my emphasis, except King Lear].

Heaven forbid that Shakespeare was thinking of conscious symbolism as he warbled his native wood notes wild! Whatever Bradley thought the distinction between allegory and conscious symbolism might be, both clearly made him nervous—enough so to diminish momentarily the persistent, reverberating allusiveness of those pelican daughters or of Lear himself—Titan, old man, father, king—and to make him forget how essentially, organically allegorical the myths of the ancient world were to begin with, let alone as they were received by later periods.[3]

Mack similarly invokes the idea of allegory to explain characterization in *King Lear* but does so only to distance the opprobrious word *allegorical*. "At any given instant," he writes, "characters may shift along a spectrum between compelling realism and an almost pure representativeness that resembles (and evidently derives from) this *esse* of the Morality play, though it is not necessarily allegorical" (67). To paraphrase Bernard Spivack, the morality character does what it is and requires no further motivation.[4] Interestingly, Mack describes a character who is conceived allegorically, albeit not necessarily allegorical, whereas Bradley and Watkins seem to describe one conceived more naturalistically but then becoming by a process of enlargement (Watkins) or decomposition (Bradley) a being more abstract, artificial, or mythic. Both conceptions—Mack's and Bradley-Watkins'—afford insight into characterization in *King Lear*, and together they cast light on the various characters—indeed the various kinds of characters—assembled in the play better than either does alone. Both conceptions are congenial to allegory and derived from it, and instances of both can be found together in a sophisticated Elizabethan allegory like *The Faerie Queene*—the latter, in the fortunes of Malbecco, the former, in those of Arthur or Artegall, for example. The fact for Bradley, Watkins, and Mack would appear to be that however non-allegorical the characters of *King Lear* are, allegory is pertinent to their conception.

When Mack turns from character to the structure of *King Lear*, one almost gets the impression that he is avoiding at all costs the risk of mentioning the word *allegorical* again and that he is substituting for it such parsonical, nonfictional terms as "homiletic" and "doctrinal." Thus in *Lear*, "we meet . . . a form of organization that is as much homiletic as it is dramatic, and sometimes more the former than the latter" (70). Elsewhere he speaks of a "homiletic structure" and of the "doctrinal relationship of one thing to another [that] embraces almost every aspect of the play" (71–72). He then describes the "cumulative effect" of "recapitulations, recurrences, and reverberations" of significance—again a persistent commitment to meaning—as "overwhelming." In *Lear*, he concludes, "significance holds plot and character in an iron grasp" (74). Allegory, anyone?

Mack's description of signification in *King Lear* sounds more "allegorical," at least in a constrictive sense, than such a description of allegorical narratives as the following:

> In the strangely fluid surfaces and insubstantial stories of these poems, ideas are transformed and systems altered. Attitudes take shape gradually, but when they do, and often as soon as they do, their shape is modified. Early events return in the poems like voices from the past to threaten, to expand, or to complete the present. Dimensions of meaning and reference shift swiftly and subtly: landscapes thicken, recede, or become interiorized; not only symbols but also words continually evolve, interact, and even merge; . . . [these] narratives contract to focus, on the . . . self and enlarge to include mankind. Through their shifting, cycling, echoing movements . . . [they] realize a process—or better, a life—of thought, of perception and recognition, in their efforts to achieve awareness of truth.

Although I am the author of this description, I composed it decades ago and in an entirely different context, a study of *Piers Plowman* and *The Faerie Queene*.[5] What is surprising even to me is the extent to which it suggests some of the more distinctive and potently memorable features of *King Lear*.[6]

My point, emphatically, is not that *King Lear* is an allegory, at least in any of the usually understood senses, but that it shares with sophisticated, problematical allegories many features which are intrinsic to its meaning and which modern criticism has identified distinctively with allegorical form. All allegories are not like *King Lear* and *King Lear* is not simply an allegory, but to insist that the play *King Lear*, whatever else it might be, is not really, vitally allegorical at its core is effectually to cut it off both from its richest contemporary analogue, *The Faerie Queene*, and from the insight of the best work on the nature of allegory itself. Such insistence isolates *Lear* from a great deal of literary history and thus, in a larger sense, from significant features of period and culture. Often we note that Shakespeare altered all his sources to turn the story of Lear to tragedy. But it has not been as often remarked that, whereas history—the "real" world—had given Lear a happy ending, his tragic ending in Shakespeare's play is a blatant fiction and, as such, either the cruelest irony or the profoundest meaning of them all, revealing itself to be mind-made, allusive as tragic form, at once reiterative and encapsulating in style and substance, and, in a word, discontinuous with a purely natural world.

Bradley's familiar, still seminal catalogue of problems and improbabilities in *King Lear* is by itself enough to whet the imagination of the most reluctant allegorist. Again and again one can substitute versions of the term *realism* for the evaluative criteria of Bradley's negative judgments, as when he complains that Shakespeare's material is "too vast" to be used "with complete dramatic effectiveness [read "realistic effect"], however essential this very vastness was for effects of another kind" (206–7). The qualifying "effects of another kind" close Bradley's sentence with an embarrassed afterthought and open its criteria themselves to question.

But a reader familiar with an older Spenserian criticism is likely to make a more specific substitution in reading Bradley on *Lear*, to have a strong sense of *déjà vu*, to fantasize that trays of type got mixed in the print shop, to wonder, in short, whether Bradley isn't really talking about *The Faerie Queene*. Thus Bradley complains about the work's crowded canvas—the "number of essential characters," the complication and compacting of their movements—so "that the reader's attention, rapidly transferred from one centre of interest to another, is overstrained" (206); he chafes at the difficulty of retracing "in memory the steps of the action," a difficulty far greater than in *Hamlet, Othello,* or *Macbeth* (209); he laments the poet's having been "exceptionally careless of probability, clearness and consistency" (208); he remarks indignantly the "insignificance" or dramatic ineffectiveness of physical battle and expresses a particular and protracted frustration with the lack of spatial, geographical, and even topographical realism in the play (206, 208–9). Bradley seems oblivious to the fact that a landscape of the mind, whether lunatic's or poet's, and one of maps and measured miles might differ radically and that a poet working in a radically significant mode might even want his audience acutely aware of this difference. But just as we shake our heads over the benighted critical past—five score years and then some past—another of Bradley's cliff-hanging afterthoughts enlarges his critical perspective. "Perhaps," he adds cryptically, Shakespeare "deliberately chose to be vague" about the physical localities and movements in *King Lear* (209). If Bradley's judgment is relentlessly "concrete"—or rather, if he thinks it ought to be—his instinct for allegory is always better. Bradley's criticism has proved enduring for good reason.

Commenting on another of Bradley's dramatic improbabilities in *King Lear*, Sheldon Zitner has argued that Shakespeare deliberately ignores realism in order to accentuate an encounter between two styles of language and thereby to contribute to a major theme or motif in the play, namely, the "validity of language."[7] The improbability in question is Gloucester's failure to show surprise when Edgar, incognito confronting Oswald, shifts abruptly into, then out of, a strong peasant dialect.[8] So pronounced a violation of dramatic realism and so radical a discontinuity in style commonly indicate the presence of allegory, and if in the unchallenged or uncompromised service of theme, the presence of an allegory that is formally naive.[9] Zitner's perceptive reading of language in *Lear* is decidedly allegorical, although he never admits the term, and yet it makes the play too unproblematical and too limited an allegory, one quite unlike *The Faerie Queene*.[10] In Zitner's view, the realistic response, whether to Edgar's dialectal transformation or to Cordelia's "Nothing" in Act I, scene i, should be discarded; whereas, to my mind, the disjunction between it and a thematic meaning—"an effect of another kind," to quote Bradley—is precisely the point. This is a disjunction that begins in the opening scene of the play, where differently conceived characters and realities confront and conflict with one another, and it is one to which I shall return.

Along with mythic characterization and persistently significant structure, disjunction is a mere appetizer to the hardy fare *Lear* affords the allegorist's active imagination: available, in addition, are allegorically significant names, topped off with radical puns and thematic words; allegorical projection of character; interiorized landscapes, including the storm and trial scenes, Dover Cliff, and Lear's prison; and permeating throughout, insistent allusion to other forms and earlier texts, from chronicle account to lyric, and from pastoral romance to fairy tale and *Faerie Queene*. Naming is an essentially allegorical act and a conspicuous, significant element in allegory proper. In *King Lear*, Cordelia's name, for example, is an allegorical tag meaning heart, possibly in combination with a glancing allusion to the sonneteers' anagram for ideal, namely, Delia, which is in any case a name of Diana, goddess of chaste purity.[11] The semi-homonymic names of Edgar and Edmund enforce comparison between them and authorize their exchange of outer identities. Fool, a character significantly without a proper name, is preeminently a function of office and plot and a hypostatized thematic word whose full meaning exceeds his own function.[12] In this respect Fool resembles his Erasmian allegorical precursor Folly, a kaleidoscopic word turned round and round until it yields the fullness and full folly of its meaning.[13]

Perhaps because Fool lacks a fully or normally characterized human identity, his figure and career afford the clearest instance of allegorical projection—not merely a technique but also a psychological conception—which, though mainly in more submerged manifestations, pervades the play. By projection allegory I mean the representation of one character's state of mind or of an aspect of his identity in a second character, who, albeit an objectively autonomous figure in the story, might at any given moment merge with or be absorbed by another like-minded figure. Fairly straightforward instances of such projection in *The Faerie Queene* occur in Book I to establish the mode there; then more complex, if less obvious, instances come in later Books—to stick to Books II and VI, those most immediately relevant to *Lear*, Guyon, Arthur, and Cymochles and Pyrochles in Book II or the poet, Colin, and Calidore in Book VI. Simpler examples in Book I include Sans Foy, who materializes like a precipitate out of Redcrosse's unfaithfulness to Una—indeed, out of the earliest stage of Redcrosse's own dissolution; Sans Joy, whose figure is interiorized, then absorbed into the consuming discontent of the Knight (and the night) of the Red Cross; and Despair, at once the intensification and the conscious recognition of such sickness within, a figure whose description closely, verbally mirrors that of the morbidly despondent Knight who emerges from Orgoglio's dungeon.

In *King Lear*, such projection allegory underlies Fool's arrival on stage to play midwife to Lear's folly, even as Lear himself begins to sense folly's presence and power, and it emerges more conspicuously on the heath when Lear first appropriates and then passes far beyond Fool's institutionalized role.[14] In the wake of Lear's storm, Fool is left a greatly diminished figure—an object of pathos, an externalized "houseless poverty" with enough sense, unlike Lear—indeed, with enough merely conventional wisdom—to come in out of the rain. Like Fool's white grease paint in a BBC production, which gradually washed off in the rain, his role washes off in the storm of Lear's greater madness, and Lear replaces Fool with Poor Tom as the alter ego of his now infinitely profounder folly. The end of the play, of course, recapitulates these allegorical movements, when in Lear's last moments his language, whatever else he means by it, identifies Cordelia with "my poor fool" and when, soon after, as before in the presence of Tom, he unbuttons.[15] Much critical discussion both of this identification and of Fool's disappearance near the end of Act III looks to me like a conspiracy of realism to avoid supremely obvious allegorical meanings. By the end of Act III, there is no place for a safely institutionalized folly, and so Fool simply drops from sight; at the end of Act V there is no longer safety in any sense or any place: "She's dead as earth," and earth as she.

Yet in the end Lear's identification of Cordelia with "my poor fool" and then, perhaps implicitly for an instant with Tom, the outcast "thing itself," is also a memory of Bradley's "effects of another kind" and more exactly of the highly fictive, fundamentally allegorical art of such merging. Zitner observes how "*Lear* ends with a stroke of art that exposes—rather than conceals—art" (4). By *art* he means language, and the wisdom he finds exposed is the deception and essential "emptiness of words" (21). But again I would go further than Zitner, since my claims both for the figuration and for the final ambivalence of *Lear* go further. I would say instead that *Lear* ends with strokes of art that insistently recall a fundamentally allegorical fiction and thereby disjoin irrevocably the realism of sense and place, of a dead earth, and the realism of what we do with it—the realism of things and the realism of any meaning, including meaninglessness. They thus disjoin the realism of one kind of effect and another.[16] Again, in other words, my allegorizing would center on the *disjunction* between two kinds of effects, whereas Zitner's would cancel one by the other, this time, fictive meaning by the realism of earth; as earlier, in Edgar's dialectal transformation, earth by meaning. Dramatically, and philosophically as well, the end of *King Lear* is not a single-minded nihilism but an ambivalent dualism: Zitner underestimates the power of words in the play.[17]

Before turning to *The Faerie Queene* as an allegorical intertext of *King Lear*, I want to raise again the broader issues of terms and categories. I have held certain pronounced elements in *Lear* to be allegorical, relying in part on my readers' general awareness of Spenser's work and of the climate of criticism on allegory in the past several decades. As I have suggested, these elements range from realistic improbability and disjunction to conspicuous mythic characterization, sustained structural significance, radical puns and thematic words, insistent reiteration of meaning, allegorical projection, interiorized landscapes, persistent allusion to the forms, images, and words of earlier literary texts, and in short, to a concern with meaning as meaning that is not naively abstracted from earth but is radically discontinuous with it. Now, one could certainly say that these "effects of another kind"—and I intend *kind* in all its senses—are not allegorical as such, although they are found in *The Faerie Queene*. But then we must ask once again, "What is allegory?" And if, as was customary in an older criticism, we define allegory reductively in terms of its lowest common denominator, then we cannot call a work like *The Faerie Queene* allegory in any meaningful way or, indeed, without essential distortion.[18] If alternatively, as earlier observed, we choose to define allegory in the very broadest sense, seeing it as a potency in most, if not all, literary art, as Paul de Man has, then all works become allegories, and we find we are really talking about the general conditions of meaning as such. This is the point at which we do well to turn, necessarily within a clarifying, comparative context, to the relevant specifics of landmark writings themselves and to attend to what they can tell us, especially about intertextual form.

Yet even nowadays such comparison is difficult to achieve because the limitations and misconceptions of our categories keep intruding. While a number of medieval and Renaissance allegories, to be sure, lack anything like the complexity of *King Lear*, a considerable body of Shakespeareans still supposes that allegory cannot be problematical, radical, historical, material, or even truly humane. They confuse allegory per se with naivety and doctrinal assertion, with merely rational world views and Christian meanings—or, still more confusingly, with both, as has an exemplary book that derides readings which send Lear off to an "allegorical heaven."[19] Such critics, in short, confuse allegory with content exclusively of a certain type, failing to recognize the entirely conceivable possibility of an allegory of nihilism. The Allegorical Beast of their critical imaginations drains tragedy of all passion, drinks dry the flowing fountains of myth, and desecrates the holy temples of verisimilitude; his feet trample probability, his breath scorches flesh, blood, and libido to cinders, and his very shadow violates Romantic sensibilities; his claws rend stage effects and prompt books, and his fearsome tail sweeps away the new unities of Shakespearean criticism as dramatically as Shakespeare swept away the old. This beast dies hard.

Regrettably, definitions of allegory in reference works as basic as *The Princeton Encyclopedia of Poetry and Poetics* have contributed to the Beast's longevity. In an early edition of this *Encyclopedia*, for example, as sympathetic a theorist of allegory as Northrop Frye, while perceptively defining allegory as a technique or "structural principle in fiction," subsequently encourages its association with simplicity and rationalism. "We have allegory," Frye explains, "when the events of a narrative obviously and continuously refer to another simultaneous structure of events or ideas."[20] It all sounds so settled, even if we assume, as we certainly need not, that Frye includes under "events" characters and poetic events in the narrative such as epic similes, lyric interludes, and digressions. Revising what Frye's statement *does* say, I would start by replacing the words "obviously" and "continuously" to define the nature of allegorical reference with words like *pronounced, persistent,* and *sustained.* Such reference in model allegories can only be described reductively as "obvious" or "continuous." A story, a metaphor, or the conceptualized tenor of an allegorical vehicle can be continued (and modified) without necessarily being continuous—unbroken and unchanging. The implications of Frye's qualifying adverbs are here mechanistic and naive.

But my replacements are only a beginning. There is no sign in Frye's definition that allegories might refer, or rather invoke, several other structures, all perhaps not entirely congenial, and that they might refer as well—and often preeminently and reflexively—to themselves, that is, to their own surfaces, methods, and structures. In fact, Frye uses complexity of reference as the criterion to distinguish *Hamlet* from an allegory of indecision. If *Hamlet* were an allegory, he adds reassuringly, "the range of commentary [on it] would be greatly limited, because the presence of allegory prescribes the direction in which commentary must go." Spenser criticism since the late 1950s might as well not have been written.

What Frye calls naive, as distinct from accomplished, allegory is said to offend fictional consistency (read "realism") in the interest of allegorical meaning, and presto! we are back in the holy temples of verisimilitude again. Quite to the contrary, sophisticated, problematical allegory—model allegory—often violates consistency in the interest of complexity and employs disjunctive effects self-reflexively to further, to interrogate, and to deepen meaning. With these effects such allegory probes the relation, acknowledges the disparity, or exposes the gap between the world within and that without us.

Perhaps allegory might be defined as an unusually direct way of conceiving and conceptualizing reality, whatever this is taken to be. While its commitment to meaning is thus radical, the meaning it represents is characteristically double and can very well prove nihilistic, as it typically does in absurdist drama.[21] Typically, allegory might also be said to reflect and to imitate the processes and products of the mind; it is explicitly and conspicuously a mental structure, fabrication, and creation. That allegory is so need exclude neither reference nor significant interaction with plot—with time, process, and history; in fact, as I have argued in my introduction, allegory as a literary form necessarily entails such interaction, which is, more precisely, the *intra-action* of its deictic and nondeictic components.

In suggesting the allegorical dimensions of *King Lear*, I do not envision a drama reduced, but one enriched. Certainly my intention is not to substitute a play of ideas or even of "kinds of effects" for human depth and horror. Although many of the problems *The Faerie Queene* examines, for example, might be no less complex and no less poetic than Shakespeare's, typically the conduct of examination is less intense—less emotional, compressed, and immediate. In Spenser's allegory, even the major characters are more openly constructs of language, and they often move in a milieu without the sharp edges and unyielding boundaries of a more nearly verisimilar world. In such allegory, conflicting forces engage more freely and extensively but also less painfully and powerfully than in *King Lear*. If, that is, *Lear* is allegorical at its core, it is also other and more: no allegory with which I am familiar "gives us a character who is objectively real and autonomously self-conscious the way King Lear [himself] . . . is."[22] But it is equally true that Lear plays his part against an allegorical ground out of which his human character emerges explosively, with which at moments he seems to coincide, and against which his final anguish is silhouetted. Far from decreasing the imaginative energy and intellectual significance of his human tragedy, the allegorical ground charges it with more. Looking ahead to chapters on Milton, I might add, with appropriate refinements to come, that broadly similar assertions apply to his major epic.

Unlike the *Purgatorio* or *Endgame*, Spenser's *Faerie Queene* was a relevant contemporary work demonstrably on Shakespeare's mind when he wrote *King Lear*.[23] The British chronicle in Spenser's second Book accounts for the form of Cordelia's name and for the manner of her death by hanging in *Lear*, and the description of the holy old hermit's dwelling in Spenser's Book VI distinctly informs the content and imagery of Lear's lyric speech to Cordelia just before their imprisonment, a speech whose "old tales" and "gilded butterflies" glance as well at Spenser's *Muiopotmos*, or "Fly-fate," an ironic, quintessentially Renaissance treatment of Ovidian myth in which "a butterfly's fate becomes the ambivalent measure of a human being's."[24]

Additionally in Book II, Spenser's imagery in recounting Lear's abdication—"when the oyle is spent, / The light goes out, and weeke is throwne away" (II.x.30)—both foreshadows and enlightens Fool's cryptic prophecy in Act I, "So out went the candle, and we were left darkling" (iv.226).[25]

Guyon's debate with Mammon outside the Cave in Book II also bears suggestively on Lear's and Gloucester's insights into the relations of true need to superfluity. On the verge of invoking the example of an ideally virtuous antiquity and thus the old tale of a golden age belonging to the world of myth, Guyon supposes that if men would "thinke, with how small allowaunce / Vntroubled Nature doth her selfe suffise, / Such superfluities they would despise" (II. vii.15).[26] In Acts II and III, Lear shifts from his still limited and ironically resonant vision of "base beggars . . . in the poorest [material][27] thing superfluous," to his recognized need of shaking "the superflux" to "naked wretches," a recognition that Gloucester's "superfluous and lust-dieted man," who "will not see / Because he does not feel" affirms in Act IV (II.iv.226–27, III.iv.28–35, IV.i.67–69). Shakespeare's incredibly detailed and assimilative knowledge of Spenser's Books II and III, which critics have established in his *Richard III*, increases the likelihood of these echoes—perhaps more accurately these relevant memories—of Book II and makes it implausible that he did not read with equal attention the second installment of *The Faerie Queene*, whose themes, forms, motifs, and even stories impinge on so many of his later plays.[28]

Conflict in *Lear* begins with *nothing*—that is, with a word that radically puns on material and immaterial reference, a word that means no thing, as well as simply nought, emptiness or silence. As I have suggested earlier, the issues of Spenser's second Book begin to take shape in a similar pun in the Proem's opening stanza—"no body." Where the "land of Faery" is, the Spenserian poet avers, "no body can know"—that is, "no one at all," "none bodily," or "none in bodily form." Throughout this Proem, he questions explicitly, if somewhat playfully, what really is true and truly real—the values of matter or of mind, of material space and physical time or of immaterial virtue and mind-made myth—and does so specifically in the context of vision, of ways of seeing or knowing: for example, "Why then should witlesse man so much misweene / That nothing is, but that which he hath seene?"[29] Whether really opposed or only apparently so, the dual values of the Proem lead in the narrative proper of Book II to impasse and total collapse just beyond the Cave of Mammon, a powerfully poetic place that Shakespeare's imagination, like Milton's and Keats's, is known to have frequented.[30] It is at the end of the Mammon episode that Guyon, described as lifeless and senseless and lying helpless on earth, becomes the "image of mortalitie," of Mortdant and Amavia, of death, love, and the human condition.

The nature of this impasse, which is Guyon's predicament, is further relevant to *Lear*. Its origins are particularly clear in the three cantos preceding the Cave of Mammon. They include the abstractive binding of Occasion—time in a female form—and subsequently the unleashing of her when her suppression itself ironically occasions inruption and strife; next, the conquest, liberation, and consequent rejection of the appetitive Pyrochles; and then, inevitably, Guyon's departure with Phaedria from his rational Palmer, who needs would keep Occasion bound and simply abandon the unruly, affective side of human nature. With each episode, Guyon is harder pressed to find a viable balance or continuity—that is, to find room for himself—between the extremes of rationality and passion, order and impulse, virtue and desire, ideal and appetite, immaterial and material, abstract and physical, fixed form and occasion—Real and real, if you will. Increasingly from this point through the Cave of Mammon, he finds, or rather loses, himself in an impasse, doomed either to deny virtue and with it his own truth and integrity or else to deny the material needs of human nature and explicitly those of the body.[31]

In Mammon's Cave, Guyon is tempted by materialism in its broadest and basest sense. Gold and other kinds of material power are just Mammon's surface. This "God of the world" who inhabits the depths of the Earth misuses, deforms, and poisons the very bases, the material elements, of life itself. At the heart of his dwelling is unrighteousness, for there lie Tantalus and Pilate, myth and history, figures alike in blood-guilt (Pelops and Christ) and in the blasphemous selfishness of pride and greed. Although Guyon resists the Cave, the sight of it debases him; denial of its power and of his own material needs exhausts his vitality. Having risen above these, he falls to earth, his immobilized figure the ironic marker of a very material impasse.

The initial conflict in *King Lear* resonates with ideas like those in Book II and dramatizes a similar confrontation of binaries and a similar impasse. Conceptually and imaginatively, it recalls Spenser's allegorical epic romance. Cordelia, though seemingly tardy in nature to advertise her love under any circumstances, utters her first aside and first commitment to silence *after* Goneril's recitation of an amatory elocution lesson, and then her second aside, much more sharply critical, *after* Regan's performance. Once Goneril and Regan have spoken, there is no way that Cordelia could say anything to express the matter of her love without sounding—and in the terms of this scene without being—as hollow and grasping as they.

Goneril's speech is full of mechanical amplification, a series of nouns, adjectives, and intensifiers. In the comparisons that loosely structure the speech—"more," "Dearer," "Beyond," "No less," "As much," "Beyond"—there is nothing positive, neither commitment nor substance. Inadvertently, her words are ironic: "I love you more than word can wield the matter; / Dearer than eye-sight, space and liberty . . . No less than life, with grace, health, beauty, honour." One begins to expect that the pointless quantification will continue indefinitely. Goneril's words not only fail to wield the matter of love but wield instead its absence. She usurps the inability topos that Cordelia sincerely affects—"A love that makes breath poor and speech unable"—and with her windy catalogues erodes its worth. She *dis-qualifies* its meaning.[32]

Like Goneril's, Regan's speech is studied, but in a plainer, more rational, more sinister way. She first appropriates what Goneril has said and then materially, indeed grossly, transforms it. Like Goneril's, her words drip irony, but her extravagant materialism is cruder, whether more cynical or simply more insensitive, than Goneril's emptiness, and it proves less comic: thus Regan is "made of that self metal" as her sister, whose insubstantial, airy mettle comes down to earth, in fact to base matter, in the pun (metal), and again when Regan, surpassing Goneril, professes "the most precious square of sense" she has joys only in paternal love. The incestuous undercurrent is palpable. Little wonder that Cordelia asks with sarcastic impatience, "Why have my sisters husbands, if they say / They love . . . [my father] all?" (99–loo).

Much as Spenser's Mammon debases the material means of living, Goneril's and Regan's misused words corrupt and debase meaning itself. From Gloucester's memorable opening play on the verb *conceive*—to form an idea or a child—to Cordelia's sharp distinction between her own "ponderous," or ponderable and profound, love, and Regan's "ponderous," or ponderable and basely weighty, tongue, material and immaterial references have been conspicuously and tensely, even uncomfortably, present in puns. Goneril's and Regan's studied rehearsals pervert both kinds of reference and with this perversion banish the possibility of expressing the "matter"—theme and substance, rationale and affection, truth and tenderness—of love. Together, Goneril's empty immateriality and Regan's gross materiality usurp not only the possibility of meaning but also the possibility of integrity, of a self-expression that is whole *and*, in Cordelia's own word for it, "true."

Siding with Lear or with Cordelia in the direct confrontation between them that follows may be hard to resist, but it is pointless. Its pointlessness is, I suspect, why the confrontation comes so suddenly and with so few and such ambiguous hints as to motivation, enough for human plausibility but not enough for a primarily realistic—Bradley's "dramatic"—understanding. Significantly, Lear's impassioned response, Kent's intervention, then France's and Burgundy's calmer assessments, all of which invite and guide our own responses, come later, disjoined from the critical moment itself: "'Nothing.' . . . 'Nothing?' 'Nothing.' 'Nothing will come of nothing.'" Cordelia may be "untender" or "true" and likely both in this confrontation, but the crucial point, floodlit and disjoined from dramatic realism, is that she is in an insoluble impasse, a no-win situation. Nothing she says—including "nothing"—will do. Moreover, the dilemma in which she is caught resides not only within what she says—that is, in the dual meaning of nothing—but also between meaning itself and the dramatically real, flesh-and-blood royal family scene. It lies between two different kinds of meanings, which fundamentally inform two different "kinds of effects," one abstract and one concrete, one pertaining to mind and one to matter.[33]

Like Guyon, Cordelia is caught between virtue and matter, rational truth and affection, self-protection and self-loss, immobilizing silence and vitiation. Like him, moreover, she is caught both in terms of action and of signification. Her crucial reply, which colors all else, is her first, namely, "Nothing," repeated once more by her and thrice by Lear and so prolonged and stressed indelibly. In voicing the word "Nothing," of course, Cordelia does say something, as she needs must. But the something, the truth she offers, is "nothing," at once materially and immaterially a negation of love—of the matter of love, theme and substance. We might say, perhaps, that instead of silence, the absence of any number at all, she speaks and says, "zero," which is a number, to be sure, but still nothing.[34] Even as Guyon resists the corruption of Mammon's Cave, which is, after all, in some sense an image of this world and this life, so Cordelia virtuously resists the corruption of herself and her meaning, but at the cost of denial and negation of these.[35]

Marvin Rosenberg describes a Norwegian staging of *Lear* in 1971 that could suggest the dramatic life latent in such an allegorized reading. In this *Lear*, armed knights, "men of stone . . . enclosing or channeling the action," formed "backdrops, corridors, courtyards, walls" (36). From the time Lear himself entered the play, they "had stood frozen . . . more decor than personae," but "at Cordelia's *Nothing* all the still faces looked up, as at some fearful violation." If language and meaning are not quite on the basic, material level of Guyon's physical needs, they are essential to human intercourse and community and, in the Renaissance, to common humanity.

While the opening scene of *King Lear* introduces a nexus of ideas that recall those in Spenser's second Book and can be illuminated by reference to them, the richest verbal memory of *The Faerie Queene* occurs in Lear's speech to Cordelia in Act V, scene iii, following their capture by the forces of Goneril and Regan. Excluding the sight of "these daughters and these sisters" after whom Cordelia asks—the sight, as it were, of malice—Lear poignantly and vividly substitutes for it life in a gilded myth. Urging Cordelia, "Come, let's away to prison; / We two alone will sing like birds i' th' cage," he imagines, or at least tries to imagine, that prison will be only a bondage of understanding and love: "When thou dost ask me blessing, I'll kneel down, / And ask of thee forgiveness" (8–11). The enclosure he envisions is a private site apart from court politics and secure from the threats of mutability—a "wall'd prison" set off from the "packs and sects of great ones / That ebb and flow by th' moon" (13–15, 18–19). He conceives a holy retreat, a place of insight into "the mystery of things," in short, a walled garden of the psyche (16–17). Like the traditional early-modern emblem of the bird-soul singing in its fleshly cage, the condition he pictures is in the world but not of it. And yet, even as Lear reaches for fairyland, his images embody his instinctive, if involuntary, awareness of caged confinement, insubstantial artifice, and death: "Upon such sacrifices, my Cordelia, / The Gods themselves throw incense" (20–21).[36] Despite Lear's defiantly hopeful vision, his words acknowledge that behind prison walls, he and Cordelia are vulnerable to fortune, time, and malice.

The content and imagery of Lear's imagined farewell to the mutable, material world recall the aged hermit's holy retreat in Spenser's Book VI, a "little Hermitage" much "like a little cage . . . Deckt with greene boughes, and flowers gay beseene" (v.34, 38). In his small house the hermit entertains his guests plainly and "with entire affection" but "Not with such forged showes, as fitter beene / For courting fooles." After a life of heroic achievement in the active world, the hermit is "now attacht with timely age, / And weary of this worlds vnquiet waies" and has therefore retired "vnto this Hermitage, / In which he liu'd alone, like carelesse bird in cage" (v.38, vi.4).

In Book VI, as I have argued elsewhere, the hermit is significantly counterpointed with Melibee, who is similarly old, artful with words, and retired from the court, and he figures in defining Melibee's significance.[37] These two aged figures function together in Spenser's exploration of the relation of fortune to human control—to human responsibility, desire, and vision—an exploration often provocatively close to that in *King Lear*. In Melibee, the theme of vision that was notably present in Spenser's Proem to

Book II and now more specifically the theme of illusion come to center stage and prove conceptually close not only to Lear's walled prison but more generally to the role of illusion in his tragedy.

The impasse on the other side of Mammon's Cave seems far distant when Melibee discounts first the value and then the reality of material fortunes. "In vaine," he explains, men accuse "The heauens of their fortunes fault," since "each [one] hath his fortune in his brest" (ix.29). Then sounding much like Boethius, his ostensible source, not to mention Hamlet, his successor, Melibee further develops the dominance of mind over matter, for

> It is the mynd, that maketh good or ill,
>   That maketh wretch or happie, rich or poore:
>   For some, that hath abundance at his will,
>   Hath not enough, but wants in greatest store;
>   And other, that hath litle, askes no more,
>   But in that litle is both rich and wise;
>   For wisedome is most riches; fooles therefore
>   They are, which fortunes doe by vowes deuize,
> Sith each vnto himselfe his life may fortunize.
>   (VI.ix.30)

To Melibee's idealized wisdom, Calidore appends the deceptive conclusion that it lies "in each mans self . . . to fashion his owne lyfes estate," to make what he *will* of it, no matter what, in fact and in material reality, it *is* (ix.31). The limitations of Melibee's insight are exposed in his capture and murder by brigands, Calidore's hopeful conclusion becoming, in ironic effect, the kindly old man's epitaph.

The landscape Melibee occupies we have seen in an earlier chapter to be an attractive site of vision, but one that is shown, like Lear's imagined prison, also to be sadly fragile, incomplete, and ephemeral. "To them, that list, the worlds gay showes I leaue, / And to great ones such follies doe forgiue," Melibee avows sincerely, but then he tries to hold on to the material world of his dreams. His is a world not truly disembodied but only displaced—in the world but not of it, mythic. He continues, describing a landscape of Hearts-desire, which is the very condition of his existence:

> Me no such cares nor combrous thoughts offend,
>   Ne once my minds vnmoued quiet grieue,
>   But all the night in siluer sleepe I spend,
>   And all the day, to what I list, I doe attend.
>   (VI.ix.22)[38]

"Sometimes," Melibee adds, he hunts the fox and other times "baytes and nets" displays

> The birds to catch, or fishes to beguyle:
> And when I wearie am, I downe doe lay
> My limbes in euery shade, to rest from toyle,
> And drinke of euery brooke, when thirst my throte doth boyle.
> (VI.ix.23)

Melibee's voice gives form to an interiorized landscape that ignores evil and specifically excludes the dangers of Book I—resting in every shade and drinking of every brook—and of Book VI, where most moments of recreation or sleep are succeeded and in fact interrupted by violence and vulnerability. Most of all he forgets Mammon, the Mammon of unrighteousness and of the unregenerate heart. Like Lear's, Melibee's lovely lyric is punctuated by such ironic memories of other, more threatening meanings and contexts, and his cruel murder at the hands of brigands makes him, like Lear, the victim of a force and reality he sought to forget. Melibee's condition in Book VI is still more complex, however. Although Melibee himself must die, a kindly but short-sighted victim of greed and malice, his pastoral landscape plays a necessary part in reaching Mount Acidale. Only through this Melibean landscape, which embodies the illusions of withdrawal and desire, does the Acidalian vision of unity between fortune and wish, between the experience given and the experience sought, become accessible.

An Acidalian vision, of course, is never achieved in *King Lear*, and yet it is ironically with reference to such vision that I would come full circle, returning to Lear himself and specifically to his last two lines, spoken as he looks at the dead and deadly silent Cordelia: "Do you see this? Look on her, look, her lips, / Look there, look there" (V.iii.310–11). The themes of vision and illusion could hardly be more searingly presented; even Cordelia's lips, from which only lines before Lear hoped for a breath or word, are now visual perceptions. Although Lear may die believing that Cordelia "lives," whether in fiction or in fact, in the mind's eye or in the body's, he may also die realizing only and finally the irrevocable fact of her death. Nothing at the end tells us exactly what or in what sense Lear "sees," and nothing will. That is the point.

Lear's last two lines recapitulate the entire theme of vision in the play, but in the context of the line that immediately precedes them—"Pray you, undo this button: thank you, Sir"—and in their own diction they recall with particular force two earlier occasions of illusion. The first is Lear's, on the heath in Act III, when he perceives "the thing itself" in Poor Tom and unbuttons (iv.109–12); the second occasion is blind Gloucester's in Act IV, when he supposes himself at Dover Cliff and having fallen to earth, hears Edgar's insistent "Look up a-height . . . do but look up" (vi.58–59), painful imperatives echoed in Lear's final lines and, a line later, in Edgar's incongruously urging, "Look up, my Lord" (V.iii.310–12). Both earlier occasions have triggered recognition and insight at odds with realism—the material truth—of what underlies them: in the first instance, a "thing itself" who is not Poor Tom but Edgar, and in the second, a Cliff that is no cliff, except in a totally interiorized landscape. On both occasions, there is thus a radical disjunction between two different kinds of perceptions, between the realism of things and the realism of what we do with them, between a cruelly farcical mistake and, whether reductive or constructive, a new kind of vision.[39]

The question of vision—of what Lear finally sees and grasps—is posed more starkly, more forcefully, and probably less optimistically at the end of this play than in any other Renaissance work I know, and yet it remains a question.[40] Only a fool would resolve its irreducible ambivalence. Pervasively in the background of *Lear*, however, *The Faerie Queene* represents the power and perhaps in some sense even the substantiality of words—by 1596 well over 33,000 lines of them. And the matter of *Lear* itself, its expanding, redefining, and contracting words and actions, gives by play's end a very different worth, indeed a fuller value and validity, to Cordelia's affirmation of love through negation alone in the opening scene. All that may still be nothing here, to paraphrase Albany on Edmund's death, but it is more, much more, than silence.

13. Venus and Adonis: *Spenser, Shakespeare, and the Forms of Desire*

In Shakespeare's *Venus and Adonis*, the switch from Venus as manhandler to Venus as the pathetic—some would say tragic—mourner over the body of dead Adonis has always been problematical. Although passion and grief are twinned conditions of want(ing), the shift in this poem from an aggressive, comic mode to a helpless, pathetic one proves larger than life and challenges credible mimesis and, otherwise put, human credibility. Or perhaps I should say balanced human credibility, since Venus' behavior makes sense as an obsessive fixation transferred from hunger to loss. Yes, Venus is a goddess and a figure of myth for whom excess is appropriate, yet her passion also verges too close to human passion and sexual realities to make such a rationalization wholly convincing. Fixation, after all, is the basic given of personification allegory and, correlatively, of the demonic, and neither designation quite suits her.

In what follows, I would suggest that, instead of a mythic rationalization, *Venus and Adonis* is a seriocomic meditation on the landscape of desire, or wanting—on passion and grief—and on the kinds of figures desire generates in the third book of Spenser's *Faerie Queene*. Shakespeare's poem explores the effects of folding into characters Spenser's multiple refractions of desire that are expressed in numerous allegorical figures and thus the effects of folding the multiple refractions of Book III into more fully and materially realized constructs. These effects and indeed this process bear on the gendered depiction of wanting, of passion and grief, over time.

The consensus of modern editors is that Shakespeare's *Venus and Adonis* was written in 1592–93, precisely the period in which Shakespeare is thought to have written *Richard III*, a play full of memories of the 1590 *Faerie Queene*, as I have earlier noted. Harold Brooks has persuasively identified recollections of Spenser's Books II and III in the terror and riches of Clarence's dream of drowning—the Cave of Mammon (II.vii), the Bower of Bliss

201

(II.xii), and Marinell's Rich Strand (III.iv)—and elsewhere I have identified a striking allusion to the Garden of Adonis (III.vi) in Richard's words to Queen Elizabeth when he seeks her daughter's hand in marriage. I have suggested as well the plausibility of another Richardian memory in the same scene of passages in Spenser's Book III concerning an unavoidable destiny.[1] The first of these passages occurs in Spenser's tale of Venus and Adonis in Malecasta's tapestry, and the second, equally relevant to the present chapter, comes in the story of Marinell's downfall for being, like Shakespeare's Adonis, "loues enimy" (III.iv.26); the story of Marinell also furnished one of the Spenserian recollections demonstrated by Brooks. All these associations and allusions indicate that Spenser's poem was much in Shakespeare's mind at this time and that his familiarity with it was extensive and detailed.

Since *Venus and Adonis* is the subject at hand, Shakespeare's allusion in *Richard III* to Spenser's Garden of Adonis, the earthly paradise where Adonis becomes "eterne in mutabilitie," is of particular interest (III.vi.47). Beyond the obvious purpose of increasing the likelihood of an intertextual relation between Shakespeare's erotic epyllion and Spenser's mythic Garden, it indicates something of Shakespeare's response to this complexly nuanced site and to the 1590 *Faerie Queene* more generally. In the fourth Act of the play, Richard replies to Queen Elizabeth's bitter rehearsal of the fates of her murdered sons that when he marries her daughter, "the liquid drops of tears that you have shed / shall come again, transform'd to orient pearl" (iv.321–22). Suggestively close to a description of Shakespeare's hopeful but apprehensive Venus, whose tears are "prison'd in her eye like pearls in glass, / Yet sometimes falls an orient tear beside," Richard's highly rhetorical promise of transformation from tears to pearl and from grief to art fails at this stage to persuade the Queen (980–81). Before long she again reminds Richard flatly, "Yet thou didst kill my children," and he quickly counters,

> But in thy daughters womb I bury them;
> Where in that nest of spicery they will breed
> Selves of themselves, to your recomforture.
> (IV.iv.423–25)

Here the memory of Spenser's Garden of Adonis is striking: the boar, Richard's heraldic device and thus metonymically Richard, would root in its fertile soil.

In the Renaissance, a Garden of Adonis, from ancient times the term for a forcing bed or place of heightened fertility (and therefore also of transience), became by etymological confusion of Adonis with Eden a "ioyous

Venus and Adonis: *Spenser, Shakespeare, and the Forms of Desire* 203

Paradize," as Spenser calls it, and the seminary of all created things.² At the center of Spenser's Garden is the mount commonly identified as a *mons veneris* and directly beneath it the deadly boar is imprisoned in a cave.³ The recycling babes returning through a gate of death "in that Garden *planted* be againe; / And grow afresh, as they had neuer seene / Fleshly corruption, nor mortall paine" (III.vi.33: my emphasis). On the Mount itself, Venus "takes her fill" of Adonis' "sweetnesse," and

> There yet, some say, in secret he does ly,
> Lapped in flowres and pretious *spycery* [my emphasis]
> By her hid from the world, and from the skill
> Of *Stygian* Gods. . . .
>
> (III.vi.46)

Similarity of situation, explicit verbal echoes, and Richard's otherwise unmotivated rhetorical flourish leave little question that Shakespeare's "nest of spicery" alludes to Spenser's Garden.

An earlier passage in the same Shakespearean courtship scene had already played on the association of womb and tomb so noticeable in the allusion to Spenser's Garden. In it, Richard objects to the resistant Queen, "Your reasons are too shallow and too quick," and she delivers the punning rejoinder, "O no, my reasons are too deep and dead—/ Too deep and dead, poor infants, in their graves" (363–63). Like Richard, Elizabeth refers to her reasons for resisting his suit, but her reasons come between the two explicit linkings of womb and tomb in the scene and evoke this link as well. Her reasons glance ironically at the Renaissance commonplace of the *rationes seminales* (seminal reasons), "the germs of those things which were to develop in the course of time"—the potentialities implanted by God in the creation to develop by temporal unfolding.⁴ In this way, they suggest a further associative link with that seminary of created forms in Spenser's Garden of Adonis, to which withered things return to be planted anew.

In the Richardian context, of course, such references to the seminary of life are heavy with negation. The point I would stress, however, is that their irony is directed not at Spenser's Garden as such but at Richard's outrageous hypocrisy and his presumption of the ultimate gullibility of the Queen. Richard's irony in this scene invites recoil by the audience rather than sympathetic (or cynical) complicity. The irony of his reference to the Garden is chilling precisely because it invokes, by *contrast*, the safety, pleasure, and renewal of Spenser's mythic site of fertility and regeneration. Yet metaphorically (or metadramatically, which amounts to the same thing), it could be said also to mock a naive misreading of the Garden. It responds to—if it also overemphasizes—the threats, darkness, chaos, and death that are in both senses *contained* in and by the Garden itself, not to mention the rest of Book III and without which an approach to the Garden violates its very nature. In question here is not merely the relation of Shakespeare's *Venus and Adonis* to Spenser's focal use of this myth but also the way Shakespeare might have read antecedent texts and in particular allegorical ones.

One method of reading—perhaps, more accurately, of utilizing—texts in this period that has lately received renewed attention involves the culling of textual nuggets, whether based on a moral, rhetorical, topical, or other principle of selection. This method, evident in the ubiquitous commonplace book and in other forms of anthologizing, can be highly insensitive to textual or historical context. But another important way of reading texts that is based on biblical interpretation and its controverted (hence publicized) methods is acutely aware of context, nuance, and detail. Here, rather than exclusively in the rhetoric books, is the parallel to modern close reading, whose popular dissemination religious training, conventicles, printed polemics, and sermons all furthered. There is, then, no necessary reason to assume that Shakespeare would have played *Venus and Adonis* off against a single episode of *The Faerie Queene* while ignoring a conspicuously relevant larger context with which we have every reason to suppose he was familiar. Within that context, the episodes to which *Venus and Adonis* is usually linked look different from the way they do in isolation, and the relation of the epyllion to the epic looks less like parody and critique and more like dialogue and complement.

The critical tradition has too often assumed rivalry or anxiety as the only possible relation between poets and precursors, whereas in a historical setting in which the mentality of a lingering manuscript culture coexisted with the incipient culture of print capitalism, there were other, more mixed and interesting possibilities. Shakespeare, after all, did not even bother to prepare his plays for publication, and his relation to his sources and analogues often looks less competitive than culturally assimilative or even comfortably dependent. As earlier mentioned, at times this relation looks like the one Gerald Bruns ascribes to a manuscript culture, in which the appropriation and "embellishment" of another text "is an art of disclosure, as well as of amplification. Or rather, amplification is not merely supplementation but also interpretation: the act of . . . eliciting from it [the earlier text] that which remains unspoken."[5] Put otherwise, it is at once an act of reading and of (in)habitation.

Venus and Adonis: *Spenser, Shakespeare, and the Forms of Desire* 205

The relation of *Venus and Adonis* to the 1590 *Faerie Queene* has certainly been explored and documented these many years. A glance at the Shakespeare *Variorum* shows that the first canto of Book III has been the primary candidate for a Spenserian analogue or occasionally for a source ("a certain resistance on the part of Adonis") simply on account of its subject matter, namely, the Ovidian rendering of Venus' love of Adonis depicted in Malecasta's tapestry.[6] Ellen Aprill Harwood also calls our attention to the 1590 ending of *The Faerie Queene* in which Scudamour and Amoret are described as if merging in a hermaphroditic union similar to that of Shakespeare's Venus and Adonis. Embracing, "lips together glued," Shakespeare's pair seems "incorporate[;] . . . face grows to face" (540, 546).[7] As thirsty as Shakespeare's Venus, Spenser's Scudamour embraces Amoret, who "in sweete rauishment pourd out her spright: / No word they spake, nor earthly thing they felt, / but like two senceles stocks in long embracement dwelt." Harwood does not notice, however, that Spenser's "senceles stocks" share with Shakespeare's images of gluing and facelessness a rejection of such amoebic blending for human beings; significantly, Britomart, Spenser's most fully realized female figure, is never allowed it.

Aside from such peripheral analogies between Shakespeare's and Spenser's poems, the fullest, most provocative essay on their relation, Harwood's, argues that Spenser actually rejects an Ovidian rendering of the sort Shakespeare was to write simply by situating his in Malecasta's lustful domain, where, I would object, Britomart, the heroine of Book III, is wounded and thus touched by and vulnerable to what this domain represents. In the main, however, Harwood concentrates her contrast not on Malecasta but on the Garden of Adonis, asserting that "much of *Venus and Adonis* can be read as a repudiation [and parody] of the erotic philosophy expounded" there (52). Considering Shakespeare the exception, Harwood notes in this essay published in 1977 that "all the critics have praised the union of Venus and Adonis in the garden as an ideal, the very image of nature"; then she marvels, "that there the 'great mother Venus' 'possesseth' and 'takes her fill' of a 'boy' produces neither the least discomfort nor the smallest giggle," responses, I hasten to add, the Garden has produced since Harwood wrote, notably from the pen of Harry Berger (53).[8] For Harwood, however, it originally took Shakespeare to appreciate the possibilities of comedy and paradox unrealized in Spenser's myth of regeneration and to combine not merely a generative Venus with a heavenly one (Venus Pandemos with Venus Urania), as Spenser does, but a generative Venus with one both passionate and sexual

(Venus vulgaris). In contrast to Spenser's, Shakespeare's Venus, she observes, would be equally at home in Acrasia's lusty Bower of Bliss or in the fertile Garden of Adonis, although she also acknowledges that his chaste Adonis would decline the pleasure of either place (59–60). That Acrasia's Bower is also and equally Spenser's Harwood seems momentarily to forget.

More recently, Gordon Williams' highly suggestive reading of the death of Shakespeare's Adonis as a "violent sexual awakening" in which sex is collocated with death—indeed, just as the familiar pun on dying would have it—conversely would signal the later poet's approval of both sites and pointedly of Spenser's Garden, where grows "euery sort of flowre / To which sad louers were transformed of yore" and where, "in euerlasting ioy," Adonis finds the continuity of dying with the perpetuation of life. (III.vi.45–47, 49).[9] Here indeed is "a life in death," though in quite a different sense from the meaningless, immediate alternation of laughter with weeping, the living death, that Shakespeare's prim Adonis has in mind (413–14). In Spenser's pleasure Garden, even more clearly than in Malecasta's tapestry, the poet of romance epic revises Ovid's story of Venus and Adonis to feature the explicit sexuality of consummation.[10]

Although Harwood ranges outside the Garden to glance at the Bower of Bliss and the figure of Mutability (not published until 1609), as well as at Malecasta's tapestry, her reading of Book III remains far too selective. While offering evidence of the bearing of the Garden on Shakespeare's poem, it neglects not only the Garden's dark shadings but also the implication of the Garden in the rest of the 1590 poem, including the rest of the canto in which it exists. Spenser's is a poem that conspicuously and often uses a kind of refraction to relate largely disparate figures to a single type, such as Venus; as Peter Hawkins has observed, in such figures we recognize less the presence of the original type than the "degrees" of its presence.[11] Whereas an older criticism at ease with oppositions and clean boundaries between them confidently saw such refractions as invitations to read *in malo* or *in bono*, more recent ones have instead seen in them complex mixtures, receding depths, and indefinition. As I have argued at length in my chapter on "Refractions of a Veiled Venus," Spenser, like his "father" Chaucer and unlike the Neoplatonizing philosophers with whom some readers of *Venus and Adonis* would *exclusively* group this filial poet, does not keep a "good" Venus and a "bad" one sharply, safely, and simplistically distinct. Instead, he insists on their connection, even while insisting on a difference between them. If briefly I might invoke a perspective beyond the publication of Shakespeare's epyllion, much of Spenser's 1609 *Faerie Queene* is set between Acrasia's

Bower and Nature's arbor, and thus between two Venerean figures, both veiled. Books III and IV, the pivotal books in the epic as we have it, most fully explore what lies beneath the veil, what relates and what differentiates these figures, which is actually the same question.

Characteristically, Spenser's cantos are units, and what is within them is in some way related. Within a single canto, the Garden of Adonis is preceded and introduced by a story that comes in two stages: the first concerns the birth of the twins Belphoebe and Amoret, and the second, which dovetails with the first, the search of Venus for a wayward Cupid, or desire. The second stage allots Belphoebe, or chastity, to Diana and allots Amoret, or love, to Venus, thus separating these consanguineous twins; Venus then takes Amoret, "in her little loues [Cupid's] stead" to the Garden of Adonis, "Where most she [Venus] wonnes, when she on earth does dwel" (III.vi.28–29). The birth of the twins is described in such a way as to ensure the *continuity* of heavenly influence with physical process—of a conception "Pure and unspotted from all loathly crime, / That is ingenerate in fleshly slime" with a very physically pregnant "belly so vpblone" (3, 9).[12] The second stage traces a Venus seamlessly and successively transforming herself from a heavenly manifestation to a more generalized social one, with more than a trace of *Venus vulgaris* evident, and in the process managing to mollify Diana, whom Actaeon-like, Venus has surprised in disarray. The first half of the canto thus shows the relatedness of higher and lower, ideal and physical, although the subsequent separation of the twins pulls against the apparently temporary rapprochement of Venus and Diana to suggest future problems for both the goddesses' young charges. Nonetheless, this entrée to the Garden emphatically *figures* relation—the desirability and actuality of a relation that is inclusive—rather than an otherworldly flight from the physical. And it remains Amoret's seemingly fortunate fate to be taken to the Garden, Venus' "ioyous Paradize."

The Garden itself, while dominantly benign, is a place that includes time and death, containing them mythically, impersonally, and cyclically. Creatively, it also draws out of "the hateful darkenesse and . . . deepe horrore, / [of] An huge eternall *Chaos* . . . The substances of natures fruitful progenyes" (36). Albeit in one aspect a Garden of forms, the Garden is preeminently an organic and physical place and therefore not one that for long respects individual subjects or gendered egos; it is, in short, a myth of generation, situated, when once the relatively more individuated figures of Venus and Adonis are reached, clearly on and in the body:

> Right in the middest of that Paradise
>> There stood a stately Mount, on whose round top
>> A gloomy groue of mirtle trees did rise,
>> Whose shadie boughes sharpe steele did neuer lop,
>> Nor wicked beasts their tender buds did crop,
>> But like a girlond compassed the hight,
>> And from their fruitfull sides sweet gum did drop,
>> That all the ground with precious deaw bedight,
> Threw forth most dainty odours, and most sweet delight.
>> (III.vi.43)

For several stanzas, the description of this landscape of erotic desire ("And from their fruitfull sides sweet gum did drop") affords a topos analogous to that of Shakespeare's Venus, who offers to be a deer park for Adonis, where he might feed at will, "on mountain, or in dale" and "Graze on . . . [her] lips, and if those hills be dry, / Stray lower, where the pleasant fountains lie" (231–34). She continues,

> Within this limit is relief enough,
> Sweet bottom grass and high delightful plain
> Round rising hillocks, brakes obscure and rough,
> To shelter thee from tempest and from rain;
>> Then be my deer, since I am such a park,
>> No dog shall rouse thee, though a thousand bark.
>> (235–40)

Shakespeare's deployment of the topos is, of course, quite different from, as well as analogous to, Spenser's: the trace of mystery, secrecy, shade, or darkness—Berger calls it gynephobia—that the Spenserian description incorporates into the landscape with such words as "gloomy" Shakespeare here embodies both in an allusion to Scylla's barking dogs and, as elsewhere, especially in the disdainful Adonis.[13] But where Spenser's landscape belongs mainly to myth and is even suggestively ambisexual, Shakespeare's belongs mainly to the social world. What the Spenserian landscape intimates, Shakespeare makes explicit, comic, and more troubling. His wily, resourceful Venus attempts to seduce Adonis with the kind of anatomical topos that many a poet has fantasied, but this youthful representative of manhood responds to her plea of "Pity . . . some favor, some remorse" by springing away in fearful disgust and hastening, ironically, to his sexually aroused horse (257–58). A final tie of Shakespeare's Venus to the Garden canto involves

Venus and Adonis: *Spenser, Shakespeare, and the Forms of Desire* 209

the likely allusion in Spenser's boar encaved beneath the *mons veneris* to the mythic *vagina dentata*. In Shakespeare, this myth reappears in Venus' fantasy that the boar's tusking of Adonis was meant as a kiss, which, had she "been tooth'd like him . . . With kissing him . . . [she would] have kill'd him first" (1114–18).[14]

Aside from the association of dying with life and of female desire with generation, the Garden also impinges on the rest of Book III and on Shakespeare's *Venus and Adonis* in the figure of a female bending over a recumbent male. This silhouetted pietà is present in *The Faerie Queene* from the Bower of Bliss at the end of Book II through nearly the end of Book III: Acrasia, Cymoent, Belphoebe, Venus (twice), Argante, and Britomart (twice) are all found in such a memorably refractive, relational, Venereal posture.[15] In a conspicuous allusion to the Bower of Bliss that is inescapable in the first canto to follow it, Venus leans over the sleeping Adonis in Malecasta's tapestry just as Acrasia leaned over the sleeping Verdant in the Bower, and as Venus will lean over Adonis' recumbent form in the Garden. While the lustful Acrasia and Venus, similarly lustful, voyeuristic, and motherly in the tapestry and dominant, contented, and contenting in the Garden, have immediate thematic relevance to *Venus and Adonis*, three of the other refractive figures, Cymoent, Belphoebe, and Argante, may be of even greater interest.

Like Shakespeare's Venus in one of her aspects and the Venus of Spenser's Garden, the sea nymph Cymoent figures motherhood. When she learns of her son Marinell's wounding, she rushes to his side, where her lament over his fallen body begins, "Deare image of myself," and suggests her possessive narcissism, which is also evident in her earlier warning to her son to avoid the love of women (III.iv.36). She subsequently takes the helpless Marinell to her own home in the sea, a state of primal flux, where he remains virtually captive until the 1596 edition, in which he is reborn in his love for a woman and reemerges from the sea of birth. Cymoent's well-meant but engulfing, infantilizing possession bears a suggestive relevance to the Shakespearean Venus' relation to Adonis, her "froward infant" and "fondling," who is "smother[ed]," "hemm'd" in, and manipulated both psychologically and physically by her (18, 229, 562). As I have earlier noted, the referent of two allusions in *Richard III* to Spenser's Book III is the story of Marinell, in which "loues enimy" Marinell is felled by Britomart, the heroine of a quest for love. Britomart spears, or symbolically tusks, him.

Spenser's beautiful Belphoebe likewise assumes the aspect of motherhood, among other aspects, in a refraction of the death of Adonis in Book

210   *Reading the Allegorical Intertext*

III. The double nature of Amoret's twin, who is also the poem's chief symbol of virginity, becomes evident when the young squire Timias, who has been wounded by a lustful forester, wakens from his swoon and, as Belphoebe bends over him, addresses her in words that align her at once with Spenser's lustful Acrasia and with Venus herself disguised as Diana in the *Aeneid*. "Mercy deare Lord," Timias asks, "what grace is this, . . . To send thine Angell from her bowre of blis," and then, echoing Aeneas, he continues, "Angell, or Goddesse do I call thee right?" (III.v.35). A strange, not fully realized amalgam of mother, lover, and virgin Queen, Belphoebe ministers to a youth who has been attacked by lustful villains armed with a boar-spear and arrows and who, Adonis-like, has been badly wounded in the thigh. So wounded, he seems about to turn into a flower, thus participating in a major motif in Book III:

> His locks [of hair], like faded leaues fallen to grownd,
> Knotted with bloud, in bounches rudely ran,
> And his sweete lips, on which before that stownd
> The bud of youth to blossome faire began,
> Spoild of their rosie red, were woxen pale and wan.
> (III.v.29)

Throughout this book, beginning with the story of Venus and Adonis in Malecasta's tapestry, characters and episodes have variously and destructively been identified with one or another bipolar term, even as the fading flower of Timias (from Greek *time* [τιμή], "honor") is here: sensuousness and brutality, withdrawal or attack, passive loveliness or hostile aggression, the Venerean flower or the boar. It is Britomart's quest as a *Venus armata* to seek their tempering and accord, not simply their suppression or separation, and in the House of Busirane, where she stands wounded but with sword erect between the captive Amoret and her felled captor Busirane, she is at once a figure of concord and yet another refraction of Venus.

The most outrageously provocative Venerean figure in Book III with respect to Shakespeare's poem is the monstrous Giantess Argante. Like her incestuous twin brother Ollyphant (destructive phantasy: Greek *ollyo* [ολλύω], "destroy," + *phantasia* [φαντασία], "imagination"), Argante shares with Shakespeare's Venus a taste for boys, ranging over the countryside to find them, and

> Whom so she fittest finds to serue her lust,
> Through her maine strength, in which she most doth trust,

Venus and Adonis: *Spenser, Shakespeare, and the Forms of Desire* 211

>She with her brings into a secret Ile,
>Where in eternall bondage dye he must,
>Or be the vassall of her pleasures vile,
>And all in shamefull sort him selfe with her defile.
>   (III.vii.50)

When first sighted in Book III, Argante has athwart her horse and "before her lap a doefull Squire"—a perverse pietà if ever there was one (vii.37). Argante is an incestuous predator like the Venus of one facet of Shakespeare's imagination, the latter of whom resembles a vulture or "an empty eagle" that tears "with her beak on feathers, flesh, and bone, / Shaking her wings, devouring all in haste" (555–57, 551). Argante, similarly compared to a hawk with a dove trembling in her talons, is forced to abandon her "quarrey," the subjected squire, to ward off the attack of the mature knight who, like an "Eagle," would capture or kill her (III.vii.39). But she soon stuns her would-be conqueror, "And on his collar laying puissant hand, / Out of his wauering seat him pluckt perforse . . . and laying thwart her horse, . . . She bore him fast away" (43). Argante's manhandling is a rare match for Shakespeare's Venus, who

>Being so enrag'd, desire doth lend her force
>Courageously to pluck him [the hapless Adonis] from his horse.

>Over one arm the lusty courser's rein,
>Under her other was the tender boy.
>   (29–32)

For those critics who suspect that Shakespeare's poem might have a satirical relation to courtship, especially under a Queen who affected a Petrarchan role, Argante's name affords further tantalizing connections with Spenser's poem: in Arthurian legend, this is the name of the Faerie Queen to whose island the mortally wounded Arthur is taken. Etymologically, the name of this legendary precursor of Spenser's Faerie figure of his own Queen could also be read as an allusion to the idle/idyll, unproductive life at court of an aspiring courtier: Greek *argos* (ἀργός).[16]

While the cast of Venerean refractions in Book III has not quite been exhausted, their range and relatedness should be evident by now. Evident as well, perhaps, is the relevance to Spenser's third book of Catherine Belsey's description of the burden of *Venus and Adonis*, namely, "an understanding of sexual desire as precisely sensual, irrational, anarchic, dangerous but also at the same time delicate, fragile, and precious."[17] Yet it would be misguided to see in Shakespeare's Venus, the major vehicle of Belsey's perception, an achieved equilibrium between life-enhancing and anarchic sex, as Harwood does, or, in Spenser's symbolic terms, to see such an equilibrium between the flower and the boar; and it would be equally misguided to see in Shakespeare's Venus merely the one or the other of these extremes. Describing *Venus and Adonis* as both polyphonic and indeterminate, Belsey is again on target, although a case with more positive and productive implications might as readily be made for over- as for indeterminacy.

Where Spenser typically channels his polyphony into separate, if also related, figures in Book III, however, Shakespeare gathers most of his into the single character of Venus. As Heather Dubrow has noted, Shakespeare's Venus speaks 537 of the poem's 1,194 lines, with the petulant Adonis speaking only 87 in my count and the narrator another 570.[18] In view of the dominance of Venus' role as a dramatized speaker, which is further augmented by the active and affective roles the poet assigns her, it is not surprising that readers tend to concentrate on her figure and to conceive of it in theatrical terms: this epyllion, after all, has even been acted, and Philip Kolin's collection of essays on it assigns a whole section to "Venus and Adonis in Production."

Just such a lingering conviction of Shakespeare's theatrical "realism," however, has led us to downplay or misjudge the relation of his poem to Spenser's. Rather than a "repudiation" of Spenser's "erotic philosophy," as Harwood would have it, *Venus and Adonis* looks like a reveling in Spenserian eros. Shakespeare's recreative poem explores the effect of transforming a number of Spenser's allegorical figures into a *relatively* more realized character—more exactly, what would result from the folding of its unfolded refractions into a more fully fleshed-out version.[19] At the same time, however, Spenser's interlaced refractions represent a variety that actually exceeds and challenges such a concentration, defying containment by it, at least until Shakespeare's creation of the infinitely various Cleopatra, in whose figure I would discern a memory of his Venus, albeit further modified in both a testimony to the poet-dramatist's own development and to that of the developing taste of the early Jacobean period.

Formally, Shakespeare's *Venus and Adonis* has a mixed genealogy that conspicuously includes both drama and allegory, and instead of suppressing the opposite impulses this genealogy implies, it flaunts them. Not surprisingly in this tale of a goddess' infatuation with the son of a tree and great-grandson of a statue, efforts to interpret intermittently symbolic characters realistically have faltered: a goddess who goes from burlesque to pathos is incongruously taken as "tragic," although thus taken she has been. Efforts to read the poem allegorically have similarly faltered, although in this instance in the face of its realism. But the poem makes a good deal of sense as a seriocomic meditation on the landscape of desire and the kinds of figures it generates in Book III of *The Faerie Queene*. Correlatively, to read *Venus and Adonis* beside this Spenserian book is to realize the nuances it highlights and the potencies it heightens within Spenser's allegory, even while appreciating the interpretive license, indeed the creativity, of such a "Shakespearean" reading. Where Shakespeare's Venus truly embodies gynephobia, as does Spenser's Argante, and Argante has a refractive relation with Spenser's Venus in the Garden, there is also a profound difference between the first two figures and the last. What is *in potentia*—barely a hint, a shadow, a memory, a refraction within the mythic Garden—is fulfilled in Argante and in Shakespeare's Venus, and, in a pun on the popular expression, it makes all the difference in the world.

14. Flowers and Boars: Surmounting Sexual Binarism in Spenser's Garden of Adonis

My story starts with two recent classroom experiences: the first concerns a class of Honors undergraduates whom I was trying to persuade to read and think more figuratively and mythically. After receiving a set of papers on sex and gender in Spenser's third book, I took a leaf, as well as a tusk, from my own past and posed for discussion the difference between an analysis of Book III in terms of male and female attributes and in terms of the flower and the boar, two symbolic referents that variously weave through the fabric of this book.[1] The students were on to the difference immediately: our class poet somewhat cryptically declared, "the allegory disappears," by which I think he meant the figural dimension; then the class queen of sex and gender surprised even herself with the discovery that flower and boar are less fixed, looser, potentially more open terms, and another bright woman suggested that there are female boars and male poets. I hasten to add, as I did in class, that I am not implying the categories *male* and *female* are not useful in reading Spenser. They are essential, if you'll pardon the word, but as we all know, they lead too easily to an offensive spinning of essence and a premature closing down of possibilities.

My second experience, which occurred in the same class, dealt specifically with the Garden of Adonis.[2] When I made a point of the *mons veneris* there, noting that this term is still a familiar one, my students were incredulous. Mounts (not to mention points) and other things that go up, they knew, are male.[3] I returned to the class with a modern desk dictionary to let them see for themselves. There, indeed, was the entry *mons veneris* and, several entries above it, *mons pubis*: belonging to the adult abdomen of either sex.[4] When we looked again at Spenser's Garden Mount, which certainly represents a *mons veneris*, it began to be clear that it also has features that could be related to either sex. Put another, better way, it appeared ambiguously, or doubly, sexed.

Spenser's "stately Mount" suggests more than a majestic ("stately") protuberance, since punningly it is also something mounted, horselike, as Adonis may well be. Myrtles, which grow on the mount, are traditionally associated with Venus and at least by one mythographer with the female pudendum, but what *is* Venus in the Garden?[5] John Hankins concludes that within the physical allegory, Venus signifies the masculo-feminine coital fluid, a conclusion that lines in *Colin Clouts Come Home Again* support: "Venus selfe doth soly couples seeme, / Both male and female through commixture joynd."[6] Similarly in Hesiod, Venus arises when the seed of (castrated) Uranus meets the sea that his mother-wife Gaea (Earth) has brought forth of herself.[7] Trees, as my students were quick to recall, have much to do with Redcrosse's sexual fleshiness in Book I, from the grove of Fradubio to Orgoglio's oak club and beyond, and the gloominess of Spenser's Venerean myrtle grove glances at the darkness and deathliness associated with the boar. Anyway, my students had me wondering, "Why should the traditionally female garden of the body have been attributed by name to Adonis, rather than to Venus?" What does "of" mean in the name "*Gardin of Adonis*": connected to, composed of, deriving from, possessed by (III.vi.29)? Should we think of Adonis, passive as he is at the climactic point in the Garden, as a tiller of its soil? *Soil*, of course, can signal sexual intercourse, and no one tills without sharp implements. But my speculative punning becomes digressive and calls for an immediate return to the Garden Mount.

Like steely sharpness, those "wicked beastes" of the *mons pubis* stanza also suggest the boar, a figure whose detailed treatment I defer for now, except to repeat that boars come in both sexes and in both genders in Spenser's third book, for that matter (vi.43). These boarish attributes may be explicitly excluded from the first stanza describing the Mount, yet by their mention they are actually also in some sense included, or accounted for, and thus as *contained* in both senses of this word-concept, as is the pun on dying throughout Spenser's account of the Garden Mount. You will recall that "sharp steele" does not lop boughs on the Mount, and beasts do not crop tender tree buds. At least in the poetry of Donne and Herbert, buds and budding are delicately and poignantly associated with male sexuality and arousal, as well as with writing: in Donne, "Gentle love deeds, as blossomes on a bough, / From loves awaken'd root do bud out now," and less openly in Herbert, "now in age I bud again, / After so many deaths I live and write; / I once more smell the dew and rain, / And relish versing."[8] Sexual puns are notoriously long-lived and deep-rooted; in any case, Donne's life overlapped Spenser's for roughly twenty-seven years. Sweetness and gentleness, often associated with buds and flowers, is not exclusively feminine in the context of sex. This is especially and characteristically true of Spenser's poetry and specifically of the stanza in question, where the "sweet gum" of the myrtle produces "sweet delight."

I have little trouble finding male as well as female suggestions in lines after the one mentioning tree buds. The first of these sequels likens the trees to "a girlond compass[ing] . . . the hight" (vi.43). If circular garlands carry female associations, heights, things that stick up, continue to carry male ones, and either sex is implied by the next two lines, particularly if Hankins' conclusion is right that in terms of the physical allegory Venus represents a mixture of coital fluids: "And from their [the trees'] fruitfull sydes sweet gum did drop, / That all the ground with pretious deaw bedight, / Threw forth most dainty odours, and most sweet delight." My interest in recognizing the extraordinary extent of bisexuality on the Mount derives from my own recent work on Britomart as an androgynous figure.[9] Androgyny need not be bisexuality, and vice versa, but the middle books of *The Faerie Queene* are intensely concerned with both and further concerned with their relation, and the Garden is central to these concerns.

In employing the term *bisexuality* to describe the pubic Mount, I should make clear, however, that I am not referring to human behavior. To do so would be a rush to premature personification in the Garden. By *bisexuality*, I refer to the defining features of a fictive Mount that is ambiguously, or doubly (ambi-), sexed. Moreover, as my discussion of mounts, budding, sweetness, and boarish traits might already have suggested, I am not simply referencing Galen's notion that the female organs of sex inversely and recessively mirror the male ones but instead describing a true, if fictive, doubleness—one that is fulfilled and positive, not failed, lesser, undeveloped, or arrested.[10] Yet this doubleness is neither that of the hermaphrodite nor of the androgyne, which is that of visual, humanized forms, although even to mention these is to recognize the relevance of the Garden to them by extension. While the Garden may glance at hermaphrodites and androgynes, these belong to the visual fixity of statues and to the landscape of quest outside its gates.[11]

The Garden is symbolic and mythic, not realistically anatomical or human in the quotidian sense. Variously drawing on many, often contradictory traditions, which have been traced to Aristotle, Plato, Galen, the encyclopedists, the Neoplatonists, biblical translation and commentary, mythography, earlier poetry, and elsewhere, the poet is not unimaginatively, ungeneratively, and unpoetically versifying an anatomical textbook, any other single source, or even any one kind of source.[12] The early modern poet at his Spenserian best is truly a maker, not just a copier.

The initial stanza describing the pubic Mount, on which I have lingered, leads into a second artful stanza that focuses on the Mount's pleasant arbor. This is made "not by art" but by an arboreal inclination that extends to the *knitting* of branches and the *fashioning* of vines, and thus through its very diction signals a human presence in nature. It concludes that neither sun nor wind—"*Phoebus* beams" nor Aeolus' blasts—can harmfully penetrate "them," momentarily an elusive pronoun in line 8 that recurs in line 9 and references the interweaving boughs and entwining vines earlier in this stanza (vi.44). Two stanzas later, looking back at this pronoun from lines that situate Venus and Adonis on the Mount, with a retrospective regard that is typically Spenserian, we might suppose "them" to anticipate this mythic couple. Also in retrospect, the masculine potential of the "trees"—indeed, of the tree, since in Spenserian orthography the plural "trees" could always pun on a singular possessive—and the traditional feminine potential of the clinging vines comes to life. This landscape is everywhere imbued with bisexuality.

Even the two successive stanzas I have touched on so far also indicate that any stage of the Garden, not just the early ones commonly remarked, can be difficult to visualize consistently and fully, taking account of multiple dimensions and perspectives.[13] As stages, those within the Garden numerically recapitulate those in the whole Garden canto: first, the myth of Chrysogne's conception, with its all-inclusive perspectives; next, Venus' Actaeon-like surprisal of the disarrayed Diana, which, in transferring the role of mythic male hunter to Venerean goddess, aptly and anticipatively mixes sexes/genders in approaching the Garden; and finally, the mythic Garden itself.

A third stanza describing the pubic Mount within the Garden concerns the flowers resulting from the metamorphosis of hapless human lovers. To these male lovers, we read, "*sweet* Poets verse hath giuen endlesse date," thus conferring on them a form of immortality symbolized by recycling plants but at once formally and materially different, since neither poems nor their readers are vegetables (vi.45: my emphasis).[14] The immortality within this stanza, like the nature of the Garden's arbor, exists as nature within art and as art within nature in much the senses that Sidney speaks of the poet as a maker of fictive nature and as one himself made by the God of all nature.[15] These flowers of metamorphosis—of *transformation* in Spenser's word and therefore of metaphor—imply the traditional flowers of rhetoric and, via the Greek word for flower, *anthos*, the idea of an anthology, or gathering, of flowers, which relates to the broadly encompassing nature of the Garden as a gathering of natural, cultural, and specifically verbal generations. Appropriately, the flowers of metamorphosis, at once of death and life, of mutability and perpetuity, on the Mount also *contain*—again in the punning sense—the jealousy, self-enclosure, grief, and despair variously found in the culturally fertile myths of Hyacinthus, Narcissus, Amaranthus, and all other sorts of floral metamorphees, as well as notably in the landscape of quest outside the Garden in Book III. Like many another figure in the Garden, the flowers of metamorphosis attest to its earthly, rather than perfect or heavenly, nature.

Art is thus conspicuous on the Mount, both as theme and as method, a juncture that can hardly be overemphasized. The coincidence of art with nature is another dimension of the Garden's inclusive commitment to conjunctive generations that at once contain and surmount doubleness and difference. I pun shamelessly with *surmount*, as well as with *generations* (physical, cultural, and historical procreation) and once more with *contain*. The very fact that an effort to discuss the Garden generates one pun after another (more in these pages than I flag) is worth further pondering. In the simultaneity of a pun, as I have observed elsewhere, the crossing of boundaries, disruption of the everyday, and doubling of reference can *trans-figure* the world that we know, rather than merely reflecting, refusing, or rising above it. By punning we approach the nature of the Garden more nearly.[16]

The central stanzas of the Mount, 45 to 48, focus on Venus and Adonis and, not surprisingly, further illuminate the limits of sexual binarism in the everyday world, as distinct from the Garden. Before I proceed to them, an explanatory sidebar is needed, however: back in stanza 33, which belongs to the first substage of the cyclic garden, the stage of seed-forms, lines referring to Old Genius tell us that he reclothes the recycling babes "Or [they are] sent into the chaungefull world agayne."[17] Hamilton's indispensable second edition encourages a problem here by taking "Or" to express a "puzzling" alternative, since, Hamilton worries, we should logically expect "and." But "Or" is actually an abbreviated form of "before" well known to the *OED*, and, in a familiar version of Spenserian compression, the phrase "they are" is understood from earlier lines to precede the participle "sent."[18] The line in question thus affords a dubious basis on which to conclude that Garden and world are the same, a proposition Harry Berger has suggested. Although the mythic Garden is earthly, its distance from everyday life is vital to its regenerative vision. The difference between its glancing at realistic worldly anxieties, such as male fear, and giving full rein to them belongs to this distance.[19] Herein paradoxically lies, yet no more than Sidneyan fiction lieth, the difference between recognizing *and* transcending or including *and* controlling threats and ceding authority to them.[20] In short, this is containment in its richest sense, with which conceptual pun, I return to the stanzas that focus on Venus and Adonis.

In the first of these, Venus is the reaper, or happy, productive, life-sustaining harvester, of "sweet pleasure" with Adonis. She reverses the destruction of the Saturnian scythe-bearer Time, whose *dis-semination* of Uranus in the familiar myth, taken by itself, intends only waste and death. True to Venus' mythic origin as *alienated*, irreparably *othered*, seed, "Born without Syre," Spenser's Venus defies both the Stygian gods of death and the saturnine scythe-bearer.[21] From them, she protects Adonis, "the wanton[, or 'lusty,'] boy" (46). Etymologically, he is the "unruly," "lacking" boy and punningly, the "wanting" boy in both senses of this word, since he lacks and wants what she offers.[22] She possesses him, taking her fill of his "sweetnesse," seemingly an obvious reference at this point to seminal fluid. Yet in this stanza, which initially stresses Venerean pleasure and joy, twice compounded, it is particularly difficult to keep various dimensions of allegory distinct. If we read in terms of character (i.e., of the deictic or real), the relation of Venus to Adonis is odd, even somewhat Acrasian, as many readers have noted. In this stanza, Spenser's relatively humanized forms, and I stress *relatively*, begin actually to invite more individualized, gendered, binary readings. If Venus and Adonis are read as female and male characters, her possessing him, however wanton this boy may be, carries a whiff of exploitation and incest. Besides, since *wanton* basically means "unruly," or "self-indulgent," it anticipates the other, less cooperative aspects of Shakespeare's more fully and dramatically individualized Adonis, a figure whose relation to Shakespeare's Venus in their eponymous epyllion recurrently looks back to Spenser's third Book, as my preceding chapter has argued.[23]

More than any other stanza, the forty-sixth thus makes an honest issue of the more nearly anthropomorphic, if still mythological, forms toward which the Garden has been moving, evolving, ascending. Yet it would be a mistake, I think, to overemphasize this issue, making an everyday, worldly context primary rather than momentarily present—fully realizing the world in the Garden rather than glimpsing it on the horizon, a horizon which, while still within the poem, remains primarily beyond the Garden in the landscape of quest. The basic issue here pertains to the nature of *containment* as merely suppression or as inclusion and constructive acknowledgment, as completion and generative surmounting, and it involves suppositions about reading and ways of reading not simply in general but in particular passages. To a very great extent such reading is what the whole *Faerie Queene* is about. Reading this poem is very much like reading the world, and our ways of reading it are variously implicated in ethics—sexual, psychological, and otherwise. To add that one person's ethics is another's politics would neither satisfy nor really suffice here. Instead, I prefer to recognize and to maintain at least a valid conceptual difference between ethics and politics, while also affirming the productive and provocative instability of their relation.

Stanza 47 shifts away from the anthropomorphic issue by insisting on Adonis' existence primarily as a principle, rather than as a character. Now he is seen as "the Father of all formes," who, though "subiect to mortalitie, / Yet is eterne in mutabilitie, / And by succession made perpetuall." Between these lines and the preceding stanza, however, come other lines indicating that Adonis "may not / For euer dye, and euer buried bee / In balefull night, where all things are forgot." While recognizing the obvious reading that Adonis cannot die forever, Berger suggests the possibility that the sexually exhausted lad may want to, and I suppose one might also read the poet's phrase "may not" as indicating some doubt about the whole proposition of perpetuity through succession: "And sooth it seemes they say," even after all that has been said, and done, to this point (114).

But at this juncture, what interests me more is the way the poem shifts from one point of view to another, using ambiguity, or doubleness, to do so. The shift in this instance is from a point of view at the end of stanza 46 that is becoming prematurely and unproductively personal and gendered to one more generalized and species-oriented. As a shift hinging on ambiguity, it is similar to that in the cyclical first stage of the Garden from the seminary of recycling forms to the eternity of matter, and it typifies progression in the Garden canto. In this first stage, the shift occurs in the word "stocke" of stanza 36, which refers equally to the preceding seed-forms and to the following material substances: "Daily they grow, and daily forth are sent / Into the world, it to replenish more, / Yet is the stocke not lessened, nor spent." With the double reference of "stocke" to form and to (material) substance, our perspective flips from one side of a single cosmic coin to the other—the view from on high to that from below, from an eternity of forms to one of matter.[24] Similarly, in the stanzas moving from Venus' possession of Adonis to his resulting perpetuity, our perspective shifts from one angle of reading to another and coincidentally once again from one more formally individuated to one more generalized and organic. The point, I think, is precisely the shift, or better, the hinge that, instead of embracing one view or the other, includes *and by succession* relates them. With an imaginative capaciousness almost incredible and seemingly inexhaustible, it thus *contains* them, while refusing containment by either one of them.[25]

With the gendering at the end of stanza 46 modified—neutralized, enlarged, and productively enriched—by stanza 47, stanza 48, which includes the encaved boar, can open with a (re)affirmation of the joy shared by Venus and Adonis: "There now he liueth in eternall blis, / Ioying his goddesse, and of her enioyd." As Hamilton and Berger explain between them, the second of these lines is susceptible of readings that make either or both Venus and Adonis the recipient of joy in significantly differing yet balanced verbal phrases.[26] Once again, I would think conjunction, inclusion, and even mutuality the point rather than the personalized male anxiety that Berger's Actaeonic essay on the Garden continues to privilege. The Spenserian stanza proceeds, referring to Adonis' situation:

> Ne feareth he henceforth that foe of his,
> Which with his cruell tuske him deadly cloyd;
> For that wilde Bore, the which him once annoyd,
> She firmely hath emprisoned for ay,
> That her sweet loue his malice mote auoyd,
> In a strong rocky Caue, which is they say,
> Hewen vnderneath that Mount, that none him losen may.
>   (III.vi.48)

Circling, not to say recycling, back to the ambisexuality of the pubic Mount, the hateful, wild Boar of winter, passion, chaos, and death within and beneath this Mount is also a bisexual figure in Spenser's artistic and thematic regeneration of the old generative myths. The boar's situation is a culminating emblem of *containment* in every sense of this fertile word. On the one hand, the gender of the Boar is pronominally masculine, and he is imprisoned beneath the pubic Mount, an obvious reference to the cave vaginal. Most traditional myths also enforce his maleness. Yet, on the other hand, Venus is his notably "firm" captor, once again giving her a dominant role, and a growing consensus of readers assents to Lauren Silberman's discovering in the figure of the boar himself the *vagina dentata*, or "an icon of fearsome venereal power" (48). The ambisexed, toothed cave is, of course, also erotically suggestive.²⁷

Although the *vagina dentata* is an obscure myth, I suspect we would find it more often if we chose to look for it: Bosch's paintings (not to mention Edward Gorey's drawings) come to mind. Shakespeare's virtual tusking of Venus in his epyllion about her frustrated seduction of Adonis relevantly gives added pause—"Had I been tooth'd like" the boar, Venus confesses, "With kissing him, I should have kill'd him first"—and thereby the epyllion suggests that both these Elizabethan poets might have encountered reference to the *vagina dentata*, unless they imagined it independently.²⁸ At the end of the central stanzas treating the Mount, as at their beginning, the totality and complexity of the depiction of Venus and Adonis is therefore emphatically ambisexual.²⁹ To be true to the succession of generations in every sense of this phrase imaginable and thus to Spenser's mythic Garden, it not only may but also *should* be, in the full sense of Sidney's ethical imperative.³⁰

Momentarily in stanza 48, even the word "cloyd" in itself may suggest the deadly (or deathly) boar's containment. As Berger observes, *cloy* can mean "glut," as well as the contextually more obvious "penetrate," and it therefore recalls the wanton boy's "expense of spirit ['semen, vitality']" to the possible point of exhaustion and disgust (114). "Life is sweet," as we say, but as the poet of the Faerie quest knew well, excess sweetness, whether in the honied words of Despair or the honied tones of Melibee, can be "deadly cloy[ing]" (vi.48). Yet I wonder whether Berger underplays another, less assuredly negative coloration even of *cloy*, when glossed as "satiate," which is glossed in turn as "satisfy (an appetite or a desire) fully," a sense whose potential lies within yet beyond, and rises above, passion's wild and hateful excesses.³¹ Satisfaction is fullness, enoughness (*satis*), and, conceivably, contentment (from *continere*: "to hold, keep together," and thus "contain"), rather than glutting, as intimated in Shakespeare's *Antony and Cleopatra*, where Antony's appetite is sharpened with "cloyless sauce" that never satiates, and Enobarbus, describing Cleopatra's "infinite variety," at once contrasts *and* rhetorically aligns "cloy" with "satisfies" to the extent that a double take is needed to separate them: "Other women cloy / The appetites they feed, but she makes hungry / Where most she satisfies" (II.i.25, ii.235–37).³² Who knows when enough is too much or, in Antony's problematical words, how "love[, or eros,] . . . can be reckoned" (I.i.15)? While not wanting to reduce the savage boar to a house pet or to discount the deadliness of his cloying, I would notice even here some blunting of a sharp edge, some trace *and* glimmer of the nearness of cloying to satisfaction. Although otherwise inflected, since in the everyday world outside a mythic *aevum*, Shakespeare's sonnet 129, invoked earlier in my paragraph by the phrase "expense of spirit," affords another telling comparison at its end, where "none knows well / To shun the heaven that leads men to this hell."[33] Even in the more worldly, relatively more negative ending of Shakespeare's sonnet, the syntactical ambiguity of the phrase "knows well," like the syntactically analogous phrase "does well," glances at the "bliss," the "joy," and the "dream" of an erotic heaven: none does well (or knows well) to shun the possibility of what *could* be.[34] In Spenser's *aevum*, taken whole, the balance is different: we glimpse the world even while recurrently and emphatically perceiving a totality that goes beyond it.

There remains one line of those I have cited from stanza 48 that seems to me to capture our final impression of the couple, or mythic principle of coupling. Venus has forever encaved the boar, "That her sweet loue his malice mote auoyd." While there may be further ambiguities to be considered in the stanza in question, the one that interests me most concerns the phrase "sweet loue" in the line just cited. "Sweet loue" (again, "sweet") refers either to the object of Venus' love, Adonis, or to the nature of her relation to him. By these readings, he *is* actually there. By yet another reading, however, if in herself she is Love (and the *if* is real), the whole idea of relation, along with Adonis, would be swallowed back into her self-enclosure and thus, in effect, either into Uranus' and Saturn's urge to suppress and consume or into her own self-mirroring. This would be a denial of her alienation from her origin in dis-semination, and a denial of her consequent otherness—a cancellation at once of her difference from destructive male gods and of the difference, the real otherness, of the wanton Adonis from her. The very succession of the central stanzas on the Mount, with their shifts in perspective and significant form, seems to me to work against such a reading, effectually having already carried us beyond its likelihood. Successive, dynamic totality, not competition; ambisexuality, not visual, humanoid hermaphroditism; the mythic *aevum*, not the everyday world—herein lie the true character and thrust of Spenser's amazing, fictive, earthly Garden.

15. *Androcentrism and Acrasian Fantasies in the Bower of Bliss*

Harry Berger's "Wring out the Old: Squeezing the Text, 1951–2001" will be a major critical statement on the Bower of Bliss for years to come, and serious work on the Bower needs to engage its generously annotated, tightly argued analysis of the structural discourse that constitutes this site.[1] In "Squeezing the Text" (is the trope laundry or lemon juice?), Berger exposes the workings of misogyny as a target, and emphatically not a given, of the Bower. He reads the Spenserian narrative as an instance of "*specular tautology,*" or self-reflection, which he also understands as an inversion of cause and effect such that the effect is misrecognized as its own cause (86).[2] In this misrecognition lies the "unconscious of the system."[3] Thus the wicked witch Acrasia is falsely projected, regarded, and bound as the "objectification of male hysteria." She "is male" because she is "placed in the position of dominance" within her Garden, and because she is "the product of male fantasy" (88). Presumably, Acrasia differs in these respects from Venus in the Garden of Adonis, but that site is at least nominally Adonis', and in light of his possession, we may have to look still further at differences and similarities between Bower and Garden.[4]

Because of the importance both of the Bower and of Berger's essay to any reading of *The Faerie Queene*, I want to raise some questions about these in accord with Berger's own critical approach to others' readings. Having forthrightly argued the insufficiency of a recent historicist interpretation, Berger observes that "critique works best when it reflects the critic's obligation to what has been critiqued—when it produces a change of mind and an idea the critic hadn't had before and thus, in serving as the prologue to appropriation, increases the target's generosity, that is, its power to generate alternative readings."[5] I intend what follows in the spirit and substance of conversation with Berger's writings that has meant much to me over many years. Where my questions existed before, his essay on the Bower has made them more urgent, and where they have not, it has provoked them.

In a whimsical, tempting touch at the end of the Bower essay, Berger wonders "what would have happened to Acrasia had the Palmer 'with his vertuous staffe her strooke'" (109). Immediately, I think to myself, "The Palmer would have been astonished by her not vanishing away." A rereading of Berger's final paragraph has indicated that my answer should have been "her replacement by Grill and, more radically, by the Guyon-Palmer composite." But for now I cling to my initial obtuseness. Without it, I am left wondering what remains of female representation in the Bower and whether a female reader like me has not, as an accidental effect, been excluded from its artistic potency. While I am not leading a chorus of "Let's hear it for Acrasia," and I am not disputing Berger's insistence that the Bower is tautologically misogynist, I am still not sure that this insistence in itself is enough. Where misogyny is brilliantly exposed and rejected, I am worried that androcentrism might still be alive and well, and, indeed, reinstated. Traditionally, androcentrism, also deeply cultural and insidiously so, swallows up the female in a telos of restoration to the male androgyne, the divine anthropos, the one, which, when gendered (and when isn't it?), is always already male: Adam's rib goes right back where it belongs.[6] Enlightened, persuaded, and provoked by Berger's reading, I wonder whether there is any female in the Bower and the rich artistic tradition it represents if "Acrasia is male," along with her agents and everything else that she apparently creates.[7] Where are the traces? A while back, I shared a playful version of my present questions with Berger by asking, "What have you done to that poor seductress?" I will return to this second question about the relation of discourse and character later, only noting at present that for me it becomes a question about form and its significance.

Both Berger's recent essay on the Garden of Adonis and his recent Bower essay render the myth of Venus' birth as "an alienated figure of the masculine role in procreation[,] . . . as a projection, an ejaculation, of male fantasy, constituted and empowered by the seminal spume of desire" (104).[8] So far so good, if mischievously high-spirited, but I want to offer a variant. In the larger version of the myth that leads to Venus' birth, Earth (Gaea), mother and wife of Uranus, arms Cronus, or Saturn, with the castrating scythe. The figure of Aphrodite, or Venus, then reverses the destruction of the Saturnian scythe-bearer Time, whose *dis-semination* of Uranus, taken by itself, only intends waste and death.[9] True to Venus' mythic origin as alienated seed, "Borne without Syre," Spenser's generative Venus defies both the Stygian gods of death and the saturnine scythe-bearer of Spenser's Garden of Adonis.[10] She may be, but she is not merely, a spume of desire; she is also truly alienated, that is, *irreparably othered*, and if her immediate cause is castrated male sexuality, her deeper cause is the desire of Gaea—Earth, matter, mother, wife—for expression and fulfillment. In the myth, Uranus has concealed Gaea's terrible children in the depths of the earth; she desires their freeing from within her, and the end result is something that male sexuality alone does not account for. When the male seed of Uranus meets the sea, which, Hesiod tells us, Gaea has brought forth of herself, Venus becomes, in Spenser's words, "male and female through commixture joynd."[11] In the Roman tradition, where Saturnus is originally a god of sowing and harvest, and Venus a goddess of flowers and vines, their cooperation in fertility and generation is apparent, although another of Venus' aspects is goddess of prostitution.[12] If all this is ideologically male, too, there are plenty of traces in it of something else.

The tradition of misogynist, male discourse in art, which is pretty various when we factor in various genres and languages, is a topos not easily evacuated or eliminated, a point Berger makes conclusively. As he puts it, causing the Bower to "vanish as a mimetic topos only ensures its continuing power over the mind as a literary topos" (108). The distance between a literary and a mimetic topos, as between the mind (THE mind?) and a place narratively and textually realized, is elusive, shifting, even tricky, however, and like the Spenserian poet's own distinctions, it easily becomes a bit fuzzy.[13] If, as Berger rightly suggests, "Maleger and his 'idle shades'" expressly displace Phantastes's 'idle phantasies' from within" the House of Alma's brain turret to forces attacking the perimeter of Alma's body, the same is true in reverse: in the narrative sequence, initial attack from without is mirrored in buzzing swarms within, and then attack from without recurs (86). What is outside, and what inside, is not easily or always distinguished here, not even as pertains to British history (II.ix–xi).[14] Renaissance theories about the leaky and permeable boundaries of the human body, about the working of the imagination, or phantasy, and about optics—poised between extra- and intromissive sight, Theresa Krier tells us—likewise erode this distinction and imply relations of reciprocity, instead.[15]

What I want to find in Berger's view that the literary topos persists in the mind when the Bower is destroyed is implicit recognition that there is much in the Bower that is not accounted for by a generic and exclusive category of misogynist, male discourse. Even within traditional (male) discourse, the mark of something female, however perverse, exists, and the same is true of (male) fantasy that is culturally and publicly intelligible. The relation of outsides to insides (and vice versa) in all its problematic, epistemological manifestations pertains here: linguistically, the problem of reference and imagistically and figurally the problem of mimesis both come to mind. For a relevant Spenserian paradigm outside the Bower, consider the depiction of hell in Book I (v), which is usually read as part of the inner landscape of Redcrosse, or Everyman. It is surely this, but at the same time, it is also more, and other. The story of Hippolytus at the very bottom of hell can be read from either the view of Redcrosse or of Una, whose presence is therefore intimated in some ironic sense (v.37–39). Read one way, Redcrosse, like Hippolytus, is "too simple and too trew," himself the chaste victim pursued by monsters rising from the deep, and Una, like Phaedra, is lustful, untrue, and treasonous (ii.45, vi.2). Read another way, Redcrosse, combining Theseus with Phaedra, is lustful, faithless, rash, jealous, and wrathful, and Una, like Hippolytus, is the chaste and innocent victim endangered by vicious forces in a hostile world. The mirror this netherworld holds up to unity and wholeness thus parodies and distorts them.[16]

While the distortion exists within the split subjectivity of what Redcrosse, together with Una, represents, it simultaneously mirrors something (or things) outside his figure alone and thereby mocks him. Herein lies the resistance of Una's figure to the attempts of Redcrosse's psyche perversely to swallow or replace it. Here, too, I take subjectivity in the broad, grammatical sense—at once agential and subjected—and not solely in the interiorized one, and I consider the major figures of Book I variously to represent its historical, social, and cultural, as well as its psychic, dimensions. In *The Faerie Queene*, a figure like Sans Joy, who becomes wholly internalized, can disappear without notice from the narrative once canto v ends, but in the central books, a figure like the somewhat more substantially developed Amoret, who has both a longer and more complicated narrative and more of a historicized dimension, turns into a liability refusing to disappear from the narrative without our notice. The symbolic absorption of Amoret's figure by Britomart's or its transcendence in the poet's lyric voice, however significant in themselves, are alike failures in the narrative mode. The abortive reunion of Scudamore and Amoret is conspicuously and significantly botched. It has content.[17]

Una, like Duessa, functions partly as an inner force and therefore as an objectification (or projection) of Redcrosse's (Everyman's) psyche, but monoscopic, static allegory, itself a contradiction in terms, is hardly typical of Spenser's poetry. Even allegory as simple as Prudentius' *Psychomachia* or *Everyman*—like personification or metaphor itself, though with the crucial, recursive-progressive addition of dramatic narrative—combines terms, levels, codes, dimensions, call them as you will.[18] If the figure Una were *merely* to fold into Redcrosse or, say, the physical, historical, theological, and cosmic dimensions of Orgoglio's figure were completely to collapse into an interior condition, then allegory, like the homologism, isomorphism, or structural parallelism Fredric Jameson critiques in *The Political Unconscious*, would indeed swallow the whole world of differences, becoming unidimensional and merely illustrative instead of relational and tensive.[19] Essential identity and stasis would replace multiplicity and process. Such allegory, by definition oxymoronic and, indeed, self-denying, belongs definitively to Milton's Satan, who, ironically, thinks his mind its own place; it does not belong to Spenser, Milton's avowed model.[20]

When I read Berger's Bower of Bliss and start thinking about Acrasia as an objectification of male discourse, I also think of the Wife of Bath and about the complexities of her subjectivity and agency, given her figuration as a virtual embodiment of misogynist writings and the resistance of her parodic figure to them.[21] We hardly need specific allusions to Chaucer in the Bower to make this intertextual connection, but there actually are some.[22] Emphatically, the purpose of my connection is not to suggest that Acrasia's figure and the Wife's are equally realized or equally complex, but first to raise the possibility of Acrasia's expression, not simply *of* male discourse but, subversively, also *from within* it—imaginatively, rhetorically, lyrically—rather than volubly and reasonably like the Wife's;[23] and second, my purpose is to bring into view the role of the narrator. Berger addresses this role specifically, remarking, for example, that the narrator's response to Phaedria in canto vi sounds "as prudish as the Palmer" and "as troubled and as ludicrously chivalrous as Guyon," a remark to which he might have added, "in a performative way worthy of Chaucer" (101). More generally, he also observes that "the male narrator's ambivalence is as much the subject of representation as is Phaedria" (99). I hope he would agree that the narrator's role in the Bower is even more thoroughly ambivalent, not simply the same as that of Guyon and the Palmer. Along with Dorothy Stephens, in particular, I also think its relation to the poet's role and its unqualified maleness, as elsewhere, are in question.[24] And where is the Spenserian poet in all this? Inside, outside, or somewhere in-between ideology? By the poet, I mean the one in the text, the only one to whom we have access, however mediated, and one who sometimes speaks from within the life of Edmund Spenser.[25] If this verbally constructed voice, or series of voices, actually believes in his poetic descent from Chaucer, his position might well be more ambivalent, more localized, and more mutable, than the absolute other side of the reigning ideology, which is male, of course. The poet's relation to the enlightened ideology of his own text would at least be an issue. But again, in referring at the outset of this paragraph to the Wife of Bath, to resistance and subversion, I have raised the specter of character, which again I shall acknowledge but defer just a little longer. Deferral, after all, is this not also something women and romance forms are always doing? Its mention brings to mind Patricia Parker's association of the Bower with lyric, romance, and suspended teleology, an association Katherine Eggert historicizes and develops: female traces, more male ideology, or, blurrily and reciprocally, maybe both?[26]

For me, *The Faerie Queene* will always be tentative and exploratory—a form of thinking. In my reading, its position regarding its own cultural traditions, gender, and the relation of mind and matter, of conceptual abstraction and embodied narrative, are ambivalent, shifting, and necessarily specific and contextual, although they are necessarily also subject to generalization, which, in my view, must always be provisional. The forms or figures that participate in the narrative are in themselves significant, much as is the vehicle of a metaphor. That is, as signifiers, aside from, and not only as, concepts signified, they have content. Here I would break from a linear telos that privileges the end or conclusion, the rational, dominant, overlying meaning, and insist on the importance of matter, earth, and surface—the underlying meaning, if you will.[27]

Not all forms, whether male or female, are the same in *The Faerie Queene*, however. I would not make quite the same argument about that iconic caricature and virtual grotesque Duessa in Book I which I float with respect to Acrasia. Lady Munera in Book V affords another exemplary variant, a kind of boundary case, humanly pitiful but furnished ambiguously with metal hands and feet.[28] Yet another variant is Charissa in the House of Holiness (I.x.29–32): I fondly recall a student who critiqued her for having so many nursing babes that she had to thrust them into the world as they grew older; she was simply a bad mother. As always, there is a grain of truth in student responses of this sort even when also erroneous or woefully incomplete. Such reading of Charissa points at once to the issue of using a female form as merely an iconic figure (a Diana of Ephesus, not to say a grotesque cow) and thus merely as a carrier of theological meaning, but also to the issue of misreading iconic depiction anachronistically and naively. Both issues, I note, involve the kind or level of human complexity of the figure involved, not just a *monoscopic translation* or a simple abstraction of the *figure*. Surface matters, and not least in the Bower of Bliss. Acrasia, whether in landscape, lyric, or figure—especially the second view of her, which is effectually free of moralistic intrusions—has substance, a word I choose for its slippery range of meaning—verbal, material and emotional, conceptual, and, broadly, historically, and ambiguously speaking, spiritual.[29] Literally, *substance* means "standing under"—subordinate, underlying, there, if also not (or nought, naught, and even knot).[30]

It seems to me important that Acrasia is a *female* figure, not *only* objectified misogyny, and that her art, perverse as it is, nonetheless has complex, synaesthetic power. Though distorted, her (mis)representation as a female registers something that has to be accounted for, that is there, even while not truly or fully there. It isn't enough to account for her by male projection, although Berger has certainly persuaded me that male misogynist discourse accounts tautologically for much of her perversion. When the Bower is desolated by our hysterical male hero, Acrasia survives, though barely and bound; Guyon and the Palmer return to the House of Alma and bundle the captive Acrasia off to Faerie Court with a strong guard (III.i.1–2). Whether Acrasia actually enters Alma's House or is summarily sent away before doing so is unclear. If only from a practical viewpoint, her summary departure seems less likely and, from an interpretive viewpoint, less interesting, since her entering the House would raise the naughty (noughty, knotty) thought that she might represent something that Alma, not to mention Faery Court, is otherwise lacking.

In the last line of the Bower canto, the Palmer advises that they all leave the ravaged garden "whilest wether serues and winde" (xii.87). At the beginning of canto xi, we heard similar words from the narrator as he watches Guyon and his Palmer sail off to the Bower—"whiles winde and wether right / Doe serue their turnes"—and before that from Phaedria in canto vi: "Who fares on sea, may not commaund his way, / Ne wind and weather at his pleasure call" (xi.4, vi.23). Varied are the ways of reading this linkage of Phaedria to narrator to the Palmer and Guyon: for example, as the exemplars of temperance exit the Bower we might glimpse in them a new openness to nature and to occasion, which have recurrently threatened Guyon; or we might find persisting misogyny in this ironized, culminating echo of the Phaedrian voice; or distantly, we just might hear Phaedria's laugh—her "honest merth," as once the poem absent-mindedly describes it (vi.21).[31]

In two especially delightful, closely-read sections of the Bower essay, Berger analytically describes and playfully animates Phaedria and the seductive bathers, whom C. S. Lewis dubbed Cissie and Flossie, thus moving them out of the garden and into the pet store.[32] Finding Phaedria "fun and funny" in canto vi, Berger reads her as "a light-hearted burlesque" of such sternly moral critiques of effeminizing Italianism ("'the Siren songs of Italy'") as Roger Ascham's:

> Outrageously but hilariously irreverent, she affords a familiar standpoint within the poem from which to smile at the principles of "Stoick" censorship Guyon and the Palmer are shown more or less hysterically, and not very effectively, to defend. Phaedria's is the standpoint of Richard Helgerson's Elizabethan prodigals. Her antics, like theirs, send up the "rugged forehead" of the civic humanism represented by the Palmer and his staff, or rod [99].

That distant Phaedrian laugh we might have thought we heard *really* was that of a prodigal male. But wouldn't this be to vaporize the surface? To have all the fun of the Phaedrian nut and then to overlook its female husk for the kernel within it? Is there a way to keep both in play? Doesn't the agency of the signifier extend to constructs of language like literary form or figure? The language of my questions signals their stakes: to overlook the husk, however enlightened the ideological goal, suggests the method of Renaissance moralism. No matter how different the goal, such methodology is anti-aesthetic, reductive, and here androcentric, to boot.

Subsequently describing the Bower's two bathers, Berger explains that they are skilled collaborators in male fantasy, and he distinguishes between their performative artifice and what Acrasia does, since, as he more or less put it in 1957, Acrasia delivers:[33]

> Under the pretext of careless abandon they watch themselves being watched, and with preemptive voyeurism stage a caricature of what it is "that men in women do require," the lineaments not of gratified desire but of men's pornographic fantasy. Theirs is a high-spirited travesty of the Acrasian nightmare that motivates and underwrites the ideology of self-restraint. But they flaunt it in a Phaedrian rather than Acrasian mode, . . . [that is, one] more theatrical and comical. [103].

I love it! But I am a little worried about that "Acrasian nightmare." If it is Guyon's and the Palmer's nightmare or, rather, that of the male discourse they, too, signify, it isn't exactly Acrasia's, although, if she witnessed the performance of her agents in action, it might tickle her silly—like Phaedria.[34] Comic theatre, like Phaedria's and the bathers', can be notoriously subversive. How about comically theatrical porn?

While I have hardly done justice to Berger's acutely perceptive treatment of these three Phaedrian figures, I hasten to its sequel, a sudden confession that the fun he has had with them "has been no different from Lewis's in one important respect." He continues, "I have been describing them as if they are independent characters, autonomous agents, when obviously they are no such thing. They are what they signify. . . . all the intentions and effects I ascribed to the bathers must be reascribed to male discourse, and this includes the illusion that the bathers are autonomous—that deliberate female provocation . . . is the cause of male prurience" (104–5). I wonder whether Berger isn't being too hard on himself, and on us, when he owns up to treating the Phaedrian figures as if they were truly *dramatis personae* or wholly autonomous agents. He has not been describing their consciousness or subconsciousness in the way that of old provoked reprimand from Paul Alpers. For heaven's sake! Captain Phaedria, whose "foamy genesis" bubbles up from stiff, patriarchal oars?! The likes of this is what we have had from him in these analyses (98–99, 104).

To read the whole of Berger's treatment, not just the nuggets I've cited, is all the more to appreciate the readerly play in his unfolding the significance of the Phaedrian figures, and I stress again, *figures*, something of which his descriptions leave little doubt.[35] These descriptions know gradations of difference between the Phaedrian figure and either an inflatable doll or a naively mimetic representation of a woman. Certainly readers of Chaucer are used to considering questions of agency (or will and responsibility) in figures as different as a rooster named Chaunticleer (prototype of the butterfly Clarion), a nameless and faceless tale-telling nun, a type, such as the old carpenter John in *The Miller's Tale*, and the fully characterized Criseyde in *Troilus*. Autonomy, like agency, is itself a situated, relative, and therefore equivocal concept, as no one knows better than Harry Berger.[36]

The alternatives of hermetic self-enclosure and reductively conceived mimesis, of total internalization and total externalization, are simply not the only possibilities. If the Bower and everything in it were translatable to a signification insensitive to surface, how could its devastation be so persistently ambivalent? The reascription of all this to male discourse need not include the illusion that is the fullness of the fiction itself in all its multiplicities of being and not being. Isn't reascription really just overwriting? Or could it be reconceived as a translation—a sublating *translatio*, or interpretive metaphor—that still retains traces of all its terms, including those that are substantively, and perhaps even subversively, female?

In a paragraph with two elusive instances of the impersonal possessive pronoun "its," Berger refers to the Phaedrian figure as "a spectral displacement [of woman] that taunts its maker." This is good! Granted the there- and not-thereness of specters and their resonance in the critical idiom, this *could* work, if only specter and maker were not to be equated absolutely and exclusively with "*male* self-mockery and self-despite," the tautological mirror again, if now a deliberated one (105: my emphasis).³⁷ In view of this possibility and of Berger's lifelong defense of the text and its openness, a defense to which I am indebted, I am not persuaded that a venturous second thought, an intuition, an idle fancy, didn't lead him to ask that final, mischievous question about the Palmer's touching Acrasia with his staff. Without it, and my momentary puzzlement, I wouldn't be causing trouble.

In a different yet relevant context, Elliot Wolfson, remarking the catch-22 of critiquing gender (in)difference in kabbalistic hermeneutics, observes that to an extent critique "enmeshes the scholar [or indeed the artist] in bolstering what is criticized, implicating one[self] in erasure and inscription simultaneously. . . . To deconstruct a text entails cracking its binding, taking apart, clearing away; but to clear away, one must take hold. How[?] . . . By letting go, withholding the appropriating, appropriating the withholding" (86). Perhaps necessarily, Wolfson's perceptive observation is somewhat elusive, since it addresses a rational impasse, but it is also quite suggestive with respect to the phenomenon of the self-contaminating critical gaze. I seize its end as an argument for provisionality and inclusiveness, for openness, as well as for a degree of *inconclusion*. In the space remaining, I want to look at the two direct views, within the fiction, that we have of the figure of Acrasia herself. Even as I wrote "herself," I considered writing "himself" and thought it both comic and unfair to do so. But why?

The first view of Acrasia is the narrator's and thence the reader's. It is denied to Guyon and the Palmer, who are still traipsing through the Bower and have not yet reached its erotic center. This view certainly has negative suggestions: Acrasia's eyes are false; she is greedy as, cow-like, she "depastures," or feeds; and she sucks Verdant's "spright," no different from the Venus of Adonis' Garden if "spright" is semen and Acrasia is Venerean, but since spright/spirit also carries its moral sense here, then also reductively, as the animal emphasis in the word "sucks" suggests.³⁸ Elsewhere, I have described the relation of Verdant and Acrasia as symbiotic: "[With] her sight beholding, his sight beheld, and his sight beholding. . . . they exist for one another in a dream."³⁹ *Symbiotic*, I realize, is not wholly accurate, yet it is arguably as close to the image as, and perhaps even closer than, the purely negative "parasitic" would be. There is a good deal of mutuality here, perverse as it might finally be, and mutuality is something not typical of parasitism. In an idiom still all too familiar, Acrasia hangs ("hong") on Verdant's sight, fixed in it, as he is fixed in hers. If he is a victim, she is "stong" by him as well and naturally goes to him for her remedy. Bedewing his lips with kisses, she fears to wake him, sighing as if she rues his situation. Her fear to wake him ambiguously and simultaneously suggests her desire to enthrall him, her fear of him once awake, and her consideration of his desire to remain sleeping. Whether waking is literal or figurative is itself ambiguous, not simply and exclusively figurative. Her sighs, "as if his case she rewd," relate her response to that desired by a Petrarchan sonnet speaker, but the conditional, tropic phrase "as if" could also suggest her assumption of a performative role—her subversive playing. Intrusively, the phrase "as if" also signals moral distancing of Acrasia by the narrator, as if he did not trust his negative indications earlier in the stanza to suffice.[40] Intrusion so notable in so erotic a context is as likely to make us suspect the intruder as to evoke agreement. The mutuality the stanza allows us to glimpse can as readily be seen as the fantasy exclusively of male discourse as of its perverse other, or, again, as something culturally more combinative and cooperative. What strikes me most, however, is the extent to which this moralizing stanza conveys something more complicated than one-sided agency or one-sided passion (II.xii.73).

Separated from our first view of Acrasia by the truly, rhythmically "louely lay" of the Rose and the unlovely creeping of Guyon and the Palmer through the bushes, our second view of Acrasia begins where the first left off, with Verdant's "sleepie head" softly positioned in her lap, following intercourse (74–76). The two stanzas describing her seem to me to speak affectively and effectively for themselves:

> Vpon a bed of Roses she was layd,
>   As faint through heat, or dight to pleasant sin,
>   And was arayd, or rather disarayd,
>   All in a vele of silke and siluer thin,
>   That hid no whit her alabaster skin,
>   But rather shewd more white, if more might bee:
>   More subtile web *Arachne* cannot spin,
>   Nor the fine nets, which oft we wouen see
> Of scorched deaw do not in th'ayre more lightly flee.
>
> Her snowy brest was bare to ready spoyle
>   Of hungry eies, which n'ote therewith be fild,
>   And yet through languour of her late sweet toyle,
>   Few drops, more cleare then Nectar, forth distild,

> That like pure Orient perles adowne it trild,
> And her faire eyes sweet smyling in delight,
> Moystened their fierie beames, with which she thrild
> Fraile harts, yet quenched not; like starry light
> Which sparckling on the silent waues, does seeme more bright.
>
> (II.xii.77–78)

Reading the first of these stanzas—performing them—in a public lecture, I was amazed fully to realize the audible attraction of their rhythm, reinforced by visual, tactile, and other sensuous and associative suggestions. Like the word "crime" at the end of the Song of the Rose, the word "sin," rhyming with "thin," "skin," and "spin" is barely distinguished in this context.[41] At the outset of the second stanza, if we actually read and listen without presuming misogyny, the narrator sounds more eager to defend this "snowy brest" and to scorn "hungry eies" that greedily seek "spoyle" than to decry Acrasia's readiness. If I affirm that the erotic appeal of both stanzas is subtle, complex, seductive, and enveloping, I am not sure what this says about Acrasia's gender or about my own implication in male discourse or even whether such discourse can remain pristinely male once it involves me. I frankly believe, however, that the appeal of these stanzas exceeds sharply defined barriers of gender and other rational determinants. More simply put, I experience some kind of exhilaration or wonder in and at these lines, whatever their origin, which have so often been likened to the description of Shakespeare's Cleopatra at Cydnus (and elsewhere), who, where "Other women cloy / The appetites they feed, . . . makes hungry / Where most she satisfies."[42] At moments the landscapes and soundscapes of the Bower evoke a similar sense of wondrous pleasure (e.g., xii.70–71).

Jean-Luc Nancy's philosophy of the image, primarily the painted image but also the literary one, is here additionally suggestive for its use of such terms as *reflection*, or mere mirroring; of *form*, or essential surface *and* force; and of affective *participation* and *contagion*. Nancy observes that "Even when the image is mimetic, it must fundamentally by itself and for itself, count for more than an image; otherwise, it will tend toward being nothing but a shadow or a reflection [a mirroring?]." "Indeed," he continues, "philosophical antimimeticism treats the image as a shadow or a reflection; in doing so, however, . . . [it actually] manifests its sensitivity to the self-affirmation of the image and to the affirmation [and exhilaration: *jouissance*] of the self in the image." For Nancy, who addresses both Renaissance and modern images, the "*mimesis* [of the image] encompasses *methexis*, a participation or a contagion through which the image seizes us." The image, and specifically its surface, is "Not an 'idea' (*idea* or *eidolon*), which is an intelligible form, but a force that forces form to touch itself."[43] Similarly, an image in allegory Acrasia may be, but as image, she, like her garden, nonetheless exceeds and surpasses rationality, or even intelligibility, alone. That an image in an allegory of temperance should do so is in some way a greater expression of artistic power than that one less morally contextualized should. Acrasia's image virtually compels participation—perhaps contagion. Truly, she *is* a-mazing.

The initial stanza describing Acrasia focuses particularly on the diaphanous veil of silk and silver thread that covers her, and the second, especially on eyes and eyesight: hungry eyes feeding on her breast, and "eyes sweet smyling in delight" to "thril[l] . . . / Fraile harts"; once again, sight reciprocally beholding but this time the sight beheld is Acrasia, "layd" on "a bed of Roses." Acrasia's veil, spun as subtly as or even more subtly than a web by Arachne, suggests arachnidan entrapment, of course, but as a woven fabric, or text (Latin *textum*: "web, fabric, text"), it also associates Acrasia with the Palmer, since he, like her—or is it she like him?—is a fabricator, a maker of nets, and elsewhere in Book II, a spinner of landscapes and stories; in short, Acrasia, like the Palmer and also like Spenser, is an artist.[44] This association could provide evidence for Berger's argument that she is male discourse in drag, but it would also appear at least potentially to implicate her poet. This appearance arguably returns us to deliberate or inadvertent male self-mockery, the tautological mirror, unless it also leads to something else. One way beyond tautological mirroring is to identify a historical dimension in the figure of Acrasia: for example, to connect her to some extent with Queen Elizabeth, as have Parker, Maureen Quilligan, and Louis Montrose, or more generally to see in the Bower multiple references to colonization and iconoclasm, as have Stephen Greenblatt and Rufus Wood.[45] Another way, according to which I have mainly operated to this point, is not without question to accept the hairy, old assumption that women's sole creative options are lies or babies, while only men can make fictions, and thus to deny art entirely to the figure of Acrasia, whether ravaging this art with Guyon or appropriating it for male discourse *tout court*. To question here is also to remember that Ovid's Arachne is a woman bold (too bold, as her tale eventuates) in protesting the violent excesses of the male gods' passions and one whose protest is depicted with positive sympathy, plus possible ambivalence, by the male Roman poet.[46] As Ovid depicts Arachne's weaving, it is deeply subversive, and to my mind, explicit reference to it in describing Acrasia conveys this suggestion as well. Arachne's eyes gaze defiantly, intertextually back from the tautological mirror, and whether they are beside or within Acrasia's, they are ostensibly, disturbingly female for those with eyes to see them.

One of Berger's much earlier essays at once affords a totalizing affirmation of his theory of spectral tautology and a final opportunity for my claim of female representation in the Bower. In "*The Faerie Queene*, Book III: A General Description," Berger characterizes the False Florimell as a figure showing that Petrarchan attitudes toward women resemble those "toward dead Things." The False Florimell

> is a magico-mechanical robot made to the specifications of the sonneteer's ideal and operated by an evil spirit (viii.5–7): the witch "in the stead / Of life, . . . put a Spright to rule the carkasse dead." The operator is a male demon, for men know best what pleases men in feminine behavior. But the creatrix is female, for women collaborate in this perversion which allows men to fulfill the desire to possess women who are basically male, who have no independence or otherness, who are therefore totally controllable machines of stimulation and pleasure. The enemy is everything in feminine nature which makes women more [other?] than this.[47]

The second half of Berger's description goes beyond the surface of Petrarchism to assert its underlying psychic and social elements, although the apparently contradictory equation in his description of (female) maleness with a lack of independence might be questioned, given Britomart's cross-dressed role in the poem.[48] Superficially, however, the False Florimell, the precipitate of the underlying elements in his assertion, resembles a tautologically male Phaedria or Acrasia insofar as he is basically male, but there also are some pretty obvious differences. Properly speaking, *the* False Florimell has no name, a lack only emphasized by the familiar addition of an objectifying "the" to de-nominate *him*. The *substance* (Spenser's word) of this parodic simulacrum actually consists of snow, mercury, and wax, and he is outfitted with lamps instead of eyes and literally with wires instead of hair, quite in contrast to Acrasia's snowy breast, moist from passion's toil, and her "faire eyes sweet smyling in delight." While it is doubtful that the witch responsible for the False Florimell wants to collaborate in perversion rather than to appease her bereaved and murderously vengeful son, she does fashion the lifeless surrogate that will content him. If (and this *if* is realistic) she is indeed responsible in some sense—ethical or legal, for instance—she, too, is in fact an agent. In conclusion, and *inconclusion*, my questions are these: is Acrasia only a like simulacrum or only a collaborator to be replicated exactly in

Book III by the triangle of witch, loutish son, and False Florimell, or are the differences between this parodic triangle and the seductive female figure at the heart of the Bower substantial and significant? Do they matter? Does ever an other's face take shape in the cultural mirror, like Eve's and Arachne's?

16. *Beyond Binarism: Eros/Death and Venus/Mars in*
Antony and Cleopatra *and* The Faerie Queene

Shakespeare's *Antony and Cleopatra*, like his earlier *Venus and Adonis*, is known to be generically mixed and even anomalous in the extent and degree to which it combines tragedy, comedy, and romance with lyric, allegory, myth, and history.[1] This is the first of several analogies I would draw between Shakespeare's play and Spenser's *Faerie Queene*, that hobgoblin's garland of epic, romance, lyric, allegory, myth, history, and more. The breaking of formal conventions beyond their generic variousness also connects these works. In Ania Loomba's view, for example, the nonteleological form of *Antony and Cleopatra* resists closure, and in Margot Heinemann's, this play refuses "a single historical or ethical center."[2] Together, these defining characteristics correspond to what Jonathan Goldberg, quoting Spenser, has described as the "endlesse worke" of *The Faerie Queene*, an endlessness more readily associated with romance and historical narrative than with classic drama.[3] Throughout Spenser's six books, refracting figures and events and reverberating words and phrases develop, modify, parody, or reverse perspectives and once stable-seeming points of reference.[4]

Like Spenser's poem, Shakespeare's play is also in good part about gender. It focally concerns one infinitely various female persona, a dramatized conception that can itself be seen as a variation on Spenser's multiple, refracted female figures. Shakespeare's leading male persona, again like Spenser's cast of refracting male figures, is also complementarily various to an extent less appreciated, I suspect, because harder to assimilate to still-conventional notions of gender. In my view, *Antony and Cleopatra* is also the pure embodiment of excess: by *pure* I mean "crystalline" or "distilled," and "concentrated absolutely," hence "conceptual." *Excess*, as I use the term here, refuses limitation by the quotidian. Virtually by definition it inheres in passion and multiplicity, and, therefore, like the imagination itself, has its basis in earthly materials. *Pure excess*, itself oxymoronic, refuses categorization and centering, and the most relevant native antecedent of Shakespeare's play that I see, besides the playwright's own *Venus and Adonis*, is Spenser's romance epic.

~

First to basics: dates and details pertaining to the plausibility of significant intertextual relations between *Antony and Cleopatra* and *The Faerie Queene*. Citations of, and allusions to, Spenser's third Book in Shakespeare's *Richard III*, a play written approximately when his *Venus and Adonis* was, establish Shakespeare's close, imaginatively processed knowledge of Spenser's 1590 volume. Evidence in *King Lear*, written relatively near but before *Antony and Cleopatra*, similarly establishes Shakespeare's reading of Spenser's second three books of 1596.[5]

In chapter 13 I have argued that Shakespeare's *Venus and Adonis* is "a seriocomic meditation on the landscape of desire and the kinds of figures it generates in Book III of *The Faerie Queene*," and I have joined earlier critics in suggesting that Shakespeare's Venus anticipates his Cleopatra. A brief recapitulation will prove useful. Aside from occasional overlaps in phrasing and imagery, the relationship between *Venus and Adonis* and *The Faerie Queene* mainly involves Spenser's Garden of Adonis and his strikingly thematized, recurrently refracted figure of a female bending over a recumbent male. This silhouetted pietà includes not only Acrasia in Book II, but in Book III also Venus (twice), Cymoent, Belphoebe, Argante, and Britomart (twice). Perspectivism, versionality, and gender are memorably written into the refractions of this figure: variously, lover, mother, virago, enchantress or witch, queen, and numerous aspects of Venus—*virgo, armata, genetrix, vulgaris*. All these topics and forms, rather than simply the focal, refracting image of the pietà itself, bear most significantly on both *Venus and Adonis* and *Antony and Cleopatra*, although the pietà notably occurs in the epyllion, as it does in Cleopatra's final scene with the mortally wounded Antony.

The further relation of *Antony and Cleopatra* to *Venus and Adonis* is well attested in critical studies and ranges from specific verbal echoes and rhetorical motifs to character and theme. For example, W. B. C. Watkins notes the extensive connection between the memorably striking "jennet and courser incident" in the epyllion and Cleopatra's imagining herself as the "happy horse, to bear the weight of Antony," an equine image of passion variously recurrent in the play.[6] Watkins also judges Antony's and Cleopatra's love, like Venus', an "obsessive disease" before describing it in phrases that suggest the Garden of Adonis, as well as other texts, since their love "can exist only by denying this world and creating a romantic paradise 'where souls

Eros/Death and Venus/Mars in Antony and Cleopatra   241

do couch on flowers,' eternally consuming each other rather than consummating something of greater importance than either" of them (35). Watkins' conclusion cites Antony's urgent, if somewhat desperate, vision—souls couching on flowers—prior to his near suicide and brief reunion with Cleopatra. It is worth note that Watkins' seemingly clinical judgment, an "obsessive disease," is basically the same, and about as trustworthy, as Octavius Caesar's.

More extensive connections between play and epyllion can be found in essays in the 1960s by J. W. Lever and Adrien Bonjour.[7] Highlights of Lever's essay include Lucretian fertility (with reference to Spenser's Temple of Venus), the striking fish imagery in *Venus and Adonis* (Adonis as immature fry) and in *Antony and Cleopatra* (angling as seduction, the salt fish on Antony's line), the pointed invocation of Venus and Mars, and the heightened antinomies, such as love and death, beauty and destruction, and creation and chaos (83–84, 87). Like other insistently thematized binaries—most obviously, Rome and Egypt, measure and measurelessness, spirit and body, eternity and time, male and female, together with the attributes conventionally associated with either—such initially seeming opposites mirror the constructs of allegorical vision, albeit not the narrative process of allegory itself, which can modify, assimilate, and exceed such binaries.[8] Bonjour, invoking specific verbal and rhetorical similarities, also relates the text of *Venus and Adonis* persuasively to Enobarbus' celebrated description of Cleopatra's barge and beyond this, to the crucial conception of her "infinite variety" (73, cf. 79).

The final piece of background I need is the acknowledged relation of *Antony and Cleopatra* to *The Faerie Queene* within modern critical studies. This relation is everywhere a point of reference in Janet Adelman's impressive study *The Common Liar*, and implicitly in her use of the myth of Isis and Osiris in *Suffocating Mothers* as well.[9] Adelman, an avowed admirer of Spenser's romance epic, refers often, at length, and in detail to Spenser's Books I through V, including the significant occurrence of the River Nile and the related imagery of serpents, crocodiles, and fertile flooding; the enchanting figure of the Faerie Queen herself; the sensuous, dominant, Venerean Acrasia and her enchanted, feminized lover Verdant; the emblematic figure of Concord, flanked by Love and Hate, and the hermaphroditic Venus in her eponymous Temple; Spenser's versions of Mars and Venus, of *Venus armata* (especially Britomart), of Isis and Osiris, and of Hercules, particularly as feminized by Omphale (a mythic precursor of Radigund); and Spenser's treatment of the virtue of Temperance.[10] Yet the characterizing appositive

Adelman uses to describe Spenser's "Palmer, that repository of common knowledge," is indicative of her carefully restricted, rather flat approach to the relation of the two works (123).

For a reader who knows Spenser well, some of Adelman's insight into *Antony and Cleopatra* actually seems to derive from her reading of *The Faerie Queene*. Yet these two works, connected by numerous common texts and commonplaces, in Adelman's seminal book also seem to be related *merely* as products of the same rich culture, as to an extent they surely are. It is finally as if even Adelman, appreciative but leery of further relation, is all too aware of critical resistance to the contamination of "poetry," particularly but not exclusively allegorical poetry, that is felt by some articulate *aficionados* of stage plays even in so egregiously anomalous a tragedy as *Antony and Cleopatra*. Adelman's phrase in *Suffocating Mothers* to describe *Timon of Athens*, namely "an almost allegorical purity," is revealing (165). I am not sure what Adelman means by "allegorical purity," but I suspect an assumed identification either between *allegorical* and *moral* or, more likely, between *allegorical* and *abstract* in the phrase. As elsewhere, I question such equations and assert that allegory, in its defining form, is never unmixed or internally unchallenged.[11] Abstraction, as well as morality, by itself is formally *other* to pure, or model, allegory, which not only has a material base but also inheres in narrative process. At this point it is useful to spotlight in my text a wise quotation from Edgar Wind, a distinguished historian of art and culture more broadly, whom I otherwise feature in endnotes: "it seems to be a lesson of history that the commonplace may be understood as a reduction of the exceptional, but that the exceptional cannot be understood by amplifying the commonplace. Both logically and causally the exceptional is crucial, because it introduces (however strange it may sound) the more comprehensive category. That this relation is irreversible should be an axiom in any study of art."[12] Wind's point effectually argues for the exemplary character of Spenserian allegory—allegory, to be sure, but also extraordinarily complex. It also attends seriously to the recognizable mutability and development that are essential to genre and to genre theory and that I have observed at appropriate moments in earlier chapters.

More recently and perhaps more notoriously than Adelman, Camille Paglia has coupled *Antony and Cleopatra* and *The Faerie Queene* in separate but adjoining chapters as expressions of Dionysian and Apollonian art, body and mind, passion and form, dissolution and definition, respectively. Paglia's broad-brushed observations deliver insight energetically, particularly regarding Cleopatra's "robustly half-masculine" persona and Shakespeare's Egypt as Spenser's Bower of Bliss.[13] "Adorne[d] with all variety," the kinetic, synaesthetically sensuous depiction of Acrasia and her Garden proves remarkably, imaginatively close to Enobarbus' vision of Cleopatra at Cydnus (II.xii.59). But Paglia's Dionysian-Apollonian binarism suffers from the kind of neat opposition that Spenser's poem and Shakespeare's play alike profoundly challenge: Apollo and Dionysius can no more be kept apart in the end (and long before the end) than can Rome and Egypt, Mars and Venus, the various forms of Venus, or, indeed, even Guyon and the Bower of Bliss—again, just for starters. If early in the play, Egypt recalls the Bower, where "nature . . . ensude / Art, and . . . Art at nature did repine," at the end it looks more like Spenser's Garden of Adonis, an earthly, mythic place "So faire . . . as Nature can deuize," where art itself is at once natural and everywhere evident.[14]

The limitations, as well as the heightened perceptions, of Paglia's discussion can be instanced in her remark that *Antony and Cleopatra* is "the most thorough of Shakespeare's replies to Spenser" or in her contrast between "the frozen iconic entrance" of Spenser's Belphoebe and Enobarbus' "answering" *depiction* of Cleopatra in her barge, the latter "Venus in motion" (213, 223). To the first, one response might be again to question—as I have in my chapter on *Venus and Adonis*—the reigning assumption that the only relationship possible between writers is mocking rivalry.[15] This assumption is simplistic, naively and narrowly gendered, and unhistorical, to boot. It often results from the habit of excising words, phrases, and short passages from their larger contexts to find quantifiable, "hard" evidence of "influence" and from the desire of an older criticism to base intertextual relations only on a writer's deliberate and specific *linguistic* allusions.

A sufficient response to Paglia's second claim would involve detailed discussion of the unfolding, fluidly perceptual description of Belphoebe, whose hair waves "like a penon wyde dispred,"

> And whether art it were, or heedelesse hap,
> As through the flouring forrest rash she fled,
> In her rude heares sweet floures themselues did lap,
> And flourishing fresh leaues and blossomes did enwrap.
> (II.iii.30)[16]

A response would also involve the relation of the description of Belphoebe to the numerous versions of Venus-Virgo to which it alludes both immediately and within the poem as a whole. Finally, it would involve enough contextualizing of the barge speech to understand its nature (both generic and specific) and its function in the play, which, in an understatement, have been variously received.[17]

I turn next to a still more recent example of reception advocating that highly rhetorical poetry and embodied drama are inimical, existing in a relation of simple, radical opposition and thereby opposed to my present argument. While not treating *The Faerie Queene* directly, *Shakespeare's Theory of Drama*, by Pauline Kiernan, considers *Antony and Cleopatra* a direct repudiation of the golden world of Sidney's *Apology for Poetry* and, correlatively, an endorsement of the real, brazen world of plain speech and physical bodies.[18] As a rejection of the highly rhetorical, written poetry salient in *Venus and Adonis*, Shakespeare's play becomes implicitly an attack on any such poem as *The Faerie Queene* and particularly on Spenser's poem, insofar as it is the major, conspicuously rhetorical, written poem of the English High Renaissance, one to which Sidney's theory of poetry is strikingly apposite.[19] Kiernan's perception of "the difference between a poetry bred by a union with the rhetorical past which is doomed to perish, and a poetry that is self-created and uncontaminated by such rhetoric" is linguistically naive and fantastically utopian. Nonetheless, it can as readily and ironically be related to the bejeweled vines and "christall running by" of Acrasia's wicked Bower as to the "ivory in an alabaster band" that, in Kiernan's view, Shakespeare's Adonis ironically becomes within the "circuit of . . . ivory" of the goddess Venus' embrace.[20] If Shakespeare is engaged in the parody of "written poetry's rhetorical excesses" in *Venus and Adonis*, he faithfully follows in Spenser's Acrasian footsteps. These steps would also have led him to the witch's creation of False Florimell in Book III, a walking parody of the sonneteer's idolized Beauty that is garnished with actual wires rather than hair and thereby a witty precursor of Shakespeare's parodic sonnet 130: "My mistress' eyes are nothing like the sun; . . . If hairs be wires, black wires grow on her head" (viii.6–8).[21]

Kiernan's argument stakes out theoretical ground that is either unspoken or spoken less provocatively in other discussions, and for this reason, I want to consider it further. Whereas Adelman discovers in Cleopatra's realization, "I am again for Cydnus," a return "to no literal Cydnus but to the Cydnus of Enobarbus' description," Kiernan finds rejection of the latter and a "triumph over" its insubstantial rhetoric (V.ii.227).[22] What we have instead at the end is "Cleopatra's body, standing on a bare stage"; it is this that is "'nature's piece, 'gainst fancy, / Condemning shadows quite'" (190). While

Kiernan's distinction between Cleopatra's "literal," physical absence in the barge speech and her presence in voicing her last, imagined destination is certainly valid in part, a single-minded focus on Cleopatra's body—her staged, boy'd presence—discounts her words and finally leaves us with a richly costumed corpse.[23] Missing from the equation of nature and body is quite simply the mind's productions and here more exactly those of the related functions of memory and imagination—the mnemonic imagination, if you will. To invoke a very different, modern context, a description of Proust that shares much with Renaissance Neoplatonism and Augustinism, "memory is active and human, at the place between fiction and desire, experience and imagination, poetry and history."[24] The functions of the mnemonic imagination are properly, if also precariously, distinguished from the delusions of *mere* fancy in sixteenth-century theories of poetry, whether dramatic, epic, or lyric. Variously conceived as the mind's eye, the sight of the soul, the icastic or the phantastic imagination, poetic wit, constructive invention, and so on, such insight is *natural* to human beings within both Aristotelian and Neoplatonic traditions of the time.[25] In Cleopatra's correction of Dolabella's commonsensible assessment of her vision—if not her waking dream—of Antony, imagination is precisely the faculty she invokes in the line above Kiernan's citation: "t'imagine / An Antony were nature's piece 'gainst fancy," quite a different piece from a body on a bare stage and necessarily, by Sidney's identification of poesy with fiction, a poetic piece realized in rhetorical language (V.ii.97–98: my emphasis).

Essentially, Cleopatra's affirmation is Sidney's position in his *Apology*, where the creative wit of the poetic maker exceeds the limits of the merely natural world, the physical "stuff" of nature, but where this human maker is also a piece of the nature that God has made. The fact of going beyond physical nature, whether by transcendence, excess, supplementation, sublation, recombination, distortion, or even reduction—"Heroes, Demigods, Cyclops, Chimeras, Furies and such like"—is basically what defines Sidney's view of the poetic imagination (100). At issue in Kiernan's theory of Shakespeare's drama are conceptions both of nature and of mimesis and fiction, and these bear on her radical opposition not only between written poetry and embodied action but also between heightened rhetoric and plain speech, the latter at base an opposition between figurative and literal dimensions that many of Shakespeare's writings engage deeply, variously, and as wholes. Kiernan's argument exposes issues that currently underlie any attempt intertextually to align Spenser's epic romance with *Antony and Cleopatra*. These include those coded "stage and page," voice and writing, "honest kersey noes" and "Taffata phrases," or, indeed, the "Three-pil'd hyperboles," that, along with paradox, Adelman sees definitively shaping form and content in *Antony and Cleopatra*.[26]

Strategically, Kiernan explains, "In the mimesis concept of art, the ideal [i.e, objective, goal] is a skilled imitation of nature that is so life-like we are deceived into thinking the imitated subject is the real thing" (8). This reductive definition of mimesis as photocopy is hardly that of an early modern Neoplatonist, let alone that of a true Aristotelian. If it is arguably Platonic, it is also already in opposition to the Platonic "ideal," and from this perspective, self-canceling. Kiernan's mimesis is a concept Spenser's Acrasia might endorse (even while seductively, subversively contesting the definition of "nature"), but, as Kiernan knows, it also opposes the mimetic conception of dramatic art in Shakespeare's *Hamlet*, where the mirror—"as 'twere," or "as if it were," and thus already a metaphorized, counterfactual surface—that is held up to "nature" registers such perceptual, interpretive, and questionably, ambiguously substantial characteristics as "form," "pressure," "feature" and "image" (III.ii.22–24).[27] Such characteristics are variously to be found in the mirror that Spenser offers his age and country, as well. Mirroring and techniques of mirroring, which include self-reflexive doubling, are everywhere in *The Faerie Queene*, conspicuous in both the Proems and the narrative.

Consider in response to Kiernan's definition, a relevant objection to the naively photographic conception of mimesis by the modern Aristotelian Paul Ricoeur, whose views have been discussed in my introduction to this volume:

> If we continue to translate mimesis by "imitation," we have to understand something completely contrary to a copy of some preexisting reality and speak instead of a creative imitation. And if we translate mimesis by "representation" . . . we must not understand by this word some redoubling of presence, as we could still do for Platonic mimesis, but rather the break that opens the space for fiction. Artisans who work with words produce not things but quasi-things; they invent the *as-if*.[28]

Kiernan presumably offers her naive definition of mimesis in order to accommodate the primacy she claims for fiction to that she claims for staged embodiment in Shakespeare's plays: Shakespeare's embodiment is not mimetic, she would argue, in order to prove it at once embodied *and* fictive. But this "no brainer" signals another purpose. In conflating the fictive with embodiment, Kiernan attempts also to claim authentic, substantial, or real fiction exclusively for voice, body, presence, and stage. Written, notably rhetorical poetry is in contrast disembodied absence. Thus Kiernan further complicates these theoretical binaries by trying, via transcoding, to equate embodied presence with the plain, worldly speech of Sidney's brazen world. All these distinctions and equations are bound for trouble, as a final example will demonstrate.

Kiernan draws the following contrast between Sidney's *Apology* and Shakespearean drama and in doing so identifies fiction with untruth, precisely the puritanical position that Sidney rejects: "Sidney claims that the poet 'nothing affirms, and therefore never lieth.' Shakespearean drama declares itself unabashedly a liar in order to affirm one unassailable truth, which is the impossibility of determining the truth. It is for this reason that its fictitiousness is the foundation for all that it attempts to achieve" (12). Sidney, of course, refers to fiction, for which his name is poesy, when he claims that the poet does not lie, and Shakespearean drama certainly more often declares its own ambiguous fictiveness than its falsehood, the latter the province of "the common liar" in *Antony and Cleopatra*.[29] Moreover, such a declaration, indeed such interrogation and exposure, of fiction is readily aligned in Spenser's nonstaged poetry with issues of representation and beyond this concern, even more self-consciously with its own frequent performance of representation, which any reading, necessarily temporal, recaptures. For a start, consider again the difference between the symbol of Christianity, the red-crossed armor at the very outset of the first canto of *The Faerie Queene*, the most obvious, trustworthy symbol imaginable, and Archimago's donning this symbolic armor early in the second canto, where the now-mock-innocent narrator's conclusive phrasing, "Full iolly knight he seemde" exactly replicates, not to say mirrors, his initial description of Redcrosse (I.i.1, ii.11). Shakespearean drama does not declare itself an unabashed, or common, liar, but like other contemporary poetic writings, and most massively, conspicuously, and relevantly *The Faerie Queene*, it raises issues everywhere about truth, about representation, and about the unstable relation between them.

Kiernan's notion of Orphic poetry, which, in the words of Gerald Bruns "seeks its transcendence not in isolation but in relation to the world of natural things," is suggestively close to Wolfgang Iser's conception of the fictive, which is not tied to "the old fiction/reality dichotomy."[30] Instead, Iser's fictive "keeps in view what has been overstepped," while it is nonetheless "an act of boundary-crossing" that at once "disrupts and doubles the referential world." The irony of my invoking Iser (another recurrent presence in my endnotes throughout) in responding to Kiernan is that his theory of the fictive and imaginary specifically references, thus privileging, Sidney's pastoral *Arcadia*—prose fiction, yet still "poesy" in Sidney's lexicon, insofar as "it is not rhyming and versing that maketh a poet" (103). Shakespeare, I suspect, would have accepted this analogy for his plays and with it the intertextual, imaginative affinity of his work with both Sidney's and Spenser's.

Turning more directly to the relation of *Antony and Cleopatra* to *The Faerie Queene*, I want to argue an imaginative affinity between them that their common cultural sources undergird—as more specifically does the combined relation of the play to *Venus and Adonis* and of this epyllion to Spenser's epic romance—but that these common cultural sources fail to account for credibly and sufficiently. This affinity is overwhelmingly thematic, although its themes extend to subtler and more specific effects: for example, in Adelman's thoroughly Spenserian word-concept, the "fusion" of Antony and Cleopatra in the end extends to the exchange of characterizing words and phrases, the symbolic blending of character that is basically allegorical in conception and a defining characteristic of *The Faerie Queene*.[31] The thematic ties that conspicuously bind these works include language and representation, as well as infinite variety, versionality, and endlessness, as I have already indicated.[32] In addition, they conspicuously include hermaphroditism and analogous composites or mergings, as opposed to, undermining, and exceeding binarism. Egregious among these composites is the oxymoronic linkage of eros and death—Spenser's Verdant and Mortdant, or fertile springtime and mortality (in both senses of this word). Another, related instance of this oxymoronic coupling in Spenser occurs in Amavia and Mortdant ("lovelife" and "death giving"), a pair impinging openly on the pun that unifies sexual and deathly dying. In terms I have used elsewhere in this volume, these thematic ties extend to the organizing, symbolic referents of Spenser's third Book, the Venerean flower and the Martian boar, and recurrently and insistently as well—Watkins might say obsessively, and Angus Fletcher "allegorically"—to thematized questions regarding the source and nature of vision.[33]

Introducing *Metaphor and Belief in "The Faerie Queene,"* Rufus Wood instances Antony's definition of the crocodile as "a telling critique of the imaginative sterility of non-metaphoric language."[34] In response to Lepidus' question, "What manner o' thing is your crocodile?" we find the following:

Antony—It is shaped, sir, like itself, and it is as broad as it hath breadth. It is just so high as it is, and moves with its own organs. It lives by that which nourisheth it, and the elements once out of it, it transmigrates.
Lepidus—What colour is it of?
Antony—Of it own colour too.
Lepidus—'Tis a strange serpent.
Antony—'Tis so, and the tears of it are wet.
(II.vii.41–50)

For Wood, this comically absurd exchange is directed less at the drunken Lepidus than at the literalism of Roman values and the perceptions of "things" informed by them. For me, it could not contrast more openly with Enobarbus' description of Cleopatra in her barge only five scenes earlier or more pointedly raise the issue of representation in language, specifically questioning the values of rhetoric and literalism, not to say of imagination and thing.[35] To remark that the same issue occurs relevantly in *The Faerie Queene* seems almost superfluous, but the significant contrast in Book II between the rhetorically heightened, sensuous Bower of Bliss and the heightened abstraction of the Castle of Medina comes quickly to mind, as do the strains "between metaphorical and material dimensions of meaning, between concept and history, and between words and things" that are thematic throughout Book V (a book that also features the myth of Isis and Osiris).[36] Along with other memories of contrast between the true and artificial Florimells in Books III to V, the metamorphosis of Malbecco in Book III (x)—an alteration which subverts his humanity (specifically his manhood) and transforms him into the monstrous figure Jealousy that his own mind makes—highlights the central concern of this book with the making of metaphors. Still more to the point is the contrast between the cannibalistic literalizers of the blazon who capture Serena and the rhetorical values of Mount Acidale, both instances in Book VI that openly, problematically, and relevantly engage the inseparability of vision from desire. Additional contrast between epic and other values significantly embodied in form comes in recurrences of pastoral (and even Langlandian) moments—for example, the future Redcrosse's being found in a furrow by a plowman or the gnats that recurrently annoy the Faerie fields; these are Spenser's nods to "russet neas" and "kersey noes," as any Elizabethan or Jacobean with a grammar-school education would have recognized, thereby avoiding confusion of such incursions of the low style with literalism.

More tellingly, however, the focusing of the issue of representation in language explicitly and insistently on the necessity, inescapability, and creative-destructive, illusory-insightful potential of metaphor is a denominator considerably closer to what ties Shakespeare to Spenser than are the common myths, as such, that they inherit. Likewise closer is the issue of moral framing, another matter of representation and interpretation. The insufficiency of such Octavian framing may need little urging in Shakespeare's play, but it should be noted that signs of it are famously numerous in Spenser's Bower as well, including the ambivalent narrator, the Palmer's interpretive commentary and woven net, Guyon's violence, the nature of this Knight's relation to the Bower, and the nature of the Bower itself.[37] The slippery, sliding relation between Acrasian beauty and Guyonic waste, as later between Busiranic form and emptiness, and the persistence of Acrasia and Busirane in what follows their apparent captures are closer to Shakespearean versions of these than any notion of "allegorical purity" would suggest.

Another specific denominator closer to what connects Shakespeare to Spenser than the rich archive of myths, the "stuff," they inherit and distinctively employ is what I have called the theme of hermaphroditism, of which the androgyne is a cultural and figurative variation not always distinguished clearly or consistently from the sexual hermaphrodite in this period.[38] No two other literary works in English in the period treat this theme more creatively, complexly, and to a more concentrated and focal extent than do the two writings in question. For Spenser, its focal treatment spans the cross-dressed Britomart's three books and then some, pertaining especially but not exclusively to her. In these books, namely III to V, it becomes evident that a binaristic conception of gender is simply inadequate; there are four terms, not two in play, or at least two in each of the major amatory players, Britomart and Artegall.

For Shakespeare, this doubling of gender involves Antony and Cleopatra equally. Consider a selection of familiar examples preceding their deaths: Antony's cross-dressing in Cleopatra's "tires and mantles," while she wears "his sword Philippan," one of several allusions to Venus and Mars in the play; or Cleopatra's startling desire that a message be "Ram[med]" in her ears, a desire doubly gendered by her possession *and* expression of its violently forceful, imagistic rhetoric (animal, gun, vagina), and her transferential relish in using her bended hook to "pierce / The . . . slimy jaws" of fishes, each of them imagined an Antony; or her desire to "Appear there for a man" in the first sea battle, "for" hovering among the meanings "as," "instead of," and "on behalf of"; or her marble-constancy, rock-hard, as death approaches.[39] Further highlighting hermaphroditic symbolism early in the play, Octavius memorably charges that the reveling Antony "is not more manlike / Than Cleopatra, nor the Queen of Ptolemy / More womanly than he"; subsequently, Antony violates his "manhood, honour" and suffers the figurative loss of his sword, or manhood, in the two battles at sea; he then dissolves or loses his firm shape even before determining on death, and dying he literally loses his sword, which is presented by one of Antony's men to Caesar, a passing of the phallus if ever there was one.[40]

As these samples suggest, instances of double gendering and cross-gendering accumulate in *Antony and Cleopatra*, and they also advance thematically as the play moves into its final Acts. Here also questions about the source and nature of vision become explicit, as they do with particular relevance in Spenser's Books III and VI, the latter taken as a whole that climaxes on Mount Acidale. Spenser's third Book centrally concerns the mind's—more exactly, the imagination's—power to project its own shapes on reality. Throughout this Book, the Venerean flower and the Martian boar, which I have earlier aligned with eros and death and with fertility and mortality, symbolically frame the quest of Britomart, the focal *Venus armata* of the poem. In the middle of Book III rises the Garden of Adonis, an earthly site where life and death co-exist eternally and spring is "Continuall" with harvest, "both meeting at one tyme" (III.vi.42).[41]

In the Renaissance, as treated in my chapter 14, a Garden of Adonis, from ancient times the term for a forcing bed or place of heightened fertility, became by etymological confusion of Adonis with Eden a "ioyous Paradize," as Spenser calls it, and the seminary of all created things (III.vi.29).[42] At the center of Spenser's Garden is a *mons pubis*, and directly beneath it the sharp-tusked boar, a traditional symbol of aggression, sexual passion, chaos, winter, and death, is imprisoned in a cave.[43] The recycling babes returning through a gate of death "in that Gardin planted bee agayne; / And grow afresh, as they had neuer seene / Fleshly corruption, nor mortall payne" (III.vi.33). On the Mount itself, Venus "takes her fill" of Adonis' "sweetnesse," and

> There yet, some say, in secret he does ly,
> Lapped in flowres and pretious spycery,
> By her hid from the world, and from the skill
> Of *Stygian* Gods. . . .
>
>   (III.vi.46)

Both in this passage and elsewhere in the Garden sex is collocated with death—much as in the pun on dying—and generation at once accompanies and alternates with exhaustion, even as spring with harvest and life with death. Mythic time here converges with mortality. Here grows "euery sort of flowre, / To which sad louers were transformde of yore," and Adonis, "in euerlasting ioy," discovers the continuity of dying with the perpetuation of life (III.vi.45–47, 49).[44] Here as well, the conventional gendering of the quotidian world is disrupted, if we believe the scholars who have studied this episode most closely and, indeed, our own commonsensible reading: Adonis lies passively and Venus takes her fill, and within his "subiect[ion] to mortalie," he experiences life "in eternall blis, / Ioying his goddesse, and of her enioyd" (III.vi.47, 48).[45] Understanding the Garden as an intense site of pleasure, knowledge, and power, Kenneth Gross describes it conclusively as at once "an ear[th]ly paradise," "an apocalypse that preserves rather than destroys the natural, and a vision of supernatural sources that survives being thrown into time, into the warring cycles of *eros* and *thanatos*" (209, cf. 200).

In the space remaining, I want to read the deaths of Antony and Cleopatra in ways that intersect with the Garden, as I have described this celebrated mythic place, which, it bears remembering, Shakespeare demonstrably knew.[46] In the fourth Act of *Antony and Cleopatra*, both after Mardian's false report of Cleopatra's death, as before it, what strikes me are Antony's repeated outcries: "Eros!" Shakespearean criticism has surely noticed these—time out of mind, however. No one recently has wanted to dwell on the obvious allegorical signal—"Eros!"—or to consider it the sign of a shift in register, a radical heightening of the mythic mode, one that is all the more noticeable for the practical Enobarbus' departure and replacement by Antony's freedman of this name.[47] That the name Eros exists in Plutarch, Shakespeare's major source, hardly diminishes the conspicuousness of this signal in the play, unless we want absurdly to pretend that Shakespeare copied history without imaginatively processing it.

To allude and refer to myth repeatedly in a play is one thing, but to bring it to life, embodying it in an actor on stage, is quite another. Antony's repeated outcries "Eros" are the equivalent of pointing fingers in the margin of a Tudor-Stuart book to attract and direct our attention to something important: "This grave charm . . . Like a false gipsy hath at fast and loose / Beguiled me to the very heart of loss. / What, Eros, Eros! . . . Ah, thou spell! Avaunt!"; "Eros, ho! / The shirt of Nessus is upon me. . . . She dies for't. Eros, ho!"; "Eros!—I come, my queen.—Eros!—Stay for me. . . .

Come Eros! Eros!" Raging like the Thessalian boar, Antony believes himself poisoned by a combination of love and betrayal, as was Hercules by the shirt of Nessus, but at the same time he turns in passionate desperation to Eros for some form of affirmation.[48] On his realization of Cleopatra's (feigned) suicide, his need quickly turns into a desire for mutual consummation. Traditionally, Eros is a god of death as well as of life, of *consummation* in both these uses of the word—*consummatum est*. In the lines I have cited, Antony's desire coincides with death, again as the pun on *die*, so dear to Elizabethans and Jacobeans, expresses this juncture.[49] Indeed, it is "with a wound [that Antony] . . . must be cured" (IV.xiv.79); with the reference to curing, one thinks both more readily of Adonis than Mars and more readily of Spenser's Adonis than Shakespeare's.

Although I am cautious, if not skeptical, of Christianizing efforts to associate Adonis with Christ in Spenser's Garden, such association certainly occurs in Christian appropriations of the classical myth, and for Antony's words it could provide another resonance that is shared by Shakespeare and Spenser.[50] Antony's curing by a wound surely glances at a sacrificial context of the sort Milton will invoke in his catalogue of devils: where "smooth *Adonis* from his native Rock / [Runs] . . . purple to the Sea, suppos'd with blood / Of *Thammuz* yearly wounded." Thammuz-Adonis, also identified with Osiris, was treated as a fertility cult by numerous, relatively popular commentators contemporary with Spenser and Shakespeare, and as later for Milton, as for many other early moderns, pagan belief is typically a deceptive shadow of truth, but nevertheless in a relation to it.[51] Again, such words as "resonance" and "glance" are appropriate to these mythic possibilities, whereas heavy-handed impositions of mythic equivalents are not. Their possible presence is as readily available to irony, moreover, as it is to the impulse of wish-fulfillment.

Antony's desire for consummation, as I have quoted it, actually frames the lines Watkins rightly, if inexplicitly, appears to have associated with the Garden of Adonis:

> Eros!—I come, my queen—Eros!—Stay for me.
> Where souls do couch on flowers we'll hand in hand
> And with our sprightly port make the ghosts gaze.
> Dido and her Aeneas shall want troops,
> And all the haunt be ours. Come Eros! Eros!
>
> (IV.xiv.51–55)

As commentators on Antony's reference to the Elysian Fields have observed, his desire notably revises Vergil on Dido and Aeneas in the netherworld, where Dido shuns her betrayer, and I would suggest he does so via a fleeting Shakespearean memory of the Garden of Adonis, which commentary has otherwise also related to Vergil's Elysium.[52] In a line from the Garden earlier quoted, which Shakespeare had already remembered in *Richard III*, Adonis lies "Lapped in flowres and pretious spycery"; and two stanzas later, "There now he liueth in eternall bliss, / Ioying his goddesse, and of her enioyed" (III.vi.46, 48). Like the contrasting frame of summonses to Eros and the imagined site in Shakespeare's lines, Antony is caught more discordantly than ever before between fleshly consummation and mythic desire. Of course he is caught as well between homoeroticism and heteroeroticism and between Roman and Egyptian allegiances.[53]

Shakespeare's character Eros kills himself out of love for Antony, a kind of total realization of his name. He becomes, like a simplified figure in allegory, exactly what he does. The sacrifice of Eros for Antony also frees, not to say forces, Antony to rise above his former self, if neither smoothly nor very effectively. In a speech initially addressed to the (allegorically) self-murdering Eros and then to himself, Antony resolves to commit suicide and then attempts it:

> O valiant Eros, what
> I should and thou couldst not! My queen and Eros
> Have by their brave instruction got upon me
> A nobleness in record. But I will be
> A bridegroom in my death and run into't
> As to a lover's bed. Come then! And, Eros,
> Thy master dies thy scholar. To do thus
> I learned of thee.
>
> (IV.xiv.97–104)

Antony wants to embrace death as a lover, indeed a bridegroom. Once again the culturally focal pun on dying is present, and he wants, in an absolute sense, to realize it. But the bridegroom Antony's running (or less climactically falling) on his sword, in view of the conspicuously phallic, often penile, symbolism of a sword in the play to this point, is remarkably hermaphroditic. If he is the bridegroom, here he is also the wounded bride.

Not surprisingly, while Antony does not finally fail to commit suicide, he certainly bungles its accomplishment in terms either of Octavian efficiency or Herculean strength. More figuratively, however, he reaches awkwardly, even with dramatic absurdity, to realize the complexity of an identity that has so far eluded him. This identity is a compound whole, a healing of systemic binaries, and of course it cannot be fully realized, as the pain of prolonged dying and the deflating falsehood of Cleopatra's feigned death cruelly bring home. As with so much in this play, however, the impossibility of such realization might be further challenged, and it is in Cleopatra's actual death. Although only Cleopatra can finish what Antony starts and close the wound he opens to view, a heightening of the mythic mode in his start is all the more emphatic precisely for its discord with physical reality, and it is also precisely what renders visible a significant, vital continuity between the two lovers' paired endings.

These endings are structurally analogous to those of *King Lear*. Antony's situation at the end inversely resembles the faux ending of *Lear*, where Edgar and Albany stand around moralizing about the justice of the gods and the wheel's coming full circle, only to have their vision shattered by that "Great thing of us forgot!"—death, in effect, cruelly real, unjust death in the fate of Cordelia, then the death of Lear himself (V.iii.237). The morality-play feint of Edgar's and Albany's reflections only heightens the tragic questions that follow it in the actual ending of the play. Where a pious vision is shattered by the end of *Lear*, however, mythic vision is reaffirmed and dramatically realized at the end of *Antony and Cleopatra*; yet with this difference: whereas Antony collocates sex and death, only to be painfully reminded of the difference, Cleopatra, making the same connection, goes beyond it to figure death effectively as (re)generation.

Antony's collocation "Eros!—I come, my queen—Eros!—Stay for me. . . . Come Eros! Eros!" cited out of its full context, is almost embarrassing, almost laughable, like his botched suicide. Perhaps another memory of *King Lear*, the notorious impulse to laughter noted at times by actors rehearsing it and by audiences in its actual performance, pertains here. Excess invites laughter and succeeds not despite but by cooperating with it, co-opting release and reality-check to vision. In this way excess can acknowledge the connection of vision with desire without simply being reduced to the latter and denying the creative value of fiction and figurative language—the as-if dimension of poesy. In effect, Antony's bungling runs interference for Cleopatra's vision by *constructive contrast*, both introducing a heightened mythic mode and providing a butt for realistic criticism that to an extent will deflect it from what is to come, even while paradoxically acknowledging the connection necessary to contrast, or meaningful difference.[54] Seen as deflection, Antony's death actually is sacrificial.

When the dying Antony is briefly reunited with Cleopatra, she bends in the familiar pietà posture over his recumbent body and wishes that he might "Die when . . . [he has] lived" and "Quicken with kissing" (IV.xv.39–40). Apparently now ceding such myths to her, he asserts in his remaining breaths, "Not Caesar's valour hath o'erthrown Antony, / But Antony's hath triumphed on itself" (IV.xv.15–16). His attention is again on Roman values. Or is it really? Given Antony's failure to commit suicide efficiently, his claim meets skepticism: his Roman valor has dubiously been reasserted. We might even consider his claim delusive or merely pathetic. Yet it might also be asked whether Caesar's conception of valor and Antony's are still the same (if they ever were) or even whether and how a Roman conception and Caesar's are identical at this moment. With the deaths of Enobarbus and Eros and the self-seeking betrayals of other followers of Antony, the nature and value of Roman valor are surely in question, and the redefining process of the entire play bears on Antony's present sense of them. Significantly, Shakespeare drops the word "other" from Antony's ambiguous claim in North's Plutarch that he is "a Roman by an other Romane" overcome, which could refer either to Antony himself or to Caesar, and instead has Antony assert that he is "a Roman by a Roman / Valiantly vanquished" (IV.xv.59–60). Shakespeare thus rewrites Plutarch to emphasize Antony's valor, but simultaneously turns this valor in on itself, making it more clearly self-referential, rather than necessarily an affirmation of a specifically Roman identity, which in fact it succeeds in extinguishing.[55] Antony's dying claim can thus be read as an affirmation of the distinction between Caesarean valor and valor of another kind. Antony's valor is now expressed not in suicide *per se* but in *dying*, a word and reality he invokes four times in his last moments with Cleopatra. As the familiar pun, this word-concept has a long history in the play, and its double-edging not only lingers, perhaps ironically, in Antony's memorably repeated line "I am dying, Egypt, dying," but in time it also merges with Cleopatra's own performance of death (IV.xv.19, 43).[56]

"Say I would die" is Cleopatra's message to Caesar once she has been captured and imprisoned in her monument, already, so to speak, a monumentalized prisoner of Roman history—unless, of course, she can find a way out of it (V.ii.69). This is the point at which she turns, as Antony did when he heard of her feigned death, to sleep and dreaming as the precursors of death and vision—on his part, a place "Where souls do couch on flowers," and on hers, "nature's piece" beyond "the size of dreaming": for Antony's plenitude—"his bounty," as she imaginatively recalls it—"There was no winter . . . ; an autumn it was / That grew the more by reaping."⁵⁷ Once again, imagination's forms touch Spenser's Garden, where male and female, life and death, spring and autumn, eternity and mortality converge. The biting of the asp, as the comic countryman will pertinently tell Cleopatra, is "immortal," a pun in which we will hear again both death and desire and with them the bonding of earthly and unearthly meanings (V.ii.245–46). Caesarean domination, which is necessarily hierarchical, fails to encompass potency: as Jean-Luc Nancy has tellingly observed, "The *imperium* is not the divine power of the pharaoh—and that is why in the end it will have divided up not so much the world as, on the contrary, the duality of world and heaven, the separation and the rivalry between two kingdoms with different forms of omnipotence."⁵⁸

"I have immortal longings in me," Cleopatra declares emphatically at the outset of her final speeches, which are punctuated by Iras' death and Charmian's choric responses (V.ii.280). While Cleopatra does not bungle her suicide, the interlude of Iras' sudden, unexpected expiration momentarily threatens the majesty of her performance, yet Cleopatra's spontaneous rescripting only enforces the easy, comic, natural nearness of life and death: "If she first meet the curled Antony, / He'll . . . spend that kiss / Which is my heaven to have" (V.ii.300–302). If this Cleopatra is newly ennobled, she is also familiar, comically human, and credibly continuous with her past—her passion to possess, however grand, little different from a milk maid's (IV.xv.77–79).

Cleopatra's words in these final speeches repeatedly imply the convergence of sex and death, recalling Antony's words when he, too, was resolving on suicide: "Husband, I come!"; "The stroke of death is as a lover's pinch / Which hurts and is desired"; "As sweet as balm, as soft as air, as gentle—/ O Antony!—Nay, I will take thee too."⁵⁹ The last two lines might even seem to gesture toward an idyllic place where lovers couch on flowers. Cleopatra's maternal image of the deadly asp likewise belongs to the matrix of generation and death—"Dost thou not see my baby at my breast / That sucks the nurse asleep?" (V.ii.308–9). The phrase "sucks the nurse asleep" can be read as "sucks to sleep" and as "sucks the nurse sleeping," either option making death gently and naturally, but only because also figuratively and creatively, continuous with life. Yet the baby's sucking the nurse sleeping is not so far removed from Acrasia's sucking Verdant's "spright" as to cancel a momently glimpsed negative nuance, the acknowledged possibility of an insidiously deadly draining of vital forces, another realistic intonation contributing to Cleopatra's final accomplishment.

The maternal and the phallic further combine in Cleopatra's image of the sharp-toothed serpent, itself an attribute of the Goddess Isis keyed already to myth. Dressed ceremonially as Isis, Cleopatra, Antony's "serpent of old Nile," figures the goddess identified by Plutarch as generation and mother of the world, whose moon-like nature is "both male and female, as she is receptive and made pregnant by the Sun, . . . [while] she herself in turn emits and disseminates into the air generative principles" (I.v.26).[60] Once again we are imaginatively and conceptually very close to the Garden of Adonis.

Cleopatra, like Antony, is "noble" in act at the end and perhaps finally truer than he to the old, "*high* Roman fashion." More than he at the end, she is also "marble-constant"—a phrase gendered stiffly, monumentally male, for she has "nothing / Of woman" in her. Even here, however, the pun on "nothing" is inescapably present—simultaneously a denial of female nature as inconstancy and a reassertion of its genital sexuality—as her climactic performance crosses the limits of sex and gender, together with those of life and death and myth and mortality.[61] Imaginatively, she meets not only Antony, but also the Venus and Adonis of Spenser's Garden.

17. *Patience and Passion in Shakespeare and Milton*

In *King Lear* and *Othello*, when Shakespeare's anguished protagonists memorably invoke patience, they do so with an unwitting irony that plays on the linguistic genealogy of this virtue, on its combination of passion and passivity. More than a half century later, Milton's poetry recalls the centrality and complexity of Shakespeare's engagement with patience but goes beyond it to render the traditional significance of this virtue dynamic and revisionary. In the unifying insight of the blind poet, patience becomes action, rather than simply giving way to action or being replaced by it. The traditional binarism of passive endurance and assertive action yields to a vision that is both unifying and originally nuanced. This is true at least until *Samson Agonistes*, whose concluding place in the 1671 volume, whatever this play's date of composition, argues for its reception as Milton's final word on the subject. In *Samson*, there is an assertion of external, historical circumstance untranscended by personal vision that is unequaled elsewhere in Milton's later poetry, and the result is a fundamental challenge to his earlier unifying vision, although not entirely a rejection of it.

There is considerable background to review here, starting with the traditional understanding of patience, then turning to its genealogy and finally to the time-honored topos of doing and suffering, of acting and enduring—*agere et pati*. This culturally fundamental topos—*agere et pati*—recurs from ancient times, especially in Homer and the Greek dramatists, through the early modern period. It consists of binary terms the nature and necessity of whose opposition both Shakespeare and Milton explore and challenge, albeit with differing results. Traditionally, the virtue of patience is the opposite of wrath, or *ira*. In the *Psychomachia* of Prudentius, for example, Patientia practices nonviolent resistance to Ira, whose many lethal weapons just slide off Patientia's armor, resulting in Ira's infuriated self-destruction. Other, more explicitly internalized treatments discuss patience as the virtue of controlling or suppressing anger. It is generally associated with monks, rather than with warriors and kings, and it tends to be gendered feminine, as mere mention of the tale of patient Griselda, popular throughout the medieval and Renaissance periods, might attest. The opposite of *patientia*, namely *ira*, although similarly feminine in the Latin language, is normatively gendered masculine as a character.[1]

Such gendering has been highlighted in recent criticism. Treating gendered heroism like Griselda's from the late sixteenth to the late seventeenth centuries in England, for example, Mary Beth Rose remarks an intense scrutiny of heroisms and the eventual "privileging [of] privacy and passive suffering" over public and military forms of heroism, and thus of "the heroism of endurance . . . over the heroics of action."[2] In her terms, this is a privileging of the female subject position over phallic heroism. More specifically in Rose's view, the subject position of Milton's Samson—his passivity, objectivity (subjected to gazing), enslavement, and garrulity—as well as his real heroism of endurance, are alike gendered female.

Etymologically, the English words *patience and patient*—the noun as well as the adjective—and the word *passion*, meaning a powerful emotion or otherwise the suffering of the crucified Christ, and the word *passivity* are all related through linguistic cognation. Their common parent is Latin *patior, pati, passus sum*, to bear, endure, or suffer. Modern students of the Renaissance are often amazed to discover the relation of passion to passivity inhering in the traditional conception of passion as something that happens or is done to you and that you control by reason, or not. In this view, instead of being either an active, defining moment of intensity or a responsible, freely chosen action, passion is simply a loss of rational control. Control itself is basically a rational act, in the fullest sense of *ratio* as not merely reason but as a system of value. Such control can certainly be a struggle. We need hardly go further than Hamlet's soliloquy about the Player's speech—"O, what a rogue and peasant slave am I!"—to register Shakespeare's probing of the traditional view of passion and thus his engagement with responses like those of modern readers and audiences. Hamlet castigates himself for his failure to respond as passionately as does the Player, thereby whipping himself into a frenzy; then he overhears and despises himself for doing so.[3] His loss of control, even if apparent in a sense, since deliberately induced, is succeeded by his reinstatement of it, once again if only apparent.

The topos *agere et pati*, to act and to suffer, to aggress and to be patient, has been studied extensively by Georgia Ronan Crampton in particular relation to Chaucer and Spenser, the former of whom she considers generally the poet of sufferance, and the latter, in contrast, the poet of active questing. As earlier noted, however, the topos *agere et pati* is at least as old as Homer, and it even aligns with the active and passive voices in grammar: either the subject acts or is acted upon, as the medieval schoolboy's "donet" or the Renaissance schoolboy's Lily both told him. *Agere et pati* also appears as a topos in rhetoric and as a category, or predicament, in logic. In philosophy, it emerges as act and potency and therefore as form and matter. A variety of authorities ranging from Plato to Boethius, St. Thomas, and Ficino exemplify its cultural embedding.[4] In short, this topos is everywhere, an outcropping of cultural bedrock.

Whereas in early modern texts, there might seem to be, as Rose asserts, "a newly and self-consciously constructed heroism of endurance that privileges the private life and pointedly rejects war," the traditional topos of action and passion perhaps suggests as much recovery and renewal as innovation (xv). Despite arguing for innovation, however, Rose also acknowledges traditional sources, such as Seneca and the Stoics and the lives of the saints and contemporary martyrs, in which general category I would include Foxe's Protestants, in addition to Loyola's Jesuits (xv). The relative salience and fixity of normative gendering in the Tudor-Stuart period is a vexed issue, of course, in which generalization must always yield both to historical and textual context, even as generalization continues to be desirable and courageous. But simply put, would medieval and early modern readers necessarily have considered the Passion of Jesus feminine? I honestly think this jury still out.

Turning to patience in Shakespeare's dramas, my purpose is not exhaustively to survey the topos *agere et pati* but to select representative passages that are particularly suggestive in relation to Milton's later poetry, that written after the loss of his eyesight. Patience in Shakespeare's *Winter's Tale*, while monumental, for example, is not to my purpose as immediately and fully pertinent as is the relation of patience to action in *King Lear* and *Othello*.[5] In King Lear, on the threshold of Lear's impetuous withdrawal into the storm, his pivotal speech "O, reason not the need!" moves from an effort to justify a need of the external trappings of status to the sudden recognition that his true need is internal: what he needs is patience, understood as emotional control, endurance, and even penitential suffering, although this last meaning is far from his fully conscious admission (II.iv.264). His recognition is partial and momentary, almost immediately giving way to self-pity, anger, and irrational futility. Toward the end of this speech, Lear talks mainly to himself, and his only choice of action has been reduced to not weeping. Where earlier he pleaded, "O, let me not be mad, not mad, sweet heaven . . . Keep me in temper, I would not be mad," now he ends his speech with the recognition, "O Fool, I shall go mad" (I.v.46–47, II.iv.286). His statement is at once declarative and promissory. That is, he seems to welcome the madness, to let it take him. His need of patience has passed into passion, imminently to be understood as the wrenching excess and anguish of the raging storm on the blasted heath.

In some sense, *King Lear* is Shakespeare's passion play, and what impels the old king into its central act begins with his half-comprehended outcry "patience, patience I need!" (II.iv.271). What is significant here for Milton's use of the same topos is the proximity, perhaps the continuity, of patience and action, *pati et agere*. In this scene, sufferance and passion are not merely successive, although they are so purely in terms of plot. In a more interpretive, more metadramatic sense, they are continuous, *beginning* to blend together. Lear's desired but unachieved sufferance in the speech becomes instead his passion, or suffering, on the heath. Yet there is still succession here, rather than union, and it is impulsive rather than fully conscious and deliberate.

In *Othello*, patience plays a less central, transformative role than in *King Lear*, but this word occurs with remarkable frequency throughout the play, and it is significantly featured in Othello's tormented and crucial speech during his only extensive interview with Desdemona alone before the scene of her murder. Othello first invokes patience as an antidote to the emotions attendant on his pain, wounded pride, and humiliation at Desdemona's imagined infidelity. Seeming to allude to biblical Job and speaking primarily, if not exclusively, to and for himself, he declares that he would have found a drop of patience had he only to deal with the raining of "sores and shames" on his "bare head" or with hopeless captivity or, in an image of submersion, with poverty up to his very lips. He adds that he could even have borne fixation as a figure of public scorn and continues,

> But there, where I have garner'd up my heart,
> Where either I must live or bear no life;
> The fountain from the which my current runs
> Or else dries up: to be discarded thence!
> Or keep it as a cestern [*sic*] for foul toads
> To knot and gender in! Turn thy complexion there,
> Patience, thou young and rose-lipp'd cherubin—
> Ay, here look, grim as hell!
>
> (IV.ii.47–64)

Patience and Passion in Shakespeare and Milton   263

By personifying Patience, Othello enacts the erotically and pathologically charged internal debate he is conducting with himself about whether to suffer Desdemona's supposed offense or to avenge it. On the one hand, personification serves to externalize and distance patience and, on the other, to make his interior debate more real to him. His feelings are conflicted to the extent that he still needs to justify his merciless plan to himself—irrevocably to tell himself that Patience herself looks grim, in effect assenting to vengeance. Patience, distractingly young and rose-lipped, is required to become fiendishly fierce and merciless, a self-canceling perversion, or turning, of this virtue (not to mention Desdemona) into its opposite vice *Ira*, traditionally, as here, associated both with rage and the devil. In Othello's monologue, female virtue and male devil, inside and outside, restraint and passion, Desdemona and Othello irrationally coalesce. Othello's labial obsession, recalling his earlier outcry—"Pish! Noses, ears, and lips"—further intimates his disintegrating, dismembering, dehumanizing vision (IV.i.42). As patience turns into destructive passion, his speech verges on the surreal. Othello's speech is the negative obverse of Lear's impetuous flight into the storm, but it is again a conjoining of patience with passion that exposes their emotional and conceptual linkage, if only making them one perversely.

With Milton, as with Shakespeare, my intention is to argue the relation of passion to passivity within the topos *agere et pati* by using sufficient examples, rather than to treat this relation exhaustively. Patience is a central concern throughout Milton's major poems, but a sonnet on his blindness provides the crucial text. In the formally Petrarchan Sonnet XIX, "When I consider how my light is spent," the octave significantly runs into the sestet with Patience's reply to prevent the speaker's murmuring, or complaining, about God's justice in giving him poetic talent and then permitting his blindness.[6] Thus overrunning the conventional break at line eight, Patience acts firmly and preemptively, as if aware of danger and urgency.

The sonnet and the famous reply of Patience together end with the recognition that while "Thousands at . . . [God's] bidding speed / And post o're Land and Ocean without rest: / They also serve who only stand and waite." This recognition seems to go out of its way to contrast rapid, restless, physical movement with "only" standing and waiting, yet the final line is oddly satisfying, conclusive, and potent. The purposeful inclusion of serving—whether understood as "making do" or as "doing something"—in the final line also connects it, despite the apparent contrast, both with the speeding and posting immediately above and with the more general recognition of the variousness of godly service earlier. Yet the truly crucial word in the final line is "stand." Simply put, this verb means more than "stand" normally does, and it does so whether or not we happen to recall the most relevant biblical text, Ephesians 6:13–14, with its martial references to the armor of God, withstanding evil, and making a stand, to which Roy Flannagan refers this line in his edition of Milton.[7] Indeed, for "fit audience" it is Milton's line that gives nonmilitary, Miltonic resonance to the contextually militarized biblical verb "stand" in the verses from Ephesians, rather than the reverse.[8] Further to assess the active significance of the verb "stand," just try omitting it from the line or else replacing it: "they also serve who only wait" or "only sit and wait." In the Miltonic context, "stand" is potent and makes even waiting, or expecting, appear so. I have often thought of Hamlet's famed declaration "the readiness is all" as an analogue to Milton's concluding verbs in the sonnet, but this parallel is not quite right: Hamlet's is a nominal readiness for action; Milton's standing is action itself—*agere*—and *pati* aligns with the waiting that ends the line.[9] Only together and with quiet strength, however, do Milton's verbs—notably, *verbs*—comprehend the conclusive answer of Patience: "stand and wait," *agere et pati*.

Briefly, in the interest of clarity and distinction, I want to engage Stanley Fish's perceptive ideas about this traditional topos, despite his not treating it as such. Fish would see the same meaning in the line "Bright-harnessed Angels *sit* in order serviceable" from Milton's "Nativity Ode" as in the lines that conclude Sonnet XIX, whereas I see a real difference in the later poem's dynamism and re-vision, quite literally, of the topos.[10] First of all, the angels in the Ode "sit"; their situation is simply more static, more in repose, even if read *in potentia*. Second, Fish repeatedly aligns Hamlet's statement "the readiness is all"—his nominal readiness, as I have termed it— with Milton's understanding of this topos. This may well be the situation before the poet's sight is gone.[11] Thereafter, however, Milton's sense of readiness becomes at once more internal *and* more active, and it cannot be both without registering a significant change of the sort to which Fish's sense of Milton's unchanging single-mindedness is inimical. I will return to Fish's arguments with my discussions of *Paradise Regained* and *Samson Agonistes* but not before touching relevant ground in *Paradise Lost* that intervenes between Sonnet XIX and these later poems.

Increasingly, Milton's major poems recall his answer in Sonnet XIX. In *Paradise Lost*, for the most familiar example, the poet praises "the better fortitude / Of Patience and Heroic Martyrdom," once more contrasting it to battles, jousts, and tournaments—to militarism in war or in peace (IX.31–32). Again, a balance of strength and passivity, agency and acceptance, is evident: *heroic* martyrdom, the *fortitude* of patience.[12] But an earlier, more tellingly defining instance is to be found in the negative example of Belial in Book II. Belial, the sensitive thinker, whose splendid poetry in the Great Consult resonates poignantly with memories of Shakespeare's Hamlet, Claudio, and Ariel contemplating death and interment, appears to worry the poet more than any of the other infernal consulters do and evokes from him more intrusively editorial warnings: "Thus Belial with words cloath'd in reasons garb / Counsel'd ignoble ease, and peaceful sloth, / Not peace" (226–28).

Not surprisingly, Belial, like all the other consulters, is a figure of perverted heroism in the face of devastating loss and thereby implicitly a negative parallel to fallen Adam and Eve, as to Milton, blind and politically impotent, and, as ever, a parallel for assessment by "fit," or enlightened, readers as well. Specifically, Belial perverts patience as endurance. Eminently, if superficially, reasonable, he is even the infernal spokesman for God's justice, observing, "To suffer, as to doe [*pati et agere*], / Our strength is equal, nor the Law unjust / That so ordains" (199–201). Belial's ostensible hope of improvement, hollowed out for the poet and his readers by an absence of interior change, is futile, merely a kind of easeful death in disguise. In a Spenserian pun, it is ironically "sensefull"—at once sensually-oriented and at least superficially commonsensible—in ways that link it to the honeyed words of Spenser's Despair.[13] The poet's harsh criticisms of Belial's sensefullness, timorousness, and sloth, and thus inclusively of his mere passivity—"Thus *sitting*, thus consulting, . . . [though] in *Arms*"—appropriately lead us to expect values at once more active *and* more interior in what the poem will finally endorse (164: my emphasis).

Another, essentially relevant passage in *Paradise Lost* highlights the *action* of standing, simultaneously combining it with the endurance and passivity that belong to patience. In this instance I conceive passivity in the grammatical sense of *pati* in which the subject is acted upon, rather than being the initiator of action. This passage occurs during the War in Heaven when the angels wearing God's armor take the hits of the diabolical cannon. The result is that

>   none on their feet might *stand*,
> Though *standing* else as Rocks, but down they fell

By thousands, Angel on Arch-Angel rowl'd;
The *sooner* for their Arms.
(VI.592–95: my emphasis)

The armor is materially confining, and because of it the interiorly unfallen Angels physically fall, in effect illustrating the nocent impact of Satanic invention on matter. Standing here is also clearly active and agential, *agere*, and, indeed, it is significantly *opposed* to armor that is martial like the armor in Ephesians earlier cited.[14] Standing is at once interior *and* an action. The verb and its essence, act and being, are one.

Paradise Regained, of course, is in good part a study of patience that is modeled on the Book of Job, as Barbara Lewalski long before has demonstrated.[15] I want only to look at the climax of the poem, the Son's stand on the highest pinnacle of the Temple, where Satan scornfully challenges him: "There stand, if thou wilt stand; to stand upright / Will ask thee skill" (IV.551–52). The taunting continues, "Now shew thy Progeny; if not to stand, / Cast thyself down; safely if Son of God," and it concludes with the devil's quoting scripture to evidence God's care for his Son. The climax comes in the Son's reply and its immediate sequel: "To whom thus Jesus: also it is written, / Tempt not the Lord thy God, he said and stood. / But Satan smitten with amazement fell . . ."(560–62). Throughout, Satan has in mind a stance that is merely physical, and his punning use of words with moral, ethical, and spiritual valence in Milton's lexicon, such as "upright" or "stand" itself, characteristically and reductively twists and limits their meaning. The Son's response atop the pinnacle restores a proper *balance* (to pun appropriately) between physical and spiritual, outer and inner, and action and passion. More exactly, it achieves a balanced synthesis of them. His reply is an imperative, yet one modified by a negative adverb and dependent on scripture: "Tempt not." More inclusively, his response is at once a physical and a spiritual act, standing, as well as a speech-act; it is potent but motionless, conclusive but unaggressive, at once simple and climactic.[16] It is effective, leading to Satan's self-destructive fall, which in contrast is neither freely active nor purely passive. Where Satan is neither in control nor not, the Son is both free subject and patient object. The Son's ambiguous—literally doubled (*ambi*, "both")—invocation of "the Lord thy God," at once actively grasps the potency of his own identity and accepts the suffering, the passive endurance, of his Passion.

While admiring the thoughtful detail of Fish's recent reading of the pinnacle scene, once again I wish to address it in the interest of clarification and distinction, since my own understanding, while different ("imperative," "potent," "climactic," above), might on quick reading seem similar. I see Milton's Son as a very human figure, as well as one divine, and his moment atop the temple as a realization at once internal and external, a kind of unified focusing *on and in* his figure of the sort of doubled projection found in Spenserian allegory: the narrative of Redcrosse and Sans Joy, Redcrosse and Despair, Redcrosse and Contemplation.[17] This is not merely a reiteration, a "jumping up and down in one place" of the sort Fish envisions; it is a realization, simultaneously subjective *and* objective, interior and embodied, and one not achieved before in this way or to this climactic extent.[18] Indeed, what may be Satan's most inadvertently ironic lines in the entirety of *Paradise Regained*, namely his own claim of sonship to God as he probes the Son's identity just before the pinnacle scene, receive their literally stunning answer when the Son takes (and makes) his *stand* atop the Temple. Explaining that the designation "Son of God . . . bears no single sence," and noting that "All men are Sons of God," Satan asserts, "The son of God I also am, or was, / And if I was, I am; relation *stands*" (IV.517–20: my emphasis). Moments later, the Son's answer, the *stand* that realizes his identity, is itself ironic by contrast. It is also intensely dramatic and quietly defining.

Analyzing the "Nativity Ode," Fish observes that the pagan deities are vanquished "not because of something the babe does (in the sense called for in this poem), but because of something he is" (321). Overlooking the parenthesis, which Fish's larger claims of consistency similarly overlook, I want to focus on the questionable distinction for this divinity of doing and being. If the babe is God in some derived yet truly agential sense, his *esse*, which is his being, will issue in an act.[19] *Esse* is a verb, and it is also God's mode of being, whether in traditional philosophy or in the Bible: "I am who am" is an utterance earlier resonant in the syntactical and lineal climax of the Son's realizing in *Paradise Regained* that "of whom . . . [the Law and Prophets] spake / I am" (I.262).[20] This active realization of verbal essence is my point.[21] The options Fish offers the Son in the pinnacle scene are Satan's pernicious alternatives, as earlier "the immolation of his own will" rather than his freedom to obey, or not, the more traditional expectation in Christology, and here the Miltonic one as well (336).[22]

Fish's options recall the false choice Satan presents the Son in the immediately preceding temptation of a kingdom either "Real or Allegoric"— earthly or unreal, historical or figurative, and in terms treated in my introduction to this volume, deictic or nondeictic (IV.390). Specifically, Fish's options now are for the Son to stand upright and prove he is divine, to fall and prove he is merely human, or to cast himself down in a willful test of scripture (383). The third option is absurd at this point, if not for Fish, or, indeed, for a desperate Satan. The other two are simply false, as is the difference here between doing and being for Jesus. Actively to stand is *to be* both divine and human, and to be both is thereby to act, thus fulfilling his identity, or being.[23]

Doubtless a major reason *Paradise Regained* and *Samson Agonistes* were originally published together is that they share a central concern with patience.[24] At the beginning of the play, however, nothing could be further from a figure of patience than blind Samson, who experiences himself "As in the land of darkness yet in light," living "a life half dead, a living death, / And buried" (99–101). The terrors of death and burial imagined by Belial return with a vengeance here, and in another memory of *Paradise Lost*, Milton's Chorus, fearful of Samson's despairing, early extolls "Patience as the truest fortitude" in an effort to counsel and comfort him (654). Much later in the play, when Samson confronts Harapha, Samson's growing self-confidence and trust in God simultaneously (and interdependently) coincide with the passing of his patience, understood only as endurance and passivity, to a notable degree into its opposites, passionate wrath and aggression. Here, his development touches that of Shakespeare's protagonists, Lear and Othello.

Particularly as a result of Samson's confrontation with Harapha, however, the Chorus' vision of patience and its traditional opposites begins to sound limited and too merely binary. Exhilarated by Samson's psychological victory over Harapha, the Chorus celebrates "invincible might . . . With plain Heroic magnitude of mind / And celestial vigour arm'd." Such godly strength can defeat "Armories" and "feats of War." Yet the Chorus goes on to describe this strength as simply the traditional opposite of patience, since "patience is more oft the exercise of Saints, the trial of their fortitude" (1268–86). Recalling for readers the pernicious, earlier alternatives—the *either/or* options—offered by Satan in *Paradise Regained*, the Chorus continues,

> *Either* of these [invincible might or patience] is in thy lot,
> *Samson*, with might endu'd
> Above the Sons of men; but sight bereav'd
> May chance to number thee with those
> Whom Patience finally must crown.
>   (1292–96: my emphasis on "Either")

The Chorus is still voting for patience, but it has clearly also registered Samson's increasingly assertive stance. Combining these possibilities or transcending their opposition is not an option the Chorus envisions, however.[25] At the same time, this is the very transcendence we have witnessed in *Paradise Regained*.

Even as Samson leaves at the end for the Philistines' assembly, he, too, thinks in binary terms: "This day will be remarkable in my life / By some great act, *or* of my days the last" (1388–89: my emphasis). Agency and death, freely elected action and the ultimate passion, still seem worlds apart. Then Samson's dramatic persona passes into the words of the messenger, who, like the poet, is inevitably now both narrator and interpreter:

> with head a while enclin'd,
> And eyes fast fixt he *stood*, as one who pray'd,
> *Or* some great matter in his mind revolv'd.
> At last with head *erect* thus cryed aloud. . . .
>   (1636–39: my emphasis)

Praying or thinking, affective faith or reason, the binaries persist for the messenger, as do literal and spiritual or physical and figurative options for reading the words "stood" and "erect." Clearly Samson's blind eyes are fixed primarily on interior concerns, however, and his physical posture, including the change from head bowed to head erect, reflects them. The relation between them appears whole.[26]

But Samson proceeds from this moment to the "horrible convulsion to and fro" that brings down the roof on himself and the hapless Philistines, "Lords, Ladies, Captains, Councellors, or Priests" (1649, 1653).[27] The savior Jesus and the slayer Samson contrast deeply in many ways, and these ways include their final fulfillment of patience, their reconciliation of action with passion, and self-assertion with obedient passivity—indeed, of life with death. Whereas Jesus' achievement realizes his identity and salvific mission, Samson's most clearly underwrites personal vindication and mass destruction. Yet symbolically, the thoroughly Spenserian series of comparisons that constitute the most telling stage of choric response signals a variety of ways to see and interpret this ending: naturally, as the "ev'ning Dragon," a serpentine predator, assailing "tame villatic Fowl"; classically, as the avenging eagle of Jove; or typologically, as the redemptive phoenix, a culmination of earlier allusions to the New Testament that invite readers to assimilate Samson's role to, or else ironically to differentiate it from, the redemptive mission of Jesus (1689–1707).[28] But to recognize the traditional redemptive potential of the phoenix simile is to notice its restriction by the Semichorus to fame and secularity, this worldliness, even if lasting for "ages of lives," that is, for all *time* and thus still worldly. It is also to note that any allusion to less worldly redemption heard by readers over the heads of the Semichorus has at present only personal, not general, application. The Philistine victims seem to have vanished from the "Holocaust" in the phoenix simile, and, with a more terrible irony than Milton could ever have imagined, Samson's tribesmen do not recognize themselves in the destruction. If they think themselves reborn in a worldly, tribal sense in Samson's sacrifice, they have failed adequately to associate themselves with its suffering. Instead, they translate and aestheticize it, along with Manoa's monumentalizing of Samson. The contrast between the perspective of the dragon simile, which is that of the slaughterhouse, and that of the phoenix simile, fundamentally lonely, worldly, and ironically distanced from the historical Redemption, sadly and fundamentally compromises the scope and character of Samson's heroism. To my mind, this is Samson's tragedy, and in Milton's play it is at once unflinching and wrenching.

While similarity of interior achievement signals essential value in *Paradise Regained* and *Samson*, in the latter, outward expression and fully historical realization call that value radically in doubt.[29] Throughout the major poems, Milton presses at the relation of the great binaries, at whose base a traditionally immaterial realm—psyche, form, and figure—conjoins with flesh, matter, and history, or else fails to do so satisfactorily. Within his 1671 volume, in the historical figure of the god-man, this juncture first gloriously satisfies, and thereafter in Samson, alive historically before Jesus but graphically, poetically, and Miltonically placed after him, it simply does not. At the outset of this chapter, I referred to the unifying insight of the blind poet, in which patience truly becomes action. Milton's printed gesture in his last major poetic volume realistically qualifies this claim.[30] Not relinquishing the achievement of interior value a whit, this volume starkly reasserts the realities of history and personal situation within it. These make a real difference, which must be faced, confronted, and acknowledged.

Milton's volume of 1671, double insofar as it contains both *Paradise Regained* and *Samson Agonistes*, eerily recalls the split reference that concludes Spenser's fifth and sixth books, as well as his Mutability Cantos, even as Spenser's final statements recall Chaucer's. Spenser's endings in the fifth and sixth books and the Cantos witness the difference between idealizing fiction and history: Arthur's triumph in Belge's land and Artegall's failure (or aborted efforts) in Irena's land and his subsequent pursuit by the Blatant

Beast; Calidore's similarly artificial, temporary triumph and the poet's vulnerability to the same Beast; the lingering loveliness of this world within its renunciation at the end of the Cantos.[31] In the multiple views, especially the epic comparisons, hence perspectives, at the end of *Samson*, we are offered only choices for reading, or interpreting, Samson's story, as we are in Spenser's final statements. In *Samson*, if we stop with the Chorus and Manoa, our choices are justifiable vengeance, traditional heroism, or tribal redemption, with the additional possibility of a typological dimension for the New Testament reader—all arguably positive, albeit with strongly ironic qualifications. But I doubt Milton does not expect us also to recognize the brutality with respect to "tame villatic Fowl" of Samson's final action, an action righteous within itself, criminal outside itself, and above all both severely and sympathetically compromised by comparison with the Son's achievement in *Paradise Regained*. Milton's two other major poems, *Paradise Lost* and *Paradise Regained*, openly oppose war, militarism, and violence. I would not expect less of Milton in *Samson Agonistes*, particularly since I honestly suspect, as have others, that in the volume of 1671 he is measuring himself against Samson and the Son, at once as pertains to the period before 1660, and to its aftermath.

18. *"Real or Allegoric" in Herbert and Milton: Thinking through Difference*

In the fourth Book of *Paradise Regained*, Satan tempts the Son with the intellectual splendors of ancient Greece, and these having been rejected, asks him in scornful frustration, "What dost thou in this World?": what connects you to history and humanity? Satan adds that his reading of heaven portends a kingdom for the Son, "but what Kingdom, / Real or Allegoric I discern not." With an irony approaching sarcasm, he goes on to say that he fails to see when the Son's kingdom will ever be at hand, since it is "eternal sure, as without end, / Without beginning."[1] By "Allegoric," Satan clearly means unreal, since merely figurative, and most editors decline to gloss the word, but Roy Flannagan offers the meaning "fabulous" and notes that elsewhere Milton relates allegory to biblical types. He then adds gratuitously that, "at least at this point," Milton "had indeed rejected allegory as a valid mode" (775*n*114). What Flannagan misses is that "Real or Allegoric," as suggested in my last chapter, is yet another of Satan's pernicious, simplistic binaries, such as heroic or holy, or, indeed, human or divine.[2] Implicitly, Satan equates allegory with abstraction, fable, and Idea alone, ignoring its defining doubleness and, in properly literary form, its necessary engagement with (dramatic) narrative.

Other commentators on Satan's "Real or Allegoric" prove more enlightening. Mindele Anne Treip explains that Satan uses *allegoric* "partly in a general sense of 'figurative' or metaphorical," and partly in "the older theological sense of 'typical' (typological)."[3] Satan thinks such figurative senses simply unreal, of course. Victoria Silver's more elaborate translation and extension of "Real or Allegoric" is similarly on target: her answer is that the Son's kingdom "is simultaneously both . . . that is, Milton's picture of the incarnation is conceptual, . . . a matter of how one envisions the experience of God; and this vision is [also] historical, . . . accommodated to time, space, and the exigencies of human being."[4] Here allegory is in danger of being conceptual and not historical, however, although Milton's vision is apparently both. Notably, Silver's larger argument will reenvision allegory as irony, another, less capacious form of double-speech, and this reinterpretive move will have broad significance: allegory, understood as an extension of metaphor, is creative; irony is skeptical and negative; characteristically, the one ventures and invents; the other undermines and exposes.[5] While all linguistic figures trope, or turn away from literalism, allegory is more directly, deeply, and fully rooted in the constructive capacity of metaphor, the arch-trope, than irony is, and the pervasive influence of allegory in Milton's major poems is crucial and defining.

A number of George Herbert's lyrics combine, while not merging, what Satan formulates as "Real or Allegoric," and for this reason they afford a clarifying point of historical comparison for Milton's practices. Often enough in Milton's as-yet-unfallen Eden, what is mimetically real coalesces with its signification, as when the serpent, possessed by Satan, rolls in tangles, to make "intricate seem strait" (IX.631–32). For the presently unsuspecting Eve, there is purposeful direction, or, iconic straightness, in the natural movement of the subtle snake; this is simply the way snakes travel.[6] Like the Miltonic narrator, however, postlapsarian readers see a danger unrecognized by Eve in this seeming straightness, and we also find coalescence between the undulating, convoluting physical movement of the snake and the deceptive Satanic intelligence now possessing it—again, an iconic correspondence, albeit one now duplicitous—doubled, or deceptive. The difference between our understanding of the snake's movement and Eve's thus coexists with contrasting correspondences for her and for us between serpentine movement and its signification. This difference, simply insofar as it involves doubling, is similar to that we get in the lyrics by Herbert I want to examine, but it is not quite the same. As fully as Herbert may materialize language in such poems as "Easter Wings" or even "Church Monuments," in the latter of which disintegrating stanzaic, syntactical, and even verbal form mirrors the dissolution of the monuments themselves, he, too, is at pains elsewhere to problematize the relation of concept to matter and word to thing.[7] While Herbert's explorations of this relation exhibit amazing variety and subtlety, only a particular, remarkable version of these concerns me at present: in this version, Herbert engages an ontological doubleness unlike that in unfallen Eden.

One of Herbert's best-known poems, "Love (III)," begins with two short sentences that quickly identify it as a love poem and as a brief allegory combining mimetic fiction with spiritual significance: "Love bade me welcome: yet my soul drew back / Guiltie of dust and sinne."[8] The unanticipated juxtaposition of "dust and sinne" is at once quite simple and quietly extraordinary. With it, the outer looks inward, and the inner outward; physical and spiritual face one another across a conjunction; the everyday and the sacred thus conjoin. Most strikingly, however, tenor and vehicle are alike on exhibit: "Guiltie of dust *and* sinne." It is as if two basic constituents of allegory were laid bare, the poet's tools given to us at the outset to employ as the poem develops.

Although "Love (III)" may be the most exquisite of Herbert's poems in this vein, his sonnet "Redemption" is another notable example of the sudden, surprising, simultaneous doubling of concrete and spiritual dimensions. In this sonnet, the speaker's resolve to sue for a new lease on the land he holds in tenancy takes him in search of his lord from heaven to "cities, theatres, gardens, parks, and courts," and then to the "ragged noise and mirth / Of theeves and murderers," where he learns that his "*suit is granted*," as, unexpectedly, his lord dies. Abruptly, this death shifts the speaker's practical concerns and businesslike manner into another register in which illogic rules and death is life. Here again in "Redemption," secular and sacred and vehicle and tenor are together openly expressed. Here, too, is the familiarizing and embodying of the spiritual and the sacralizing and spiritualizing of the everyday that are hallmarks of reformed Christianity, as well as of readings of Herbert. But as Herbert's sonnet also makes strikingly evident, here also is difference. Commerce and religion do not really merge, and sacrificial death is no more a renegotiation of commercial tenancy than dust is sin. "Dust and sinne" may be conjoined by *and*, but syntactically and grammatically these elements *openly* stop short of merging. Their difference is, in fact, also on display.

Close to Herbert's practice in the lyrics I've cited is a line within an early passage in *Paradise Regained* in which we read that the Son, "Musing and much revolving in his brest" how he might begin his salvific work,

> One day forth walk'd alone, the Spirit leading;
> And his deep thoughts, the better to converse
> With solitude, till far from track of men,
> Thought following thought, and step by step led on,
> He entred now the bordering Desert wild.
>   (I.185, 189–93)

"Thought following thought, and step by step led on" has the kind of noticeable doubleness found in the lyrics by Herbert I have cited, but again with a significant difference. As in "Love (III)," inner and outer, psychic and physical, conceptual and mimetic alike are not merely represented but openly and equally so. That "Thought [should] follow . . . thought" into the wilderness, thereby not only preceding physical movement but also preempting its customary idiom (foot following foot, like "foot after foot" or, indeed, "step by step"), is at least noticeable, if not slightly odd. "Thought [first] follow[s] . . . thought," only then to be mirrored in the Son's physical movement, and in this way it emphasizes and prioritizes his inner directive, even while harmonizing the one with the other. An interior sequence leads to an actual place, the "Desert wild," yet simultaneously triggers and neutralizes the shift in orientation from inside to outside and psychic to physical. The Son's apparently physical steps are easily read metaphorically as well, however—as steps in meditation rather than only in the flesh. This notable, if unassuming, line thus pointedly connects the Satanic binaries real and allegoric, historical and figurative, mimetic and conceptual, and does so without also making them markedly distinct. The Wilderness ("Desert wild"), the actual, outer place to which the Son's thoughts lead, is, for that matter, also a topos, a rhetorical and mental place, familiar to any reader of the Bible. In sum, consonance, more than difference, is remarkable even in these early actions of God's Son.

Before leaving Herbert, I want to look at what has always struck me as an open allusion in *Paradise Regained* to the end of Herbert's "Love (III)." This allusion, or series of allusions, further suggests that the differences in technique I have traced have content, as we have learned to expect in artful writing of this period. Put otherwise, these technical differences are themselves iconic. Not once, or twice, but three times in close proximity in *Paradise Regained*, Book II, Satan's words, offering a sumptuous banquet to the fasting Son, recall the memorable ending of "Love (III)," in which Herbert's speaker, responding to Love's invitation to "sit down . . . and taste my meat," simply reports, "So I did sit and eat."[9] Satan's invitation is first to "deign to sit and eat," then more earnestly, "What doubts the Son of God to sit and eat?" and finally with more force, "What doubt'st thou Son of God? sit down and eat." Like the ending of Herbert's poem, Satan's repeated invitation recalls Luke 12.37, although parodically in Satan's mouth: when the Lord comes he shall make those he finds watching "to sit down to meat, and will come forth and serve them." "Love (III)" is clearly a poem that suggests the sacramental supper, and in this context, it also glances in its final lines at the marriage supper of the Lamb in Revelation 19.9 and at John 6.54–55: "Whoso eateth my flesh and drinketh my blood, hath eternal life. . . . For my flesh is meat indeed, and my blood is drink indeed."[10] In view of the feminization of Herbert's figure of Love, it glances distantly as well at the Song of Solomon 4.16: "Let my beloved come into his garden, and eat." Satan's splendidly overwrought banquet is interpreted primarily as a temptation to gluttony and to sensual indulgence more generally, and like his other attempts, it is a temptation to doubt that ironically recalls the affirmation of faith over doubt in Herbert's lyric.[11] But it also participates overtly in the confrontation of plain and rich styles—the formal tension—that recurs throughout *Paradise Regained*, which David Loewenstein suggestively aligns with that between Quaker austerity and Cavalier or French courtliness, to the latter of which, I would add, high-church sacramentalism.[12] The insistent allusions to the sacramental matrix of Herbert's lovely lyric that frame Satan's temptation not only add outrageous blasphemy to it but also signal that sacramental ritual, with its traditional differences between surface and significance, material sign and inner faith or inner reality, may be inherently blasphemous. Such differences ill suit the Son's holistic identity in Milton's brief epic, the Son's divinity and humanity, and his restorative mission in the world.

In *Paradise Lost*, within the context of *unfallen* Eden, the Archangel Raphael speaks to Adam of the "transubstantiation" of material fruit to spirit in angelic digestion, and this passage has become a touchstone for Milton's monism.[13] In *fallen* Eden, Adam later learns that the obedience, faith, and charity of the New Adam, God's son, will enable the paradisal "New Heav'ns, new Earth" in an indefinite future (XII.549). This time when time ends will bring full "*respiration* to the just"—Latin *re*, "back," and *spiro*, "blow, breathe"—the recreative, re-breathing, reanimating of the material world and the full recovery of the progressive monist potency that Raphael envisions for humankind before the Fall and that the Son at once realizes in his own incarnate life on earth and universally and allegorically portends (XII.540: my emphasis).[14]

Leaving Herbert's lyrics with Milton's monism in mind, I want to look at the culminating images of *Paradise Lost* that combine real with allegoric by recollecting large patterns of the poem and thus exceeding the more localized terms I have examined to this point. Insistently meaningful, such patterns participate in the highly configured history of created being *Paradise Lost* has invented. They variously invite, persuade, and seduce us to expect significance, which they nonetheless deliver in cumulative rather than finalized form. They might be said to convey a perceptual process and a configuring vision experientially, and in this way, to enable its realization.

Like the "paradise within" and, indeed, as an expression from within its Miltonic precinct, the familiar images of the final verse paragraph of Milton's grand epic express a unified vision neither *Satanically* separable into spiritual and material or figurative and literal, nor reducible to one or the other term. At the same time, they remain in the end conspicuously open and unfinished. In them, the Cherubim descend to the Garden of Eden,

> on the ground
> Gliding meteorous, as Ev'ning Mist
> Ris'n from a River o're the marish glides,
> And gathers ground fast at the Labourers heel
> Homeward returning.
> (XII.628–32)

This pastoral scene is saturated with positive and negative memories of earlier passages, through several of which play patterns of fire and mist and light and darkness: the "dewie Mist" that rises from earth to water the ground on the third day of Creation, or Satan, "involv'd in rising Mist" as he reenters Eden through a river and then "Like a black mist low creeping" searches by night for the serpent; perhaps, in a typically Miltonic swipe at Establishment religion, even the mist that is "the common gloss / Of Theologians" or the mist that dims the inward shining of "Celestial light," both related, if less mythic, corruptions in the inclusive allegorical patterning of the poem. "The Labourers heel" at which the mist "gathers ground fast" recalls the cursed fruits of the Fall—the sweaty labor enjoined on Adam, and the painful labor of childbirth on Eve, as well as the serpent's bruising the heels of their offspring, itself a memory reinforcing that of Satan's involution in mist when he seeks the serpent. But the laborer's returning homeward, a secure and comforting destination not yet reached, also recalls the complexly suggestive image of the worrisomely belated peasant at the end of Book I and the related comparison in Book IX of Eve misled by Satan to an "amaz'd Night-wanderer" led to destruction by a phosphorescent swamp fire, or illusive *ignis fatuus*.[15]

The fiery exhalations attending the descent of the Cherubim at the end of *Paradise Lost* further invite mnemonic association with this deluded Night-wanderer. Recollection of the belated peasant of Book I comes with "calling shapes and beckning shadows dire," with memories of joy and fear, at once the exhilaration and the danger of the demonic.[16] Since this peasant "sees, / Or [only] dreams he sees," the Faerie Elves reveling by moonlit night to whom Milton's simile compares his demons, the peasant's uncertain perception casts momentary doubt on these devils' reality, disorienting and displacing our sense of Hell itself, where we have, so to speak, just spent

Book I. Thus this memory conclusively recalls the poet's recurrent distancing of his myths, his thoroughly Spenserian exposure of them as being precisely that—mythic. John Rogers' recognition of the two types of motion evident in Milton's imagery of expulsion, namely, "the celestial descent of the angels and the autochthonous ascent of the mist," to which Milton compares them, gets at the core of Milton's pervasively allegorical patterning of reality itself (172–73). These motions also recall the movement up and down in Incarnation and Redemption that is emphasized in God's final speech to the Son in Book III, a speech that witnesses the wedding of renewal to metaphorizing allegory, as I argue in the next chapter of this volume. Coming from above and from below, the cherubic and natural influences pointedly bring spirit together with matter, and form with content, simultaneously urging the laborer homeward and threatening to obscure his way. All this junctional doubling is at once conclusive and open-ended. The world it recalls and extends at the end is suffused with moral and spiritual meaning—simultaneously real and allegoric, and in the terms of my introduction, deictic and nondeictic, physical and psychic, real and Real. An artfully made world, it offers itself at once to belief and existence.

While less overtly figurative, the last four lines of the epic similarly render what is real, and what allegoric, at once integral *and* distinct, coherent *and* identifiable:

> The World was all before them, where to choose
> Their place of rest, and Providence their guide:
> They hand in hand with wandring steps and slow,
> Through *Eden* took thir solitarie way.

The joining of Adam's and Eve's hands, a motif signaling their relationship from our first sight of them, offsets the uncertainty of their "wandring steps," as Providence offsets the solitariness of their way. Their choosing where to rest recalls the role of free will, or truly rational choice, in the poem, and balances it with the reminder of providential guidance. It does so in a context saturated with reminders of Milton's view that memory is "essential to moral decision making."[17] The simple word "rest" is particularly resonant, since it suggests at once residence, repose, and death. The "World . . . [that is] all before them" awaits human shaping, but at the same time, for a reader of *Paradise Lost*, even more than for Adam and Eve, it is a world prefigured by patterns whose full significance still waits.

Stephen Fallon observes that in light of Milton's monist metaphysic, in *Paradise Lost* "the gap between image and idea [repeatedly] narrows, and

"Real or Allegoric" in Herbert and Milton: Thinking through Difference 279

metaphor verges on metonymy." While Fallon does not specify what he intends by metonymy here, in my lexicon, it is a form of homology and ideological coding that denies significant difference. It reasonably applies to what he describes as a poetic "world . . . not divisible into discrete categories of being, but rather a continuum of the one first matter," the world "of kind the same" that is envisioned in unfallen Eden by the Archangel Raphael.[18] In comparison to such metonymic substitution, I consider Milton's epic less settled and more dynamic, less static conceptually and more exploratory in form. The metaphoric patterns of *Paradise Lost*, at once constructive and uncontained, trump its metonymy, not to deny Edenic monism but in a fallen world to surround it with constantly shifting and thoroughly real questions of moral agency, origin, value, and final end.[19] Whereas metonymic monism is merely natural, constructive allegory is deliberative; like the apple tree, or indeed, the knowledge of good and evil, it involves moral choice.[20] Rather than undermining our confidence in the productivity of such a process, as would pervasive irony, however, Milton's allegorized reality everywhere intimates its ever-unfinished shaping of what he calls truth.[21] My next chapter will address these differences further, tracing them in the allegorical intertext of Milton with Spenser.

19. Spenser and Milton: The Mind's Allegorical Place

Of relatively recent studies of Milton's poetics, Mindele Anne Treip's *Allegorical Poetics and the Epic: The Renaissance Tradition to "Paradise Lost"* remains, for my purpose, the most historically significant.[1] In the Renaissance, Treip explains, Salutati's theoretical discussions of poetry anticipate "a practical paradigm of epic allegory of the kind Tasso would evolve, suggesting how the poet may weave together the entire linguistic surface of a poem, along with its narrative substructure, so that 'all' in it ('deeds', 'figures', 'things') will hang together in one subtle system as forms of 'translated' discourse, together signalling the presence of an underlying Idea or further sense" (22).[2] In such a paradigm, "extended allegorical metaphor" is the "'Idea,' 'Foreconceit,' or very long '*continued* dark conceit', working itself out across an entire poetical narrative" (23). While the foreconceit is primary and essential, it is embodied in "a text and aesthetic in which the juncture of narrative form and latent figurative meaning is indissoluble" (12, cf. 3, 42–45).

Treip insists on the importance of a line of influence running from Tasso to Spenser to Milton, one in which Spenser's poetry is a virtual "compendium of both all available recent and some older literary theories and forms of allegory." She adds that "Recognition of Spenser as an advanced theorist of allegory in Renaissance modes . . . puts Milton's tacit allegorical dialogue with Spenser into a correct and more contemporaneous perspective" (105). In these observations, Treip especially has in mind the major narrative structures of *The Faerie Queene*, but elsewhere she suggests that "Milton's most eloquent debt to Spenser lies in the verbal texture of his rhetoric . . . the constantly self-reflexive, self-echoing texture of . . . allusively allegorical language." Such striking and deliberate "evocation in *Paradise Lost* of Spenserian linguistic resources, as well as direct echo of *The Faerie Queene* and overt imitation of Spenserian allegorical devices . . . [thus] constitute Milton's true debt to Spenser." Among Spenser's allegorical effects and devices that Milton adopts, Treip lists "emblems, icons, dream-visions, allegorical landscapes, metamorphoses, . . . allegorical personifications, and allegorical 'Houses'" (135).³ The two instances of "Spenserian verbal-allegorical methods" enacted in *Paradise Lost* that she elaborates, if briefly, are the motifs of error and death, in which the "bare word [expands] to fictive depiction to allegorical figure" or, alternatively, contracts, I would add (136–37).⁴ Repeatedly, Treip acknowledges that Milton's plot is more "literal" or "verisimilar" than Spenser's and that his epic as a whole is more "neoclassically unified," with Spenserian techniques "more in the background" and "more strictly controlled" (135, 137). The final result for her, in fact, seems to be that "much of Spenser's influence on *Paradise Lost* lies beneath the verbal surface" (149). By the time Treip has finished with Spenser, she has managed to argue both the great extent of Milton's debt to him and its evident elusiveness. This is not an unreasonable position.

I have two reservations about Treip's admirable study, however, both relating to the level of generality on which it is understandably conducted, given its primary focus on Renaissance theory. Despite a variety of observations about the unity of form, content, and theory, this focus leads to her endorsement of Tasso's view that "'Words [always] follow concepts,'" and allegory itself becomes Idea rather than the tensive, evolving interaction of concept and embodied narrative for which I have often argued in this volume. As Treip amplifies Tasso's view, "Body and thought, dress and Platonic Idea, concrete particulars and allegory, mesh in an indivisible perfection of transcendental thought given palpable and visible form" (74).⁵ Meshing of terms aside, the first of each set she enumerates is subordinate to the second, and the description as a whole is both too simply binaristic and, paradoxically, too simply harmonious adequately to characterize the kind of provisional and open-ended allegory that Spenser practices. Expression merely as dress (in a twentieth-century amplification) and allegory as abstraction, here the opposite of body and concrete particulars, seem to me fundamentally misconceived.⁶ Formulations like these miss the shaping value, or influence, of language and the agency of the signifier itself, whether understood as a single word, a figure, or an image in the writing of Spenser and Milton alike, an agency that is swept into the process of their poems, enlarging, modifying, surprising, shifting, and ostensibly subverting this process on numerous occasions. Allegorical process, particularly through embodied narrative, modifies and destabilizes initially contained, abstract identities, such as holiness, temperance, reason, or, indeed, error and death, and the essentially, irreducibly coupled terms of literary allegory—*deictic* and *nondeictic*, particular and universal, concrete and abstract, material and moral, natural and emblematic, real and Real—are also never wholly free of contradiction, which is a given, seemingly an inescapable condition, at once of language itself, more specifically of fictive language, and supremely of hyperlinguistic allegorical form.[7] This is as true for expressions of Milton's monism in the fallen world, which is the only one we have, as of Spenser's similarly qualified Neoplatonism.

Good and evil, as Milton well knew, are joined at the hip, and truth is a streaming fountain—always moving, always changing, never wholly stable or fixed.[8] Their relation to matter is problematic, moreover, as he also knew. Materially, any being can potentially move up to heaven's rarity and down to hell's density on a dynamic continuum, but categories other than exclusively material ones, such as good, evil, justice, and freedom exist within culture, faith, and ideology, and they radically affect the evaluation and therefore the (tricky) reality of material movement, equivocal or mediating spirit(s) notwithstanding. The problematical relations of matter and morality, indeed, of material substance and faith, extend to language and rhetoric. If everything is absolutely material, then, as Hobbes knew, nothing at all is truly figurative, an assumption whose inherent, self-canceling ambiguity is blatant. Indeed, is not nothing itself always already a figure? Even a dead metaphor such as "the book says" is untrue for Hobbes, while everywhere and otherwise in culture it pertains intuitively.[9] If allegory is basically "continued metaphor," the common Renaissance perception that I find undeniable, then it is a contiguous form in which tension between its dual elements (tenor and vehicle, concepts and narrative embodiments) is defining, as Paul Ricoeur has extensively and persuasively argued regarding metaphor. Their common identity will always be and not be; at their most concordant, they will join fictively, that is, *as if*.[10] Having argued at length in two of my recent books—*Words That Matter* and *Translating Investments*—for a complexity of linguistic, as well as specifically rhetorical, perception and practice in the sixteenth and seventeenth centuries, I confess that I do not consider Treip's more idealized and, correlatively, less problematized sense of these any more historical or theoretical than my own.[11]

My second reservation about Treip's study relates to the first. A study of influence punctuated by recognition of a need to demonstrate it in greater detail and by apologies for not doing so has a curiously mixed effect. Enumerations of similarities have a kind of weight, but they are likely to leave a reader somewhat skeptical: "emblems, icons, dream-visions, allegorical landscapes, metamorphoses, . . . allegorical personifications, and allegorical 'Houses'" are to be found in many poetic narratives in the medieval and

Tudor periods, some arguably more allegorical than others, and whether and where they are found in *Paradise Lost* and how they function there surely need to be laid out in greater detail. How is Spenser's hell or, perhaps, his Cave of Mammon, "That to the gate of Hell . . . [is] next adioyning," similar to Milton's hell, for example, or if (emphatic *if*) Milton's God is "one of his [Milton's] most radically allegorical constructs," is he so in specifically Spenserian ways (238)?[12] Does the double vision of Milton's Edenic landscapes resemble the great variety of allegorical landscapes in *The Faerie Queene* in specific or only in generic ways (246–47)? Without close textual engagement, Milton's relation to Spenser remains too general, too abstract, insubstantial, and unrealized to be persuasive, despite the many verbal echoes of Spenser that editions of Milton duly remark. At the end of Treip's study of historically theorized Renaissance allegory, Spenser's and Milton's major poems may still seem as different as their surfaces can seem on first impression. Like Treip, I am skeptical of such a first impression, which too often is the result of misunderstandings of allegory, realism, and symbolism that still linger in our culture.[13] With the assistance of her efforts, I hope to get beyond it by looking at the mind's own place in these two broadly ideational—in Treip's sense, "allegorical"—epics in question. The "mind's own place," the title of this chapter, is a phrase that obviously derives from Satan's celebrated declaration of solipsism, and it necessarily entails a focus on Satan in the pages to follow. This focus will prove no more limited to him, however, than are evil, its effects, and its relation to God in Milton's grand epic.

In a paradigm of poetic development, the opening verse paragraph of *Paradise Lost* is a genesis for poet, poem, and reader. It moves from past to present and from history to conviction and thus from outer, historical events like the Creation and Fall, to inner ones: "What in me is dark / Illumin, what is low raise and support."[14] Further developing this paradigm, the poet's voice next moves directly to question his Muse, or S/spirit, both an outer and inner influence, and his questions implicitly issue in inspired responses to generate the *ground-plot* of the poem: "say first what cause / Mov'd our Grand Parents . . . to fall off / From thir Creator . . . Who first seduc'd them to that foul revolt? / Th' infernal Serpent; he it was, whose guile / . . . deceiv'd / The Mother of Mankind" (I.27–36).[15] Pertinently, as Forrest G. Robinson explains, the term *ground-plot*, a concept used famously by Sidney in his *Apology for Poetry*, is a metaphor at once with architectural, literary, pictorial ("ground"), mathematical, scientific, rhetorical, and logical connections; as such, its reference to Milton's purpose is almost perfect. Here, *in nuce*, must truly be the Idea of the poem, which, like the "plot" of a Renaissance mathematician, collocates "ideas or intellectually determinate relationships presented in visible form."[16]

Even while making a connection here between the ground-plot and the all-encompassing Idea of an allegorical epic, as expounded by Treip, however, I want once more to register a brief demurrer. The plot, or relational ground-plot, of an epic is not quite the same as an Idea, no matter how universal. As Ricoeur, interpreting Aristotle's *Poetics*, indicates, the plot of a story is an organization of action and events; it is narrative, not theme, and it is progressive and recursive, not simply thetic and static. Allegory is both, as I have additionally argued in my introduction to this book in relation to Ricoeur's theory of historical time. Potentially, moreover, allegory itself evolves as a form within and between poems: interextual allegorical form is dynamic.

By line 84 of *Paradise Lost*, the ground of immediate action in the poem has been established, and Satan first speaks. He does so already in a ventriloquized, or borrowed, voice—"If thou beest he; But O how fall'n! How chang'd / From him who in the happy Realms of Light / Cloth'd with transcendent brightness didst out-shine / Myriads though bright." Echoing the words of Vergil's Aeneas to the ghost of Hector on the night Troy falls, Satan quickly assumes the dress of traditional heroism.[17] He addresses Beelzebub, his closest subordinate, as if the latter were a mirror image in whom Satan either does not or cannot recognize himself.[18] In doing so, he also assumes the most strikingly characteristic situation of Spenser's Redcross Knight, for whom many of the other figures of Book I are mirror images, or his own projections, unrecognized by this ever more errant knight: Fradubio, Sans Joy, Orgoglio, Despair, to instance only some of the more obvious.

Between the outline of the ground-plot and Satan's opening exclamation, the poet begins to give more substantial expression to the ground of Satan's heroic figure, or, as yet only his heroic voice, setting the opening scene and establishing its site in a way that quickly activates the trademark Spenserian play on the concept of "sight"—a place both topographical and rhetorically topical, and at once a percept and a perceiving. In a paradigmatic episode early in the first book of *The Faerie Queene*, for example, Redcrosse, aroused by Archimago to witness the lust of the impersonating false Una and her false squire, experiences the "bitter anguish of his guilty sight," simultaneously the guilty sight seen and his guilty sight seeing (ii.6). Outside and inside mirror one another, and the question of which is originary begins to become unendingly recessive: Redcrosse, in abandoning Una, is soon to fly "from his thoughts and gealous feare"; the false lust he has witnessed has arisen at once from within him and through the diabolical machinations of Archimago, "the old man," the *vetus homo*, whose body is that of this death, and thus at once a reality and a nonentity and at once within and without him (I.ii.5, 12).[19] This is the Bible's Old Man who has failed to put on the New, as urged in Ephesians 4:22–24, and he is also the shadow, indeed the infernal shade, who, we come to realize, accompanies Satan from our first sight—more exactly, our first sound—of him, resonant with the memory of Hector's death. Of course "the body of this death" leads back, unerringly, to the story of the Fall, and thence to Satan's rebellion and the origin of evil, and thus returns us to Milton's *ground-plot*.

Spenser's plot is broadly similar. From the point at which Redcrosse flies from Una (oneness, unity) into an illusory condition of duplicity—double vision, double language, double being, *Duo-esse*—until his rescue by Arthur, reformation in the House of Holiness, and fight with the hell-mouthed dragon, which is a huge accretive, climactic image of evil, the knight wanders primarily in a landscape in which death, "a shade . . . Vnbodied, vnsoul'd, vnheard, vnseene," takes ever more substantial forms: Lucifera's morally and physically diseased counselors, Orgoglio's castle and dungeon, Despair (I.ii.6, VII.vii.46). This landscape the knight traverses is at once real, that is, temporally and epistemologically existent in the space/time of narrative, as well in the world of history to which it alludes, and it is illusory, a mirror of morally diseased vision. In a word, it is double, and it is also and inseparably progressive, evolving.

The infernal site, or "Situation waste and wilde," into which Satan—proleptically already the "Serpent"—falls is from its first mention marked by ambiguity, indefinition, oxymoron, and illogic (I.34, 60). Having just read that Satan's pride casts him out of heaven, we next learn that God's power is what drives him hellward: "Him the Almighty Power / Hurld headlong flaming from th' Ethereal Skie / With hideous ruine and combustion down / To bottomless perdition" (I.44–47). Moreover, until we reach lines subsequent to the ones just cited, we could take the participle "flaming" to modify "Almighty Power" rather than "Him," Satan. For a moment God's powerful wrath, like Jovian thunderbolts, seems to co-operate in the fiery descent of Satan to a perdition that is bottomless, rendering a single cause of his fall less assuredly clear and therefore, if fleetingly, already doubtful.

From the outset, noticeably unstable syntax, which, insofar as syntax is the rational ordering of language, intimates irrationality, accompanies Satan's open-ended and never ending descent to "bottomless perdition." As diction, "bottomless perdition" is both marvelously, imaginatively expansive and further irrational—inherently contradictory, since bottomlessness is intelligible only through its relation to the positive, visual, concrete conception of a bottom, or limit. In "bottomless perdition," concrete and abstract, tangible and intangible, thingness and nothingness thus already merge in *unwholly* union.[20] Much the same might be said of the even more celebrated phrase "darkness visible" later in the same verse paragraph and also of such phrases as the "vast abrupt" or the "palpable obscure" in Beelzebub's subsequent depiction of the chaotic space Satan will traverse from hell to earth. In these last two Miltonic phrases, the further substantive instability of adjective for noun, or, indeed, in traditional, categorical terms, of accident for essence, is added (I.63, II.406, 409). Such signature phrases by Milton feed the imagination while, paradoxically, resisting visualization. They brilliantly substantialize nothingness, not unlike evil itself.[21] A specifically hellish place in *The Faerie Queene* offers an affectively applicable description, since in this place, "darkenesse dred and daily night did houer / Through all the inner parts, wherein they dwelt . . . which delt / A doubtfull sense of things, not so well seene, as felt." Surrounded by "griesly ['horrible, terrible'] theeues," Spenser's character thinks "her self in hell, / Where with such damned fiends she should in darknesse dwell" (VI.x.42–43).

In both Spenser's and Milton's epics, a resistance to visualization can, like most techniques, be turned to positive or negative effect: for a positive example in Spenser, the Garden of Adonis, where this resistance ensures an imaginative distance from everyday reality, or, for a negative one, at moments in the highly visual tempting of the House of Busirane, where the marchers fade in and out of pictorial realization and intense looking amazes Britomart, "The whiles the passing brightnes her fraile senses dazd" (III.xi.49); for examples in Milton, negatively not only at times in hell, but also positively in our first view of heaven, where concept and voice, not *visual* image, are realized, and, when rarely seeming otherwise, the "Fountain of Light" still sits invisibly "Amidst the glorious brightness" of his throne, through a cloud shading "The full blaze . . . of [his] beams" so that, "like a radiant Shrine, / Dark with excessive bright . . . [his] Skirts appeer, / Yet dazle Heav'n" (III.375–81). Metaphorical imagery gives the impression of substance to invisible being. In using the word "metaphorical," I speak from a fallen perspective, of course; for Milton, this biblically informed imagery is arguably metonymic and thereby visionary. Such differences will return for discussion near the end of this chapter.

Still within the second verse paragraph of *Paradise Lost*, which occurs right before Satan's first words, another series of lines more insistently exhibits an irrational surface. They convey Satan's sight, at once what he sees and the experience of his seeing:

> At once as far as Angels kenn he views
> The dismal Situation waste and wilde,
> A Dungeon horrible, on all sides round
> As one great Furnace flam'd, yet from those flames
> No light, but rather darkness visible
> Serv'd onely to discover sights of woe,
> Regions of sorrow, doleful shades, where peace
> And rest can never dwell, hope never comes
> That comes to all.
>
> (I.59–67)

The pun on "sights" and "sites" is explicit in the sixth line. As Alastair Fowler, among others, has noted, expression in the first four lines of this passage is also exceedingly irrational.[22] To begin with, "kenn" is either a verb or a noun, which might be glossed with fitting ambiguity as "view," and "Angels" could be a plural subject of verbal "kenn" or a singular or plural possessive of nominal "kenn." "A Dungeon horrible" could be an appositive to "Situation waste and wilde" or, with deletion of the comma after "horrible" on grounds of the unreliability of accidentals in the poem, "Dungeon" could be the subject of "flamd" as an intransitive verb. Alternatively, "flam'd" could be a participle modifying "Furnace"—"Furnace flam'd," or "fired up," "roaring." Irrationality so conspicuous asks for attention. One line later in the passage, "darkness visible" serves as the immediate gloss: instability and paradox are distinctive characteristics of this landscape, this topos or place, this mirror of the mind perceiving, which is that of Milton's character Satan. He sees (and, through his eyes, we see) without seeing. Here rational distinctions themselves are elusive, shifting, and unreliable.

Hell is indeed the mind's own place, at once a classic instance of projection allegory and, in modern terms, a kind of objective correlative: that is, the expression of a state of mind, an attitude, or a condition as an externalized object or a place.[23] In such projection or objectification, however, the vehicle and not only the interior condition or concept has substantive existence—thereness.[24] Such substantive existence does not extend merely to abstractive translations and transcodings of the vehicle, such as those typically belonging to psychoanalytic theory. Spenser's hell in Book I is likewise strikingly such a correlative, as is his glittery, discontented, diseased House of Pride, which is revealed to be merely hell's surface, pridefully emergent in what only appears to be the waking world. Paradoxically, this surface also alludes openly to the historical world, as the court of the maiden Queen Lucifera inescapably aligns with that of Elizabeth I, whether potentially, partially, or fully. Satan's hell has similarly been aligned with tyrannical rule, and Satan himself either with Charles I or Oliver Cromwell or with other political players, all seen as real-world expressions of Milton's ideational narrative.[25] Coincidentally, a multiplicity of possible and actual references is typical of historical allegory, insofar as this form variously embodies and situates generalized concepts in narrative: like Satan, Duessa (duplicity or doubleness) has many historical faces and occasions that enable the exploration of relationships among them, the reassessment of values, or the production of meaningful possibilities.

The most immediately accessible instance, since brief, of a paradigmatic parallel in Spenser to the content-laden form of the lines that substantiate the landscape of Milton's hell may come at the end of the Fradubio episode in Spenser's first book. In this episode, Redcrosse hears from the tree-man Fradubio, a human figure rooted in the arboreal matter that symbolizes flesh, his own story of doubt and betrayal as it is presently occurring and fails utterly to recognize its pertinence to himself. Intent on distracting Redcrosse from the warning embedded in Fradubio's story, the disguised Duessa feigns a faint:

> Her eyelids blew
> And dimmed sight with pale and deadly hew
> At last she vp gan lift: with trembling cheare
> Her vp he tooke, too simple and too trew,
> And oft her kist. At length all passed feare,
> He set her on her steede, and forward forth did beare.
> (I.ii.45)

Ambiguities of syntax and reference in this passage mirror the duplicities of Redcrosse's situation, much as those in Satan's hellscape mirror his.

Whether Duessa's "deadly hew" is simply a sign of her own approaching death or is fatal to another is unclear, as is the referent of the phrase "too simple and too trew," which is equally applicable to the melodramatic excess of the swooning witch or to the inexperienced Redcrosse, who, only a canto earlier, is said to know "no'vntruth" (i.53). "Trembling cheare," a phrase that reflects the motif of "trembling" leaves in the grove of Fradubio, also refers either to Duessa or to Redcrosse, either and both of whose miens reflect the grove as these two characters ominously seem to merge together (ii.28). The phrase "all passed feare" is a virtual encapsulation of ambiguity and merging: "all fear is past"; "she is past fear"; "he is past fearing." This verbal and syntactic surface is as treacherous as quicksand; its instability resembles the confused irrationalities of Redcrosse's situation with a closeness that bears Spenser's imprint. Medium is indeed message in such writing, as remarkably and relatedly they will be again in Spenser's description of the hellish House of Pride and its patron Lucifera, and in Milton's description of Pandemonium, both sites being virtual soundscapes, as well as sites/sights, of excess.[26]

Satan's third and finest speech in Milton's opening book, which occurs right after comparison of him to the huge but ungainly Leviathan, contains what might be his most famous lines: "The mind is its own place, and in it self / Can make a Heav'n of Hell, a Hell of Heav'n" (I.254–55). The *ambiguity* of Satan's defiance of anything outside the mind's self, such as place, time, change, or God, usually goes unremarked: "in itself" can be read not only as "inside itself" and thus as solipsistic self-enclosure but also as "by itself" and thus as a claim to transform what is outside it, too, or perhaps merely to destroy what is outside by swallowing it, Saturn- or Zeus-like, and thereby to return the seeming doubleness of the statement to solipsistic singularity: in short, a Cartesian circle. Satan's declaration focuses and greatly reinforces the "doubtfull sense of things, not so well seene, as felt," which, in Spenser's words, characterizes Milton's hell.

Stephen Fallon suggests an allusion to the title of Hobbes's masterpiece and its philosophy of inert materialism in Milton's striking comparison of Satan to Leviathan, and in Satan's declaration of solipsism, a complementary allusion to the mind/body split in the philosophy of Descartes, who considers himself a substance "whose whole essence or nature is simply to think, and *which does not require any place*, or depend on any material thing, in order to exist." In the familiar Cartesian circle, from which the mind never escapes, God also guarantees the distinct ideas from which the idea of God itself derives.[27] As Fallon notes, Hobbes and Descartes, though at first glance an odd couple, share several fundamental beliefs: both found "in geometry a foundation for natural philosophy, banished formal and final cause . . . and argued for a mechanistic universe driven by material and efficient cause alone," hardly the same as Milton's animist materialism (31).

Spenser's best known depiction of hell comes in the fourth and fifth cantos of Book I, in which Redcrosse and Duessa enter the House of Pride, where Redcrosse battles Sans Joy, at once a projection of his joylessness and a mirror of himself, whom he wounds, suppresses, but fails to destroy; then Redcrosse 's companion Duessa (Doubleness) by night conveys Sans Joy, to hell, where this psychic sickness within Redcrosse (and the House of Pride) recovers strength. Hell, we thus recognize, is within the Redcross Knight, an inner place that is the mind's. Yet Redcrosse's inner hell, which will eventually issue into the wakeful, or seemingly wakeful, world, as "That cursed wight . . . A man of hell, that calls himselfe *Despayre*," is simultaneously a substantive place in the poem, in history, and in myth (I.ix.28). Redcrosse's hell is specifically a classical topos, from its outset alluding to Servius' influential gloss on Vergil's *silva* ("wood, forest"), through which descent to the netherworld is accomplished and which establishes a tradition associating such descent with flesh, the physical world, and matter as such.[28] At the very nadir of this Spenserian hell, the story of Hippolytus, whose unsituated and unbodied speaker is best described as a suddenly arresting cultural voice, pertains either to Redcrosse or, read differently, to Una, whose presence is therefore ironically and perversely intimated in both its psychic and historical dimensions, indeed, in its continuity and potential unity (v.37–39).[29] In this story, Redcrosse and Una thus meet parodically in hellish, unwholly union.

The unsituated speaker, or disembodied cultural voice, that is suddenly met, or heard, in the story of Hippolytus at the bottom of Spenser's hell, is as cultural voice, actually without bottom, receding limitlessly into past myth. Another way of approaching the effect of this voice is to notice that a narrator in any way explicit, for example, flashing contextual signals or referring to his own *dramatis personae* in the larger narrative, simply drops from sight.[30] The story of Hippolytus therefore comments on Redcrosse's lust and/or Una's innocence only by being itself. It *is* their mutual condition, separated as they now are "into double parts," split at once within themselves and from one another, divided within and without (I.ii.9). At the same time, it is also an expression of the poet's narrative presence momentarily so direct that his voice has actually become the ground and immediate source of experience, a typically Spenserian effect to which the Miltonic narrator of hell must have attended closely.

Other hell-like (and some pleasurable or heaven-like) places in Spenser are similarly direct, immediate, and ambiguously and inclusively situated with respect to the insides and outsides of perception and experience. Spenser's Cave of Mammon is at once a depiction of worldly materialism, whose references range from Machiavellian expediency to Spanish mines in the New World, and, pertinently, a depiction of moral darkness, the Bible's wicked Mammon. By this Mammon's own account, he is "God of the world and worldlings," but his "'secret place,' his home, is the heart of unrighteousness, . . . which embraces misuse, deformity, distortion, and injustice, for it finds its roots in an immoral materialism that suffocates the spirit; historically, it deadens truth, as 'th'vniust *Atheniens* made to dy / Wise *Socrates*,' and it kills 'Life,' as Pilate, 'the falsest Iudge . . . And most vniust . . . Deliuered vp the Lord of life to die.'"[31] The reason Guyon, who has assumed the burden of Mortdant, or mortality, early in Book II, must see this Mammonic place is that it exists in human history and European society, in myth, and, of course, in the Bible. It is within the nature Guyon has assumed on shouldering the burden of fallen humanity (Mortdant's armor, and, with his Palmer, Mortdant's and Amavia's blood-stained child), and it is also visibly outside and everywhere around him.[32]

Taken together, Mammon and his Cave, which Spenser's narrator explicitly calls Mammon's "house," resemble the "God of the world"—known also as *Mundus*—housed on his scaffold in the old morality plays, as well as a house or topos in the rhetorical sense (II.viii.3). The list of houses, or cultural topoi, is readily expanded: Alma's House recreates the medieval castle of the body, and its brain turret contains, reflects, processes, and continually intersects with what happens in British and Faerie history, in real and mythic time, beyond its castle walls; Busirane's House is blatantly a rhetorical place, where Petrarchan and Ovidian *abusio* ("abuse, catachresis") reigns and Ciceronian *boldness* weighs in the balance. The Temple of Venus derives from the medieval Courts of Love, inherited and embedded—"yfounded stronge" in Chaucer's phrasing; Isis Church is built on Plutarchan ethnology and medieval saints' lives; Mount Acidale, draws extensively on the iconography of the Graces, and the Pageant of Mutability, on the calendrical tradition.[33] By no means exhaustive, my list sufficiently indicates that these Faerie houses, familiar topoi all, are constructs on the cultural landscape, at once inner and outer, psychological and social, mythic and historical, and no one of these descriptive terms to the exclusion of the others. They are also allegorical constructs, *deictic* and *nondeictic*, particular and universal, concrete and abstract, natural (or social) and emblematic, material and moral, real and Real. The hell of Milton's Satan has much in common with them.

The question of Milton's philosophical monism and animist materialism, or scientific vitalism, pertains here, as it will again in later stages of my argument. Allegory as encompassing Idea or, indeed, as encompassing monist materialism, skirts the issue of doubleness—double speech, bifocality, or even what Auerbach terms *konkret Innergeschichtlichen* ("concrete inner history"), his key term for typology, or *figura*.[34] Doubleness characterizes literary allegory as a concept or abstraction that is in various ways subject to the embodied, temporal process of narrative, as I have recurrently argued. A fully singular, nontensive, nonmetaphorical allegory is simply not allegory; it is instead substitution, metonymy, and coding, or else it is mystical vision—identity, or sameness.[35] Whether mystical or metonymic, such unified, singular vision effectually denies the translative (i.e., metaphoric) and constructive function of language, which is characteristic of any human language I know. Fundamentally, it also denies significant difference.

Put simply, Satan's sin changes everything, a proposition seeming so obvious that I hardly dare offer it. The extenuating condition and contingent cause of the human Fall are found in Satan's willful disobedience and resulting descent to hell, as God explains in Book III: it is because humankind is first deceived by Satan that they will find mercy, in contrast to Satan and his followers, who are "Self-tempted, self-depraved"—perverse, morally corrupt, and, since *depraved* derives from Latin *de*, "completely," and *parvus*, "crooked," also "deviant, oblique" (129–32).[36] It can further be argued (and often is) that Satan's corrupt (and corrupting) actions lead back to the manifestation and elevation of the Son, and thence to the Father's *conception* in all the ambiguity of this generative word—objective and subjective, substantive and ideational. Such conception is simultaneously idea and action, groundplot and realization. In it, as I have already suggested, normative allegory passes beyond doubleness and into vision. Again, these are points to which I shall subsequently turn, but my present focus must remain Satan's sinning and its noxious effects.

Once Satan sins, evil in some sense exists, whether defined, as by Milton in *Christian Doctrine*, as an oblique or perverse *action*, which can include words, thoughts, or even the omission of good action, or whether understood as privation, which is the resulting *punishment* of evil, or sin, in Milton's view. Evil, moreover, exists both in and along with its ultimate manifestation death, a substantive experience that denies act and substance alike.[37] More properly, evil denies the *vitality*—the animating spirit—of matter and becomes an illogical, perceptual, oxymoronic condition of "darkness visible" and "bottomless perdition."[38]

According to the chronology (as well as the narrative order) of events in *Paradise Lost*, Satan's rebellion and fall occur prior to the Creation described by Raphael in Book VII.[39] Since the personified figure Chaos reports that he has witnessed Satan's fall and complains about the encroachment on his domain by hell first and then by Earth, chaos (as phenomenon, lowercase *c*, but not necessarily as personified abstraction, uppercase *C*) apparently exists prior to the hell into which Satan falls. This hell is characterized paradoxically as being itself "A Universe of death, which God by curse / Created evil, for evil only good" (II.622–23). Albeit created thus by curse and good for evil, God's creating anything evil—depraved, deviant, defective, diseased—is a terrible thought: hell, the Satanic mind's own place, like everything else that is, or even that apparently also is not, is God's—punningly "for good," that is, "forever" and "beneficently"—and not merely Satan's. If the darkness, disorder, and ill will of Chaos, Satan's sinning, and the creation of hell all precede the created human world, then the discord that ceases, the light that springs "from the Deep" to displace total "Darkness profound," and "the black tartareous cold Infernal dregs / Adverse to life" that are "downward purg'd" but nonetheless present at the moment of Creation do not seem so surprising.[40] Satan's evil, no matter how oblique in origin and how privative as result, is already a fact of existence and influential. It might be compared to the introduction of the *figure* zero, the Hindu number that at once denies number and paradoxically enables further numeration, which was introduced into Europe in the thirteenth century.[41]

The dregs that are "Adverse to life" at the Creation are *adversus*: "adversarial," like the eponymous Satan, whose name means "Adversary."[42] Such dregs are "turned in hostility toward" (*adversus*) and thus actually against and away from life, vitality, and they are thereby oblique, evil, and deathly. In short, Satan's evil is contagious, although also subject to infernal containment by God. Still, what is it to know evil as fully as Milton's God must? Is the difference between knowing, and being, evil complete? Is this God innocent—*in*, "not" and *nocere /-ent(em)*, "harm/harmed"—that is, always already unharmed? Unfallen Adam assures Eve that "Evil into the mind of God or Man / May come and go, so unapprov'd and leave / No spot or blame behind"; at least this is his intuitive belief, still in his innocence (V.117–19).

Satan's sin, from his first conception of her, overwrites Edenic monism with metaphorical tension, which, when continued, becomes openly allegorical. Again, his sin affects everything subsequent to it. We enter Eden with Satan and never see it without an awareness of his predatory, allegorical presence, which both narratively and conceptually frames the initial description of Adam and Eve.[43] His very presence brings doubleness and perceived dualism with it. The humanized, hairy sides of the Edenic mount, whose head is crowned with the paradisal garden, recalls the sexually charged imagery of Spenser's similarly "stately," pubic Mount in the Garden of Adonis, and, as well recognized, Milton's narrator signals explicitly in approaching Eden (e.g., "grottesque," "Silvan Scene," "woodie Theatre," "enameld colours") and then repeatedly, insistently within the Garden itself that this is art's creation (IV.131–42).[44] Simultaneously, the entire initial description of Mount and Garden, not unlike Spenser's, insists on bifocality, and more specifically on the perception that Eden is simultaneously and inseparably an ideal and an awareness at once of its loss and of the necessarily fictive nature of its topography.[45]

Moreover, only the Miltonic narrator, his character Satan, and we can be fully aware in Book IV of Adam and Eve's innocence, their lack of *nocence*, of harm and ultimately of death, which is otherwise present in the gazes of those who observe them: only the narrator and Satan will use the word *innocence* with self-consciousness of loss until much later in the poem, and when, before the Fall, Adam finally uses this word twice, his doing so signals his significant growth in degree and kind of awareness. Even so, his last unfallen use refers to Eve's "native [inborn, natural] innocence," and not to a death penalty that remains for him, as in some sense it must, an unfathomable concept—bottomless.[46] His last use refers specifically to Eve's innocence rather than self-reflexively to his own, yet his heightened sense of its precarious contingency and of the real possibility of its loss is crucial and momentous, as hers should also be after their intense dialogue, which has clearly defined the real danger to *right* reason and *moral* choice.[47] Such concepts as reason, choice, and innocence have themselves evolved along with Adam's and Eve's understanding of them in the course of Milton's narrative. This growth has coincided with an increasing awareness of evil—of Satan's past actions and present intentions.

The echo-chamber of Milton's poem at this stage, as at others, resounds convolutely, much as does Spenser's. For a large, complex, and particularly relevant example of Spenserian convolution treated earlier in this volume, consider the celebrated lyric moments in Book VI that are variously embedded in the larger narrative, even as Book VI is embedded in history, the poetry of past times included. Hellish by descent and symbolically hellmouthed, the Blatant Beast that rends the poet's rhymes at the end of Book

VI aligns allegorically with the diabolical thieves who despoil Melibee's pastoral idyll in its tenth canto; this is the very canto in which the Graces appear on Mount Acidale, and thus, in a series of frames or concentric circles, the poem as a whole becomes analogous to the Melibean cantos.[48] What is at stake in these cantos involves their relationship not merely to idyllic pastoral and to an Edenic landscape of desire but also to Melibean innocence, moral choice, and guilt, and in a broader sense to memory, to allegorical narrative, and to history. Melibee strikingly resembles a belated Adam.[49] The interwoven threads, circles, and frames of Milton's text, notably including the recurrent, allegorized presence and awareness in Eden of Satan, and, indeed, the structural complexity of Milton's unfolding ground-plot again and again urge layered memories of Spenser's. At this point, I want to return once more to the chronology of events in *Paradise Lost* and specifically to Satan's crucial rebellion, which chronologically precedes and affects Milton's initial depiction of Eden in Book IV, but in the narrative order of the poem is only shown to originate as deviant agency, or evil, in Raphael's account of the War in Heaven in the fifth and sixth books.

The *adverse* effect on matter of Satan's rebellion, his sin and consequent falling, is conspicuous throughout the War in Heaven in Book VI. For example, Satan's followers demonstrate the corrupting effect of Satanic invention on matter when they "reduce" the very elements beneath heaven's soil to gunpowder and when their cannon balls fell the unfallen angels "The *sooner for* thir Arms," which have been rendered materially confining— harmful, nocent, no longer innocent—by Satan's reductive invention and destructive assault (VI.514, 595: my emphasis). Not unlike Spenser's Mammon, whose "yron cote [is] . . . ouergrowne with rust" in a sign of his corrosive effect on natural materials, Satan's effect on "Th' originals of Nature" is corrupting—similarly corrosive, reductive, and destructive.[50] In an explicit attack on monism, it renders matter inimical to spirit: the faithful angels fall physically *because* of their armor: "unarm'd they might / Have easily as Spirits evaded swift" the diabolical cannonade (595–96). The same effect that day is evident in the gamesome *double entendres* of Satan and Belial, which, in a paradigm of sustained verbal duplicity, set the material, physical, or literal senses of words and phrases against civilized, sublated, or figurative senses in order to mock and discredit the latter (e.g., VI.558–67, 620–27).[51]

Such Satanic *reduction* is pointedly included in, and contrasted with, divine reduction, as expressed by God and by his faithful servant Abdiel, who tries to explain to Satan that the elevation of the Son actually enhances the nearness of the angels to God, making them more "*illustrious*" and "*exalt[ed]*," since the Son "One of our number thus reduc't becomes."[52] Divine reduction thus raises, or sublates, while also including and effecting change. As God has earlier put the matter, "under thee . . . Thrones, Princedoms, Powers, Dominions I reduce: . . . For regal Scepter then no more shall need, / God shall be All in All."[53] Simultaneously, the Son's elevation reduces, or supersedes, the community of angels, and the angels are reduced, or elevated, to the Son; that is, they are led back (Latin *re*, "back," and *ducere*, "lead") more nearly to their origin in God. They become more "illustrious," more radiantly in God's image, more godlike.

In modern terms, as my own terminology has already suggested, what is at issue in divine versus Satanic reduction looks like the philosophical and linguistic issue of the Hegelian *Aufhebung*, a concept that is variously rendered "sublation," "raising," or "supersession" and one that in our world is accompanied both by memory and loss, by partial preservation and partial cancellation.[54] In sum, divine reduction is preeminently elevation and fulfillment; Satanic reduction is preeminently either (self-)loss or else resistant (self-)preservation; they split the effects, the entailments, of *Aufhebung* between them, so to speak. In both divine and Satanic versions of reduction, however, there is interpretive room to notice the remainder, the trace, what either version leaves, or tries to leave, behind: losing the self to find the self is two-sided in this adversarial encounter.[55] The very nature of human language renders it so.

As I have argued at length elsewhere, this proto-Hegelian problematic, which moderns tag with the term *Aufhebung*, is fundamentally linguistic; as such, it was demonstrably evident in the Renaissance and available to anyone with even a rudimentary awareness of the etymological basis of abstract English words in roots signifying a physical or material sense: for example, *idea* from Greek *eido*, "to see"; *concept* from Latin *com* + *capere*, "to seize together." Examples are legion. This awareness was fairly common in the period, given widespread training in Latin, with its pedagogical emphasis on morphology; the enormous influx of new words from other languages into English, and the absence of monolingual dictionaries like our own to stabilize their significations and, in effect, fully to acculturate them.[56]

The debate between Satan and Abdiel, God's faithful servant, regarding *reduction* is, in small, also the familiar, twentieth-century debate between Paul Ricoeur and Jacques Derrida about *Aufhebung* and, more exactly, about whether the meaning of a word is tied to the implications of its material origin or whether, within a conceptual, syntactic, or temporal structure, it can truly rise above, exceed, or transcend its strictly or densely material roots: Milton's God thinks it can; his Satan does not.[57] In a strictly monist universe and particularly within a materialism animated by God, this debate should not occur, nor should tensive allegory, but both do recurrently in *Paradise Lost*, once given Satan, the adversary, the evil impulse downward—infernal dregs. As perhaps is already evident, free will proves a sticking point on the Edenic, metonymic, monist continuum and, as will eventually be evident, it aligns suggestively with both the doubleness of allegory and of moral choice. As the leveling Giant learns in Spenser's fifth Book, the principles of truth and falsehood, like good and evil or right and wrong, simply slide off a pair of scales that is calibrated only for the weighing of matter.[58]

In Milton's Book V, his God anticipates the Satanic *double entendres* of Book VI, reducing civilized, sublated, figurative senses to merely physical and literal ones. For a prime example, God tells his Son in derision that they must take measures to defend themselves "lest unawares we lose / This our high place, our Sanctuarie, our Hill" (V.731–32). Aside from the blatant joke about godly lack of awareness, the progressively material and thus descending order of God's triple series—place (superior status), sanctuary (sacred site), hill (material site)—proleptically mirrors and mocks Satan's verbal play in the War in Heaven. God himself mimics the reduction of meaning to material reality and finally to the hill claimed here by the feistiest cock on the block. But what differentiates God's heavy irony, his near-sarcasm, from Satan's?[59] Is the difference that tells us not to take God literally only attributable to faith or, alternatively, to historically contextualized reading?

In Book VI, Satan's hilarious *double entendres* are debasing, but they are not primarily personal. They concern war, peace, negotiation, diplomacy, understanding, agency, and force. God's *double entendres* concern his own power, authority, and place; his smirking derision ridicules the undercutting or debasing of his position.[60] God's *double entendres* might further be said to elevate by distinction, and they are preemptive, since their priority in the narrative puts God in control of Satanic irony, insofar as Satan's irony subsequently becomes merely a perverse inversion of God's. God speaks literally of a hill, but his meaning is ironically figurative; it is raised, or sublated, the irony of its raising the more striking because it is climactically a hill, a material elevation, that is thus so serenely sublated. The wordplay with *hill* also anticipates (and foresees) both the chaotic, material highpoint of the War in Heaven when "Hills amid the air encounter . . . Hills" and the subsequent restoration of divine order, with the hills returning "Each to his place" (VI.664, 781–82).

In a fanfaronade of ironic duplicity, Satan only appears to speak figuratively of *overtures* (implicitly to peace: etymologically from Latin *apertura*: "opening"), of the free *discharge* of a part (implicitly sincere fulfillment of responsibility in negotiation: from Old French *deschargier*, "unloose"), of *propounding* a matter (implicitly offering a proposal: from Latin: *proponere*, "put forth"), and so on, meaning, respectively, force from the opening of cannon, with a further play on "over," as in a cannonade; the firing or unloosing of a weapon or projectile; the unrestrained (physically "free") putting forward, or forth, of cannon balls. Although Satan appears to speak figuratively, his meaning is thus ironically literal and literally material. Where God sublates, Satan again reduces or lowers, flipping, as it were, the ironical coin to its other side. But the difference between their utterances remains precarious, both because its contrasting extremities are on a rhetorical continuum and because its recognition relies on readerly faith, rather than on something more, or otherwise, substantive, such as contrasting rhetorical structures. Like so much in this poem, this final lack of substantive difference is disturbing, unless, of course, we are ready to marry "real" substance to faith with St. Paul or to equivocate regarding spirit(s).[61] The lack of difference is both another testimony to the insidiousness of Satan's corrupting sin, and an invitation further to consider moral, ethical, and religious distinctions that fit less easily into a monism that is *only* material: it is, after all, or rather, first of all, Milton's God who breathes life, word, creativity—*vitality*, or vitalizing spirit—into the abyss and makes it pregnant. His inspiriting makes all the difference. My further consideration of such distinctions will necessarily be somewhat circuitous, not unlike Satan's journey from hell though chaos to Earth, on which note I now leave the chronology of Satanic influence and return to the narrative sequence of the poem.

Satan's journey through chaos additionally instances his initial situation in the poem, namely hell, as an interior place, at once an inner projection and a topos belonging to larger social, mythic, and historical contexts. His journey references those of Jason and Odysseus and alludes more than once to the Redcrosse Knight's climactic battle with his dragon: for example, Fowler notes the parallel between the dragon's "Halfe flying, and halfe footing in his haste" and Satan's nigh foundering "half on foot, / Half flying." I can add in a proximate remembrance that the "flaggy winges" of Spenser's dragon are also "like two sayles" or are, indeed, "broad sayles," and that

Milton's Satan spreads his "Sail-broad Vannes" for flight.[62] Milton thus appears to have had Spenser's dragon fight in mind at this stage of Satan's journey. Redcrosse's epic battle with the serpentine dragon (or draconic serpent) recapitulates much of his journey through Book I, as well as a broad sweep of salvific history.[63] It is at once interiorized and historical, personal and general, figurative and physical, spiritual, moral, and embodied. Recalling it, I am struck the more by the Miltonic narrator's reporting, after Chaos' final declaration of resistance to anything encroaching on his realm to weaken "the Scepter of old *Night*," that "*Satan* staid not to reply, / But glad that now his Sea should find a shore . . . Springs upward" (II.1002, 1010–13). That "his Sea," Satan's sea, the medium through which he has been swimming, sinking, wading, creeping, and flying, should belong to him signals clearly that it, too, is within him, and *not merely* without (II.948–50).[64] Given this signal, the pun on "sea," another of Spenser's favorites, explicitly raises the issue of perception. The relation of what is perceived, or seen, to the mind perceiving is again ambiguous, or doubled.[65]

The chaos Satan traverses in Book II, which supplies the material of divine creation and, according to *Christian Doctrine*, derives from God's own substance, has been variously interpreted, and with good reason.[66] Regina Schwartz finds it preeminently evil (11); John Peter Rumrich proposes that it "represent[s] the material dimension of God's own being" and therefore participates "in the fullness of divinity as neither the Son nor the Holy Spirit do"; Michael Lieb considers it neutral, "the Womb of nature and perhaps her Grave," a potent source for good or evil (II.911); John Rogers, distinguishing this chaos from the vital matter of creation, calls it "specifically Hobbesian"; David Norbrook finds in Chaos "the cosmos's default mode," and "a cosmic civil war," although Milton's Chaos is nonetheless "not inherently evil."[67] I simply want to emphasize that chaos, like hell itself, is, after Satan's rebellion and descent, not only the womb of creation but also the place, or superficially another place, of Satan's mind. It is what he sees or experiences. Even from the outset of the Miltonic narrator's description of chaos, it is said to be "Before th[e] . . . eyes" of Satan and Sin, his offspring (II.890).[68] This is why Chaos (uppercase C), enthroned beside his consort Night, irrationally takes shape as the hypostatized "Ancestor . . . of Nature," as "Umpire," or ironic, oxymoronic patron, of strife, and as dubiously moral "Anarch" of this contradictory "Realm."[69] Chaos as personification is Satan's projection, one that ascribes (im)moral intent to this place and that becomes another instance of Satan's corrupting effect on matter: it is Chaos who, with a parodic and corrosive glance at the expression "Godspeed," bids Satan imperatively, "go and speed"; who provides helpful directions to him, and whose implicit gloss on the elision of God in his parting imperatives is "Havock and spoil and ruin are my gain" (II.1008–9).[70] This personified Chaos thus sounds like a one-dimensional devil or demonic villain straight out of the moral plays. A suggestive parallel might also be found in Spenser's personified Night, who is the "most aunciet Grandmother of all . . . Which was begot in Daemogorgons hall / And sawst the secrets of the world vnmade." Night's nephew is Redcrosse's San Joy, the Knight's morally diseased double, and Night addresses Duessa as daughter and child when this duplicitous figure asks for Night's assistance (I.v.22, 25, 27). Spenser's personified Night is clearly not only a natural phenomenon, a time of darkness, but also a moral darkness within the Knight of the Redcross. Milton, conspicuously like Spenser, layers differences in figuration, such as personification, with significance.

For my purpose, Rumrich's discussion of Satan's initial rebellion in heaven affords an insight he does not specifically intend into Milton's use of significant form in personifying Chaos and Night. Rumrich argues that the angels' goodness prior to the elevation of the Son is "natural," as this word is understood—in a relevant but merely *representative* example—in the terminism (incipient nominalism) of the Franciscan Duns Scotus, whose familiarity to and influence in the seventeenth century is considerable (157–58).[71] Scotus, like his more clearly nominalist successor William of Ockham, writes in a modified Augustinian tradition (as later do Martin Luther and John Calvin). Scotus and the nominalist tradition descending from him give primacy to the will over knowledge, contrasting in this respect with the thinking of Thomas Aquinas and the Thomist tradition in general.

Prior to the Reformation, of course, the dominant, or at least the established, Roman Catholic, view is that the will is free. As Heiko Augustinus Oberman has conclusively shown, however, the primacy of the will informs the inverted voluntarism of much Reformation theology, in which the primacy of will over knowledge perversely becomes an argument for the overwhelming bondage of the will.[72] Such bondage is merely the flip side of the voluntarist coin and looks like a classic case of the son's futile effort to forget the father. As Rumrich observes, Milton, who in *Areopagitica* mentions Scotus, along with Aquinas, as a teacher inferior to Spenser, could hardly have avoided acquaintance with Scotism and the nominalist tradition at Cambridge (148–59).[73] Milton's distinction in his tract between Spenser and two leading Scholastics is not an attack on the latter, as Rumrich also notes, but instead a privileging of *affective* Spenserian poetry, indeed of allegory, over the intellectual dryness of philosophy, and therefore one that also might suggestively recall the emphasis on the will and the motivating power of poetry in Sidney's *Apology*.[74]

As Rumrich argues, in Scotistic terms, before the Son's elevation angelic wills are naturally disposed to choose the good, and what is good is not distinguished from what is most advantageous for each angel. In elevating the Son, however, God acts to transform a natural order into a moral one in which good is chosen for its own sake and thus, from a moral perspective, freely (161–62, 172–73).[75] The difference is that between a natural order or innate law and a moral order and positive law imposed by God, like the command to Adam and Eve not to eat of the apple.[76] As my wording indicates, relevant connections might also be drawn to discussions of law from ancient times to Milton's present, albeit with various results.[77] While I do not agree with Rumrich's virtually exclusive attribution to God of what is represented by C/chaos in Book II, I find his distinction between natural and moral orders applicable to the significance of such personified figures there as Chaos and Night.[78]

The same distinction illuminates the first passage in Paradise *Lost* that requires knowledge of Milton's theory of creation *ex Deo*. This passage describes the former behavior in heaven of Mammon, who now mines gold in hell for the building of Pandemonium, Satan's palace.[79] Mammon is

> the least erected Spirit that fell
> From heav'n, for ev'n in heav'n his looks and thoughts
> Were always downward bent, admiring more
> The riches of Heav'ns pavement, trod'n Gold,
> Then aught divine or holy else enjoy'd
> In vision beatific.
>
> (I.679–84)

Notably, Mammon, although presumably a lower order of angel and, in his own right, also the "least erected" angel in heaven, is nonetheless unfallen, indeed, presumably innocent, before he commits himself to Satan's rebellion and thus falls. His "downward bent" behavior in heaven is habitual ("always") and apparently perfectly natural for him. It pokes fun at the notion of will within Hobbesian materialism, since Hobbes's reductive word for will is often "inclination," or appetite, in effect.[80] In heaven, Mammon is literally and figuratively inclined to denser, heavier forms of matter than beatific visions. His inclination is at once spiritually inferior and, ironically and literally, also materially so. It is not immoral or sinful, however, as it will become when he chooses to cast his lot with Satan and against God. It is this choice, and I emphasize choice, that might be said to cast him into a landscape newly allegorical, in which downward-bent behavior has become disloyal and immoral. Like several of Spenser's characters—Serena and Melibee in Book VI, for example—his figure suddenly finds itself fallen into moral allegory and doubleness.[81] Of course he simultaneously falls into other forms of allegory, as well: historical (work ethic), psychological (obsessive fetishizing), and ideological (inert, dis-spirited materialism), just for example and argument. In sum, Satan's sinful rebellion adversely affects Edenic monism, innocence, language, and perception. Perhaps most simply and fundamentally, it taints matter and the forms that matter takes.

Following the Great Consult and prior to traversing chaos, Satan encounters the personified figure Sin, who is his daughter-wife, and Death, their equally incestuous son, who is also the rapist of his sinful mother and the father of her tormenting hell-hounds. A Cartesian circle, if ever there was one. Sin, self-tortured and self-destructive, is gnawed viscerally by the howling hounds that are ever reborn from within her as the "conscious terrors" surrounding her on the outside: inside and outside both, like the doubled meaning of Satan's "mind . . . *in itself*" that I addressed earlier in this chapter.[82] Thus the unceasing, temporal circularity of Sin's birthing, her hounds "hourly conceiv'd / And hourly born," is spatially duplicated in the "cry [howling pack] of Hell Hounds" encircling her middle and later reduplicated in the compulsive, despairing circularity of Satan's affecting soliloquy at the outset of Book IV: "Which way I flie is Hell; myself am Hell."[83] Very much like the progressive emergence of Redcrosse's unconscious hell in Book I's fifth canto into the conscious figure of Despair in its ninth, the hell within Satan, which is defined—*de* + *finis*, literally "de-limited"—and contained by Sin and Death in hell, rises into conscious despair in this soliloquy. Now horror and doubt

> from the bottom stirr
> The hell within him, for within him Hell
> He brings, and round about him, nor from Hell
> One step no more then from himself can fly
> By *change of place*: Now *conscience wakes despair*
> That slumberd, wakes the bitter memorie

Of what he was, what is, and what must be
Worse.
                    (IV.19–26: my emphasis)

Conscience is also awareness, or consciousness, in this period and, as anciently observed by Plotinus, "awareness of self is the foundation of memory."[84] Here this proves to be the case for Satan when he recalls his relation to God and his willful rebellion: even so, the fully conscious Despair of Spenser's Redcrosse preys relentlessly on his guilty memories of betrayal and flight (I.ix.45–46). Self-awareness and memory are conspicuously lacking, however, when Satan, seeking egress from hell, confronts Sin and Death and initially neither recognizes nor remembers them.[85] The futility of a "Change of place," whether topographical or rhetorically topical, outer or inner, is another ironic touch in the Miltonic passage cited just above: all places are essentially the same within Satanic circularity, much like the interchangeability of the hell hounds within his Sin or without her in both the adverbial and prepositional senses of the word *without*—that is, either "outside her" or "in the absence of her figure." As if in application of my pun, Satan may leave Sin's figure in hell, but not really.

Sin's account of her birth and relation to Satan is not only a telling return to Satan's past, but also a history lacking in the angel Raphael's account of events leading to the outbreak of War in Heaven. From Raphael we hear nothing of "th' Assembly . . . Of all the Seraphim" who side with Satan's rebellion and who, according to Sin, witness her birth from Satan's head, in a well-recognized parody of the birth of Athena, goddess of wisdom, from Zeus's (II.749–58).[86] Conceivably, Raphael's omission of this account indicates that Sin's birth, her realization and epiphany, occurs after Abdiel's departure from the rebels and is unknown to Raphael for this reason; traditionally, God alone can know another's inmost thought. But for a reason thematically more significant and specifically relevant to the treatment of knowledge in Milton's epic, the unfallen Raphael could only know Sin's birth vicariously, by report. Presumably, only the liked-minded angels loyal to Satan witness the birth of Sin's figure into being, insofar as she can be said to be. The absence of her birth from Raphael's account suggests that the substance of sin, as apart from its essence as act, is simply not something unfallen angels see as a personified entity.[87] Abdiel's dialogue with Satan before departing from the rebels participates, as Stella Revard showed long ago, in the *progressive* paradigm of Satan's sinning—a narrative *movement* from withdrawal, separation, and secession from God to a more direct challenge to his authority and then to an active assault on it.[88] Again, the distinction Milton draws in *Christian Doctrine* between evil as action and privation as its consequence is relevant. Raphael's account, reflecting Abdiel's experience, dramatizes Satan's deviant, oblique, perverse *act* of sinning, and Sin herself is the figurative embodiment, the verbal substance, the resulting, manifest brainchild of Satan's sinful action. She, along with Death, is what Joseph H. Summers has fittingly termed a "real nonentity."[89]

Real, however, in any number of senses, excluding ontological and metaphyical ones: for example, a real consequence of Satan's evil action, really there in living experience and as a figure in the poem, and really fertile, if only generative of self-plaguing agony and Death. Like Sin, the figure of Death is a contradiction, a "shape, / If shape it might be call'd that shape had none / Distinguishable in member, joynt, or limb, / Or substance might be call'd that shadow seem'd" (II.666–69). Milton's son of Satanic Sin is at once the Pauline "body of this death," and a memory of Spenser's Maleger (Latin *mal*, "evil," and *aeger*, "diseased, dejected, sorrowful"), who leads the attack on Spenser's House of Alma (the healthy body) in Book II and is finally suppressed with extreme difficulty by Prince Arthur.[90] I can hardly do better in short space with respect to Maleger's pertinence than first to quote James Carscallen's telling description of him:

> in this adversary [Maleger] Arthur has met the body of death itself, man's own substance as man's enemy. And while the body of death must continually die, it is also in a spectral way as powerfully tempered and as enduring as the House of Alma.... The standing [i.e., stagnant] lake in which Maleger finally perishes is like the negative eternity from which the Sons of Acrates [Greek ἀκρατής, "lacking control"] take their descent. We might call it "non-being," the final opposite of any goodly frame [healthy body, or House of Alma] to which even chaos must come in the end.[91]

In a sampling of Spenser's own words in the episode, which afford a striking commentary on Milton's figure of Death, Maleger appears to be "some magicall / Illusion . . . Or wandring ghost, that wanted funerall, / Or aery spirite vnder false pretence, / Or hellish feend raysd vp through diuelish science." He also proves to be an effective contradiction: "Flesh without blood, a person without spright . . . That could doe harme, yet could not harmed bee, / That could not die, yet seemd a mortall wight, /That was most strong in most infirmitee" (II.xi.39–40). The power of Impotence and the persistence of Impatience are the defining attributes of two hags who accompany Maleger and assist his vicious attacks. Assertive negations, they perversely embody the traditional topos of doing and suffering, of acting and enduring—*agere et pati*.⁹²

If read allegorically, Sin's role in Milton's Book II is supremely obvious. Sin, as Satan's sin projected directly from his head, holds the key to hell, and therefore he is self-confined, albeit evidently with God's active co-operation, as I have earlier suggested. When Sin opens the gates of hell in response to Satan's request, Satan sins again, presumably with God's permissive will, and his doing so thrusts him into a worse hell, the one about which he soliloquizes so eloquently and acutely at the outset of Book IV.⁹³ To my mind, Milton uses literary allegory (and not merely personification) in this hellish episode in Book II because it has a history of association with self-projection, one especially conspicuous for its significant exploration *and* exposure in Milton's Spenserian model—again, his Spenserian "Original," as Milton acknowledged to his fellow poet John Dryden.⁹⁴

Aside from the prominence of projection allegory in Book I of *The Faerie Queene*, the other most celebrated assessment and critique of its psychic and epistemological dangers comes with the metamorphosis of Malbecco, the evil he-goat, January figure, and lecherous old man of Book III, into the personification Jealousy.⁹⁵ Malbecco's dehumanization as the emblematic, avian abstraction Jealousy, is simultaneously the personification, or humanizing, of an Idea—in Malbecco's instance, an obsessive jealousy, or Mammonic possessiveness. His change foreshadows the turning of passions into persons, persons into passions in the pageant of Busirane's House of horrors. This sort of behavior is self-enclosed, compulsive, and demonic, as Angus Fletcher long since characterized it, and it certainly anticipates Satan's.⁹⁶ Before Milton saw the demonic potential of allegory, Spenser had already done so in a self-conscious form of allegory that Milton knew well. Malbecco literally runs away with himself—he "ran away, ran with him selfe away" to such an extent that anyone seeing him "From Limbo lake him late escaped sure would say." As he runs, "Griefe, and despight, and gealosy, and scorne / Did all the way him follow hard behynd" and "as a Snake, still lurked in his wounded mynd" (III.x.54–55). His "selfe-murdring thought" so wastes him that all his human "substance . . . [is] consum'd to nought," and he morphs into a monstrous personification of Jealousy: as Spenser sums up his change, he "Is woxen so deform'd that he has quite / Forgot he was a man, and *Gelosy* is hight (x.57, 60).⁹⁷ In short, Malbecco memorably becomes a real nonentity.

Milton's figure of Sin has long been recognized as an allusion to Spenser's Error, as well as to the long tradition of serpentine women to which Spenser's Error herself alludes.[98] What interests me about this connection is less the generic similarity or the similarity of specific details of the two figures than the similarity in their significant functions within either poem. Herein, as in many other instances, lies the most meaningful relation within the Spenser-Milton intertext. This is a truly textual relation, an integrally interwoven one that involves narrative action, not simply personified Idea(s), and it sharply contrasts with an inert coincidence of words and phrases. Like Sin, Spenser's Error has diabolical, religious, and biblical credentials, but her ties to natural philosophy are even more conspicuous, since they suddenly and surprisingly erupt into extended epic similes and interrupt Redcrosse's battle with her to demand our attention. She is revealed to be a corruption of fertility, as Satan's Sin is, since she is conspicuously associated with the rising of the Nile and the generative source of nature itself, as well as later with the naturalized landscape of pastoral, the generic rhetorical "place" in and with which traditional Renaissance poets begin their making (I.i.21–23).[99]

Of even greater significance for the Spenser-Milton intertext, Redcrosse's escape from Error, whom he only defeats with supreme effort, is as illusory as Satan's from hell. The battle of Redcrosse with Error generates and releases themes and images that reappear within this Knight and his night of temptation spent at Archimago's hermitage. Ironically, it is Una who counsels Redcrosse to get some sleep at the hermitage, since to do so is as natural as the sun's resting "his steedes the *Ocean* waves among" (I.i.32). Within a few stanzas, "a murmuring winde, much like the sowne / Of swarming Bees" blows through the cave of sleep and recalls the noisome gnats whose memorable "murmurings" mar the pastoral landscape that intervenes conspicuously in Redcrosse's battle with Error (i.23, 41). As Spenser, recalling Chaucer, openly explains in his fourth Book, "The things that day most minds, at night doe most appeare": whatever it is of which you are *mind-full* in the daytime, you dream about at night (v.43).[100] Through the memory of murmuring *flies* (generically insects in the Renaissance, potentially alluding to the eponymous Beelzebub, "Lord of the Flies") and through other, similar verbal parallels, the poem signals that Redcrosse's battle with Error is unfinished and, in fact, that it has now moved, like Sin's hell hounds and Satan's soliloquized nihilism and despair, from primarily without Redcrosse to primarily within him. Once again the unfolding ground-plot of Spenser's epic suggestively and specifically foreshadows Milton's.

Milton characterizes the *place* of Satan conclusively in his tale of the metamorphosis of the devils to serpents in the middle of Book X. This hellish place in the poem, like the earlier expressions of hell, belongs to mind and body alike; it is interior condition and objectified landscape, simultaneously and reciprocally inner and outer—real delusion, real torment, Realized Evil. It is also the fulfillment of the allegory specifically of Satan that has spanned ten books of the poem, although it is not yet the end of God's allegory, which unfolds typologically in the concrete, biblical history of the last two books.[101] Again back in hell in Book X, Satan morphs into the snaky emblem and abstraction Evil much as Spenser's Malbecco morphs into the avian emblem and abstraction Jealousy.[102] Real nonentities both.[103]

Prior to metamorphosis, Satan revels in his account of the marvelous joke he has played on God's human creatures with a mere apple. His literalist perspective first denies the symbolic value of the apple as "sign," or "Pledge of . . . [their] Obedience *and* . . . [of their] Faith," and then, in effect, it *reduces* the enmity of God and humankind to a bruised serpent.[104] Satan misrecognizes the actuality of his own imbruting, his carnal descent, his snakishness, and whether he does so through a deliberate refusal or through a failure of awareness is unclear. The levity of his account suggests the latter. Pointedly, his levity recalls Eve's inebriate jocundity (and materialist tree worship) after her fall, along with Adam's witty, reductive, inebriate sensuality immediately after his own fall.[105] Like them, he knows "not eating death," although he is soon to experience it—in fact, to "savour" it in his favorite form of knowledge, not to say, in his merely materialized "Sapience" (IX.792, 1018–20).

In a sibilating soundscape of hisses, Satan falls into the form of "A monstrous Serpent on his Belly prone," as before he was prone like Leviathan, now coming full circle. But a "greater power" rules him now (or is it just again?), and he is fittingly "punisht in the shape he sin'd" (X.514–16). He and his disciples "fix[ate]" their eyes on "A Grove hard by, sprung up with this thir change, / His will who reigns above," and they perceive its trees to be laden with apples, "imagining / For one forbidden Tree a multitude / Now ris'n." Their bodies "parcht with scalding thurst and hunger fierce," they cannot "abstain, / But on they rould in heaps, and up the Trees / Climbing, sat thicker then the snakie locks that curld *Megaera*." Their greedy imaginings are grounded in, and reduced to, purely physical compulsion, a total enslavement to delusive lust: "fondly thinking to allay / Thir appetite" with gusto, they chew bitter ashes instead of fruit, again and again writhing "thir jaws /With soot and cinders fill'd" (548–70). As Fowler notes, the ashes, soot, and cinders fulfill the curse on the snake in Genesis 3:14, "dust shalt thou eat," and glance as well at the sentence of death on humankind in Genesis 3:19, "dust thou art, and unto dust shalt thou return."[106] I would add that they also parody traditional signs of penitence (Ash Wednesday, sackcloth and ashes, and the like).[107] If Satan's consorting with repentance in his soliloquy at the outset of Book IV were to be seen as the extension and refusal of prevenient grace, this last touch of parody would become sadly mnemonic and sardonically reiterative.

The most conspicuous Spenserian parallel to the suitability, or poetic justice, of Milton's metamorphic snakes occurs in the earlier poet's Book of Justice (V), in which the first two cantos exhibit instances of fittingly tailored symbolic penalties, which are actualized and embodied in the narrative. The brutal knight who beheads a lady gets to wear her head, albatross-like, hanging from his neck. The ambiguously metallic hands and feet of Lady Munera (rewards, gifts, bribes) are summarily chopped off and hung as a warning on high.[108] The leveling Giant of materialism, who materializes ironically out of Lady Munera's punishment, is himself cast down, or leveled, and his reliance on physical sight and measurement is eliminated when he is fittingly drowned, with accompanying pun, in the "sea." But what specifically connects these sorts of typically Renaissance, symbolically fitting but savage penal rituals and their parodic appropriation by Spenser, to that which Milton visits on his devils, is their embedding in a larger context of qualification, critique, and exposure. The steps of Artegall, Spenser's Knight of Justice and judicial imposer of punishment in Book V, are insistently dogged by parody in the early cantos; his justice is questioned, distanced, and, on occasion, openly mocked.[109]

In a thoroughly Spenserian gesture, the Miltonic narrator no sooner triumphs in the metamorphic tour de force that imposes punishment on his devils than he, too, qualifies it. His climactic, poetic realization of the mind's own place, as Satan parodically and holistically experiences it in Book X, is distanced and its reality questioned. "Long" the diabolical serpents hunger, chew, and hiss, until "thir lost shape, permitted, they resum'd, / Yearly enjoynd, some say, to undergo / This annual humbling" (X.573–77).[110] The poet might as well have put a pointing finger with the tag "self-conscious fiction" in the margin as to have written "some say" here. At similar moments in *The Faerie Queene*, the Spenserian narrator sends this signal or close variants of it that are tantamount to a trademark. For example, four times within seven stanzas in recounting the fabulous story of Merlin, Spenser writes, "some say," "(they say)," "(they say)," "men say"; three times within three stanzas on the mythic, pubic Mount in the Garden of Adonis, "some say," "they say," "they say"; again in the Temple of Venus in reference to the statue of Venus, who has, "they say, . . . both kinds [sexes] in one." A further sampling includes the occurrence of this signal in reference to the holy grail in the British Chronicle, and in a description of "Old *Cybele*" in the Pageant of Rivers, in Books II and IV, respectively. In Book V, the signal comes in the story of Diomedes' flesh-eating horses and the metamorphosis of Adicia into a tiger ("to proue her surname [Injustice] true"), and four times in the account of Geryoneo and his monstrous idol.[111] While my sampling is not exhaustive, it indicates Spenser's use of this distancing signal especially for fabulous and mythic contexts. Some occur, however, in conjunction with real history, past and present—the British Chronicle in Book II or the defeat of the Spanish Armada and the English campaign in the Netherlands in Book V, for instance—and it is always worth remembering that myth had long been considered variously to carry real historical significance. Typically, and well before Giambattista Vico, Francis Bacon, like the poets contemporary with him (1561–1626), recognized both in theory and in practice that symbols themselves, like battles, have histories that are significant aesthetically, culturally, and, in fact, historically. Symbolic language informs and shapes, rather than simply expressing, history as event and as account, and this fact makes a difference.[112] Spenser's distancing, like Milton's allusion to it, is not a denial of validity to fiction even of a fabulous sort, but it is, like Sidney's *Apology*, a specifying and delimiting of its literal, objective, and historical claims.

Another form of Spenserian distancing or self-conscious qualifying of the truth-claims of fiction is his denial of closure to endings—his characteristic "vnperfiting" of them—as Milton imperfects the climactic finish of Satan not only by invoking the distancing allusion "some say," but also by reporting an alternative myth concerning it. Milton depreciates this alternative as merely "tradition" and "fable": "However some tradition they [the devils] dispers'd . . . And fabl'd" about their triumphant ascent of Olympus in the form of the Serpent Ophion (X.578–84). Even the rest of this fable, the subsequent defeat of Ophion by successor gods, discounts it. But the most telling qualification of the poetic justice imposed on the metamorphosed Satan may come at the very end of the same, seamlessly long verse paragraph that recounts his snaky metamorphosis: "Mean while in Paradise the hellish pair / Too soon arriv'd, *Sin* there in power before, / *Once actual, now in body*" (X.585–87: except *Sin*, my emphasis). The figure of Satan may be finished, but not really. Even as his metamorphosis occurs, he returns to Earth in his descendants Sin and Death, nonentities, to be sure, but ever more real ones. The Miltonic distinction between sin, as deviant, evil act and its resulting embodiment, a privation, is notably present in the lines last cited as well: power, potency, act, as distinct from body, substance, entity. I have often had occasion to remark this significant distinction.

Both with emphasis on the body of sin and death and with the conspicuous qualification of poetic triumph, the end of Satan's allegory circles back to its beginning, the introduction of the substantive figures of Sin and Death in Book II and the qualification of another poetic tour de force in the series of epic similes that close, or nearly close, Book I. This circle is what Ricoeur would consider a healthy one that, through narrative emplotment, extracts a configuration from a succession, as treated in my introduction. Lens-like, the similes with which Book I draws to its close play variously with perception, reducing the Titanic size and correspondent enormity of the demons: first these similes diminish the demons to swarming bees, whose "russling wings" resonate mnemonically with the wings of the "murmuring" gnats and the "murmuring winde," like the sound of "swarming Bees," of Spenser's interlaced figures of Error and Morpheus (sleep); then, with further distancing, they compare the demons to faraway dwarfs and "Faerie Elves" whose reality is dreamlike and elusive. Yet the Miltonic narrator's power so to invoke allusive Spenserian memories and to manipulate the threatening reality of the demons is brought up short in the reminder that follows these focal similes that "far within . . . And in thir own dimensions like themselves" sit "The great Seraphic Lords and Cherubim / In close recess and secret conclave" (767–95). These cautionary lines signal that the real threat remains within, at once unchanged and unaffected by the narrator's play with perspective.

The very end of *Paradise Lost*, with its pun on "rest," suggesting residence, repose, and death, recalls the final stanza of the Mutability Cantos, not only Spenser's use of this word itself but also his thrice repeated play on *Sabbath*, God's day of rest. In a larger sense, Milton's final verse paragraph, like Spenser's Cantos, recalls his whole poem as well, as my preceding chapter has shown, and again, like so many of Spenser's endings, it at once imperfects and open-ends Milton's ending.[113] The Spenserian word "vnperfite" appears in the heading of the last, two-stanza Canto of Mutability, but it captures and encapsulates a Spenserian signature writ large, namely, the poet's persistent commitment to what I have elsewhere in this volume called punningly *inconclusion*, an ending that is also not an ending, as it turns out. Again, examples in *The Faerie Queene* abound at the ends of books and in retrospective revisions at the beginnings of subsequent books. In addition to refusing closure, such examples qualify, without denying and indeed, while also continuing, the claims of fiction—Sidney's *poesy*—to power and truth. Archimago may be jailed and fettered in the final canto of Book I, for example, but he is loose again at the beginning of Book II. Una may represent Unity, but in the end Redcrosse has again to leave her. In Book II there is the memorable demurrer of Grill when offered morality, and at the beginning of Book III, in allusive recall of Acrasia's lover Verdant, Guyon, the erstwhile hero of Temperance, tries to spear the female Knight of Chastity, while the fiery feet of his steed burn the "verdant gras" and make the return of the repressed more than a little difficult to ignore (i.5). At the beginning of Book IV, it is clear that Busirane's abusive masking has ironically rubbed off on his conqueror Britomart and that the hermaphroditic silhouette of Britomart and Amoret together on a single horse, which has been precipitated right out of the final cantos of Book III, is what remains of Busirane's erotic site when all his other art forms have vanished.[114] At the very end of Book IV, moreover, Florimell's masking in "modestie" can hardly be innocent of the thematic ambivalence of acculturated masking throughout Spenser's central books (xii.35). Books V and VI both end with pointed contrasts between idealized and actual history, as well as with the envious barking and biting of the Blatant Beast, and each of the Cantos of Mutabilitie ends inconclusively: canto vi with a *pourquoi* fable about wolves and thieves that roam unchecked through Ireland; canto vii with the vanishing of Nature, whose very disappearance makes a point of her fictitiousness; and the "vnperfite" canto viii with verbal ambiguity about the nature of this world and poignant equivocation about that of the next.

Two loose ends of my topic "the mind's allegorical place" remain: the relation of Milton's initial depiction of God and the Son in Book III, which pointedly asks that readers remember Satan's hellish, allegorical place in Books I and II, and the "paradise within" conditionally promised Adam and Eve near the end of *Paradise Lost*. The latter pertains to the mind's place insofar as any inner paradise in the fallen world must be psychic, a word I choose for its straddling the distinction between mind and soul, intellectual and moral being (XII.587). Since the nature of the "paradise within" is well recognized and I have little to add at this point except a Spenserian analogue, I shall start with it, although I shall want to circle back to it at the end of my argument.

The familiar difference between Satan's ringing cry of solipsism in Book I, "The mind is its own place, and in it self / Can make a Heav'n of Hell, a Hell of Heav'n," and the "paradise within" the human psyche that is available to faith, patience, temperance, and charity, "the soul / Of all the rest," amounts both to a difference in what we might call attitude, and also to the achievement of this inner paradise simultaneously with awareness, acknowledgment, and direct experience of fallen reality, specifically of pain, death, and other deprivations (XII.584–85). The Spenserian analogue to the "paradise within" is a place incredibly, hence with blatant fictionality, called "Eden" in the final canto of Book I. Of course, Spenser's Eden, where a dead dragon and "heauenly noise" like that of angels singing before the throne of God are both to be found, must be, whatever its potential for historical and prophetic allusion, preeminently an interior condition, as are Lucifera's palace, hell, or the House of Holiness. Momentarily, such seemingly Edenic joy is also disrupted by Archimago, the emissary of duplicity, and, as earlier noted, Archimago, though apprehended and bound, escapes his prison in Eden to reemerge in the next Book, that is, once again in narrative space/time. Spenser's Eden exists as a place of "ease and . . . rest" in the narrative that Redcrosse, the questing Knight, must physically leave at the end, and that Arthur, who similarly belongs to the landscape of quest, will (and must) never reach (xii.17). In a fallen world, such an Eden is obviously also an idealized fiction of the happy earthly kingdom, in comparison to which Milton's "paradise within" looks, while refusing self-enclosure, less hopeful for society as a whole.

Milton's depiction of God, my other loose end, has been characterized by Treip as "one of his most radically allegorical constructs" (238). Others, notably Kenneth Borris, have agreed.[115] The similarities of the depiction of God and the Son in Book III to Satanic projection allegory are also well recognized, the Son being the image of the Father, not entirely unlike Sin's relation to Satan—but again, by no means entirely like.[116] From beginning to end, Satan, the Adversary and ultimately the serpentine embodiment of Evil, is enmeshed in the doubleness of literary allegory, as I have argued throughout this chapter. My present question is simply whether or to what extent God and his Son, both of whom the figure of Satan so often deliberately or inwittingly mimes, are similarly so. Is Milton's depiction of God and his Son in Book III—crucially his first and arguably his most lasting depiction of them—literary allegory, as is his depiction of the unholy Trinity in hell?

This is a formal question with real, substantial consequences. It is more structural and fundamental than are the more obvious, yet still important, ideational differences between Satan's and the Son's missions: for example, their motivations, Satan's envy, destruction, and self-glorification, and the Son's charity, salvation, and self-sacrifice. A thematized, stylistic difference also exists in the highly rhetorical language of Satan in hell and God's painfully plain speaking in much of Book III, which is especially, mnemonically impressive in his first speech. The difference between the relation of the Son to the Father in Book III and that of the devils to Satan and Beelzebub in the "great consult" of Book II is further relevant. The great consult turns out to be a performance staged by Satan and his chief henchman Beelzebub. Its result is determined beforehand, according with their plan: this is already a parody of divine providence and of freedom and agency, as well as of the relation of Father and Son in Book III.[117]

The conversation between the Father and Son in the third book corrects the diabolical debasing of agency in hell. Treip has described their conversation as a "ritualized representation, . . . with . . . liturgical rhythms, of the dual nature of the Godhead," that is, of justice and mercy (235).[118] While recognizing something of the effect to which she responds, I worry about ascribing duality so bluntly to Milton's Godhead and the unqualified appreciation of ritualized liturgy to Milton.[119] I also consider the conversation between God and the Son a notably intellectual exchange, quite in contrast to the affective but surely less rational intoning of ritual.[120] Borrowing a metaphor from music, I would describe their amicable debate as a contrapuntal duet, ending in complex harmony. In this respect, it could not contrast more thoroughly with the specious harmonies of hell.

Allegorically minded though I am, I am not inclined to see Milton's depiction of God and the Son in Book III specifically as allegory, although one might make a case for sublated (and sublating) metaphor. The striking, if finally and necessarily relative, absence of defining doubleness in heaven, whether in descriptions or speeches, is telling for me. This is the duplicity Spenser embodies perversely in Duessa, and it is also a feature of human language that is especially concentrated in complex allegory, such as his. In God's conversation with the Son, however, puns, metaphors, and epic similes are notably missing; more precisely, given the metaphorical condition of human language, they are inconspicuous and suppressed until the exchange between Father and Son nears its conclusion, and thereafter in its celebration by the angels: "Dark with excessive bright thy Skirts appear," for my favorite moment of Miltonic vision. The features of figurative language and rhetoric that I have specified are forms of doubleness characteristic of literary allegory, which is itself a definitively extended form of metaphor, the arch-trope that is and/or is not.

Qualification of literal language in God's speech, if not exceptions to it, merit attention, however. Christopher Ricks, having indicated that he is not sure whether he is looking at metaphor or not, discusses the word *transport* in God's first speech in Book III: "Onely begotten son, seest thou what rage / Transports our adversarie. . . ." (80–81)? Ricks's uncertainty is justified, since he responds to what I consider metaphor *in potentia*—potential metaphor that is hinted, implied, foreshadowed, and also foreshadowing. What Ricks observes is the setting of this word "in a context which stresses the physical roots of the emotional meaning, so that we see a *transport* [Latin: *transportare*, "carry across"] as something that does literally and powerfully *move* you" (47, 59–60). This is actually a reliteralizing of the word and a return to its basic, etymological meaning—what John Leonard might call its natural meaning, momentarily unaffected by Satan's rage here. Yet *transport* IS a pun for the postlapserian reader (Ricks in this instance) and presumably for this eternal, omniscient deity as well when he remarks Satan's journey toward earth, although it is also iconic with respect to Satan's condition and its doubleness arguably contained (included and controlled) by God's specific application of its iconicity to the already-fallen Satan.

Other words in God's speech, twice notably *pervert*—"By some false guile pervert; and shall pervert" (92)—are similarly inflected and subtly "infected," to use Ricks's term, upon which Leonard greatly enlarges.[121] Thus God's first speech might be said not only to announce the coming Fall of humankind in conspicuously plain and direct terms but also verbally to foreshadow the metaphorizing of language that will accompany the Fall. *Transport*, "carry across," is virtually a stand-in for *translate*, "carry across" or, in its rhetorical sense, "metaphorize," and *pervert* (from Latin *pervetere*) signifies "turned away, around, about" or "athwart," hence "tropic" (Greek *tropos*, "turn"). Both words encapsulate *in potentia* the linguistic, along with the moral, effect of sin. For a modern reader, *pervert* resonates further with Paul Ricoeur's definition of metaphor as a "deviant predication"—one that turns away from the literal sense, troping into the simultaneity of being and not being, or, as-ifness.[122] Again, such explicit troping at this point is potential—there and not there—rather than fully realized, and it is intimated rather than explicit. It could well result from the perversity, the tropic deviance, of human language itself and thereby express the agency of the signifier, rather than of the poet, or it could be some combination of these—for example, a fortuitous word or phrase (*transport*) whose potential is heard by the poet and then reinforced or developed (*pervert*).[123] If briefly and tangentially I might reintroduce an intertextual point bearing on alternative agencies, readers need to go beyond the imposition of rigid, hard-edged categories on imaginative writings, which, in effect, deny their distinctive, metaphorical mode of *cognition*, a mode simultaneously continuous with and different from that of more purely abstractive systems.

Perhaps the closest the divine conversation gets to conspicuous doubleness, however, comes in the notorious ambiguity of the word "ingrate" within the Father's first speech: "whose fault? / Whose but his own? ingrate, he had of mee /All he could have" (III.96–98). The ambiguity here does not consist primarily in signification *per se*, that is, in the meaning of *ingrate*, which is "ungrateful" or, as noun, "ungrateful Man," even though the latter, nominal reading cooperates more readily with rhythmic doubleness. Essentially, the problem lies in accent and rhythmic performance and therefore in reading. If "ingrate" is accented on the first syllable (íngrate), it sounds indignant, if not contemptuous, and angry or even defensive, and the intralineal pause at the end of the question just before it ("whose but his own?") invites the trochaic substitution that would ask for this initial accentuation of "ingrate"—with or without the nominalizing capitalization of this word that editors occasionally elect.[124] Accentuation of the first syllable would also invite interpretation of "ingrate" as a noun. But if "ingrate" is read with the Latinate accent on the second syllable (ingráte, from Latin *ingrātus*), it sounds calmer, unworried, relatively unemotional and a-tonal, and, in these senses, Olympian.[125] If the dominant iambic meter of the poem is maintained in reading the line in question, it would also invite the latter, adjectival alternative, as it does in the less ambiguous rhythmic context of Abdiel's use of the word "ingrate" to rebuke Satan in Book V, an echo that many novice readers quite tellingly miss at first: the poem makes it easy in the later passage to overlook the connection of an ungrateful, rebellious angel with the likes of us (V.811).

In particular, then, I do not consider the conversation of God with his Son an allegory of the divine mind's place, properly, structurally, and formally speaking, since it lacks the verbal and rhetorical doubleness that would identify it as such. Nonetheless, this conversation is a representation and expression of divine thought and intention in our language and, as such, necessarily approximate and imperfect. Milton, true to his Spenserian model, ensures our awareness of imperfection virtually from the outset of the conversation, with puns *in potentia* and more certainly with the single, focalized, deliberately troublesome word "ingrate." This is not suddenly to deny that allegory as a duplex, doubled, duplicit form has a noticeable affinity to Satan's hellish place in Milton's epic, but, rather, to insist on it and simultaneously to assert the distancing of divine conversation from allegorical form as fully as human language allows—that is, to a notably significant extent, yet still incompletely. The difference, observed in my introduction, between the perception that all language is allegorical and that allegory is a specific literary form pertains to this imperfection: there can be no clean and clear separation between these perceptions; eventually, the one will slide into the other. At the same time, however, merely collapsing the one into the other eventuates in an undifferentiated blur—a terrible sameness. This is one way of framing the problem of representing the Godhead in Book III.

In Milton's hell, Satan, Sin, and Death combine in a notorious parody of the Trinity to raise further issues about the unity or duplicity of Milton's representation of the Godhead in Book III and specifically about its visualization. Saint Bonaventure's influential formulation of the Trinitarian view of Father, Son, and Spirit remarks the traditional correspondence between the Trinity and the human psyche in a way that seems made for Milton's Satanic version: "Just as the Father engenders the eternal knowledge of the Word who expresses Him, and as the Word is in turn united with the Father by the Holy spirit, so memory or thought, big with the ideas which it encloses, engenders knowledge of the intellect or word, and love is born from both as the bond that unites them. It is no accidental correspondence that is here described; the structure of the creative trinity conditions and therefore explains the structure of the human soul."[126] Outrageously parodying this view, Sin, engendered by Satan, reunites with him, and their offspring Death (rather than love) is born from the bond that unites them. Milton is hardly a traditional Trinitarian, however, and what strikes me most is the obvious gap between his depictions of the unholy Trinity in hell and of the Father and Son in heaven.

God's Son is the "radiant image of . . . [the Father's] Glory" and also the Father "visibly" and "Substantially express'd"; in addition, he is the Father's "word . . . wisdom, and effectual might," who speaks the Father's thoughts and purpose (III.63, 140–41, 170). Perhaps most provocatively, he is, if only in the angels' choric song of praise, the "Divine Similitude, / In whose conspicuous count'nance, without cloud / Made visible, th' Almighty Father shines" (384–86). Treip takes "Similitude" to mean not only "likeness" but "metaphor" here (203). I think the latter unlikely and allegory even less so.[127] Within the rhetorical tradition tracing back to the Romans, a *similitudo* is simply a likeness, although it is open to various extensions and applications.[128] It certainly need not be metaphor, and still less, continued metaphor, or allegory.

As I read the likeness of the Son to the Father in Book III, it lacks tropic tension, the denial of likeness that would accompany its assertion if the likeness were truly metaphor, rather than, say, *illustration* (from Latin *in* and *lustrare*, "make bright," or, perhaps, "radiant," as in "radiant image").[129] The Neoplatonic (and notably Spenserian) notion of emanation, a vital flowing out, a radiating, is also suggestive with respect to the Son's likeness, particularly as distinguished from something illusorily projected onto a screen—a Platonic shadow on the wall of an enclosing cave, say—again a distinction that glances at Satan's situation in hell. In short, the likeness of the Son to the Father appears preeminently verbal, nonfigurative, and truly substantive, whereas metaphor both is and is not and is also *as if*, that is, fictive and hypothetical. If the Son voices the value of mercy in counterpoint to the Father's stern justice, his view turns out to be exactly the Father's thought after all. It is not partly, conditionally, or as if so. If they are two, in this respect they are also one.

We call a portrait photograph or portrait painting a likeness or a resemblance without thinking it metaphorical, and if it is a metaphor, it arguably enters another order of representation and, indeed, of signification. Normally a likeness is not an allegorical projection, either—that is, a narcissistic psychic image that in whole or in part really is, or else is interchangeable with, oneself. Nor is the reflected likeness in the mirror of my medicine cabinet what I would normally consider a similitude, although it might be, insofar as it only approaches the reality of my face: as a similitude, the Son is not the same as, or identical to, the Father, but he is nonetheless still *like* him.[130] But the very idea of an image may be distracting in Book III if we think of it in pictorial terms; we certainly have no idea of what Milton's God looks like and we really do not have one of his radiant image the Son, either. Although Milton uses the word "visibly" to characterize the relation of Son to Father, vision in *Paradise Lost* is hardly limited to physical sight except in Satanic reasoning, and "image," *imago*, the product of the imagination, which accesses the inner cave of memory as well as images from the immediately sensory world, can be purely and substantively verbal.[131] Both Father and Son are primarily words, attitudes, and values in Book III, and, taken together, they are distinct voices—at least at one moment, already discussed, an ambiguous voice on the part of the Father.[132]

God's final speech in this book makes explicit and deliberate use of figurative language, however: first, in modern terms, it uses simile, with the explicit marker *as*, here short for "as if," and then it uses a continuation of simile that opens into metaphor, the arch-trope, with its more direct and immediate translational claim.[133] Significantly, God refers here to the Incarnation and Redemption, both of which involve conceptual and physical movement vertically, the one down, the other up.[134] He employs a traditional image to explain that as all the descendants of Adam perish in him, so in the Son, "as from a second root" as many as are to be restored will be so (III.287–89).[135] God's rhetoric, not to mention his logic, could have come right out of a handbook. Aristotle describes the metaphorical transference—the translation (*translatio*: "carrying across")—that results from proportional analogy as being "possible whenever there are four terms [old Adam and fallen descendants, New Adam and restored descendants] so related that the second is to the first as the fourth to the third; for one may then put the fourth in place of the second, and the second in place of the fourth."[136] This transference of first to third and fourth to second goes beyond merely associative relation to *near* identity. Emphasizing similarity, it invites substitution *yet* structurally recognizes difference nonetheless. It is a transfer, a translation, a carrying across that is categorically metaphorical within the rhetorical tradition extending from antiquity through the Renaissance. It is and is not, unless it is by faith absolutely, that is, by *vision*. Read solely in light of Reality, God's allegory and his translational power in the world are wholly real: just think of the *translations* of Enoch or Elijah to heaven (III.522, XI.664–71).

Within several lines, God returns explicitly to his metaphorical logic. He adds that to Adam's redeemed sons the sacrificial merit of God's Son is to be imputed, or credited, as if to a financial account: Latin *imputare*, "enter into the account," combining *in*, "into, to, towards" and *putare*, "cleanse, clear up, count, reckon." In this way, Adam's elected sons shall be "absolved" (Latin *absolvere*, "loosen from," "set free"), provided that they also disclaim their own deeds:

And live in thee [the incarnate Son] *transplanted*, and from thee
Receive new life. So Man, as is most just,
Shall satisfie for Man, be judg'd and die,

And *dying rise, and rising* with him *raise*
His Brethren.
(III.293–97: my emphasis)

Talionic justice (an eye for an eye) will at once be satisfied and transmuted to redemption. It will be transplanted, translated, carried across to another place, a redemptive place, through the potency of self-sacrificing charity—love. The language is partly legal here, but the underlying logic and the imagery are metaphorical. Like the figure of the root before, here the organic, arboreal metaphor may be materially substantive, but it works tropically.[137] "Dying rise, and rising . . . raise": this is the active work and the working activity of metaphorized sublation—raising, cancelling, and, in the new Adam's Manhood (humanity), also continuing. This is, moreover, profoundly the action of the substantive w/Word.

Finally, this action encapsulates God's allegory, here the *continued metaphor* of root and tree, that is incident, significantly so, on incarnation and redemption, the movement down, then up. This is not materially monist identity but near identity that must recognize the difference between the organically natural and the fictively, constructively, creatively moral that truly defines the similitude, or the likeness, of Man to God and distinguishes it from the purely, yet merely, natural innocence that was (or here in God's timeless eternity also is and will be) lost. As metaphor, it includes doubleness, along with difference, however limited, and where there is doubleness and difference, there will always also be some leap from logic and rhetoric and from structure and material substance, to faith. If an animist, divinely inspired materialism were somehow to deny this leap, this gap, this translation, it would refuse the consequence of sinning and falling, which even in those redeemed still coexists in this world with death. If death is a Real nonentity, it is nonetheless real, and its reality ensures the necessary bifocality of human experience. Far from being merely identical with insubstantiality and illusion, allegory's intersecting dimensions of real and Real are the true way of our world.[138]

The tale Milton's nephew Edward Phillips tells about the occasioning of *Paradise Regained* by Thomas Ellwood's question to Milton after reading *Paradise Lost* may have puzzled Milton at first, since he is reported initially to have met it with silence.[139] Ellwood's question was simply, "what hast thou to say of *Paradise found*?" While Milton is said later to have told Ellwood that he had not thought of this question, I suspect he had not done so only because he supposed it obvious that, in some sense, he had already addressed the recovery of paradise in his epic and that he took Ellwood's question to require something more. In *Paradise Lost*, Milton's two accounts of the Incarnation and Redemption and his concluding focus on a "paradise within" certainly speak to recovery and renewal. His allegorized history in the final books of the epic, which simultaneously prepares for and leads into his conception of the "paradise within," does so as well. Drawing extensively on the Bible, this account sweeps into its allegorical plot even the Incarnation and Redemption as crucially defining, yet still unfinished, events in what Auerbach has characterized as *konkret Innergeschichtlichen*, "concrete inner history." The "paradise within," whose Miltonic "soul," or animating spirit, is charity, in the end may also be an actual grasp of the Augustinian threefold present discussed, along with Auerbachian typology, in my introduction to this volume (XII.583–87). The three stages of this dynamic and dialectical present correspond to the distension (*distentio*) of past and future, their extension as memory and expectation, that is presently held in continuity within the attentive mind, the *intentio*. With respect to history, such a view includes not only past wars and reigns and past sins, punishments, and sacrifices, but also includes past myths and poetic models. Comprehensively, it endeavors to balance history with significant emplotment, the reality of flesh and worldly event with that of the creatively metaphorizing and, more exactly, the constructively allegorizing mind. Within human history and human language, which participates in history, such a mind gratefully acknowledges doubleness, and especially the potential of tropic doubleness for evil or good, and it never stops trying to rise above it.

Notes

Introduction: Reading the Allegorical Intertext

1. Michael Riffaterre also uses the term *intertext*; he, too, considers it a relationship and aligns it with an act of reading: *Semiotics of Poetry* (Bloomington: Indiana University Press, 1978), e.g., 2, 42, 165–66. Riffaterre's sense of a poem as primarily metonymic code(s) and riddle and of the intertext as a word game may be apt for nineteenth- and twentieth-century French lyrics, but, aside from occasionally provocative resonances, it does not fit mine (137, 164). My designs are also more historical and less global than his. The specifically allegorical intertext I address involves a base text that is less self-sufficient, more mimetic (as subsequently discussed), and more open than is his conception of textuality. Gérard Genette relevantly criticizes Riffaterre's definition of intertextuality for its *de facto* limitation to "semantic-semiotic microstructures" rather than to "the work considered as a structural whole": *Palimpsests: Literature in the Second Degree*, trans. Channa Newman and Claude Doubinsky (Lincoln: University of Nebraska Press, 1997), 2–3. On Riffaterre, see also Jay Clayton and Eric Rothstein, eds., *Influence and Intertextuality in Literary History* (Madison: University of Wisconsin Press, 1991), 23–24; and Graham Allen, *Intertextuality* (London: Routledge, 2000), 115–32, esp. 115, 119–20, 124, 132; Mary Orr, *Intertextuality: Debates and Contexts* (Cambridge, U.K.: Polity, 2003), 37–40.

2. Orr, 1–2, 29, 31–32, 66. The phrase "a mosaic of quotations" appears in Kristeva's "Word, dialogue, novel," translated in 1980 from the 1969 French version in *Semeiotikè: recherches pour une sémanalyse* (Paris: Points), chap 4; two years earlier, Kristeva had published the essay as "Bakhtin, le mot, le dialogue et le roman," *Critique*, no. 239 (1967), 438–65 (Orr, 21, 185*n*6). For the translation, see Kristeva's *Desire in Language: A Semiotic Approach to Literature and Art*, ed. Leon S. Roudiez, trans. Thomas Gora, Alice Jardine, and Leon S. Roudiez (New York: Columbia University Press, 1980), 64–91, here 66, where "intertextuality" and "a mosaic of quotations" occur in consecutive sentences. Noting that Kristevan intertexuality "involve[s] the components of a *textual system* such as the novel," Roudiez glosses her intertextuality "as the transposition of one or more *systems* of signs into another, accompanied by a new articulation of the enunciative and denotative position" (15). *Transposition* is Kristeva's subsequent (1974) term for *intertextuality* and at once an effort to distance the latter from simple source-study and to tie it to subjectivity in both the psychological and social senses (i.e., positionality): see *Kristeva's Revolution*

in *Poetic Language*, trans. Margaret Waller (New York: Columbia University Press, 1984), 59–60; also Clayton and Rothstein, eds., "Figures in the Corpus: Theories of Influence and Intertextuality," 3–36, here 21; and Tilottama Rajan, "Intertextuality and the Subject of Reading/Writing," in *Influence and Intertextuality*, ed. Clayton and Rothstein, 61–74, here 63 (transposition); while recognizing the generative energy of Kristevan intertextuality, Rajan cautions against its "dynamics of negativity" (65).

3. In the interest of consistency, I have substituted the letter "X" for Allen's letter "A."

4. Paul Ricoeur, "The Metaphorical Process as Cognition, Imagination, and Feeling," in *On Metaphor*, ed. Sheldon Sacks (1978; rpt. Chicago: University of Chicago Press, 1979), 141–57, here 151; also his *Rule of Metaphor: Multi-disciplinary Studies of the Creation of Meaning in Language*, trans. Robert Czerny with Kathleen McLaughlin and John Costello (1977; rpt. Toronto: University of Toronto Press, 1987), 224, 256; and Judith H. Anderson, *Translating Investments: Metaphor and the Dynamic of Cultural Change in Tudor-Stuart England* (New York: Fordham University Press, 2005), 7, 218n7. Further, see Wolfgang Iser, *The Fictive and the Imaginary: Charting Literary Anthropology* (Baltimore: Johns Hopkins University Press, 1993), xiv–xv, whose language my description also invokes: like Ricoeur's Majorcan tales, Iser's category of the fictive is not tied to "the old fiction/reality dichotomy." The fictive "keeps in view what has been overstepped," but it is nonetheless "an act of boundary-crossing" that at once "disrupts and doubles the referential world." In the simultaneity of Ricoeur's split reference, as in the pastoral narratives that Iser privileges, the crossing of boundaries, disruption of the everyday, and doubling of reference actually *trans-figure* the world that we know, rather than merely reflecting, refusing, or rising above it.

5. Gregory Machacek usefully discusses Kristevan *intertextuality* in an essay on "Allusion," *PMLA*, 122 (2007), 522–36, here 523–25: for Kristeva, the term "denotes . . . the semiotic principles and presuppositions that lie, as it were, between texts from a given culture." It indicates a text's "'participation in the discursive *space* of a culture'" (citation from Jonathan Culler, "Presupposition and Intertextuality," *The Pursuit of Signs: Semiotics, Literature, Deconstruction* [Ithaca, N.Y.: Cornell University Press, 1981], 100–18, here 103: Machacek's emphasis). Machacek rightly rejects the view that synchronic and diachronic forms of intertextuality are antithetical or that the relationship of a text to a prior text or texts is a-cultural—readerless, as well as writerless, in effect (531, 533–34).

6. Cf. Rajan, 61, for a similar view. On the extension of the intertextuality of the signifier to whole texts, Vincent B. Leitch analyzes Joseph N. Riddel's theory of the literary text as a play of textual differences that radically displaces and reappropriates other texts: in Leitch's words, "Riddel merges intertextuality with textuality; that is, he presents the literary text as irreducibly infiltrated by previous texts. . . . The predecessor-texts themselves operate intertextually." Texts are thus "uncontrollably permeated with previous texts"; "In place of pure signifiers . . . we have

here contaminating pieces of various intertexts": *Deconstructive Criticism: An Advanced Introduction* (New York: Columbia University Press, 1983), 98. Rajan accuses Leitch of "unwittingly" conceding that this conception mixes textuality with intertextuality (63). I find more revealing the values of purity and contamination—textual versus intertextual hygiene, or ascetism—at once in Leitch's description and Rajan's criticism of it. Their interpretive, metaphorical binaries oversimplify the issue. (For the relevant passages by Riddel, see *Martin Heidegger and the Question of Literature: Toward a Postmodern Literary Hermeneutics*, ed. William V. Spanos [Bloomington: Indiana University Press, 1979], 247–49; and Riddell's "Interpreting Stevens: An Essay on Poetry and Thinking," *Boundary 2*, 1 [1972], 79–97.)

7. *The Faerie Queene*, ed. A. C. Hamilton, with text by Hiroshi Yamashita and Toshiyuki Suzuki, 2nd ed. (Harlow, U.K.: Pearson, 2001), IV.ii.34, VI.Pro.2. Subsequent reference in my introduction is to this edition.

8. Genette's poetics of transtextuality relates suggestively to my project, but, like Riffaterre's poetics, only to an extent. For Genette, transtextuality includes, among other textual variations, intertextuality, understood specifically as quotation, plagiarism, and allusion; architextuality, understood as genre, mode, and the like; and hypertextuality, understood to involve whole texts and variously to embrace imitation (1–7). The structuralism he envisions is open, social, and conscious or deliberate; it is typified by (satiric) parody and pastiche (9). My own sense of the hypothetical intertext is more receptive to the agency of the signifier as a subversive potency, more historically and formally grounded, and more rhetorically oriented. My claims are still more pragmatic and less grandly inclusive than Genette's. For other assessments of Genette, cf. Allen, 95–115; Orr, 106–112.

9. For example, see Andy Clark's *Being There: Putting Brain, Body, and World Together Again* (Cambridge, Mass.: MIT Press, 2001), 32–33.

10. Ricoeur, *Time and Narrative*, trans. Kathleen McLaughlin and David Pellauer, 3 vols. (Chicago: University of Chicago Press, 1984). Ricoeur argues both that "the world unfolded by every narrative work is always a temporal world" and that "time becomes human time to the extent that it is organized after the manner of a narrative" (I, 3).

11. See my *Growth of a Personal Voice: "Piers Plowman" and "The Faerie Queene"* (New Haven, Conn.: Yale University Press, 1976), e.g., 4–5.

12. Marcus Tullius Cicero, *De Oratore*, ed. G. P. Goold, trans. E. W. Sutton, completed H. Rackham, 2 vols. (1942–49; rpt. London: Heinemann, 1976–78), II: Bk. III.xli.166. I want to keep at a distance Roman Jakobson's dubious transfer of distinctions in structuralist linguistics to rhetoric, specifically the identification of the paradigmatic/associative with metaphor and the syntagmatic/contiguous with metonymy: see Jean-François Lyotard's critique, "The Dream-Work Does Not Think," trans. Mary Lydon, in *The Lyotard Reader*, ed. Andrew Benjamin (Oxford: Blackwell, 1989), 19–40, here 30–40: "Jakobson starts off from a notion of substitution based on a strictly structuralist concept of language, and proceeds (unjustifiably, as we will see) to a rhetorical meaning of metaphor which is applied to discourse"

(34). Lyotard exposes as erroneous not only this Jakobsonian transfer, but also that from linguistics to psychology as an "imprecision [that] results from applying to one field of expression [I would add, metonymically substituting from one to another] categories borrowed from another, quite different field (33).

13. Carolynn Van Dyke, *The Fiction of Truth: Structures of Meaning in Narrative and Dramatic Allegory* (Ithaca, N.Y.: Cornell University Press, 1985), 40.

14. Alastair Fowler, *Kinds of Literature: An Introduction to the Theory of Genres and Modes* (Cambridge, Mass.: Harvard University Press, 1982), 56, 106, 191–95.

15. Cf. Fowler, 20, 37; all of chaps. 2–3 is relevantly suggestive.

16. Stephen A. Barney, *Allegories of History, Allegories of Love* (Hamden, Conn.: Archon, 1979), 29.

17. Van Dyke, 37. Frye, "Allegory," in *Princeton Encyclopedia of Poetry and Poetics* (enlarged edition), ed. Alex Preminger, with Frank J. Warnke and O. B. Hardison (Princeton, N.J.: Princeton University Press, 1974), 12–15.

18. On Prudentius, see Van Dyke, 46–67; on *Everyman*, see her "The Intangible and Its Image: Allegorical Discourse and the Cast of *Everyman*," in *Acts of Interpretation: The Text in Its Contexts, 700–1600*, ed. Mary J. Carruthers and Elizabeth D. Kirk (Norman, Okla.: Pilgrim, 1982), 311–24.

19. Gordon Teskey, *Allegory and Violence* (Ithaca, N.Y.: Cornell University Press, 1996). The following sentence in my text is based on Teskey's chap. 1, esp. 14–18.

20. Surprisingly, Hamilton, ed., takes "stocke" exclusively to mean "matter," evidently connecting "For" in line 6 with line 3 alone, whereas, it readily connects with line 2 as well (347n36.3–9). In the same note, he also assumes an exclusively material meaning of the word "substances" in line 9, but *substance* is a highly controverted term with multiple possible meanings in this period, more than one of which is relevant here: on *substance*, see my *Translating Investments*, 49–51. John Erskine Hankins, *Source and Meaning in Spenser's Allegory* (Oxford: Clarendon, 1971), 259–60, and Humphrey Tonkin, "Spenser's Garden of Adonis and Britomart's Quest," *PMLA*, 88 (1973), 408–17, here 411, similarly recognize the ambiguity, or doubled reference, of "stocke." For further discussion of Spenser's Garden, see chapter 14 in this volume: "Flowers and Boars: Surmounting Sexual Binarism in Spenser's Garden of Adonis."

21. *The Ground of the Image*, trans. Jeff Fort (New York: Fordham University Press, 2005), 9, 20. On "exhilaration," see, for example, "jouissance" (9).

22. Erwin Panofsky, "The Neoplatonic Movement and Michelangelo," *Studies in Iconology: Humanistic Themes in the Art of the Renaissance* (1939; rpt. New York: Harper and Row, 1962), 171–230, here 181.

23. In a discussion of early medieval literature with wide ramifications, Christopher Cannon observes that Thomas Aquinas, "understood better than most that . . . form described the borderline between thought and things." He adds that a history of forms "would be a history of the tension between idealism and materialism as general views": *The Grounds of English Literature* (Oxford: Oxford University Press, 2004), 8–9. Form might be said both to materialize thought and to formalize matter.

For a brief, classic exposition of Aristotle's hylomorphism, see William B. Hunter, Jr., "Milton's Power of Matter," *Journal of the History of Ideas*, 13 (1952), 551–62.

24. Thomas H. Luxon, *Literal Figures: Puritan Allegory and the Reformation Crisis in Representation* (Chicago, Ill.: University of Chicago Press, 1995), 43; Erich Auerbach, *Figura*, trans. Ralph Mannheim, in *Scenes from the Drama of European Literature* (New York: Meridian, 1959), 11–76. For Auerbach's original German text, see his *Neue Dantestudien, Instanbuler Schriften*, 5 (Istanbul: Robert Anhegger, Walter Ruben, Andreas Tietze, 1944), 11–71. When I cite both languages, I shall give parenthetical, paginal references in English first, German second.

25. Barbara Kiefer Lewalski, *Protestant Poetics and the Seventeenth-Century Religious Lyric* (Princeton, N.J.: Princeton University Press, 1979), chap. 4, e.g., 111.

26. Auerbach, *Figura*: English, 54; German, 48. On "Innergeschichtlichkeit" here, given the somewhat open-ended translation "historicity," see the discussion later in my introduction.

27. Luxon rightly observes that Auerbach makes an ontological distinction between allegory and history, but the latter does not stop with this distinction; frequently he refers to a teleological difference as well (Luxon, 44; Auerbach: English, 54; German 48). Auerbach apparently considers all forms of "allegory" static. He does not conceive of allegory as narrative or temporal process, which is fundamental to my own view of literary allegory.

28. Auerbach was a German-Jewish refugee from Nazi Germany when he wrote *Figura*. Luxon presents Auerbach as one who would (unknowingly?) evacuate Jewish reality, or biblical history. The Auerbach I read in the German text is an accomplished cultural historian, who is aware of his terms and their implications, which the English translation, good as it is, flattens out. Auerbach's insistence on the concreteness of Old Testament history complexly and therefore realistically recognizes its continuity and preservation, despite an overlay of Christian ideology: cf. Hegel's *Aufhebung*—simultaneously, paradoxically "raising," "canceling," and "preserving." (I treat *Aufhebung/aufheben* in subsequent paragraphs, as well as in later chapters.) But compare Rachel J. Trubowitz's argument that Milton, the last two books of whose epic are full of typology, is ambivalent "about the concreteness of the biblical Israel, about the Hebraic/Judaic past, and, more broadly, about the very matter of historical memory itself": "Body Politics in *Paradise Lost*," *PMLA*, 121 (2006), 388–404, here 390–91. Perhaps by explicating Pauline duality, Auerbach, for all his insistence on materiality, indicates a similar ambivalence or, in his case, a loss of ethnic identity. On such a contaminating critical gaze, however, consider Elliot R. Wolfson's trenchant remarks in *Language, Eros, Being: Kabbalistic Hermeneutics and Poetic Imagination* (New York: Fordham, 2005), 86: critical engagement "enmeshes the scholar [or the artist] in bolstering what is criticized, implicating one in erasure and inscription simultaneously."

29. Auerbach's *Mimesis*, originally published in German, was translated into English by Willard Trask in 1953: the edition of this translation to which I refer is New York: Doubleday (1957).

30. At a later stage of argument not concerned specifically with Augustine, Auerbach discusses the difference between figural and modern interpretations of historical persons and events and again refers to an ideal model, or prototype, situated in the future. This model, he continues, which is "imitated in the figures [one is reminded of the phrase "*imitatio veritatis*, 'imitation of the truth' '": Auerbach, 44] recalls Platonistic notions" (59). Another point: Auerbach's *transposition* ("*versetzt*") in the immediately preceding, indented citation resonates both with Kristeva's substitution of *transposition* for *intertextuality*, either of which is basically a metaphorical concept, and with the Latin term for metaphor, *translatio/transferre*, "to carry across, transfer," or indeed, "transpose," as noted earlier in this chapter.

31. Thanks to Breon Mitchell and Fritz Breithaupt, my colleagues in German, for reassuring me on this point. I should add that I alone am responsible for renderings of Auerbach's meaning in the context of *Figura*.

32. Ricoeur, *Time and Narrative*, I, chap. 1, esp. 9, 11, 21. Ricoeur's major text in the chapter is Book 11 of Augustine's *Confessions*.

33. On *aufheben/Aufhebung*, see my *Translating Investments*, 1, 17, 217n1.

34. Luxon, 59, also notices the importance of Auerbach's reference to "concrete dramatic actuality," but he opposes "dramatic" to "actual" by limiting "actual" exclusively to the material and merely literal and again supposes that Auerbach is fumbling rather than breaking ground.

35. Auerbach, *Figura*: for example, English, 16, 55 (2), 58, 59 (2); German, 16, 49 (2), 52, 53 (2).

36. Treating the reemergence of an Aristotelian concept of mimesis in the Renaissance, Janet Leslie Knedlick argues that Tasso and Mazzoni (not to mention Sidney and Milton) understood and applied "the fundamental point of Aristotle's *Poetics*: that in the process of structuring the artistic mimesis, the poetic maker works in a mode intrinsically valid as a way of knowing. . . . Generative mimesis [becomes] a 'middle term' between literal inspiration and autonomous imagination"—that is between biblical prophesy and the post-Kantian Romantic imagination: "Fancy, Faith, and Generative Mimesis in *Paradise Lost*," *Modern Language Quarterly*, 47 (1986), 19–47, here 24–25, 27, 30.

37. Ricoeur, *Time and Narrative*, I, 181; cf. 180–82, 186, 196. Ricoeur recognizes the circularity in his position but argues that this circle is healthy, not vicious. He indicates that he would prefer to speak of an endless spiral, and he endeavors to refute the two relevant versions of circularity, the first emphasizing violence, and the second redundancy (or tautology): see 72–76. His arguments merit consideration.

38. Ricoeur's major writings on metaphor are *The Rule of Metaphor* and "The Metaphorical Process," earlier cited.

39. See my *Translating Investments*, chap. 2. I have used my own formulations here, only to an extent adopting Ricoeur's, because, simply put, I have Auerbachian reservations about the extent to which he would *at moments* cancel descriptive, direct, or literal reference by raising and transposing it. Cancellation or annulment

is only partial in my view. Metaphorical reference is always bifocal, doubled (at least).

40. The subject of mimesis returns explicitly in my chapter 16, on Shakespeare's *Antony and Cleopatra*.

41. Rajan, 66–74 (esp. 66), offers a telling critique of the shortcomings of Kristeva's conception of intertextuality/transposition with respect to readers and reading.

42. T. S. Eliot, *Selected Essays*, new edition (New York: Harcourt Brace, 1950), 3–11, here 5.

43. The art historian Michael Baxandall pertinently remarks the "wrong-headed" view of influence in which agent and patient are always frozen into a single position, the earlier X acting on the later Y, whereas Y's relation to X is active and almost infinitely diverse: *Patterns of Intention: On the Historical Explanation of Pictures* (New Haven, Conn.: Yale University Press, 1985), 58–59.

44. I hardly want to deny that poetry, or, indeed, imaginative writing in general, heightens figuration, word-play, and the like. Spenser's *Faerie Queene* even uses deliberate archaism, albeit limited in extent and less wholly archaic in his time than in ours, especially given the existence of medieval English in linguistic pockets of early modern Ireland. (Willy Maley remarks the Middle English spoken by the Old Irish in *Salvaging Spenser: Colonialism, Culture and Identity* [London: Macmillan, 1997], 34.) What I would deny is that the medium of poetry is as unique as a critic like Riffaterre would make it. It is not a different kind of language, although it is *distinctively* heightened within and as a part of a given text. Literary language is on a continuum with ordinary language. For a different view, see Riffaterre, 88–89, 125, 138. Had Riffaterre understood medieval and Renaissance allegory, he might not so readily (and wrongly) have separated mimesis from semiosis and syntagm from paradigm.

45. My sense of *sharing* readings is reciprocal, at least in a classroom, and, if less immediate, in published engagements with others' views as well. Such sharing works against exclusivity of the sort of which an intertextualist like Riffaterre is quickly and generally accused. The textual community I have in mind, moreover, is knowledge-specific, but it is not my intention to imply that it is closed, unique, or superior to others. My present project may imply general applications, insofar as a reader grants that allegory is in some sense basic to signification, but it nonetheless focuses on particular textual relationships and kinds of intertextual relationships and not on universal ones: the latter have their place and their appeal, but also their losses of specificity, historicity, and ultimately, in my view, of persuasive power.

46. A personal anecdote: the last time my department seriously discussed the status and content of the traditional survey course, I recall that one my colleagues, a woman of Asian descent whose expertise lies in modernity, remarked, in defense of the survey, "I need it." Opposition needs an opponent, although this is hardly the only way of perceiving the past or those who evaluate it.

47. Quotation from *The Parliament of Fowls*, in Geoffrey Chaucer's *Works 1532, supplemented by material from the editions of 1542, 1561, 1598, and 1602* (1968; rpt. London, 1976), cclxxx^v. For discussion, see my chapter "Chaucer's *Parliament of Fowls* and Refractions of a Veiled Venus in *The Faerie Queene*."

48. Anne Davidson Ferry, *Milton's Epic Voice: The Narrator in "Paradise Lost"* (Cambridge, Mass.: Harvard University Press, 1963), chaps. 4–5, here 89; Mindele Anne Treip, *Allegorical Poetics and the Epic: The Renaissance Tradition to "Paradise Lost"* (Lexington: University Press of Kentucky, 1994), esp. chaps 4, 12, 20–21 (see also my final chapter); Kenneth Borris, *Allegory and Epic in English Renaissance Literature: Heroic Form in Sidney, Spenser, Milton* (Cambridge: Cambridge University Press, 2000), esp. parts 1 and 4. Walter Benjamin also characterizes the allegorical *Trauerspiel* (mourning play) as a Platonized idea that implies a metaphysics of form: *The Origin of German Tragic Drama*, trans. John Osborne (1998; rpt. London: Verso, 2003), 38, 46, 48.

49. Catherine Gimelli Martin, *The Ruins of Allegory: "Paradise Lost" and the Metamorphosis of Epic Convention* (Durham, N.C.: Duke University Press, 1998), introduction and chap. 1; on Spenser, see, for example, 33, 75, 125, 158, 196, 286. Martin speaks of "the static homologies of allegory" and generally identifies allegory simply with abstraction (e.g., 230–31). Martin's predecessor in this vein is Herman Rapaport, *Milton and the Postmodern* (Lincoln: University of Nebraska Press, 1983), 24–25. Rapaport explicitly rejects analogy with the "veiled" truths of Spenserian allegory, only to replace such a veil at a later point with the hymeneal veil of deconstruction (25–26, 82–83). The threefold present of Augustine's *intentio* and *attentio* (alert, inward present) might also be said to become for him the hymeneal dream of Jacques Derrida and Jacques Lacan (83–84).

50. See Borris, 2; Teskey, *Allegory and Violence*, 12; Benjamin, 57–235. Benjamin, Teskey's avowed inspiration, characterizes the baroque mourning play (*Trauerspiel*) as Platonized Idea (38, 46, 48, 169); he finds its spiritual source in emblem books, hieroglyphs, *tableaux vivants*, and triumphs (*trionfi*)—in subjective forms that torment flesh and rule arbitrarily over material things (220, 233). I have earlier characterized such forms as motionless "boundary cases," distinct from narrative allegory (162–63, 169, 175–76, 192–96). Refreshingly, William Kolbrener considers relevant to Milton the Walter Benjamin in whom he finds a grasp of *discordia concors*, rather than the Benjamin of mourning and nostalgia: *Milton's Warring Angels: A Study of Critical Engagements* (Cambridge: Cambridge University Press, 1997), 135. Kolbrener ascribes a poetics of complexity, polvalency, and paradoxical inconsistency to Milton, for whom "the incompleteness of representation does not so much signal a lack, but rather a perfection" (142).

51. Victoria Silver, *Imperfect Sense: the Predicament of Milton's Irony* (Princeton, N.J.: Princeton University Press, 2001), 26–54, e.g., 30, 210–25; see also my discussion of allegory and irony in the penultimate chapter. Cf. as well Peter Herman's argument for "incertitude," which shares ground with Silver's perception of irony in Milton: *Destabilizing Milton: "Paradise Lost" and the Poetics of Incertitude* (New York: Palgrave Macmillan, 2005). In *Delirious Milton* (Cambridge, Mass.: Harvard University Press, 2006), Gordon Teskey does not address allegory relevantly. He finds Spenser and Milton incomparable, however, the one a poet of hallucination and the other a poet of delirium; yet he also contrasts them, insofar as Spenser thinks archeologically through the layers of the past, whereas Milton is a thinker of the

arche itself, "of the origin and governing principle" (6, 14–15); as Fredric Jameson has observed, contrast implies at least some general identity between two things, without which meaningful differences could not be enumerated: *The Political Unconscious: Narrative as a Socially Symbolic Act* (1981; rpt. Ithaca, N.Y.: Cornell University Press, 1988), 41–42. My reference to Milton's *Paradise Regained*, IV, 390, is to the edition of Roy Flannagan, *The Riverside Milton* (Boston: Houghton Mifflin, 1998).

52. Susanne Lindgren Wofford, "Britomart's Petrarchan Lament: Allegory and Narrative in *The Faerie Queene* III, iv," *Comparative Literature*, 39 (1987), 28–57; Teskey, *Allegory and Violence*, esp. chap. 2.

53. Sayre N. Greenfield, *The Ends of Allegory* (Newark, N.J.: University of Delaware Press, 1998), chaps. 1, 3, 6, esp. 136–43. On distinguishing metaphor from metonymy, see also my *Translating Investments*, 1–4, 21–22, 61–62, and the rest of chap. 4.

54. See Barbara K. Lewalski, *The Life of John Milton: A Critical Biography* (Oxford: Blackwell, 2000), 508: John Dryden reports that Milton acknowledged Spenser to be his model, or "Original."

PART 1: Allegorical Reflections of *The Canterbury Tales* in the *Faerie Queene*

Chapter One: Chaucer's and Spenser's Reflexive Narrators

1. *The Faerie Queene*, IV.ii.34: all references to Spenser's writings in this chapter are to *The Works of Edmund Spenser: A Variorum Edition*, ed. Edwin Greenlaw et al, 11 vols. (1932–57; rpt. Baltimore: Johns Hopkins Press, 1966), cited as *Var*. Subsequently, *The Faerie Queene* is cited as *FQ*.

2. This is the reading of Lee Patterson in "'What Man Artow?': Authorial Self-Definition in *The Tale of Sir Thopas* and *The Tale of Melibee*," *Studies in the Age of Chaucer*, 11 (1989), 117–75, e.g., 123. See also Alfred David, *The Strumpet Muse: Art and Morals in Chaucer's Poetry* (Bloomington: Indiana University Press, 1976), chap. 15, esp. 215–21, on *sentence* and *solas* in *Melibee* and *Sir Thopas*.

3. See also my discussions of *Thopas* and *Melibee* elsewhere in this volume, namely, chapter 3, "'Pricking on the plaine': Spenser's Intertextual Beginnings and Endings," chapter 6, "Spenser's Use of Chaucer's *Melibee*: Allegory, Narrative, and History," and chapter 9, "Chaucer's *Parliament of Fowls* and Refractions of a Veiled Venus in *The Faerie Queene*."

4. E.g., *Colin Clouts Come Home Again*, vs. 652–87; and *FQ*, VI.ix.24–25, x.2–3.

5. Harry Berger, Jr., "'Kidnapped Romance': Discourse in *The Faerie Queene*," in *Unfolded Tales: Essays on Renaissance Romance*, ed. George M. Logan and Gordon Teskey (Ithaca, N.Y.: Cornell University Press, 1989), 208–56; "Narrative as

Rhetoric in *The Faerie Queene*," *English Literary Renaissance*, 21 (1991), 3–48. For discussions related to Berger's, albeit also distinguished from his, see David Lee Miller's argument for Spenserian "authorship under erasure": "The Earl of Cork's Lute," in *Spenser's Life and the Subject of Biography*, ed. Judith H. Anderson, Donald Cheney, and David A. Richardson (Amherst: University of Massachusetts Press, 1996), 146–71. Cheney's Afterword in the same volume pertinently describes a "dialogic" Spenser (172–77).

6. All Chaucerian references in this chapter are to *The Works 1532, with Supplementary Material from the Editions of 1542, 1561, 1598, and 1602* (1969; rpt. London: Scolar, 1976), here Bvi^r. I have expanded the contractions in Thynne's text and changed the solidi to commas; in the interest of clarity, I have also added minimal modern punctuation, which is enclosed within brackets. Unless otherwise noted, reference to Chaucer's texts is to this edition. Although A. Kent Hieatt (*Chaucer, Spenser, Milton: Mythopoeic Continuities and Transformations* [Montreal: McGill-Queen's University Press, 1975], 19–24) offers speculations regarding the specific edition of Chaucer that Spenser uses, his hard evidence—the word "checklatoun"—establishes only that this was one of the Thynne family of editions. I cite the facsimile of Thynne's 1532 edition for three reasons: (1) its wide availability, (2) the irrelevance to my argument of the texts added to later editions, (3) the absence of substantial variants among the Thynne editions that relate to my citations, and, indeed, in my experience, of substantial textual variants among these editions in general. Craig A. Berry's welcome discovery that Spenser might have known more than one edition of Chaucer—and an earlier edition than Thynne's at that—does not cancel Hieatt's evidence that Spenser knew one or more Thynne editions: "'Sundrie Doubts': Vulnerable Understanding and Dubious Origins in Spenser's Continuation of the Squire's Tale," in *Refiguring Chaucer in the Renaissance*, ed. Theresa M. Krier (Gainesville: University Press of Florida, 1998), 106–27, here 112 and 124n14.

7. In the main, I am following—and indebted to—the reading of H. Marshall Leicester, Jr., *The Disenchanted Self: Representing the Subject in the "Canterbury Tales"* (Berkeley: University of California Press, 1990), 383–417, here 397–98, 400–405. But see also David Lawton, *Chaucer's Narrators* (Cambridge: D. S. Brewer, 1985), 1–8, 102; and E. Talbot Donaldson's classic essay "Chaucer the Pilgrim," *PMLA*, 69 (1954), 928–36. For an illuminating update on the current status of the Chaucerian (and Donaldsonian) persona, see the recent issue of *The Chaucer Review* devoted to this subject, namely, 41.3 (2007).

8. Harry Berger, Jr., *Revisionary Play: Studies in the Spenserian Dynamics* (Berkeley: University of California Press, 1988), 59–60, has a provocatively entertaining discussion of the irony in this passage. My *Growth of a Personal Voice: "Piers Plowman" and "The Faerie Queene"* (New Haven, Conn.: Yale University Press, 1976), 97–98 and 219–20n3, is skeptical about Spenser's ironical treatment of Una in a way that I no longer embrace, although I continue to find this treatment problematical. On irony in the Proem to Book V, see my *Growth of a Personal Voice: "Piers Plowman" and "The Faerie Queene"* (New Haven, Conn.: Yale University Press, 1976), 184–86.

9. While recent criticism has considerably qualified the Knight's ideality and the Pardoner's degeneracy, the general moral contrast between them remains obvious.

10. Stephen A. Barney's *Allegories of History, Allegories of Love* (Hamden, Conn.: Archon, 1979), 17–18, 20–21, is pertinent; but also Joel Fineman, "The Structure of Allegorical Desire," in *Allegory and Representation*, ed. Stephen J. Greenblatt (Baltimore: Johns Hopkins University Press, 1981), 26–60, esp. 31–36.

11. Paul de Man, "The Rhetoric of Temporality," in *Interpretation: Theory and Practice*, ed. Charles S. Singleton (Baltimore: Johns Hopkins University. Press, 1969), 173–209, here 194–95. Cf. de Man on "Pascal's Allegory of Persuasion," in *Allegory and Representation*, ed. Greenblatt, 1–25. On the debate about the *dédoublement* of de Man's own life and its bearing on authorship, see the prologue of Séan Burke's *Death and Return of the Author: Criticism and Subjectivity in Barthes, Foucault and Derrida* (Edinburgh: Edinburgh University Press, 1992).

12. Gordon Teskey, "Irony, Allegory, and Metaphysical Decay," *PMLA*, 109 (1994), 397–408.

13. Responding to my essay, Alfred David asks whether this reference to Chaucer by the Man of Law makes "the narrator a different person" or whether it indicates his failure to recognize Chaucer as pilgrim. In any case, the ironic effect is to destabilize the subject, as David and I would agree. (David, 231, also suggests a Chaucerian signature in *The Second Nun's Prologue*, when the narrator, presumably the second nun, prays Mary, "though that I, unworthy sone of Eve, / Be synful, yet accepte my bileve": cited from *The Riverside Chaucer*, ed. Larry D. Benson, 3rd ed. [Boston, Mass.: Houghton Mifflin, 1987], 263, vs. 62–63. Insofar as the Thynne editions of Chaucer that Spenser used change "sone" to "doughter," my present concern, the question of whether this self-assertive filiation differs from the momentary blending of narrator with character that suggests self-projection, is moot as regards Spenser: lxv^v. In Caxton's 1478 edition, which Spenser might have seen, the word "sone" remains, however, and it could be read as an authorial signature, albeit a notably indirect one.)

14. In Gérard Genette's now familiar terminology, a paratext is "a title, a subtitle, intertitles; prefaces, postfaces, notices, forewords, etc.; marginal, infrapaginal, terminal notes; epigraphs; illustrations, blurbs, book covers, dust jackets, and many other kinds of secondary signals, whether allographic or autographic": *Palimpsests: Literature in the Second Degree*, trans. Channa Newman and Claude Doubinsky (Lincoln: University of Nebraska Press, 1997), 3.

15. I regard as an exception the occurrence of "Edmundus" in Spenser's Latin verse epistle "Ad Ornatissimum virum . . . G. H.," vs. 233, where Spenser's first name is ventriloquized as issuing from Gabriel Harvey's mouth (*Var.*, X, 11). Like Milton, Spenser appears to have felt Latin not only an intimate form but also a protecting (and mediating?) one. Insofar as John Donne and Ben Jonson are contemporaries of Spenser, in both cases writing during the 1590s, Spenser's evident avoidance of explicit nomination other than in Latin, for a dedication, or on a title page or such a letter as that to Ralegh (belatedly introducing *The Faerie Queene* at the end

of Book III in 1590 and not at all in 1596) is all the more noticeable: but see Joseph Loewenstein, "Spenser's Retrography: Two Episodes in Post-Petrarchan Bibliography," in *Spenser's Life and the Subject of Biography*, 99–130. Jonson, of course, employs his name explicitly in his poetry, and Donne plays openly on his.

16. On the cultural difference between history and poetry, truth and fiction, see chapter 10, on "The Antiquities of Fairyland and Ireland."

17. Bialostosky's statement is taken from an unpublished paper cited in Gerald Graff's *Professing Literature: An Institutional History* (Chicago: University of Chicago Press, 1987), 257, 303n.

18. Since the writers on whom I focus are men, I am not going regularly to use the phrase "he or she" or the pronoun "she" when in fact I am referring to "him." In a less specific discussion, I will operate otherwise.

19. Susan Frye's *Elizabeth I: The Competition for Representation* (Oxford: Oxford University Press, 1993), 124–35, instances a relevant effort to identify Spenser and his narrator with Busirane's perversions. A number of Frye's fascinating readings are questionable, however, and her assumptions about the relation of poet to poem need fuller theorization.

20. I might well be reading Chaucer as Spenser's poetry suggests he might have read him. The point is that the Chaucerian text accepts—indeed invites—such a reading.

21. According to the *OED*, *mask* is usually thought to have been adopted from French *masque*, in turn an adaptation of the synonymous Spanish *máscara* and Italian *maschera*. But the *OED* also suggests a connection between *mask* and medieval Latin *mascus, masca* "mask" or "specter." Slavoj Žižek describes a suggestively similar phenomenon in *The Sublime Object of Ideology* (London: Verso, 1989), 193–94: "If, behind the phenomenal veil, there is nothing, it is through the mediation of this 'nothing' that the subject constitutes himself in the very act of his misrecognition. The illusion that there is something hidden behind the curtain is . . . reflexive . . . what is hidden behind the appearance is the possibility of this very illusion." Likewise suggestive in relation to my argument are Judith Butler's theories about the performativity of identity: e.g., *Gender Trouble: Feminism and the Subversion of Identity* (New York: Routledge, 1990), 128–49; and her *Bodies That Matter: On the Discursive Limits of "Sex"* (New York: Routledge, 1993), 1–23.

22. Cf. the use of *mask* in *Amoretti* LIV:

> Of this worlds Theatre in which we stay,
>   My loue lyke the Spectator ydly sits
>   beholding me that all the pageants play,
>   disguysing diuersly my troubled wits.
> Sometimes I ioy when glad occasion fits,
>   and mask in myrth lyke to a Comedy. . . .

23. Discussing the social fashioning of identity in the Renaissance, Stephen Greenblatt observes that Thomas Hobbes (1588–1679) derives the English word *person* from Latin *persona*, "'*disguise, or outward appearance* of a man, counterfeited on

the stage; and sometimes more particularly . . . a Mask or Visard.'" Glancing at Shakespeare and Spenser, Greenblatt continues, "for Hobbes there is no person, no coherent, enduring identity beneath the mask. . . . Identity is only possible as a mask, something constructed and assumed": "Psychoanalysis and Renaissance Culture," in *Literary Theory / Renaissance Texts*, ed. Patricia Parker and David Quint (Baltimore: Johns Hopkins University Press, 1986), 210–24, here 221–23.

24. Curiously, the word *impersonation*, as distinct from the conception, does not appear until the the early decades of the seventeenth century and does not occur in a specifically theatrical sense until the eighteenth: OED, s.v. *Impersonate/-ion*. The OED records occurrences in 1598 and 1602 of the verb *personate*, from Latin *persona* ("mask"), meaning "to act or play the part of (a character in a drama or the like)." Spenser employs this verb in the dedication to "Mother Hubberds Tale," where he refers to "the simplicitie and meannesse thus personated"—that is, "thus represented as a person."

25. See Gail Kern Paster, *The Body Embarrassed: Drama and the Disciplines of Shame in Early Modern England* (Ithaca, N.Y.: Cornell University Press, 1993), 1–15, here 9; and Mikhail Bakhtin, *Rabelais and His World*, trans. Hélène Iswolsky (Cambridge, Mass.: M.I.T. Press, 1968), 26. Additional warrant for such blending might be found in the various philosophic ideas concerning a common human nature, which were often developed more confidently and consensually than were those concerning individuation.

26. In this line, after "byd" I have replaced Thynne's solidus with a question mark rather than a comma, and I have capitalized the *h* in "howe."

27. Leicester, 387, makes the same point, one that is generally familiar.

28. On the bearing of the Parson's portrait on other narrative personae in *The General Prologue*, see E. Talbot Donaldson, "Adventures with the Adversative Conjunction in the General Prologue to the *Canterbury Tales*; or, What's before the *But*?" in *So meny people longages and tonges: philological essays in Scots and mediaeval English presented to Angus McIntosh*, ed. Michael Benskin and M. L. Samuels (Edinburgh: by the eds., 1981), 355–66, here 355–56; and in chapter 2 of the present volume, my relation of Donaldson's essay to Spenser: "What Comes After Chaucer's *But* in *The Faerie Queene*."

29. My definition of *expression* has been adapted from OED, s.v. *Express, v*. *Express* derives from Latin *exprimere*: "to press out," "to form (an image) by pressure," "to represent in sculpture or painting," "to represent or set forth in words or actions."

30. In this connection, cf. the envoy to *The Shepheardes Calender* in which the poet dares not match his poem "with Tityrus hys style, / Nor with the Pilgrim that the Ploughman playde a whyle." The pilgrim playing plowman (or plowman playing pilgrim) alludes to a similar technique: see *Growth of a Personal Voice*, 1–2.

31. The remainder of this paragraph draws on my discussion of the Giant in the final chapter of *Words that Matter: Linguistic Perception in Renaissance English* (Stanford, Calif.: Stanford University Press, 1996), 171–72, 185–86.

32. My discussion of the Temple draws on a more detailed and contextualized discussion in "Chaucer's *Parliament of Fowls* and Refractions of a Veiled Venus in *The Faerie Queene*," chapter 9 in this volume.

33. On Orpheus in *Epithalamion*, see Joseph Loewenstein, "Echo's Ring: Orpheus and Spenser's Career," *English Literary Renaissance*, 15 (1986), 287–302; and on Spenser as Orphic poet more generally, see Thomas H. Cain, *Praise in "The Faerie Queene"* (Lincoln: University of Nebraska Press, 1978), 14–24, 169–73; and Patrick Cheney, *Spenser's Famous Flight: A Renaissance Idea of a Literary Career* (Toronto: University of Toronto Press, 1993), chap. 1.

34. In the *Prologue* to Chaucer's *Miller's Tale*, compare the slipping of the pilgrim's mask in the line "Turne ouer the lefe, and chose another tale" (xiii^v). See David, chap. 8, esp. 120.

35. *Roland Barthes by Roland Barthes*, trans. Richard Howard (New York: Hill and Wang, 1977), 168. The original French reads, "pourquoi ne parlerais-je pas de 'moi', puisque 'moi' n'est plus 'soi'?" and "le sujet se prend *ailleurs*": *Roland Barthes par roland barthes* (Paris: Seuil, 1975), 171. "Apprehends" is a sensitive translation of "se prend" in this context. See also Paul Smith, *Discerning the Subject* (Minneapolis: University of Minnesota Press, 1988), 6: "the singular is not necessarily to be conceived of as a unity: to think of it as such would be to posit it as purely the effect of the ideological processes in which it lives." Likewise, Burke, *Death and Return of the Author*, 27: "Observing light passing through a prism . . . we do not deny its effect upon the light, still less call for the death of the prism. . . . One must, at base, be deeply *auterist* to call for the Death of the Author"; cf. 25, 154, 167. Cf. Christopher Norris, *Derrida* (Cambridge, Mass.: Harvard University Press, 1987), 213; also Donna J. Haraway, *Simians, Cyborgs, and Women: The Reinvention of Nature* (New York: Routledge, 1991), 191: "The alternative to relativism is partial, locatable, critical knowledges sustaining the possibility of webs of connections. . . . Relativism is a way of being nowhere while claiming to be everywhere equally. . . . [It is the] twin of totalization . . . both deny the stakes in location, embodiment, and partial perspective."

36. Cf. *FQ*, II.xii.70–71, 77 with Chaucer's *Parliament*, cclxxx^{r-v}.

37. I return to the description of Acrasia in part 3, chapter 15, of this volume, "Androcentrism and Acrasian Fantasies in the Bower of Bliss." Acrasia and her garden also appear in chapter 9, "Chaucer's *Parliament of Fowls* and Refractions of a Veiled Venus in *The Faerie Queene*."

38. Manfred Frank, *What Is Neostructuralism?*, trans. Sabine Wilke and Richard Gray; foreword by Martin Schwab (Minneapolis: University of Minnesota Press, 1989), lectures 25–27, esp. 408, 424, 432–33, 436–37; cf. xxxix, xxxiv–xxxv. Frank's theory of individuality as difference/*différance* in these lectures is also pertinent. Cf. the mathematician Brian Rotman's *Signifying Nothing: The Semiotics of Zero* (1987; rpt. Stanford, Calif.: Stanford University Press, 1993), 105: "the very function which zero enjoys within mathematics as the mark of an origin requires there to be . . . a certain sort of subject present, a conscious intentional agency, whose 'presence' at the initiation of the process of counting is precisely what zero signifies."

Chapter Two: What Comes after Chaucer's But *in* The Faerie Queene

1. *Chaucer's Poetry: An Anthology for the Modern Reader*, ed. E. Talbot Donaldson, 2nd ed. (New York: Ronald Press, 1975), lines 142, 74, 448. Subsequent references in this chapter to *The General Prologue* are to this edition.

2. Quotations are from the first paragraph of Donaldson's article on *But* in *So meny people longages and tonges*, ed. Michael Benskin and M. L. Samuels (Edinburgh: by the eds., 1981): for the full reference, see chapter 1*n*28, just above.

3. My emphasis. All references to *The Faerie Queene* in this chapter are to *The Works of Edmund Spenser: A Variorum Edition*, ed. Edwin Greenlaw et al, 11 vols. (Baltimore: Johns Hopkins Press, 1932–57); cited as *Var.*

4. Donald Cheney has noted the ambiguity of the phrasing "with paine / Planted in earth" (discussion sponsored by the Spenser Society, New York, December, 1978).

5. OED, s.v. *But*, headnote and note following examples under A.3; C.I.1.b (b.), 3, 4.

6. In the Proem to Book III, as in earlier Proems, the poem continues to mirror the Queen, and although she is now invited to see herself "In mirrours more then one" (i.e., in Gloriana or Belphoebe), both glasses are essentially virtuous. But in this Proem the present embodiment also begins to vie with the antique image, living Queen with antiquity. Uneasy nuances cluster around the word "living" (1, vs. 8–9; 2, vs. 1–2, 6; 3, vs. 5–9; 4, vs.1–3). Adversatives (five in stanzas 2–5) begin to sound every bit as subjective as strictly logical. The poem becomes a slightly compromised "coloured" show that shadows the Queen's "glorious pourtraict" and fits "antique praises" to "present persons," a process of tailoring neither so close nor so natural as the unbroken continuity of bright reflections in Proems 1 and 2. The poem is uneasily differentiated from the "liuing colours" and "right hew" of Sir Walter Ralegh's *Cynthia*. With the reference to Ralegh we are getting closer to the real, historical Elizabeth, whose relation to the Faerie Queen is to become increasingly discontinuous.

7. *Spenser's Courteous Pastoral: Book Six of the "Faerie Queene"* (Oxford: Clarendon Press, 1972), 24.

8. For statements of an opposite view of Proem VI, see Thomas H. Cain, *Praise in "The Faerie Queene"* (Lincoln: University of Nebraska Press, 1978), 155–56; and Daniel Javitch, *Poetry and Courtliness in Renaissance England* (Princeton, N.J.: Princeton University Press, 1978), 143–44. Trenchant as both these writers are, they read Proem VI selectively and appear to overlook its syntactical, verbal, and logical complexities.

9. In the phrase "It showes," the word *it* could conceivably, if less logically, refer to "praise of Princely curtesie," which is virtually identical with "patterne" in line 2. Since *praise* occurs in a clause subordinate to *patterne*, the latter is the logical referent of *it*. In any case, the less likely reading of *praise* as the referent would not significantly alter the preceding discussion except to make *praise of Princely curtesie*

both the subject of *meriteth* and an important part of the object in line 8: "an higher name [than 'praise of Princely curtesie']." If anything, this reading would strengthen the ironical undertones of lines 8 and 9.

   10. *Var.*, VI, 186: Church suggests that the word *name* means "appellation" in line 8 and "character" in line 9. *Var.*, VI, 459, notes that four of Spenser's editors or commentators (the earliest in 1758) have emended "name" to "fame" in line 9. Their emendation—interpretive at best and at worst arbitrary—has not been generally accepted. The editions both of A. C. Hamilton (*The Faerie Queene* [London: Pearson, 1977; 2nd ed.2001, with text by Hiroshi Yamashita and Toshiyuki Suzuki]) and of Thomas P. Roche, Jr. (*The Faerie Queene* [Harmondsworth, Middlesex, U.K.: Penguin, 1978]) read *name* in line 9.

Chapter Three: "Pricking on the plaine": Spenser's Intertextual Beginnings and Endings

   1. All Spenserian references in this chapter are to *The Works of Edmund Spenser: A Variorum Edition*, ed. Edwin Greenlaw et al, 11 vols. (Baltimore: Johns Hopkins Press, 1932–1957), cited as *Var.*; *The Faerie Queene* is cited as *FQ*.
   2. *OED*, s.v. *Prick v*, 11.
   3. Cf. *FQ* I.i.8. *OED*, s.v. *Shroud v^1*, 2c, 3–7.
   4. *OED*, s.v. *Prick v*, 10.
   5. *OED*, s.v. *Courage sb*, 1, 3, 4. Unless otherwise specified, all Chaucerian references in this chapter are to *The Works 1532, supplemented by material from the editions of 1542, 1561, 1598, and 1602* (London: Scolar, 1969): I have changed the solidi to commas and expanded the contractions in Thynne's text.
   6. See Lucretius, *De Rerum Natura*, trans. W. H. D. Rouse (London: Heinemann, 1924), 2–4, esp. vs.12–13, 18–20 of Book 1. Cf. also J. A. W. Bennett, *The Parlement of Foules: An Interpretation* (Oxford: Clarendon, 1957), 119–20.
   7. *OED*, s.v. *Jollity*, 1, 3, 5.
   8. *Shakespeare's Bawdy*, rev. ed. (New York: E. P. Dutton, 1969), 167 (*prick, n, v; prick out*), 176 (rose), 153 (needle).
   9. *The Riverside Shakespeare*, ed. G. Blakemore Evans et al. (Boston, Mass.: Houghton Mifflin, 1974).
   10. The March Eclogue rhymes aabccb. In Thynne's edition, the first stanza of *Sir Thopas* rhymes aabaab; vs. 79ff. rhyme aa^c/bccb (tail rhyme added to verse 3, i.e., c-rhyme internalized in verse 3); vs. 142ff. rhyme aabccb. (Thynne's vs. 142 is vs. 146 in Donaldson's 2nd edition and vs. 857 in Robinson's 2nd edition.) See *Var.*, III, 267; VI, 225–26, and A. Kent Hieatt, *Chaucer, Spenser, Milton: Mythopoeic Continuities and Transformations* (Montreal: McGill–Queen's University Press, 1975), 19–24. (On page 23, Hieatt mistakenly assumes that the rhyme scheme of *Sir Thopas* is uniform.)
   11. *Var.*, IV, 170–71. Ollyphant signifies "elephant" and "destructive fantasy."
   12. *FQ* III.vii.48, vs. 4; *Var.*, III, 412.
   13. Edwin Greenlaw, "Britomart at the House of Busirane," *Studies in Philology*, 26 (1929), 124–27, suggests that Arthur of Little Britain is the source of Prince

Arthur's dream in *The Faerie Queene*. A glance at Arthur's dreams in chapters 16 and 46 of *Little Britain* will show that, while they might be a distant analogue to Spenser's episode, they are an unlikely source: *The History of the Valiant Knight Arthur of Little Britain*, trans. John Bourchier, Lord Berners ([1555?]; rpt. London: White, Cochrane, 1814). The motto of an older generation of Spenserians appears to have been "anything but Chaucer": cf. chapter 9 on "Chaucer's *Parliament of Fowls* and Refractions of a Veiled Venus in *The Faerie Queene*" in part 2 of this volume.

14. See Josephine Waters Bennett, *The Evolution of "The Faerie Queene"* (1942; rpt. New York: B. Franklin, 1960), 11–15. For Drayton, see also *Works*, ed. J. William Hebel (Oxford, Shakespeare Head, 1961), I, 88–91; V, 11–12. On Chaucer's humor in *Sir Thopas*, see E. Talbot Donaldson, "The Embarrassments of Art: *The Tale of Sir Thopas*, 'Pyramus and Thisbe,' and *A Midsummer Night's Dream*," in *The Swan at the Well: Shakespeare Reading Chaucer* (New Haven, Conn.: Yale University Press, 1985), 7–29. (Shakespeare's *MND* is indebted to John Lyly's *Endymion*, whose comic *Sir Thopas* derives from Chaucer's.)

15. Bennett, 15; also *Gabriel Harvey's Marginalia*, ed. G. C. Moore Smith (Stratford-upon-Avon, U.K.: Shakespeare Head, 1913), 228.

16. J. A. Burrow, citing Bennett, implies that Harvey's marginalium confirms a strictly "morall" interpretation of *Sir Thopas* by Spenser: "*Sir Thopas* in the Sixteenth Century," in *Middle English Studies Presented to Norman Davis*, ed. Douglas Gray and E. G. Stanley (Oxford: Clarendon, 1983), 81–88, esp. 87. Unfortunately, electronic searches turn up Burrow's essay, since it exists in an anthology analyzed by bibliographies such as the MLA's, without turning up corrections of it in other essays that do not feature *Sir Thopas* in their titles.

17. Patricia A. Parker, *Inescapable Romance: Studies in the Poetics of a Mode* (Princeton, N.J.: Princeton University Press, 1979), 83–86.

18. See *Troilus and Criseyde*, lxxi–lxxii (Bk. I.183–239, 316–57, in E. T. Donaldson's or F. N. Robinson's 2nd editions).

19. *Var.*, I, 267.

20. "Arthur and Argante: Parodying the Ideal Vision," part 2, chapter 8, in this volume, returns to ambivalent nuances that accrue to Arthur's figure, exploring these in other passages of Book I.

21. Again, "grand finale": in 1596, Spenser also published *Fowre Hymnes*, two of which are earlier pieces, and the occasional *Prothalamion*.

22. "The Existential Mysteries as Treated in Certain Passages of Our Older Poets," in *Acts of Interpretation: The Text in Its Contexts 700–1600*, ed. Mary J. Carruthers and Elizabeth D. Kirk (Norman, Okla.: Pilgrim, 1982), 345–62, here 345–47, 360–62. Pope quotes E. Talbot Donaldson's "Ending of 'Troilus,'" in *Speaking of Chaucer* (London: Athlone, 1970), 98: "All the illusory loveliness of a world which is man's only reality is expressed in the very lines that reject that loveliness."

23. The interpretive quotation earlier in this sentence is from E. T. Donaldson, ed., *Chaucer's Poetry: An Anthology for the Modern Reader*, 2nd ed. (New York: Ronald, 1975), 1144.

24. In the preceding line, I have eliminated the comma after *tickle* in *Var.* In these profoundly ambiguous lines, *loath* is either an adjective or a verb, and *vain* is either an adjective modifying *love* or *things* or else it is an adverb modifying the infinitive *to cast*: see Harry Berger, Jr., "The *Mutabilitie Cantos*: Archaism and Evolution in Retrospect," in *Spenser: A Collection of Critical Essays*, ed. Harry Berger, Jr. (Englewood Cliffs, N.J.: Prentice-Hall, 1968) 146–76, esp. 172–73; and my *Growth of a Personal Voice: "Piers Plowman" and "The Faerie Queene"* (New Haven, Conn.: Yale University Press, 1976), 200–202, cf. 48–49.

25. My position differs from Jonathan Goldberg's sense of Spenser's helplessness—indeed, his dark despair—in the face of time: *Endlesse Worke: Spenser and the Structures of Discourse* (Baltimore: Johns Hopkins University Press, 1981). Goldberg's book greatly renewed interest, including my own, in the relation of Spenser to Chaucer.

Chapter Four: Allegory, Irony, Despair: Chaucer's Pardoner's *and* Franklin's Tales *and Spenser's* Faerie Queene, *Books I and III*

1. Lynn Enterline has suggested how a figure like Ovid's suffering Hecuba could become "a 'mirror' or 'example' "—to which I would add, a rhetorical "place"—"for pupils to imitate," ostensibly to develop their own styles but inevitably with further "social, imaginary, and personal" impact. Both Shakespeare's Lucrece and his Hamlet, she notes, use Ovid's Hecuba as just such a mirror "in and through which to understand and to express what they claim to be their 'own' emotions": *The Rhetoric of the Body from Ovid to Shakespeare* (Cambridge: Cambridge University Press, 2000), 19, 25–26.

2. Gerald L. Bruns, *Inventions: Writing, Textuality, and Understanding in Literary History* (New Haven, Conn.: Yale University Press, 1982), 55–56.

3. A. C. Hamilton, ed., *The Faerie Queene*, 2nd ed. (Harlow, U.K.: Pearson, 2001), 428, note on stanza 1.

4. Citations of *The Faerie Queene* in this chapter, unless otherwise specified, are from the *Variorum* edition: *The Works of Edmund Spenser*, ed. Edwin Greenlaw et al, 11 vols. (Baltimore: Johns Hopkins University Press, 1932–57), vols. 1–6. Each citation has been checked for variants against the Yamashita–Suzuki text of 1590 in A. C. Hamilton's second edition. With a single possible exception, noted below, the variants involve insignificant differences in spelling, most commonly the interchangeable letters *i* and *y*.

5. *The Faerie Queene*, I.ix.46–47. *The Riverside Chaucer*, ed. Larry D. Benson, 3rd edition (Boston, Mass.: Houghton Mifflin, 1987), 199, vs. 729.

6. Theresa M. Krier, *Birth Passages: Maternity and Nostalgia, Antiquity to Shakespeare* (Ithaca, N.Y.: Cornell University Press, 2001), 210–12. Quotation from *Faerie Queene*, IV.ii.32.

7. H. Marshall Leicester, Jr., *The Disenchanted Self: Representing the Subject in the Canterbury Tales* (Berkeley: University of California Press, 1990), 39. Leicester cites

Robert P. Miller, "Chaucer's Pardoner, the Scriptural Eunuch, and the *Pardoner's Tale*," *Speculum* 30 (1955), 180–99. For the "body of this death," see Romans 7:24.

8. Leicester, 46. Donald R. Howard, *The Idea of the Canterbury Tales* (Berkeley: University of California Press, 1976), 357–58, 361; also Alfred Kellogg, "An Augustinian Interpretation of Chaucer's Pardoner," in his *Chaucer, Langland, Arthur: Essays in Middle-English Literature* (New Brunswick, N.J.: Rutgers University Press, 1972), 245–68, here 257. Carolyn Dinshaw credits the Pardoner with more awareness than do most, since she finds in the "olde man" not an ironic, sub- or semiconscious reflection of the Pardoner's imagination but a self-knowing one. For her, the "olde man" is "an incarnation of the Pardoner's anguished knowledge of his fragmentariness": *Chaucer's Sexual Poetics* (Madison: University of Wisconsin Press, 1989), 179.

9. Unless otherwise specified, subsequent citations of Chaucer in this chapter are to *Works 1532, supplemented by material from the editions of 1542, 1561, 1598, and 1602* (1968; rpt. London: Scolar, 1976). The present reference to *The Pardoner's Tale* is on folio lxxviii^r. Throughout I have changed solidi to commas and have expanded contractions in Thynne's text of Chaucer.

10. On the relation of pride to despair, besides Kellogg (note 8, above), see Harry Rusche, "Pride, Humility, and Grace in Book I of *The Faerie Queene*," *Studies in English Literature*, 7 (1967), 29–39: "Despair, like all the sins that threaten the Christian's quest for salvation, is a result of the egocentrism created by pride" (38–39). For a more extensive and learned examination of "The Left Hand of God: Despair in Medieval and Renaissance Tradition," see Susan Snyder's essay in *Studies in the Renaissance*, 12 (1965), 18–59: e.g., "Augustine points out the paradox of the travelers to Emmaus who walked with the risen Christ without recognizing him: the living walked with the dead but bereft of hope *they* were in fact dead, while he was Life itself" (58). Throughout the essay, Snyder keys her discussion to Spenser's rendering of despair in Book I, canto ix.

11. E.g., Howard, 357: "taking the personification literally, they attempt to 'slay' Death"; Dinshaw, 178: "The three [rioters], of course, take this talk [the boy's] literally." On use of the Platonized real in allegory, see Stephen A. Barney, *Allegories of History, Allegories of Love* (Hamden, Conn.: Archon, 1979), 22–23.

12. See Carolynn Van Dyke's semiotic characterization of literary allegory as a "synthesis of deictic and nondeictic generic codes": *The Fiction of Truth: Structures of Meaning in Narrative and Dramatic Allegory* (Ithaca, N.Y.: Cornell University Press, 1985), 40. As explained in my introduction to this volume, I follow Van Dyke in using *deictic* and *nondeictic* as convenient, summary terms for the various binaries in her argument (or in mine), such as particular and universal, concrete and abstract, natural and emblematic, real and Real. *Deictic* itself signifies "directly pointing out" or "demonstrative." In a linguistic context, it indicates a word that particularizes and points, such as the demonstrative pronoun *this*. By "genre," Van Dyke intends "a set of conventions based on an inferable semiotic code" *and* "the texts that realize the code—or realize it to a significant degree" (20–21).

13. *MED*, s.v. *Aspien*, 2.(a), 4b, 4c; *OED*, s.v. *Espy, sb.*, 1.b.

14. On Servius' gloss, see William Nelson, *The Poetry of Edmund Spenser: A Study* (New York: Columbia University Press, 1963), 159: Servius' commentary on *silva*, namely, "that in which beastliness and passion dominate," was standard throughout the Middle Ages and in the Renaissance entered the dictionaries. Now linked with *hyle*, the "Vergilian forest . . . becomes a figure variously signifying the material stuff upon which the divine ideas are impressed, the activities of this world, the passions of the body, the earthly or fleshly aspect of human life."

15. "Refraction," a term I use here to describe the relation between two different poems, occurs in Spenser criticism to describe the recurrence within and between different parts of *The Faerie Queene* itself. Spenser's poem often uses a kind of refraction to relate largely disparate figures to a single type, model, or, as I would argue here, to a nondeictic abstraction; as Peter Hawkins has observed, in such phenomena we recognize less the presence of the original than the "degrees" of its presence: "From Mythography to Myth-making: Spenser and the *Magna Mater Cybele*," *Sixteenth-Century Journal*, 12 (1981), 51–64, here 57, 59.

16. See my "Redcrosse and the Descent into Hell," *ELH*, 36 (1969), 481–85.

17. Despair's cave is "Darke, dolefull, drearie, like a greedie graue" (I.ix.33).

18. For additional discussion of this unholy communion, see Anderson, "Redcrosse and the Descent," 487–88.

19. The Yamashita-Suzuki text in Hamilton, ed., has "trauailes" rather than "trauels"; either spelling enables the pun, although the former may do so more insistently for a modern reader.

20. My source for this eyewitness story is the late Charles Boxer, an officer in the British Army in World War II and subsequently an academic historian.

21. Compare *The Franklin's Tale*, lx[v]: "Loue wol not be constrayned by maistry / Whan maistrye cometh, the god of loue anon / Beateth his wynges, and farewel he is gon."

22. For *The Tale of Sir Thopas* in Book III, see my chapter 9 in this volume, "Chaucer's *Parliament of Fowls* and Refractions of a Veiled Venus in *The Faerie Queene*." Book III.x,10, vs. 1–3, also recalls both I.ix.11, vs. 1–4, and The Wife's Prologue, 263–64 (lineation of Benson, ed., *The Riverside Chaucer*).

23. See Snyder, 18, 54, 58: Snyder specifies Augustine's commentary on Psalm 101 and Gregory's *Moralia* for the imagery of storm and shipwreck. Augustine, Chrysostom, Gregory, Bernard, and Bonaventura are among those referring to despair as a deep abyss (related is the image of despair as a prison). I have combined "profundum marum" and abyss, perhaps the most common image of despair. In connection with Britomart's sea imagery, Hamilton, ed., *The Faerie Queene*, cites Psalm 69:15 (the Vulgate's 68:16), which is clearly related as well.

24. I am not suggesting the absence of rocks from Petrarch's *Rime sparse* by noting their presence in *The Franklin's Tale*. My point is simply that the rocks are not in Spenser's immediate subtext, sonnet 189, and anything less immediate lacks its *prima facie* force. For the combination of rocks and boats in the *Rime sparse*, see, for example, poems 80 ("Chi è fermato di mensar sua vita /su per l'onde fallaci et per li scogli / scevro da morte con un picciol legno . . . (He who has decided to lead

his life on the deceiving waves and near the rocks, separated from death by a little ship . . .)," 135, 235 ("Né mai saggio nocchier guardò da scoglio / nave did merci preziose carca (Nor did ever a wise helmsman keep from the rocks a ship laden with precious merchandise)," 264: *Petrarch's Lyric Poems: The "Rime sparse" and Other Lyrics*, trans. and ed. Robert M. Durling (1976; rpt. Cambridge, Mass.: Harvard University Press, 1995). None of these parallels is psychologically or emotionally as close to Britomart's as are Petrarch's sonnet 189 and the complaint of Dorigen, Chaucer's notably and relevantly *female* speaker. On sonnet 189 as the immediate subtext, see note 28 below.

25. On the well-established connection between suicide and despair, see Snyder, 50–57.

26. Elaine Tuttle Hansen, *Chaucer and the Fictions of Gender* (Berkeley: University of California Press, 1992) also notices this pun (279).

27. Citations respectively are Hansen, 272, 277; E. T. Donaldson, ed., *Chaucer's Poetry: An Anthology for the Modern Reader*, 2nd ed. (New York: Ronald Press, 1975), 1088; Stephen Knight, "Ideology in The Franklin's Tale," *Parergon*, 28 (1980), 3–35, here 23.

28. On the Petrarchan circle and Britomart's lament, see Susanne Lindgren Wofford, "Britomart's Petrarchan Lament: Allegory and Narrative in *The Faerie Queene* III.iv," *Comparative Literature*, 39 (1987), 28–57, esp. 34–43. Behind Wofford's view of this circle is John Freccero's classic discussion "The Fig Tree and the Laurel: Petrarch's Poetics," in *Literary Theory/Renaissance Texts*, ed. Patricia Parker and David Quint (1975; rpt. Baltimore: Johns Hopkins University Press, 1986), 20–32.

29. Mark Rasmussen has also remarked this similarity between Arthur's and Dorigen's complaints in a paper read at The New Chaucer Society conference in July, 2002.

30. E.g., Spenser's III.iv.53, 61, and Arthur's intervening fantasy associating Florimell with his elf queen (iv.54), and *Tale of Sir Thopas*, vs. 778–803 (lineation of Benson, ed., *The Riverside Chaucer*). But see also note 22, above. My argument is a close one spanning two pages, and it benefits from the larger context of discussion in chapter 9, on "Refractions." Relevantly, one of these memories of Sir Thopas simultaneously recalls the Redcross Knight when he disarms in Book I, an action soon followed by Orgoglio's capture of him.

31. I did find it of interest in *The Growth of a Personal Voice: "Piers Plowman" and "The Faerie Queene"* (New Haven, Conn.: Yale University Press, 1976), 110–13. What is especially notable about the passage is its representing a movement from affective personal experience to the mythologizing imagination.

32. Quotations from Daniel S. Murtaugh, "The Garden and the Sea: The Topography of *The Faerie Queene*, III," *ELH*, 40 (1973), 325–38, here 336.

33. Mark Rasmussen, having read this essay, in personal correspondence suggests that the "excessive, or willful, grief" of Cymoent and her companions "may be in part [Spenserian] self-parody." He has in mind the echo of "The Teares of the Muses," vs. 229–32, in *The Faerie Queene*, III.iv.35.

34. I disagree with Stephen Knight (27) here, who finds Dorigen's initial examples irrelevant to her situation since they concern virgins who choose death over defilement. Perhaps I am being too Spenserian in seeing the possibility of chaste love within marriage—that is, faithful love or "wifely chastyte" in Dorigen's words—and not identifying the *chastity* of Dorigen's exemplary virgins only with virginity. A corrective Spenserian perspective does appear apposite.

35. Robert Burlin, *Chaucerian Fiction* (Princeton, N.J.: Princeton University Press, 1977), 200: Burlin cites Germaine Dempster's "Chaucer at Work on the Complaint in the Franklin's Tale," *Modern Language Notes*, 52 (1973), 16–23, quotation at 22. On page 199, Burlin speaks of the "bathetic inconsistency" of the exempla with Dorigen's immediate dilemma. Rhodogone killed her nurse for suggesting that she marry again; Valeria was faithful to her husband's memory in refusing to remarry. Trying to justify Dorigen's use of Bilia as an example, Gerald Morgan explains that Bilia's endurance of "her husband's bad breath is merely one reason she acquired so great a reputation (the other is her unawareness of the fact that not all men have bad breath)": "A Defence of Dorigen's Complaint," *Medium Aevum*, 46 (1977), 77–97, here 93. Morgan seems to be saying that Bilia's heroic defense of womanly honor was to endure her husband's unspeakable halitosis in uncomplaining *ignorance* of other men.

36. Janet Levarie Smarr's article on "Anacreontics" in *The Spenser Encyclopedia*, ed. A. C. Hamilton et al (Toronto: Toronto University Press, 1990), 39, provides helpful background to Spenser's use of this poetic form.

Chapter Five: Eumnestes' "immortall scrine": Spenser's Archive

1. See, for example, John Guillory, *Poetic Authority: Spenser, Milton, and Literary History* (New York: Columbia University Press, 1983), chaps. 2–3; and Maureen Quilligan's response to Guillory in *Milton's Spenser: The Politics of Reading* (Ithaca: Cornell University Press, 1983), 157–71.

2. *FQ* VI.ii.32. Citations of Spenser in this chapter are to *The Works of Edmund Spenser: A Variorum Edition*, ed. Edwin Greenlaw et al, 11 vols. (Baltimore: Johns Hopkins Press, 1932–57); cited as *Var*. Quotation of Chaucer's poetry in this chapter is from *Works 1532, with Supplementary Material from the Editions of 1542, 1561, 1598, and 1602* (London: Scolar, 1969).

3. See *FQ*, II.vii.i, vs. 5, 7; IV.ii.32, vs. 8. I discuss Spenser's image of antiquity in further detail in chapter 10, "The Antiquities of Fairyland and Ireland."

4. Thomas H. Cain, *Praise in "The Faerie Queene"* (Lincoln: University of Nebraska Press, 1978), 49–50, argues that *scrine* in Proem I transfers to Elizabeth I a phrase used in reference to papal authority, namely in *scrinio pectoris omnia*. While this meaning may also be present in Proem I, Cain presses its claims too far, treating them as primary and exclusive. Parodic reference to papal authority is already too narrow a meaning for *scrine* in Proem I and much too narrow for Spenser's second use of the word in II.ix.56, examined later in this chapter.

5. Thomas Cooper, *Thesaurus linguae romanae & britannicae* (London: Henry Bynneman, 1584). Cf. Thomas Thomas, *Dictionarium linguae latinae et anglicanae* (London: Richard Boyle, [1588?]).

6. Robertus Stephanus, *Thesaurus linguae latinae* (Basel: Froben, 1576–78).

7. *OED*, s.v. *scrine*; Charles du Fresne Du Cange, *Glossarium mediae et infimae Latinitatis*, rev. Léopold Favre, 10 vols. (Paris: Libraire des Sciences et des Arts, 1937–38), s.v. *scrinium*.

8. Catullus, ed. Elmer Truesdell Merrill (Cambridge, Mass.: Harvard University Press. 1893), XIV.17–18 and notes, 33: for my purpose the notes in this edition are most pertinent, but for more recent corroboration see *Catullus: A Commentary*, by C. J. Fordyce (Oxford: Clarendon Press, 1961), 137–38nn17–18.

9. Lewis and Short, s.v. *scrinium*.

10. Du Cange, s.v. *scrinium*; also Ronald E. Latham, *Revised Medieval Latin Word-List* (London: Oxford University Press, 1965). See Mary J. Carruthers, *The Book of Memory: A Study of Memory in Medieval Culture* (Cambridge: Cambridge University Press, 1990), 39–40.

11. Du Cange, s.v. *scrinium*.

12. Sir Philip Sidney, *An Apology for Poetry*, in *Elizabethan Critical Essays*, ed. G. Gregory Smith (Oxford: Oxford University Press, 1904), I, 182. Cf. Thomas Wilson, *Arte of Rhetorique*, ed. Thomas J. Derrick (1553; rpt. New York: Garland, 1982), 415: "The memorie [is] called the Threasure of the mynde." Francis MacDonald Cornford, *Plato's Theory of Knowledge* (1934; rpt. New York: Liberal Arts Press, 1957), 2, 27–28; Étienne Gilson, *The Christian Philosophy of Saint Augustine*, trans. L. E. M. Lynch (1960; rpt. New York: Random House, 1967), 71–76, 99–105. In *Aristotle on Memory* (Providence, R.I.: Brown University Press, 1972), Richard Sorabji asks "why Aristotle should have devoted half his treatise" on memory to recollection or reminiscence (*anamnesis*) and then explains that "recollection played a major role in Plato's metaphysics and epistemology. And though Aristotle did not accept the metaphysics and epistemology, he did inherit [from Plato] the interest in recollection" (35).

13. Harry Berger, Jr., *The Allegorical Temper: Vision and Reality in Book II of Spenser's "Faerie Queene"* (New Haven, Conn.: Yale University Press, 1957), 79, makes a similar observation about the written documents in Eumnestes' chamber. Likewise, Michael Murrin, *The Veil of Allegory: Some Notes toward a Theory of Allegorical Rhetoric in the English Renaissance* (Chicago: University of Chicago Press, 1969), 82.

14. Francis Bacon, *Works*, ed. James Spedding, Robert Leslie Ellis, and Douglas Denon Heath, 15 vols. (Boston: Brown and Taggard [imprint varies; vols. 6–10: Taggard and Thompson], 1860–64), VI, 182; VIII, 408, 426, 433; II, 187–88, 206, 214–15. Aristotle, *Works*, ed. Jonathan Barnes, rev. Oxford trans. (Princeton: Princeton University Press, 1984): *Metaphysics* I.i.980b26–981a21, 981b30–982a2; *Nicomachean Ethics* II.i.1103a14–16; *Poetics* IX.1451b5–9. Saint Thomas Aquinas, *The "Summa Theologica,"* trans. Fathers of the English Dominican Province, 2nd rev. ed. (London: Burns Oates and Washbourne, 1929), X, II–II.47.16, 49.1; also *Summa theologiae*, Blackfriars Edition (London: Eyre and Spottiswoode, 1974),

XXXVI: "Sed ad generationem prudentiae necessarium est experimentum, quod fit ex multis memoriis, ut dicitur in princ. *Meta.*" (II–II.47.16); "Quid autem in pluribus sit verum oportet per experimentum considerare. Unde et Philosophus dicit quod *virtus intellectualis habet generationem et augmentum ex experimento et tempore.* Experimentum autem est ex pluribus memoriis, ut patet in I *Meta.*, unde consequens est quod ad prudentiam requiritur plurium memoriam habere" (II–II.49.1). On Spenser's allegory of prudence, see *Books I and II of "The Faerie Queene,"* ed. Robert Kellogg and Oliver Steele (New York: Odyssey, 1965), 343n47.8–9, and the references in note 25 below.

15. (London: Richard Grafton, 1542), 145ᵛ: I have expanded ampersands in the passage. Cf. Wilson, 414: "The same is memorie to the mynde, that life is to the body."

16. Whether the muse of *The Faerie Queene* is Clio or Calliope is a perennially vexed question. I suspect that Spenser saw his muses as he saw his Venuses, as so many expressions of a single power–related, continuous, and often blending–in the muses' case, the power of mnemonic song. When Spenser does not specifically name his muse, she is likely to be a composite figure, as in the first Proem and in the present quotation (VI.Pro.2–3), where the "muse" is the focal referent for the power of the "sacred ymps, that on *Parnasso* dwell." In any event, the material I present argues strongly against the exclusion of Clio and her concerns from the figure Spenser identifies as the "Muse," or inspiration, of his poem, "this famous antique history." It argues instead for the likelihood of her conflation at some crucial points with Calliope. A useful discussion of the Classical muses is Wesley Trimpi's *Muses of One Mind: The Literary Analysis of Experience and Its Continuity* (Princeton: Princeton University Press, 1983), i, xvii. Referring to Hesiod's *Theogony*, Trimpi observes that the poet's office embodies "the collective activities of the Muses," who themselves exist as "various aspects" of each other, "one implying all the others."

17. On the word *still* in the Mutability Cantos, see my *Words That Matter: Linguistic Perception in Renaissance English* (Stanford, Calif.: Stanford University Press, 1996), 133–34: "Frequently a pun in the Cantos, *still* is a primary intensifier of their central paradox of stability in flux."

18. In this volume, see part 1, chapter 3, "'Pricking on the plaine': Spenser's Intertextual Beginnings and Endings."

19. *Webster's New World Dictionary*, s.v. *manor*; Lewis and Short, s.v. *maneo*.

20. See Ernest Weekley, "Our Early Etymologists," *Quarterly Review*, 257 (1931), 63–72; also A. C. Hamilton, "Our New Poet: Spenser's 'well of English undefyld,'" in *A Theatre for Spenserians*, ed. Judith M. Kennedy and James A. Reither (Toronto: University of Toronto Press, 1973), 101–23; and K. K. Ruthven, "The Poet as Etymologist," *Critical Quarterly*, 11 (1969), 9–37.

21. Varro, *De lingua latina*, trans. Roland G. Kent, 2 vols. (London: Heinemann, 1938), VI.49: "Meminisse a memoria cum [in] id quod remansit in mente rursus movetur; quae a manendo." Cf. Thomas, s.v. *maneo*: "To tarie, staie, stand still, remaine, continue, or persist . . . also to stick to, or to stick at: to remember, not to

forget." Thomas has obviously been reading Varro, whether directly or through an intermediary.

22. Ibid.: "Itaque Salii quod cantant: 'Mamuri Veturi,' significant memoriam veterem." See also Lewis and Short, s.v. *ancile* and *Mamurius Veturius*.

23. Erwin Panofsky, "Et in Arcadia Ego: On the Conception of Transience in Poussin and Wateau," in *Philosophy and History: Essays Presented to Ernst Cassirer*, ed. Raymond Klibansky and H. J. Paton (1936; rpt. New York: Harper and Row, 1963), 223, 230, 232. Cf. *The Confessions of Saint Augustine*, trans. E. M. Blaiklock (New York: Thomas Nelson, 1983), 261 (X.21): "And since no one can say that they [*sic*] have not had the experience [of happiness], it is recognised because it is found in the memory."

24. Du Cange, s.v. *scrinium*. Cf. Thomas, s.v. *recordor* and *permaneo*: "To abide till the end, or till all be done: to remaine still, to continue, to tarrie."

25. See, for example, Jerry Leath Mills, "Spenser, Lodowick Bryskett, and the Mortalist Controversy: *The Faerie Queene*, II.ix.22," *Philological Quarterly*, 52 (1973), 173–86; Robert L. Reid, "Alma's Castle and the Symbolization of Reason in *The Faerie Queene*," *JEGP*, 80 (1981), 512–27.

26. Cf. Harry Berger, Jr., "Archaism, Immortality, and the Muse in Spenser's Poetry," *Yale Review*, 58 (1969), 214–31: Berger's argument is more critical of primitivism in recorded or antique resources of memory than mine is; where he emphasizes a theory of evolution, I emphasize recovery and renewal; both emphases involve poetic revision. Mine might be compared to a spiral, his, perhaps, to a straight line. In "A Secret Discipline: *The Faerie Queene*, Book VI," Berger mentions *anamnesis* relevantly, but he is not concerned with its connection to sources, to texts, to recorded memory in *The Faerie Queene*; he locates reminiscence more exclusively in a self: *Form and Convention in the Poetry of Edmund Spenser*, ed. William Nelson (New York: Columbia University Press, 1961), 73. Cf. Murrin, 90–97; also Gerald L. Bruns, *Inventions: Writing, Textuality, and Understanding in Literary History* (New Haven, Conn.: Yale University Press, 1982.), 49–59. Bruns distinguishes between the imitation of a text and the "imitation of antique authority . . . that incarnates [and continues] rather than replicates," the latter of which he finds in a manuscript culture (52, cf. 49).

27. Alastair Fowler, *Spenser and the Numbers of Time* (London: Routledge and Kegan Paul, 1964), 99–100; Macrobius, *Commentary on the Dream of Scipio*, trans. William Harris Stahl (New York: Columbia University Press, 1952), 133–37 (chap. XII). See also *FQ*, VII.vii.2.

28. In the Thynne family of editions of Chaucer's works, "well" here reads "wyll." Since "wyll" fails to rhyme with "tell," it is unlikely that the correct reading "well" did not occur to the poet Spenser, especially if he recognized the source of the Knight's "well" in Chaucer's translation of Boethius, which is also to be found in the Thynne family of editions.

29. Varro, V.123: "Fons unde funditur . . . aqua viva"; cf. Isidori Hispalensis Episcopi, *Etymologiarum sive originvm*, ed. W. M. Lindsay (Oxford: Clarendon Press,

1911), XIII.21.5; Thomas, s.v. *fons*: "A fountain or water spring: a well: *per translationem*, the head, roote, principall cause, and beginning of a matter: also water."

30. I discuss *Sir Thopas* as the Chaucerian source of Arthur's dream in Book I in chapter 3, "'Pricking on the plaine.'"

Chapter Six: Spenser's Use of Chaucer's Melibee: *Allegory, Narrative, History*

1. Paul Alpers, "Spenser's Late Pastorals," *ELH*, 56 (1989), 797–817, here 797–99. Alpers cites observations of Harry Berger and of Humphrey Tonkin to represent negative assessments of Melibee (797).

2. Paul Alpers, "Pastoral and the Domain of Lyric in Spenser's *Shepheardes Calender*," in *Representing the English Renaissance*, ed. Stephen Greenblatt (1985; rpt. Berkeley: University of California Press, 1988), 163–80.

3. Alpers, "Pastoral and the Domain of Lyric," 174–75, and *OED*, s.v. *Demesne*.

4. Alpers, "Late Pastorals," 798.

5. *The Faerie Queene*, VI.x.6, in *Works: A Variorum Edition*, ed. Edwin Greenlaw et al, 11 vols. (1938–57; rpt. Baltimore: Johns Hopkins Press, 1966). Subsequent reference in this chapter is to this edition (*Works*). *The Faerie Queene* is cited as *FQ*.

6. *Pastoral and Ideology: Virgil to Valéry* (Berkeley: University of California Press, 1987), 119, 123.

7. *The Tale of Melibee*, *The Riverside Chaucer*, 3rd edition, ed. Larry D. Benson (Boston, Mass.: Houghton Mifflin, 1987), lines 1409–11. In the present chapter, I have chosen to cite quotations of Chaucer from this edition, rather than from an early modern one, because the lines in it are numbered, an aid to precise reference in a piece of medieval prose. But I have also checked the quotations against the Renaissance edition accessible in a facsimile, whose folio page is cited after each reference; any significant discrepancy between the two editions is noted. Folio references are to *Works 1532, with Supplementary Material from the Editions of 1542, 1561, 1598, and 1602* (London: Scolar, 1969), here xci^r.

8. I have discussed the religious dimensions of Book VI, including nuances pertaining to Melibee, in *The Growth of a Personal Voice: "Piers Plowman" and "The Faerie Queene"* (New Haven, Conn.: Yale University Press, 1976), 157–59, 173–77, 177–84. In view of my previous work on Spenser's Melibee, on which the present chapter draws, I have treated the textual details of his depiction only to the extent needed to argue the full pertinence of Chaucer's *Melibee* to Spenser's.

9. Paul Strohm, "The Allegory of the Tale of Melibee," *Chaucer Review*, 2 (1967), 32–42; and Charles A. Owen, Jr., "The Tale of Melibee," *Chaucer Review*, 7 (1973), 267–80, have admirably treated the allegorical inconsistencies in Chaucer's *Tale*. At bottom, however, both consider these apparent rather than significant, as they become when they are viewed through the interpretive lens of *The Faerie Queene*. Following Donald R. Howard's distinction between the sources (world, flesh, and devil) and the human perpetrators of Melibee's misfortune (*The Idea of the Canterbury Tales* [Berkeley: University of California Press, 1976], 312), John M. Hill

defends the rational consistency of the passages at issue, but he also acknowledges that, in the allegorical terms the *Tale* employs, the analogy they imply is flawed: *Chaucerian Belief: The Poetics of Reverence and Delight* (New Haven, Conn.: Yale University Press, 1991),

10. *Melibee*, 969–72, 1423; lxxxv^v, xci^r. At the outset, the text identifies Sophie's feet rather than her eyes as the site of one wound; *feet* (Fr. *piez*) is an error for *eyes* (Fr. *yeux*) in Chaucer's immediate source: *Riverside Chaucer*, 925n972.

11. Both Marlowe's and Ralegh's poems are available in Agnes M. C. Latham's edition of the *Selected Prose and Poetry* of Sir Walter Raleigh (London: Athlone, 1965), 30–32.

12. Paul J. Alpers, *The Poetry of "The Faerie Queene"* (Princeton: Princeton University Press, 1967), 382.

13. *OED*, s.v. *List v.*^{1}, Forms; 1; s.v. *Lust v.*, 1–4; s.v. *Lust sb.*, 1.

14. Alpers, "Late Pastorals," 812–13.

15. For more detailed discussion of these similarities, see my *Growth of a Personal Voice*, 191–97.

16. In the 1590s the unrest in Ireland worsened. Kilcolman, Spenser's estate in Cork, was burned by insurgents in 1598.

17. On connections between Chaucer's *Sir Thopas, Melibee,* and large, symbolic patterns in *The Faerie Queene*, as well as on poetic identity within the Chaucer-Spenser intertext, see chapter 1, part 1, in this volume, "Chaucer's and Spenser's Reflexive Narrators."

18. *Nicomachean Ethics*, in *Introduction to Aristotle*, ed. Richard McKeon (New York: Modern Library, 1947), 428–29, 433: VI.5 (1140a–b), 8 (1142a): I have capitalized the text's "man" in order to signal its old, inclusive meaning.

19. See also St. Thomas Aquinas, *Basic Writings*, ed. Anton C. Pegis, 2 vols. (New York: Random House, 1945), II, 436–37; and *Summa theologiae*, Blackfriars Edition, 60 vols. (London: Eyre and Spottiswoode, 1964–76), XXIII, 54–57 (Pt. I–II.57.5); XXXVI, 50–51 (Pt. II–II. 47.16); and *Cicero*, 28 vols., *De inventione*, trans. H. B. Hubbell (1949; rpt., London: Heinemann, 1976), II, 326–27 (II.liii.160); see also *Ad Herennium*, trans. Harry Kaplan (1954; rpt., London: Heinemann, 1981), I, 162–65 (III.ii.3).

20. The quotations are from Aquinas, *Summa theologica*, trans. Fathers of the Dominican Province, 2nd rev. ed., 22 vols. (London: Burns, Oates and Washbourne, 1916–29), X, 27 (Pt. II–II.47.16, 49.1); see also *Summa theologiae* (note 19), XXXVI, 50–51, 60–63: "Sed ad generationem prudentiae necessarium est experimentum, quod fit ex multis memoriis, ut dicitur in princ. *Meta*. [Now to produce prudence experience is necessary, and this is formed of many memories, as remarked at the beginning of the *Metaphysics*]" (Pt. II–II.47.16); "Quid autem in pluribus sit verum oportet per experimentum considerare. Unde et Philosophus dicit quod *virtus intellectualis habet generationem et augmentum ex experimento et tempore*. Experimentum autem est ex pluribus memoriis, ut patet in 1 *Meta.*, unde consequens est quod ad prudentiam requiritur plurium memoriam habere [Now to know what is true in the majority of cases we must be empirical; Aristotle says that intellectual

virtue is produced and developed by time and experience. Experience is stocked with memories, as noted in the *Metaphysics*; consequently recalling many facts is required for prudence]" (Pt. II–II.49.1). See also Aristotle, (note 18), 433: VI.8 (1142a). Mary J. Carruthers' linking of prudence with memory is pertinent: *The Book of Memory: A Study of Memory in Medieval Culture* (Cambridge: Cambridge University Press, 1990), 65–67.

21. Aquinas, *Basic Writings* (note 19), II, 436; *Summa theologiae* (note 19), XXIII, 54–57 (Pt. I–II.57.5); XXXVI, 4–7 (Pt. II–II.47.1).

22. Cicero, *De inventione* (note 19), II, 326–27 (II.liii.160).

23. Lee Patterson, "'What Man Artow?': Authorial Self-Definition in *The Tale of Sir Thopas* and *The Tale of Melibee*," *Studies in the Age of Chaucer*, 11 (1989), 117–75, here 147. *Melibee*, 1315, 1318, lxxxx^r; 1587, xciii^r; 1553, xcii^v. The 1532 edition renders *weleful*, "a very foole," and in doing so leaves the saying incongruously framed by contradictory sentiments.

24. Matt. 22:21: "Reddite ergo quae sunt Caesaris, Caesari: et quae sunt Dei, Deo."

25. Carruthers, 65–71, and L. Patterson, 147. The critics who complain repeatedly about Prudence's "relentless" lectures may be overlooking the nature of prudence, which is, in terms of cultural nuggets, copious. They may also be displaying some discomfort with female talkativeness.

26. Carruthers, 35–39, discusses the traditional association of bees, honey, and hives with memory and implicitly with prudence.

27. These examples are drawn from the compilation of Charles G. Smith, *Spenser's Proverb Lore* (Cambridge, Mass.: Harvard University Press, 1970).

28. *Var.*, VI, 240. *Juvenal and Persius*, trans. G. G. Ramsay, rev. ed. (London: Heinemann, 1940), vs. 365–66: Ramsay translates *prudentia*, "wisdom," which could be misleading in the context of my argument.

29. *Works*, VI, 239–40; cf. Torquato Tasso, *Jerusalem Delivered*, trans. Edward Fairfax (New York: Capricon, n.d.), VII.vi–xvii.

30. L. Patterson, 147–51, 157–59; Judith Ferster, *Chaucer on Interpretation* (Cambridge: Cambridge University Press, 1985), 19–22. Against Patterson's view, Hill urges a more positive reading of the *Melibee* and finds in it a realistic embrace of prudence: 123–24, 182n9.

31. On the role of proverbs in humanist practice, see Mary Thomas Crane, *Framing Authority: Sayings, Self, and Society in Sixteenth-Century England* (Princeton: Princeton University Press, 1993), esp. chaps. 1, 3; also my *Words That Matter: Linguistic Perception in Renaissance English* (Stanford, Calif.: Stanford University Press, 1996): *Sententiae* in the index.

32. Cicero's definition of history is a commonplace in the early modern period: see *De oratore*, II.ix.36. The translation is mine; the Latin is cited from the edition of E. W. Sutton, in *Cicero*, 28 vols. (1942; rpt., London: Heinemann, 1988), III, 224.

33. On the relation of fortune to desire in Book VI, see my discussion in *Growth of a Personal Voice*, 173–77; also Michael Steppat, *Chances of Mischief: Variations of Fortune in Spenser* (Köln: Böhlau, 1990), chap. 6.

34. Alpers restricts the limitations of pastoral to Coridon, while distributing its powers equally to Colin and Melibee. I find Melibee's powers more seriously compromised than Colin's: "Late Pastorals," 811–12.

PART 2: Agency, Allegory, and History Within the Spenserian Intertext

Chapter Seven: Spenser's Muiopotmos *and Chaucer's* Nun's Priest's Tale

1. *Muiopotmos: or The Fate of the Butterflie*, ed. C. G. Osgood and H. G. Lotspeich, in *Works: A Variorum Edition* (Baltimore: Johns Hopkins Press, 1947), VIII, 610. References to *Muiopotmos* are to this edition (*Var.*). References to *The Nun's Priest's Tale* (B) are to *The Works of Geoffrey Chaucer*, ed. F. N. Robinson, 2nd ed. (Cambridge, Mass.: Riverside, 1957), cited as NPT.

2. See Thomas William Nadal, "Spenser's *Muiopotmos* in relation to Chaucer's *Sir Thopas* and *The Nun's Priest's Tale*," *PMLA*, 25 (1910), 640–56, esp. 650 ff.; Hallett Smith, "The Use of Conventions in Spenser's Minor Poems," in *Form and Convention in the Poetry of Edmund Spenser*, ed. William Nelson (New York: Columbia University Press, 1961), 128.

3. Quotation from E. Talbot Donaldson on *NPT* in *The Norton Anthology of English Literature*, ed. M. H. Abrams et al; rev. ed. (New York: W. W. Norton, 1968), I, 175*n*.

4. My discussion of *NPT* is indebted to E. T. Donaldson in his edition *Chaucer's Poetry: An Anthology for the Modern Reader* (New York: Ronald, 1958), 940–44; Charles Muscatine, *Chaucer and the French Tradition* (Berkeley: University of California Press, 1957), 237–43; Charles A. Owen, Jr., "The Crucial Passages in Five of the *Canterbury Tales*: A Study in Irony and Symbol," *JEGP*, 52 (1953), 305–9. The phrase quoted in the next sentence is Owen's, 307.

5. *MED*, s.v. *Malkin*: (a) "often used as jocular or contemptuous term for a servant woman, a young woman of the lower classes, or a woman of loose morals."

6. Cf. Muscatine, 238, 242; David Holbrook, "The Nonne Preestes Tale," in *The Age of Chaucer*, ed. Boris Ford, rev. ed. (Harmondsworth, Middlesex, U.K.: Penguin, 1959), 118.

7. Cf. Charles A. Watkins, "Chaucer's Sweete Preest," *ELH*, 36 (1969), 465: "the sharp tone" the Priest uses to disavow theories about the will "reveals his true interest. . . . Clearly the 'fruyt' of the Priest's *Tale* is his disclosure of the kind of human freedom available to man, the use to which he may put it, and the consequences of failing to use it properly."

8. See esp. Donaldson, *ed., Chaucer's Poetry*, 941–42.

9. I do not imply an equation between the views of will in *NPT* and everywhere else in Chaucer's writing, specifically not in the far more complex *Troilus*. Nor are views in *Muiopotmos* the necessary equivalents of those in *The Faerie Queene*.

In *The Growth of a Personal Voice: "Piers Plowman" and "The Faerie Queene"* (New Haven, Conn.: Yale University Press, 1976), I have argued for an evolution of the treatment of the will within Spenser's romance epic itself (chap. 7, e.g., 175–76).

10. Don Cameron Allen's chapter on *Muiopotmos* in *Image and Meaning: Metaphorical Traditions in Renaissance Poetry* (Baltimore: Johns Hopkins University Press, 1960), 20–41; and the comments of Robert L. Kellogg and Oliver L. Steele in their edition of *The Faerie Queene: Books I and II, "The Mutability Cantos," and Selections from the Minor Poetry* (New York: Odyssey, 1965) 525–26, have been useful in framing my argument. William Nelson's reading of *Muiopotmos* in *The Poetry of Edmund Spenser* (New York: Columbia University Press, 1963), 71–74, has proved indispensable. Franklin E. Court, "The Theme and Structure of Spenser's *Muiopotmos*," *Studies in English Literature*, 10 (1970), 1–15, helpfully summarizes older criticism (1–4), as more recently do William A. Oram et al, eds. *The Yale Edition of the Shorter Poems of Edmund Spenser* (New Haven, Conn.: Yale University Press, 1989), 810; Hugh Maclean and Anne Lake Prescott, eds., *Edmund Spenser's Poetry*, 3rd ed. (New York: W. W. Norton, 1993), 558–59, 837. For a current, well-documented treatment, see Ayesha Ramachandran, "Clarion in the Bower of Bliss: Poetry and Politics in Spenser's 'Muiopotmos,'" *Spenser Studies*, 20 (2005), 77–106.

11. E.g., *Var.*, 599–608. There have, of course, been efforts to read *NPT* as a historical, social, or even personal allegory: e.g., J. Leslie Hotson, "Colfox vs. Chauntecleer," *PMLA*, 39 (1924), 762–81; D. W. Robertson, Jr., *A Preface to Chaucer* (Princeton: Princeton University Press, 1962), 250–51, 376; Judson Boyce Allen, "The Ironic Fruyt: Chauntecleer as Figura," *Studies in Philology*, 66 (1969), 25–35. These readers are admittedly looking, via analogues, for significance *additional* to the moral meaning of *NPT*. In contrast, readers of *Muiopotmos* have turned to allegory because they have first found the tone and moral meaning of this poem puzzling.

12. See Nelson, 71–72: Spenser "sets against each other not two realms but two proportions, that between gods and men and that between men and insects."

13. Cf. Court, 4: *Muiopotmos* has a "general mood of disillusionment—an atmosphere of hopelessness, of futile struggle." For similar conclusions, see Eric F. Taylor, "*The Knight's Tale*: A New Source for Spenser's *Muiopotmos*," *Renaissance Papers* (1965), 60, 62–63.

14. Cf. Nelson, 71: "Clarion is too beautiful to be absurd and though he is little he is not contemptible. . . . the tragedy of his end is tempered only by his distance from us."

15. Court holds a somewhat similar view, but he identifies Clarion too closely and simply with Eve (11). Clarion moves in a fallen context, and, of course, Clarion *is* an insect. Simply put, the allegorical vehicle in a poem does not disappear into its tenor, as arguably it might in the abstractive simplicities of allegoresis.

16. On the medicinal and culinary significance of these herbs and flowers, see *Var.*, 398–99. The gardens are especially comparable to the trees in the Wandering Wood of worldly experience in *The Faerie Queene*, I.i.8–9; variously, they might also be compared and contrasted with the plants in the Bower of Bliss, and, in the

main, contrasted with the unwholesomeness of those in the Garden of Proserpine within the Cave of Mammon.

17. E.g., the astronomical telling of time in *NPT*, 4377 ff.

18. John Calvin, *The Institution of Christian Religion*, trans. Thomas Norton (London: Bonham Norton, 1599), III.x.2, I.i.2: I have modernized long *s* in the citations.

19. Touchstones of Calvin's thought might be found in *Institution*, II.xvi.16, III.i.1, IV.xvii.5; in Paul Van Buren, *Christ in Our Place: The Substitutionary Character of Calvin's Doctrine of Reconciliation* (Grand Rapids, Mich.: Eerdmans, 1957), 50, 87–88; and in T. F. Torrance, *Calvin's Doctrine of Man* (Westport, Conn.: Greenwood, 1952), 138–39. For a concise example of similar thought in a reformer who was a Lutheran rather than a Calvinist, see "A Prologue Upon the Epistle of St. Paul to the Romans," in *The Work of William Tyndale*, ed. G. E. Duffield (Philadelphia: Fortress, 1965), 130–31.

20. Cf. Court, 5.

21. Cf. Kellogg and Steele, eds., 525–26; D. C. Allen, 37–38, 40.

22. Cf. Nelson, 74; Kellogg and Steele, eds., 534. Court, 13, inexplicably finds Spenser "firmly on the side of Arachne; she does what few mortals dare—she challenges divinity." This may be Spenser's view elsewhere, but it is not so here, where he rewrites Ovid at Arachne's expense.

23. *Metamorphoses*, trans. F. J. Miller, Loeb (Cambridge, Mass.: Harvard University Press, 1916), Vol. I, Bk. VI, 129–45. Spenser calls the reader's attention to his Ovidian source in *Muiopotmos*, 258. Significantly, the butterfly is not to be found in Ovid's version of the myth.

24. See D. C. Allen, 30–31.

25. The impasse is remarkably close to those described by Erasmus in *De libero arbitrio diatribe sive collatio*, in *Omnia Opera* (Basel: Froben, 1540), IX, 1023.

26. Cf. Harry Berger, Jr., "Two Spenserian Retrospects: The Antique Temple of Venus and the Primitive Marriage of Rivers," *Texas Studies in Literature and Language*, 10 (1968), 5–25. With a more complex emphasis on "the act of revision whereby the poet moves back in time to recapitulate the antique and primitive sources of his own vision," Berger has analyzed a movement in *The Faerie Queene*, Book IV, which could be seen as bearing a relationship to *Muiopotmos* (8).

27. Spenser's attitude toward will is reformed but also eclectic. It would be difficult on the grounds stated here, for example, to maintain that his position is closer to Calvin, II.iii.13 (based on Augustine), than to Erasmus, 1021–22, or to Richard Hooker, *Of the Laws of Ecclesiastical Polity*, in *Works*, ed. John Keble, 7th ed. (Oxford: Oxford University Press, 1888), Vol. I, Bk. I.viii.11.

28. *Muiopotmos*, vs. 277–78, 305–6, 326, 328.

29. Cf. Sir Philip Sidney on the poet, or maker, in *An Apologie for Poetrie*, in *Elizabethan Critical Essays*, ed. G. Gregory Smith (London: Oxford University Press, 1904), I, 155–58; on page 195, Sidney associates Athena with poetry. *OED*, s.v. *Figure*, 2, reads, "To represent in a diagram or picture," and cites *Muiopotmos*, 277, as an instance of this meaning. The border of Arachne's tapestry, formed solely of

352 Notes to Pages 124–127

ivy leaves, perhaps suggests the merely natural order to which her artistic vision is bound.

30. *OED*, s.v. *Wantonly*: "a. Lewdly, lasciviously; voluptuously; b. Frolicsomely, sportively, playfully, light-heartedly; c. Recklessly, unadvisedly; without proper excuse or motive; without regard for right or consequences . . . wilfully." See also *OED*, s.v., *Wanton*, A.1–4.

Chapter Eight: Arthur and Argante: Parodying the Ideal Vision

1. All Spenserian references in this chapter are to *The Works of Edmund Spenser: A Variorum Edition*, ed. Edwin Greenlaw et al, 11 vols. (Baltimore: Johns Hopkins Press, 1932–57), cited as *Var.*; *The Faerie Queene* is cited as *FQ*. The present reference is to *FQ*, III.vii.37.

2. Edmund Spenser, *The Faerie Queene*, ed. A. C. Hamilton (London: Longman, 1977), 373. Hamilton glosses Ollyphant as "elephant," referencing Chaucer's *Sir Thopas* (373n48.2); the name also suggests "destructive fantasy": from Greek *ollyo* (ολλύω), "destroy" + *phantasia* (φαντασία), "imagination." *Faute de mieux*, I use the term *parody* throughout this essay to approximate the phenomenon of reflection in a fun-house mirror—in this case a reflection often more sobering than comic. To my mind, one can parody a person's status or behavior and, indeed, a person's identity or style of life. Indeed, one can parody any manner or form that the mind has fashioned. Parody of Elizabeth I, the virgin Queen, is the parody of an image, idea, or conception of Elizabeth. Spenserian parody typically and ironically reflects actual texts—Chaucer's or Spenser's own, for example—and textualized ideas, such as those embodied in the figures of the virgin Queen or Belphoebe.

3. In the 1590 *Faerie Queene*, "Chylde Thopas" is the confounder of Ollyphant (III.vii.48, *Var.*, III, 412). See also note 2, right above.

4. *Var.*, I, 168.

5. Hamilton, ed., 373n47.2; Joel Jay Belson, "The Names in *The Faerie Queene*" (Ph.D. Columbia University), 1964: 35. Liddell and Scott, s.v., ἈΡΓΌΣ, ἀργής, ἀργᾶς. On the relationship of these Greek words, see Julius Pokorny, *Indogermanisches etymologisches Wörterbuch* (Bern: Francke, 1959), 64–65, who discusses their proto-Indo-European root, *arg-*. Hamilton cites only *argos* to gloss Argante's name. Belson cites both *argos* and *arges* but not *argas*. For the reference to Tasso, see *Var.*, 265nxl.

6. *FQ*, III.vii.39, vs. 8; 49, vs. 8; 40, vs. 4; 37, vs. 3.

7. *FQ*, III.vii.50. Liddell and Scott, s.v. ἀργός.

8. "Layamon's *Brut*," in *Arthurian Chronicles Represented by Wace and Layamon*, intro. Lucy Allen Paton (1912; rpt. London: J. M. Dent, 1928), 264. Laȝamon, *Brut*, ed. G. L. Brook and R. F. Leslie, EETS 227 (London: Oxford University Press, 1978), II, 750:

> And ich wulle uaren to Aualun.ˊ to uairest alre maidene.
> to Argante þere quene.ˊ aluen swiðe sceone.
> & heo s[c]al mine wunden.ˊ makien alle isunde.

Notes to Pages 127–130   353

al hal me makien.´ mid halewei3e drenchen.
. . . .

Bruttes ileueð 3ete.´ Þat he bon on liue.
and wunnien in Aualun.´ mid fairest alre aluen.
(14277–80, 14290–91)

9. Galfrido Monemutensi, *Brittannie vtriusq[ue] regu[m] et principium origo et gesta insignia* ([Paris]: Jo. Badius Ascensius, 1517), Fo. xci^v, VII.vii: "in insulam Auallonis"; Geoffrey of Monmouth, *The Historia Regum Britanniae*, ed. Acton Griscom (London: Longmans, Green, 1929), 501.

10. Belson, 35–37; Lewis Spence, *The Minor Traditions of British Mythology* (London: Rider, 1948), 27–28. There is no foundation in Spence for Belson's suggestion that the morgans of Ushant live "on" the island.

11. For example, Lucy Allen Paton, *Studies in the Fairy Mythology of Arthurian Romance*, 2nd ed. (1903; rpt. New York: Burt Franklin, 1960), 26–28; J. D. Bruce, "Some Proper Names in Layamon's *Brut* Not Represented in Wace or Geoffrey of Monmouth," *MLN*, 26 (1911), 65–68.

12. J. S. P. Tatlock, *The Legendary History of Britain: Geoffrey of Monmouth's Historia Regum Britanniae and Its Early Vernacular Versions* (Berkeley: University of California Press, 1950), 483–531, esp. 515–29; Spence, 27; Paton, 26–34; Bruce, 65–69. For a relatively more recent assessment, see *Dictionary of the Middle Ages*, ed. Joseph R. Strayer (New York: Scribner's, 1983), II, s.v. *Brut*.

13. *Dictionary of the Middle Ages*, II, s.v. *Brut*. Cf. Carrie Anna Harper, *The Sources of the British Chronicle History in Spenser's Faerie Queene* (1910; rpt. New York: Haskell House, 1964), 24–27.

14. Rosemond Tuve, "Spenser and Some Pictorial Conventions" and "Spenserus," in *Essays by Rosemond Tuve*, ed. Thomas P. Roche, Jr. (Princeton: Princeton University Press, 1970), 112–62, esp. 112–18.

15. The Welsh words occur in *FQ* II.x.24: "That not *Scuith guiridh* it mote seeme to bee, / But rather *y Scuith gogh*, signe of sad crueltee." See also Charles Bowie Millican, *Spenser and the Table Round: A Study in the Contemporaneous Background for Spenser's Use of the Arthurian Legend* (Cambridge, Mass.: Harvard University Press, 1932), 202n5; cf. 78.

16. On the allusion to Ralegh, see James P. Bednarz, "Ralegh in Spenser's Historical Allegory," *Spenser Studies*, 4 (1983), 49–70.

17. Edmond Huguet, *Dictionnaire de la langue française du seizième siècle* (Paris: Didier, 1925), s.v. *Argente, Argenté*. Lewis and Short, s.v. *Argentum*, relate *arges* and *argas* etymologically to *argentum*. Henry Gibbons Lotspeich, *Classical Mythology in the Poetry of Edmund Spenser* (1932; rpt. New York: Gordian, 1965), s.v. *Giants*, suggests that Argente, "an alternative name for Luna, daughter of Hyperion," in Boccaccio's *De genealogia deorum gentilium* (IV.16) may account for the name and size of Spenser's Argante. But the name remains Argente, not Argante, in Boccaccio, and, as Belson observes, the incidental size of Argente does not persuasively account for "the psychotic lustfulness which Argante typifies [for this] is, by nature, of monstrous and gigantic proportions" (35–37).

18. Cf. the reference to Merlin's death in *FQ* III.iii.10.

19. I have treated this dream more fully in part 1, chapter 3, "'Pricking on the plaine': Spenser's Intertextual Beginnings and Endings." See also Patricia A. Parker, *Inescapable Romance: Studies in the Poetics of a Mode* (Princeton: Princeton University Press, 1979), 83.

20. On these ambivalences, see Kenneth Gross, *Spenserian Poetics: Idolatry, Iconoclasm, and Magic* (Ithaca: Cornell University Press, 1985), 128–43, esp. 133. In Gross's reading, parodic elements reflect the poet's concern with idolatry, with the threat and power of the image as image.

21. On the dragon, see Hamilton, ed., 103. On serpentine forms, cf. Jane Aptekar, *Icons of Justice: Iconography and Thematic Imagery in Book V of "The Faerie Queene"* (New York: Columbia University Press, 1969), 87–107, esp. 103; 125–39.

22. For a similar view, see Kathleen Williams, *Spenser's Faerie Queene: The World of Glass* (London: Routledge and Kegan Paul, 1966), 22. Gross, 133–34, gives short shrift to the positive force of the description of Arthur. His suggestion that a positive reading is moralistic fudges the fact that the moralism, if that's what it is, is Spenser's. *The Faerie Queene* is much more than simply, or simplistically, moralistic, but moral it sometimes—indeed, more than sometimes—is.

23. *OED*, s.v. Haughty, 1–3.

24. *OED*, s.v. Pride sb^1, II.7, 9.

25. On Belphoebe's "ensample dead" and the "queane" Slander, see my essay "'In liuing colours and right hew': The Queen of Spenser's Central Books," in *Critical Essays on Edmund Spenser*, ed. Mihoko Suzuki (New York: Simon and Shuster Macmillan, 1996), 168–82.

Chapter Nine: Chaucer's Parliament of Fowls *and Refractions of a Veiled Venus in* The Faerie Queene

1. A notable exception is the discussion of A. Kent Hieatt, *Chaucer, Spenser, Milton: Mythopoeic Continuities and Transformations* (Montreal: McGill-Queen's University Press, 1975), 47–58, 95–113. Numerous parallels between *The Faerie Queene* and the *Parliament* are cited in *The Works of Edmund Spenser: A Variorum Edition*, ed. Edwin Greenlaw et al, 11 vols. (Baltimore: Johns Hopkins Press, 1932–1957). J. A. W. Bennett, *The Parlement of Foules: An Interpretation* (Oxford: Clarendon, 1957), 112–21, deals briefly with many of these parallels. Most critical attention has focused exclusively on the relation between the *Parliament* and the appearance of Nature in the Mutability Cantos: e.g., Alice S. Miskimin, *The Renaissance Chaucer* (New Haven, Conn.: Yale University Press, 1975), 35–54; John Guillory, *Poetic Authority: Spenser, Milton, and Literary History* (New York: Columbia University Press, 1983), 57–67; Maureen Quilligan, *Milton's Spenser: The Politics of Reading* (Ithaca, N.Y.: Cornell University Press, 1983), 157–66. The quotation in my text is from *The Shepheardes Calender*, June, vs. 8. All references to Spenser's poetry in this chapter are to the *Variorum* edition of *Works*, cited as *Var.*

2. As will be apparent in succeeding pages, my view both benefits and differs from Harry Berger's, whether in the 1968 or the 1989–1991 version. For references, see note 36 below.

3. Gilles Deleuze and Felix Guattari, *A Thousand Plateaus: Capitalism and Schizophrenia*, trans. Brian Massumi (Minneapolis: University of Minnesota Press, 1987), 1–25, esp. 6–9, 21.

4. *FQ* VII.vii.8. Unless specified otherwise, all references to Chaucer's poetry in this chapter are to *Works 1532, Supplemented by Material from the Editions of 1542, 1561, 1598, and 1602* (1968; rpt. London, 1976). The present reference to the *Parliament* is on folio cclxxx^v. Throughout, I have changed solidi to commas and have expanded contractions in Thynne's text of Chaucer. Hieatt, 19–29, demonstrates that Spenser is likely to have used one of the Thynne family of Renaissance editions of Chaucer.

5. Josephine Waters Bennett, "Spenser's Venus and the Goddess Nature of the *Cantos of Mutabilitie*," *Studies in Philology*, 30 (1933), 160–92, here 179.

6. *Var.*, II, 391. See also the useful edition of the *Parliament*, ed. D. S. Brewer (London Thomas Nelson, 1960), 138–40; and the edition of Walter W. Skeat, in *Works*, 2nd ed. (Oxford: Clarendon, 1899), I, 68–73. The sentence in my text immediately below quotes "subtyl coverchef," the reading modern editors consider authoritative, from *The Riverside Chaucer*, ed. Larry D. Benson et al, 3rd ed. (Boston, Mass.: Houghton Mifflin, 1987), 389, vs. 272.

7. Alternatively, Spenser could also have seen a more accurate manuscript of the *Parliament*, or he could have rediscovered Chaucer's adjective on his own, since subtle, meaning "thin," "tenuous," is a word he uses with some frequency and often associates with a web (elsewhere, too, one woven by Arachne) or with other woven matter: e.g., see *FQ*, I.ii.3; II.vii.28, xi.20, xii.81; IV.vi.20; V.v.52; *Muiopotmos*, vs. 369, 429.

8. Useful discussions of Renaissance imitation (embellishment, amplification, translation) as a form of interpretation and invention are available in Terence Cave, *The Cornucopian Text: Problems of Writing in the French Renaissance* (Oxford: Clarendon, 1979), esp. chap. 2; Gerald L. Bruns, *Inventions: Writing, Textuality, and Understanding in Literary History* (New Haven, Conn.: Yale University Press, 1982), 49–59; and Thomas M. Greene, *The Light in Troy: Imitation and Discovery in Renaissance Poetry* (New Haven, Conn.: Yale University Press, 1982), chaps. 1–3. Greene argues that a literary work affirms "its own historicity" through a deliberate allusiveness; in his terms, Spenser's assimilation of Chaucerian texts would be considered "ostentatiously diachronic" (16, 37). Cf. also David Quint, *Origin and Originality in Renaissance Literature: Versions of the Source* (New Haven, Conn.: Yale University Press, 1983), xi, 7, 19–23, 157–66.

9. See Robert A. Pratt, "Chaucer's Claudian," *Speculum*, 22 (1947), 419–29; here 422–23. Originally, Claudian's lines, which the medieval compilers adapted to their own purposes in the schoolbook *Libri Catoniani*, came from his poem *Panegyricus de sexto consolatu Honorii Augusti*.

10. I particularly have in mind the psychic dismemberment in I.v, which I have discussed in detail in "Redcrosse and the Descent into Hell," *ELH*, 36 (1969), 470–92.

11. Joseph Loewenstein's fine essay "Echo's Ring: Orpheus and Spenser's Career," *English Literary Renaissance*, 15 (1986), 287–302, informs my observation.

12. My third chapter, part 1, "'Pricking on the plaine': Spenser's Intertextual Beginnings and Endings," considers *Sir Thopas* in relation to Arthur's dream in greater detail, as well as the connections between this dream and Redcrosse's experiences. The relationship between Arthur and Scudamour discussed in the next paragraph of the present chapter also recalls Redcrosse: see *FQ*, I.vii.2, vs. 6–9 ("forage"), and note 13 below.

13. See J. A. Burrow, "*Sir Thopas* in the Sixteenth Century," in *Middle English Studies Presented to Norman Davis in Honour of his Seventieth Birthday*, ed. Douglas Gray and E. G. Stanley (Oxford: Clarendon, 1983), 69–91; here 82–84. Burrow, however, characteristically assumes that Spenser missed Chaucer's joke, whereas the paired contexts I have cited suggest that he was aware of it. Spenser's only other use—and, it would seem, deliberate misuse—of *forage* occurs in a similar description of the dismounted, disarmed, and imminently dissolute Redcrosse, about to succumb to Duessa and Orgoglio (I.vii. 2).

14. After losing Serena, Calepine also searches primarily for a woman, but the reader observes little of the process or stages of his search. On *clomb*, just above, cf. A. C. Hamilton's note on III.iv.61, vs. 6, in his edition of *The Faerie Queene* (London: Longman, 1977); Hamilton refers to the contrasting context of III.iii.61, but the expertise of young Britomart's and old Glauce's maiden mounting of steeds is open to question; similarity, not contrast, might be the point.

15. I am grateful to Michael Hanrahan for noticing Spenser's echo of this passage in IV.x and for his permission to refer to it.

16. Jonathan Goldberg, *Endlesse Worke: Spenser and the Structures of Discourse* (Baltimore: Johns Hopkins University Press, 1981), 63, suggests that the travelers' importuning Scudamour to tell his tale also "echoes" the Prologue to *The Squire's Tale*. For two reasons, this resemblance seems to me unlikely: it is not verbally persuasive, and, as Goldberg earlier acknowledges (35–36*n*), the Prologue in question is missing from Renaissance editions of Chaucer.

17. Boccaccio's *Teseida* is the source of the Temple in *The Knight's Tale*, as well as in the *Parliament*. A taxonomy of generic resemblances between Spenser's Temple of Venus, Chaucer's *Parliament*, and numerous other works is available in Earle Broadus Fowler's *Spenser and the Courts of Love* (Menasha, Wis.: G. Banta, 1921).

18. I have borrowed two of J. A. W. Bennett's adjectives, 91. I also agree with Charles Muscatine's endorsement (*Riverside Chaucer*, 998*n*260–79) of Bennett's observation that the "ambivalence of the concept [that Venus embodies in the *Parliament*] is part of the very theme" of the poem (98).

19. "Try and try" comes from Emerson Brown, "Priapus and the *Parlement of Foulys*," *Studies in Philology* 72 (1975), 258–74, here 262.

20. Some critics (e.g., Brewer, ed.) would like the formel's words and the invocation of the goddess who causes the dream to refer to a Venus different from the one in the Temple. Such special pleading is unpersuasive, however. In the invocation, Venus' "fyre bronde"—right out of the erotic ending of the *Romance of the Rose* and anticipating the description of Venus at January's wedding in *The Merchant's Tale*—seems to me to speak for itself; there is also no reason to suppose that the formel does not mean exactly what she says.

21. In describing "dame Nature," Spenser, too, invokes Alanus, or, since he did not have access to a printed copy of Alanus' *De planctu naturae* and the availability to him of a manuscript copy is in question (Quilligan, 157–66), at the very least he invokes Chaucer's invocation of it. See also Edwin Greenlaw, "Some Old Religious Cults in Spenser," *Studies in Philology*, 20 (1923), 216–43; here 219–31.

22. "Horns Away," in *The Minor Poems of John Lydgate*, ed. Henry Noble MacCracken, EETS, o.s. 192 (London: Oxford University Press, 1934). J. A. W. Bennett mentions this reference unsympathetically, 211 (read "192" for the misprinted "92").

23. OED, s.v. *Slender*: 2. "Of things: Small in . . . width in proportion to length; long and thin; attenuated." 3.a. "Having little thickness or solidity in proportion to extent of surface; slight or slim in size or structure." Cf. Hamilton, ed., 488n40.8–9: "thin" and "long."

24. It is unclear whether the breasts of Chaucer's Venus ("naked from the brest vnto the hede": cclxxx^v) are uncovered, though I take them to be. Spenser does not specify whether the breast of his Venus is uncovered, presumably because "both kinds in one" would challenge visual representation of this anatomical feature.

25. See *Var.*, IV, 229–31; Josephine Waters Bennett, 169–70; Peter S. Hawkins, "From Mythography to Myth-making: Spenser and the Magna Mater Cybele," *Sixteenth-Century Journal*, 12 (1981), 51–64; Greenlaw, 228, 235; Henry Gibbons Lotspeich, *Classical Mythology in the Poetry of Edmund Spenser* (1932; rpt. New York: Gordian, 1965), 115–16. John Erskine Hankins, *Source and Meaning in Spenser's Allegory: A Study of "The Faerie Queene"* (Oxford: Clarendon, 1971), 246, suggests that the double sex of Venus is "a reference to her as the masculo-feminine fluid resulting after coitus has taken place."

26. Plutarch's *Moralia*, trans. Frank Cole Babbitt (Cambridge, Mass.: Harvard University Press, 1957), V, 23–24: Babbitt translates πέπλον "robe"; I follow *Var.*, IV, 231, in reading "veil."

27. Greenlaw, 231; Vincenzo Cartari, *Le Imagini de i Dei de gli Antichi* (1571; rpt. New York: Garland, 1976), 552–53; see also 550–51: cited by Josephine Waters Bennett from another edition (166–69).

28. Hawkins, 57, 59. Just above, I have cited the authoritative Chaucerian reading "subtyl coverchef," as well as the reading of the Renaissance editions, in accordance with my view, expressed earlier, that Spenser followed both Chaucer and Boccaccio, Chaucer's own source, in describing Venus' covering. On Spenser's use of precursor texts, see also my fifth chapter, part 1, on "Eumnestes' 'immortall scrine': Spenser's Archive."

29. On generative eros in the broadest of senses, see my chapter 14, part 3, on "Flowers and Boars: Surmounting Sexual Binarism in Spenser's Garden of Adonis."

30. The quotation is from *FQ*, II.Pro.5, where it refers to the "antique Image" of Elizabeth I. *OED*, s.v. *Covert*, gives the adjectival meanings "concealed," "hidden," "secret" and the substantive meaning "a covering." While the adjectival meaning "covering" or "concealing" affords the best sense for Spenser's phrase, "concealed" is also a sense appropriate to his half-hidden refractions of Chaucer's veiled Venus. At least one critic, Philippa Berry, glances at an allusion to Elizabeth's mythic powers in the hermaphroditic Venus (*Of Chastity and Power: Elizabethan Literature and the Unmarried Queen* [London: Routledge, 1989], 153–54); other readers have associated Elizabeth with Isis, and Patricia Parker has seen an allusion to the Queen in Acrasia: *Literary Fat Ladies: Rhetoric, Gender, Property* (London: Methuen, 1987), 54–66. Renaissance mythographers included, rather than excluded, multiple meanings, and the imaginatively potent figures they depicted were, like Spenser's, often richly ambivalent: see Hawkins, 57–60.

31. On the figures drawn from Dante's circle of the lustful (*Inferno*, v.58–69), see Brewer, ed., 111–13.

32. The complexities of the innocence of Milton's Eve come to mind. See also part 2, chapter 7, on *Muiopotmos*, in this volume.

33. *OED*, s.v. *Soil sb.*³, III.5

34. For an extensive discussion of Spenser's intertextualized use of the deer image in the *Amoretti*, see Anne Lake Prescott, "The Thirsty Deer and the Lord of Life: Some Contexts for *Amoretti* 67–70," *Spenser Studies*, 6 (1985) 33–76.

35. For a positive reading of the Temple episode, see, for example, Thomas P. Roche, Jr., *The Kindly Flame: A Study of the Third and Fourth Books of Spenser's "Faerie Queene"* (Princeton: Princeton University Press, 1964), 128–33; for a negative one, Goldberg, 88–92.

36. Harry Berger, Jr.'s 1968 treatment of the Temple has been reprinted in *Revisionary Play: Studies in the Spenserian Dynamics* (Berkeley: University of California Press, 1988), 195–202; see 277–79, 289 on the "paradise principle." For his later treatment of narrator and narrative, see his provocative essays " 'Kidnapped Romance': Discourse in *The Faerie Queene*," in *Unfolded Tales: Essays on Renaissance Romance*, ed. George M. Logan and Gordon Teskey (Ithaca, N.Y.: Cornell University Press, 1989), 208–56, and "Narrative as Rhetoric in *The Faerie Queene*," *English Literary Renaissance*, 21 (1991), 3–48. Page 48 of the latter affords a succinct example of his position on the play of discourses within the poem.

37. C. S. Lewis, *The Allegory of Love: A Study in Medieval Tradition* (1936; rpt. New York: Oxford University Press, 1958), 341.

38. Cf. "emboldened," reiterated in IV.x.56, vs. 5; also IV.x.19 (Scudamour's resolve "to assault" Daunger, or fear of dominion, "with manhood stout, / And either beat him in, or driue him out") and IV.x.55 (Scudamour's showing Womanhood his shield "On which when *Cupid* with his killing bow / And cruell shafts emblazoned she beheld, / At sight thereof she was with terror queld"). On boldness (*audacia*) in the Classical tradition and its inheritors and in *The Faerie Queene*, Book

III (House of Busirane), see my *Translating Investments: Metaphor and the Dynamic of Cultural Change in Tudor-Stuart England* (New York: Fordham University Press, 2005), chaps. 6–7.

Chapter Ten: The Antiquities of Fairyland and Ireland

1. On my use of "Spenser" and "poet," see chapter 1, part 1, of this volume, "Chaucer's and Spenser's Reflexive Narrators." I often use "Spenser" in the present chapter to designate the figure we identify metonymically with the poet (the Faerie poet, the Spenserian poet, etc.) in *The Faerie Queene* or to specify his other prose and poetic writings and the relatively slender biographical traces we have of him.

2. Elizabeth L. Eisenstein, *The Printing Press as an Agent of Change: Communications and Cultural Transformations in Early-Modern Europe* (Cambridge: Cambridge University Press, 1979), I, 183–95. Eisenstein does not distinguish, however, between an awareness of temporal distance (simple age) and of obsolescence or obsoleteness (worthlessness or irrelevance).

3. I do not consider negative OED, s.v. Antiquity, I.2, 1596 Shakes. *2 Hen. IV*, I.ii.208: "Is not your voice broken? . . . and euery part about you blasted with Antiquity." The paradoxical combination of "blasted" and "Antiquity" sharpens the ironic edge of the Judge's question to Falstaff; substitution of a more neutral term like "old age" for the more awesome and positive "Antiquity" would blunt this edge. See also OED, s.v. Antique *a.* and *sb*. My citations are to the original edition of the OED, but an online check of the 1989 (2nd ed.), with additions of 1993 and 1997, has not altered my conclusions.

4. OED, s.v. Antiquate *ppl. a.* In glossing this word, the OED fails to discriminate between obsolescence or desuetude and simple age or antiquity: see citations dated 1657 and 1706, which follow citation of Tyndale. The OED also dates the citation of Tyndale "1537(?)" but actually cites Day's 1573 edition of Tyndale, as found in the Parker Society Vol. 43: William Tyndale, *Expositions and Notes on Sundry Portions of the Holy Scriptures, together with the Practice of Prelates*, ed. Henry Walter (Cambridge: Cambridge University Press, 1849), 174. Walter's notes on Day's edition indicate that *antiquate* reads *waxen old* in an older edition with which Day's has been collated, and they raise the possibility that *antiquate* may be editorial (134, 174). This is unlikely, however, since *antiquate* is the reading of the 1531 edition of the same work: *The Exposition of the fyrste epistle of seynt Jhon* (Antwerp: M. Lempereur), D3^r. The relevant passage of Tyndale (1573) can be found in the penultimate paragraph of my present essay. All further reference is to Walter's edition of Tyndale's *Exposition of I John*.

5. *Middle English Dictionary*, s.v. Antiquat *adj.*: the medieval occurrence of this word is not in the OED.

6. OED, s.v. Antiquate *v*. *A View of the Present State of Ireland*, in *The Works of Edmund Spenser: A Variorum Edition*, ed. Edwin Greenlaw et al, 11 vols. (Baltimore: Johns Hopkins Press, 1932–57), X, 75 (my emphasis); all further reference in this

chapter to Spenser's work is to this edition, cited as *Var.* On dating *A View,* see Gottfried, *Var.* X, 505.

7. In my count, Shakespeare uses cognates of *antique/antiquity* 23 times. Seven of these instances, often ambivalent or negative, occur in the sonnets and one in *Lucrece,* all of which could have been influenced by the first installment of Spenser's romance epic. Relative dating with respect to Spenser's second installment and his *View* and to Shakespeare's sonnets is less clear, however. Relative range, focus, and novelty, rather than strict priority, in Spenser's writings are again what I would emphasize.

8. *Var.,* vii, 8–9. *OED,* s.v. *Obsolete a.,* 1.

9. For a variety of approaches to the roots and implications of such a distinction, cf. Myron P. Gilmore, "The Renaissance Conception of the Lessons of History" in *Facets of the Renaissance,* ed. William H. Werkmeister (1959; rpt. New York: Harper and Row, 1963), 95–98; Charles Trinkaus, "The Problem of Free Will in the Renaissance and the Reformation," *Journal of the History of Ideas,* 10 (1949), rpt. in *Renaissance Essays from the "Journal of the History of Ideas,"* ed. Paul Oskar Kristeller and Philip B. Wiener (New York: Harper and Row, 1968), 194; William Nelson, *Fact or Fiction: The Dilemma of the Renaissance Storyteller* (Cambridge, Mass.: Harvard University Press, 1973), 1–2, 8.

10. E.g., Sir Philip Sidney, *An Apology for Poetry or The Defence of Poesy,* ed. Geoffrey Shepherd (1965; rpt. Manchester: Manchester University Press, 1973), 103: "it is not rhyming and versing that maketh a poet." All further reference in this chapter is to Shepherd's edition of the *Defence.* Francis Bacon, *Works,* ed. James Spedding, Robert Leslie Ellis, and Douglas Denon Heath (Boston: Taggard and Thompson, 1863), VI, 202–3: Poesy "is taken in two senses, in respect of words or matter. . . . In the later [and pertinent] sense, it is . . . Feigned History, which may be styled as well in prose as in verse." Bacon's statement is from the *Advancement of Learning,* 1605; further reference is to this edition of the *Advancement.* Rudolf Gottfried concludes an otherwise helpful note to his edition of *A View* by suggesting that the distinction in question is one between "the truth of poetry" and "the truth of prose" (*Var.,* X, 310).

11. *Var.,* X, 82: apparatus, line 1152.

12. *Var.,* X, 85–86: apparatus, lines 1215–1330; see also Appendix III, *Var.,* X, 511, 516–18, regarding the Ms.

13. *Var.,* X, 309–10, line 1152n.

14. *Var.,* X, 82, 110. Asked elsewhere whether the antiquities of Ireland are to his purpose in the *View,* Irenius answers, "Trulye verye materiall for if ye marked the Course of all that speache well it was to shewe by what meanes the Customes that now are in Ireland beinge some of them indede verie strange and allmoste heathenishe weare firste broughte in[.] And that was as I saide by those nacions from whom that Countrie was firste peopled, for the difference of manners and Customes dothe followe the difference of nacions and people" (97).

15. E.g., *Var.,* X, 81–82, 230–31.

16. Gottfried, *Var.,* X, 502–3.

17. Appendix III, *Var.*, X, 509–10.

18. Gottfried notes these expansions (Appendix III, *Var.*, X, 510) but seems to overlook their relevance to his belief that the antiquities are merely decorative in the *View*. See *View*, apparatus on 82, line 1152, and on 85–86, lines 1215–1330, revised on 89–90; also apparatus on 92, lines 1383–1451, revised on 92–95; also Smith, *Var.*, X, 320, first note on lines 1383–1451.

19. See part 1, chapter 2, "What Comes after Chaucer's *But* in *The Faerie Queene*," an essay on adversative construction in Spenser's sixth Proem and thus on the poet's shifting perspective. From different vantage points, Eamon Grennan ("Language and Politics: A Note on Some Metaphors in Spenser's *A View of the Present State of Ireland*," *Spenser Studies*, 3 [1982], 106–9) and Jonathan Goldberg ("The Poet's Authority: Spenser, Jonson, and James I and VI," *Genre* 15 [1982], 89–90) both address the tensions in Spenser's *View*.

20. Smith, ed., *Var.*, X, 319; Gough on vii.3. *Var.*, V, 194.

21. See Berger's "Two Spenserian Retrospects: The Antique Temple of Venus and the Primitive Marriage of Rivers," *Texas Studies in Literature and Language*, 10 (1968), 21; also Gordon Braden, "Riverrun: An Epic Catalogue in *The Faerie Queene*," *English Literary Renaissance*, 5 (1975), 31–35.

22. Cf. *OED*, s.v. *Still a.* and *sb.*², A.1, 2, 3.c, 4.d, 5, 7; *adv.*, 1, 1.b, 2, 3, 4.a, c. The meaning of "hidden still," as glossed here, bears a suggestive, though limited, relation to Jan Karel Kouwenhoven's description of Glory in *The Faerie Queene* as attained "already-not yet" (*Apparent Narrative as Thematic Metaphor: The Organization of "The Faerie Queene"* [Oxford: Clarendon Press, 1983], 20); I also note my rejection, in a review in *JEGP* (84 [1985], 423) of Kouwenhoven's premises, methodology, and conclusions aside from this point.

23. *Faerie Queene*, II.ix.59; III.ii.2, vi.6; IV.xi.10, 48–52, xii.1–2; VII.vi.2.

24. Whether the Muse of *The Faerie Queene* is Clio or Calliope is a very old and still current question. I expect that Spenser is most often deliberately vague—or, rather, inclusive—in his designation of her. The material I present argues against the *exclusion* of Clio, in any case.

25. *OED*, s.v. *Scrine*.

26. On Eumnestes, see Robert L. Reid, "Alma's Castle and the Symbolization of Reason in *The Faerie Queene*," *JEGP*, 80 (1981), 512–27, esp. 517–18; Reid's article affords a useful summary of earlier scholarship. On the traditional relation of memory to history, see, for example, Bacon, *Advancement*, 182: "The parts of human learning have reference to the three parts of Man's Understanding, which is the seat of learning: History to his Memory, Poesy to his Imagination, and Philosophy to his Reason." On Memory, see especially Frances A. Yates, *The Art of Memory* (Chicago: University of Chicago Press, 1966), 299: "The conviction that it [truth] is within, in the inner images which are nearer to reality than the objects [or events] of the outer world, that reality is grasped and the unified vision achieved, underlies the whole" art of memory. Also, Yates's *Giordano Bruno and the Hermetic Tradition* (Chicago: University of Chicago Press, 1964), 66: "for a Renaissance Neoplatonist an 'ancient' image, one that reached him from traditions going back, so he believed,

into a remote past, did actually have within it the reflection of an Idea. An ancient image of Justice was not just a picture but actually contained within it some echo, taste, substance, of the divine Idea of Justice." Yates cites E. H. Gombrich, "*Icones Symbolicae*: The Visual Image in Neo-Platonic Thought," *Journal of the Warburg and Courtauld Institutes*, 11 (1948), 163–92, esp. 169–70. Relatively more recently, John Guillory (*Poetic Authority: Spenser, Milton, and Literary History* [New York: Columbia University Press, 1983], chs. 2–3), has treated the subject of authorizing power in Spenser's poetry, although at a theoretical remove from the present argument. More relevant to it is the paralleling of proverbial wisdom and the wisdom of the ancients in Mary Ann Cincotta's "Reinventing Authority in *The Faerie Queene*," *SP*, 80 (1983), esp. 34–35.

27. Cf. the famous instance of "nothing" and "no thing" in *King Lear* and part 3, chapter 12, on this play in the present volume.

28. Eumnestes' materials include "The warres . . . Of king *Nine*, / Of old *Assaracus*, and *Inachus* diuine" (ix.56). Arthur and Guyon also find "*Briton moniments*" and the "*Antiquities of Fairy lond*" in Eumnestes' library (ix.59–60).

29. In *Clio Unbound: Perception of the Social and Cultural Past in Renaissance England* ([Durham, N.C.: Duke University Press, 1979], 36), Arthur B. Ferguson observes that Spenser saw in such stories as that of Brutus "something of value as metahistory." (*Just*, meaning "only," does not occur until 1665 or relevantly until 1785, according to the *OED*, s.v. *Just adv.*, 5. If this meaning were contemporary with Spenser, it would make the second Proem considerably more ambivalent.)

30. *OED*, s.v. *Antic a.* and *sb.*; s.v. *Antique a.* and *sb.*: preliminary matter. *Faerie Queene*, II.iii.27, vii.4; III.xi.51.

31. Appendix I, *Var.*, X, 472.

32. *Letter-Book of Gabriel Harvey*, 1573–1580, ed. Edward John Long Scott, Camden Society, n.s. 33 (Westminster: Nichols, 1884), 82–83. I have silently expanded contractions in citing this edition.

33. *The Poetry of Edmund Spenser: A Study* (New York: Columbia University Press, 1963), 302. Guillaume Budé's Latin is quoted from St. Thomas More, *Utopia*, ed. Edward Surtz and J. H. Hexter, in *Works* (New Haven, Conn.: Yale University Press, 1965), IV, 12; the translation is mine.

34. Cf. Michael Murrin, *The Allegorical Epic: Essays in its Rise and Decline* (Chicago: University of Chicago Press, 1980), 133–34, 139, but also 141.

35. See part 1, chapter 2, "What Comes after Chaucer's *But* in *The Faerie Queene*."

36. See my *Growth of a Personal Voice: "Piers Plowman" and "The Faerie Queene"* (New Haven, Conn.: Yale University Press, 1976), 52–61, esp. 56. Mammon's argument in II.vii.18 is at once Mercantilist (i.e., Bullionist) and Machiavellian (213n12).

37. In *The Past That Poets Make* ([Cambridge, Mass.: Harvard University Press, 1981], 120), Harold Toliver describes Spenser's view of the past as more static and one-dimensional. He argues that it is generally "optimistic about blending history, fiction, and religious myth and thus about renewing past ideals not merely in the

poem but in society" (cf. 129). For a different view, see my *Biographical Truth: The Representation of Historical Persons in Tudor-Stuart Writing* (New Haven, Conn.: Yale University Press, 1984), 1–8, 69–71, 124–25, 157–69, the last a discussion of Bacon's sense of history, poetry, and truth.

38. "Queene Elizabeth I as *Astraea*," in *Astraea: The Imperial Theme in the Sixteenth Century* (London: Routledge and Kegan Paul, 1975), 87. Yates refers to the contrast between symbol and history in Shakespeare's plays.

Chapter Eleven: Better a mischief than an inconvenience: *"The saiyng self" in Spenser's* View of the Present State of Ireland

1. "To the Reader," in Udall, ed. and trans., *Apophthegmes* (London: John Kingston, 1564), *iii[r]. I wish to thank Vincent Blasi of the Columbia University Law School, my fellow fellow at the National Humanities Center, for reading and commenting on the legal nuances of this chapter.

2. Reference to Spenser's work in this chapter is to *The Works of Edmund Spenser: A Variorum Edition*, ed. Edwin Greenlaw et al, 11 vols. (Baltimore: Johns Hopkins Press, 1932–57), cited as *Var.* The present reference is to X, 80. *A View of the Present State of Ireland*, X, special ed. Rudolf Gottfried, is cited as *View*.

3. See my *Words that Matter: Linguistic Perception in Renaissance English* (Stanford, Calif.: Stanford University Press, 1996), 21–23, 25–26, 33–42; Roland Barthes, *Elements of Semiology*, trans. Annette Laves and Colin Smith (New York: Hill and Wang, 1974), 19, 62; and John Hoskyns, *Direccions for Speech and Style. The Life, Letters, and Writings of John Hoskyns, 1566–1638*, ed. Louise Brown Osborn (New Haven, Conn.: Yale University Press, 1937), 153–54. I borrow the analogy between a saying and a "prefabricated unit" from Nigel Barley, "A Structural Approach to the Proverb and Maxim with Special Reference to the Anglo-Saxon Corpus," *Proverbium*, 20 (1972), 737–50, here 740.

4. Erasmus, cited in *Erasmus on His Times: A Shortened Version of the Adages of Erasmus*, trans. Margaret Mann Phillips (London: Cambridge University Press, 1967), 3; see also Roland Barthes, *S–Z*, trans. Richard Miller (New York: Hill and Wang, 1974), 100; Barley, 740–41; Mary Thomas Crane, *Framing Authority: Sayings, Self, and Society in Sixteenth-Century England* (Princeton: Princeton University Press, 1993), chap. 1; and part 1, chapter 6, in the present volume on "Spenser's Use of Chaucer's *Melibee*: Allegory, Narrative, History."

5. J. H. Baker, *Manual of Law French*, 2nd ed. (Aldershot, Hants, Eng: Scolar, 1990), s.v. *enconvenient*: "absurd, unfitting, logically inconsistent, unnecessary, undesirable."

6. *OED*, s.v. *Inconvenience*, 3.c (Malynes); *Mischief n.*, 3.b (Spenser's *View*).

7. For the relevant quotation from Jean Bodin, see *Var.*, X, 297, lines 648–62; and for incisive remarks about Bodin's treatment of natural law, see Debora Kuller Shuger, *The Renaissance Bible: Scholarship, Sacrifice, and Subjectivity* (Berkeley: University of California Press, 1994), 78.

8. *The Statutes of Ireland* (Dublin: Society of Stationers, 1621), 286–87: from Pollard and Redgrave 1072: "Ireland, Laws and Statutes" (Ann Arbor: University Microfilms).

9. See *Statutes of the Realm* (London: Dawsons of Pall Mall, 1810–22), IV, 365 (1 Eliza., chap. 5); 526 (13 Eliza., chap. 1), cf. 657 (23 Eliza., chap 1); 705 (27 Eliza., chap. 1). Also John Bellamy, *The Tudor Law of Treason* (London: Routledge and Kegan Paul, 1979), chap. 2.

10. The Irish parliament that met in the second year of Elizabeth's reign (1560) passed the treason legislation making a second offense capital. Although Irish parliaments also met in 1569–71 and in 1585–86, they failed to enact specific legislation pertaining to capital treason against the crown. During the sixteenth century the relation of English to Irish parliamentary law is unsettled and evolving both theoretically and practically. For a sampling of diverse views of the legal situation, see Ciaran Brady, "Court, Castle and Country: The Framework of Government in Tudor Ireland," in *Natives and Newcomers: Essays on the Making of Irish Colonial Society, 1534–1641*, ed. Ciaran Brady and Raymond Gillespie (Dublin: Irish Academic Press, 1986), 22–49, here 22–30, 40–41; Steven G. Ellis, *Tudor Ireland: Crown, Community and the Conflict of Cultures, 1470–1603* (London: Longman, 1985), 178–79, 192–95; and his "Henry VIII, Rebellion and the Rule of Law," *The Historical Journal*, 24 (1981), 513–31, esp. 516, 520, 531; Nicholas P. Canny, *The Elizabethan Conquest of Ireland: A Pattern Established, 1565–76* (New York: Barnes and Noble, 1976), 61, 102–3, 117–20; his *From Reformation to Restoration: Ireland, 1534–1660* (Dublin: Helicon, 1987), 22, 75; and his "Edmund Spenser and the Development of an Anglo-Irish Identity," *Yearbook of English Studies*, 13 (1983), 1–19, esp. 3–4; Brendan Bradshaw, *The Irish Constitutional Revolution of the Sixteenth Century* (Cambridge: Cambridge University Press, 1979), 263–67, 282, 287–88; G. J. Swift MacNeill, *The Constitutional and Parliamentary History of Ireland Till the Union* (1917; rpt. Port Washington, N.Y.: Kennikat, 1970), 1–8. Also, Jon G. Crawford, *Anglicizing the Government of Ireland: The Irish Privy Council and the Expansion of Tudor Rule, 1556–78* (Dublin: Irish Academic Press in association with the Irish Legal History Society, 1993), 41; J. C. Beckett, *The Making of Modern Ireland, 1603–1923* (London: Faber and Faber, 1966), 18–19, 22–23; Cyril Falls, *Elizabeth's Irish Wars* (London: Methuen, 1950), 18–23, 64–65. A sampling of relevant documents can be found in *Elizabethan Ireland*, ed. Morton Grenfell (London: Longman, 1971), 112–23.

11. See *The Oxford Dictionary of English Etymology*, ed. C. T. Onions (Oxford: Clarendon, 1966), s.v. *Mischief*.

12. *OED*, s.v. *Inconvenience*, 1.

13. Annabel Patterson offers a review of the place of Spenser's tract in the valuable historical work on sixteenth-century Ireland done by Nicholas Canny, Brendan Bradshaw, and Ciaran Brady: *Pastoral and Ideology: Virgil to Valéry* (Berkeley: University of California Press, 1987), 82–86. None of these writers, including Patterson, directly address the proverbial saying in question, although the passage in which it occurs at times proves of interest to them.

14. Personal correspondence, for which I am grateful to Professor J. H. Baker, and Baker's introduction to his edition of *The Reports of Sir John Spelman*, 2 vols. (London: Selden Society, 1977–78), II, 38; cf. also Baker's *Manual of Law French*, s.v. *enconvenient, enconvenientise*.

15. By "late medieval" Doe mainly means the fifteenth century, but he includes Christopher St. German's *Doctor and Student* (1529–31) and corroborating Renaissance citations to the writings of such figures as Thomas Smith and Richard Hooker. For *Doctor and Student*, see *The Secunde dyaloge in Englysshe bytwene a doctour of dyuyntye and a student in the lawes of Englande* (Southwarke: P. Treuerys, 1530).

16. Chap. xlvi (mislabeled xlv). The rest of this paragraph derives from the same chapter of *Doctor and Student*, its customary title.

17. Stephen D. White, *Sir Edward Coke and "The Grievances of the Commonwealth," 1621–28* (Chapel Hill: University of North Carolina Press, 1979), 80n199.

18. Although *Lex Mercatoria* (Amsterdam: Theatrum Orbis Terrarum, 1979) was published in 1622, I consider the thinking of Malynes (on record from 1586—1626) roughly contemporary with that at the turn of the century; he also treats a subject steeped in custom and precedent, as the full title of his treatise indicates. See, for example, the sixteenth-century petitions to the Privy Council regarding marine insurance in Harold E. Raynes' *A History of British Insurance*, rev. ed. (London: Sir Isaac Pitman, 1950): " 'the order of assurance is not grounded upon the laws of the realm but [is] rather a civil and maritime cause to be determined and decided by civilians,' . . . 'forasmuch as the matter . . . consisteth and standeth much upon the order and usages of merchants by whom rather than the course of law it may be forwarded and determined' " (29).

19. The context of the proverb is somewhat ambiguous: more exactly the statement that "the last assurors which haue subscribed to the Policie, shall enioy the benefit thereof, as hath beene declared" (161). The problem is the referent of "thereof." The only explanation I have found for this benefit comes on page 156: "those Assurors that have last subscribed to the Policy of Assurance, bear not any adventure at all." Instead, Malynes continues, they refund the premium to the holder of the policy, but they also take a cut of it because they are *ipso facto* subscribers to it. I thus take the Assurors' being bound "*ipso facto* to the said Assurance" (161) to indicate not merely the fact of having signed a document but the fact of the declared value of the cargo in question. See also note 18, just above.

20. Cf. a bill regarding marine insurance introduced into Parliament in 1601: "our Courts have not the knowledge of their [merchants'] terms, neither can they tell what to say upon their causes, which be secret in their science proceeding out of their experience" (Raynes, 56).

21. Rpt. *A Discourse Upon Usury*, ed. R. H. Tawney (London: G. Bell, 1925).

22. John Bridges, *The Supremacie of Christian Princes* (London: H. Bynneman for H. Toye, 1573), 1058: for this reference and those that follow, I have consulted *The Oxford Dictionary of English Proverbs*, 3rd ed., rev. F. P. Wilson (Oxford: Clarendon, 1970); Morris Palmer Tilley, *A Dictionary of Proverbs in England in the Sixteenth and Seventeenth Centuries* (1950; rpt. Ann Arbor: University of Michigan Press, 1966);

R. W. Dent, *Proverbial Language in English Drama Exclusive of Shakespeare, 1495–1616* (Berkeley: University of California Press, 1984); and *Var.*, X, 297.

23. *The Resurrection of Our Lord*, Malone Society Reprints (Oxford: Oxford University Press, 1912), 15–16: I have assumed some corruption in the text, which initially seems to make the discrediting of Mosaic law a mischief rather than an inconvenience (lines 462–64). But the surrounding context clearly indicates that this discrediting is the larger concern or "inconvenience."

24. *The Complete Works of John Lyly*, ed. R. Warwick Bond (1902: rpt. Oxford: Clarendon, 1967), III, 216: *Bombie* V.ii.26–27; and II, 457: *Gallathea* IV.i. 38–39.

25. T[homas] Middleton and T[homas] Dekker, *The Roaring Girl*, ed. John S. Farmer (1611; rpt. Amersham: Tudor Facsimile Texts, 1914), F4. Andor Gomme, ed., *The Roaring Girl*, by Middleton and Dekker (London: Ernest Benn, 1976), follows the earlier dating of R. C. Bald, 1608, for the play; he offers no annotation for the inverted proverb in question (III.ii.135–36); Paul A. Mulholland, ed., *The Roaring Girl*, by Middleton and Dekker (Manchester: Manchester University Press, 1987) dates the play 1611 (12–13); he cites Tilley's listing of the proverb "Better once a mischief than always an inconvenience" without further comment (III.ii.139–40).

26. *OED*, s.v. *Inconvenience n.*, 2; *Mischief n.*, 1.a, 2.a–b: with the phrase "evil consequences" I borrow a later refinement in the *OED*'s equivalence because it accounts for the "evil arising out of or existing in certain conditions" (2.b).

27. Brian Melbancke, *Philotimus: The Warre betwixt Nature and Fortune* (London: Roger Warde, 1583), 173. *OED*, s.v. *Inconvenience n.*, 2, 4. Although the meaning "discomfort" is not recognized by the *OED* until 1653, a case can be made for it in this earlier citation.

28. *The Riverside Shakespeare*, ed. G. Blakemore Evans (Boston, Mass.: Houghton Mifflin, 1974). R. W. Dent, *Shakespeare's Proverbial Language* (Berkeley: University of California Press, 1981), 143, notes the relevance of *Better a mischief than an inconvenience* to *Merry Wives*.

29. "A New Letter of Notable Contents, 1593," in *The Works of Gabriel Harvey*, ed. Alexander B. Grosart, 3 vols. (1884; rpt. New York: AMS, 1996), I, 284. On relevant details of the Harvey-Nashe feud, see Thomas Nashe, "To the Reader," *Christs Teares over Jerusalem*, 1593, 1595, in *The Works of Thomas Nashe*, ed. Ronald B. McKerrow, 5 vols., with corrections and supplementary notes by F. P. Wilson (1958; rpt. Oxford: Basil Blackwell, 1966), II, 12–13, 179–81; and discussion of the Harvey-Nashe feud in Nashe, *Works*, V, 66–67, 90–105. Also Virginia F. Stern, *Gabriel Harvey: His Life, Marginalia and Library* (Oxford: Clarendon, 1979), 106–8, 110–13.

30. Cf. Doe, 169: "[legal] usages of mischief and inconvenience reflect two fundamentally opposing concerns."

31. *A Discourse upon the Exposicion and Understanding of Statutes, with Sir Thomas Egerton's Additions*, ed. Samuel E. Thorne (San Marino: Huntington Library, 1942), 79n165.

32. *OED*, s.v. *Mischief n.*, 1.a–c, 2.a–b, 4.b, 6, 7.

33. OED, s.v. Inconvenience n., 1–3, 4.b.

34. See Doe, 163; View, e.g., 52, 60, 74–75, 198–200.

35. View 100, 118; cf. 75, 225–26; for the meaning "harm," "trouble," "injury[ous]," see, e.g., 176, 214, 226, 229.

36. Raymond Jenkins, "Spenser: The Uncertain Years 1584–1589," *PMLA*, 53 (1938), 350–61, here 350; also his "Spenser and the Clerkship in Munster," *PMLA*, 47 (1932), 109–21; for Judson, see *Var.*, XI, 113–16.

37. Chaucer, *General Prologue*, vs. 639–41, *The Canterbury Tales*, in *The Riverside Chaucer*, ed. Larry D. Benson, 3rd ed. (Boston, Mass.: Houghton Mifflin, 1987).

38. On discomfort, see Annabel Patterson, *Reading Between the Lines*, (Madison: University of Wisconsin Press, 1993), 110. For a provocative exchange regarding dialogue in the *View*, see John M. Breen, "Imagining Voices in *A View of the Present State of Ireland*: A Discussion of Recent Studies concerning Edmund Spenser's Dialogue," *Connotations* 4 (1994–95), 119–32, esp. 123–24; and Andrew Hadfield, "Who Is Speaking in Spenser's *View of the Present State of Ireland*? A Response to John Breen," *Connotations* 4 (1994–95), 232–41, esp. 236–37. While the tenor of my chapter and the possibilities considered here are at odds with those of Anne Fogarty's provocative essay "The Colonization of Language: Narrative Strategy in *A View of The Present State of Ireland* and *The Faerie Queene*, Book VI," there is much in her essay that I admire and find generally relevant to my concerns: *Spenser and Ireland: An Interdisciplinary Perspective*, ed. Patricia Coughlan (Cork, Ireland: Cork University Press, 1989), 75–108. Cf. Also David J. Baker, "'Some Quirk, Some Subtle Evasion': Legal Subversion in Spenser's *A View of the Present State of Ireland*," *Spenser Studies*, 6 (1985), 147–63.

39. Cf. my earlier discussion of this proverb in part 1, chapter 2, "What Comes after Chaucer's *But* in *The Faerie Queene*": in the Proem to Book VI, the poet seems to have swallowed the opposed voices of Burbon and Artegall.

40. See *Copia: Foundations of the Abundant Style*, trans. Betty I. Knott, ed. Craig R. Thompson. *Collected Works of Erasmus* (Toronto: University of Toronto Press, 1978), XXIV, 646–48; I thank Kathy Eden for suggesting the relevance of Erasmus' text. Victoria Kahn's discussion of training in the Renaissance to argue *in utramque partem*, "on both sides," of a question is also pertinent: *Rhetoric, Prudence, and Skepticism in the Renaissance* (Ithaca, N.Y.: Cornell University Press, 1985), 11, 38–39, and chap. 4. On Chaucer's use of proverbs in *Troilus and Criseyde*, see Karla Taylor, "Proverbs and the Authentication of Convention in *Troilus and Criseyde*," in *Chaucer's Troilus: Essays in Criticism*, ed. Stephen A. Barney (Hamden, Conn.: Archon, 1980), 277–95, esp. 286–87.

41. Shuger, *Renaissance Bible*, 81, 87, and chap. 2.

42. See Brian Tierney, "Origins of Natural Rights Language: Texts and Contexts, 1150–1250," *History of Political Thought*, 10 (1989), 615–46; also his "Aristotle and the American Indians—Again," *Cristianesimo nella Storia*, 12 (1991), 295–304, 315–22. My qualification "at least" is based on Fred D. Miller, Jr., *Nature, Justice, and Rights in Aristotle's "Politics"* (Oxford: Clarendon, 1995), 87–139, 373–78. Shuger declines to call the "oscillation" or "differentiation" (her preferred word)

between "autonomous subject" and common weal a tension, which she describes as an "achieved polarization" (53). Tensions are arguably more subtle. This one in question already has a persistent, not to say an abiding, shape. Additional definition of it can be found in Cynthia B. Herrup's investigation of law enforcement in England during the late sixteenth and seventeenth centuries, which, in her view, attempted to balance absolute considerations of justice with individuating history and circumstances and public order with personal error: *The Common Peace: Participation and the Criminal Law in Seventeenth-Century England* (Cambridge: Cambridge University Press, 1987).

43. Anthony Giddens, *Modernity and Self-Identity: Self and Society in the Late Modern Age* (Stanford, Calif.: Stanford University Press, 1991), e.g., 1–9, 32–36, 52–55.

44. Willy Maley and Andrew Hadfield, among others, have suggested that Spenser had Republican sympathies, possibly derived from the writings of Bodin, Buchanan, and Machiavelli: respectively, *Salvaging Spenser: Colonialism, Culture and Identity* (London: Macmillan, 1997), 115; and "Was Spenser a Republican?" *English*, 47 (1998), 169–82. My findings regarding Spenser's deployment of the maxim "Better a mischief than an inconvenience" could be used to support this suggestion. To it, I would add one consideration, however: the questioning of monarchical absolutism and the revaluation of individual right are historically related—and thoroughly intertextualized.

PART 3 Spenserian Allegory in the Intertexts of Shakespeare and Milton

Chapter Twelve: The Conspiracy of Realism: Impasse and Vision in The Faerie Queene *and Shakespeare's* King Lear

1. In order, A. C. Bradley, *Shakespearean Tragedy: "Hamlet," "Othello," "King Lear," "Macbeth"* (1904; rpt. Cleveland: World Publishing, 1955); W. B. C. Watkins, *Shakespeare and Spenser* (1950; rpt. Cambridge: Walker-de-Berry, 1961); Maynard Mack, *King Lear in Our Time* (1965; rpt. Berkeley: University of California Press, 1972). Quotations of the text of *King Lear* in this chapter are from Kenneth Muir's edition (1952; rpt. New York: Vintage, 1964). Quotations of Spenser's works in this chapter are from the *Variorum* edition, ed. Edwin Greenlaw at al, 11 vols. (Baltimore: Johns Hopkins Press, 1932–57).

2. See Paul de Man, "The Rhetoric of Temporality," in *Interpretation: Theory and Practice*, ed. Charles S. Singleton (Baltimore: Johns Hopkins University Press, 1969), 173–91, esp. 191.

3. On allegory in myth, see, for example, John MacQueen, *Allegory* (London: Methuen, 1970), 1–17. Also two classics on the subject: Jean Seznec, *The Survival of the Pagan Gods: The Mythological Tradition and Its Place in Renaissance Humanism and Art*, trans. Barbara F. Sessions (1953; rpt. New York: Harper, 1961); and Edgar

Wind, *Pagan Mysteries in the Renaissance*, rev. ed. (Harmondsworth, Middlesex, U.K.: Penguin, 1967).

4. Bernard Spivack, *Shakespeare and the Allegory of Evil: The History of a Metaphor in Relation to His Major Villains* (New York: Columbia University Press, 1958), 127. On characters as allegorical projections of Lear, cf. Richard Fly, *Shakespeare's Mediated World* (Amherst: University of Massachusetts Press, 1976), 109–10; and Robert B. Heilman, "The Unity of King Lear," in *Shakespeare: "King Lear,"* ed. Frank Kermode (London: Macmillan, 1969), 169–78, esp. 175, 178.

5. Judith H. Anderson, *The Growth of a Personal Voice: "Piers Plowman" and "The Faerie Queene"* (New Haven, Conn.: Yale University Press, 1976), 5.

6. Cf. the description in Peter Brook's film script (1970) for the opening of *Lear*: "'On a blank screen, dots and blotches slowly materialize. What are they? . . . the disconnected patches are tantalizingly enigmatic . . . then suddenly from the chaos a coherent shape emerges. A pair of eyes. . . . For a moment they are sharp and clear . . . then they dissolve away again. . . . Now faces, old and young, men and women: characters we do not know yet, but will identify later. Slight sounds and voices fade in and die away. Always, the very first or the very last shapes to resolve into sense are the eyes'": from Marvin Rosenberg, *The Masks of King Lear* (Berkeley: University of California Press, 1972), 38.

7. "King Lear and Its Language," in *Some Facets of "King Lear": Essays in Prismatic Criticism*, ed. Rosalie L. Colie and F. T. Flahiff (Toronto: University of Toronto Press, 1974), 10.

8. Bradley, 207. Leo Kirschbaum finds in Edgar's dialect a recurrence of the theme of the good servant: *Character and Characterization in Shakespeare* (Detroit: Wayne State University Press, 1962), 66–74. Kirschbaum calls Edgar a "dramatic device" and a "dramatic function"—a figure primarily in the service of (allegorical?) meaning (51–2, 61, 75).

9. E.g., cf. Stephen A. Barney, *Allegories of History, Allegories of Love* (Hamden, Conn.: Archon, 1979), 16–21. Also my chapter on "*Muiopotmos* and *The Nun's Priest's Tale*" in this volume: part 2, chap. 1.

10. Similarly for Zitner in *Lear*, I.i, any questioning of the tenderness or indeed of the adequacy of Cordelia's *Nothing* is irrelevant to the question of language and to what seems to be his ideal of plain-talk (7). For another, stimulating but finally too unproblematical response to the presence of allegory in *Lear*, see Nicholas Brooke, *King Lear* (Great Neck, N.Y.: Barron's Educational Series, 1963), esp. 59–60.

11. Latin *cor/cordis* signifies "heart." If Shakespeare was aware of Delia as an anagram for ideal, this meaning might further have influenced his choosing the form "Cordelia," which he found in *The Faerie Queene*. See Arthur F. Kinney, "Lear," *Massachusetts Review* 17 (1976), 684.

12. Rosenberg, 102, 107.

13. See William Empson's discussion of the word "Fool in Lear" in *The Structure of Complex Words* (1951; rpt. Totowa, N.J.: Rowman and Littlefield, 1979), 125–57.

14. Cf. Rosenberg. 192, 228: my conception of Fool has been influenced by Rosenberg's insight, 101–239, esp. 101–17.

15. On the ambiguities of Lear's final reference to fool," see Stephen Booth, *"King Lear," "Macbeth," Indefinition, and Tragedy* (New Haven, Conn.: Yale University Press, 1983), 32–33.

16. Cf. Mack, 117: "*King Lear* . . . begs us to seek the meaning of our human fate not in what becomes of us, but in what we become." Similarly, Susan Snyder, *The Comic Matrix of Shakespeare's Tragedies: "Romeo and Juliet," "Hamlet," "Othello," and "King Lear"* (Princeton: Princeton University Press, 1979), 170. Like Zitner and Brooke (note 10, above), Fly recognizes that "quasi-allegorical" elements (109–10) are present in *Lear* but finally denies that they signify anything, whether this signification is absence and negation or something more constructive. Such a conclusion simplifies the intellectual and ideological complexities demonstrably present in *Lear* that pertain to the meaning of art and the meaning of meaning.

17. Zitner, 12, 14, implies an ideal of plain speech in IV.vii, the early stages of Lear's return to sanity. This ideal seems to me too much that of a broken old man, at once powerless and pathetic. Celebration of it as a final answer is equivalent to our getting Lear into a nice, comfy nursing home, where Cordelia can visit him once a week. What is wrong is its lack of energy and its empty identity: this, in a word, is and is not Lear.

18. Cf. Wind, 238: "the commonplace may be understood as a reduction of the exceptional, but . . . the exceptional cannot be understood by amplifying the commonplace. Both logically and causally the exceptional . . . introduces . . . the more comprehensive category." Moreover, as observed in my introduction, artistic form, including but not limited to genre, is developmental; indeed, again to invoke Alastair Fowler, literary forms "continuously undergo . . . metamorphosis," and the very "character of genres is that they change," without becoming unrecognizable, however: *Kinds of Literature: An Introduction to the Theory of Genres and Modes* (Cambridge, Mass.: Harvard University Press, 1982), 18, 23; cf. 20, 37; all of chaps. 2–3 is relevantly suggestive.

19. William F. Zak, *Sovereign Shame: A Study of "King Lear"* (Cranbury, N.J.: Assoc. University Presses, 1984), 77, criticizes "redemptionist readings . . . that tend to lift Cordelia out of her very human predicament and place her safely in an allegorical heaven."

20. S.v. *Allegory*, by Northrop Frye, 12–15, here 12: I have expanded the abbreviation of *allegory* in Frye's entry.

21. See the discussion of metaphor and allegory (a form of metaphor) in my introduction. The absurdist I particularly intend is Beckett, but Albee, early Stoppard, and Ionesco also come to mind.

22. From my *Growth of a Personal Voice*, 5.

23. Snyder, 179, compares *Purgatorio* and *Endgame* to visions between which Lear's tragedy is enacted. For an absurdist's *locus classicus*, see Jan Kott, *Shakespeare*

our Contemporary, trans. Boleslaw Taborski, 2nd ed. (London: Methuen, 1967), 100–133: "'King Lear', or Endgame."

24. See *Narrative and Dramatic Sources of Shakespeare*, ed. Geoffrey Bullough (New York: Columbia University Press, 1973), VII, 276, 332–34; also J. C. Maxwell, in Muir, ed., *King Lear*, 199 (citation of *The Faerie Queene*, VI.vi.4, vs. 9). For relevant discussion of *Muiopotmos*, see my chapter "*Muiopotmos* and *The Nun's Priest's Tale*," whence the concluding description I quote here.

25. See Bullough, ed., VII, 276; Muir, ed., 4.

26. William R. Elton aligns these lines with Lear, II.iv.266–67: *King Lear and the Gods* (San Marino: Huntington Library 1966), 228.

27. In the course of Lear's speech "O! reason not the need" (II.iv.266–88), his understanding of true need begins to shift, so that by speech's end, he is not so sure that the "poorest thing" the base possess is material. Nor are we.

28. On Shakespeare's use of *The Faerie Queene* in *Richard III*, see my *Biographical Truth: The Representation of Historical Persons in Tudor-Stuart Writing* (New Haven, Conn.: Yale University Press, 1984), 118, 223–24nn.23–24, 26; and in the present volume, my chapter "'*Venus and Adonis*'": Spenser, Shakespeare, and the Forms of Desire." Also Harold F. Brooks, "'Richard III': Antecedents of Clarence's Dream," *Shakespeare Survey*, 32 (1979), 145–50. Cf. also *Lear*, V.iii.2 ("men of stones") and I.iv.262 ("Degenerate bastard") with *Faerie Queene*, V.Pro.2:

> For from the golden age, that first was named,
>   It's now at earst become a *stonie* one;
> And men themselues, the which at first were framed
> Of earthly mould, and form'd of flesh and bone,
> Are now transformed into hardest *stone*:
> Such as behind their backs (so backward bred)
> Were throwne by *Pyrrha* and *Deucalione*:
> And if then those may any worse be red,
> They into that ere long will be *degendered*.
>   (My emphasis, excepting proper names)

The common source is Ovid, but the rest of Spenser's fifth Proem—the bearing of the erratic revolutions of the heavens on worldly justice and injustice—enforces the verbal relevance of this stanza to *King Lear*. (Note also the general relevance of pastoral motifs in Spenser's Book VI to *Lear*—e.g., the bear-baby in canto iv and Melibee's retreat, the latter discussed later in the present chapter.)

29. Within this volume, I have further treated the dual values of Spenser's second Proem in "The Antiquities of Fairyland and Ireland" (part 2, chapter 10). Notably the juxtaposition of physical with mythic space/time recurs in *Faerie Queene*, II.x (the chronicles of Britain and Fairyland), wherein Spenser's tale of Lear and Cordelia—an acknowledged Shakespearean source—is also found. Space precludes my discussing here the ties between the second Proem and canto x, which are pronounced and specific, both including, for example, references to America.

30. See note 28, above: Brooks refers to the Cave of Mammon. Milton mentions this Cave in *Areopagitica* (*Complete Prose Works*, ed. Don M. Wolfe et al, vol. 2, ed. Ernest Sirluck [New Haven, Conn.: Yale University Press, 1959], 516). Keats finds in the Cave what Paul Alpers has described as "a metaphor for the poet's activity": *The Poetry of The Faerie Queene* (Princeton: Princeton University Press, 1967), 264; and *The Letters of John Keats 1814–21*, ed. Hyder Edward Rollins, 2 vols. (Cambridge, Mass.: Harvard University Press, 1958), II, 322–23.

31. This paragraph and the following one are based on my conclusions in "The Knight and the Palmer in *The Faerie Queene*, Book II," *Modern Language Quarterly*, 31 (1970), 160–78, and in my *Growth of a Personal Voice*, 51–65, 75–76.

32. Book II of *The Faerie Queene* is full of the elemental symbolism of water, wind, fire, and earth that pertains so fundamentally to Mammon's Cave: see James Carscallen, "The Goodly Frame of Temperance: The Metaphor of Cosmos in *The Faerie Queene*, Book II," *University of Toronto Quarterly*, 37 (1968), 136–55. In connection with Goneril's speech, cf. also her claim in *The True Chronicle Historie of King Leir*, a Shakespeare source: "my zeale to you . . . cannot be in *windy* words rehearst" (*Narrative and Dramatic Sources*. 343, lines 238–39: my emphasis). A Shakespeare play is nothing if not intertextually eclectic.

33. Cf. *Othello*, III.iii.157: "Who steals my purse steals trash; 'tis something, [that is] nothing" (cited from *The Riverside Shakespeare*, ed. G. Blakemore Evans et al [Boston, Mass.: Houghton Mifflin, 1974]).

34. Cf. *Lear*, I.iv.200–201: "now thou art an O without a figure." Although Ralph Berry's original interpretation of Lear's division of the kingdom is much more one-sidedly critical of Cordelia and more sympathetic to Goneril and Regan than mine, even he must acknowledge Shakespeare's efforts to ensure the immediacy and ambivalence of our response to Cordelia's "Nothing": "Lear's System," *Shakespeare Quarterly*, 35 (1984), 421–29, esp. 427.

35. Cf. Elton's provocative treatment of "Nothing," 180–88. My reading by no means excludes resonances of the sort Elton discusses; one of the beauties of allegory is its expansiveness; its inclusive multiplicities are another. Yet I must also note that Elton's sources in this instance are not so demonstrably and specifically relevant to *Lear* as is *The Faerie Queene*. More generally, I find astonishing the common assumption that Shakespeare was more likely to have known well tenth-rate dramas and theological tracts than the central poetic statement of the Elizabethan period. Where such an assumption exists it is usually based on a misconceived reading of Spenser. On "Nothing," see also Kinney, 687.

36. See Carol L. Marks's (Sicherman's) perceptively balanced essay " 'Speak what we feel': The End of King Lear," *English Language Notes*, 5 (1968): 163–71, esp, 167; also Elton, 240. Elton is right to remind us of the negative implication of a caged bird, but I find him mistaken in trying to cancel the positive implications (Spenserian and emblematic) in the negative one and, indeed, the mythic in the merely natural one. The more pertinent of Elton's negative analogues, the caged bird in Sir

Philip Sidney's *Arcadia*, Book I, is infinitely less relevant verbally and contextually to *Lear* than is the Spenserian source in *Faerie Queene*, VI; see *The Countesse of Pembrokes Arcadia*, in *Prose Works*, ed. Albert Feuillerat, 4 vols. (Cambridge: Cambridge University Press, 1912), I, 139. Elton fails to take Spenser's image in its context in Book VI and therefore supposes that it is simplistically positive and holy. More generally on negation in the final Act of *Lear*, see, for example, Nicholas Brooke, "The Ending of *King Lear*," in *Shakespeare 1564–1964*, ed. Edward A. Bloom (Providence, R.I.: Brown University Press, 1964), 71–87; and Brooke's *King Lear*, 47–55; also Fly, 87–115, esp. 97–99. My point, I stress again, is not that some sort of purgatorial, redemptive, or even affirmative reading of *Lear* should be substituted for a desperate or nihilistic one, or vice-versa, but that the ending of *Lear* truly denies us the comfort of closure (and catharsis). This is a point that Fly, among others, makes but then, it seems to me, thoroughly undermines. Booth's recent work on *Lear* affords an impressive and persuasive exception to readings that enclose and limit its ending: see 5–57. Yet Booth finds an infinity of meaning, where I find a disjunction in meaning. If such disjunction invites choice and challenges invention, Booth accepts the constructive challenge. I stop where I think *Lear* does—with the spotlight on disjunction.

37. This paragraph, like the two preceding ones, draws on my earlier essay, "'Come, let's away to prison': Fortune and Freedom in *The Faerie Queene*, Book VI," *Journal of Narrative Technique*, 2 (1972), 133–37. For additional discussion of Melibee in the present volume, see part 1, chapter 6, "Spenser's Use of Chaucer's Melibee: Allegory, Narrative, History."

38. Cf. Kott, 226–27, on the land of Hearts-desire (in this case the Forest of Arden).

39. Cf. as well Lear's illusory rebirth to new life in IV.vii, a rebirth that is actually just a waking from sleep.

40. With four dead bodies and three major spectators on stage, the end of *Lear* is essentially a spectacle, and the spectators' comments are notoriously inadequate to distract us from, or to substitute for, what—in every sense of the word—we finally *see*. Absurdly, the ending of *Muiopotmos* ("Fly-fate") comes to mind, namely, "that his deepe groning spright / In bloodie streames foorth fled into the aire, / His bodie left the spectacle of care." In this volume, chapter 7, part 1, on "*Muiopotmos*," explores relevant contemporary issues of agency, fate, and determinism.

Chapter Thirteen: Venus and Adonis: *Spenser, Shakespeare, and the Forms of Desire*

1. *Richard III*, IV.iv.218, and *The Faerie Queene*, III.i.37, vs. 9; iv.27, vs. 1; Shakespeare's allusion to the Garden of Adonis is discussed in the following paragraph. Reference to Shakespeare in this chapter is to the 2nd Riverside edition, ed. G. Blakemore Evans et al (Boston, Mass.: Houghton Mifflin, 1997). Reference to *The Faerie Queene* in this chapter is to A. C. Hamilton's edition (London: Longman, 1977). I have discussed the Spenserian allusions in *Richard III in Biographical Truth:*

The Representation of Historical Persons in Tudor-Stuart Writing (New Haven, Conn.: Yale University Press, 1984), 118–20.

2. See Hamilton, ed., 360n30–50.

3. I argue the bisexuality of the Garden's *mons pubis* in part 3, chapter 14: "Flowers and Boars: Surmounting Binarism in Spenser's Garden of Adonis."

4. Frederick Copleston, *A History of Philosophy* (1950; rpt. New York: Newman, 1971), II, 76–77. Cf. Hamilton, ed., 360n30–50. For numerous additional examples of the seminal reasons in Renaissance thought, see James Nohrnberg, *The Analogy of "The Faerie Queene"* (Princeton: Princeton University Press, 1976), 537–54, and John Erskine Hankins, *Source and Meaning in Spenser's Allegory: A Study of "The Faerie Queene"* (Oxford: Clarendon, 1971), 234–86.

5. Gerald L. Bruns, *Inventions: Writing, Textuality, and Understanding in Literary History* (New Haven, Conn.: Yale University Press, 1982), 55–56.

6. *A New Variorum Edition of Shakespeare: The Poems*, ed. Hyder Edward Rollins (Philadelphia: J. B. Lippincott, 1938), 390–405, here 400.

7. "Venus and Adonis: Shakespeare's Critique of Spenser," *The Journal of the Rutgers University Library*, 39 (1977), 44–60, here 52.

8. "Actaeon at the Hinder Gate: The Stag Party in Spenser's Gardens of Adonis," in *Desire in the Renaissance: Psychoanalysis and Literature*, ed. Valeria Finucci and Regina Schwartz (Princeton: Princeton University Press, 1994), 91–119.

9. Gordon Williams, "The Coming of Age in Shakespeare's Adonis," *Modern Language Review*, 78 (1983), 769–76, here 770, 775.

10. Cf. Lauren Silberman, "Singing Unsung Heroines: Androgynous Discourse in Book 3 of *The Faerie Queene*," in *Rewriting the Renaissance: The Discourses of Sexual Difference in Early Modern Europe*, ed. Margaret W. Ferguson, Maureen Quilligan, and Nancy J. Vickers (Chicago: University of Chicago Press, 1986), 259–71, here 271. On sexuality and passion in the Garden, cf. also Katherine Eggert, "Spenser's Ravishment: Rape and Rapture in *The Faerie Queene*," *Representations*, 70 (2000), 1–26.

11. See Peter S. Hawkins, "From Mythography to Myth-making: Spenser and the *Magna Mater Cybele*," *Sixteenth-Century Journal*, 12 (1981), 51–64, here 57, 59.

12. According to the Vulgate reading of Genesis 2:7, "Adam's fall infected the substance of which he was made, the *limus terrae*, or slime of the earth": John Erskine Hankins, *Source and Meaning in Spenser's Allegory: A Study of "The Faerie Queene"* (Oxford: Clarendon, 1971), 137.

13. See also Eggert's discussion of "rapture" (in opposition to gynephobia) in the Garden, 9.

14. On the *vagina dentata*, "an icon of fearsome venereal power," in Spenser's Garden cave, see Lauren Silberman, *Transforming Desire: Erotic Knowledge in Books III and IV of "The Faerie Queene"* (Berkeley: University of California Press, 1995), 48.

15. Northrop Frye observes the pietà analogue in relation to Spenser's Venus and Adonis: *Fables of Identity: Studies in Poetic Mythology* (New York: Harcourt, Brace and World, 1963), 82; *Anatomy of Criticism: Four Essays* (Princeton: Princeton University Press, 1957), 205.

16. See part 2, chapter 8, in this volume on "Arthur and Argante: Parodying the Ideal Vision" for further discussion.

17. Catherine Belsey, "Love as Trompe-L'oeil: Taxonomies of Desire in *Venus and Adonis*," in *Venus and Adonis: Critical Essays*, ed. Philip C. Kolin (New York: Garland, 1997), 281.

18. Heather Dubrow, *Captive Victors: Shakespeare's Narrative Poems and Sonnets* (Ithaca, N.Y.: Cornell University Press, 1987), 537.

19. Pauline Kiernan's view in *Shakespeare's Theory of Drama* (Cambridge: Cambridge University Press, 1996) superficially resembles mine: Shakespeare's "narrative poems are a dramatist's way of working out his relationship to non-dramatic poetry" (24). Her sense of this relationship is exclusively parodic and satiric, however. In some areas Kiernan's insight is excellent, but her notions of mimesis, invention, rhetoric, and fiction are dubious, as I argue in the present volume: part 3, chapter 16, on *Antony and Cleopatra*

Chapter Fourteen: Flowers and Boars: Surmounting Sexual Binarism in Spenser's Garden of Adonis

1. The past to which I refer is my *Growth of a Personal Voice: "Piers Plowman" and "The Faerie Queene"* (New Haven, Conn.: Yale University Press, 1976), 98–113.

2. No Spenserian approaches the Garden of Adonis without having incurred a huge debt to the rich critical tradition. I gratefully acknowledge mine over many decades, particularly to John Erskine Hankins, *Source and Meaning in Spenser's Allegory: A Study of "The Faerie Queene"* (Oxford: Clarendon, 1971), 228–86; James Nohrnberg, *The Analogy of "The Faerie Queene"* (Princeton: Princeton University Press, 1976, 490–569; Harry Berger, Jr., "Spenser's Garden of Adonis: Force and Form in the Renaissance Imagination" (1961), rpt. in *Revisionary Play: Studies in the Spenserian Dynamics* (Berkeley: University of California Press, 1988), 131–53; and "Actaeon at the Hinder Gate: The Stag Party in Spenser's Garden of Adonis," in *Desire in the Renaissance: Psychoanalysis and Literature*, ed. Valeria Finucci and Regina Schwartz (Princeton: Princeton University Press, 1994), 90–119; Jon A. Quitslund, *Spenser's Supreme Fiction: Platonic Natural Philosophy and "The Faerie Queene"* (Toronto: University of Toronto Press, 2001), esp. 184–266; Kenneth Gross, *Spenserian Poetics: Idolatry, Iconoclasm, and Magic* (Ithaca, N.Y.: Cornell University Press, 1985), 181–209; Humphrey Tonkin, "Spenser's Garden of Adonis and Britomart's Quest," *PMLA*, 88 (1973), 408–17; Maureen Quilligan, *Milton's Spenser: The Politics of Reading* (Ithaca, N.Y.: Cornell University Press, 1983), 190–97; Donald Cheney, *Spenser's Image of Nature: Wild Man and Shepherd in "The Faerie Queene"* (New Haven, Conn.: Yale University Press, 1966), 117–45; Alastair Fowler, *Spenser and the Numbers of Time* (London: Routledge and Kegan Paul, 1964), 132–44; Thomas P. Roche, Jr., *The Kindly Flame: A Study of the Third and Fourth Books of Spenser's "Faerie Queene,"* (Princeton, N.J.: Princeton University Press, 1964), 117–28; Stevie Davies, *The Feminine Reclaimed: The Idea of Woman in Spenser, Shakespeare, and Milton* (Lexington: University Press of Kentucky, 1986), 77–93; Theresa M.

Krier, "Mother's Sorrow, Mother's Joy: Mourning Birth in Spenser's Garden of Adonis," in *Grief and Gender, 700–1700*, ed. Jennifer C. Vaught, with Lynne Dickson Bruckner (New York: Palgrave Macmillan, 2003), 133–47; David Lee Miller, *The Poem's Two Bodies: the Poetics of the 1590 "Faerie Queene"* (Princeton, N.J.: Princeton University Press, 1988), esp. 261–81; Lauren Silberman, *Transforming Desire: Erotic Knowledge in Books III and IV of "The Faerie Queene"* (Berkeley: University of California Press, 1995), 35–48.

3. Visually represented mounts, as Leah Marcus has remarked to me, are often peaked, pointed, or sharply protuberant in Tudor times, although they could also be given a more gently rounded contour.

4. *Webster's New World Dictionary*, 3rd ed. (1988; rpt. New York: Macmillan, 1997); *The American Heritage College Dictionary*, 3rd ed. (1993; rpt. Boston, Mass.: Houghton Mifflin, 1997). The definition I offer is a compressed composite.

5. On the myrtle, see Fowler, 137; cf. Hankins, 240.

6. Hankins, 246, cf. 255. For the reference to *Colin Clouts Come Home again*, see *The Yale Edition of the Shorter Poems of Edmund Spenser*, ed. William A. Oram, et al (New Haven, Conn.: Yale University Press, 1989), 527–62, here 801–2; further reference to the shorter poems in this chapter is to this edition. Cf. *The Faerie Queene*, IV.x.41. Unless otherwise noted, reference to *The Faerie Queene* in this chapter is to the second edition of A. C. Hamilton, with text edited by Hiroshi Yamashita and Toshiyuki Suzuki (Harlow, U.K.: Pearson, 2001).

7. *Theogyny*, in *Hesiod and Theognis*, trans. Dorothea Wender (Harmondsworth, U.K.: Penguin, 1973), 27–29.

8. "Loves Growth," in *The Elegies and the Songs and Sonnets* of John Donne, ed. Helen Gardner (Oxford: Clarendon, 1965), 76–77; "The Flower," in *The Works of George Herbert*, ed. F. E. Hutchinson (1941; rpt. Oxford: Clarendon, 1959), 165–67. See also the association by François Rabelais of codpieces (and their contents) with sap, moisture, verdancy, flowers, fruit, delight: *Gargantua and Pantagruel* (London: Penguin, 1955), I.8 (55). Rabelais was a physician, as well as a monk.

9. My essay "Britomart's Armor in Spenser's *Faerie Queene*: Reopening Cultural Matters of Gender and Figuration" is forthcoming in *English Literary Renaissance* (2008).

10. Thomas Laqueur's one-sex, unimorphic, structural, and fundamentally Galenic model of sexuality could be seen as an inspiration for Spenser, as it were, and, at some level, I consider it so: *Making Sex: Body and Gender from the Greeks to Freud* (Cambridge, Mass.: Harvard University Press, 1990). But Laqueur's model is composite and interpretive. For example, while concluding that "a two-sex and a one-sex model had always been available," he invests strongly in the one-sex model for early periods, neutralizing the two-sex view, specifically Aristotle's, by reading it both interpretively and holistically (viii, 28–43, 114; cf. 124). It does not take much awareness of the variety of reading and other interpretive practices in the Renaissance or of the availability of reliable texts (not to mention the questionable reliability of human memory) to have reservations about philosophic holism. Spenser did not have the benefit of Laqueur's composite, which, in interpreting

Spenser, cannot be imposed without benefit of the careful words of Spenser's own text. Spenser's mythic model is actually more complex, inclusive, and layered than Galen's, and it belongs to a realm of writing other than science, although it is also deeply touched and intellectually provoked by the science of the time. Grant Williams' caveat in "Early Modern Blazons and the Rhetoric of Wonder" (*Luce Irigaray and Premodern Culture: Thresholds of History*, ed. Theresa M. Krier and Elizabeth D. Harvey [New York: Routledge, 2004], 126–37) is notable as well: "early modern culture's dependence on Galenic homology necessitated the exaggeration of anatomical distinctions" in order to exclude women from dominant social and discursive positions (126). Another touchstone for me in the context of sex and gender has been Valerie Traub's introduction in *Desire and Anxiety: Circulation of Sexuality in Shakespearean Drama* (London: Routledge, 1992), 1–22.

11. Thanks to Jerry Findley and Mary Ellen Lamb for asking questions that led me to clarify this paragraph.

12. Hankins, Norhnberg, and Quitslund provide the most extensive review of sources and analogues. Both Hankins and Norhnberg find these enormously eclectic; Quitslund more narrowly privileges Neoplatonic sources. A fairly recent and relevant discussion of matter and specifically of vitalism is Philippa Berry's in her introduction to *Shakespeare's Feminine Endings: Disfiguring Death in the Tragedies* (London: Routledge, 1999), 12–20, esp 13–14.

13. See Roche, 118–19.

14. In a paper delivered to a conference of the International Spenser Society in Toronto, 2006, David Wilson-Okamura relevantly noted that "sweet" is a traditional descriptor for poetry written in the middle style. In his view, Spenser is characteristically a poet of the middle voice.

15. Sir Philip Sidney, *An Apology for Poetry*, ed. Geoffrey Shepherd (1965; rpt. Manchester, U.K.: Manchester University Press, 1973), 101, lines 14–24.

16. For a broadly based discussion of punning that includes philosophical and psycholinguistic reference, see my essay "Donne's (Im)possible Punning," *John Donne Journal*, 23 (2004), 59–68. My words here, as at the end of the essay on Donne, reflect those of Wolfgang Iser, *The Fictive and the Imaginary: Charting Literary Anthropology* (Baltimore: Johns Hopkins University Press, 1993), xiv–xv. Referring to the simultaneity of a pun, I have in mind both its existence as text, and as read text, but primarily and definitively as text. Responding to my present argument, for a pertinent example, Lauren Silberman has asked whether a pun might be successive, and I certainly accept this possibility in reading: some puns in some readings might occur sequentially or even belatedly; moreover, one reader's simultaneity might be experienced by another reader as succession.

17. On the stages of the Garden, see Cheney, 129–31; Silberman, 45.

18. Hamilton, ed., 347n33.7; *OED*, s.v. *Or, conj.* (or *conjunctive adv.*) C.b; cf. B.b.

19. While Berger, "Actaeon," tries not to give rein to these anxieties, the thrust of his argument is to do so. Evidently endorsing Hamilton's reading, he concludes "that the garden and the world must be the same" (107). This "dissolution of

boundaries" is important to his carefully crafted and productive argument. But gendered egos preeminently belong to this world, rather than to the *aevum*: cf. Gross, 195–98; Silberman, *Transforming Desire*, 40; Quitslund, 217–18. Gross's explanation and qualification of the use of the term *aevum* are alike pertinent (195–96), but the concept of a liminal *aevum* suspended between binary terms, realms, realities, or the like remains useful only as long as we remember that Spenser rarely leaves an inherited concept as he finds it. In Nohrnberg's observing the *"symbolic* reversibility of the garden-world into a world-garden," his word "symbolic" also maintains a significant distinction (530: my emphasis). The concept of the *aevum* within commentary on the Garden of Adonis traces back to Frank Kermode's *The Sense of an Ending: Studies in the Theory of Fiction* (New York: Oxford University Press, 1967), 74. Of course the concept has longer, more complicated roots as well.

20. Sidney, 123, lines 38–39.

21. For the quotation, see *Colin Clouts Come Home Again*, vs. 800. Notably, in the myth leading to Venus' birth, Gaea (Earth), mother and wife of Uranus, arms Cronus (subsequently known as Chronos: "Time"), or Saturn, with the scythe. The Roman Saturnus was a god of sowing. Berger's spin on the mythic birth of Venus ("Actaeon," 112–13) differs considerably from mine. His resists the irreparable alienation of the sperm and the consequent otherness of Venus; in part 3, see my chapter fifteen on the Bower of Bliss.

22. *Wan* is "a prefix, expressing privation or negation," i.e, "want" (*OED*, s.v. *Wan*). The other element in *wanton* is Old English *towen/togen*, "to discipline, train (*OED*, s.v. *Wanton, a.* and *sb.*). See also *MED*, s.v. *Wantoun*, adj: "unregulated," "recalcitrant," "rebellious," "willful," "lascivious," "lustful."

23. See part 3, chapter 13, "*Venus and Adonis*: Spenser, Shakespeare, and the Forms of Desire." Modern editors generally agree that Shakespeare's epyllion was written in 1592–93.

24. Surprisingly, Hamilton, ed., takes "stocke" exclusively to mean "matter," evidently connecting "For" in line 6 with line 3 alone, whereas it readily connects with line 2 as well (347*n*36.3–9). In the same note, he also assumes an exclusively material meaning of the word "substances" in line 9, but *substance* is a highly controverted term with multiple possible meanings in this period, more than one of which is relevant here: on *substance*, see my *Translating Investments: Metaphor and the Dynamic of Cultural Change* (New York: Fordham University Press, 2005), 49–51. Hankins, 259–60, and Tonkin, 411, similarly recognize the ambiguity, or doubled reference, of "stocke." Not without pertinence, in relation to Milton, Christopher Hill notes Spenser's and his friend Lodowick Bryskett's deep interest in the mortalist controversy (i.e., death of the soul, along with the body): *Milton and the English Revolution* (London: Faber and Faber, 1977), 74; cf. *The Faerie Queene*, VII.19: "Ne doe their bodies only flit and fly: / But eeke their minds (which they immortall call)." According to the critical consensus, Milton was a mortalist.

25. Cf. Miller, 272; Fowler, 136; Gross, 196; Silberman, *Transforming Desire*, 47–48. References could be multiplied.

26. Hamilton, ed., 350*n*48.2; Berger, "Actaeon," 114 and 119*n*39.

27. Cf. Quitslund's observation that Cupid's wanton play with Adonis in Spenser's Garden is homoerotic, keeping "Venus's consort ready for her" (208).

28. *Venus and Adonis*, in *The Riverside Shakespeare*, ed. G. Blakemore Evans, et al, 2nd ed. (Boston, Mass.: Houghton Mifflin, 1997), pages 1797–1813, here verses 1117–18; cf. vs. 1105–16: unless otherwise noted, reference to Shakespeare in this chapter is to this edition. In a discussion I led at Vanderbilt University, I found reassuring Lynn Enterline's quickly connecting the *vagina dentata* in the Garden's cave with Shakespeare's virtual tusking of Venus.

29. Cf. Davies' observation that "Venus and Adonis in the act of coition make up an androgyne within the feminine gender" (89). Together, they more fully and frankly represent bisexuality in my view. Spenser's androgynes belong to the landscape of quest. Davies goes on to characterize Adonis as "transformed matter" (89).

30. Sidney's "right poet" considers "what may be and should be": 102, lines 21–37.

31. I actually quote a modern definition of *satiate* from *The American Heritage College Dictionary*, s.v. *Satiate*, 1, but its historicized equivalents can be found less succinctly in *OED*, s.v., *Satiate v.* 1, cf. *Satiate ppl.* and *ppl. a.*

32. John Wilders, ed., glosses "cloyless" in the first of these quotations as sauce "that never cloys (or satiates)": *Antony and Cleopatra* (London: Routledge, 1995), 126n25. Likewise, David Bevington, ed., *Antony and Cleopatra*, updated ed. (Cambridge: Cambridge University Press, 2005). Reviewing the *OED*'s definitions of *cloy*, I notice another Shakespearean example that is at least ambiguous: Richard II asks, "who can . . . cloy the hungry edge of appetite / By bare imagination of a feast?" (I.iii.294–97). In addition to *OED* examples, the alignment of *cloy* with *satiate* and *satisfy* is marked in *Cymbeline*, I.vi.47–48: "The cloyed will—/ That satiate yet unsatisfied desire. . . ."

33. On *aevum*, see note 19, above.

34. Reverse the order of Shakespeare's phrase, making it "well knows," and the syntactical ambiguity is gone. For anyone aware of the several Renaissance editions and printings of *Piers Plowman*, the focal term, name, and virtual character Do-well (Dowel) bears on the syntactical pun *does well / knows well*. Memory of Langland thus supports the early modern currency of the phrase, or saying, *do[es]-well*.

Chapter Fifteen: Androcentrism and Acrasian Fantasies in the Bower of Bliss

1. *Spenser Studies*, 18 (2003), 81–121; see 81–86 (and the extensive notes throughout) for a relevantly selected survey of criticism on the Bower. Unless otherwise indicated, parenthetical citation of Berger's words will be from this essay.

2. Berger further generalizes these principles in his "Gynephobia and Culture Change: An Irigarayan Just-So Story," in *Luce Irigaray and Premodern Culture: Thresholds of History*, ed. Theresa M. Krier and Elizabeth D. Harvey (London: Routledge, 2004), 138–45, here 143: the quotation in the next sentence of my chapter is from this same page.

3. The "unconscious of the system" is a particularly resonant phrase for a reader of Fredric Jameson's *Political Unconscious: Narrative as a Socially Symbolic Act* (1981; rpt. Ithaca, N.Y.: Cornell University Press, 1988), a book to which I shall subsequently refer.

4. Berger elsewhere treats the Garden of Adonis, as do I: see note 8, below, and in part 3, chapter 14, of this volume, my "Flowers and Boars: Surmounting Sexual Binarism in Spenser's Garden of Adonis."

5. Harry Berger, Jr., "Sexual and Religious Politics in Book I of Spenser's *Faerie Queene*," *English Literary Renaissance*, 34 (2004), 201–42, here 219. The well-regarded historicist rendering that Berger tactfully, but directly, critiques is Claire McEachern's second chapter in *The Poetics of English Nationhood, 1590–1612* (Cambridge: Cambridge University Press, 1996).

6. For a fascinating discussion of cultural androcentrism, which includes parallels with Christianity and Sufism, as well as with modern philosophies and psychoanalytics, see Elliot R. Wolfson, *Language, Eros, Being: Kabbalistic Hermeneutics and Poetic Imagination* (New York: Fordham University Press, 2005), esp. chaps. 2–4.

7. Camille A. Paglia describes Acrasia with Verdant as "a form of hermaphroditism"; Acrasia is "masculine of will" as she hovers seductively over Verdant "with a languorous possessiveness": "The Apollonian Androgyne and *The Faerie Queene*," *English Literary Renaissance*, 9 (1979), 42–63, here 62. If Acrasia is male, is Verdant female, or is each both? And are we dealing with metaphor or metonymy here?

8. Cf. "Actaeon at the Hinder Gate: The Stag Party in Spenser's Garden of Adonis," in *Desire in the Renaissance: Psychoanalysis and Literature*, ed. Valeria Finucci and Regina Schwartz (Princeton: Princeton University Press, 1994), 90–119, here 112–13.

9. The name of Cronus gets conflated with Chronos, or Time, and in this way Cronus/Saturn becomes the god of time: Oskar Seyffert, *Dictionary of Classical Antiquities*, rev. and ed. Henry Nettleship and J. E. Sandys (1956; rpt. Cleveland, Oh.: World, 1963), 167–68.

10. For the quotation, see *Colin Clouts Come Home Again*, in *The Yale Edition of the Shorter Poems of Edmund Spenser*, ed. William A. Oram et al (New Haven, Conn.: Yale University Press, 1989), 527–62, here vs. 800. Further reference to the shorter poems in this chapter is to this edition.

11. *Colin Clouts Come Home Again*, vs. 802. Hesiod, *Theogyny*, in *Hesiod and Theognis*, trans. Dorothea Wender (Harmondsworth, Middlesex, U.K.: Penguin, 1973), 27–29.

12. Seyffert, 681. A recent historicist argument has connected the Bower of Bliss with actual prostitution in Spenser's time: Matthew A. Fike, *Spenser's Underworld in the 1590 "Faerie Queene"* (Lewiston, N.Y.: Edwin Mellen, 2003), chap. 4. In reference to Phaedria (vi.16), Fike mentions a notorious brothel in medieval Southwark called the "Floure-deluce." Historical notoriety often turns into legend in traditional societies.

13. For a definition of mimesis by a modern Aristotelian, see Paul Ricoeur, *Time and Narrative*, I, trans. Kathleen McLaughlin and David Pellauer (Chicago, Ill.: University of Chicago Press, 1984), 45. Mimesis is treated more extensively in my introduction and in the following chapter (part 3, chapter 16) on *Antony and Cleopatra* and *The Faerie Queene*.

14. Lewis H. Miller, Jr., for example, argues a parallel between the battle with Maleger and that of Locrine with Humber in *The Faerie Queene*, II.x.14–16: "Arthur, Maleger, and History in the Allegorical Context," *University of Toronto Quarterly*, 35 (1966), 176–87. Similar words and images recurrently signal reciprocal relations between inside and outside in cantos ix–xi of Book II (Maleger's attack on the periphery of the House of Alma, chronicles of British and Faerie history within the House, Arthur's issuing from the House to battle Maleger and his forces). Unless otherwise indicated, reference to *The Faerie Queene* in this chapter is to the second edition of A. C. Hamilton, with text edited by Hiroshi Yamashita and Toshiyuki Suzuki (Harlow, U.K.: Pearson, 2001).

15. Theresa M. Krier, *Gazing on Secret Sights: Spenser, Classical Imitation, and the Decorums of Vision* (Ithaca, N.Y.: Cornell University Press, 1990), 84. On the porous body, see Gail Kern Paster, *The Body Embarrassed: Drama and the Disciplines of Shame in Early Modern England* (Ithaca, N.Y.: Cornell University Press, 1993), e.g., 8–16; and, on the tempered body, Michael C. Schoenfeldt, *Bodies and Selves in Early Modern England: Physiology and Inwardness in Spenser, Shakespeare, Herbert, and Milton* (Cambridge: Cambridge University Press, 1999), e.g., 14–16. On imagination, or fantasy, see Robert L. Reid, "Spenserian Psychology and the Structure of Allegory in Books 1 and 2 of *The Faerie Queene*," *Modern Philology*, 79 (1982), 359–75; and his "Alma's Castle and the Symbolization of Reason in *The Faerie Queene, JEGP*, 80 (1981), 512–27; additionally useful background is found in Mary J. Carruthers, *The Book of Memory: A Study of Memory in Medieval Culture* (Cambridge: Cambridge University Press, 1990), 52–55. Imagination receives sense impressions and combines these into images; its function is both reflective and creative. Again, my chapter 16 is further relevant.

16. See my fuller treatment of hell in *The Growth of a Personal Voice: "Piers Plowman" and "The Faerie Queene"* (New Haven, Conn.: Yale University Press, 1976), 39–40.

17. For discussion of Amoret's fate, see my *Translating Investments: Metaphor and the Dynamic of Cultural Change in Tudor-Stuart England* (New York: Fordham University Press, 2005), 127–28 and 255nn30, 32.

18. On Prudentius, see the discussion of Carolynn Van Dyke, *The Fiction of Truth: Structures of Meaning in Narrative and Dramatic Allegory* (Ithaca, N.Y.: Cornell University Press, 1985), 46–67; on *Everyman*, see her essay "The Intangible and Its Image: Allegorical Discourse and the Cast of *Everyman*," in *Acts of Interpretation: The Text in Its Contexts, 700–1600*, ed. Mary J. Carruthers and Elizabeth D. Kirk (Norman, Okla.: Pilgrim, 1982), 311–24.

19. For Jameson's critique, see his *Political Unconscious*, 40–44, and Anderson, *Translating Investments*, 173–74, for discussion.

20. Barbara K. Lewalski, *The Life of John Milton: A Critical Biography* (Oxford: Blackwell, 2000), 508: Milton told John Dryden, his contemporary and fellow poet, that Spenser was his "Original."

21. For a relevant, recent, and excellent discussion of the Wife, see Carolynn Van Dyke, *Chaucer's Agents: Cause and Representation in Chaucerian Narrative* (Madison, N.J.: Fairleigh Dickinson University Press, 2005), 184–98.

22. See part 2, chapter 9, "Chaucer's *Parliament of Fowls* and Refractions of a Veiled Venus in *The Faerie Queene*"; the specific connections are Venerean.

23. On subversive resistance from within, see Judith Butler, *Gender Trouble: Feminism and the Subversion of Identity*, rev. ed. (New York: Routledge, 1999), 184–87; and Michel de Certeau, *The Practice of Everyday Life*, trans. Steven Rendall (Berkeley: University of California Press, 1984), e.g., 29–42, 96.

24. Dorothy Stephens is particularly interesting regarding the Spenserian narrator's "flirtation" (à la Adam Phillips) with gender possibilities, which are such that we cannot assume that "its speaking voice is purely masculine": *The Limits of Eroticism in Post-Petrarchan Narrative: Conditional Pleasure from Spenser to Marvell* (Cambridge: Cambridge University Press, 1998), 52 (citation), 106–7, 117, cf. 14, 73. See also part 1, chapter 1, of this volume on "Chaucer's and Spenser's Reflexive Narrators."

25. E.g., "*Mulla* mine"; "my mother Cambridge" (IV.xi.34, 41); also my first chapter, "Reflexive Narrators."

26. Patricia Parker, *Literary Fat Ladies: Rhetoric, Gender, Property* (London: Methuen, 1987), chap. 4: "Suspended Instruments: Lyric and Power in the Bower of Bliss"; Eggert, *Showing Like a Queene: Female Authority and Literary Experiment in Spenser, Shakespeare, and Milton* (Philadelphia: University of Pennsylvania Press, 2000), chaps. 1–2.

27. Not so paradoxically, surface underlies the higher, more rational, and more teleologically oriented meaning(s).

28. On Munera's ambivalence, see my *Words That Matter: Linguistic Perception in Renaissance English* (Stanford, Calif.: Stanford University Press, 1996), 169–71. Munera's metallic extremities can be understood literally or symbolically—her hands gold-dispensing and her fingers richly adorned (like those of her prototype Lady Meed) and her feet similarly furnished with jewelry or net-work slippers of "trye" (choice) silver (170).

29. On *substance*, see my *Translating Investments*, 49–51, and *Words That Matter*, 8–9, 14–19, 63–70, 94–96.

30. Alignment of what is "not there" with a Lacanian conception of the phallus is conceivable, since symbolically the phallus is "a sign that coincides with its own impossibility inasmuch as it embodies the representation of the nonrepresentational" and inasmuch as "it signifies the signification of the feminine lacking signifier": Wolfson, 131. But I am reluctant to foreground this all-too-often thinly veiled

and thickly mystified phallic conception because of the seemingly inevitable confusion of gender identification in language with the Oedipal drama that it entails: Wolfson, 129; Ellie Ragland-Sullivan, *Jacques Lacan and the Philosophy of Psychoanalysis* (Urbana: University of Illinois Press, 1986), 55; and more tellingly, Judith Butler's reasoned objections to representation of the feminine as the Phallic not-there: *Gender Trouble: Feminism and the Subversion of Identity*, (New York: Routledge, 1990), 43–57, esp. 44 (the Phallic Other as reflection of Phallic power and significance, as absence, lack, and "dialectical confirmation of . . . [Phallic] identity"); 48 (Lacan's unnamed, fetishized [Phallic?] "organ"); 56 ("the structure of religious tragedy [before the Law] in Lacanian theory").

31. Cf. James Carscallen, "Time in a female form . . . is the witch who has opposed Guyon early and late": "The Goodly Frame of Temperance: The Metaphor of Cosmos in *The Faerie Queene*, Book II," in *Essential Articles for the Study of Edmund Spenser*, ed. A. C. Hamilton (Hamden, Conn.: Archon, 1972), 347–65, here 363.

32. With the names Cissie and Flossie, bunnies come especially to mind, not to mention Playgirl Bunnies. (By coincidence, Lewis, author of *The Chronicles of Narnia*, was taken with personified animal characters.)

33. Harry Berger, Jr., *The Allegorical Temper: Vision and Reality in Book II of Spenser's "Faerie Queene"* (New Haven, Conn.: Yale University Press, 1957), 226.

34. As Van Dyke (*Chaucer's Agents*, 16–22) observes, the word "agent" has a broad range of meaning. Consider "bleaching agent" or "travel agent," for example. Many are the kinds and gradations of agency between an indistinguishable, wholly dependent, or inaminate agent and a wholly autonomous, wholly responsible, and fully conscious one. Within different fields of activity, further differences also pertain: as one of several cases in point, Van Dyke discusses law.

35. For a provocative treatment of the difference between discourse and figure, see Jean-François Lyotard, "The Dream-Work Does Not Think," trans. Mary Lydon, in *The Lyotard Reader*, ed. Andrew Benjamin (Oxford: Blackwell, 1989), 19–55. Lyotard rejects the Lacanian view that dream-work is a form of discourse and argues instead for its substantive figurality; for Lyotard, however, "an imaged text is a discourse which is very close to the figure." Its proximity inheres in "the figurative power of a word, of course, but also the rhythmic power of syntax, and at an even deeper level, the matrix of narrative rhythm, what Propp called form. . . ." (29, cf. 31). The figure, as form, "jam[s]" the communicative constraints inscribed in "any *language*. . . . [b]y virtue of the fact that it sets up a closed circuit intercom system of the work with itself." He concludes that "language, at least in its poetic usage, is possessed, haunted by the figure" (30).

36. See Berger, *Situated Utterances: Texts, Bodies, and Cultural Representations* (New York: Fordham University Press, 2005).

37. Referring to "the movement between the represented and unrepresented female subject of male discourse," as Teresa de Lauretis has described it, Berger approaches the thereness and not-thereness to which I refer here: *The Absence of Grace: Sprezzatura and Suspicion in Two Renaissance Courtesy Books* (Stanford, Calif.:

Stanford University Press, 2000), 94–95. He focuses on "the renewed desire and anxiety" and the "potential trauma" that destabilizes male efforts "to penetrate the veil" of representation, rather than on the "excess" of representation itself. Earlier, he highlights his own shifting of attention from subjective to discursive agency, and thus from the psychology *of* subjects to the psychology *in* discourse (76). In this way, discourse itself develops a consciousness and subconsciousness, agency, personality, and subjecthood. What seems missing in this latter day Leviathan (the collective Hobbesian image comes to mind) is ironically the body, an existent, physically and historically material dimension, and what I might call the matter of reference. For the views of de Lauretis that Berger invokes, see her *Technologies of Gender: Essays on Theory, Film, and Fiction* (Bloomington: Indiana University Press, 1987), 25–26.

38. Each discharge of semen, an expenditure (or expense) of spirit, was popularly thought to shorten one's life by a day. Aristotle describes semen as a substance between body and (sometimes ambiguously) incorporeal *psyche*: "All have in their semen that which causes it to be productive[,] . . . the breath [*pneuma*] included in the semen and the foam-like [stuff], and the natural principle in the breath, being analogous to the element of the stars" (*Generation of Animals*, 736b30–737a1, in *The Complete Works of Aristotle*, ed. Jonathan Barnes, rev. Oxford translation, 2 vols. (Princeton, N.J.: Princeton University Press, 1984), I, 1143.

39. Again, see also part 1, chapter 1, "Reflexive Narrators."

40. *OED*, s.v., *Rue v.*[1] II.8: "To regard with pity or compassion; to feel sorry for (a person, etc.)." *Obs. OED* cites as an example *The Faerie Queene*, I.i.51: "Die is my dew: yet rew my wretched state." Cf. *Rue*, I.4 and *Faerie Queene*, I.ii.21, vs. 8. The verb is also associated with regret and sorrow, further implying some degree of human agency.

41. On the words "crime" and "sin," see Stephen Greenblatt, *Renaissance Self-Fashioning: From More to Shakespeare* (Chicago: University of Chicago Press, 1980), 172.

42. William Shakespeare, *Antony and Cleopatra*, ed. John Wilders (London: Routledge, 1995), II.ii.245–47. My use of the word *wonder* might well recall Longinus' treatise *On the Sublime*, first printed at Basle in 1554 but both generally and erroneously still thought to be unknown in England until Gerard Langbaine's edition in 1636: William Ringler, "An Early Reference to Longinus," *Modern Language Notes*, 53, no. 1 (1938), 23–24. Ringler finds knowledge of Longinus' treatise in a lecture on rhetoric by John Rainolds at Oxford in 1573/4. Langbaine (1608/9–1658) also reports that it was his old Oxford tutor who urged him to publish his edition and that his attention was also drawn to a Cambridge manuscript of the treatise, "probably that of Andreas Dudith who came to England with Cardinal Pole in 1554": T. J. B. Spencer, "Longinus in English Criticism: Influences before Milton," *Review of English Studies*, 8 (1957), 137–43, here 142. For recent and relevant critical interest in wonder (albeit with the mistaken assumption that Longinus is unknown in England in the Tudor period), cf. the perceptive essay of Grant Williams, "Early Modern Blazons and the Rhetoric of Wonder: Turning towards an Ethic of Sexual Difference," in Krier and Harvey, eds., 126–37, esp. 137 (Longinus);

and the essay of Adam McKeown, "Looking at Britomart Looking at Pictures," *Studies in English Literature*, 45 (2005), 43–63, esp. 48–49 (Longinus).

43. *The Ground of the Image*, trans. Jeff Fort (New York: Fordham University Press, 2005), 9, 20. On "exhilaration," see, for example, "jouissance" (9).

44. On the Palmer as an artist, a spinner of myth, see my article "The Knight and the Palmer in *The Faerie Queene*, Book II," *Modern Language Quarterly*, 31 (1970), 160–78, esp. 162–65. The Palmer is a rational, and sometimes a rationalizing, spinner; even his "subtile" net is "formally," or regularly, rationally, logically "frame[d]" (II.xii.81).

45. Parker, chap. 4; Maureen Quilligan, *Milton's Spenser: the Politics of Reading* (Ithaca, N.Y.: Cornell University Press, 1983), 69; Greenblatt, chap. 4; Montrose, "Spenser and the Elizabethan Political Imaginary," *ELH*, 69 (2002), 907–46, here 925–35 (including Elizabeth's eye-catching, "hideous large black spider" brooch: 930); Rufus Wood, *Metaphor and Belief in "The Faerie Queene"* (London: Macmillan, 1997), 141–56.

46. For example, see Leonard Barkan, *The Gods Made Flesh: Metamorphosis and the Pursuit of Paganism* (New Haven, Conn.: Yale University Press, 1986), 2–5; Ann Rosalind Jones and Peter Stallybrass, *Renaissance Clothing and the Materials of Memory* (Cambridge: Cambridge University Press, 2000), chap. 4, esp. 89–97; Heather James, "Ovid and the Question of Politics in Early Modern England," *ELH*, 70 (2003), 343–73, here 358–63; Syrithe Pugh, *Spenser and Ovid* (Aldershot, Hants., U.K.: Ashgate, 2005), 146, 214, 266. In the poem *Muiopotmos*, Spenser's use of the myth of Arachne is quite different, as discussed in part 2, chapter 7, of this volume. I have treated Spenser's *various* allusions to Arachne in *The Faerie Queene* and in his shorter poems in *Translating Investments*, 115–19; cf. also Pamela Royston Macfie, "Text and *Textura*: Spenser's Arachnean Art," in *Traditions and Innovations: Essays on British Literature of the Middle Ages and the Renaissance*, ed. David G. Allen and Robert H. White (Newark, N.J.: University of Delaware Press, 1990), 88–96.

47. Berger's essay can be found in *Essential Articles*, ed. Hamilton, 395–424, here 423–24.

48. I do question the possibility that Britomart, too, is always already another manifestation of male discourse in "Britomart's Armor: Reopening Cultural Matters of Gender and Figuration," forthcoming in *English Literary Renaissance*, 38 (2008).

Chapter Sixteen: Beyond Binarism: Eros/Death and Venus/Mars in Antony and Cleopatra *and* The Faerie Queene

1. On genre, see Sara Munson Deats, "Shakespeare's Anamorphic Drama: A Survey of *Antony and Cleopatra* in Criticism," in Deats, ed., *Antony and Cleopatra: New Critical Essays* (London: Routledge, 2005), 1–93, here esp. 12–14. Deats's review of ethos (Rome/Egypt), characters (Cleopatra, Antony, Octavius Caesar), and performance is also excellent. For discussion of *Antony and Cleopatra* as mannerist, anamorphic tragi-comedy, see Pauline Blanc, "'All Joy of the Worm': Tragi-Comic Tempering in Shakespeare's Antony and Cleopatra," *Q/W/E/R/T/Y*, 10 (2000), 5–18.

2. See Jyotsna G. Singh, "The Politics of Empathy in *Antony and Cleopatra*: A View from Below," in *A Companion to Shakespeare's Works*: Vol. I: *The Tragedies*, ed. Richard Dutton and Jean E. Howard (Oxford: Blackwell, 2003), 411–29, here, 413, 419–20: Singh quotes Loomba, "'Travelling Thoughts': Theatre and the Space of the Other," in *New Casebooks: Antony and Cleopatra*, ed. J. Drakakis (London: Macmillan, 1994), 279–307, here, 281; and in Dutton's and Howard's volume, Margot Heinemann, "'Let Rome in Tiber Melt': Order and Disorder in *Antony and Cleopatra*," 166–81, here 177.

3. Jonathan Goldberg, *Endlesse Worke: Spenser and the Structures of Discourse* (Baltimore: Johns Hopkins University Press, 1981).

4. *Spenser: The Faerie Queene*, ed. A. C. Hamilton, 2nd ed., with text edited by Hiroshi Yamashita and Toshiyuki Suzuki (Harlow, U.K.: Pearson, 2001). Unless otherwise specified, reference to Spenser in the present chapter is to this edition; *The Faerie Queene* is cited as *FQ*.

5. Further evidence exists in other plays, *Midsummer Night's Dream* being an obvious candidate. For discussion of the evidence in *Richard III* and in *King Lear*, see, respectively, in part 3 of this volume, chapter 13, "*Venus and Adonis*: Spenser, Shakespeare, and the Forms of Desire," and chapter 12, "The Conspiracy of Realism: Impasse and Vision in *The Faerie Queene* and Shakespeare's *King Lear*." On dating, I have followed *The Riverside Shakespeare*, ed. G. Blakemore Evans et al, 2nd ed. (Boston: Houghton Mifflin, 1997), 78–87; supplemented by reference to Antony Hammond, ed. *King Richard III* (London: Methuen, 1981), 54–61; John Roe, ed., *The Poems* [of William Shakespeare] (Cambridge: Cambridge University Press, 1992), 1, 12–15; David Bevington, ed., *Antony and Cleopatra*, updated ed. (Cambridge: Cambridge University Press, 2005), 1–2; and John Wilders, ed., *Antony and Cleopatra* (London: Routledge, 1995), 69–75.

6. E.g., *AC*, I.v.22; cf. III.vii.7, x.10–15; IV.viii.14–16: for *Antony and Cleopatra*, unless otherwise specified, I cite the third Arden edition, by John Wilders, as *AC* in this chapter. Watkins, *Shakespeare and Spenser* (1950; rpt. Cambridge, Mass.: Walker-de-Berry, 1961), 25.

7. Respectively, "Venus and the Second Chance," *Shakespeare Survey*, 15 (1962), 81–88; and "From Shakespeare's Venus to Cleopatra's Cupids," *Shakespeare Survey*, 15 (1962), 73–80.

8. On the constructs of allegorical vision, Paul de Man's seminal essay "The Rhetoric of Temporality" remains useful: *Interpretation: Theory and Practice*, ed. Charles S. Singleton (Baltimore: Johns Hopkins University Press, 1969), 173–209.

9. Respectively, Janet Adelman, *The Common Liar: An Essay on "Antony and Cleopatra"* (New Haven, Conn.: Yale University Press, 1973); and *Suffocating Mothers: Fantasies of Maternal Origin in Shakespeare's Plays, "Hamlet" to "The Tempest"* (New York: Routledge, 1992); see also Barbara J. Bono, *Literary Transvaluation: From Vergilian Epic to Shakespearean Tragicomedy* (Berkeley: University of California Press, 1984), 176–82. On the various mythic associations of Cleopatra and Anthony, see also Deats's survey, 20–21, 29–33.

10. Adelman, *Common Liar*, e.g., 62, 65–66, 83–88, 90–93, 123; on Isis and Osiris, although not Spenser, cf. Adelman, *Suffocating Mothers*, 183–84. Katherine Eggert compares Cleopatra to Acrasia in order to differentiate them: *Showing Like a Queen: Female Authority and Literary Experiment in Spenser, Shakespeare, and Milton* (Philadelphia: University of Pennsylvania Press, 2000), 144, 153. Adelman characterizes her academic life as a Shakespearean as "a kind of forty-year-long hiatus from Spenser": Hugh Maclean Memorial Lecture: "Revaluing the Body in *The Faerie Queene*," *The Spenser Review*, 36 (2005), 15–25, here 15.

11. For a sophisticated discussion of allegory, see Carolynn Van Dyke, *The Fiction of Truth: Structures of Meaning in Narrative and Dramatic Allegory* (Ithaca, N.Y.: Cornell University Press, 1985), 15–46.

12. Edgar Wind, *Pagan Mysteries in the Renaissance*, rev. ed. (Harmondsworth, Middlesex, U.K.: Penguin, 1967), 238. Cf. Walter Benjamin, *The Origin of German Tragic Drama*, trans. John Osborne (1998; rpt. London: Verso, 2003), 44: "A major work will either establish the genre or abolish it; and the perfect work will do both."

13. Camille Paglia, *Sexual Personae: Art and Decadence from Nefertiti to Emily Dickinson* (1990; rpt. New York: Random House, 1991), 213, 216–19.

14. *FQ*, II.xii.59, III.vi.29. In the Garden, the arbor on the Mount is "not by art, / But of the trees owne inclination made" (III.vi.44). Aside from the fact that the inclination of the trees is naturally artful, the whole Garden canto is egregiously so. It is a lyrical myth that includes the generativity of art and specifically the mythic transformations to which "sweet Poets verse hath giuen endlesse date" (45). Acrasia's art is artificial in a sense that a reader of Baudrillard might appreciate.

15. See also part 1, chapter 4, "Allegory, Irony, Despair: Chaucer's *Pardoner's* and *Franklin's Tales* and Spenser's Books I and III." The issue recurs in various essays and contexts in the present volume.

16. The waving of Belphoebe's hair "like a penon wyde dispred" irresistibly calls to mind the illustration of a title that is "deformed in such a way as to give the impression that a wind is blowing the flat surface on which they [the letters in the title] are written," which Jean-François Lyotard uses to suggest "how language, at least in its poetic usage, is possessed, haunted by the figure": "The Dream-Work Does Not Think," trans. Mary Lydon, in *The Lyotard Reader*, ed. Andrew Benjamin (Oxford: Blackwell, 1989), 19–55, here 27, 30. Belphoebe is a figure in Lyotard's sense.

17. The indispensable place to start a consideration of the description of Belphoebe remains Harry Berger, Jr.,'s detailed analysis in *The Allegorical Temper: Vision and Reality in Book II of Spenser's "Faerie Queene"* (New Haven, Conn.: Yale University Press, 1957), 120–49.

18. Pauline Kiernan, *Shakespeare's Theory of Drama* (Cambridge: Cambridge University Press, 1996).

19. Kiernan, 174 ("written poetry's rhetorical excesses"); cf. chaps. 2–3. Patrick Cheney, while acknowledging that Goddard might not have "got the 'story' right" in asserting a "'gradual subjection of the theatrical to the poetical'" in Shakespeare's

plays, embraces Goddard's view if poetry is understood as lyric: *Shakespeare, National Poet-Playwright* (Cambridge: Cambridge University Press, 2004), 275–76; Harold C. Goddard, *The Meaning of Shakespeare* (1951; rpt. Chicago: Chicago University Press, Phoenix ed., 1960), II, 203. Cheney's embrace is too restrictive.

20. Kiernan, 47, 51, 174 (cited in the following sentence); *The Faerie Queene*, II.xii.54–55, 58; cf. "sparkling [or crystallizing] face," xii.68; *Venus and Adonis*, 230, 363 (passages in the epyllion referenced by Kiernan). For Shakespeare's writings other than *Antony and Cleopatra*, I cite *The Riverside Shakespeare* in this chapter unless otherwise specified.

21. For relevant discussion of Acrasia and False Florimell in the present volume see part 3, chapter 15, "Androcentrism and Acrasian Fantasies in the Bower of Bliss."

22. Adelman, 150; cf. 161; Kiernan, 190. Cf. Marguerite A. Tassi, "O'erpicturing Appelles: Shakespeare's *Paragone* with Painting in *Antony and Cleopatra*," in Deats, ed. 291–307, here 303–4. Also Philippa Berry, *Shakespeare's Feminine Endings: Disfiguring Death in the Tragedies* (London: Routledge, 1999), 87: "the enigmatically obscure spectacle of Cleopatra on Cydnus reminds us" that tragedy directs "our attention precisely towards those aspects of experience which elude absolute comprehension."

23. A more persuasively balanced antecedent of Kiernan's argument is W. B. Worthen's essay "The Weight of Antony: Staging 'Character' in *Antony and Cleopatra*," *Studies in English Literature*, 26 (1986), 295–308, esp. 301–3, 305. Referring to Cleopatra's return, as it were, to Cydnus, Worthen argues that "the play forces us to negotiate the difficulties of its own representation, the 'restoration' of an inaccessible, nearly unimaginable greatness—one known to us only through words, as a text—to the stage ... [where] there will be no barge burnishing, no music, no Cupids and Nereides, only a barren platform and two weeping servants" (305). A successful negotiation, he adds, will accept Cleopatra's rhetoric and staged pathos as efficacious play. See also Carol Cook, "The Fatal Cleopatra," in *Shakespearean Tragedy and Gender*, ed. Shirley Nelson Garner and Madelon Sprengnether (Bloomington: Indiana University Press, 1996), 241–67, here 245: in V.ii, the "boy actor, speaking the lines of the male playwright, draws our attention to the absence of Cleopatra from this scene, the absence which constitutes Cleopatra, constitutes the unrepresentable woman, the unassimable other." Cook's Irigarayan reading of the play rightly places a high value on fluidity. A more positive balance to Cook's notthereness might be found in the thoughtful discussion of early modern "vitalism" by Berry, however, 12–20, esp. 13–14.

24. Mary Orr, *Intertextuality: Debates and Contexts* (Cambridge, U.K.: Polity, 2003), 57.

25. Imprecise or unstable terminology obscures similarities and differences, but a selection of relevant views can be found in Sir Philip Sidney, *An Apology for Poetry*, ed. Geoffrey Shepherd (1965; rpt. Manchester, U.K.: Manchester University Press, 1973), 125; George Puttenham, *The Arte of English Poesie* (1589; rpt. Kent, Oh.: Kent State University Press, 1988), 34–35; Allan H. Gilbert, ed., *Literary Criticism:*

Plato to Dryden (1940; rpt. Detroit, Mich.: Wayne State University Press, 1962), 305–7, 312, 324 (Lodovico Castelvetro); 360–62, 367–70, 386–88 (Jacopo Mazzoni); 472, 474, 476–81, 492–94 (Torquato Tasso). On Tasso's views, see also the excellent discussion of Mindele Anne Treip, *Allegorical Poetics and the Epic: The Renaissance Tradition to "Paradise Lost"* (Lexington: University Press of Kentucky, 1994), 45–49 and chaps. 5–8, esp. 67, 74–79, 82–85, 91–94. While the Aristotelian Pietro Pomponazzi does not address poetics in his treatise *On the Immortality of the Soul*, his argument that "in all cognition, however far abstracted, we form some bodily image," or, as Aristotle himself had put it, "'knowing is either imagination, or is not without imagination,'" is likewise suggestive regarding the status of poetic imagery: *The Renaissance Philosophy of Man*, ed. Ernst Cassirer, Paul Oskar Kristeller, John Herman Randall, Jr. (1948; rpt. Chicago, Ill.: University of Chicago Press, 1956), 257–381, here 305, 319. See also Janet Leslie Knedlick, "Fancy, Faith, and Generative Mimesis in *Paradise Lost*," *Modern Language Quarterly*, 47 (1986), 19–47: as noted in my introduction, Knedlick argues that in the Renaissance Tasso and Mazzoni (not to mention Sidney and Milton) understood and applied "the fundamental point of Aristotle's *Poetics*: that in the process of structuring the artistic mimesis, the poetic maker works in a mode intrinsically valid as a way of knowing . . . between literal inspiration and autonomous imagination" (24–25, 27, 30).

26. Adelman, 121–22. *Love's Labor Lost*, V.ii.406–7, 413. On stage and page, see Harry Berger, Jr. "Bodies and Texts," in *Situated Utterances: Texts, Bodies, and Cultural Representations* (New York: Fordham University Press, 2005), 99–128; also his *Imaginary Audition: Shakespeare on Stage and Page* (1989; rpt. Berkeley: University of California Press, 1991). Cf. Kiernan, 10–11, 15, for example.

27. The phrase "as 'twere" conceivably can be taken either with the verb "hold" that precedes it or, more likely, with the "mirror" that follows it: the purpose, or end, of playing is "to hold as 'twere the mirror up to nature." Either way, the statement is counterfactual, and the act of holding or else the reflecting surface is conceived metaphorically. On this speech by Hamlet, cf. Robert Weimann, "Mimesis in *Hamlet*," in *Shakespeare and the Question of Theory*, ed. Patricia Parker and Geoffrey Hartman (New York: Methuen, 1985), 275–91, esp. 278–80: Shakespeare's "uses of mimesis cannot be formulated in (let alone reduced to) either a representational or nonrepresentational theory of dramatic language" (278). Cf. Also Weimann's "Towards a literary theory of ideology: mimesis, representation, authority," in *Shakespeare Reproduced: The Text in History and Ideology*, ed. Jean E. Howard and Marion F. O'Connor (1987; rpt. New York: Routledge, 1993), 265–72, here 268. In this more recent essay, Weimann's observation that "there is no point in minimizing the actually existing contradiction between mimesis and the sign," true as it is, reflects his apparent identification of mimesis with referentiality and of signification with semiotics (266). Dichotomous terminology, while clear, seems inescapably problematical. I doubt Aristotle meant mimesis in as limited a sense as Weimann's here, but my doubt immediately opens the meaning of referentiality to question, as does Weimann's own discussion of *mimesis* in his distinguished *Shakespeare and the Popular Tradition in the Theater: Studies in the Social Dimension of Dramatic Form and*

Function, ed. Robert Schwarz (Baltimore: Johns Hopkins University Press, 1978), 2–3: here, while Weimann emphasizes the interpretive role of the actor (*hypokrites*), for whom the Ionian equivalent was *exegetes* (exegete), he notes from earliest times basic aspects of *mimesis* not derived from the object imitated: so how do we distinguish the dancer from the dance?

28. *Time and Narrative*, I, trans. Kathleen McLaughlin and David Pellauer (Chicago, Ill.: University of Chicago Press, 1984), 45. See also Orr, chap. 3: "Imitation," esp. 96–106, and the discussion of mimesis in my introduction.

29. Sidney,123; Shakespeare, I.i.61.

30. Kiernan, 13; Kiernan cites Gerald L. Bruns, *Modern Poetry and the Idea of Language: A Critical and Historical Study* (New Haven, Conn.: Yale University Press, 1974), 1–5. Wolfgang Iser, *The Fictive and the Imaginary: Charting Literary Anthropology* (Baltimore: Johns Hopkins University Press, 1993), xiv–xv. On the relation of Sidney's *Apology* to *Antony and Cleopatra*, see also Bono, 141, 150–51, 219.

31. Adelman, *Suffocating Mothers*, 189; *Common Liar*, 161. On the blending of character in Shakespeare and Spenser, see my examples in "Conspiracy of Realism" (*King Lear*) in part 3, chapter 12, of the present volume, and in *Translating Investments: Metaphor and the Dynamic of Cultural Change in Tudor-Stuart England* (New York: Fordham University Press, 2005), 29–30 (*1* and *2 Henry IV*). Early instances of the merging of different speakers' statements can be found in the Despair and Contemplation episodes of Spenser's first Book of *The Faerie Queene* (I.ix.41–42, x.62) and in the replies of the Palmer and Guyon to Atin in Book II.iv.44.

32. James Hirsch remarks the Egyptian, or infinitely various, structure of this play, whose scenes number more than forty, some "absurdly brief": "Rome and Egypt in *Antony and Cleopatra* and in Criticism of the Play," in Deats, ed., 175–91, here 189. Hirsch's review of the Rome/Egypt binarism in criticism of the play nicely supplements Deats's survey (note 1 of this chapter). On the spatial politics of the play, see also Ania Loomba, "Theatre and the Space of the Other in *Antony and Cleopatra*," in *Shakespeare's Late Tragedies'': A Collection of Critical Essays*, ed. Susanne L. Wofford (Upper Saddle River, N.J.: Prentice Hall, 1996), 235–48, here 237–40.

33. In *Allegory: The Theory of a Symbolic Mode* (Ithaca, N.Y.: Cornell University Press, 1964), Angus Fletcher aligns allegory with obsessive-compulsive neurosis: chap. 6. His argument merges individual with broadly historico-cultural explanation and medical pathology with ideological hegemony. Quite a few controversial assumptions and transcodings here.

34. Rufus Wood, *Metaphor and Belief in "The Faerie Queene"* (Houndmills, Basingstoke, Hants., U.K.: Macmillan, 1997), 2–3.

35. The contrast is heightened by further parallels: Enobarbus describes from land a boat-scene, while Antony, situated on a boat (tenuously tied to land), describes an amphibian. What is striking about both is their amphibiousness. Cf. Cook, 249, who reads the crocodile exchange as mockery of the Roman "logic of identity," or sameness.

36. Altering the conjunction "or" to "and," I quote from my *Words That Matter: Linguistic Perception in Renaissance English* (Stanford, Calif.: Stanford University Press,

1996), 168: this book is concerned throughout with the relations of words to things and offers relevant cultural context: rhetorics, logics, dictionaries, grammars, treatises, sermons, etc.

37. On the Palmer's spinning of yarns, see my essay "The Knight and the Palmer in *The Faerie Queene*, Book II," *Modern Language Quarterly*, 31 (1970); and chapter 15 in part 3 of the present volume, "Androcentrism and Acrasian Fantasies in the Bower of Bliss."

38. Background for my argument can be found in Thomas Laqueur, *Making Sex: Body and Gender from the Greeks to Freud* (Cambridge, Mass.: Harvard University Press, 1990), preface and chaps 1–2, e.g., viii, 8, 11, 30–31. Another important touchstone is Valerie Traub's thoughtful, precise introduction in *Desire and Anxiety: Circulation of Sexuality in Shakespearean Drama* (London: Routledge, 1992), 1–22.

39. *AC*, II.v.12–14, 21–24; III.vii.18, V.ii.239. On hermaphroditism and androgyny in relation to Cleopatra, cf. Michael Payne's "Erotic Irony and Polarity in *Antony and Cleopatra*," *Shakespeare Quarterly*, 24 (1973), 265–79, esp. 271–74.

40. *AC*, I.iv.5–7, III.x.23, IV.xiv.10–14, 23, 113–14. Heather James treats another exchange of gender in Cleopatra's ambivalent observation that Antony is one way painted "like a Gorgon," that is, like the female Medusa (II.v.116): "The Politics of Display and the Anamorphic Subjects of *Antony and Cleopatra*," in Wofford, ed., 208–34, here 212.

41. On the imagination's power to project its own shapes on reality and on the symbols of flower and boar in Book III, see my *Growth of a Personal Voice: "Piers Plowman" and "The Faerie Queene"* (New Haven, Conn.: Yale University Press, 1976), 98–113.

42. See Hamilton, ed., 346nn30–50. Also John Erskine Hankins, *Source and Meaning in Spenser's Allegory: A Study of "The Faerie Queene"* (Oxford: Clarendon, 1971), 277–86; and James Nohrnberg, *The Analogy of "The Faerie Queene"* (Princeton, N.J.: Princeton University Press, 1976), 516. Of course traditionally the Garden of Adonis also implied ephemerality and triviality: for example, see Nohrnberg, 493–94, who suggests that Spenser put the negative associations of the Garden of the Adonis into the Bower of Bliss. Kenneth Gross qualifies Nornhberg's observation, maintaining that Spenser both cancels and preserves the negative associations within the Garden: *Spenserian Poetics: Idolatry, Iconoclasm, and Magic* (Ithaca, N.Y.: Cornell University Press, 1985), 201–2. I would add, in a word, that he simultaneously raises, or *sublates*, them as well, a form of translation to reappear in part 3, chapter 19, on *Paradise Lost*.

43. Traditionally the Garden Mount is considered a *mons veneris*, and it is this, although this is not all that it is. I argue for the bisexuality of the Mount in part 3, chapter 14, "Flowers and Boars: Surmounting Sexual Binarism in Spenser's Garden of Adonis."

44. On the dying Adonis, cf. Gordon Williams, "The Coming of Age in Shakespeare's Adonis," *Modern Language Review*, 78 (1983), 769–76, here 770, 775. Nohrnberg, 532, aligns the combining of womb and tomb in the Garden with the

act of sex when he observes, "Although a man cannot re-enter the womb except symbolically, he can do so seminally."

45. On the subordination of Adonis to Venus, see the discussion of Jon Quitslund, *Spenser's Supreme Fiction: Platonic Natural Philosophy and "The Faerie Queene"* (Toronto: University of Toronto Press, 2001), 211–19. For a historicist's approach to such subordination in Tudor society, see Lisa Celovsky, "Early Modern Masculinities and *The Faerie Queene*," *English Literary Renaissance*, 35 (2005), 210–47, here 212–17. Further relevant are the differing analyses of the Garden canto by Harry Berger, Jr.: "Spenser's Gardens of Adonis: Force and Form in the Renaissance Imagination" (1961), in his *Revisionary Play: Studies in the Spenserian Dynamics* (Berkeley: University of California Press, 1988), 131–53, and "Actaeon at the Hinder Gate: The Stag Party in Spenser's Gardens of Adonis," in *Desire in the Renaissance: Psychoanalysis and Literature*, ed. Valeria Finucci and Regina Schwartz (Princeton, N.J.: Princeton University Press, 1994), 91–119.

46. See part 3, chapter 13, on "*Venus and Adonis*," for Shakespeare's allusion to Spenser's Garden in *Richard III*. Shakespeare's *1 Henry VI*, I.vi.6, also refers to "Adonis' garden," and *The Riverside Shakespeare* notes in this reference the possibility of yet another Spenserian allusion.

47. Again, "dwell": various recent commentators on the play mention allegory at this point but do little more with it. Coppélia Kahn, for example, confines it to a local effect, "a signifier of love specifically between men": *Roman Shakespeare: Warriors, Wounds, and Women* (London: Routledge, 1997), 130. While astutely recognizing the allegorical binarism of other critics, James Hirsch remains anxiously suspicious of allegory itself: "Allegorical figures usually represent fixed abstractions, whereas Cleopatra strives for variety, change, originality, and individuality. And yet there is something obsessive about this striving," and "She, too, presents herself as an allegorical figure, although a paradoxical one, the embodiment of Infinite Variety, the antithesis of allegorical reductionism." Similarly, for Hirsch, the individualized Antony is no Everyman, "and yet, like a morality-play character, he does make a fateful choice between incompatible alternatives" (188). See also Cook, 253–54: "*Antony and Cleopatra* . . . is in many ways closer to something like allegory or dialectic than to psychological drama"; Benjamin, 228, on the prevalence of ideational allegory in Shakespeare, particularly in *Hamlet* (136–37).

48. *AC,* IV.xii.25–30, 42–49, xiii.2, xiv.51–55. In *Richard III*, Richard's heraldic device, a boar, presumably triggers Shakespeare's allusion to Spenser's Garden of Adonis. In the fourth Act of *Antony and Cleopatra*, while Antony's descent from Hercules triggers reference to the Thessalian boar, in the present context of love and death, memories of the boar beneath Spenser's Garden Mount are plausible as well. On the boar, cf. Anne Lake Prescott, "The Equinoctial Boar: Venus and Adonis in Spenser's Garden, Shakespeare's Epyllion, and Richard III's England," forthcoming in *Shakespeare and Spenser: Attractive Opposites*, ed. J. B. Lethbridge (Manchester, U.K.: Manchester University Press, 2008).

49. Cf. Wind, chap. 10: "Amor as a God of Death." John 19:30.

50. On the identification of Adonis with Christ, see, for example, Syrithe Pugh, *Spenser and Ovid* (Aldershot, Hants., U.K.: Ashgate, 2005), 55–57; also Gross's precariously balanced assessment in which Adonis is at once "the fallen Adam *and* the redemptive Christ," and yet however much he combines them, "he sustains a crucial measure of difference from both"(197–98). Lisa Hopkins neatly sums up the many biblical associations of Antony and Cleopatra: "Cleopatra and the Myth of Scota," in Deats, ed., 231–42, here 235. In the twentieth century, the association of Antony with Christ goes back at least to John Middleton Murry (1936), who took it seriously, and to Roy Battenhouse (1969), who thought it ironic: see Deats, 8, 28.

51. *Paradise Lost*, I.450–52, in *John Milton: Complete Poems and Major Prose*, ed. Merritt Y. Hughes (New York: Odyssey, 1957): also 222–23nn446, 458–60. Cf. as well Richard T. Neuse's discussion of "*Adonis, gardens of*" in *The Spenser Encyclopedia*, ed. A. C. Hamilton, et al (Toronto: University of Toronto Press, 1990).

52. Hankins observes the bearing of Vergil's Elysian Fields on Spenser's wheel of death and regeneration, 274. Also Nohrnberg, 503, 514, 517. In the November Eclogue of Spenser's *Shepheards Calender*, E. K.'s gloss on line 179 describes the Elysian Fields as "a place of pleasure like Paradise": *The Yale Edition of the Shorter Poems of Edmund Spenser*, ed. William A. Oram, et al (New Haven, Conn.: Yale University Press, 1989), 198. Heather James, 229, pertinently considers Antony's seeming mistake regarding Dido a deliberate act of "resistance to Caesar's ideological appropriation of him."

53. On homoeroticism in Spenser's Garden, see Quitslund, 208.

54. Related techniques occur in *The Faerie Queene*, for example, in the contrast, already mentioned, between the vision of sonneteering cannibals and that of Mount Acidale in Book VI. Another, analogous kind of example can be found in Spenser's basing Arthur's dream of the Faerie Queen on Chaucer's parodic *Sir Thopas* or the embedding of allusions to *Troilus* and to *The Wife of Bath's Prologue* in Arthur's account of this dream. Instead of destroying Arthur's vision, these allusions bring it momentarily into relation with less idealized experiences. Their point is connection, not identity–difference and similarity at once. In this volume, see part 1, chapter 3, "'Pricking on the plaine': Spenser's Intertextual Beginnings and Endings" and part 2, chapter 8, "Arthur and Argante: Parodying the Ideal Vision."

55. "The Life of Marcus Antonius," from *Plutarch's Lives of the Noble Grecians and Romanes*, trans. Sir Thomas North, in *Narrative and Dramatic Sources of Shakespeare*, ed. Geoffrey Bullough (London: Routledge and Kegan Paul, 1964), V, 254–321, here 310. Plutarch's final evaluation of Antony's suicide is also mixed: Antonius "slue him selfe . . . cowardly, and miserably, to his great paine and griefe: and yet was it before his bodie came into his enemies hands" (321). Cf. Robert A. Logan's argument that Shakespeare, in contrast to Plutarch, his main source, gives more space to Antony's heroism: "'High Events as these': Sources, Influences, and the Artistry of *Antony and Cleopatra*," in Deats, ed., 153–74, here 159–61. For a sympathetic explanation of Antony's final actions, cf. also Jacqueline Vanhoutte, "Antony's 'secret house of death': Suicide and Sovereignty in *Antony and Cleopatra*," *Philological Quarterly*, 79 (2000), 153–75, esp. 160–61, 166–69; also Bono, 187.

For a defense of Antony's stature and "weight," or "greatness," that is oriented to performance, cf. Michael Goldman, "*Antony and Cleopatra*: Action as Imaginative Command," in Wofford, ed., 249–67, here 255–57, 259–60; and for an unqualifiedly negative view of Antony's end, cf. Julia M. Walker, *Medusa's Mirrors: Spenser, Shakespeare, Milton, and the Metamorphosis of the Female Self* (Newark, N.J.: University of Delaware Press, 1998), 139–41.

56. Cf. Cook: Antony's loss of "'visible shape' . . . follows from the nature of his desire and seems requisite for its consummation. . . . The annihilation of separateness comes to entail the annihilation of bodies" (259, IV.xiv.14). Cook's comment pertains to Antony's desire before his attempted suicide, but it applies ironically here as well. Cf. also Lisa S. Starks, "'Immortal Longings': The Erotics of Death in *Antony and Cleopatra*," in Deats, ed., 243–58: "The death of desire" becomes "the ecstatic *desire of death*, a longing beyond the pleasure principle, a fusion of the destructive and regenerative forces of Thanatos and Eros" (245).

57. *AC*, IV.xiv.36, 52; V.ii.85–87, 96, 98. Carol Thomas Neely (*Broken Nuptials in Shakespeare's Plays* [1985; rpt. Urbana: University of Illinois Press, 1993], 160) characterizes the "reciprocal opposites" of male and female sexuality in the complementary visions of Enobarbus (of Cleopatra) and Cleopatra (of Antony) in terms that resonate with Spenser's Garden: "infinite variety and eternal bounty, magnetic power and hyperbolic fruitfulness, stasis and motion, art and nature."

58. Jean-Luc Nancy, *The Ground of the Image*, trans. Jeff Fort (New York: Fordham University Press, 2005), 133; see also 137: "The conjunction of power and *jouissance* corresponds to the withdrawal of the sacred foundation of authority: in the pleasure of power and in the power of pleasure—the chiasmus of a double autotelos—is indicated an unfathomable double secret that no sacred certainty can resolve . . . neither sovereignty nor love owes anything to anyone or to anything other than itself, and this unparalleled sufficiency is also their extraordinary fragility. They are, each of them, what they are only inasmuch as they renounce their own ground and therefore are capable, ultimately, of renouncing themselves." Nancy's essay treats representations of Cleopatra, including Shakespeare's.

59. *AC*, V.ii.286, 294–95, 310–11.

60. Plutarch, "Marcus Antonius," 291: "she did not onely weare at that time (but at all other [public] times els . . .) the apparell of the goddesse Isis." For the quotation about Isis' double nature, see Plutarch, *Moralia*, trans. Frank Cole Babbitt (1936; rpt. Cambridge, Mass.: Harvard University Press, 2003), V, 105 (368.43D).

61. *AC*, IV.xv.90–91 (my emphasis), V.ii.237–39, 284. Berry (6, 17–18, 155) finds other sexual references and exquisite puns in Cleopatra's urging the asp to untie "this knot intrinsicate" (V.ii.303) and, after Cleopatra's death, in Octavius' observation that she would "catch another Antony / In her strong toil of grace"—that is, the grease of carnival pleasures, those genital in particular (ii.346–47)—and finally in other Romans' noting the "vent of blood, and something blown" and the aspic's slimy trail at the scene of Cleopatra's suicide (ii.347–52). While assenting to these, I consider them less focal than the familiar pun on "nothing."

Chapter Seventeen: Patience and Passion in Shakespeare and Milton

1. See *Anger's Past: The Social Uses of an Emotion in the Middle Ages*, ed. Barbara H. Rosenwein (Ithaca, N.Y.: Cornell University Press, 1998), esp. Rosenwein's introduction, 1–6 and conclusion, 233–47; Lester K. Little, "Anger in Monastic Curses," 9–35; and Gerd Althoff, "*Ira Regis*: Prolegomena to a History of Royal Anger," 59–74. Also, William V. Harris, *Restraining Rage: The Ideology of Anger Control in Classical Antiquity* (Cambridge, Mass.: Harvard University Press, 2001).

2. Mary Beth Rose, *Gender and Heroism in Early Modern English Literature* (Chicago: University of Chicago Press, 2002), xii; my next sentence is based on Rose's pages 89–90, 96–99. Thanks to Jennifer Vaught for calling Rose's argument to my attention.

3. *The Riverside Shakespeare*, ed. G. Blakemore Evans et al, 2nd ed. (Boston, Mass.: Houghton Mifflin, 1997): II.ii.550–87: the Player performs a single speech (from Aeneas' tale to Dido), which is interrupted occasionally by his auditors. His role is representative of professional actors and their acting. Subsequent reference to Shakespeare's writing in this chapter is to the Riverside edition, unless otherwise noted.

4. See Georgia Ronan Crampton, *The Condition of Creatures: Suffering and Action in Chaucer and Spenser*, (New Haven, Conn.: Yale University Press, 1974), chap. 1. Also William Lily, *A Shorte Introduction of Grammar* (New York: Scholars' Facsimiles and Reprints, 1943): "Verbum . . . esse aliquid, ageréue, aut pati significat" (C.ii.^{v}). I have elaborated on Crampton's binaries, adding Lily and extending act and potency to form and matter. For Crampton's conclusions regarding Spenser and Chaucer, which my first sentence in this paragraph invokes, see page 201. Her discussion of individual texts of both poets is more nuanced than her conclusion.

5. Another example of monumental patience is to be found in Queen Katherine in Shakespeare's *Henry VIII*. But even in such a comedy as *Twelfth Night* it makes an appearance when Cesario/Viola describes her imagined sister sitting "like Patience on a monument, / Smiling at grief" (II.iv.114–15). Examples abound in Shakespeare's plays.

6. Unless otherwise indicated, reference to Milton's writings in this chapter is to *The Riverside Milton*, ed. Roy Flannagan (Boston, Mass.: Houghton Mifflin, 1998).

7. Ephesians reads, "Wherefore take unto you the whole armour of God, that ye may be able to withstand in the evil day, and having done all, to stand. Stand therefore, having your loins girt about with truth, and having on the breastplate of righteousness." Flannagan, ed., cites the discussion of James L. Jackson and Walter E. Weese, "'. . . Who Only stand and Wait': Milton's Sonnet 'On his Blindness,'" *Modern Language Notes*, 72 (1957), 91–93. Of course the idea of standing firm, fast, or steadfast is common in the Bible, but in the fifty-odd instances I have checked, it is not as clearly associated with service as in the verses from Ephesians. For other relevant examples, see 1 Thess. 3:8, 1 Cor. 16:13, Coloss. 4:12.

8. For "fit audience," see *Paradise Lost*, VII.31. Another context the Miltonic standing invokes for a modern reader is Roland H. Bainton's popular *Here I Stand: A Life of Martin Luther* (1950; rpt. New York: Penguin, 1995). The official record of Luther's examination at Worms does not include the words "Here I stand," but they appear in the first printed account of his responses: "Hie stehe ich / ich kan nicht anders / Got helffe mir [Here I stand. I cannot do otherwise. God help me]" (Bainton, 144–45: *sic*). Milton could have read Luther's words in a Latin version. Although Bainton's title might skew a current historical response, it is also notable that recent criticism has made much of Milton's Lutheran affiliations: for instance, Victoria Silver, *Imperfect Sense: The Predicament of Milton's Irony* (Princeton, N.J.: Princeton University Press, 2001): see references under the entry *Luther* in Silver's index, and 183–87 for discussion of Sonnet XIX. (Emphasis on the influence of Luther appears to be a current trend: for Shakespeare, cf. Lisa Freinkel, *Reading Shakespeare's Will: The Theology of Figure from Augustine to the Sonnets* [New York: Columbia University Press, 2002].)

9. Discussing works of faith, as distinct from works of law, Mary Ann Radzinowicz relevantly cites *De Doctrina Christiana* (vi, 490): "the only living faith is a faith which acts" (*Toward "Samson Agonistes": The Growth of Milton's Mind* [Princeton, N.J.: Princeton University Press, 1978], 245). In *Theaters of Intention: Drama and the Law in Early Modern England* (Stanford, Calif.: Stanford University Press, 2000), 13–16, Luke Wilson briefly aligns Donne's "Satire III" ("'To will implies delay, therefore now do'" or "'To stand inquiring right is not to stray'") with Milton's Sonnet XIX. But Wilson describes this "Christian ethic of service" as "alert inaction" in an effort to capture its active passivity. I would shift emphasis, definitively seeing it is as a form of *action*.

10. My emphasis on "sit." Stanley Fish, *How Milton Works* (Cambridge, Mass.: Harvard University Press, 2001), 39–40, 323.

11. See, for example, Fish, regarding the angels in the "Nativity Ode" who are "content merely to be ready" (40), whose "'harnass'd' ability, a power that in its readiness for action is the essence of action, at least as the poem has defined it" (323). Fish continues to see Milton's beliefs as fundamentally static, "'jumping up and down in one place,'" a perception he has earlier shared to an extent with K. G. Hamilton's view of Milton "'as a dialectician . . . at times'": *Self-Consuming Artifacts: The Experience of Seventeenth-Century Literature* (Berkeley: University of California Press, 1972), 271. Suffice it for the moment to say that I see the point and have benefitted from it but that I do not finally agree with it.

12. Milton's connection of patience with fortitude is traditional, although its extent is not: e.g., see Étienne Gilson, *The Christian Philosophy of St. Thomas Aquinas* (New York: Random House, 1956), 285–95, esp. 294: "Like magnificence . . . [patience for Aquinas] is a secondary virtue attached to the principal virtue of fortitude. By fortitude, we hold firm against fear. By patience, we support grief." Milton identifies the two virtues more closely and values patience more highly.

13. The pun occurs memorably in *The Faerie Queene*, VI.ix.26; for discussion of Melibee's use of it and its link to Spenser's Despair, see my *Growth of a Personal Voice:*

"Piers Plowman" and "The Faerie Queene" (New Haven, Conn.: Yale University Press, 1976), 178–79.

14. Relevant annotation here ranges widely, though none has my particular focus: cf. Arnold Stein, *Answerable Style* (Minneapolis: University of Minnesota Press, 1953), 17–37; Catherine Gimelli Martin, *The Ruins of Allegory: "Paradise Lost" and the Metamorphosis of Epic Convention* (Durham, N.C.: Duke University Press, 1998), 325 and chap. 5.

15. Barbara Lewalski's entire discussion of *Paradise Regained* remains an indispensable point of reference: *Milton's Brief Epic: The Genre, Meaning, and Art of "Paradise Regained"* (Providence, R.I.: Brown University Press, 1966). Cf. Silver, 26–44; also cf. Peter C. Herman, *Destabilizing Milton: "Paradise Lost" and the Poetics of Incertitude* (New York: Palgrave Macmillan, 2005), 111–14: Herman remarks increased interest in the seventeenth century in Job as a focus for questions not only about predestination but also about England's condition and God's justice.

16. Cf. Silver, 28: "the words—'Tempt not the Lord thy God'—here express the value of attitude over action, the implied over the demonstrable, the groundlessness of faith over mythic spectacle." To my reading, even this perceptive view is too binary, too much involved in the either/or that Jesus, Word made flesh, must surmount. Cf also R. A. Shoaf's view that the Son obeys in perfect faith "by simply refusing to tempt the Lord God": *Milton, Poet of Duality: A Study of Semiosis in the Poetry and Prose* (New Haven, Conn.: Yale University Press, 1985), 166.

17. Cf. *Christian Doctrine, Complete Prose Works of John Milton*, VI, ed. Maurice Kelley, trans. John Carey (New Haven, Conn.: Yale University Press, 1973), I.xiv: "His Nature is double, divine and human" (418); "Christ, then, although he was God, put on human nature, and was made flesh" (420). References to *Christian Doctrine* in this chapter, unless otherwise indicated, are to Kelley's edition. If Carey's translation significantly modifies the Latin original (edition cited below), I shall note the Latin. On the authorship of *Christian Doctrine*, compare William B. Hunter, *Visitation Unimplor'd: Milton and the Authorship of "De Doctrina Christiana"* (Pittsburgh, Penn.: Duquesne University Press, 1998), who disputes it, with the arguments of those who accept it: e.g., Barbara Lewalski, *The Life of John Milton* (Oxford: Blackwell, 2000), 415–41; and the extensive critiques of Hunter's argument in *Studies in English Literature*, 32 (1992) and 34 (1994), esp. Lewalski (142–54) in 1992 and Christopher Hill (165–93) in 1994. In *Milton's Warring Angels: A Study of Critical Engagements* (Cambridge: Cambridge University Press, 1997), 64–65, William Kolbrener provides a credible assessment of Hunter's claims: "the inherited weight of *De Doctrina* as part of the Milton canon has created a reality among Milton scholars which has been shaken, though certainly not shattered by Hunter's arguments." Kolbrener's demonstration of the polyvalence and perspectivism of Milton's views in *De Doctrina* and *Paradise Lost* might be seen as his more extensive answer to Hunter. In the same year as Kolbrener's book, conclusions in the fifty-page essay on "The Provenance of *De Doctrina Christiana*, by Gordon Campbell, Thomas N. Corns, John K. Hale, David I. Holmes, and Fiona J. Tweedie, are consonant with his assessment: *Milton Quarterly*, 31 (1997), 67–117, esp. 42–43. The authors conclude that

De Doctrina is Milton's revision of a separate manuscript, whether his own or another's, which was "halted before completion"; much of the work on the manuscript "may well" have been done "during the late 1650s" (43).

18. For the quotation, see note 11 of this chapter. In a provocative discussion of negative (apophatic) theology in *Paradise Regained*, Regina Schwartz challenges the emphasis on the unfolding or discovery of the Son's identity to be found in Lewalski's and many another subsequent reading. She considers the Son's role *radically passive*: "Redemption and *Paradise Regained*," *Milton Studies*, 42 (2002), 26–49, here esp. 38. In a related connection, medieval studies of the psychology of Christ in the Hypostatic Union, both those in the Dominican tradition of Aquinas and those in the Franciscan tradition of Duns Scotus, whose work Milton knew, make it unlikely that he did not think about the psychological relation of Jesus to the Godhead, disinclined as he might have been to speculate about it in prose. The humanity of Jesus within Milton's proto-subordinationism (or *sui generis* Arianism, if *subordinationism* is too modern a term) makes this consideration more likely. Consider *Paradise Regained*, I.192, "Thought following thought," and the metaphor in I.196–97, "O what a multitude of thoughts at once / Awakn'd in me *swarm* " (my emphasis). As Michael Lieb has argued, in *Paradise Lost*, Milton "does not hesitate to concern himself with the states [even] of God's mind": "Reading God: Milton and the Anthropopathetic Tradition," *Milton Studies*, 25 (1989), 213–43, here 227. For a persuasive consideration of Milton's acquaintance with Duns Scotus (not specifically with his Christology), see John Peter Rumrich, *Matter of Glory: A New Preface to Paradise Lost* (Pittsburgh, Penn.: University of Pittsburgh Press, 1987), 148–65; and for discussion of the psychology of the Son within a Scotistic system, see my *Growth of a Personal Voice*, 136–42, 224–27nn20–43: the context is Langland's portrayal of Piers/Christ in *Piers Plowman*, a poem thought to herald the Reformation and one that Milton evidently read, according to his *Apology against a Pamphlet* . . . , etc. (i.e., *Apology for Smectymnuus*), in *Prose Works*, vol. 1, ed. Don M. Wolfe (New Haven, Conn.: Yale University Press, 1953), 868–953, here 915–16.

19. The noun *act* derives from *agere/actus*; the noun *agent* and the adjective *agential* derive from *agens/agent-*, the present participle of *agere*.

20. Milton glosses "*I am who I am*" first as a Spirit and then as "nothing but that most perfect *essence by which God exists* from himself, in himself, and through himself. . . . Therefore, just as God is an utterly simple essence, so he is an utterly simple subsistence": *Prose Works*, VI, 140–42 (I.ii): my emphasis.

21. In *Christian Doctrine*, 145–46 (I.ii), Milton rejects the Aristotelian/Thomist exclusion of potentiality (realization *in potentia*) in characterizing God: "God cannot rightly be called Actus Purus, or pure actuality, . . . for thus he could do nothing except what he does do, and he would do that of necessity." Simply put, God can will the begetting of the Son when he will do so, rather than from eternity (cf. Kelley, ed., 145–146n47). Since my point is the realization in action of the Son's being *in potentia*, it is not opposed to divine actuality, as Milton conceived it. God is; as Milton describes him, he truly exists and acts freely. See also Michael Lieb, *Theological Milton: Deity, Discourse and Heresy in the Miltonic Canon* (Pittsburgh,

Penn.: Duquesne University Press, 2006), 99–100: in Milton's *De Doctrina*, the result of his theological method "is a composite God, one in whom the metaphysical notions of *entelecheia* and *dynamis* [i.e., *actus* and *potentia*] are present, but in whom the culture of the . . . [Bible] reign[s] supreme."

22. My terms attempt both to observe Milton's distinction between God and his Son and the very special relation between them. In *Christian Doctrine*, 211 (I.v), Milton explains that "God imparted to the Son as much as he wished of the divine nature, and indeed of the divine substance also." He then adds, "do not take *substance* to mean total essence," thus at once connecting and distinguishing their natures in a way that rejects traditional Trinitarianism: Kelley, ed., takes Milton to have "avoided" Arianism by having God create the Son (directly? immediately?) out of his own substance, rather than from the dust of the earth (71), a qualified avoidance, as commonly observed, since all substance ultimately derives in some way from Milton's God. Milton's distinction carefully limits the extent of divinity imparted to the Son (i.e., its *totality*, in Carey's interpretive addition to the Latin text, perhaps to neutralize his equally interpretive imperative "do not take"), but his distinction does not preclude realization of such divinity as is imparted, of its agency (in a *factor* or *agent*, a "doer") and, above all, of its existential mode: *esse* as *existere, extare* (see my discussion of *esse* in *Translating Investments: Metaphor and the Dynamic of Cultural Change in Tudor-Stuart England* [New York: Fordham University Press, 2005], 26–42). The Latin text of *De Doctrina Christiana* that Carey's translation dramatizes reads simply, "nec tamen inde sequitur eiusdem esse cum Patre: Yet it does not follow from hence that the Son is co-essential [*esse*: co-existent?] with the Father": *The Works of John Milton*, XIV, ed. James Holly Hanford and Waldo Hilary Dunn, trans. Charles R. Sumner (New York: Columbia University Press, 1933), 186–87; amplifying this point, Milton denies that the Son is coeval ("coaevus") with the Father or that he has the same numerical essence ("eiusdem numero essentiae"). Although I consider Milton mainly the author of *Christian Doctrine*, I nonetheless find Hunter's remarks about the ambiguity of the term *essence* provocative in reference to the distinctive, relative divinity of the Son in Milton's poetry (1998: 115–16). See also Campbell, et al, 35–36 (item iv: discrepancies between *De Doctrina* and *Paradise Lost*), and most especially, Lieb, *Theological Milton*, chaps. 1–3, 8.

23. Modifying the common opinion that Milton adopts Augustine's view of sin, or evil, as merely privation of entity, Mindele Anne Treip relevantly cites Milton's designation of sin (evil) in *Christian Doctrine*, I.xi, as *active* obliquity, deviation, perversion from right and good, and privation as only its (passive) consequence: *Allegorical Poetics and the Epic: The Renaissance Tradition to "Paradise Lost."* (Lexington: University Press of Kentucky, 1994), 315n3; *Christian Doctrine*, 388–91, here 391. If sin is active, obedience is presumably active as well in the Son's dramatic and climactic stand.

24. Derek N. C. Wood affords a comprehensive review of approaches to *Samson Agonistes: "Exiled from Light": Divine Law, Morality, and Violence in Milton's "Samson Agonistes"* (Toronto: University of Toronto Press, 2001). Wood reads Samson as "the example not to be imitated" (191); his is "the tragedy of fallen humanity, of

the stunted and darkened moral consciousness of the fallen human spirit" (164–65). My own reading, as argued, is less negative. For another provocative review of recent readings of *Samson*, see Feisal G. Mohamed, "Confronting Religious Violence: Milton's *Samson Agonistes*," *PMLA*, 120 (2005), 327–40. Mohamed disputes Fish's separation of Samson's regeneration from his slaughter of the Philistines; instead, "Milton shows us a hero of faith achieving the saintly militarism ["spiritually justified militarism": 333] described by [Henry] Lawrence and [Henry] Vane" (336). For Mohamed, our facing the "religious extremism and political radicalism" evident at times in Milton's writing can lead us to "interrogate the coding of high Western culture as fundamentally rational and nonviolent" and the privileging of "the freedoms of the elect above those of the marginal" (337).

25. On alternatives in *Samson*, cf. Herman, 171–72, and for a more general consideration of the conjunction *or*, 43–49.

26. Noting that Samson's head inclines in prayer or meditation immediately prior to his pulling down the pillars, Fish observes that Samson is unlikely to have vengeance in mind (420). Samson, with arms outstretched to grasp the pillars on either side of him, may even suggest the image of the crucified Christ, whether straightforwardly or ironically. With Fish, I see a split between Samson's interior state and the violence of his final action that is everywhere evident at the end of the play.

27. Peter Herman asks rhetorically, "Is everyone in the theater equally guilty? . . . Does the simple fact of one's identity as a Philistine condemn one"? (174, cf. 176). Citing Franz Rosenzweig and Walter Benjamin, Brendan Quigley argues cogently for the defining character of Samson's heroic silence: "The Distant Hero of *Samson Agonistes*," *ELH*, 72 (2005), 529–51, here 543. He misses the connection between silence and patience, since "Patience is [merely] a bore" (537, 549*n*14).

28. On the potential range of allusions in the phoenix simile, see Christopher Hill, *Milton and the English Revolution* (London: Faber and Faber, 1977), 445–46. As John Carey, ed., notes (*Milton: The Complete Shorter Poems*, 2nd ed. [Harlow, U.K.: Pearson, 2007], 411*n*1692), a dragon is a serpentine form that can be considered a snake: representation of Satan as a dragon is recurrent in *Paradise Lost* (e.g., IV.3, X.529) and recalls the Satanic dragon of Rev. 12:3. Despite these associations or possibly an alternative association of the dragon with the dreadful power of a primitive God (Lieb, *Theological Milton*, 189–90), nagging doubts about "tame villatic Fowl" remain. Such mocking, trivializing detail redounds on the dragon, whose figure otherwise suggests such vindictive night-ravages as those of the flaming dragon near the end of *Beowulf*.

29. Cf. Achsah Guibbory, *The Map of Time: Seventeenth-Century English Literature and Ideas of Pattern in History* (Urbana: University of Illinois Press, 1986), 203: "In *Samson Agonistes*, and indeed in all the major poems published late in Milton's life, only the individual actually fulfills the ideal of progress Milton had entertained for England." Kolbrener, examining Milton's *Readie and Easie Way* (1660), relevantly observes Milton's increasing isolation and the widening fissure between public and private domains: chap. 2, esp. 44–49.

30. I have discounted the (re)publication of *Paradise Lost*, albeit in twelve books, in 1674, the year of Milton's death.

31. For discussion, in this volume see part 1, chapter 3, " 'Pricking on the Plaine': Spenser's Intertextual Beginnings and Endings" and part 2, chapter 10, "The Antiquities of Fairyland and Ireland." Also my *Growth of a Personal Voice*, 171–73, 196–97.

Chapter Eighteen: "Real or Allegoric" in Herbert and Milton: Thinking through Difference

1. Quotations of Milton's writings in this chapter are from *The Riverside Milton*, ed. Roy Flannagan (Boston, Mass.: Houghton Mifflin, 1998): here *Paradise Regained*, IV.372, 389–92.

2. Cf. Stephen Fallon, *Milton among the Philosophers: Poetry and Materialism in Seventeenth-Century England* (Ithaca, N.Y.: Cornell University Press, 1991): "From the time of *Eikonoklastes* Milton was done with fiction; his later poems are records of truth delivered directly, not through the mediation of allegories" (163). For a different view, see especially part 3, chapter 19, "Spenser and Milton: The Mind's Allegorical Place."

3. Mindele Anne Treip, *Allegorical Poetics and the Epic: The Renaissance Tradition to "Paradise Lost"* (Lexington: University Press of Kentucky, 1994), 171–72.

4. Victoria Silver, *Imperfect Sense: the Predicament of Milton's Irony* (Princeton, N.J.: Princeton University Press, 2001), 30.

5. Cf. Silver, 13: "if allegory can . . . bowdlerize the sense of a text, . . . irony can . . . deracinate it"; and "where allegory complicates the sense . . . , irony criticizes" it. The implications of Silver's choice of words are loaded, however. How bowdlerization is a complication of sense, and deracination merely a criticism, is quite beyond me.

6. Cf. John Leonard, *Naming in Paradise: Milton and the Language of Adam and Eve* (Oxford: Clarendon, 1990), 199: "Adam and Eve are represented as speaking a natural language" in *Paradise Lost*, that is, a language in which words correspond to natures, or defining essences. Leonard's whole book is relevant.

7. On Herbert's "Church Monuments," see Joseph H. Summers, *George Herbert: His Religion and Art* (1954; rpt. Binghamton, N.Y.: Center for Medieval and Early Renaissance Studies, 1981), 129–35; and my *Words That Matter: Linguistic Perception in Renaissance English* (Stanford, Calif.: Stanford University Press, 1996), 17–18.

8. Quotations of Herbert's poetry are from *The Works of George Herbert*, ed. F. E. Hutchinson (1941; rpt. Oxford: Clarendon, 1959). Helen Vendler, for one, emphasizes the presence of allegory in "Love (III)": *The Poetry of George Herbert* (Cambridge, Mass.: Harvard University Press, 1975), 274–76.

9. *Paradise Regained*, II.336, 368, 377.

10. Richard Strier observes that there is a problem in taking "Love (III)" to be "*primarily* Eucharistic in reference," insofar as only Puritans sat and ate at Communion: *Love Known: Theology and Experience in George Herbert's Poetry* (Chicago: University of Chicago Press, 1983), 78*n*41 (my emphasis). Two points: more than one

communal banquet is referenced in "Love (III)"; it seems unlikely that the saints will kneel at the marriage supper of the Lamb. Moreover, Herbert's freedom of thought in his poetry is not to be underestimated; in "Aaron," for example, he does not endorse a Laudian point of view with respect to vestments: for discussion see my *Translating Investments: Metaphor and the Dynamic of Cultural Change in Tudor-Stuart England* (New York: Fordham University Press, 2005), 108–11.

11. Although Michael C. Schoenfeldt does not remark the bearing of "Love (III)" on the Satanic banquet in *Paradise Regained*, he connects Milton and Herbert biographically: "Like Herbert, Milton was led by ill health to a deep personal engagement with the quotidian regimes of temperance" and to link "the highest of spiritual aspirations with the most mundane physiological operations": *Bodies and Selves in Early Modern England: Physiology and Inwardness in Spenser, Shakespeare, Herbert, and Milton* (Cambridge: Cambridge University Press, 1999), 132. Milton had numerous reasons to attend to Herbert's poetry. As William B. Hunter, Jr., observes, "one forgets [Herbert's] . . . public attack on a royalist position which may have cost him his career"; Hunter adds that Milton, unlike Herbert, had to cope with Laud in his prime, making all "the difference": "Herbert and Milton," *South Central Review*, 1 (1984), 22–37, here 22, 36. Hunter relates Herbert as an innovator in sonnet-form at some length to Milton (30–36).

12. David Loewenstein, *Representing Revolution in Milton and His Contemporaries: Religion, Politics, and Polemics in Radical Puritanism* (Cambridge: Cambridge University Press, 2001), 249.

13. *Paradise Lost*, V.468–503, cf.438. On this monist touchstone, see Regina M. Schwartz, "Real Hunger: Milton's Version of the Eucharist," *Religion and Literature*, 31 (1999), 1–17; also John Rogers, *The Matter of Revolution: Science, Poetry, and Politics in the Age of Milton* (Ithaca, N.Y.: Cornell University Press, 1996), 110–11.

14. See the discussion of history and allegory in Erich Auerbach's *Figura* in my introduction to this volume, and for a different view of the relation of allegory to universality, Fallon, 176; cf. 173–75.

15. In order, *Paradise Lost*, VII.333, IX.75, 180–81 (cf. 158–59); V.435–36; III.53–55 (cf. XI.412–18); I.781–88; IX.638–42. Most, but not all, of the associations in my paragraph are regularly noted in editions of *Paradise Lost*: e.g., Alastair Fowler, ed., *Paradise Lost*, rev. 2nd ed. (Harlow, U.K.: Pearson, 2007); and Flannagan, ed.

16. Quotation borrowed from *Comus*, vs. 207, insofar as it expresses my point better here than a paraphrase would. Cf. *Paradise Lost*, I.788.

17. Gregory Machacek, "Allusion," *PMLA*, 122 (2007), 522–36, here 531.

18. Fallon, 254–55; *Paradise Lost*, V.490. Cf. to Fallon's view Catherine Gimelli Martin's misconception that allegory consists of "static homologies": *The Ruins of Allegory: "Paradise Lost" and the Metamorphosis of Epic Convention* (Durham, N.C.: Duke University Press, 1998), 230. On the relation and distinction between metaphor and metonymy, see my *Translating Investments*, esp. chaps. 1, 4, 7: e.g., metonymy is "referential, substitutive, coded, ideological;" metaphor is "deviant,

constructive, creative–code-breaking" (4); on homologism, or "transcoding," as Fredric Jameson terms it, see *Translating Investments*, 172–74, and Jameson's *The Political Unconscious: Narrative as a Socially Symbolic Act* (1981; rpt. Ithaca: Cornell University Press, 1988), 40–44.

19. For a fascinating and largely persuasive approach to the ambivalence of Milton's shifting positions on monism, see Rachel J. Trubowitz, "Body Politics in *Paradise Lost*," *PMLA*, 121 (2006), 388–404. Similarly and more extensively, William Kolbrener considers Milton's views both "monist and dualist": *Milton's Warring Angels: A Study of Critical Engagements* (Cambridge: Cambridge University Press, 1997), 85, 108, 137–43; all of chap. 5 is relevant.

20. For further development, see John Peter Rumrich, *Matter of Glory: a New Preface to "Paradise Lost"* (Pittsburgh, Penn.: University of Pittsburgh Press, 1987), 148–63, 172–73, and my adaptation of his argument in part 3, chapter 19.

21. Familiar passages in *Areopagitica* are pertinent: 1017–18 (gathering up the limbs of Osiris/Truth) and 1015 (Truth as a perpetually progressive, streaming fountain, opposed to conformity, stasis, and stagnation). Cf. Kolbrener, 23–24; also Rumrich, *Milton Unbound: Controversy and Reinterpretation* (Cambridge: Cambridge University Press, 1996), 22, 24, 138 (coincidence of opposites), 145. Rumrich finds a "poetics of *becoming*" in Milton (24). His is a Milton tolerant of "indeterminacy" and "uncertainty, doubt, and division in seeking truth" (22, 24). David Norbrook largely agrees, but he cautions as well that "For all his championing of an open religious public sphere, Milton saw it as a means to an end," namely, "the revelation of a single, absolute truth": *Writing the English Republic: Poetry, Rhetoric, and Politics, 1627–1660* (Cambridge: Cambridge University Press, 1999), 480. Cf. Christopher Hill's less skeptical take on this point, however: "Milton's encyclopaedic learning, his emphasis on the oneness of truth, his desire to synthesize all knowledge, associate him with those [Fludd, Winstanley, the Hermeticists, the Comenians] who wanted to preserve a unified concept of culture against the growing specialization and fragmentation of the age, just as his insistence on creation *ex deo* links him with the mystical tradition of some of the sects, in conscious opposition to a mechanical universe": *Milton and the English Revolution* (London: Faber and Faber, 1977), 401. Rogers would add to Hill's "sects," scientific vitalism, which, like alchemy, had its share of mysticism, too.

Chapter Nineteen: Spenser and Milton: The Mind's Allegorical Place

1. Mindele Anne Treip, *Allegorical Poetics and the Epic: The Renaissance Tradition to "Paradise Lost"* Lexington: University Press of Kentucky, 1994. For a brief review of other relevant studies of Milton's allegorical poetics, see my introduction to this volume. I want to thank Stella Revard for reading a draft of this essay. Her very helpful comments led me to clarify numerous passages.

2. Michael Riffaterre's conception of a matrix as a sentence or a word that actualizes a structure curiously resembles Treip's Idea: *Semiotics of Poetry* (Bloomington:

Indiana University Press, 1978). For Riffaterre, "Matrix, model, and text are variants of the same structure" (19, cf. 13). As earlier remarked, literary allegory challenges the wall he erects between mimesis and semiosis and between syntagm and paradigm (e.g., 88–89). (Riffaterre makes several appearances in the notes to my introduction.)

3. For examples of Miltonic emblems, see Treip's " 'Reason is Also Choice': The Emblematics of Free Will in *Paradise Lost*," *Studies in English Literature*, 31 (1991), 147–77.

4. Cf. R. A. Shoaf, *Milton, Poet of Duality: A Study of Semiosis in the Poetry and Prose* (New Haven, Conn.: Yale University Press, 1985), 17–23; Maureen Quilligan, *The Language of Allegory: Defining the Genre* (Ithaca, N.Y.: Cornell University Press, 1979), 33–42, esp. 37; Martha Craig, "The Secret Wit of Spenser's Language," in *Elizabethan Poetry: Modern Essays in Criticism*, ed. Paul J. Alpers (New York: Oxford, 1967), 447–72. John Leonard, *Naming in Paradise: Milton and the Language of Adam and Eve* (Oxford: Clarendon, 1990), 20–21, notes Spenser's greater freedom than Milton's in inventing names to suit natures by playing upon etymological roots, and throughout this subtle, perceptive book, he emphasizes the significance of Milton's timing in the use and withholding of names. Timing is essential for Spenser as well: for example, his typically naming a character in Books I–III *after* an extensive description of characteristics that are more complex than is the bare label itself (e.g., Lucifera, Orgoglio, or, the Redcross Knight, exclusively so nominated until canto x). With additional significance, Spenser modifies his dominant practice early in Book IV when he gives the name first and generates an extensive characterization from it (e.g., Ate): see my *Growth of a Personal Voice: "Piers Plowman" and "The Faerie Queene"* (New Haven, Conn.: Yale University Press, 1976), esp. 116–17.

5. Treip cites Tasso's *Discourses on the Heroic Poem* (1594), trans. Mariella Cavalchini and Irene Samuel (Oxford: Clarendon, 1973), V, 170; and *Discorsi del poema eroico* (1594), in *Prose*, ed. Ettore Mazzali (Verona, Milan, and Naples: Ricciale editore, 1959), 487–729. On Milton's sense of the Platonic Idea, Treip (150) references Irene Samuel, *Plato and Milton* (Ithaca, N.Y.: Cornell University Press, 1947), chap. 6. Samuel identifies Milton's view with the Augustinian understanding of Platonic Ideas as the archetypes of creation in the mind of God. Augustine's view is commonly cited in the sixteenth and seventeenth centuries. As noted (and criticized) in my introduction, Walter Benjamin also characterizes the allegorical *Trauerspiel* (mourning play) as a Platonized Idea: *The Origin of German Tragic Drama*, trans. John Osborne (1998; rpt. London: Verso, 2003), 38, 46, 48, 169.

6. In an unqualified modern context, the metaphor of clothing for expression, style, or rhetoric normally signals the assumption that language is *merely* an external adornment and not constitutive of meaning. In the Renaissance the same metaphor is likely to be materially defining in broad and basic ways: see my *Translating Investments: Metaphor and the Dynamic of Cultural Change in Tudor-Stuart England* (New York: Fordham University Press, 2005), e.g., 24–25.

7. On *deictic* and *nondeictic*, see my introduction.

8. *Areopagitica*, vol. 2, ed. Ernest Sirluck, in *Complete Prose Works of John Milton*, (New Haven, Conn.: Yale University Press, 1959), 480–570, here 514–15, 543. Unless otherwise indicated, quotations of Milton's prose in this chapter are from *Complete Prose Works of John Milton*, gen. ed. Don M. Wolfe, 8 vols. (New Haven, Conn.: Yale University Press, 1953–82), cited hereafter as *Prose Works*. Citation of Milton's Latin text of *De Doctrina Christiana* is from the edition of James Holly Hanford and Waldo Hilary Dunn, trans. Charles R. Sumner, in *The Works of John Milton*, ed. Frank Allen Patterson et al, 18 vols. (New York: Columbia University Press, 1931–40): XIV–XVII, cited hereafter as *De Doctrina*.

9. Thomas Hobbes, *Leviathan*, ed. Richard E. Flathman and David Johnston (New York: W. W. Norton, 1997), 28 (I.v).

10. Paul Ricoeur, *The Rule of Metaphor*, trans. Robert Czerny, with Kathleen McLaughlin and John Costello (1977; rpt. Toronto: Toronto University Press, 1987), 83–90, 125–33, esp. 131–32; Max Black, *Models and Metaphors: Studies in Language and Philosophy* (Ithaca, N.Y.: Cornell University Press, 1962), chap. 3, cf. chap. 13.

11. Judith H. Anderson, *Words That Matter: Linguistic Perception in Renaissance English* (Stanford, Calif.: Stanford University Press, 1996); for *Translating Investments* see note 6, above.

12. Reference to *The Faerie Queene* in this chapter is to the second edition of A. C. Hamilton, with text edited by Hiroshi Yamashita and Toshiyuki Suzuki (Harlow, U.K.: Pearson, 2001), here II.vii.24. Spenser's romance epic will be cited as *FQ*.

13. On these misunderstandings, see, for example, Paul de Man's fundamentally important "Rhetoric of Temporality," in *Blindness and Insight: Essays in the Rhetoric of Contemporary Criticism*, 2nd ed., rev. (Minneapolis: University of Minnesota Press, 1983), 187–228.

14. Unless otherwise specified, reference to Milton's poetry in this chapter is to *The Riverside Milton*, ed. Roy Flannagan (Boston, Mass.: Houghton Mifflin, 1998), here *Paradise Lost*, I.22–23: Milton's epic will be cited as *PL*. I also consult the edition of Merritt Y. Hughes, *John Milton: Complete Poems and Major Prose* (New York: Odyssey, 1957) and that of Alastair Fowler, *Paradise Lost*, rev. 2nd ed. (Harlow, U.K.: Pearson, 2007). For Milton's other poems, I also consult *Milton: The Complete Shorter Poems*, ed. John Carey, rev. 2nd ed. (Harlow, U.K.: Pearson, 2007).

15. On Milton's conception of the (Holy) Spirit, see *Christian Doctrine*, in *Prose Works*, vol. 6, ed. Maurice Kelley, trans. John Carey, 280–92, esp. 280–87, 298 (I.vi).

16. Forrest G. Robinson, *The Shape of Things Known: Sidney's Apology in Its Philosophical Tradition* (Cambridge, Mass.: Harvard University Press, 1972), 122–28, citation at 124. Reference to *An Apology for Poetry* is to Geoffrey Shepherd, ed. (1965; rpt. Manchester, U.K.: Manchester University Press, 1973), 124 ("ground-plot"). Shepherd glosses *ground-plot* as "the 'seat of argument' (Quintilian, *Institutes*, V, x, 1), where material is hidden and whence it is sought in the process of 'invention'" (201n25f.). Treip suggests that the Idea of *Paradise Lost* is the "'Justification' of the

ways of God." While this may be Milton's goal, I don't see how it is, in itself, a *ground-plot* (151). Treip goes on to identify Milton's "subject" as "the Fall of Man" and his "action" as "the revenge of Satan upon Man" (152). Kenneth Borris, whose argument builds on Treip's, locates Milton's Idea in the corporate body (a version of the traditional *corpus mysticum*) of the Son: *Allegory and Epic in English Renaissance Literature: Heroic Form in Sidney, Spenser, Milton* (Cambridge: Cambridge University Press, 2000), esp. parts 1 and 4. John Rogers observes that animist materialism (vitalism) is "the old medieval metaphor of the *corpus mysticum*, stripped of its mysticism, . . . [and] made flesh": *The Matter of Revolution: Science, Poetry, and Politics in the Age of Milton* (Ithaca, N.Y.: Cornell University Press, 1996), 10. Shoaf variously centers *Paradise Lost* in the words *justify, pair, partner,* and *repetition,* and in additional puns on the notion of "faith"; to an extent, his argument, too, like Treip's but only partially so, recalls Riffaterre's riddles and verbal keywords in *Semiotics of Poetry*.

17. As Fowler, ed., 65n84, observes, Satan's opening response also recalls Isaiah 14:12, though secondarily, in my view.

18. Cf. Leonard, 77–78, on Satan's confusion and his significant lack of a name for Beelzebub.

19. Romans 7:24.

20. The phrase "bottomless perdition" also combines a word having a native English root (Old English *botm*) with a word having Latin roots (*per-* + *dare*). To my ear, such native English/Latin combinations contribute to the special effects of phrases employing them; they are also frequent in the sermons of Donne: see my *Words That Matter*, 204–5.

21. Stephen M. Fallon notes that the conception of *substance* is "one of the central preoccupations of seventeenth-century philosophy": *Milton among the Philosophers: Poetry and Materialism in Seventeenth-Century England* (Ithaca, N.Y.: Cornell University Press, 1991), 3. This concern is also a feature of the intellectual culture of the sixteenth century, and it is a familiar keynote of theological debate about the Eucharist throughout both centuries. On the controversy over *substance* and the many possible meanings of this word-concept from Aristotle onward, see my *Translating Investments*, 49–51: conflations of essence and substance might be said to litter the entire philosophic tradition of the West. Cf. also my *Words That Matter*, indexical entry for *Substance*.

22. Fowler, ed., remarks most of the ambiguities of these lines: 63nn59, 60. His notes indicate that the lines are ambiguous rather than specifically irrational.

23. The term "objective correlative" is T. S. Eliot's: "Hamlet and His Problems," in *The Sacred Wood: Essays on Poetry and Criticism* (1920; rpt. London: Methuen, 1960), 95–104, here 100. Cf. also Regina M. Schwartz, *Remembering and Repeating: On Milton's Theology and Poetics,* with a new preface (1988; rpt. Chicago: University of Chicago Press, 1993), xiii: Milton's "cosmic spaces, like Dante's, are also the interior spaces of the subject."

24. In Milton's *Christian Doctrine*, hell is said to be both an internal state of loss and a "place" that is "situated outside this world": *Prose Works*, VI, 628–30

(I.xxxiii). See also John Gillies' analysis of "Space and Place in *Paradise Lost*," *ELH*, 74 (2007), 27–57: instead of embracing the space of the new philosophy, Gillies argues, Milton intuits "place as a property of the body" (32).

25. E.g., David Norbrook thinks the rhetoric of Satan more likely to allude to Cromwell than to either Charles I or II, but he also finds the Great Consult sending both royalist and republican signals: *Writing the English Republic: Poetry, Rhetoric, and Politics, 1627–1660* (Cambridge: Cambridge University Press, 1999), 442, 445–46, 452, 485. Likewise, Christopher Hill finds "the Satanic" in Royalists, Ranters, and major-generals: *Milton and the English Revolution* (London: Faber and Faber, 1977), 343, 365–75, esp. 367; Hill is unclear regarding historical allegory itself, however: he first describes allegory simplistically, then declares that Satan "is not a flat allegorical figure," and eventually, having remarked the political mirroring throughout *Paradise Lost*, refers to it as "political allegory" comparable to that found in Spenser, Bunyan, or Swift (342–43, 390–91). Joan S. Bennett sees Satan as a portrait of Charles I: *Reviving Liberty: Radical Christian Humanism in Milton's Great Poems* (Cambridge, Mass.: Harvard University Press, 1989), chap. 2. David Loewenstein, who favors the term "mythic" where others use "allegorical," finds no need to align the political rhetoric of Satan's revolt with a single figure or group, whether Charles I, Laudian prelates, Cromwell, Army leaders, Presbyterian clergy, Irish rebels; cautiously, he also suggests that reference to the Presbyterians might be dominant in this rhetoric, however: *Representing Revolution in Milton and His Contemporaries: Religion, Politics, and Polemics in Radical Puritanism* (Cambridge: Cambridge University Press, 2001), e.g., 203–8. Cf. also Sharon Achinstein, *Milton and the Revolutionary Reader* (Princeton: Princeton University Press, 1994), 200, 222; Michael Bryson, *The Tyranny of Heaven: Milton's Rejection of God as King* (Newark, N.J.: University of Delaware Press, 2004), 28, 43, 114 ; Peter C. Herman, *Destabilizing Milton: "Paradise Lost" and the Poetics of Incertitude* (New York: Palgrave Macmillan, 2005), 37–38.

26. For another particularly striking example of duplicitous Spenserian syntax, see part 1, chapter 2, "What Comes after Chaucer's *But* in *The Faerie Queene*." This chapter demonstrates that the theme of perception in the sixth Proem is a Spenserian corollary of illogical syntax.

27. Fallon, 22–23, 204 (citation), 207, cf. 81, 107: since I disagree strongly with Fallon's assumptions regarding allegory, I want to make clear that otherwise I value, and have greatly benefitted from, his important study. Stephen B. Dobranski, "Pondering Satan's Shield in Milton's *Paradise Lost*, *English Literary Renaissance*, 35 (2005), 490–506, suggests that Satan, with his shield ingloriously hung on his back and as Leviathan, resembles the serpentine, hence scaly, form of a tortoise, insofar as the term *leviathan* designates any " 'large water animal or sea monster' " (501): on *leviathan* Dobranski cites Karen L. Edwards: *Milton and the Natural World: Science and Poetry in "Paradise Lost"* (Cambridge: Cambridge University Press, 1999), 108. Dobranski pertinently aligns bifocality in *Paradise Lost* with Satan's "amphibious nature" (504).

28. On Servius' gloss, see William Nelson, *The Poetry of Edmund Spenser: A Study* (New York: Columbia University Press, 1963), 159.

29. As observed in part 3, chapter 15, "Androcentrism and Acrasian Fantasies in the Bower of Bliss," the story of Hippolytus can be read from either Redcrosse's or Una's point of view. Read through the illusory lens of Redcrosse himself, he, like Hippolytus, is "too simple and too trew," himself the chaste victim pursued by monsters rising from the deep, and Una, like Phaedra, is lustful, untrue, and treasonous (ii.45, vi.2). Read through the lens of Una, or truth, Redcrosse, combining Theseus with Phaedra, is lustful, faithless, rash, jealous, and wrathful, and Una, like Hippolytus, is the chaste and innocent victim endangered by vicious forces in a hostile world. In other words, Redcrosse's illusion exists in the mythic mirror along with the true state of affairs.

30. See my *Growth of a Personal Voice*, 38–40.

31. *FQ*, II.vii.8, 20, 52, 62. Framing quotation from my *Growth of a Personal Voice*, 54–55, modified by the addition of "historically"; on Machiavelli and Mammon, see 58–61 and 213n11. On Spanish mines in the Mammon episode, see Thomas H. Cain, *Praise in "The Faerie Queene"* (Lincoln: University of Nebraska Press, 1978), 94–96.

32. On what is interior and what exterior, see also part 2, chapter 15, "Androcentrism and Acrasian Fantasies" in this volume.

33. On the House of Alma, see part 2, chapter 15, "Androcentrism and Acrasian Fantasies" in this volume; on the House of Busirane, see my *Translating Investments*, chaps. 6–7; on the Temple of Venus, see part 2, chapter 9, "Chaucer's *Parliament of Fowls* and Refractions of a Veiled Venus in *The Faerie Queene*," in this volume; on Isis Church, see Plutarch, *Moralia*, trans. Frank Cole Babbitt (1936; rpt. Cambridge, Mass.: Harvard University Press, 2003), V, 6–191; Alice Miskimin, "Britomart's Crocodile and the Legends of Chastity," *JEGP*, 77 (1978), 17–36; and my "Spenser's *Faerie Queene*, Book V: Poetry, Politics, and Justice," in *A Companion to English Renaissance Literature and Culture*, ed. Michael Hattaway (Oxford: Blackwell, 2000), 195–205, here 201–2; for the extensive background of Spenser's Acidalian Graces, see Edgar Wind, *Pagan Mysteries in the Renaissance*, rev. ed. (Harmondsworth, Middlesex, U.K.: Penguin, 1967); on the calendrical tradition in the Mutability Cantos, see Sherman Hawkins, "Mutabilitie and the Cycle of the Months," in *Form and Convention in the Poetry of Edmund Spenser*, ed. William Nelson (New York: Columbia University Press, 1961), 76–102, here 88–98.

34. On Erich Auerbach, see my introduction to this volume, which also treats allegory more generally.

35. On the relation and distinction between metaphor and metonymy, see my *Translating Investments*, esp. chaps. 1, 4, 7: e.g., metonymy is "referential, substitutive, coded, ideological;" metaphor is "deviant, constructive, creative–code-breaking" (4); on transcoding, or, homology, see 172–74. Cf. Rachel J. Trubowitz's view that Milton is both a monist and a dualist and that he is ambivalent both about the concreteness of the past and about the allegorized future; she makes a good case for opposing Hebraic monism to Pauline dualism: "Body Politics in *Paradise Lost*," *PMLA*, 121 (2006), 388–404.

36. Leonard, 147–48, questions the views of a number of critics who have argued against God's claim that the angels are "Self-tempted, self-depraved." His third chapter (147–91), which argues that the angels fall by their own "suggestion," assesses and persuasively supports God's assertion. Cf. Loewenstein, 218–19, 223–24. In *Christian Doctrine, Prose Works*, VI, 160–67, esp. 164 (I.iii), Milton makes clear that angels and human beings were free to stand or fall. Bryson, 93–95, vigorously objects to the decree of Milton's God to elevate the Son; he considers it an unfair temptation of Satan, a provocation meant "to drive dissent out into the open, to create dissent in the first place" (93). But cf. *Christian Doctrine*, 338 (I.viii), where Milton distinguishes between good and evil temptations by God and declares both kinds just. His example of an evil temptation is one used by God to unmask hypocrisy. Bryson's argument against the Father's justice is overstated and overly selective. For a good résumé of various, mainly positive understandings of Milton's God, see Jeffrey Shoulson, *Milton and the Rabbis: Hebraism, Hellenism, and Christianity* (New York: Columbia University Press, 2001), 98; Shoulson's own view is that "both the rabbis and Milton . . . enlist God's unreadability," his "excessively human traits," in their projects, while insisting "on the justice of his ways" (98–99). See also Michael Lieb, "Milton's 'Dramatick Constitution': The Celestial Dialogue in *Paradise Lost*, Book III," *Milton Studies*, 23 (1987), 215–40, here 218, 233; and his *Theological Milton: Deity, Discourse and Heresy in the Miltonic Canon* (Pittsburgh Penn.: Duquesne University Press, 2006), 96–97.

37. Cf. Treip, 315n3; Milton, *Christian Doctrine, Prose Works*, VI, 388–91, here 391 (I.xi). In *De Doctrina*, the Latin reads, "sola eius [i.e., actionis] obliquitas sive anomalia a legis norma proprie mala est" (XV, 198). Carey's translation (the more accurate one this time) reads, "it is only its [the action's] misdirection or deviation from the set course of law which can properly be called evil" (391).

38. For background, see *Christian Doctrine*, VI, 317–22 (I.vii): the creation by God of a *"living soul"*; also 399–401 (I.xiii), on the inseparability of body and soul (or body, spirit, and soul) in death. In *De Doctrina*, XV, 40, Milton describes the breath of life as follows: "halitumque illum vitae nec divinae partem essentiae, nec animam quidem fuisse, sed auram quandam sive virtutem divinam efflatam," which I would render, "and that breath of life was neither part of the divine essence nor itself the soul but a certain wind [cf. modern English *aura*] or divine virtue [power] breathed forth": Milton seems to know more clearly what the breath is not than what it is.

39. Fowler, ed., 31, offers a convenient outline of the chronology of events, as distinct from the order in which they are narrated in the poem.

40. *PL*, VII.233, 237–39, 245. Rogers (135) notes that in Paracelsus, tartar is evil generated with the Fall (of Adam and Eve), but in Milton is evident before the Fall. He is not concerned by the effect of Satan's rebellion and fall and its implications for matter prior to the creation of Earth. On the religious associations of alchemy more generally, see William R. Newman, *Promethean Ambitions: Alchemy and the Quest to Perfect Nature* (Chicago: University of Chicago Press, 2004), e.g., 171–73. Norbrook connects the same "cold Infernal dregs" with "the masses . . . calling for

a return to monarchy" (471). Eric B. Song argues for a connection of the "tartareous" dregs with the Tartar people: "Nation, Empire, and the Strange Fire of Tartars in Milton's Poetry and Prose," *Milton Studies*, 47 (2008), 118–44. Without reference to Milton, Walter Benjamin notes the gnostic-manichean doctrine that "matter was created to bring about the 'de-Tartarization' of the world, and was destined to absorb everything devilish" (227).

41. See Brian Rotman, *Signifying Nothing: the Semiotics of Zero* (1987; rpt. Stanford, Calif.: Stanford University Press, 1993), 1. Cf. Fallon, 185: Fallon's view of negative numeration is, well, more simply negative. Properly (or mathematically), *zero* is cultural rather then physical, and epistemological rather than ontological (105).

42. *PL*, II.629, VI.282 (Adversary); and James P. Boyd, *Bible Dictionary* (New York: Ottenheimer, 1958), 84. Of course, Satan is also called, "Enemy," "Foe," and the like. In *PL*, VI.262–64, Satan becomes, by syntactical blurring, not only the "Author of evil," but also e/Evil itself.

43. E.g., John Peter, *A Critique of "Paradise Lost"* (New York: Columbia University Press, 1960), 87.

44. Commentary on the hairy hillside of the Mount famously goes back to C. S. Lewis, *A Preface to "Paradise Lost,"* (1942; rpt. New York: Oxford, 1961), 47–50. On the imagery of Spenser's Garden, see part 3, chapter 14, "Flowers and Boars: Surmounting Sexual Binarism in the Garden of Adonis" in this volume; on the resemblance between Spenser's Garden Mount and Milton's, also Fowler, ed., 222n135. On the resemblance between Spenser's Melibean landscape in Book VI.x and Milton's Eden, see part 1, chapter 6, "Spenser's Use of Chaucer's *Melibee*: Allegory, Narrative, History."

45. The current *locus classicus* for the double perspective of Milton's presentation of Eden may well be Stanley E. Fish's *Surprised by Sin: The Reader in Paradise Lost* (London: Macmillan, 1967), e.g., 136; cf. 129, 156. Among Fish's acknowledged antecedents are Arnold Stein, *Answerable Style: Essays on "Paradise Lost"* (Minneapolis: University of Minnesota Press, 1953), 52–74; and Christopher Ricks, *Milton's Grand Style* (Oxford: Clarendon, 1963), 109–17. Fish's "monolithic" emphasis on the fallen reader, whose only recourse is mindless doctrine, has been roundly criticized in recent years: e.g., William Kolbrener, *Milton's Warring Angels: A Study of Critical Engagements* (Cambridge: Cambridge University Press, 1997), 128–29, 132, 134; and John P. Rumrich, *Milton Unbound: Controversy and Reinterpretation* (Cambridge: Cambridge University Press, 1996), 1–23, 60–64; also Herman, 1–8, 16–19. Joanna Picciotto criticizes Fish for erecting "a *rigid* boundary" between Eden and fallen experience instead of seeing Eden as "an alien [othered or doubled?] experience of the world we already know": "Reforming the Garden: The Experimentalist Eden and *Paradise Lost*," *ELH*, 72 (2005), 23–78, here 40 (my emphasis).

46. For pertinent uses by Milton and Satan, see *PL*, IV.318, 388; and for Adam's two uses, *PL*, VIII.501, IX.373. Adam's first use comes in conversation with Raphael and refers to Eve's turning away from him because of her "Innocence and Virgin Modestie" when first she sees him; the meaning of *innocence* here is a blend

of "integrity, purity, sexual inexperience," and it raises the knotty issues about purity and experience that both Adam's impassioned perception of his relation to Eve and morally loaded words always raise for readers of the poem. The roots of Latin *nocere*, "to harm, injure"—whence, with the negative *in*, English *innocence* is derived via cognates—are entangled in a nexus of related words: e.g., Latin *necare*, "to kill," and *nex*, "(violent) death," and Greek *nekros*, "corpse": that death is finally an unfathomable concept for unfallen Adam and Eve hardly justifies their fall, unless we base knowledge on loss and faith on fear of punishment. John Peter treats the character of Adam and Eve's innocence suggestively: e.g., 92–96, 99–103, 133–34; cf. also James Grantham Turner, *One Flesh: Paradisal Marriage and Sexual Relations in the Age of Milton* (Oxford: Clarendon, 1987), 308–9. In the present volume, discussion of natural innocence and wantonness in part 1, chapter 6, and part 2, chapter 7, on Spenser's Melibee (Book VI) and *Muiopotmos*, respectively, relates quite suggestively to these subjects in *Paradise Lost*.

47. See *PL*, III.108: "Reason is also choice." Such a basic description of right reason as Douglas Bush's remains useful: "the candle of the Lord is the *recta ratio* of the humanistic tradition, and *recta ratio* is found . . . where *fides* is found. . . . [For] Milton and others, reason signifies not the mere logical and critical faculty but the Platonic capacity for attaining divine truth, the whole unified personality, the philosophic conscience, of the well-disposed man": *English Literature in the Earlier Seventeenth Century, 1600–1660*, 2nd ed. (Oxford: Oxford University Press, 1962), 360–61.

48. The brigands who spoil Melibee's landscape and swarm around Calidore like "flyes" are pointedly described as "theeues," one of the most traditional figures for sinners, the Old Adam, and Satan himself in theological writings and one invoked earlier by Spenser (VI.xi.41, 48). Calidore's rescue of Pastorella alludes to the Harrowing of Hell: see my *Growth of a Personal Voice*, 181–83. Sure signs of the paradisal nature of Mount Acidale are evident in Spenser's initial description:

> It was an hill plaste in an open plaine,
> That round about was bordered with a wood
> Of matchlesse hight, that seem'd th' earth to disdaine,
> In which all trees of honour stately stod,
> And did all winter as in sommer bud. . . .

At the foot of the Mount a river "His siluer waues did softly tumble downe, / Vnmard with ragged mosse or filthy mud, / Ne mote wylde beastes . . . Thereto approach, ne filth mote therein drowne" (VI.x.6–7). Fowler, ed., 222–23nn135, 136–37, 138–43, cites resemblances between this and other Spenserian landscapes and Milton's descriptions of Eden.

49. To expand this description of Book VI, see part 1, chapter 6, "Spenser's Use of Chaucer's *Melibee*: Allegory, Narrative, History."

50. *FQ*, II.vii.4; *PL*, VI.512; cf. II.983–84, Satan's offer to Chaos to "reduce [the created world] / To her original darkness and your sway."

51. As Leonard has observed, "The War in Heaven is in large part a struggle for Heaven's language" (186). It is equally a struggle over matter and, perhaps most inclusively, over *substance*, in all its senses, which include linguistic/rhetorical, philosophical, and scientific ones. Cf. also Robert L. Entzminger, *Divine Word: Milton and the Redemption of Language* (Pittsburgh, Penn.: Duquesne University Press, 1985), chap. 2, esp. 52, 58.

52. *PL*, V.829–30, 843–44: my emphasis. Commenting on God's becoming "All in All," John T. Shawcross remarks Michael's reduction of his army to the Son in the War in Heaven and reduction of the devils' size in the concluding similes of Book I: see his contribution to "Forum: Milton's *Christian Doctrine*," *Studies in English Literature*, 32 (1992), 155–62, here 157–58. On God's reduction, cf. Norbrook's perceptive discussion: 475–77.

53. *PL*, III.319–20, 340–41: my emphasis. On the exquisite linguistic subtleties at the conclusion of God's statement, see Albert C. Labriola, "'All in All' and 'All in One': Obedience and Disobedience in *Paradise Lost*," in *"All in All": Unity, Diversity, and the Miltonic Perspective*, ed. Charles W. Durham and Kristin A. Pruitt (Selinsgrove, Penn.: Susquehanna University Press, 1999), 39–47.

54. Shoaf appears to understand *Aufhebung* merely as cancellation and raising, overlooking preservation, continuity, and, indeed, trace in this instance (47). In effect, he also reads *Paradise Lost* as an allegory of language (although he avoids the term *allegory*), and he seriously underestimates other investments evident in the poem—in morality and history, for example. He wants to see God's Son as a metaphor and as not one, that is, apparently, as a metonymy (102). His reading of Calvin puzzles me; indeed, I find his seventh chapter questionable: e.g., propriety, impropriety, and metaphor, Calvin—all subjects I discuss in *Translating Investments*, chaps. 3 and 7. Even as I express strong reservations, however, I think there is much in Shoaf's book that provokes in the better sense. I also (and relatedly) find provocative Herman Rapaport's *Milton and the Postmodern* (Lincoln: University of Nebraska Press, 1983), chaps. 2–3. Rapaport is clearly engaged in translation himself, but his transfers are often interesting ones.

55. Lexically, the German verb *aufheben*, cognate of the noun *Aufhebung*, variously signifies "lift," "raise"; "keep," "preserve"; "abolish," "suspend."

56. I have discussed the historical context of signification at length in *Words That Matter* and *Translating Investments*, both of which further explain and expand on my statements here.

57. See *Translating Investments*, 17–22, for relevant analysis of the Ricoeur-Derrida debate.

58. When Michael Lieb, *The Sinews of Ulysses: Form and Convention in Milton's Works* (Pittsburgh, Penn.: Duquesne University Press, 1989), 19, argues on the basis of *Christian Doctrine* that for Milton "there is simply no dichotomy between 'body' and 'spirit,'" I assume this also applies to darkness and light for Milton, but I wonder (with Milton's devils) whether it extends as well to good and evil. For discussion of the interestingly analogous attempt of Spenser's materialist Giant to weigh words, including *true* and *false*, see my *Words That Matter*, 167–89, esp. 180–85.

59. Philip J. Gallagher observes suggestively that without God's irony, "you [would simply] have . . . Hesiod's Zeus": "*Paradise Lost* and the Greek Theogony," *English Literary Renaissance* 9 (1979), 121–48, here 140.

60. Bryson's argument (132–47) that representation of the Son develops in the poem—in chronological rather than narrative order, i.e., from Books V–VI to Book III—might be applied to the Father as well, particularly since the narrator of the War in Heaven in V–VI is Raphael, whose voice is elsewhere subject to question (e.g., his characterization of Eve in responding to Adam: VIII.561–94). *Paradise Lost* affords a variety of representations (images, conceptions) of God the Father.

61. See Hebrews 11:1: "faith is the substance of things hoped for, the evidence of things not seen." William B. Hunter, *Visitation Unimplor'd: Milton and the Authorship of "De Doctrina Christiana"* (Pittsburgh, Penn.: Duquesne University Press, 1998), chap. 8, makes a case for Milton's having attempted, through Raphael's monist pronouncements, to resolve mind-body dualism "at the expense of confusing two different meanings of spirit." He finds a "concomitant failure" in *Christian Doctrine* (133, cf. 130–32). *Spirit*, like *substance*, is a highly variable word-concept in the period. Is a vapor a material spirit or spiritual matter in the same sense that God is spirit? Do the same powers (e.g., omnipresence, omniscience) pertain to these?

62. *FQ*, I.xi.8, 10, 18; *PL*, II.927, 941–42.

63. Traditionally interchangeable, serpents and dragons are often referred to synonymously in the Renaissance and Middle Ages: cf. Revelation 12.7–9.

64. *PL*, II.948–50; cf. IV.15–16, 114–20.

65. An especially striking instance of Spenser's use of the sea/see pun can be found in *FQ*, Book V.ii.37, on which see my *Words That Matter*, 171–72, 185.

66. William B. Hunter, Jr., "Milton's Power of Matter," *Journal of the History of Ideas*, 13 (1952), 551–62, is a basic reference for the material of Milton's chaos, which has much exercised Miltonists in recent decades.

67. Schwartz, *Remembering and Repeating*, 11; John Peter Rumrich, *Matter of Glory: A New Preface to "Paradise Lost"* (Pittsburgh, Penn.: University of Pittsburgh Press, 1987), 7–8; Michael Lieb, *The Dialectics of Creation: Patterns of Birth and Regeneration in "Paradise Lost"* (Amherst: University of Massachusetts Press, 1970), 16–17; Rogers, 219; Norbrook, 472. In *Milton Unbound*, Rumrich more recently has described chaos as representing "a principle of indeterminacy and randomness essential to divine power," and functioning as "God's womb" (141). Rumrich considers the views in his two books on Milton in general unchanged (*Milton Unbound*, vi). Unless otherwise noted, *parenthetical* reference to Rumrich's argument from this point forward is to *Matter of Glory*. Hunter agrees with Lieb that chaos is neutral: *Visitation Unimplor'd*, chap. 8, here 25. (In notes to part 3, chapter 17, in this volume, "Patience and Passion," I have indicated my rejection of Hunter's view that Milton is not responsible for *De Doctrina*.)

68. Cf. Norbrook, 472: "the viewpoint in Book II is Satan's."

69. *PL*, II. 895, 907, 972, 988. Rumrich, too, distinguishes a "malignant" Chaos from chaos, but he never adequately explains why: *Milton Unbound*, 118–19, 127. He accepts Fallon's stunted view of allegory and associates allegory merely with

abstraction and frozen stasis (128, 130, 140). He also identifies chaos (but not allegory) as a state of "as yet unrealized potential for being, the precondition of creation" (128). Elsewhere it is "the as yet unrealized capacity for otherness" (145).

70. Flannagan, ed., 410n256, observes the play on "God-speed."

71. My summary of part of Rumrich's argument borrows from my review of his *Matter of Glory* in "Recent Studies in the English Renaisssance," *Studies in English Literature*, 29 (1989), 157–99, here 184–85.

72. Heiko Augustinus Oberman, *The Harvest of Medieval Theology: Gabriel Biel and Late Medieval Nominalism* (Cambridge, Mass.: Harvard University Press, 1963): e.g., 1–9, 249–80. Besides the privileging of the will in Scotistic writings, Scotus' wondering, "Can matter think?" might have caught Milton's attention: Christopher Cannon, *The Grounds of English Literature* (Oxford: Oxford University Press, 2004), 7.

73. Rumrich, *Matter of Glory*, 148–49; *Areopagitica*, *Prose Works*, II, 516. Archbishop Thomas Cranmer, a major architect of the Reformation in England, and his close associates were trained in the nominalist tradition: e.g., see my *Translating Investments*, 49–50, 55.

74. Illuminating Milton's interest in Spenser's poetry, Hill, *English Revolution*, 27, 39, observes the devotion to it of the elder Alexander Gil, High Master of St. Paul's School during Milton's years there. As Classical as Milton's learning was, and as broadly European his interests and acquaintances, in both prose and poetry he was emphatically aware of himself as an *English* author. The dedicatory poems that appeared in 1668 with the reissue of *Paradise Lost* both observe this nationalism: thus Samuel Barrow—"Et tamen haec hodie terra Britanna legit [And yet the British land reads them today]"—and John Dryden: "Three poets, in three distant ages born, / Greece, Italy, and England did adorn" (Fowler, ed., 51–52, 55).

75. Rumrich, *Matter of Glory*, 161–62, 172–73. Rumrich, 158, relevantly cites *Christian Doctrine*, *Prose Works*, VI, 353 (I.x). Suggestively, Fowler, ed., also notes a scholastic distinction between "*pura naturalia* (properties of human nature *per se*)" and "*donum supernaturale*," the "super-added 'original righteousness'" of Adam and Eve, which was contingent on their obedience to God's decree concerning the apple (604n98).

76. Cf. Hill, *English Revolution*, 367: Milton appears to have invented the exaltation of the Son "in order to have an *unexplained divine decree* leading to the fall of the angels analogous to that which led to the Fall of Man" (my emphasis). Also, *Christian Doctrine*, *Prose Works*, VI, 338 (I.viii): "Good temptations are those which God uses to tempt even righteous men, in order to prove them. . . . either to exercise or demonstrate their faith or patience, as in the case of Abraham or Job, or to lessen their self-confidence and prove them guilty of weakness, so that they may become wiser and others may be instructed." Milton subsequently adds, "Good temptation, then, is . . . to be desired" (339). Earlier in the same chapter, he writes, "Even in sin, . . . we see God's providence at work, not only in permitting it or withdrawing his grace, but often in inciting sinners" (331); yet, "it must not be concluded that he [God] is the originator even of the very smallest sin" (332).

77. Rumrich, *Milton Unbound*, 47, considers Presbyterians generally inclined to history and legal precedent, and Independents inclined to seeing the future in terms of an ideal order that "transcend[s] previous laws and institutions." Noting that "innovation in law [especially if sudden] is a bad thing," Herman aligns God's elevation of the Son and Satan's response with "the legal, philosophical, and political conflicts that led to the English Revolution" (100). Norbrook, 476–77, argues conversely that "Satan's resistance to innovation" aligns him with "defenders of a traditional constitution who fail to see the need for periodic change"; he also suggests that "Milton's God . . . is a king with distinct overtones of a republican founding legislator"; see also 478, however. As often in *Paradise Lost*, more than one reading pertains to passages that are densely significant: partial resemblances of Satan to participants in "*the good Old Cause*" and of God to a Stuart monarch complicate, without canceling, the moral reading on which my argument focuses: quotation from *The Readie and Easie Way*, 2nd ed., in *Complete Prose Works*, rev. ed., vol. 7, ed. Robert W. Ayers (New Haven, Conn.: Yale University Press, 1980), 462. Examining *The Readie and Easie Way*, Kolbrener finds Milton by 1660 skeptical of all political models (23–24; cf. 102, 135).

78. I have used the qualification "virtually" because in *Milton Unbound*, Rumrich belatedly suggests that "In the frame of prelapsarian allegorical narrative, Chaos appears as Satan's material accomplice, hostile to God's actual creation"; he then aligns the divine substance of chaos with the capacity for free will (145). His admirably fertile explanations—indeed, his multiple translations of chaos—become somewhat dizzying, however. Satan himself, moreover, is already fallen, not prelapsarian, in Milton's narrative rendering of chaos, a further complication for Rumrich's argument.

79. Fowler, ed., 101n678, observes that Spenser's Mammon "similarly presides over gold smelting" in an episode admired by Milton (*Areopagitica*, *Prose Works*, VI, 516).

80. Fallon, 215.

81. See my comments in this volume on Serena in part 1, chapter 6, "Spenser's Use of Chaucer's *Melibee*: Allegory, Narrative, History"; also, more generally on Serena, in *Growth of a Personal Voice*, 174–77.

82. *PL*, I.254: my emphasis; II.798–801.

83. *PL*, II.654, 796–97; IV.75.

84. Quotation from G. J. Whitrow, *The Natural Philosophy of Time* (1961; rpt. New York: Harper and Row, 1963), 111. See Plotinus, *The Six-Enneads*, trans. Stephen Mackenna and B. S. Page, *Great Books of the Western World*, vol. 17 (Chicago: Encyclopedia Britannica, c. 1952), *En*.IV.iii.24–32, iv.1–8. A similar discovery of awareness and recovery of memory occurs in the quest of Spenser's Artegall in Book V: see my discussion in "'Nor Man It Is,': The Knight of Justice in Book V of Spenser's *Faerie Queene*," in *Essential Articles for the Study of Edmund Spenser*, ed. A. C. Hamilton (Hamden, Conn.: Archon, 1972), 447–70, here 462–63.

85. Leonard's ingenious argument, against most critics' views, that Satan does recognize Sin, although not as his daughter, strikes me as special pleading. It assumes

that the figure of Sin has not changed for the worse since her birth, first pregnancy, and fall into hell, as well as that Satan's powers of recognition, including self-recognition, are not fundamentally in doubt (120–24).

86. Cf. *PL*, I.794: many a seraph and cherub apparently fell into hell with Satan. In any event, Milton is inconsistent with respect to angelic orders, referring to Raphael as both Seraph and Virtue, for example (V.277, 371). He appears not to follow any authority on angelic hierarchy closely.

87. *Christian Doctrine*, *Prose Works*, VI, 211 (I.v): my distinction uses Milton's language (as Carey renders it) in his discussion of the distinction of God from his Son: "do not take *substance* to mean total essence"; cf. *De Doctrina*, 192: "modo ne substantia pro essentia tota accipiatur." Philip J. Gallagher argues that "Raphael's ignorance of the painful birth of Sin establishes the satanic authorship of Athena's birth in ... [Hesiod's] *Theogony*": "'Real or Allegoric': The Ontology of Sin and Death in *Paradise Lost*," *English Literary Renaissance*, 6 (1976), 317–35, here 332. For Gallagher, the whole point of this birth in Milton's poem is to criticize the Greek myth and to rationalize its origin. For a more recent and broader version of this point, see Pitt Harding, "Milton's Serpent and the Birth of Pagan Error," *Studies in English Literature*, 47 (2007), 161–77; and relatedly, Gregory Machacek, "Allusion," *PMLA*, 122 (207), 522–36, here 531–32. On the uniqueness of God's knowledge of the heart's thoughts, see Helen Gardner, ed., *The Elegies and the Songs and Sonnets of John Donne* (1965; rpt. Oxford: Clarendon, 1970), 210n16: Gardner cites Aquinas and a sermon by Donne that invokes biblical authority. See also the angel Uriel's inability to discern Satan's hypocrisy (the thoughts of his heart) in *PL*, III.681–84.

88. Stella Revard, "Milton's Critique of Heroic Warfare in *Paradise Lost* V and VI," in *Studies in English Literature*, 7 (1967), 119–39, here 129–31; for more extensive discussion, see also Stella Purce Revard, *The War in Heaven: "Paradise Lost" and the Tradition of Satan's Rebellion* (Ithaca, N.Y.: Cornell University Press, 1980), e.g., chap. 1. Cf. Loewenstein, 228; also Labriola's analysis of (dis)obedience in Book V and elsewhere ("'All in All,'" 39–47). For relevant discussion of Spenser's Despair, see part 1, chapter 4, "Allegory, Irony, Despair: Chaucer's *Pardoner's* and Franklin's *Tales* and Spenser's *Faerie Queene*, Books I and III," in this volume.

89. *The Muse's Method: An Introduction to "Paradise Lost"* (Cambridge, Mass.: Harvard University Press, 1962), 39. Fallon discusses Summers' term (184). Rapaport pertinently observes Satan's "desire to infuse Sin with his own seed, to inseminate her with a Satanic being that will prove . . . that Satan, consequently, has the power to create life" (27).

90. For extensive consideration of bases for a poetic intertext when a common biblical referent (e.g., *vetus homo*, "the old man," or "body of this death") is involved, see part 1, chapter 4, in this volume, "Allegory, Irony, Despair," especially the discussion of the Pardoner and Book I. Other chapters engaging the issue of common sources—such as the Bible and Classical myth—that underlie intertextual relations are chapter 9, part 2, "Chaucer's *Parliament of Fowls* and Refractions of a Veiled Venus," and chapter 16, part 3, "Beyond Binarism: Eros/Death and Venus/

Mars." Discussion of this issue recurs in various other contexts throughout the present volume.

91. James Carscallen, "The Goodly Frame of Temperance: The Metaphor of Cosmos in *The Faerie Queene, Book II*," in *Essential Articles*, ed. Hamilton, 347–65, here 360–61. For Paul's desire to be delivered from "the body of this death," again see Romans 7:24.

92. On the topos *pati et agere*, see part 3, chapter 17, on "Patience and Passion in Shakespeare and Milton."

93. On God's permissive will, see, for example, *PL*, III.685. This will, as well as God's omniscience, is recurrently in evidence in Book III, e.g., 78–92.

94. Barbara K. Lewalski, *The Life of John Milton: A Critical Biography* (Oxford: Blackwell, 2000), 508.

95. For a moment, Satan's "jealous leer maligne" comes to mind; in a verbal echo of the jealous Malbecco's behavior, Satan also eyes Adam and Eve "askance" in the same passage (*PL*, IV.503–4; *FQ*, III.ix.27). Cf. the related descriptions of Suspect's "looking still askaunce" in Spenser's Masque of Busirane (III.xii.15.2), and of Malecasta's wanton looks "askaunce" in Castle Joyous (III.1.41). Cf. also Turner, 262, on Satan's being driven partly "by thwarted love of Eve."

96. Angus Fletcher, *Allegory: The Theory of a Symbolic Mode* (Ithaca, N.Y.: Cornell University Press, 1964), e.g., chap. 1. Fletcher's theory of allegory makes all expressions of this form compulsive and demonic. As indicated earlier, I consider such extension heady but unsound.

97. Cf. Linda Gregerson on Malbecco in her "Protestant Erotics: Idolatry and Interpretation in Spenser's *Faerie Queene*," *ELH*, 58 (1991), 1–34; Gregerson revisits and revises the concerns of her article in *The Reformation of the Subject: Spenser, Milton and the English Protestant Epic* (Cambridge: Cambridge University Press, 1995), chap. 2. I still find the article useful, however.

98. For an extensive list of sources and analogues for the serpent woman, see Hamilton, ed., *FQ*, 35*n*14.7–9; Fowler, ed., 142–43; John Steadman, "Error," in *The Spenser Encyclopedia*, ed. A. C. Hamilton, et al (Toronto: Toronto University Press, 1990), 252–53.

99. See my "Redcrosse and the Descent into Hell," *ELH*, 36 (1969), 470–92, here 471–74.

100. That Spenser's line suggestively recalls Chaucer's *Parliament of Fowls* would have made it more, not less, attractive to Milton. On Spenser and *The Parliament*, again see part 2, chapter 9, "Chaucer's *Parliament of Fowls* and Refractions of a Veiled Venus in *The Faerie Queene*."

101. On typology as allegory, see the discussion of Erich Auerbach in my introduction.

102. Hamilton, ed., *FQ*, 387*n*57, mentions avian associations in Malbecco's metamorphosis. Malbecco's claws, his life in darkness, his (jealous) wakefulness, and his diet of toads and frogs might suggest an owl. The association of another bird, a cock, with jealous wakefulness might have reinforced the avian association: John M.

Steadman, "Spenser's House of Care: A Reinterpretation," *Studies in the Renaissance*, 7 (1960), 207–24, here 223–24. See my following note, as well.

103. As earlier noted, in the War in Heaven Satan thus retrospectively becomes, by significant syntactical blurring that foreshadows the eventual realization of his fate in Book X, not only the "Author of evil," but also e/Evil itself: "Author of evil, unknown till thy revolt / Unnam'd in Heav'n, now plenteous, as thou seest / These Acts of hateful strife" (VI.261–63). The ambiguous modifier "unknown" effectually merges author with evil act and hateful results. Leonard discusses this syntactical blurring in connection with the naming of Satan, concluding, "Since Michael goes on to speak of Satan's unprecedented evil acts, the prime meaning is that 'evil' was unnamed" (119). See also *PL*, IX.463–64: "That space the Evil one abstracted stood / From his own evil."

104. *PL*, IV.428, VIII.325 (my emphasis), X.485–501.

105. *PL*, IX.792–801, 1008, 1017–28.

106. Fowler, ed., 548–49n175–81, 550n203–8, 570n566–70.

107. A. J. A. Waldock notoriously considers the metamorphosis of the devils "the essence of cartoon-technique": *Paradise Lost and Its Critics* (1947; rpt. Cambridge: Cambridge University Press, 1961), 92; cf. his cry of indignation: "It was mean of Milton to use his Satan so"(87). Waldock's characterizing as a cartoon Satan's snaky metamorphosis is actually perspicacious; Milton's century, like the one before, was much taken with *cartoons*, understood as allegorical and satirical drawings, although, until quite late in the seventeenth century, they used other words for them, including *emblem* and *grotesque*. The illustrations in the borders of manuscripts come to mind, as do the pictures of Arcimboldo, grotesque, half-bird or half-beast cartoons of Queen Elizabeth I, Rabelaisian drolleries, illustrated Ovids, and the like. (Illustrations and discussions of Rabelaisian drolleries are available in Anne Lake Prescott, *Imagining Rabelais in Renaissance England* [New Haven, Conn.: Yale University Press, 1998]).

108. See Hamilton, ed., *FQ*, for the gloss on *Munera*: 517n9.9.

109. On the ritual nature of much physical punishment in the early modern period, see Michel Foucault, *Discipline and Punish: The Birth of the Prison*, trans. Alan Sheridan (New York: Random House, 1979), chaps. 1–2. Foucault cites Vico's remark that "this old jurisprudence was 'an entire poetics'" (45). He also makes a point relevant to Spenser's depiction of Artegall that is often overlooked, namely, "the great spectacle of punishment ran the risk of being rejected by the very people to whom it was addressed" (63, cf. 59–60). On Artegall's justice in Book V, see my *Words That Matter*, 167–89. In an unpublished essay, Luke Wilson draws provocative analogies between "Poetic Justice" (his title) in law and in literature: cited with permission. Like my examples from Spenser, his discussion qualifies and updates Foucault's seminal treatment.

110. Cf. Hill, *English Revolution*, 408–9: on the use of *some say* and *perhaps* in Milton's poetry.

111. *FQ*, II.x.53; III.iii.7–13, vi.46–48; IV.x.41, xi.28; V.viii.31, 49, x.9–10, 29, xi.20.

112. On Bacon's historiography and practice of history in his *Henry VII*, see my *Biographical Truth: The Representation of Historical Persons in Tudor-Stuart Writing* (New Haven, Conn.: Yale University Press, 1984), chaps. 9–10, esp. 164, 178–81. On euhemerism, or the interpretation of myth as veiled history, see Jean Seznec's classic discussion in *The Survival of the Pagan Gods: The Mythological Tradition and Its Place in Renaissance Humanism and Art*, trans. Barbara F. Sessions (1953; rpt. New York: Harper, 1961), esp. chap. 1. More recently, Bart van Es has studied *Spenser's Forms of History* (Oxford: Oxford University Press, 2002): cf. his treatment of euhemerism, 112–38. In van Es's argument, Spenser "demonstrates a profound awareness of historical forms"—all contemporary varieties of them (vi).

113. For fuller discussion of the final verse paragraph of *Paradise Lost*, see part 3, chapter 18, of this volume.

114. On the House of Busirane and the beginning of Book IV, see my *Translating Investments*, chap. 6, and my essay "Britomart's Armor in Spenser's *Faerie Queene*: Reopening Cultural Matters of Gender and Figuration," *English Literary Renaissance* (forthcoming 2008).

115. Borris describes Milton's "cosmos *ex Deo*" as "a general allegoresis of his God" and, thinking Miltonic allegory metonymic, a matter of analogical correspondences and ideologized substitutions, he appears also to conflate it with allegoresis (252). For me, these categorical terms are misleading. As practiced by a medieval exegete, allegoresis typically involved identification of abstract ideas or transcendent referents in a passage thought to be allegorical. Such allegoresis is notorious for its insensitivity to sensory vehicle and temporal narrative and thus to significant form—to "substance" in any but a spiritual or abstract sense: e.g., Orpheus' looking back at his wife Eurydice when he rescues her from the underworld, interpreted as his desire for the sins of his past life: on allegoresis, cf. Carolynn Van Dyke, *The Fiction of Truth: Structures of Meaning in Narrative and Dramatic Allegory* (Ithaca, N.Y.: Cornell University Press, 1985), 44–45, 203; Stephen A. Barney, *Allegories of History, Allegories of Love* (Hamden, Conn.: Archon, 1979), 43–47; Quilligan, 29–32; Robert W. Hanning, "No [One] Way to Treat a Text: Donaldson and the Criticism of Engagement," *Chaucer Review*, 41 (2007), 261–70, here 262.

116. Shoaf comments helpfully on the contrast between the narcissistic relation of Satan to Sin and the Son's freely filial relation to the Father: "Narcissism . . . is the illusion of two where, in reality, there is only one. Equality [as asserted by the Father with respect to the Son] . . . obtains only where there are 'two or more essences' (or so Milton understood the matter)" in *Christian Doctrine*. "Real equality, then, is the impossibility of narcissism and incest, even as it is also the impossibility of identity" (129–30). Arguably, moral freedom, rather than equality, is the more basic issue, however.

117. Herman, 94–95, doubts that Beelzebub fronts for Satan, finding instead an instance of incertitude in Beelzebub's performance. In agreement with the critical consensus, I accept the Miltonic narrator's indication that Beelzebub and Satan had their strategy in place before the great consult began: *PL*, II.378–85.

118. Lieb, "Milton's 'Dramatick Constitution,'" 220–22, 232, relates the dialogue between Father and Son to the medieval debate among the Four Daughters of God (Mercy, Truth, Righteousness, Peace) that allegorizes Psalm 85. Likewise Barbara Kiefer Lewalski, *"Paradise Lost" and the Rhetoric of Literary Forms* (Princeton: Princeton University Press, 1985), 118–19; Lewalski is typically careful, however, to try to distance allegory from Milton's use of the tradition. Janet Leslie Knedlick, "Fancy, Faith, and Generative Mimesis in *Paradise Lost*," *Modern Language Quarterly*, 47 (1986), 19–47, observes that "the Son's speeches remain not ceremonial iteration but generative process of thought" (33). For her, the Son's first response to the Father is an act of *reading* with "sympathetic imagination" (31). Knedlick's characterization of divine speech is integral to her understanding of mimesis as generative in Tasso, Mazzoni, and Milton.

119. See Milton's negative statements about liturgy, as assembled by Christopher Hill in "Professor William B. Hunter, Bishop Burgess, and John Milton," *Studies in English Literature*, 34 (1994), 165–93, here 172.

120. On such qualities of ritual, see my *Words That Matter*, 175–76, and Maurice Bloch, "Symbols, Song, Dance and Features of Articulation," *European Journal of Sociology*, 15 (1974), 55–81.

121. Ricks, 112; Leonard, e.g., 177 ("The infection of language"), also chaps. 3–4.

122. Ricoeur, "The Metaphorical Process as Cognition, Imagination, and Feeling," in *On Metaphor*, ed. Sheldon Sacks (Chicago: University of Chicago Press, 1979), 141–57, here 143, 151. Also his *Rule of Metaphor*, 248, 254–56. Cf. Shoulson's perceptive discussion of transparency and mediation, literalism and literariness, in Milton's representation of God in Book III (chap. 3, esp. 104, 107, 115). Shoulson, 108, notes that the first simile in Milton's initial representation of heaven occurs in III.60–61 ("the Sanctities of Heaven / Stood thick as Starrs") and rightly considers it metonymic rather than metaphorical; monist substitution is apt here.

123. Where I find an openness of possibilities, another reader might see in God's opening puns *in potentia* merely the undermining of Milton's depiction of the deity, whether inadvertent or deliberate: e.g., William Empson's *Milton's God*, rev. ed. (London: Chatto and Windus, 1965); notoriously comparing Milton's God to Stalin (146), Empson intends to expose the evils of Christianity. Empson's work on Milton has gained new respect in recent decades (e.g., Rumrich, *Milton Unbound*; Kolbrener, Bryson, Herman).

124. E.g., Fowler, ed.: of course Fowler's modernized spelling requires the capitalization of *ingrate*.

125. Typically and tellingly, Irene Samuel characterizes the Father's first speech as "passionless logic" and the "toneless voice of the moral law." She sees it as *enabling* the "compassionate tone" of the Son, and, anticipating recent arguments (e.g., Bryson, 131), she treats the *development* of the Father's view in interaction with the Son's: "The Dialogue in Heaven: A Reconsideration of *Paradise Lost*, III, 1–417," in *Milton: Modern Essays in Criticism*, ed. Arthur E. Barker (New York: Oxford,

1965), 233–45, here 235. More recently, cf. Shoulson, 108–110, 115. Lieb, "Milton's 'Dramatick Constitution,'" 216, disagrees with Samuel's characterization of the Father's first speech, instead considering it impassioned, righteously indignant, morally outraged (224–25). I am persuaded, on the basis both of the text and of performance, that the speech can legitimately be read (or heard) more than one way and that it participates in a representation of the Godhead that is developmental and various, whether within Book III or elsewhere in the poem. It thus participates in "the personalities in the Godhead," albeit not entirely in the dramatic sense Lieb (218) invokes in citing a longer form of this Miltonic phrase from Sumner's translation of *De Doctrina*, namely, "the drama of the personalities in the Godhead": *De Doctrina*, XIV, 196–97 (I.v). In context, the longer phrase is part of Milton's refusal *advocare* ("to summon," whence English "to advocate") "that whole drama of personalities" ("personalitatum illud totum drama advocem": my translation) and therefore equivocal evidence for Lieb's dramatic reading, which, however, has other bases meriting consideration.

126. Étienne Gilson, *The Philosophy of St. Bonaventure.*, trans. Illtyd Trethowan and F. J. Sheed (New York and London: Sheed and Ward, 1938), 224.

127. Treip, 203, also suggests "symbol." How symbol differs from metaphor (outside the ideology of Romanticism) is unclear: see de Man, "Rhetoric of Temporality, 187–228. Cf. Michael Lieb, "Reading God: Milton and the Anthropopathetic Tradition," *Milton Studies*, 25 (1989), 213–43, here 234: "the Son is not simply metaphor (similitude). Or if he is metaphor, he represents an entirely different order of troping from that customarily associated with rhetoric as a secular enterprise." Useful as I find Lieb's argument, I am not sure what this different order is. Denying conspicuous doubleness to it, I am again tempted to call it metonymy in some contexts or, in others, vision. Elsewhere in this article, Lieb opposes "real meaning" to metaphor and to rhetoric too simply, perhaps (e.g., 222–23, 224–26).

128. See my *Translating Investments*, chap. 7.

129. On metaphor, see my introduction to this volume, and *Translating Investments*, esp. chaps. 1–2, 4, 7.

130. Whether Milton's view of the Son should be considered "subordinationist," or Arian (or even Socinian) is a perennial issue. For a discussion of Milton's Arianism or Socinianism that I find persuasive, see Lieb, *Theological Milton*, chaps. 7–8: on the basis of *De Doctrina*, "we are not at liberty to conclude . . . that Milton is [properly and precisely speaking] an Arian [let alone a Socinian]" (272, 277; see 245–46 on Socianism). Cf. Gordon Campbell, Thomas N. Corns, John K. Hale, David I. Holmes, and Fiona J. Tweedie, "The Provenance of *De Doctrina Christiana*," *Milton Quarterly*, 31 (1997), 67–117, here 35–36 (item iv: on contradictions within *De Doctrina* regarding the Son's relation to the Father) and the notes in my "Patience and Passion," where I refer (*faute de mieux*) to Milton's proto-subordinationism (or *sui generis* Arianism) to register how he is not a traditional Trinitarian anymore than he is a traditional Calvinist, a traditional sectarian, or a traditional heretic of any stripe.

131. For a classic example, see Augustine on the cave of memory in the tenth book of the *Confessions*, ed. Michael P. Foley, trans. F. J. Sheed (1942; rpt. Indianapolis, Ind.: Hackett, 2006), 195–210; and in *The Trinity* (trans. Stephen McKenna,

The Fathers of the Church [Washington, D.C.: Catholic University of America Press, 1963], vol. XLV, 475, 506–10 (chap. xv.10, 2–23). For the Aristotelian view, see Richard Sorabji, *Aristotle on Memory* (Providence, R.I.: Brown University Press, 1972).

132. The entirety of Kolbrener's chap. 7 is illuminating with respect to Milton's representation of God.

133. On metaphor as arch-trope (arch-*translatio*), see my *Translating Investments*, chap. 7, and indexical entries for "Arch-Trope" and "Rhetorical Taxonomy." Simile, defined most commonly in modern terms as a comparison using *like* or *as*, was not recognized in these terms by the Roman rhetoricians and their Renaissance heirs: see *Translating Investments*, 256n7.

134. Cf. the relevant, intertextual movement up and down in the writings of John Calvin and of John Donne: *Translating Investments*, chap. 4, esp. 67–76.

135. Cf. vegetable imagery in the passage that is a touchstone for Milton's monism in *PL*, V.479–82: "So from the root / Springs the green stalk, from thence the leaves / More aerie, last the bright consummate floure / Spirits odorous breathes."

136. Aristotle, *Poetics*, 1457b7–24, here 16–18; *Rhetoric*, 1407a14–17, 1411a1–3, 1411b24–25: *The Complete Works of Aristotle*, ed. Jonathan Barnes, rev. Oxford translation, 2 vols. (Princeton, N.J.: Princeton University Press, 1984), II. See also my *Translating Investments*, 180–81: from merchants to painters and architects in the Renaissance, a trained eye for proportion was crucial. Bruce G. Carruthers and Wendy Nelson Espeland argue the "cognitive aspects" of such skills: "Accounting for Rationality: Double-Entry Bookkeeping and the Rhetoric of Economic Rationality," *American Journal of Sociology*, 97 (1991), 31–69. Chap. 7 of *Translating Investments* is also relevant for its contextualized examination of similitudes in rhetoric from the Romans through the end of the sixteenth century, including Erasmus, Melanchthon, and Talon (popularizer of Ramus), as well as a clutch of English rhetoricians.

137. Cf. Shoaf, 53–54.

138. Versus the too simply ontological view of Fallon, 182–83. Cf. Fallon's assertion that "From the time of *Eikonoklastes* Milton was done with fiction; his later poems are records of truth delivered directly, not through the mediation of allegories" (163). For Fallon, if not for Milton, language has apparently become transparent.

139. The story of Ellwood is recounted by Flannagan, ed., 711.

Index

Acrasia, 20, 311; and *Antony and Cleopatra*, 240–41, 243–44, 246, 250, 257, 380*n*7, 387*n*14; in the Bower of Bliss, 39–40, 119, 138–39, 148, 153, 219, 224–38; and *Venus and Adonis*, 206, 209–10
Adelman, Janet, 241–42, 244, 246, 248, 386*n*9, 387*n*10
adversative conjunction, 42–53, 158, 335*n*6
agency, 4, 19–20, 27, 134, 168, 373*n*40, 383*n*34, 399*n*22; authorial, 2, 20, 27, 228, 334*n*38; in *Muiopotmos*, 113, 121, 125; and *Paradise Lost*, 279, 295, 297, 313; and reascription in the Bower of Bliss, 228, 232–34, 383–84*n*37; of the signifier, 2, 19, 231, 281, 315, 323*n*8; and *standing* (concept), 265–66, 269
agere et pati, 259–64, 305. See also passion; patience
Alanus de Insulis, 90, 146, 357*n*21
allegory, conception of, 2, 5–8, 17–22, 105, 227–28, 236, 325*n*7, 328*nn*48–51, 390*n*33, 403–4*n*2; and allegorical projection, 36, 227, 267; and *Antony and Cleopatra*, 239, 241–42, 248, 250–54, 392*n*47; of authorship, 39–41, 95; and Chaucer, 29–31, 64–66, 69–70, 73, 93–95 (Melibee); and *figura*, 9–15; and the Garden of Adonis, 214–16, 219; and irony, 69, 272–73, 401*n*5; and *King Lear*, 183–92, 196, 370*n*16, 372*n*35; and Milton's adversarial Satan, 291–97, 307; and Milton's God, 311–19, 412*n*54, 419*n*115, 420*n*118; and Milton's landscape of hell, 286–91, 302, 307–8, 413–14*n*69; and Milton's "Real or Allegoric," 272–79, 402*n*118, 407*n*25; and Milton's Sin and Death, 302–6; and Spenser's *Muiopotmos*, 116, 350*n*11, 350*n*115; and *Venus and Adonis*, 201, 204, 212–13. See also duplicity and doubleness; form; landscape; metaphor
Allen, Graham, 3, 322*n*3, 323*n*8
Alpers, Paul J., 91–92, 94–95, 104–5, 232, 346*n*1, 349*n*34, 372*n*30
androcentrism, 224–38, 380*n*6
androgyny, 216, 225, 250, 379*n*29, 391*n*39. See also hermaphroditism
antiquity, 19–20, 43–46, 49–50, 79–80, 82–83, 85–86, 154–67, 193; ideal image of, 86, 161, 163, 167, 335*n*6
Aquinas, Saint Thomas, 261, 324*n*23, 398*n*18, 416*n*87; Duns Scotus and, 300; on patience, 396*n*12; on prudence, 81, 98, 343*n*14, 347*nn*19–20
Archimago, in *Faerie Queene*, Book I, 58, 62, 66–67, 69, 132, 141; and *Paradise Lost*, 284–85, 306, 311–12; as symbol, 34, 247
Aristotle, 3, 8, 87, 216, 318, 324–25*n*23, 376*n*10, 384*n*38; and Milton, 389*n*27, 398*n*21, 406*n*21; *Poetics* (mimesis), 5–6, 13–14, 245–46,

424 Index

284, 326n36; on prudence, 81, 97–98, 343n12, 347–48n20
Artegall, 37–38, 50–51, 71, 165, 177, 418n109; and Milton, 270, 308; and Shakespeare, 184, 250
Auerbach, Erich, 9–15, 292, 320, 325nn27–28, 326nn30–31, 326n34, 326n39, 402n14, 408n34, 417n101
aufhebung/aufheben (word-concept), 12, 14, 296, 325, 412nn54–55
Augustine, Saint, 65, 120, 300, 320, 328n49, 399n23, 404n5; Auerbach on, 10–11, 13; on despair, 63, 71; on memory, 81, 245, 345n23, 421n131; Ricoeur on, 15

Bacon, Sir Francis, 81, 156, 164–66, 309, 360n10, 361n26, 419n112
Bainton, Roland H., 396n8
Baker, J. H., 170, 363n5, 365n14
Bakhtin, Mikhail, 2, 333n25
Barley, Nigel, 363nn3–4
Barney, Stephen A., 6, 22, 331n10, 339n11, 419n115
Barthes, Roland, 2, 39, 334n35
Baxandall, Michael, 327n43
Beckett, J. C., 364n10
Beckett, Samuel, 20, 183, 370n21
Belsey, Catherine, 211–12
Belson, Joel Jay, 127–28, 352n5, 353n10, 353n17
Benjamin, Walter, 21, 328n48, 328n50, 387n12, 392n47, 400n27, 404n5, 409–10n40
Bennett, J. A. W., 146, 336n6, 354n1, 356n18, 357n22
Bennett, Joan S., 407n25
Bennett, Josephine Waters, 58, 137, 337n16, 357n25
Berger, Harry, Jr., 20–21, 28, 159, 343n13, 345n26, 378n21, 383–84n37; on the Bower of Bliss, 224–33, 236–37; on the Garden of Adonis, 205, 218, 220–21, 377–78n19; on gynephobia, 208; on the Temple of Venus, 152, 351n26, 358n36; on Venus and Adonis, 222
Berry, Craig A., 330n6
Berry, Philippa, 358n30, 377n12, 388nn22–23
Berry, Ralph, 372n34
Bialostosky, Don, 33
binaries and binarism, 2, 322–23n6; allegorical, 5–6, 20, 22; in the Garden of Adonis, 22, 214–23; in Milton, 259, 269–70, 272, 275, 281; in Shakespeare, 194, 239–58
Bloch, Maurice, 420n120
boars, 202–3, 209–10, 212, 214–23 passim, 248, 251, 253, 392n48
Boccaccio, Giovanni, 138–39, 353n17, 356n17, 357n28
Bodin, Jean, 169, 363n7, 368n44
Boethius, 87, 90, 116, 198, 261, 345n28
Bonaventure, Saint, 316, 340n23
Bonjour, Adrien, 241
Bono, Barbara J., 386n9, 390n30, 393n55
Booth, Stephen, 370n15, 372–73n36
Borris, Kenneth, 21, 312, 405–6n16, 419n115
Bosch, Hieronymus, 222
Bower of Bliss, 20–21, 39, 41, 119, 137–38, 144, 148, 224–38; in *Antony and Cleopatra*, 243–44, 249–50; in *Venus and Adonis*, 201, 206, 209
Bradley, A. C., 183–84, 186–87, 189, 196
Bradshaw, Brendan, 364n10, 364n13
Bradwardine, Thomas (archbishop), 112, 116
Brady, Ciaran, 364n10, 364n13
Breen, John M., 367n38
Brewer, D. S., 355n6, 357n20, 358n31
Bridges, John (bishop), 173
Britomart, 18, 30, 143, 216, 227, 237, 286, 311; and *Antony and Cleopatra*, 240–41, 250–51; in *Faerie Queene*,

Book III.iv, 70–75, 77–78; and
  Venus and Adonis, 205, 209–10
Brook, Peter, 369n6
Brooke, Nicholas, 369n10, 370n16,
  372–73n36
Brooks, Harold F., 201–2, 371n28,
  372n30
Bruns, Gerald, 61, 69, 204, 247, 345n26,
  355n8
Brutus, 128–29, 156–57, 161, 362n29
Bryskett, Lodowick, 378n24
Bryson, Michael, 407n25, 409n36,
  413n60
Budé, Guillaume, 163
Bunyan, John, 9–10, 407n25
Burke, Séan, 331n11, 334n35
Burlin, Robert, 76, 342n35
Burrow, J. A., 58, 337n16, 356n13
Bush, Douglas, 411n47
Butler, Judith, 332n21, 382n23,
  382–83n30

Cain, Thomas H., 334n33, 335n8,
  342n4, 408n31
Calvin, John, 109, 119–20, 300, 351n19,
  351n27, 412n54, 422n134
Campbell, Gordon, 397n17, 399n22,
  421n130
Cannon, Christopher, 324n23, 414n72
Canny, Nicholas, 364n10, 364n13
Carey, John, 397n17, 399n22, 400n28,
  409n37, 416n87
Carruthers, Bruce G., 422n136
Carruthers, Mary J., 343n10, 347–
  48n20, 348nn25–26, 381n15
Carscallen, James, 304, 372n32, 383n31
Cartari, Vincenzo, 357n27
Catullus, Gaius Valerius, 80
Cave, Terence, 355n8
Caxton, William, 331n13
Celovsky, Lisa, 392n45
Charles I (king of England), 288, 407n25
Chaucer, Geoffrey, 2, 8, 260, 270; inter-
  textuality and, 15, 17–19, 53, 177,
  228, 206. *See also* allegory;
  intertextuality
Book of the Duchess, 66
The Franklin's Tale, 18, 61, 70–78,
  134, 340–41nn21–29 passim,
  342nn34–35
General Prologue, 17, 28–37, 42–45,
  48, 55–56, 75, 134, 176, 333n28
The House of Fame, 32, 143
The Knight's Tale, 79, 87–89, 143,
  356n17
The Man of Law's Tale, 31–32, 331n13
The Merchant's Tale, 70, 357n20
The Miller's Tale, 232, 334n34
The Monk's Tale, 112
The Nun's Priest's Tale, 19, 22, 109–24
  passim
The Pardoner's Tale, 18, 61–70, 339n8
Parliament of Fowls, 19, 39, 66, 87,
  135–53, 291, 417n100
The Squire's Tale, 89, 356n16
The Tale of Melibee, 18, 27–28, 31, 33,
  92–101, 104–5, 346–47nn9–10,
  348n30
The Tale of Sir Thopas, 27–31, 54–59,
  70, 74, 89, 97, 126, 131, 136, 139–
  44, 153, 336n10, 341n30
Treatise on the Astrolabe, 57
Troilus and Criseyde, 18, 59–60, 84–
  87, 131, 134, 144, 232, 349n9,
  367n40, 393n54
The Wife of Bath's Prologue, 59, 70,
  131, 144, 393n54
Cheney, Donald, 329–30n5, 335n4,
  375n2, 377n17
Cheney, Patrick, 334n33, 387–88n19
Church, Ralph, 336n10
Cicero, 5, 21, 61, 98, 101, 291, 348n32
Cincotta, Mary Ann, 361–62n26
Clark, Andy, 4, 323n9
Cleopatra, 20, 150, 212, 222–23, 235; in
  Antony and Cleopatra, 240–45,
  248–53, 255–58
Coke, Sir Edward, 171

426 Index

containment (conceptual pun), 2, 77–78, 204, 207, 212, 215, 218–22, 293, 302, 314
Cook, Carol, 388*n*23, 390*n*35, 392*n*47, 394*n*56
Cooper, Thomas, 80
Corns, Thomas N., 397–98*n*17, 421*n*130
Cotton, Sir Robert, 128
Crampton, Georgia Ronan, 260, 395*n*4
Crane, Mary Thomas, 348*n*31, 363*n*4
Cranmer, Thomas (archbishop), 414*n*73
Cromwell, Oliver, 288, 407*n*25

Dante Alighieri, 10, 15, 20, 150, 183, 358*n*31, 406*n*23
David, Alfred, 329*n*2, 331*n*13, 334*n*34
Davies, Stevie, 375*n*2, 379*n*29
death, 21, 113, 131, 169, 171, 203–4, 225, 265, 268–69, 274, 278; in *Antony and Cleopatra*, 20, 241, 248, 251–58, 394*n*56; of the author, 2–3, 26, 334*n*35; in *King Lear*, 192, 194, 197, 199–200; Milton's figure of, 22, 302–4, 310, 316; in Spenser, 214–15, 218–19, 221–22, 225; in Spenser-Chaucer, 62–65, 67–71, 74–75; in Spenser-Milton, 281, 292–94, 285, 307–8, 312, 319, 409*n*38, 410–11*n*46, 416–17*n*90; in *Venus and Adonis*, 206–7, 209. *See also* despair; puns and punning: on dying; *vetus homo*
de Certeau, Michel, 382*n*23
de Lauretis, Teresa, 383–84*n*37
de Man, Paul, 31, 183, 190, 331*n*11, 386*n*8, 405*n*13, 421*n*127
Deats, Sara Munson, 385*n*1, 386*n*9, 390*n*32, 393*n*50
Dekker, Thomas, 174, 366*n*25
Deleuze, Gilles, 136
Dempster, Germaine, 76, 342*n*35
Dent, R. W., 365–66*n*22, 366*n*28
Derrida, Jacques, 296, 328*n*49, 412*n*57

Descartes, René, 289, 302
despair (in Spenser), 18, 28, 61–78, 96–97, 177, 188, 222, 339*n*10; and Milton, 265, 267, 284–85, 302–3. *See also* death; *vetus homo*
Dinshaw, Carolyn, 339*n*8, 339*n*11
Dobranski, Stephen B., 407*n*27
Doe, Norman, 170–71, 175, 365*n*15, 366*n*30
Donaldson, E. Talbot, 42–44, 48, 60, 72, 330*n*7, 333*n*28, 337*n*14, 337*n*22
Donne, John, 215, 331–32*n*15, 377*n*16, 396*n*9, 406*n*20, 416*n*87, 422*n*134
dragons, 131–33, 269–70, 312, 354*n*21, 400*n*63; Spenser-Milton, 285, 298–99. *See also* serpents
Drayton, Michael, 57, 337*n*14
Dryden, John, 305, 329*n*54, 382*n*20, 414*n*74
Du Cange, Charles du Fresne, 343*n*7, 343*nn*10–11, 345*n*24
Dubrow, Heather, 212
Duns Scotus, John, 300, 398*n*18, 414*n*72
duplicity and doubleness, 3, 21, 133, 191, 210, 250–51, 320, 322*n*4, 326–27*n*39; Chaucerian, 60, 143, 146, 153; as *dédoublement*, 29–39, 177, 246; and Duessa, 67, 285; in the Garden of Adonis, 214–20, 324*n*20, 378*n*24; in *Faerie Queene* Proem VI, 42, 45–48, 51–55; in Milton, 266–67, 270, 272–74, 278, 288–302, 312–16, 320. *See also* binaries and binarism

Eggert, Katherine, 229, 374*n*10, 374*n*13, 382*n*26, 387*n*10
Eisenstein, Elizabeth L., 154, 359*n*2
Eliot, T. S., 15, 406*n*23
Elizabeth I (queen of England), 169, 364*n*10, 418*n*107; and Spenser, 28, 45, 126–30, 133, 165, 236, 288, 335*n*6, 342*n*4, 352*n*2, 358*n*30

Elton, William R., 371*n*26, 372–73*nn*35–36
Empson, William, 369*n*13, 420*n*123
Enterline, Lynn, 338*n*1, 379*n*28
Entzminger, Robert L., 412*n*51
Erasmus, Desiderius, 82, 168, 177, 188, 351*n*25, 351*n*27, 367*n*40, 422*n*136
Espeland, Wendy Nelson, 422*n*136
Everyman, 7, 227, 324*n*18, 381*n*18

Fallon, Stephen M., 278–79, 289, 401*n*2, 402*n*18, 406*n*21, 407*n*27, 410*n*41
Ferguson, Arthur B., 362*n*29
Ferry, Anne Davidson, 21
Ficino, Marsilio, 261
fiction, 2, 6, 32, 219, 401*n*2 ; antiquity as, 159; and *Antony and Cleopatra*, 245–48, 255; in the Bower of Bliss; contrast with history, 104, 156, 163–66, 270, 322*n*4; Elizabeth I as, 51–53; and *King Lear*, 186, 189–91; self-conscious, 308–12
figura, 9–13, 15
Fike, Matthew A., 380*n*12
Fish, Stanley E., 264, 266–68, 396*n*11, 399–400*n*24, 400*n*26, 410*n*25
Flannagan, Roy, 264, 272, 395*n*7, 414*n*70, 422*n*139
Fletcher, Angus, 248, 305, 390*n*33, 417*n*96
Fly, Richard, 369*n*4, 370*n*16, 372–73*n*36
form, 4, 7–9, 14, 45, 135–36, 153, 194, 220, 261; in *Antony and Cleopatra*, 239–42, 246, 249–50, 257; content of, 2, 21–22, 65, 94, 225, 229–32, 323*n*8, 324*n*23, 328*nn*48–50, 383*n*35; history of, 69, 77; in Milton, 270, 272–79; in *Paradise Lost*, 280–85, 288, 300–2, 304, 307, 309–10, 313–16, 419*n*115. *See also* allegory; genre; metaphor
Foucault, Michel, 418*n*109

Fowler, Alastair, 6, 87; on *Paradise Lost*, 287, 298, 308, 376*n*5, 406*n*17, 406*n*22, 411*n*48, 414*n*75, 415*n*79, 420*n*124
Fowler, Earle Broadus, 138, 356*n*17
Foxe, John, 261
Frank, Manfred, 41, 334*n*38
Freccero, John, 341*n*28
Freinkel, Lisa, 396*n*8
Frye, Northrop, 6, 22, 190–91, 374*n*15
Frye, Susan, 332*n*19

Galen, 216, 376–77*n*10
Gallagher, Philip J., 413*n*59, 416*n*87
Garden of Adonis, 20, 129, 149, 214–25, 286, 294, 375–76*n*2; in Shakespeare, 202, 205–9, 222–23, 240, 243, 251–54, 256
Gardner, Helen, 416*n*87
Gathelus, 156, 158, 161
gender, 20–21, 23, 259–61; in *Antony and Cleopatra*, 239–43, 250–52, 254, 258, 382–83*n*30, 391*n*40; in the Bower of Bliss, 224–38, 382*n*24; in the Garden of Adonis, 214–23, 376–77*n*10, 379*n*29; in Spenser, 74, 141–42, 151. *See also* androcentrism; androgyny; binaries and binarism; hermaphroditism
Genette, Gérard, 321*n*1, 323*n*8, 331*n*14
genre, 4, 70, 75, 89, 101, 109, 239, 242–43, 370*n*18; concept of, 6, 323*n*8, 387*n*12
Geoffrey of Monmouth, 127
Giddens, Anthony, 179
Gil, Alexander, 414*n*74
Gillies, John, 406–7*n*24
Gilson, Étienne, 343*n*12, 396*n*12
Goddard, Harold C., 387–88*n*19
Goldberg, Jonathan, 150, 239, 338*n*25, 356*n*16, 358*n*35, 361*n*19
Goldman, Michael, 393–94*n*55
Gottfried, Rudolf, 157, 359–60*n*6, 360*n*10, 361*n*18

428 Index

Greenblatt, Stephen J., 236, 332–33*n*23, 384*n*41, 385*n*45
Greene, Thomas M., 355*n*8
Greenfield, Sayre N., 22
Greenlaw, Edwin, 336–37*n*13, 357*n*21, 357*n*25
Gregerson, Linda, 417*n*97
Gross, Kenneth, 252, 354*n*20, 354*n*22, 375*n*2, 377–78*n*19, 391*n*42, 393*n*50
ground-plot, 283–85, 292, 295, 306, 405–6*n*16
Guattari, Felix, 136
Guibbory, Achsah, 400*n*29
Guillory, John, 342*n*1, 354*n*1, 361–62*n*26
Guyon, 101–2, 138, 163–64, 243, 250, 390*n*31; in the Bower of Bliss, 39–40, 225, 228, 230–31, 233–34, 236; and *King Lear*, 188, 193–94, 196; and *Paradise Lost*, 291, 311. See also Mammon

Hadfield, Andrew, 367*n*38, 368*n*44
Hale, John K., 397–98*n*17, 421*n*130
Hamilton, A. C., 61–62, 340*n*23, 352*n*2, 354*n*21, 417*n*98, 417*n*102; on Argante, 126–28, 218, 352*n*5; on the Garden of Adonis, 221, 324*n*20, 377–78*nn*18–19, 378*n*24; on names, 352*n*2, 352*n*5
Hankins, John Erskine, 215–16, 324*n*20, 357*n*25, 374*n*4, 374*n*12, 375*n*2, 377*n*12, 393*n*52
Hansen, Elaine Tuttle, 72, 76, 341*n*26
Haraway, Donna J., 334*n*35
Harvey, Gabriel, 58, 162, 174–75, 331*n*15, 337*n*16, 366*n*29
Harwood, Ellen Aprill, 205–6, 212
Hawkins, Peter S., 148, 206, 340*n*15, 357*n*28, 358*n*30
Hegel, Georg Wilhelm Friedrich, 12, 296, 325*n*28
Heinemann, Margot, 239
Helgerson, Richard, 231

Herbert, George, 215, 272–79, 401*nn*7–8, 401–2*nn*10–11
Herman, Peter C., 328*n*51, 397*n*15, 400*n*25, 400*n*27, 415*n*77, 419*n*117
hermaphroditism: in *Antony and Cleopatra*, 241, 248, 250–51, 254, 391*n*39; in Spenser, 147–48, 216, 223, 311, 358*n*30, 380*n*7; in *Venus and Adonis*, 205. See also androgyny; gender
Herrup, Cynthia B., 367–68*n*42
Hesiod, 215, 226, 344*n*16, 413*n*59, 416*n*87
Hieatt, A. Kent, 152–53, 330*n*6, 336*n*10, 354*n*1, 355*n*4
Hill, Christopher, 378*n*24, 397*n*17, 400*n*28, 403*n*21, 414*n*74; on *Paradise Lost*, 407*n*25, 414*n*76, 418*n*110, 420*n*119
Hill, John M., 346–47*n*9, 348*n*30
Hippolytus, story of, 67, 227, 260, 290, 408*n*29
Hirsch, James, 390*n*32, 392*n*47
history, 5, 18, 20, 30, 32, 226, 236, 355*n*8, 360*n*10, 419*n*112; and antiquity, 154–79, 361*n*26, 362*nn*37–38; and *Antony and Cleopatra*, 239, 245, 249, 252; Auerbach on, 9–15, 325*nn*26–28; in Chaucer and Spenser, 27–28; in *Faerie Queene* Book VI, 81, 83, 88, 91–105; and *King Lear*, 186, 191; in Milton, 259, 270, 272; in *Muiopotmos*, 122, 125; in *Paradise Lost*, 276, 283–85, 288, 290–95, 309, 311, 407*n*25; Ricoeur on, 14–15; and Spenserian parody, 129–34
Hobbes, Thomas, 282, 289, 299, 301, 332–33*n*23, 383–84*n*37
Holmes, David I., 397–98*n*17, 421*n*130
Homer, 60, 75, 259–60
Hooker, Richard, 351*n*27, 365*n*15
Hoskyns, John, 363*n*3

Howard, Donald R., 339*n*8, 339*n*11, 346–47*n*9
Hunter, William B., Jr., 324–25*n*23, 397*n*17, 399*n*22, 402*n*11, 413*n*61, 413*nn*66–67

imitation, 1, 4–5, 14, 61, 109, 246, 280, 323*n*8, 338*n*1, 345*n*26, 355*n*8. See also mimesis
influence, 3–5, 19, 69, 136, 143, 243, 280–83, 298, 327*n*43
intertext (term), 1–3, 15–23, 321*n*1, 323*n*8; biblical, 416–17*n*90; Chaucer-Spenser, 43, 53–54, 58, 60, 135, 148; Spenser-Milton, 279, 306; Spenser-Shakespeare, 189. See also intertextuality
intertextuality (concept), 1–5, 17–22, 33, 134, 162, 190, 315, 321–22*nn*1–2, 322*nn*5–6, 323*n*8, 327*n*30, 327*n*41, 327*n*45; in the Bower of Bliss, 228, 236; in Chaucer-Spenser, 54, 61, 69, 77, 139; in Spenser (prose-poetry), 156, 167, 170, 175, 368*n*44; in Spenser-Shakespeare, 190, 202, 240, 243, 245, 248. See also intertext; landscape
Irigaray, Luce, 388*n*23
Iser, Wolfgang, 247, 322*n*4, 377*n*16
Isidore of Seville (Isidori Hispalensis Episcopi), 80, 345*n*29

Jakobson, Roman, 323–24*n*12
James, Heather, 385*n*46, 391*n*40, 393*n*52
Jameson, Fredric, 228, 328–29*n*51, 380*n*3, 382*n*19, 402–3*n*18
Jenkins, Raymond, 176, 367
John, Saint, 166–67
Jonson, Ben, 331–32*n*15
Judson, Alexander, 176
Juvenal, 100

Kahn, Coppélia, 392*n*47
Kahn, Victoria, 367*n*40

Keats, John, 193, 372*n*30
Kelley, Maurice, 398–99*nn*21–22
Kellogg, Robert, 350*n*10
Kermode, Frank, 377–78*n*19
Kierkegaard, Søren, 63, 68
Kiernan, Pauline, 244–48, 375*n*19, 389*n*26
Kinney, Arthur F., 369*n*11, 372*n*35
Kirschbaum, Leo, 369*n*8
Knedlick, Janet Leslie, 326*n*36, 388–89*n*25, 420*n*118
Knight, Stephen, 72, 76–77, 342*n*34
Kolbrener, William, 328*n*50, 397*n*17, 400*n*29, 403*n*19, 415*n*77, 422*n*132
Kolin, Philip C., 212
Kott, Jan, 370–71*n*23, 373*n*38
Krier, Theresa, 61–62, 226, 375–76*n*2
Kristeva, Julia, 2–4, 321–22*n*2, 322*n*5, 326*n*30, 327*n*41

Laȝamon, 19, 127–30, 134, 352–53*n*8
Labriola, Albert C., 412*n*53, 416*n*88
Lacan, Jacques, 328*n*49, 382–83*n*30, 383*n*35
landscape, 144, 249, 281–83, 291, 311; of desire, 201, 208, 213, 229, 235, 240, 295, 409*n*44, 411*n*48; Melibee's pastoral, 92, 94–95, 103–5, 198–99; of the mind, 185–89, 200, 227, 285–88, 302, 306–8; of quest, 216, 218–20, 379*n*29
Langbaine, Gerard, 384*n*42
Langland, William, 249, 379*n*34, 398*n*18
Laqueur, Thomas, 376–77*n*10, 391*n*38
Lawton, David, 330*n*7
Leicester, H. Marshall, 62–63, 330*n*7, 333*n*27, 338–39*n*7
Leitch, Vincent B., 322–23*n*6
Leonard, John, 314, 401*n*6, 404*n*4, 406*n*18, 409*n*36, 412*n*51, 415–16*n*85, 418*n*103
Lever, J. W., 241
Lewalski, Barbara Kiefer, 9, 266, 329*n*54, 397*n*15, 397*n*17, 398*n*18, 420*n*118

430 Index

Lewis, C. S., 152, 230–31, 383*n*32, 410*n*44
Lieb, Michael, 299, 398*nn*18–22 passim, 412*n*58, 420–21*nn*118–30 passim
Lily, William, 261, 395*n*4
Livy, 61, 155
Loewenstein, David, 276, 407*n*25, 409*n*36, 416*n*88
Loewenstein, Joseph, 331–32*n*15, 334*n*33, 356*n*11
Logan, Robert A., 393*n*55
Longinus, 384–85*n*42
Loomba, Ania, 239, 386*n*2, 390*n*32
Lotspeich, Henry Gibbons, 353*n*17, 357*n*25
Lucretius, 55, 149, 152, 241
Luther, Martin, 300, 351*n*19, 396*n*8
Luxon, Thomas H., 9, 325*nn*27–28, 326*n*34
Lydgate, John, 146
Lyly, John, 57, 173–74, 337*n*14
Lyotard, Jean-François, 323–24*n*12, 383*n*35, 387*n*16

Macfie, Pamela Royston, 385*n*46
Machacek, Gregory, 322*n*5, 402*n*17, 416*n*87
Machiavelli, Niccolò, 172, 291, 362*n*36, 368*n*44, 408*n*31
Mack, Maynard, 183–85, 370*n*16
MacQueen, John, 368*n*3
Macrobius, 87, 90
Malbecco, 70, 184, 249, 417*n*97; and Milton's Satan, 305, 307, 417*n*95, 417–18*n*102
Maley, Willy, 327*n*44, 368*n*44
Malynes, Gerard de, 172, 365*nn*18–19
Mammon, 101, 155, 161, 163–64, 201, 283, 291, 295, 305, 362*n*36, 372*n*30; in *King Lear*, 193–99; in Milton, 301, 408*n*31, 415*n*79
Marlowe, Christopher, 94, 100
Marot, Clément, 92

Martin, Catherine Gimelli, 21, 328*n*49, 397*n*14
masks and masking, 33–37, 39, 69, 131, 311, 332–33*nn*21–24, 334*n*34, 369*n*6. *See also* persona
materiality and materialism, 37, 87, 164, 273, 324–25*n*23, 406*n*21, 412*n*58; animist materialism, 290, 292, 319, 406*n*16; and history, 9–10, 15, 325*n*28; in *King Lear*, 194–95; and *Paradise Lost*, 289–92, 301–2, 307–8. *See also* monism; vitalism
Mazzoni, Jacopo, 326*n*36, 389*n*25, 420*n*118
McEachern, Claire, 380*n*5
McKeown, Adam, 384–85*n*42
Melanchthon, Philipp, 422*n*136
Melbancke, Brian, 174
Melibee, 18, 20, 27–28, 31–32, 346*n*9; in *Faerie Queene* Book VI, 91–105; and *King Lear*, 197–99, 222; and *Paradise Lost*, 295, 302, 411*n*48
metaphor, 21–22, 217, 227, 229, 232, 246, 248–50, 320, 323–24*n*12, 389*n*27; continued, 5, 7, 191, 278–83, 292–93; and *figura*, 10–13, 326*n*30; and intertextuality, 3–5; and irony, 272–73; and metonymy, 22, 286–87, 380*n*7, 402–3*n*18, 412*n*54, 420*n*122; and Milton's God, 313–19, 421*n*127; Ricoeur on, 15; specific intertextual instances of, 305, 309–10 (bees), 116, 125, 192, 306 (flies). *See also* metonymy
metonymy, distinguished from metaphor, 22, 279, 292, 323–24*n*12, 380*n*7, 402–3*n*18, 412*n*54, 420*n*122, 421*n*127; and Milton's God, 419*n*115; and monism, 297; and Riffaterre, 321*n*1; and vision, 287. *See also* metaphor
Michelangelo, 8, 11, 15
Middleton, Thomas, 174, 366*n*25

Miller, David Lee, 330n5, 376n2
Mills, Jerry Leath, 345n25
Milton, John, 2; allegory and, 10, 20–23, 192, 228, 328–29nn48–51; intertextuality and, 17, 49, 95–96, 100, 124, 163, 193, 404nn3–5; mortalism of, 378n24; nationalism in, 414n74; patience and, 396n12. *See also* allegory; intertextuality
Apology Against a Pamphlet (*Smectymnuus*), 398n18
Areopagitica, 300, 372n30, 403n21
Eikonoklastes, 401n2, 422n138
A Maske Presented at Ludlow Castle (*Comus*), 402n16
"Nativity Ode," 264, 267, 396n11
On Christian Doctrine (*De Doctrina Christiana*), 21–22, 292, 299, 304, 396n9, 397–99nn17–23, 406n24, 409nn36–37, 409n38, 412n58, 413n61, 414n76, 416n87, 419n116, 420–21n125, 421n130
Paradise Lost, 253, 264–68, 271, 276–320, 325n28, 358n32, 398n18, 400n28, 401n6, 401n30, 403n19, 405–6nn16–18, 406–7nn24–25, 407n27, 410–11nn45–48, 412n54, 413nn59–60, 415n77, 415–16nn85–89, 418n107, 419–20nn117–18, 420–21nn122–25, 421n130
Paradise Regained, 21, 264, 266–76, 319, 398n18, 402n11
The Readie & Easie Way to Establish a Free Commonwealth, 400n29, 415n77
Samson Agonistes, 259–60, 264, 268–71, 399–400nn24–29
Sonnet XIX ("When I consider how my light is spent"), 263–64, 396n9
mimesis, 9, 13, 201, 420n118; and *Antony and Cleopatra*, 245–46, 389–90n27; Aristotelian, 5–6, 14–15, 321n1, 326n36, 327n44; and the Bower of Bliss, 226–27, 232, 235; and fiction, 273–75; and poet figures, 31–32, 35, 37. *See also* imitation
Miskimin, Alice S., 354n1, 408n33
Mohamed, Feisal G., 400n24
monism, 276–79, 282, 292–98, 302, 319, 403n19, 408n35, 413n61, 420n122, 422n135. *See also* materiality and materialism; vitalism
mons veneris, 203, 209, 214, 391n43. See also *vagina dentata*; Venus
Montrose, Louis, 236, 385n45
More, Sir Thomas, 163, 170
Morgan, Gerald, 76, 342n35
Mount Acidale, 27–28, 87, 91, 96, 104–5, 199
Murrin, Michael, 343n13, 345n26, 362n34
Murtaugh, Daniel S., 341n32
Muscatine, Charles, 349n4, 349n6, 356n68

Nancy, Jean-Luc, 8, 235, 257, 394n58
narrative, 44–45, 54–55, 59–60, 226–29, 239–42, 323n10, 383n35; and allegory, 5–9, 12, 14, 22, 65, 101, 105, 185, 325n27, 328n50; and allegory in Milton, 272, 280–85, 294–97, 303–4, 415n78, 419n115; of the Bower of Bliss 228, 230, 233–35, 250, 382n24; Chaucer's and Spenser's, 8, 27–41, 48, 75, 114–15, 118, 141, 143–47, 152–53, 331n13, 358n36; Frye on allegory in, 190–91; and narrator, 18, 75, 413n60; in Spenser and Milton, 290–91, 308–10. *See also* history; persona
Nashe, Thomas, 174, 366n29
Neely, Carol Thomas, 394n57
Nelson, William, 96, 163, 340n14; on *Muiopotmos*, 350n10, 350n12, 350n14

Index

Neoplatonism, 8–9, 81, 87, 206, 216, 245–46, 282, 317, 361–62n26, 377n12. *See also* Platonism
Nohrnberg, James, 374n4, 375n2, 378n19, 391n42, 391–92n44, 393n52
Norbrook, David, 299, 403n21, 407n25, 409–10n40, 412n52, 413n68, 415n77

Oberman, Heiko Augustinus, 300
Orr, Mary, 2, 4–5, 388n24, 390n28
Ovid, 99, 122, 136, 141, 192, 205–6, 236, 291, 338n1, 351nn22–23, 371n28, 418n107
Owen, Charles A., Jr., 346n9, 349n4

Paglia, Camille A., 242–43, 380n7
Panofsky, Erwin, 8, 86
Parker, Patricia A., 59, 229, 236, 354n19, 358n30, 385n45
Partridge, Eric, 56
passion, 143, 145, 150, 153, 194, 201, 221–22, 234, 239–42, 259–71, 340n14, 420–21n125. *See also agere et pati*; patience
Paster, Gail Kern, 333n25, 381n15
patience, 145, 259–71, 312, 395n5, 396n12, 400n27, 414n76. *See also agere et pati*; passion
Paton, Lucy Allen, 353nn11–12
Patterson, Annabel, 92, 364n13, 367n38
Patterson, Lee, 98, 101, 329n2, 348n23, 348n25, 348n30
Paul, Saint, 10, 12–13, 15, 111, 298, 304, 408n35, 417n91
persona, 17, 28–34, 42, 48, 99, 173, 332–33nn23–24; of Colin Clout, 91, 96; in drama, 239, 242, 269; in *A View of the Present State of Ireland*, 155–56, 168, 177–78. *See also* personation and impersonation
personation and impersonation, 33–34, 37–39, 66, 132, 284, 332–33nn23–24

personification, and allegory, 6–7; in Chaucer, 62, 64–65, 144–45, 339n11; in Milton, 281–82, 293, 299–303, 305–6; in Shakespeare, 184, 200, 263; in Spenser, 216, 227, 229–30, 232, 237. *See also* allegory; form
Peter, John, 410n43, 411n46
Petrarch (Francesco Petrarca), 61, 71, 340–41n24
Petrarchism, 71, 73, 150, 211, 234, 237, 263, 291, 341n28
Phillips, Adam, 382n24
Phillips, Edward, 319
Picciotto, Joanna, 410n45
Plato, 8, 15, 81, 216, 261, 328n50, 343n12
Platonism, 15, 63, 87, 317, 326n30, 339n11, 404n5, 411n47; allegory and, 7–8, 281; Benjamin and, 21, 328n48, 328n50; mimesis and, 246. *See also* Neoplatonism
Plautus, 100
Plotinus, 8, 303
Plutarch, 147, 252, 256, 258, 291, 393n55, 394n60, 408n33
Pomponazzi, Pietro, 389n25
Pope, John, 60, 337n22
Pratt, Robert A., 355n9
Prescott, Anne Lake, 358n34, 392n48, 418n107
Proust, Marcel, 245
proverbs, 36, 361–62n26; and Melibee, 96, 99–101, 104; in *A View of the Present State of Ireland*, 19, 168–79, 363n3. *See also* prudence
prudence, virtue of, 81, 97–98, 100–2, 105, 125, 168, 347–48nn20–30 passim; in Chaucer, 92–93, 97–102, 348n25
Prudentius, 7, 227, 259, 324n18, 381n18
Pugh, Syrithe, 385n46, 393n50
puns and punning (concept), 2, 8, 72, 203, 377n16; on *dying*, 206, 215,

220, 248, 250–58; and the Garden of Adonis, 212, 214–22, 344n7; and *King Lear*, 187, 189, 193, 195, 199–200; in Milton (selected instances), 277–78, 287, 293, 295–98, 310–16, 405–6n16; on *nothing*, 84, 193, 258; in Spenser (selected instances), 34, 41, 56, 89, 127, 151, 161, 164; on *standing*, 263–66, 269; syntactical, 47, 379n34

Quigley, Brendan, 400n27
Quilligan, Maureen, 236, 342n1, 354n1, 357n21, 375n2, 404n4, 419n115
Quitslund, Jon A., 375n2, 377n12, 378n19, 379n27, 392n45, 393n53

Rabelais, François, 376n8, 418n107
Radzinowicz, Mary Ann, 396n9
Ragland-Sullivan, Ellie, 382–83n30
Rainolds, John, 384n42
Rajan, Tilottama, 321–22n2, 322n6, 323n6, 327n41
Ralegh, Sir Walter, 32, 94, 126, 129, 331–32n15, 335n6, 353n16
Ramachandran, Ayesha, 350n10
Ramsay, G. G., 348n28
Ramus, Peter (Pierre de la Ramée), 422n136
Rapaport, Herman, 328n49, 412n54, 416n89
Rasmussen, Mark, 341n29, 341n33
Raynes, Harold E., 365n18, 365n20
reading (concept and practice), 1–2, 15–17, 33, 61, 77, 115, 125, 179, 214, 220, 278, 327n45; historically, 69, 134, 167, 297; refractive, 148, 201; sequential, 42, 247. *See also* history
Redcrosse, 38, 70, 131–32, 165, 188, 215, 404n4; and despair, 62–63, 66–69; and Hippolytus, 226–28, 284–85, 408n29; and Milton, 267, 284–85, 289–90, 299–300, 304, 306, 311–12; and pricking, 28, 54–56, 58–59; and reading, 7, 247–48; and Scudamour, 139, 141
refraction, 19, 97, 135–53, 201, 206, 209–13, 239–40, 358n30; concept of, 148, 340n15
Reid, Robert L., 345n25, 361n26, 381n15
Renwick, W. L., 96, 157
Resurrection of Our Lord, The, 173, 366n23
Revard, Stella Purce, 303, 403n1, 416n88
Ricks, Christopher, 314, 410n45
Ricoeur, Paul: on Aristotle's *Poetics* (mimesis), 5, 14–15, 246, 284, 310, 323n10, 326nn37–39; on metaphor, 3, 282, 296, 314, 322n4, 420n122
Riddel, Joseph N., 322–23n6
Riffaterre, Michael, 321n1, 323n8, 327nn44–45, 403–4n2, 406n16
Ringler, William, 384n42
Robinson, Forrest G., 283
Roche, Thomas P., Jr., 358n35, 375n2, 377n13
Rogers, John, 278, 299, 402n13, 403n21, 406n16, 409n40, 413n67
Rose, Mary Beth, 260–61, 395n2
Rosenberg, Marvin, 196, 369n6, 369n12, 370n14
Rotman, Brian, 334n38, 410n41
Roudiez, Leon S., 321n2
Rumrich, John Peter, 299–301, 403n21, 413n67, 413–14n69, 415nn77–78
Rusche, Harry, 339n10

Samuel, Irene, 404n5, 420–21n125
Sans Joy, 67, 69, 188, 227, 267; and *Paradise Lost*, 284, 290
Satan, 228; and allegory, 22; and binarism, 21, 272–73; in *Paradise Lost*, 277, 283–89, 191–99, 302–17, 400n28, 407n25, 409n36, 411n48, 415n77, 416n87, 417n95, 418n103; and *Paradise Regained*, 266–68, 272,

275–76; and Spenser's *Muiopotmos*, 121–22
Saussure, Ferdinand de, 2
Schoenfeldt, Michael C., 381n15, 402n11
Schwartz, Regina M., 299, 398n18, 402n13, 406n23, 413n67
serpents, 66, 132, and *Antony and Cleopatra*, 241, 249, 258; and *Paradise Lost*, 273, 277, 283, 285, 299, 306–9, 312, 400n28, 407n27, 413n63, 417n98. See also dragons
Servius, 65, 67, 290, 340n14, 407n28
Seyffert, Oskar, 380n9, 380n12
Seznec, Jean, 368n3, 419n112
Shakespeare, William, 2, 20–23, 57, 100, 155, 219; intertextuality and, 15, 17. See also allegory; intertextuality
    Antony and Cleopatra, 20, 222–23, 235, 239–58, 379n32, 385–94nn1–61 passim
    Hamlet, 186, 191, 198, 246, 260, 264–65, 338n1, 389–90n27, 392n47, 395n3
    Henry VIII, 395n5
    King Lear, 20, 23, 84, 183–200, 255, 259, 261–62, 268, 362n27, 368–73nn1–40 passim, 386n5
    Lucrece, 338n1
    Merry Wives of Windsor, 174, 366n28
    A Midsummer Night's Dream, 337n14
    Othello, 186, 259, 261–63, 268, 372n33
    Richard II, 379n32
    Richard III, 193, 201–4, 209, 240, 254, 371n28, 373n1, 386n5, 392n48
    Romeo and Juliet, 56
    Sonnet 129 ("The expense of spirit in a waste of shame"), 223, 379n34
    Twelfth Night, 395n5
    Venus and Adonis, 20, 201–13, 217–22, 240–41, 243–44, 248, 379n28
Shawcross, John T., 412n52
Shepherd, Geoffrey, 405n16
Shoaf, R. A., 397n16, 404n4, 406n16, 412n54, 419n116, 422n137
Shoulson, Jeffrey, 409n36, 420n122, 421n125
Shuger, Debora Kuller, 178, 363n7, 367–68n42
Sidney, Sir Philip, 81, 217, 222, 301, 379n30; on fiction, 219, 244–48, 311; on the ground-plot, 283–84; on poetic imagination, 326n36, 351n29, 388–89n25, 390n30; on poetry and history 156, 164–66, 309, 360n10
Silberman, Lauren, 221, 374n10, 374n14, 377nn16–17, 378n19
Silver, Victoria, 21, 272, 328n51, 396n8, 397nn15–16, 401n5
Smarr, Janet Levarie, 342n36
Smith, Paul, 334n35
Snyder, Susan, 339n10, 340n23, 341n25, 370n16, 370n23
Song, Eric B., 410n40
Sorabji, Richard, 343n12, 422n131
Spence, Lewis, 353n10, 353n12
Spenser, Edmund, 2, 4, 260, 265, 317, 328–29n51, 331–32n15, 332–33nn23–24; allegory and, 7–8, 301; intertextuality and, 15, 21, 35, 269, 278–81, 300, 304, 307–11, 315–16. See also allegory; intertextuality; reading
    Amoretti and Epithalamion, 32, 38–39, 77, 83–85, 136, 141, 151–52, 332n22, 334n33, 358n34
    Colin Clouts Come Home Again, 28, 96, 215, 224–26
    Faerie Queene Book I, 18, 28, 30–31, 34, 45, 54–70, 77, 80, 96–97, 101, 126, 130–37, 159, 162, 177, 188, 215, 227, 229, 247, 284–85, 288–90, 299–300, 303, 305–6, 311–12, 339n10, 341n30, 356n13, 390n31

Faerie Queene Book II, 55, 85–88, 98, 101–2, 137–38, 157, 159–66, 188, 192–94, 197–98, 201–2, 233–37, 240, 243, 249, 291, 304, 309, 311, 342n4, 343n13, 353n15, 358n30

Faerie Queene Book III, 18, 38, 57, 61, 70–79, 85, 126–30, 134, 137, 141–42, 149, 157, 193, 201–15, 218, 221, 230, 237–38, 240, 244, 249–54, 286, 305, 311, 335n6, 341n30, 356n14, 417n95

Faerie Queene Book IV, 28, 30, 34, 38, 55, 61–62, 73–74, 85, 89, 95, 134–53, 159, 207, 309, 311, 351n26, 358–59n38, 404n4

Faerie Queene Book V, 19, 30, 34, 37–38, 50, 159, 161, 164–65, 177–78, 229, 249, 270, 297, 311, 371n28, 415n84

Faerie Queene Book VI, 17–18, 42–53, 57, 83, 89–105, 164–65, 192, 197–99, 249, 270, 286, 294–95, 311, 335n8, 344n16, 357n21, 373n36, 411n48

Faerie Queene Book VII (Mutability Cantos), 17–18, 59–60, 83–89, 135–37, 153, 270, 285, 291, 310, 344n17, 354n1, 378n24, 408n33

Muiopotmos, 19–20, 22, 109–25, 134, 192, 349–52nn1–30 passim, 373n40, 385n46

The Shepheardes Calender, 57, 60, 91, 97, 104, 152, 333n30; and "E. K.," 155–56, 160, 393n52

A View of the Present State of Ireland, 19, 102, 155–56, 159, 168–79, 367n38

Spivack, Bernard, 184
St. German, Christopher, 171, 365n15
Starks, Lisa S., 394n56
Steadman, John M., 417n98, 417–18n102
Steele, Oliver, 350n10
Stein, Arnold, 397n14, 410n45

Stephanus, Robertus, 80, 82
Stephens, Dorothy, 228, 382n24
Strier, Richard, 401n10
Strohm, Paul, 346n9
Stuart, Mary (queen of Scotland), 177
Summers, Joseph H., 304, 401n7, 416n89

Talon, Omer, 422n136
Tasso, Torquato, 21, 40, 100, 127, 138–39, 280–81, 326n36, 389n25, 420n118
Teskey, Gordon, 7, 22, 31, 328–29nn50–52
Thomas, Thomas, 343n5, 344–45n21
Thynne, William, 57–58, 330n6, 336n10
Tierney, Brian, 367–68n42
Tilley, Morris Palmer, 365n22, 366n25
Toliver, Harold, 362–63n37
Tonkin, Humphrey, 50, 324n20, 346n1, 375n2, 378n24
Traub, Valerie, 377n10, 391n38
Treip, Mindele Anne, 21, 272, 280–84, 312–13, 316–17, 388–89n25, 399n23, 403nn2–3, 405–6n16, 421n127
Trimpi, Wesley, 344n16
Trubowitz, Rachel J., 325n28, 403n19, 408n35
Turner, James Grantham, 411n46
Tuve, Rosemond, 129
Tweedie, Fiona J., 397–98n17, 421n130
Tyndale, William, 154, 166–67, 359n4

Udall, Nicholas, 82, 168

vagina dentata, 209, 221–22, 374n14, 379n28. See also mons veneris; Venus
Van Dyke, Carolynn, 6–7, 12, 21–22, 339n12, 381n18, 382n21, 383n34, 387n11, 419n115
van Es, Bart, 419n112

Vanhoutte, Jacqueline, 393n55
Varro, 85–86, 345n21
Vendler, Helen, 401n8
Venus, 19–20, 233, 309, 344n16, 357nn24–25, 374n14, 378n21; aspects and names of, 205–7, 210, 240, 243, 251; Chaucer's compared to Spenser's, 112, 117, 119, 122–23, 135–53; in the Garden of Adonis, 214–23, 379n29, 392n45; in Shakespeare, 201–13, 224–26, 239–44, 248, 250–52, 258; Spenser's Temple of, 31, 38, 55, 291, 358n30
Vergil, 65, 67, 91–92, 110, 254, 284, 290, 340n14, 393n52
vetus homo (Old Man), 58, 62–66, 285, 304–5, 416–17nn90–91. *See also* death; despair
Vico, Giambattista, 309, 418n109
vitalism, 8, 292, 377n12, 388n23, 403n21, 405–6n6. *See also* materiality and materialism; monism
Wace, 128
Waldock, A. J. A., 418n107
Watkins, Charles A., 349n7

Watkins, W. B. C., 183–84, 240–41, 248, 253
Weimann, Robert, 389–90n27
Williams, Gordon, 206, 391n44
Williams, Grant, 377n10, 384n42
Wilson, Luke, 396n9, 418n109
Wilson, Thomas, 172–73, 343n12, 344n15
Wind, Edgar, 242, 368–69n3, 370n18, 392n49, 408n33
Wofford, Susanne Lindgren, 21, 341n28
Wolfson, Elliot R., 233, 325n28, 380n6, 382–83n30
Wood, Derek N. C., 399–400n24
Wood, Rufus, 236, 248–49
Worthen, W. B., 388n23
Wyatt, Sir Thomas, 57

Yates, Frances A., 166, 361–62n26, 363n38

Zak, William F., 370n19
Zitner, Sheldon, 187, 189, 369n10, 370nn16–17
Žižek, Slavoj, 332n21

www.ingramcontent.com/pod-product-compliance
Lightning Source LLC
Chambersburg PA
CBHW022024290426
44109CB00014B/739